CHRISTIANITY
AND
NATIVE CULTURES

Perspectives from Different Regions of the World

CHRISTIANITY
AND
NATIVE CULTURES

Perspectives from Different Regions of the World

Edited by
Cyriac K. Pullapilly
Bernard J. Donahoe, C.S.C.
David Stefancic
Bill Svelmoe

Foreword by
Patrick White

Volume XIII: The Church and The World Series
Cyriac K. Pullapilly, General Editor
Saint Mary's College, Notre Dame, Indiana

Cross Cultural
PUBLICATIONS, INC.

The Church and The World Series

Dedicated to the scholarly investigation of Christianity's interaction with the non-Christian world. This includes the Church's initial encounters with the civilizations of the ancient world, its influence on the tribal nationalities of the medieval times and its missionary impact in more modern times. Included also are Christianity's ideological and institutional impacts on the secular worlds of science, technology, politics, economics and the arts.

Authors who wish to publish in the series are requested to contact the General Editor at the address below:

Editorial Board:
Cyriac K. Pullapilly, General Editor
Saint Mary's College, Notre Dame, Indiana

Cover Art by Mary Beth Dominello
Cover Design by Joan Addison

Printed in the United States of America. *1ˢᵗ Edition*

Published by Cross Cultural Publications, Inc. Cross Roads Books

Library of Congress Catalog Number: 2003099563
ISBN: 0-940121-77-8

TABLE OF CONTENTS

INTRODUCTORY ESSAYS

PART I

**Aspects of Christian Inculturation in Southern Europe,
the Middle East and Africa**

**Edited by David Stefancic
Saint Mary's College**

PART II

**The State of Christian Inculturation with the Native Cultures of
South Asia, The Far East, Polynesia, Melanasia and Australia**

**Edited by Cyriac K. Pullapilly
Saint Mary's College, Notre Dame, Indiana**

PART III

Seeing Eye to Eye: The Struggle of Inculturation Between European Christian Views and the Native American Cultures of North America

Edited by Bernard J. Donahoe, C.S.C. Saint Mary's College, Notre Dame, Indiana

PART IV

Christian Inculturation with the Cultures of Central and South America

Edited by Bill Svelmoe
Saint Mary's College, Notre Dame, Indiana

PART V

Interaction of Christian Theology and Ethics with Native Arts and Literature

Edited by Cyriac K. Pullapilly
Saint Mary's College, Notre Dame, Indiana

FOREWORD

The essays brought together in this valuable collection had their origin in the rich and varied conference *Christianity and Native Cultures* held at Saint Mary's College in September 2002. For three days scholars focused new attention on multiple points of interaction between Christianity and indigenous cultures throughout the world.

In recent decades scholarly and public discourse has become awash with commentary and analysis of cross-cultural contact, multicultural engagement, ethnicity and religion, globalization and its discontents. In this flurry much valuable work has been produced. In some cases, however, the actual distinctiveness, particularity, and complexity of the encounters between Christianity and native cultures have become obscured. In this collection, though, the papers are anchored in time and place, in the particular and specific conditions and experience of contact. These essays thus keep us close to the ground – helping us all see how the multiple encounters between the seemingly abstract entities of Christianity and native cultures have been played out in a variety of ways, times, and places.

By this grounding these essays can inform theory, analysis, and commentary with a vital understanding of the complexity of these interactions. Further, the scholars in this collection come from a variety of disciplines to share an understanding of the ways in which literature, art, religion, economics, psychology, women's studies, philosophy, political science, and other fields offer valuable perspectives on the contact of Christianity and native cultures and are themselves informed and transformed by that encounter. We at Saint Mary's College are proud that this conference originated under the leadership of Dr. Cyriac Pullapilly and his colleagues in the Department of History, but we are even more proud that the conference became a campus-wide event and engaged faculty from throughout the College. The interdisciplinary diversity evident in these essays is one more distinctive value of this collection.

Though anchored in the particular, these essays go far beyond the merely parochial; they are more than specialized analyses of worlds, issues, and artifacts of human experience remote in time and space. The writers evidence an understanding of the ongoing relevance of the encounters they describe and analyze. The permutations of the encounter of Christianity and native cultures form a complex web of engagements that has shaped world cultures for many, many centuries, and, if anything, is even more intense and involving in this new millennium.

The conference was an exhilarating event characterized by a lively exchange of ideas and questions. By collecting these essays, we hope to give others the opportunity to engage in the conversation across diverse perspectives. The ideas and questions here assembled continue to animate our public, political, and religious discourses. They are alive every day in our world and are of stupendous importance. The millions of points of ongoing contact and reciprocal influence between a complex Christianity and a myriad of native cultures continue to demand our attention and shape our experience.

1492 brought new worlds to Europe together with powerful questions that continue to bedevil us. These new people encountered by the voyages of Columbus, were they human beings, were they animals? This is not an inconsequential question, of course. If they were animals, they could be brutalized and exterminated without guilt; if they were human, they thus had souls and must be capable of receiving the faith. This for a large part of Catholic Christianity was decided in 1537 through the bull *Sublimis Deus* of Pope Paul III that declared, "The Indians are true men." That this declaration did not, nor still does not protect indigenous peoples from brutalization and extermination must not completely negate its fundamental insight and its revolutionary character, for within this declaration is a world shaking understanding of commonality within difference that continues to shape our hearts and minds. The essays here collected help us see the long history and ongoing interaction of Christianity and native cultures in new and complex ways. In this they not only contribute to a vital interdisciplinary discourse but also illuminate some of the most necessary and profound questions facing human culture in our time.

> Patrick E. White
> Vice President and Dean of Faculty
> Saint Mary's College

ACKNOWLEDGEMENTS

The editors of this volume are indebted to many colleagues and friends who, in various ways, helped us along the way. The first among them are several generations of alumnae of the Department of History at Saint Mary's College whose restricted gifts to the Department at Christmases over many years made the International Conference on Christianity and Native Cultures, held at Saint Mary's College in September 2002, possible. Nearly all the essays in this volume were initially presented at the conference.

Next, our gratitude goes to Dr. Marilou Eldred, the President of Saint Mary's College, and Dr. Karen Ristau, our former Vice President, for their moral support. Dr. Patrick White, who took over as interim chair of the History Department during the Conference and subsequently became Vice President and Dean of Faculty, was a source of inspiration and logistical support not only for the conference but also for the publication of this book, for which we are most grateful.

Our special thanks are due to the following colleagues who delivered plenary addresses at the conference: Professor Tod Swanson of Arizona State University; Professor Amanda Porterfield, University of Wyoming and 2001-2002 President of the American Society of Church History; and the New York film maker Judith Gleason, who screened and lectured on her film, *This Trowel in My Hand Facilitates the Miracle*, which focused on indigenous religious devotions in Mexico.

We thank the following members of the clergy who offered liturgies of different rites / denominations at the conference. They are: Reverend Robert Rabbat, pastor of several Byzantine parishes in the Chicago area (Liturgy of St. John Chrisostom, Catholic); Reverend Roy Thomas, pastor, Malankara Mar Thoma Syrian Church, Chicago (Liturgy of Saint James, Orthodox); and His Excellency Mar Jacob Angadiath, Bishop, Syro Malabar Catholic Diocese of Chicago and Permanent Apostolic Visitor to Canada (Liturgy of the Syro Malabar Church of India, Catholic).

We are grateful to Rev. Robert Trisco, Editor, The Catholic Historical Review and Professor Patrick Carey, 2001-2002, President of the American Catholic Historical Association for the official endorsement of the conference by the ACHA. To Barbara De Concini, Executive Director, American Academy of Religion; to Professor Pamela Gleason, Secretary, College Theology Society; to Professor Dolores Christie,

President, Catholic Theology Society of America; and Mr. Henry W. Bowden, Executive Secretary, American Society of Church History, we extend our thanks for their help with the publicity for the conference. To Professor Lawrence Sullivan, Director, center for the Study of World Religions, Harvard University, for his counsel on various aspects of the conference, we are grateful.

We want to thank Drs. Kelly Hamilton, Mark Stein and Carol Meaney of our Department who contributed significantly to the success of the conference.

Richard Baxter, Director of Special Events at Saint Mary's and his staff were meticulous in providing all the space and technical assistance for the conference. Similarly, Amanda Weber of the Food Service at the College took excellent care of the catering for the conference. To them, we are very thankful.

The one person whose expertise and attention to detail were crucial to the success of the conference and this publishing effort was Mrs. Mary Beth Dominello, Administrative Secretary of the Department of History. When things became tight, Mary Beth and we could count on the cheerful and friendly assistance of Mrs. Celia Fallon, Secretary of the Center for Academic Innovation. We are most grateful for the invaluable help of these two generous persons.

Finally, to Kavita Pullapilly, who put her career plans on hold and took on the responsibility for all aspects of the publication of this volume, we express our gratitude and wish her well in her Peace Corps work in the Ukraine for the next two years.

The Editors

INTRODUCTORY ESSAYS

I

INCULTURATION AND THE MOTHER CHURCH: AN OVERVIEW FROM APOSTLE PETER TO JOHN PAUL II

Cyriac K. Pullapilly[*]

Among the celebratory events held to mark the fourth centenary of the arrival of Matteo Ricci, "the great Italian missionary, humanist and man of science," in Beijing, China were two conferences, one held in the Chinese capital (October 14-17, 2001) and the other in Rome, at the Pontifical Gregorian University (October 24-25, 2001). Pope John Paul II sent messages to both conferences in which he stated:

"After twenty-one long years of avid and intense study of the language, history and culture of China, Father Ricci entered Beijing, the city of the Emperor, on January 24, 1601. Received with every honor, held in high regard and frequently visited by men of letters, mandarins, and those desiring to learn the new sciences of which he was an acknowledged master, he lived the rest of his days in the imperial capital, where he died a holy death on May 11, 1610, at the age of fifty-seven years, almost twenty-eight of which he had spent in China, his merit lay above all in the realm of inculturation. Father Ricci forged a Chinese terminology for Catholic theology and liturgy, and thus created the conditions for making Christ known and for incarnating the Gospel message and the church within Chinese culture. From his first contacts with the Chinese, Father Ricci based his entire scientific and apostolic methodology upon two pillars, to which he remained faithful until his death, despite many difficulties and misunderstandings, both internal and external: first the Chinese neophytes, in embracing Christianity, did not in any way have to re-

[*] Cyriac Pullapilly is a Professor of History at Saint Mary's College. He holds a Ph.D. in history from the University of Chicago and his researches and publications are in the areas of Catholic Reformation and Indian History and Religions.

nounce loyalty to their country; second, the Christian
revelation of the mystery of God in no way destroyed
but in fact enriched and complemented everything beautiful and good, just and holy, in what had been produced
and handed down by the ancient Chinese traditions...Father Ricci made this insight the basis of his
patient and far-sighted work of inculturation of the faith
in China, in the constant search for a common ground of
understanding with the intellectuals of that great land."[1]

Pope John Paul's lavish praise for Matteo Ricci's work of inculturating Western Christian theology and liturgy with Chinese philosophy,
customs and rituals is in sharp contrast to the severe condemnation several eighteenth century Popes issued against Ricci and his work.[2] In fact,
it was not Ricci alone who came under scrutiny and condemnation during the notorious "Rites Controversy" of the early eighteenth century, but
also his near-contemporary and fellow Italian Jesuit Robert de Nobili,
who did exactly the same type of inculturation in India as Ricci did in
China. By adopting the customs and manners of high caste Hindus and
by becoming conversant in Sanskrit language and Hindu sacred texts, de
Nobili gained the trust and respect of elite Hindu Brahmins of South India. And by incorporating many Hindu symbolisms and customs into
Catholic liturgy and devotions, he made it possible for high caste Hindus
to become Christians without losing their social status. Criticisms against
de Nobili's unorthodox practices were leveled in early seventeenth century itself by missionaries of different religious orders and nationalities,
especially the Portuguese. However, de Nobili and his practices were
vindicated first by the Grand Inquisitor of Portugal in 1621 and some of
his main innovations received formal approval from Pope Gregory XV
himself in 1623.[3] This was not the end of the controversy, however. Rivals of the Jesuits, primarily the Capuchins, started to lodge complaints
against them in Rome. When such complaints became intense, Rome
sent an emissary, Charles Thomas Maillard de Tournon (1668 – 1710), a

[1] Quoted in *Catholic Historical Review*, Vol. LXXXVIII, No.1, January 2002.
Notes and Comments, 179-181.
[2] The Papal bull "Romanae Sedis Antistites," in L.M. Jordao and P. Manso, eds.,
Bullarium Patronatus Portugaliae Regum, 32-34.
[3] Joseph Thekkedath, *History of Christianity in India from the Middle of the Sixteenth Century to the End of the Seventeenth Century*, Vol. II (Bangalore, India:
The Church History Association of India, 1997), 212-214.

Savoyard bishop and titular Latin Patriarch of Antioch, to both China and India in early 1703. De Tournon investigated the Jesuit missionary practices in liturgy and devotions as well as in personal attire and manners in both China and India. He found all practices different from the rubrics of sacraments and sacramentals followed by the Latin Church objectionable and issued decrees to cease their observances forthwith. Response from the Jesuits was predictable. They reacted with fury and determination. As one Jesuit wrote from India to his confreres in the West, "The Patriarch of Antioch lit in India a fire which shall not be quickly put out."[4] It quickly turned into a power struggle between Rome's Propaganda Congregation and Portugal's Padroado Authorities. Many representations were sent to Rome by both sides, many memoranda were submitted, many meetings were held by the Holy Office in Rome and five Popes intervened in this matter—Clement XI, Innocent XIII, Benedict XIII, Clement XII and Benedict XIV. It was the last of them, Benedict XIV, who ended the controversy on "Chinese Rites" and "Malabar Rites" with his bull "Omnium Sollicitudinum" in 1744. The "inculturation" Matteo Ricci and Robert de Nobili pioneered, the object of great admiration and lavish praise from Pope John Paul II in the year of Christ 2001, was severely condemned by Pope Benedict XIV in the year of Christ 1744. No serious attempt towards "inculturation" occurred from 1744 until after Pope John XXIII allowed fresh air to get in by opening the windows of the church through Vatican Council II.

I started this paper on inculturation with Pope John Paul II's stance on the issue and the contrasting pronouncements of the 18th century popes to demonstrate that the church's highest leadership has been divided on this matter from time to time and that the church has to revisit the issue as she constantly confronts ever-changing cultural milieus. The very first controversial matter that the first apostles had to resolve, the one that pitted Peter and Paul against each other, was the question whether non-circumcised gentiles should be admitted into the Christian community. Peter's bull headedness was mellowed only by a direct intervention from God, the basket that was lowered from heaven with unclean things in it and the voice from God ordering Peter to pick and eat

---

[4] Jesuit Guy Tachard's letter to his superiors in France, February 18, 1706, Archiepiscopal Archives, Madras-Mylapore, AMMSJ-MC Doc.I.n.51. See for details E.R. Hambye, S.J., *History of Christianity in India in the Eighteenth Century* Vol. II (Bangalore: The Church History Association of India, 1997), 216-227.

from them. Unfortunately, Peter's successors have not always been beneficiaries of visions and voices from heaven. The story of Christianity's
inculturation with native cultures has been one of intermittent successes
and failures. What I propose to do now is to present an overview of such
failures and successes in different periods of history.

To start with the Apostolic age, in the first council (held 49/50
AD; see Acts, 15:29) at the recommendation of Peter and at the motion
of James, it was resolved that no burden should be imposed on the converted Gentiles other than to abstain from sacrificing to idols, from
blood, from things strangled and from fornication. All other cultural
practices of the Gentiles were made acceptable to the Christian community. It was true, however, that despite this decision of the Council, many
Jewish Christians, sympathetic to Peter's old position, were hesitant to
mingle with the Gentile converts. Paul, who in all his apostolic journeys,
through so many places, held faith as the only condition to baptism,
fought back this prejudicial attitude and obviously won. Then, when Jerusalem was destroyed by the Romans, a tragedy which some Gentile
Christians thought of as punishment from God for the Jewish Christians'
narrow-mindedness, such prejudices seem to have entirely disappeared.
Christians of all nationalities and all religious backgrounds were united
by the common bond of their faith.[5, 6]

When Christianity started to spread and make a visible presence
in the Roman Empire, critics such as Fronto, Celsus, Lucian and Porphy-
rius leveled literary attacks against the new religion. Christian apologists
such as Justin and Minucius Felix, instead of attacking Roman religions
and cultures as pagan, praised the noble aspects in them and established
links between them and the Christian faith, thereby extending an implicit
invitation to the Romans to come aboard.[7]

From the first through the third centuries, Christianity had to
confront and compete with three new religions that were making inroads
into the Roman Empire – Gnosticism, Mithraism and Manichaeism.
Gnosticism, propounding an elaborate theology systematically dealing
with the fundamental issues of the nature of man and God and the way to
obtain salvation posed a serious challenge to Christianity, even claiming

---

[5] Adolph Harnack, *The Mission and Expansion of Christianity in the First Three Centuries* (New York: Harper Torchbooks, 1961), chaps. II – VI, 19-83.
[6] Joseph Schmidlin, *Catholic Mission History*, Matthias Braun, edit & trans. (Techny, IL: Mission Press SVD, 1933), 40-60.
[7] Ibid., 66.

some of her leading intellectuals such as Basilides, Valentine and Tertullian. However, sifting through some of the most sophisticated concepts proposed by this religion of intellectuals the church, thanks to the clear minds of leaders such as St. Irenaeus of Lyons, discarded all that were inconsistent with apostolic teaching and assimilated into itself all that were compatible to biblical theology and conducive to spiritual growth. The presence of the personal soul, the indwelling of the divine in man, contemplation as the way of reaching and touching that divine in you; these were all, to a large measure, Gnostic contributions to Christianity and they, in time, became the inspiration for Christian hermitic and monastic traditions.

Mithraism, the Persian religion that swept into the Roman Empire soon after Rome conquered Persia had a rich mythology and eschatology more elaborate than any other religion of the time. There is remarkable similarity between the basic tenets and rituals of Mithraism and Christianity: salvation through the sacrifice of the mediating figures (Mithra and Christ), beliefs in the immortality of the soul (heaven and hell), bodily resurrection, last judgment, second coming of the savior, baptism, communion with bread and water / wine, Sunday as the day of worship, and the birthday celebration of the Savior on December 25 in the winter solstice and celibate priesthood. Despite the vehement denial by Christian apologists and historians such as Pere Lagrange and the University of Notre Dame's Father Philip Hughes,[8] in the middle part of this century, and by many before them, the phenomenon does not seem to have any plausible explanation other than a massive adaptation of many aspects of the older religion, Mithraism, by the younger one, Christianity.

Manichaeism was founded by the Persian Mani, who drew his inspiration from Zoroaster, Buddha and Jesus, but based his religion on the central principle of the continuing struggle between good and evil, the good god and the bad god. Having framed his teachings on sound logic and keen observation of the human nature Mani attracted the community of intellectuals in the eastern half of the Roman empire, including one of the greatest, Saint Augustine. Seeing it as a serious threat, Mani's religion was severely rejected by Christians, Zoroastrians and Mithaists, but at least one of Mani's central teachings gained a permanent place in the Christian economy of salvation, that is the need for systematic asceti-

---

[8] Philip Hughes, *A History of the Church*, Vol. I (New York, Sheed and Ward, 1952), 128-130.

cism, which it enshrined in the Christian monastic ideal. Once the edict of Milan by the triumphant Caesars Constantine and Licinius liberated Christianity in 313, the nascent Christian monastic tradition was nurtured by the preachings and writings of Sts. Jerome, Ambrose, Basil, Martin of Tours, Chrisostom, Hyppolitus and a host of others. It was this monastic movement that was in the forefront of the de-paganization of the Empire, more so in the East as Constantinople had become the center of the Empire with Constantine.

The fourth and fifth centuries of the Christian era were marked by tragic events in both the Western and Eastern Empires. While emperors in Constantinople held precarious control over their people, in the West the last of the emperors, the young boy Romulus Augustulus was forced to hand over his crown to Odovacar the Barbarian in 476. Then the Vandals took over North Africa and that church became Arian; the Arian Visigoths took Spain but within a century they became Catholic; Arian Burgundians gradually embraced Catholicism; Clovis, the chief of the Franks, was made Catholic by his nagging wife Clotilda; and the Arian Ostrogoths held sway in central Italy. The important thing for us to consider here is that church life, including rituals and ceremonies followed the contours of local cultures rather than governed by centrally established formulae. Even when an indigenous monastic movement was initiated in Celtic lands by Sts. Columba and Columban, both Irishmen, they did not follow either the pattern of the Byzantine monastic orders or the rules of St. Benedict already in effect in Monte Casino and other Benedictine houses in Italy; rather, they followed a pattern uniquely Celtic.

It was also in the fifth and sixth centuries that the basic curriculum for education was established by Boethius. By adding to the curriculum containing grammar, rhetoric and logic (the Trivium-inherited from the ancients) four more disciplines (arithmetic, music, geometry and astronomy: the quadrivium), Boethius not only established a fuller curriculum for contemporary schools but also foreshadowed the syllabi of medieval universities, the first of which, the University of Paris, was formally chartered only in 1210, 714 years after his death.[9] He also translated Aristotle's *Categories* together with Porphyry's introduction starting a trend of introducing classical learning into Christian culture that gained momentum only in the mid 1300s with the first generation

---

[9] William R. Cannon, *History of Christianity in the Middle Ages* (New York, Abington Press, 1960), 21.

Renaissance Humanists, Dante, Petrarch and Boccacio.

Boethius' friend and fellow courtier at the court of the Barbarian King Theodoric, Cassiodorus, wrote the History of the Goths and several theological treatises and, after becoming a Benedictine monk, established a syllabus of studies for the monks based on the seven arts of antiquity.[10]

Gregory of Tours wrote the History of the Franks and liturgical manuals in crude Latin, in contrast to his more erudite contemporaries, Boethius and Cassiodorus, but his contribution was, in a sense, more significant as he incorporated local legends (about miracles), customs and values into the religious life of fellow Franks.[11]

In the sixth century the universal church was divided into five Patriarchies —Rome, Constantinople, Alexandria, Antioch and Jerusalem—each following its own established customs in worship, ecclesiastical administration and church law, even allowing a good measure of flexibility in these matters to provincial churches within these Patriarchies. Even though the promulgation of the Code of Justinian took place in 529, which included also laws governing church life and rituals, they never came into effect in the West and in the East they were enforced with plenty of margin for local customs. In other words, nowhere in the Christian world, local customs and tastes were rejected in favor of uniformity in the church universe.

At the death of Justinian, the Byzantine Emperor, in 565, the East slowly descended into a state of dissention, decay and destitution. The West, leaderless after the deposition of Romulus Augustulus in 476, had been divided into several kingdoms by the occupying Barbarian tribes, most of them non-Christians. It was Gregory I (The Great) who initiated the movement to convert these barbarian nations to Christianity. Elected by acclamation of the people of Rome to be Pope on February 7, 590, the same day Pope Pelagius II died, and consecrated against his will (he had run away but the people found him in his hiding place, dragged him to Rome and crowned him Pope) on September 3, 590, Gregory sent his first missionary, Augustine, in 596, to convert the Anglo-Saxons in Britain. With the baptism of Ethelbert, the ruler of the Jutes, Augustine started the conversion of the people of Britain. The Anglo-Saxon monk Willibrod became the apostle to the Netherlands and his friend Winifred (nicknamed Boniface, doer of good) became the apostle of Germany.[12]

---

[10] Ibid., 21-22.
[11] Ibid., 21, 30.
[12] Schmidlin, 126-180.

It did not take much more than two centuries from Boniface's apostolate in southern Germany, the torch was carried to the north by Saint Asgar, nicknamed the "Boniface of the North," and further north into Scandinavia by new generations of missionaries like Bishop Ebbo of Reims, to Denmark; Archbishop Unni of Hamburg, to Sweden; by King Haakon the Good himself, to Norway (himself having been converted to Christianity in England); by Olaf Tryggvason, to Iceland; and by Leif the Happy, to Greenland and Vinland. Leif's activities were in the concluding years of the first millennium of the Christian era (1000).[13]

Christianity was introduced into the Eastern European regions about the same time as in Western Europe, but from the Byzantine Empire. The Serbs were the first to accept Christianity in connection with an alliance agreed upon between them and Emperor Heraclius in 630. The Croations were converted as their prince Porga was influenced by Roman missionaries around 680. The Bulgarians accepted Christianity in 864 as their prince Boris was converted through the influence of his sister who had been a prisoner in Constantinople. However, Bulgaria became the first battleground between Byzantine and Latin Missionaries as Boris (who assumed the Christian name of Michael) became unhappy with Constantinople and invited missionaries from the West. Pope Nicholas I obliged him and sent missionaries in 867. In the end, though, Bulgaria went back to Byzantium.[14]

Moravia, too became a battleground between Byzantium and Rome. The Moravian prince Radislav who shifted his alliance between Latin King Louis the German and Emperor Michael III of Byzantium finally settled with the East. Emperor Michael sent the two brothers Cyril and Methodius to Moravia. These two brothers introduced Slav language into the liturgy and translated the Bible into the vernacular, having invented a new alphabet for this purpose. This infuriated the Latin missionaries who complained to Rome. Pope Nicholas I summoned them to Rome in 867. Methodius returned to Moravia with papal approval for his work and blessing for himself. Subsequently he went back to Rome and was consecrated bishop by the Pope. Back in Moravia, he was hauled to ecclesiastical court by the Latin Archbishop of Salzburg and was threatened with physical punishment. Again called back to Rome, he was exonerated by Pope John VIII and sent back to Moravia, and spent the rest of his years without aggravation from his Latin rivals. Both

---

[13] Cannon, 90-91.
[14] Schmidlin, 157-172.

brothers, Cyril and Methodius, are now in the roster of Saints of the Catholic Church. But the persecution of those two brothers by their Latin rivals in the 9th century gives us a foretaste of the troubles Matteo Ricci and Robert de Nobili had to endure in the 18th century at the hands of their own Latin brothers from different religious orders.[15, 16]

Christianity spread into the land of the Czechs or Bohemia from Moravia and was helped along by the German population there and the intervention of German Kings Louis the German in 845 and Otto the Great in 943. Prague became a Christian city and the seat of an archbishopric.

From Bohemia, Christianity was introduced into Poland. Duke Mieceslav (Misika) became a Christian in 966 due to the influence of his wife Dobrawa, the daughter of Bolslav I, King of Bohemia and at the urging of Otto I of Germany. Benedictine and Camaldulensian monks from Germany converted the population and established a well-organized church by year 1000.[17]

Christianity was introduced into Russia by the efforts of Greek Patriarchs Photius and Ignatius in the early part of 900. By 945 there existed a large Christian community in Kiev under Grand Duke Igor. Igor's widow, Olga, was baptized by the Patriarch in Constantinople in 955 and was given the Christian name of Helena. She made a valiant effort to Christianize all Russians, with the support of Otto I of Germany but with no great success. Her grandson Vladimir married Greek princess Anna and was baptized in 988. His enthusiasm for Christianizing his people earned him the title the Apostolic. His successor Yaroslav I continued his work and by the early part of 1000, old Russia was pretty much Christian with an established ecclesiastical organization.[18]

The Magyars, originally of Mongolian or Tartar origin, occupied Hungary towards the end of the 9th century after having killed or driven out the Slavic Christian settlers there. Towards the middle of the 10th century, Christian Germans entered Hungary as colonists or conquerors. Two Magyar princes, Bulosudes (Bulcsu) and Gylas (Gyula) were baptized by Patriarch Theophylactus. The patriarch also sent Hierotheus as their bishop. Gylas' daughter, Sarolta, influenced her husband, Duke Geisa (Giza) to become Christian in 972. Geisa requested Otto II of

---

[15] Ibid., 190-215.
[16] Cannon, 118-119.
[17] Schmidlin, 190-215.
[18] Ibid.

Germany to send missionaries. Bishop Adalbert of Prague also sent missionaries. Geisa's son Stephen (St. Stephen, 997-1038) requested the hand of Gisela, Henry II's sister, which request was granted on condition that he would Christianize the whole country. That he did and established the church in Hungary with ten bishoprics under the Archdiocese of Gran.[19]

The Baltic lands of Livonia, Estonia, Courland, Prussia, Finland and Lithuania were the very last European territories to become Christian. Missionary activities, military expeditions and marriage alliances from Germany, Poland and Sweden were instrumental in converting these Baltic peoples between late 1100 and early 1400.[20]

Spread of Christianity to the Orient had a very different history. China, the heavenly empire, kept all outsiders out by an ideological barrier of imagined superiority over the rest of the human race and the physical barrier of the Great Wall. It was during the brief period of openness provided by the benevolent T'ang Dynasty Christianity, along with a host of other religions such as Judaism, Islam, Zoroastrianism and Buddhism entered in the "Heavenly Empire." Nestorian missionaries from the Middle East established themselves in Changan, with a substantial church and many converts in 781, but within a short time they were wiped out during the religious persecutions between 841 and 845. The next opening for Christianity occurred when China fell to the Mongols and Kublai Khan became the emperor in 1260. A few years later, he requested Pope Nicholas IV to send 100 scholars / priests. The Franciscan John of Monte Corvino whom the Pope sent, in 1294 was successful in converting many Chinese, thus establishing a large Christian community in Beijing. In 1303 John received Papal appointment as Archbishop of Khanbuluc (Peking) and Patriarch of the entire orient with seven Franciscan bishops. Christianity flourished in China all through the Mongol rule but when the Mongols were driven out in 1368 the new Ming rulers of China suppressed all foreign religions, including Christianity.[21, 22]

In the Western Mongol Empire, stretching from the borders of china westward all the way to the borders of Europe, Christianity was welcomed also in 1260, with the conversion of Il-Khan Hulagu (Jalue)

---

[19] Ibid.
[20] Ibid.
[21] Ibid., 317-338
[22] John K. Fairbank, Edwin O. Reischauer, Albert M. Craig, *East Asia: Tradition and Transformation* (Boston: Houghton Mifflin, 1973), 111-115.

the Mongol Emperor. At the request of Hulagu's son and successor, Abaka, Pope Nicholas III sent Franciscan missionaries who baptized many and established a vibrant church. But with the ascension of a new line of Il-Khans, starting with Ghazan, in 1295, the Persian church fell into hard times. Christians were forcibly converted to Islam and their churches were turned into mosques.

Christianity was more than likely introduced in India by St. Thomas the Apostle. There are two living traditions attributing Thomas' entry point into India at two different regions separated by several thousand miles. The first is that Thomas came through central Asia, evangelizing Persia, converting king Gundaphorus of Bactria, the Greek Kingdom, a remnant of Alexander the Great's invasion of India in the 4th century B.C. The second places Thomas traveling by sea to Cranganor, the ancient seaport on the Malabar coast in South India, converting the local Chola King and the Brahmin Hindu priests by force of many miracles, establishing seven churches, some of them converted Hindu temples, then moving on along the east coast towards today's Madras, where he was martyred and buried. This second tradition seems to have more validity as living legend is supported by physical remnants of the churches Thomas supposed to have built in Malabar and his tomb in Madras, though they have not been verified scientifically.[23]

I have sketched the evangelizing activities of the church from Apostolic times to the end of early the middle ages to demonstrate one point. That is the first Apostles and the missionaries of subsequent centuries had a singular focus which was to convey the true and authentic message of the Gospels to the nations they addressed and to insure that those who accepted the faith followed its basic tenets in their ways of living and their ways of worship. The only things they objected to were sinfulness in life and superstitions in worship, an example of which was the Frisian worship of the old oak tree which St. Boniface miraculously split in four pieces. Outside of these there seems to have been no rules or restrictions imposed on the way the new converts lived their religion, that is their liturgical services, including eucharistic celebration, administration of sacraments and personal devotional practices. There were no rubrics and no special liturgical language.

It was Charlemagne, crowned Holy Roman Emperor by Pope Leo III on Christmas day in 800 A.D. who for the first time decreed uniform rules concerning, liturgy, lifestyle of the clergy, and church

---

[23] Schmidlin, 288-307.

administration.[24, 25, 26]

The establishment of the Holy Roman Empire in the West as a dependant of the papacy and the separation of Eastern Christendom and the Patriarchate of Constantinople from the West as a result of the Great Schism in 1054 led to an increase in the power and prestige of the papacy. The destruction of the Byzantine Empire by the Ottoman Muslims in 1453 and the diminished existence of the Eastern Church allowed Rome virtual dominance over the entire Christian World. The Romanization or Latinization of local churches, including Oriental churches that remained in obedience to Rome, became inevitable. As a corollary, a stern attitude also developed towards the new converts in the mission fields, against their adoptation of indigenous cultural norms in their liturgical and devotional practices.

Despite this pronounced retrenchment of the church from local cultures as a result of the Carolignian era consolidation of power by the Roman Church, the Carolignian Renaissance itself, especially the introduction of parochial and cathedral schools, had a very positive impact. The cathedral schools were the spawning grounds for the great medieval universities and the parochial schools provided them prospective students. Even though these universities did not have any direct impact on the church's inculturation with native cultures in the mission fields, their openness to include in their curriculum works of pre-Christian pagan and even medieval Islamic scholars, in the ivory tower situation of the academia though it was, still affected the outlook of the church toward non-Christian scholarship and cultures. The study of Aristotle, Plato, Cicero, Tacitus, as well as Al Ghazali, Avicenna, and Averroes in the Academy did have a spill over impact on the every day European world outside.

It was this spill over effect and the powerful impression that the economically prosperous and scientifically advanced Islamic world left on the psyche of the European elite when they encountered each other in the Middle East during the Crusades that brought about a drastic change in the European attitude towards economics, social structure, politics, religion and world view. European nobles who had never been outside their manors or small towns were dazzled by the world beyond Europe

---

[24] L. Duchene, *Christian Worship: Its Origin and Evolution*, M.L. McClure, trans., (1919), 403.
[25] E.Baluze, *Capitularia Regum Fancorum Ab Anno 742 Ad Annum 922*, I.P. 503, 779.
[26] *Acta Sanctorum Bollandina*, Antwerp and Brussels, 1643-1931, Vol. I, 416.

and they wanted to explore and exploit that world. The great discoveries of Columbus and Vasco da Gama followed. Europeans reached out eastward and westward. The discoveries of the New World and the sea route to the Orient were accompanied by equally dramatic and revolutionary discoveries of the correct orbital revolutions of the planets in the solar system and the discovery or rediscovery of Europe's classical heritage. Together these discoveries and the Renaissance movement turned the medieval Christian world view upside down and sent Western Christian value system into a tailspin. Popes and prelates became promoters of pagan classical learning, collectors of ancient artifacts, makers of world maps (Pope Pius II, a pioneer mapmaker whose map of the world made Columbus end up in the wrong continent), and patrons of banks, once considered worthy of only Jews and devils. It was a time of discoveries, great openness and great creativity. Philosophers such as Pico Della Mirandola argued for eclectic learning, including the languages, religions and philosophies of the Orient—India, China—and the Islamic world. While Rome, the center of the Christian world, was experiencing the greatest creativity in arts and letters, ironically enough, the church's leadership in Rome seemingly lost its moral compass. The result was, of course, the breakup of the church with the Protestant Reformation.

Shocked by the violent breakup of the church and chastised by its own internal critics, the Christian Humanists, the Roman church began to reform itself through what we know as the Catholic or Counter Reformation. With the Counter Reformation, the greatest wave of missionary activity, since Gregory the Great's time in the late 6th century was initiated. The pioneers were the Jesuits, although the older orders of the Franciscans and Dominicans also followed suit. These missionaries became partners with the Portuguese explorers and traders in the East and their counterparts, the Spaniards, in the Western hemisphere. Both had great successes. St. Francis Xavier's success in India and Japan are legendary and, though less dramatic, equally effective were the Spanish missionaries in the New World. However, these Counter Reformation missionary efforts did not reflect the openness to other cultures that was characteristic of the European Renaissance or that of the medieval missionaries. Rather, they were reflective of the centralized Latin domination of the Carolignian era. More than that, they were driven by a mistrust of the Renaissance worldview, disaffection for the art and literature of the Renaissance and fear for the Devotio Moderna and the anti-institutionalism of the Christian Humanists.

The next generation of Jesuits were of a different ilk, however.

Much more exposed to non-Western and non-Christian religions and cultures, these second generation Jesuits approached them with respect, openness and compassion. The works of Matteo Ricci in China and Robert de Nobili in India, which we have already discussed, and the works of Spanish Jesuits in Paraguay setting up the so called "Christian Republic" and the "Reductions" for the Native Indians were classic examples of this noble and generous approach. But alas, the works of these noble souls were thwarted by other religious orders who set themselves up as rivals of Jesuits, in the guise of protecting the orthodoxy of the church, by selfish Spanish colonists who could not enslave the Indians anymore, by absolutist monarchs worrying about the growing power of the Jesuits and finally by weak and thoughtless popes. Eventually the Jesuit order itself was suppressed. Ironically, the only monarchs who extended welcome to the disbanded Jesuits, the master educators and missionaries of the time, were Frederick II The Great of Prussia and Catherine The Great of Russia, neither of whom had any interest in religion but valued the services of the Jesuits as educators.

The late 18th century witnessed the flowering of the Enlightenment movement with its noble ideals of liberty, equality and fraternity. Coming in direct conflict with the absolutist regimes, these ideas burst out into the American and French revolutions. In Europe the French Revolution was followed by the Napoleonic era and that was followed by the Metternichan era of conservative reaction. Culturally, the political conservatism was accompanied by the Romanticist movements in literature, music, theatre and the arts. Religion and emotion became fashionable again and along with this came the birth of the evangelical movement in England and, its parallel, the Great Awakening in America. Associated with these were also the Utilitarian movement headed by Jeremy Bentham and James and John Stuart Mills. These religious and political ideals jelling together spawned the outwardly moral precept of the "White Man's Burden." It is true, that inspired by the utilitarian ideals, the British Parliament enacted political reforms in Britain's colonies. The colonial peoples were allowed limited participation in their governments. This was not meaningful or significant, but still a small step forward.

However, the overall impact of the evangelical movement and the "White Man's Burden" concept was extremely destructive. Under pressure from the Evangelicals, Britain and Holland, who up until 1813 had not permitted missionaries to enter their colonies and interfere in their commercial enterprises, finally gave in. Driven by the conviction that they had the mandate to save the souls of the brown, black and yellow races of Asia and Africa, hosts of missionaries of all denominations descended on every colony and every "sphere of influence" of European powers. Using every tactic possible, tasteful and distasteful, ethical and unethical, these pseudo-apostles effected the so-called "conversion" of masses of people, mostly from the lower classes, in many parts of the non-Western world. The reaction of the people in these lands with long histories and highly advanced cultures was predictable and swift. In China, it manifested in the Taiping Rebellion and in the Nien and Moslem Rebellions.[27] Hung Hsiu-chüan, the leader of the Taiping Rebellion, fancied himself to be the younger brother of Jesus Christ, preached his own Gospel message, emphasizing many noble principles, including equality of all races, equal rights to women, just distribution of wealth, and the like, thus becoming extremely popular with the masses. Critical of the Western missionaries and colonial powers and the Manchu government, he posed a serious threat to both. The years of combined efforts of the Western powers and the Chinese government to suppress the Taiping followers in practically all provinces of China caused the destruction of at least 20 million Chinese lives.

In India the tactics of the new missionaries disillusioned the Western educated Hindu elite of India, such as Ram Mohun Roy and Keshab Chander Sen. They had formed the progressive organization, the Brahmo Smaj, to institute reforms in Hindu society, for example, the abolishment of Sathi (widow burning) and caste system, which were inspired by Christian principles taught by revered early missionaries such as Robert de Nobili, the Jesuit, and William Carey, the Baptist. Similar reactions by native elites were manifested in the Dutch colony of Indonesia and in several European colonies in Africa. Certainly, these "White Man's Burden" missionaries did not serve the cause of Christianity, nor did they do any good to the native populations.

Unfortunately, a new wave of pseudo-missionaries are descending on many parts of the Third World today, creating worse havoc than the "White Man's Burden" missionaries ever did. Basically self-serving and affiliated to fringe churches or with no affiliation at all, they operate in the slums of many Third World countries, in South America, the Caribbean, Asia and Africa. Taking advantage of the desperation among the poor, caused by the negligence and inaction of mainline churches, both in spiritual and social welfare issues, these pseudo messengers of the

---

[27] Fairbank, Reischauer, Craig, 469-475.

Gospel attract the disadvantaged in the urban ghettos and villages through a variety of devices. Among the tactics they use are donations of food, clothing and money; denigration of local cultures, customs and religions; and threat of everlasting hell fire if their beneficiaries did not convert to their type of "Christianity." With no significant exposure to biblical or theological studies, these so-called missionaries are incapable of conveying to their converts the true message of the Gospel. Nor are they interested in it. Their main interest is to affect the largest number of "conversions" possible in order to maximize the material support from their sponsoring congregations back home, equally ignorant of the Gospel message as they are.

The crudeness of conversion efforts by the pseudo missionaries invites severe reactions from various local sources in many countries. First of all from wealthy land holders and industry magnates who stand to loose their cheap labor force because once the poor or low caste convert, they often break their ties with local employers who have been exploiting them for generations. For example, the recent waves of violence against missionaries in Northern India are in large part, initiated by disgruntled land owners. Leaders of local religions and cults who are enraged by the erosion of their followers are another source. Finally, political leaders who are always weary of disruptions in the social order that can impact their fortunes, especially those among them who are also members of fanatic religious groups who want to promote their own agendas.

As the mother church and other mainline Christian churches are experiencing the largest erosion of their membership since the massive desertion of European laborers to Communism in the second half of the 19th century, the leaders of these churches are busy resolving the problem of sexual abuse among their clergy and wrestling with modern issues of priestly celibacy, ordination of women and gay men, same sex marriage, abortion and birth control. The crises in the mission fields are largely neglected.

In order to remedy this situation, it is imperative of the dioceses to take on more responsibilities in the mission fields instead of delegating all the work to religious congregations. All seminaries should include substantive courses on world religions and multicultural issues. Seminaries that specialize in training personnel for the missions must take special care in imparting sufficient knowledge of the religions and cultures they are destined to encounter and adequate skills to treat them with respect, sympathy and understanding. Most importantly, all priests and missionaries, regardless of where they work, must be made to realize that their mandate is to proclaim the good news of the Gospel to all nations, not to persuade them, through ways of the world, to become Christians.

As Christian missionary activities have become not just a religious, but also a social and political issue in many parts of the world, the Academy should have a legitimate interest in them as well. Instead of merely discussing the philosophy, theology and history of world religions, the courses in religious studies should engage students in the discussion of contemporary developments in world religions including the rising tides of fundamentalisms and the nature and impact of Christian missionary activities around the world. As a disinterested party, only the Academy will have the credibility to bring such issues for open discussion in the public forum.

I believe that through such open discussions, the mother church, the mainline churches and the academy, together, can bring about a new era of proclaiming the good news of the Gospel to the nations of the world, an era reminiscent of the time of Robert de Nobili and Matteo Ricci.

CHRIST AND CULTURE: THREE MODELS OF INCULTURATION — RICHARD NIEBUHR, EUGENE HILLMAN, AND PAUL TILLICH

Michael S. Casey*

God created a world full of little worlds.
Yiddish Folk Saying

In *Christ and Culture*, published in 1951, H. Richard Niebuhr develops a "typology" with which to categorize certain theological thought into one of five groupings. Niebuhr then uses his categorization to reach a more thorough understanding of the relationship between, on the one hand, Christ (as defined by Niebuhr), and, on the other, civilization or more specifically, various cultures recognized by Niebuhr.

Niebuhr's types include "Christ against Culture," "The Christ of Culture," "Christ above Culture," "Christ and Culture in Paradox," and "Christ the Transformer of Culture."[1] Niebuhr acknowledges that not every theological, philosophical, social, or political approach may fit one of these categories perfectly, and that occasionally a position may actually fit into more than a single type. Unfortunately, he then proceeds to use a "shoehorn" to fit his examples more or less snugly into his typology. Given the total control Niebuhr had over choosing his historical examples, this turns out to look surprisingly difficult.

While Niebuhr's typology is fairly straightforward, the key to its applicability lies in the underlying definitions of "Christ" and "culture" which Niebuhr makes operative for his study. If one changes any of Niebuhr's definitions, the utility of the typology is altered proportionately. In other words, the farther one strays from "mainstream" Judeo-Christian

---

* Michael S. Casey is an associate professor at Graceland University in Iowa, where he teaches the Humanities and History. He previously taught at the Naval War College and holds a Ph.D. from Salve Regina University. He wrote *America's Technological Sailor: A Retrospective on a Century of "Progress" in the United States Navy* (1998) and co-authored, with his spouse, *Teaching the Korean War: An Instructor's Handbook* (2003).
[1] H. Richard Niebuhr, *Christ and Culture* (New York: Harper, 1951), 11-39.

thought, tradition, and culture, the less applicable becomes Niebuhr's typology. When discussing a society in which there is no Christ, only God, and in which culture, if defined at all, does not necessarily fit seamlessly into Niebuhr's definition, one must use this typology with a high degree of caution. That said, whether or not one agrees totally with Niebuhr's system, his typology provides a useful methodology for analyzing and discussing works of other authors. Such is the objective of this paper, but it strives to go deeper, as well, by further comparing and contrasting to Niebuhr two noteworthy Christian scholars.

By way of background, Christian approaches to native cultures tend to fall along a broad spectrum of possible relationships. While we cannot see either end of the spectrum, the visible portion runs from total, albeit unintended, destruction of native religion on one side to complete acceptance of native religion as an equal on the other. Significant Christian theologians fall at various points along this spectrum though historically, Christian missionary activity has, in practice if not theory, leaned more toward the former rather than the latter. As a tool, Niebuhr's typology could become our "yardstick" with which to pinpoint the spot along that spectrum at which one or another view would lie.

The two Christian authors under discussion at the moment are, relatively speaking, far apart on this theoretical framework. For philosophical purposes, the dialectic this creates allows us to better explore and comprehend the differences between the two writers, while the commonalities tend to be overlooked or go unspoken. In a sense, then, to approach the issue with Niebuhr as a yardstick turns our exploration into a conflict. If we can have only two points on a line, and only a yardstick as a tool, we can only measure how far apart those points lie from each other.

If Niebuhr's theory is seen as a lens, however, and his typology becomes a microscope, use of this new tool offers promising insights. Thus, despite the appearance of confrontation between our two authors, the prime objective here is to better comprehend both, not to necessarily refute one or the other. With Niebuhr's typology as an optical instrument, the picture of Christianity's essential relationship to native cultures comes into sharper focus.

The first author is Father Eugene Hillman. Hillman is the author of a series of theological studies that relate to the same general question: what should be the relationship between Christianity and other, "alien" religions? Within Niebuhr's typology, Hillman's writings, on the surface at least, fit rather well into the second category, The Christ of Culture.

Hillman sees no basic tension between Christ (God) and culture, wherever that culture is found and no matter how much it appears to differ from Western Christian culture.

In Hillman's view, Christ is accepting of all cultures, or more specifically, of all peoples whatever their culture. To use Hillman's analogy of language, Christ is multi-lingual. He can speak to a people through whatever language (and religion) they have; the basic message of spirituality is unchanged. As Hillman put it in "Cross-cultural Ministry in Crisis":

> God's word comes to a people where they are historically and culturally: not where they are not. Nor does it come to a people through a process of substituting for their traditional ways of being human and religious the ways of some other ethnic group with an entirely alien culture and history. If God speaks to people in their own situations, and in their terms, then also he allows them to respond through the relevant communication systems available to them... God can and does converse with all peoples through their respective religious symbol systems, historically conditioned, socially constructed and culturally colored as they are.[2]

Before continuing, it bears noting that Niebuhr's typology was designed primarily to consider the relationship between Christ and Christian culture, not the "alien" cultures about which Hillman speaks. With that in mind, one could just as easily say that Hillman's works fit into the "Christ above Culture" or even the "Christ against Culture" types depending on exactly what kind of "spin" one wanted to attach to Hillman's writing. If cultures and their respective religions are more or less relative, and thus God will in effect "sort everyone out in the end," then Christ is above culture; there is an inherent duality of the "God of a thousand faces" who interacts with men daily through their cultures and the "One Supreme Being," who does not take an "active" role until approached on his throne on Judgment Day.

This is very similar to what is found in the Koran regarding the relationship between Islam (as both religion and culture simultaneously)

---

[2] Eugene Hillman, "Cross-cultural Ministry in Crisis," in *Religious Life Review*, Vol. 30 No 149 (July-August 1991): 62-63.

and all other religions and cultures:

> For every nation We have ordained a ritual which they
> observe. Let them not dispute with you concerning this.
> Call them to the path of your Lord: you are rightly
> guided. If they argue with you, say: 'Allah knows best
> all that you do. On the Day of Resurrection He will
> judge all your disputes.'[3]

If, on the other hand, by Christ we mean Christianity and, further, we knowingly accept Hillman's underlying assumptions, then attempting to "convert the heathens" is clearly a case of Christ against (native) culture. Both of these perspectives are supportable positions to varying degrees, but the "Christ of Culture" approach is the position of greatest merit and utility for the current discussion.

Hillman's basic premise is that religion, like language, is a cultural construct, not a single (Christian) way of life created and directed by God. Thus Christ, or God by any and every other name, is as integral to culture as is "humanly" possible. The role of divine intervention is inherently minimized and the historico-cultural aspects of a people are strongly emphasized in Hillman's approach to religion, as he explained in *Many Paths*.

> Religions, like languages, are cultural inventions; they
> are human-made and handed on from generation to generation. As products of human creativity, religious
> forms, structures, rites and beliefs are variously modified
> as they are appropriated and reassessed by subsequent
> generations borrowing continuously and sometimes extensively from both the creativity of their own respective
> generations and from the genius of other peoples. Human beings become religious in a manner similar to their
> achieving fluency in a language... For most people the
> religions they follow, like the languages they call their
> own, are determined for them by their place of birth and
> by obscure political events in the remote historical past
> of their progenitors.[4]

---

[3] *The Koran*, N.J. Dawood, trans. (New York: Penguin Books, 1968), 395-6.
[4] Eugene Hillman, *Many Paths: A Catholic Approach to Religious Pluralism*

Combined with his operative definition of religion, Hillman subsequently defines culture as "everything created by human beings and handed on from generation to generation...all learned behaviors."[5] This is essentially identical to Peter Berger's definition from *The Sacred Canopy*: "Culture consists of the totality of man's products."[6]

Hillman's definition of culture also appears to fit quite well with Niebuhr's more lengthy definition and discussion of culture as "the artificial, secondary environment which man superimposes on the natural." Niebuhr quickly adds that culture "comprises language, habits, ideas, beliefs, customs, social organization, inherited artifacts, technical processes, and values."[7]

Niebuhr further identifies several significant aspects of culture that include its social nature, its basis in human achievement, and its total immersion in the world of values. Niebuhr goes on to discuss the pluralism inherent in cultural values. For Niebuhr, the pluralism he saw involved the various dichotomies present in a specific culture, dichotomies between male and female, young and old, or rulers and ruled.[8] This differs significantly from the pluralism about which Fr. Hillman speaks in "Authentic Spirituality," a pluralism centered on the inherent differences between one culture and another.

> Like religion or ethics, language, law or aesthetics, therefore, spirituality is a cultural creation, humanly constructed and historically conditioned, hence ephemeral. Since cultures are, like God's creation, gloriously pluriform and perennially changing, spirituality is also unavoidably multiform. Its humanly prescribed forms are all transitory, relative and dispensable.[9]

Significantly, Niebuhr leaves the door open to later value judgments of specific religions by including the requirement that cultural values be "good for man."[10] This runs counter to Hillman's position in

---

(Maryknoll, NY: Orbis Books, 1989), 5.
[5] Ibid., 4-5.
[6] Peter L. Berger, *The Sacred Canopy* (New York: Doubleday, 1990), 6.
[7] Niebuhr, 32.
[8] Ibid., 38.
[9] Eugene Hillman, "Authentic Spirituality," in *New Blackfriars*, Vol. 72 No 846, (February 1991): 200.
[10] Niebuhr, 35.

"Pluriformity in Ethics" that judgment is more or less impossible since there is no pre-ordained "moral high-ground" from which to judge.

> If all morality is culturally formed and historically conditioned, always and only in the terms of some concrete society, then no particular ethical system stands, in some kind of abstract Platonic objectivity, over and above all human behavior. For this behavior, and therefore all morality, is real only where men actually live, in the diversity of their particular historico-cultural experiences.[11]

Niebuhr's discussion of culture certainly stressed its social aspects, culture being "inextricably bound up with man's life in society; it is always social."[12] Given that, one could logically expect that he and Hillman would arrive intellectually at the same position. They have not, however, because Niebuhr adds some "small print" that reverses the meaning of his original statement: "The culture with which we are concerned cannot be simply that of a particular society," he says, "such as the Graeco-Roman, the medieval, or the modern Western."[13] Niebuhr never explains how culture can be social and yet does not apply to the society in which one lives, which is where the values and beliefs are to be found, as Hillman correctly points out. Thus Niebuhr significantly weakens his overall argument, at least relative to Hillman's position.

The second author to be considered using Niebuhr's typology is Paul Tillich, author of *Theology of Culture* from 1959. Tillich's work, at least in this particular instance, falls squarely in the "Christ against Culture" type. For Tillich there can be no accommodation or compromise. Each so-called Christian is forced to choose; will it be Christ or will it be culture?

> The question implied in this chapter is not: What is the Christian message? Rather it is: How shall the message (which is presupposed) be focused for the people of our time?...We are asking: How do we make the message

---

[11] Eugene Hillman, "Pluriformity in Ethics: A Modern Missionary Problem," in *Irish Theological Quarterly*, Vol. XL No 3 (July 1973): 272.
[12] Niebuhr, 32.
[13] Ibid., 30.

heard and seen, and then either rejected or accepted?...
To communicate the Gospel means putting it before the
people so they are able to decide for or against it. The
Christian Gospel is a matter of decision. It is to be accepted or rejected.[14]

Based on this quotation, Tillich's approach looks straightforward, but it has a few hidden twists and turns. Almost simultaneously,
Tillich outwardly appears to approach Hillman by clearly acknowledging
the importance of cultural context with regard to religion, and he does so
in largely the same terms Hillman uses.

The first thing we must do is to communicate the Gospel
as a message of man understanding his own predicament....We can speak to people only if we participate in
their concern, not by condescension, but by sharing in
it.[15]

Additionally, both Tillich[16] and Hillman[17] devote attention to the
meanings of signs and symbols, another apparent similarity between the
two. Both would likely agree with Mircea Eliade who, in *Images and
Symbols*, argues persuasively that symbols "...are part and parcel of the
human being, and it is impossible that they should not be found again in
any and every existential situation of man in the Cosmos."[18]

In both of these above cases, however, there are critical differences between what Tillich and Hillman expect from their consideration
of cultural context and symbolism. For Hillman, understanding these religious symbols (both Christian symbols and others) would be the end or
goal, hard-earned insight, into the human condition, in effect a dialogue
between "fellow travelers." Ian Barbour would call this same phenomenon "Pluralistic Dialogue," the middle ground between absolutism and
relativism, recognition that God is present in the faith and lives of people

---

[14] Paul Tillich, *Theology of Culture* (New York: Oxford University Press, 1959),
201.
[15] Ibid., 203.
[16] Ibid., 53-67.
[17] Hillman, *Many Paths*, 9-12.
[18] Mircea Eliade, *Images and Symbols: Studies in Religious Symbolism*, Philip
Mairet, trans., (New York: Sheed and Ward, 1969), 25.

of other traditions.[19] To borrow from Eliade's work again:

> ....the West is now compelled to accept a dialogue with
> the other, the 'exotic' or 'primitive' cultures. It would be
> regrettable indeed if we entered upon this without having
> learnt anything from all the revelations vouchsafed to us
> by the study of symbolisms.[20]

The understanding of a people's culture through their symbols, however, is not Tillich's end; it is only his means. He intends to use that understanding to tailor his Gospel "sales pitch" to make it more effective. Thus, in many respects, Tillich's approach embodies the historically ubiquitous "Colonial Model" of the Christian mission that Hillman correctly looks on with suspicion in *Toward an African Christianity.*[21]

As an aside, the legal scholar Stephen L. Carter argues in *The Culture of Disbelief* that American law and politics trivialize the Christian religion in our culture.[22] If true, and Carter makes a very persuasive and compelling argument, it still pales by comparison to Tillich's interpretation of native religions. Taken in that light, Tillich's approach seems arrogant and potentially devastating to native cultures. One, albeit unfavorable, critical interpretation of Tillich, in everyday language, is this:

> Every culture and religion but mine has it wrong. More-
> over, those primitive people out there are so misguided
> that their lives consist of asking the wrong questions en-
> tirely, questions to which Christianity does not provide
> the answers. The solution is to educate these primitives
> until they are conditioned to ask the questions for which
> Christianity does have the answers. That will solve their
> problems and make my One True God happy, to boot.

While it was never Niebuhr's specific purpose to categorize the several possible relationships between Christ and native cultures, his method nonetheless serves as a ready-made tool for performing that task.

---

[19] Ian G. Barbour, *Religion in an Age of Science* (New York: Harper and Row, 1990).
[20] Eliade, 175.
[21] Eugene Hillman, *Toward an African Christianity: Inculturation Applied* (New York: Paulist Press, 1993), 7.
[22] Stephen L. Carter, *The Culture of Disbelief* (New York: Basic Books, 1993).

Today, we live in a world that is infinitely more culturally "sensitive" than it was when Niebuhr did his writing. Tension between and among Christianity and native cultures around the globe is now more prevalent, and more potentially destructive or beneficial, than ever before.

Our technologies, primarily modern communications and transportation, make it inevitable that our cultures and religions will abut with increasing frequency. Further examples of how these interactions might play out can be found in the historical studies conducted by Andrew Walls.[23] Moreover, given the culturo-religious aspects of the ongoing "War on Terror" and, especially, the underlying motives of that conflict, the goals of religious inculturation or, at least religious accommodation, become imperatives.

Up to this point, this exploration of the opportunities and pitfalls of inculturation has been purely intellectual in nature. From the perspective of a native religion, unfortunately, this is not simply an academic or philosophical matter of "Christ against Culture," their culture. Instead, it is, arguably, a fight to the death! As Bernard Lonergan pointed out in *Method in Theology*:

> In so far as one preaches the gospel as it has been developed within one's own culture, one is preaching not only the gospel but also one's own culture. In so far as one is preaching one's own culture, one is asking others not only to accept the gospel but also to renounce their own culture and accept one's own.[24]

Fortunately, having recognized the destructive tension of the traditional Christian approach to missionary activity, we are in a much better position to now apply our "lessons learned." Our progress in the 21st century need not be as culturally-destructive as were so many of our religious "advances" of the 16th through the 20th centuries. Many might agree that one of our main goals is to "save" souls, regardless of however foreign or unfamiliar their cultures may be to us. The trick, as Hillman so persuasively advocates, is to do so without erasing native culture and re-

---

[23] Andrew F. Walls, *The Cross-Cultural Process in Christian History: Studies in the Transmission and Appropriation of Faith* (Maryknoll, NY: Orbis Books, 2002).
[24] Bernard Lonergan, *Method in Theology* (New York: Herder and Herder, 1972), 362-363.

ligion in the process. This new model offers hope for the future and, moreover, that those with the expertise in a region are in the best position to apply such an enlightened strategy.

For an example of how this new strategy can be applied in the geographic region of Africa, consider Father Hillman's *Toward an African Christianity: Inculturation Applied*, published in 1993, which deals in detail with his long experience among the Maasai and other East African peoples.[25] David Bosch's discussion of "mission as inculturation," from *Transforming Mission: Paradigm Shifts in Theology of Mission*, while only an abbreviated treatment of the subject, also offers several key insights that show promise for further development, especially in Africa, by thoughtful missionaries.[26]

The desired relationship between Christianity and native cultures during the 21st century requires much additional thought. There are far more possible approaches than the few discussed here. An oft-ignored aspect of the 21st century is that Christianity will once again face stiff competition from global Islam for the hearts and minds of native peoples. Lamin Sanneh, based on his own first-hand experience in Africa, provides an exceptionally clear and concise analysis and discussion which ably frames this impending, if not already on-going, struggle between Christianity and Islam in his study, *Translating the Message: The Missionary Impact on Culture*.[27] While he believes that Christianity offers a compelling counterpoint to the attractions of Islam, the competition will go on for decades at least. The effect of such competition must be factored into any contemporary Christian missionary strategy that hopes to be effective.

Islam aside, while there may be, in some respects, a single "Christianity," there is certainly no one "native culture." We may quickly discover that our approaches as Christians, to have any hope of success, must be hand-tailored to each actual native people. Additionally, the discussion to this point has assumed that Christianity and native culture interact in a vacuum. In reality, this interaction takes place in shifting geo-political, social, and economic contexts that interact among them-

---

[25] Hillman, *African Christianity*, 1993.

[26] David Jacobus Bosch, *Transforming Mission: Paradigm Shifts in Theology of Mission*, American Society of Missiology Series, No. 16 (Maryknoll, NY: Orbis Books, 1991), 447-456.

[27] Lamin Sanneh, *Translating the Message: The Missionary Impact on Culture*, American Society of Missiology Series, No. 13 (Maryknoll, NY: Orbis Books, 1989).

selves, transmitting cultural "shockwaves" that routinely and problemati-
cally supersede theological considerations. How we *should* interact may
be up to us to determine, but how we *can* interact is often the prerogative
of the bureaucrat or the warlord, not the Christian missionary. How to be
most effective under this constraint, then, merits careful consideration.

In *Transforming Mission: Paradigm Shifts in Theology of Mission*, Bosch examines the evolutionary "revolutions" in thinking on the
Christian mission. The latest shift in perspective, though undoubtedly not
the final one, Bosch calls the "Ecumenical Missionary Paradigm," an
outgrowth of the post-modern era which is only in its initial, ill-defined
stages.[28] This paradigm is characterized not by a single, rigid definition
of mission, but rather a "separate but equal" arrangement that essentially
synthesizes the most prominent but previously incompatible earlier definitions of mission. The parallel definitions include "mission as evangelism," "mission as liberation," "mission as inculturation," and "mission as
witness to people of other living faiths."[29]

Allowing, indeed encouraging, a native people to translate Christ
culturally is clearly called for here. The validity and long-term viability
of letting a native people translate Christ into their culture on their own,
with some reinterpretation to be expected, already has a strong historical
precedent in Christian history. Philip Jenkins, in *The Next Christendom:
The Coming of Global Christianity*, carefully analyzed one of the first inculturation processes of Christ by soon-to-be Christians.

Specifically, Jenkins explores the process and outcome when
Mediterranean Christianity was brought to the woodland peoples of
northern Europe. The end result should come as no surprise, as Jenkins
notes, "European Christians reinterpreted the faith through their own
concepts of social and gender relations...."[30] He also acknowledges that,
"Christianity was profoundly changed by the move to the Northern forests." Given that it is the very same profoundly changed European Christian church to which we in the West belong today, it would be illogical to
argue that inculturation and incipient reinterpretation are inherently inappropriate or inapplicable in places like Africa today.[31]

Finally, and perhaps most significantly, the future relationship

---

[28] Bosch, 368.
[29] Ibid., 409, 432, 447, 474.
[30] Philip Jenkins. *The Next Christendom: The Coming of Global Cristianity*
(New York, NY: Oxford University Press, 2002), 6.
[31] Ibid., 6.

between Christianity and native cultures is not simply for Christians to decide. Native peoples will determine for themselves how they will approach Christ and Christians, at the same time we are trying to grapple with how to approach their cultures individually and collectively. If Christian missionaries of the 21st century attempt to force a single, rigid approach, however well intentioned, on these native peoples, they would be just as shortsighted as some of those missionaries who came before them.

PART I

Aspects of Christian Inculturation in Southern Europe, the Middle East and Africa

Edited by
David Stefancic
Saint Mary's College

ANGELS, SCROLLS, DEACONS AND ROLLS: THE EXULTET AND THE UNIQUE FUNCTION OF THE DEACON IN THE EASTER VIGIL SERVICE OF TENTH TO THIRTEENTH CENTURY SOUTHERN ITALY

Christopher F. Smith[*]

Around the millennial year 1000, Southern Italy was situated at the crossroads of many Byzantine trade routes. Thus, to a great degree, the culture of the region was influenced by the wide variety of people from the Byzantine Empire who would have passed through the area. In spite of, or more likely because of this great mix of individuals and cultures, Southern Italy produced the singular phenomenon of religious, material, and liturgical culture known as the Exultet Roll.

The Exultet Roll was used in the Easter Vigil Service of Southern Italy. One of the distinctive moments in this liturgical event is the lighting of an Easter Candle, which is carried by a deacon. The lighted Paschal candle symbolizes the resurrected Christ as the Light of the World as well as the Pillar of Fire, which went before the Israelites in the wilderness.[1] The blessing of the candle is wrought by a sung benediction known as the *Exultet*. A deacon sings this benediction. In southern Italy, the deacon himself actually blessed the candle. The text and music for the singing of the Exultet were placed upon the Exultet Roll, which was often illustrated with related illuminations. During the singing of the Exultet, the roll is unfurled vertically.

The rolls are an excellent example of a native culture's interaction with Byzantium, for the Byzantine church also used vertical rolls during its regular mass. However, Exultet Rolls are also culturally

---

[*] Christopher Smith is currently pursuing a Ph.D. in Liturgical Studies at The Catholic University of America in Washington, DC. He holds a Master of Music from Westminster Choir College, Princeton, NJ, and the Master of Divinity and Master of Sacred Theology degrees from Yale University. Prior to his theological studies he was engaged as a choral conductor, church musician and tenor soloist. Aside from his interest in the medieval deacon, he has an active interest in the use of the Easter Vigil Service by "Reformed" Protestant traditions in the United States.

[1] Marion J. Hatchett, *Commentary on the American Prayer Book* (San Francisco: Harper Collins, 1995), 244.

unique, for Southern Italy is the only place that utilized and produced rolls for the Easter Vigil Service with illuminations of the type that I shall discuss. Therefore, I discuss these rolls for two reasons. First, they are the result of a native culture's interaction with the larger world of Byzantine Christianity. Second, this interaction resulted in a unique cultural and liturgical expression that existed in Southern Italy and nowhere else: the Exultet Roll and its use by a deacon in the Southern Italian Easter Vigil Service.

In this paper I shall give a brief overview of these so-called Exultet Rolls, twenty-eight of which have survived.[2] I will then offer some possible reasons for their use by a deacon and his prominent role as the singer of the Exultet. Finally, I shall suggest reasons for the deacon's unique function as the one who actually blesses the Paschal Candle.

Exultet Rolls

A roll, properly called a *rotulus*, is the means by which thoughts were preserved prior to the advent of the bound book. An Exultet roll is unique among liturgical rolls, however, because its text is arranged upon a roll that is spread out vertically. Even more interesting is that the pictures on the majority of these rolls are inverted in relation to the text. Thus, if one were to read the text right side up, the pictures would be upside down! (See *Illumination 1*) When used, the Exultet Roll is unfurled upon an ambo or pulpit. Thus, those on the other side of the ambo will see the illustrations right side up. (See *Illumination 2*)

When inverted, the pictures are often placed significantly ahead of the text to which they refer. It has been traditionally thought that the reason for such placement of the pictures is so that as the roll is unfurled over an ambo, those in close proximity might view the pictures while the text to which they refer is being proclaimed. Thus, when placed over an ambo, the roll becomes a medieval music video of sorts, since the illuminations accompany the sung text of the Exultet! This reverse arrangement of the pictures is the best known feature of the Exultet Rolls and the one that captures the imagination of the person who wonders what it must have been like to have experienced such a ceremony during the time in question.[3]

---

[2] M. L. Wurfbain, "The Liturgical Rolls of South Italy and their Possible Origin." in *Essays Presented to G. I. Lieftinck, IV.* (Amsterdam: A. L. Van Gendt & Company, 1976), 9-15.

[3] Thomas Forrest Kelly, *The Exultet in Southern Italy* (Oxford: Oxford Univer-

As noted above, the moment during the Easter vigil in which the roll would be used is the singing of the Exultet. The Exultet is an ancient Easter hymn in which the resurrection of Christ and his triumph over darkness and death is proclaimed. The hymn is known to have been in existence at least as early as the fourth century. The hymn is divided into two parts; the prologue and the preface. The prologue calls for angelic choirs, the earth, and Mother Church to rejoice along with the great body of the people. The deacon then asks for God's mercy so that the candle might be praised. This is followed by a Trinitarian closing and an *Amen*.

The second part, or preface, sings the praises of Christ who has brought light to the night and has trampled sin.

The space above each line of the Exultet text contains musical notation. The notation guides the singing deacon. Thus, the roll itself contains words, pictures, and music. Among the rolls, there are iconographic similarities, but the majority of the rolls are unique stylistic examples. The diversity of styles, combined with thematic continuity, lends credence to the idea that the rolls were produced for distinguished individual owners such as Bishops or an institution such as a monastery. The final outstanding feature of these rolls is that they were produced and used exclusively in Southern Italy and nowhere else in the Western church.[4] Except for two rolls of Pisa, they do not exist outside of Campania and Apulia.[5] It is important to note that the Byzantine church also made use of vertical rolls for liturgical purposes. However, Byzantine rolls most often contain a specific liturgy such as that of St. Basil and normally contain the text to be said by the one celebrating mass. In contrast, Exultet Rolls are used by a deacon once a year during a specific

---

sity Press, 1996). Kelly suggests that the rolls were created for the pleasure of the bishop and that the bishop would be the one who would likely view the pictures since he would be close at hand during the proclamation of the Exultet. (see pp. 199-206) I agree with Kelly. Standing a mere twelve feet away from one representative roll, I found it difficult to discern its illuminations with much clarity. Thus, only someone fairly close at hand could benefit from these illuminations.

[4] Myrtilla Avery, *The Exultet Rolls of Southern Italy, vol. II: Plates* (Princeton: Princeton University Press, 1936), plate LXXXI and plates. XCVIII-CIII. All of the Exultet rolls, except two (Pisa 1 and 3) were manufactured in Southern Italy. These two non-southern rolls are preserved in the Museo San Mateo in Pisa. Pisa 1 dates from the eleventh century and Pisa 3 dates from the end of the thirteenth century. They come from central Italy and Lucca respectively.

[5] Wurfbain, 14.

moment in the Easter Vigil Service.

Miniatures / Pictures

The illuminations on the rolls portray a wide variety of subjects. Like most manuscripts of the time, they contain decorated initials. The two initials that are commonly seen are the *"E"* for *Exultet*, which begins the text, and a *"V"* for *Vere Dignum*, which begins the preface. If the initial E is not the first illuminated item, then it is often preceded by frontispiece illuminations such as *Christ Enthroned*, the *Lamb of God*, *Christ Crucified*, or a depiction of a bishop consigning an Exultet Roll to a deacon. One often encounters Old Testament scenes such as the crossing of the Red Sea, or New Testament scenes such as the raising of Lazarus, which are reflective of the readings of the Easter Vigil Service.

Illustrations of textual subjects and themes in the Exultet text often occur. They might be depictions of concepts such as *Mother Church* or depictions of a single word drawn from the text such as *Populus* (the people) or *Tellus* (earth). One depiction often encountered is that of the bees (*apus*). *Angelica Turba Caellorum* (a throng of heavenly angels) is another common depiction. (See *Illumination 3*)

On some rolls one encounters pictures of secular and ecclesiastical authorities. This is not surprising given that prayers for the temporal and ecclesiastical authorities are encountered at the end of the Exultet text.

Some of the more interesting depictions are those of liturgical events, particularly in relation to the ceremony surrounding the Paschal Candle and the deacon's role in that portion of the liturgy. The depictions include the deacon singing the Exultet, and the lighting, blessing and censing of the candle. Many of these depictions include the deacon making a gesture of benediction. In most liturgical depictions, the deacon figures quite prominently. (See *Illuminations 4 & 5*)

Liturgy

In the Middle Ages as today, Easter, the Resurrection of Christ, was the pinnacle of the church year. In the Western church, the Easter Vigil was the time when new members were received into the church and baptized. This liturgy generally took place on Holy Saturday Night.

Central to this liturgy, then as now, was the lighting of a New Flame outside the church; after which the deacon, processing into the darkened church, would carry a candle lit from the New Flame while chanting *the Light of Christ*. In response, the congregation would chant *Thanks be to God*. This action took place three times in three locations: when entering the church, when the procession was midway into the church and upon reaching the main altar. The deacon raised the starting pitch each time he intoned *the Light of Christ*. When he reached the main altar, the deacon would commence with the Exultet.[6] The general shape of the Liturgy continued with litanies, readings with canticles and prayers, procession to the font, baptisms and Mass. Among the readings were the stories of Creation, the Fall, the Flood, the Sacrifice of Isaac, the Passover, the Crossing of the Red Sea, the Entry into the Promised Land, the Valley of Dry Bones, and Jonah.

Although this is the basic form of the liturgy, there are some minor regional variations. Unique to the Beneventan Vigil, for example, is the placement of the Exultet just prior to the final scripture reading instead of at the beginning of the service as was done everywhere else.[7]

Monte Cassino, where the majority of the extant rolls were produced, provides us with a slightly different Liturgy (The Desiderian). In the Desiderian manner, the ministers first process into the church. The deacon asks a blessing from the priest and then takes the text for the candle blessing from the altar. The deacon proceeds to the ambo led by two subdeacons and an acolyte carrying a candle. When he arrives at the ambo, he says *the Light of Christ* three times and the people reply *Thanks be to God* three times. The acolyte then lights the great Paschal candle, which is to be blessed, and the deacon proceeds with the blessing that begins *Rejoice now heavenly choir of angels*.[8] This is the service for which rolls produced at Monte Cassino were designed.[9] Unlike the Beneventan ritual, it places the Exultet at the beginning of the rite. Unique to this ritual is the acolyte bearing the candle, the placing of the

---

[6] A.J. MacGregor, *Fire and Light in the Western Triduum: Their Use at Tenebrae and at the Paschal Vigil* [Alcuin Club Collection Number 71] (Collegeville, Minnesota: The Liturgical Press, 1992). For general information about the processional itself see, pp. 291-295. For information about the candle and its origins see pp. 299-308.

[7] For further elaboration upon the Beneventan Vigil see Kelly, pp. 135-137, 139-140.

[8] Kelly provides a translation of a Holy Saturday Ordo of Monte Cassino, pp. 149. For a brief treatment of the processional and the singing of the Light of Christ see also MacGregor, pp. 281-290.

[9] Kelly, 149.

roll upon the altar and the removal of the roll, which has not been previ-
ously displayed. Moreover, the deacon sings *the Light of Christ* from the
ambo and not in procession as is done everywhere outside of Southern
Italy. Usually, the deacon sings *the Light of Christ* while he is touching
or holding the candle to be blessed. It is likely that the singing of both
The Light of Christ and the Exultet from the ambo reflects the fact that
Southern Italy is the only place that made use of the Exultet Roll in its
Easter Vigil Liturgy.[10]

In Beneventan practice, the bishop lights the candle and places
oil or chrism upon it, after which the deacon sings *the Light of Christ.*[11]
Many of the depictions on the rolls show the deacon in the ambo with the
bishop lighting a very tall and large candle. (See *Illumination 6*) Indeed,
over time, the candle used in the liturgy seems to have increased in
physical size. In later rolls, the candles depicted are considerably larger
and the deacon has made his way into the ambo. It seems that as the candle grew larger, it necessitated that the deacon proclaim the hymn and
bless the Paschal Candle from the ambo. Thus, the illustration reflects a
change in the actual liturgy as it was practiced in the Desiderian manner.

Although in some roll depictions one sees the deacon blessing
the candle from a center area of the church, the greater part of the depictions show him blessing and singing over the candle from an ambo. In
many Italian churches, the ambo was a rather large and tall structure that
was exquisitely constructed and well adorned.[12]

Why the Deacon?

In his thorough treatment of Exultet Rolls, Thomas Kelly observes that
one of the most difficult problems concerning the Exultet is the question
of why it is sung by the deacon.[13] This fact is indeed puzzling, for the
Exultet is not merely a hymn, but also a candle blessing. Generally, the
blessing of people or objects is not one of the deacon's responsibilities.
Yet, during the Easter Vigil, the deacon performs a blessing over the
candle with the bishop's approval. During the most sacred event of the
Christian year, the deacon performs a duty that would normally be per-

---

[10] For Further elaboration upon the Desiderian manner of the liturgy see Kelly,
pp. 148-150.
[11] For further elaboration upon the Beneventan practice see Kelly, pp. 150-151.
[12] For a general treatment of the positioning of the candle throughout Italy see
MacGregor, pp. 320-326.
[13] Kelly, 192.

formed by the highest-ranking cleric present, usually the bishop. Why?

One possible answer to this question lies in the fact that the Exultet is a *sung* blessing. While it is arguable that the ability to sing was a requirement in some sense for all orders at this time, it seems that by the fifth century the ability of deacons to sing had become a "positive attribute" and perhaps even a criterion for their selection.[14] Indeed, a letter of Pope Gregory the Great (590-604) gives support to this notion:

> A very reprehensible custom has arisen whereby certain cantors are chosen for the ministry of the altar and are constituted in the order of deacons for the modulation of their voice...[I]n this See ministers of the altar are not to sing, and during mass let them only sing the Gospel. Psalms and other readings should be recited by subdeacons or if necessary, by those in minor orders.[15]

Moreover Gregory indicated that:

> The reason for this reform was that the deacons had paid more attention to the cultivation of their vocal powers than their morals, also to the neglect of their more important duties; and it happened that whilst they delighted the people with their singing, they offended God with their ill living.[16]

Evidently, the deacons composed an elite group of singers. Despite Gregory's great displeasure, deacons continued to sing in the church and the deacon chanting and blessing the candle during the Exultet became a fixed feature of the Easter Vigil.

We know from an early letter of St. Jerome (c. 347-420) that the

---

[14] Jeannine E. Olson, *One Ministry Many Roles: Deacons and Deaconesses through the Centuries* (St. Louis: Concordia Publishing House, 1992), 57.

[15] *Conc. Rom.* 595, Can. I. See also Edward P. Echlin, *The Deacon in the Church, Past and Future* (Staten Island, NY: Alba House, Society of St. Paul, 1971), 68, 79.

[16] *Conc. Rom., 595, Can I.* This can be found translated in Vernon Staley, ed. *Ordo Romanus Primus* in *The Library of Liturgiology and Ecclesiology for English Readers* (London: Alexander Moring, Limited The De La More Press, 1905), 41.

custom of the deacon singing the Exultet goes back at least as far as the fourth century. This famous letter was written to a deacon named Prae-sidius, who served in Northern Italy. Praesidius was to sing over the Paschal candle during the coming Easter Vigil and had asked Jerome to write the Exultet hymn which he was to sing. Jerome declined to do so, but the letter testifies to the fact that the deacon sang the Exultet within the ceremony from a very early time.[17]

If one considers the origins of the deacon's liturgical role, it is even less surprising to think of deacons as singers. Their liturgical role is modeled after the Levites of the Jewish Temple. In fact, by the beginning of the second century[18] it was common to compare bishops, priests and deacons with the three Jewish Temple (Old Testament) orders of high priest, priest, and Levite.[19] The Levites were those who functioned as as-sistants to the high priest. Thought to be among the duties of the Levite was the performance of sacred music.[20] Indeed, while singing the Exultet hymn, the deacon thanks God for numbering him among the Levites![21]

The notion of deacons being particularly gifted singers is lent further support by the fact that in Rome, under each of seven district dea-cons, there was a subdeacon who chanted the lessons and the liturgical epistles at stational masses. These subdeacons would likely become dea-cons, further implying a necessity for vocal skill in spite of Gregory's desires. In addition to these subdeacons, there were seven others who belonged specifically to the *Schola Cantorum*; and by the eleventh cen-tury there were also seven palatine subdeacons whose duties were con-fined to the Lateran Basilica.[22] Consequently, it seems that vocal

---

[17] Jerome, *Letter to Praesidius [English and Latin]*, Charles Francis Cave. Trans. (Thesis Catholic University of America, 1983), 38-50. See also *Epistle 28, Ad Praesidium, De Cereo paschali*, ed. Jacques Paul Migne, *Patrologia cur-sus completus*, Series latina, Tomus 30, *S. Hieronymi, Tomus undecimus* (Paris: n.p., 1846). This letter also supports the idea that the Exultet was often com-posed anew. For further elaboration one might see James Monroe Barnett, *The Diaconate* (New York: Seabury Press, 1981), 79.

[18] 107 CE

[19] 1 Clement 40.

[20] "Levite" *Encyclopedia of The Jewish Religion*, 1986 ed.

[21] *Ut qui me non meis meritis in levitarum numero dignatus est aggregare lumi-nis sui gratiam infundens cerei huius laudem implere precipiat.* [So that he who not through my merits has deigned to number me among the Levites, pouring the grace of his light, may direct me to accomplish the praise of the candle]

[22] Staley, 38. The term *palatine* is both a geographic and a vocal reference.

proficiency did become an expectation of the deacon. Although vocal skill may not have been a stated requirement, it does seem to have been assumed of deacons since Gregory's letter indicates that many deacons belonged to an elite class of singers. Extending this line of reasoning, we can conclude that the deacon was likely chosen as the one to sing the Exultet for the mere fact that he had a more pleasing voice than other clerics. On no occasion was an aesthetically pleasing voice more desirable than during the central hymn of the first service on the greatest holiday of the church year. It is not surprising then that a lower ranking cleric with a pleasing voice was called upon to sing the Exultet.

This idea is given credence by present day practice. Lay cantors of exceptional skill are often called upon to sing the Exultet during the Easter Vigil Service, even when there are deacons present. The reason being that a pleasing voice ought to proclaim the great hymn. Continuing this line of thought, it is logical to consider that the bishop would have likewise delegated the deacon to perform the sung blessing of the candle. Deacons were often allowed to bless bread at a non-Eucharistic agape meal with the bishop's approval, so why not a candle, especially if the deacon is to be in close proximity to it anyway? Two pictorial themes support the idea of the bishop delegating the physical blessing of the candle to the deacon: first, depictions of the bishop handing the deacon the roll, and second, depictions of the deacon with his hand making a gesture of blessing upon the candle, often in the presence of the bishop. (See *Illuminations 7 & 8*) If events transpired as suggested here, it would make sense that the gifted singer would perform the Exultet and bless the candle. This could all be done by delegation of the bishop.

Kelly states that the Exultet is not a chant for specialist singers.[23] After examining the chants on some rolls, I am quite inclined to agree with Kelly's assessment; it is indeed not a chant of sufficient technical difficulty to require a specialist. Nevertheless, in view of the nature of the Exultet's subject and the occasion on which it is performed, it would still be logical to have it performed by the most aesthetically pleasing voice, the voice of the deacon! Like the roll, which was not technically necessary, but rather a beautiful object belonging to the bishop used to add solemnity to the occasion,[24] it was equally desirable to have a simi-

---

Geographically, the term refers to one of the Seven Hills of Rome. Vocally the term refers to the palate.

[23] Kelly, 10.

[24] Ibid., 194-196, 204.

larly beautiful voice to enhance the solemnity.

Kelly argues that the roll was created for the pleasure of the bishop. He states that the bishop consigned the roll to the deacon and that the Exultet was sung in the bishop's stead and was in fact directed towards the bishop.[25] We can conclude that if the bishop were to have a text performed, on his behalf, from an unusually beautiful document, it is likely that this text was going to be proclaimed by an equally beautiful voice. The singing of the Exultet is a unique liturgical moment. Even today, it is the lighting of the candle and the singing of the Exultet that greatly capture the attention of the congregation.

Angels, Scrolls, Deacons and Rolls

Exultet Roll illuminations of the deacon, placed on high, proclaiming the Exultet from an unfurled roll, remind one of the many depictions in other mediums of angels proclaiming messages from scrolls. Some of the more common motifs in this tradition are the Annunciation to Mary, the Annunciation to the Shepherds, and Nativity Scenes in which an angel is seen proclaiming the joyous event with a scroll unfurled in its hands. Although the scroll is not an actual script for the angel, the scroll communicates the angel's message to the subjects in the picture and serves to inform the viewer of the event depicted. Further, the scroll indicates that the angel is delivering a message from someone other than himself, namely God. Likewise, the deacon is consigned a roll which is not his, in order to deliver a message on behalf of another (the bishop). The Exultet Roll thus functions in the same way as the angel's scroll. Like the angelic text from which the birth of Jesus is proclaimed at Christmas, the deacon's Exultet text proclaims Christ's redemptive act at Easter. The Incarnation is depicted in art with angels utilizing scrolls to proclaim the birth of Christ at Christmas. At the Easter Vigil, we see deacons proclaiming Christ's death and resurrection from rolls.

Since the scroll is a common artistic device used to proclaim the birth of Christ from heaven, it is not surprising then that an actual roll is used in the physical proclamation of Christ's resurrection. To appreciate this idea, it is helpful to look at the illustrations of angels with scrolls in *Figure 1*. Then, if one looks at *Figures 2 & 3*, taken from an Exultet Roll, one will see some interesting parallels. Viewing the Annunciation and Nativity scenes on this roll, one sees an angel speaking to Mary with

---

[25] Ibid., 193.

an outstretched right hand. Below this depiction is a Nativity scene with an angel holding an unfurled scroll. Not far down on the same roll is a picture of a deacon blessing a paschal candle. In *Figure 4*, the unfurled scroll and the hand gesture of the deacon in the ambo are somewhat similar to the angelic depictions in *Figures 2 & 3*. The roll becomes the device containing the textual proclamation of the beginning and the end of Jesus' earthly work among humanity. Like the words on the angel's scroll, which help the subjects and the viewer of the painting to understand the event, the pictures upon the Exultet Roll help those people in proximity to comprehend the joyous mystery being proclaimed.

In his 1998 publication, Maurice McNamee developed the idea that in late Medieval Netherlandish arc angels are often vested as the sub-ministers at an eternal Mass celebrated by Christ in heaven. The most common vestment seen is that of the deacon.[26] According to McNamee the "usual costume of angels in the art of the Western world before the thirteenth century was derived from the Byzantine tradition of the East or was based on an adaptation of the Roman toga or of the tunic actually worn by men in the Middle Ages."[27] In the Byzantine representation of the "eternal liturgy" angels are vested as deacons participating with Christ in the Mass. In many depictions, Christ is vested as a bishop. McNamee points to a Western adaptation of this Eastern motif that may be observed on the exterior of the apse of the Rheims Cathedral. Angels appear there vested in tunics, holding items associated with the Mass, such as missals and scrolls. One angel, on the exterior of the apse of Rheims Cathedral wears the alb and dalmatic of the deacon.[28] McNamee states that "in Italy, what developed into the Byzantine garb for angels is also in evidence in all media of artistic expression from the third to the thirteenth century." [29] Since Byzantine rolls influenced the Exultet Rolls, it is not surprising to see that other Byzantine concepts, such as diaconal dress for angels, made their way into the illustrations with a Western adaptation.[30] One illumination taken from an Exultet Roll depicts a group of angels in dalmatics, a vestment worn only by deacons. (See *Illumination 3*) It is apparent that the tradition of angels vested as deacons was

---

[26] Maurice B. McNamee, *Vested Angels: Eucharistic Allusions in Early Netherlandish Paintings* (Leuven: Peeters, 1998).
[27] Ibid., 43.
[28] For a photograph, see McNamee, figure 11, p. 271.
[29] Ibid., 47.
[30] Ibid., 43, 47.

not unknown to the illustrators of some of the rolls.

Outside of visual art, one can look to the medieval liturgical dramas of the church and find precedent for the tradition of earthly deacons portraying angels. When watching a liturgical drama, it would not be surprising to see deacons identified with angels.[31] In some of the more developed Easter plays "Christ himself appeared in a chasuble, while the angel, or in some instances two angels, were vested in dalmatics." [32]

I do not raise these ideas in order to say that deacons are perfect angels, but rather to say that at the time of the design of these rolls there was already an association with angels and deacons in the medieval imagination.

At the time the Exultet Rolls were produced, the deacon played an important part in the life of the church. In many ways the deacon's role was parallel to the role of an angel. The deacon was literally the bishop's emissary. Deacons were ordained by the bishop alone. Deacons assisted bishops in the administration of a diocese and were in some ways the power behind the throne, controlling large bodies of the church's charitable lands. In the popular imagination, the angel is likewise an emissary of God. It is an angel who delivers the message to Mary that she will bear the divine child, and an angel who greets the mourners at the tomb of Jesus. Likewise, it is the deacon who proclaims the risen Christ at Easter. The idea of the angel and deacon as emissaries is supported by the many illustrations of Christ flanked by angels and likewise a number of illustrations of bishops flanked by deacons. When one considers the deacon and his role as the bishop's messenger it is not surprising to find the deacon proclaiming the bishop's gospel news of Christ's resurrection via the Exultet at the Easter Vigil service.

In short, to consider the deacon as earthly angel, one should consider the following ideas from art and the temporal realm. Christ is often vested like a bishop. Angels are vested like deacons. Angels function as God's emissaries. Moreover, deacons functioned as the bishop's emissaries and were answerable to the bishop alone. Deacons served as bishop's representatives to church councils and meetings, and also served as messengers and intermediaries between the bishop and the people, just

---

[31] Karl Young, *The Drama of the Medieval Church* 2 vols. (Oxford: Clarendon Press, 1933). In those plays in which Young prescribes dress for angels he prescribes the vestments of sub-ministers of the Mass: albs, stoles, dalmatics, or copes.

[32] McNamee, 53.

as angels serve as messengers and intermediaries between God and humanity. Along with these duties, deacons were involved with charitable institutions. It was because of these duties that the church of late antiquity compared deacons to angelic orders and clothed them in white albs or tunics at liturgy.[33]

In consideration of the question of why the deacon would be the one appointed to bless the candle and sing the Exultet, I reiterate two possibilities. First, the deacon was given this honor due to the quality of his singing voice. Second, it is likely that the deacon, as the bishop's messenger, blessed the candle and delivered the Easter Proclamation in his stead. If one considers this angel-like duty to be the charge of the bishop, then one is not surprised to find at the end of one Exultet Roll, at the point where the Exultet proclamation ends, an illustration of a little deacon offering the roll to Christ, the one whom he ultimately serves as the bishop's earthly delegate. (See *Illumination 9*) Perhaps he is not offering the roll, but rather returning the words and the scroll to the heavenly place from which they came.

---

[33] Olson, 57.

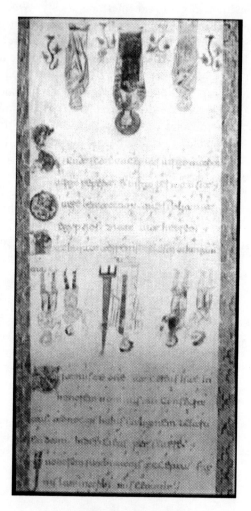

Illumination One
Pisa, Museo Dell'Opera Del Duomo,
Exultet 2 (circa. 1059-1071) Capua

Illumination Two
Prayer of the Deacon
Virgin Mary
Pisa, Museo Dell'Opera Del Duomo,
Exultet 2 (circa. 1059-1071) Capua

Illumination Three
Throng of Heavenly Angels,
© Biblioteca Apostolica Vaticana (Vatican)
Città del Vaticano, Vat. Lat. 3784, Exultet
(circa. 1060-1070, Montecassino)

Illumination Four
Fratres Carissimi,
© Biblioteca Apostolica Vaticana (Vatican)
Città del Vaticano, Vat. Lat. 3784, Exultet. (circa. 1060-1070, Montecassino)

Illumination Five
Fratres Carissimi,
© Biblioteca Apostolica Vaticana (Vatican)
Città del Vaticano, Vat. Lat. 9820, Exultet
(circa. 981-987, Benevento)

Illumination Six
Lighting of the Candle,
© Biblioteca Apostolica Vaticana (Vatican)
Città del Vaticano, Vat. Lat. 9820, Exultet. (circa. 981-987, Benevento)

Illumination Seven
Consignation of the Exultet Roll to the Deacon (frontispiece),
© Biblioteca Apostolica Vaticana (Vatican)
Città del Vaticano, Vat. Lat. 9820-1a, Exultet
(circa. 981-987, Benevento)

Illumination Eight
Blessing of the Candle,
© Biblioteca Apostolica Vaticana (Vatican)
Città del Vaticano, Vat. Lat. 9820
(circa 981-987, Benevento)

Illumination Nine
Offering of the Roll by Boniface the Deacon (an accretion)
Montecassino, © Archivio Dell'Abbazia, Exultet 2
(circa. 1105-1110, Sorrento)

Figure 1
Robert Campin, *The Nativity,* © Musée des Beaux-Arts de Dijon
(Cliché R. Remeyn Dijon).

Figure 2 (upper) *The Annunciation*
Figure 3 (lower) *Nativity*
Troia, © Archivio Capitolare, Exultet 3 (circa.1145-1155)

Figure 4
Consecration of the Candle
Troia, © Archivio Capitolare, Exultet 3. (circa. 1145-1155)

Primary Manuscripts

Vatican City, Biblioteca Apostolica Vaticana: *MS Barb lat. 592.*
Vatican City, Biblioteca Apostolica Vaticana: *MS Vat. lat. 3784.*
Vatican City, Biblioteca Apostolica Vaticana: *MS Vat. lat. 3784a.*
Vatican City, Biblioteca Apostolica Vaticana: *MS Vat. lat. 9820.*

Other Primary Sources

Avery, Myrtilla, *The Exultet Rolls of Southern Italy*, II: Plates (Princeton: University Press, 1936).

British Museum, *An Exultet Roll Illuminated in the XIth Century at The Abbey of Monte Cassino*, Reproduced from ADD. MS 30337 (London: 1929).

The Divine Liturgy According to St. John Chrysostom (South Canaan, PA: St. Tikhons Seminary Press, 1994).

Exultet: Rotoli liturgici del medioevo meridionale (Roma: Istituto Poligrafico e Zecca Dello Stato, 1994).

The Roman Missal: Compiled by lawful authority from the Missale Romanum (New York: The Macmillan Company, 1951).

Secondary Sources

Avery, Myrtilla, "The Relation of St. Ambrose to the 'Exultet' Hymn," Dorothy Miner, ed., *Studies in Art and Literature for Belle da Costa Greene* (Princeton: Princeton University Press, 1954).

Bannister, H.M., "The Vetus Itala Text of the Exultet," *Journal of Theological Studies*, XI (1910): 43-54.

Barracane, Gaetano, *Gli Exultet di Bari* (Bari: Edipuglia, 1994).

Cappelli, Adriano, *Lexicon abbreviaturarum : dizionario di abbreviature latine ed italiane, usate nelle carte e codici, specialmente del Medio-Evo, riprodotte con oltre 14000 segni incise*, 6th edition (Milano: Hoepli, 1961).

Cappelli, Adriano, *The Elements of Abbreviation in Medieval Latin Paleography* (Brachigrafia Medioevale), David Heimann and Richard Kay. Lawrence, trans. (Kansas: University of Kansas Libraries, 1982).

Deacons in the Ministry of the Church, A Report to the House of Bishops of the General Synod of the Church of England (London: Church House Publishing, 1988).

Ferguson, George, *Signs and Symbols in Christian Art* (London: Oxford University Press, 1954).

Hughes, Andrew, *Medieval Manuscripts for Mass and Office: A Guide to Their Organization and Terminology* (Toronto: University of Toronto Press, 1982).

Jasper, R.C.D. and G.J. Cuming, eds. *Prayers of the Eucharist: Early and Reformed* (Collegeville, Minnesota: The Liturgical Press, 1990).

Masetti, Anna Rosa Calderoni, Cosimo Fonseca, and Guglielmo Cavallo, *L'Exultet <<Beneventano>> del duomo di Pisa* (Galatina: Congedo, 1989).

O'Shea, W.J., ed., "Easter Vigil," *New Catholic Encyclopedia* 1967, ed.

Romagosa, Guillermo, Telephone interview. 8 November 1998.

Strittmatter, A., "Exsultet Iam Angelica Turba," *New Catholic Encyclopedia*, 1967, ed.

Thurston, Herbert, *Lent and Holy Week: Chapters on Catholic Observance and Ritual* (London: Longmans, Green and Company, 1904).

Whitehill, W.M., "A Twelfth Century Exultet Roll at Troja." *Speculum*, 2, (1927): 80-84.

THE *FIESTA DE MOROS Y CRISTIANOS* IN SPAIN

Jerry T. Farmer[*]

An Historical Overview

The *Fiesta de moros y cristianos* is a social , economic and entertaining event that today takes place annually in many cities and towns in the Spanish Provinces of Murcia, Albacete, Alicante and Valencia. Its main elements consist of the "entrance" (*entradas*) or formal parading into the city or town of both the Moors and Christians, the "conquest" and subsequent "reconquest" of a castle, and the dramatization of the struggle by means of the respective groups (*comparsas)* attired in ornate and elaborate dress, involving the various Moorish and Christian military units or bands.

It is important to look at the term itself: *moro* (Moor). Titus Burckhardt, gives the following perspective:

> ...it would be more accurate to refer to "Arabic" culture in Spain, since its language was predominantly Arabic, or even "Islamic" culture, since it actually belonged to the Islamic world. The word "moorish" derives from the Spanish word, *moros*, that is "Moors" or "Mauretanians." "Moorish" culture in the literal sense does not exist any more than does "Gothic" architecture. Yet the word "Moorish" has become synonymous with "Arab-Islamic." The Moors were simply Maghrebins, inhabitants of the *maghreb*, the western part of the Islamic world, that extends from Spain to Tunisia, and represents a homogeneous cultural entity.[1]

[*] Dr. Jerry T. Farmer is an Associate Professor of Theology at the Historically Black and Catholic Xavier University in New Orleans, Louisiana. Born in Covington, Kentucky and raised in California, he is married to Dr. Ángeles Pla Farmer, who is from Almeria, Spain. His theological writing and research has centered on the theology of Karl Rahner. He has both the M.A. as well as the Ph.D in Religious Studies from the Katholieke Universiteit Leuven, Belgium. He has also studied issues of popular religiosity, in both the U.S. Hispanic / Latino context as well as in Spain, and he has been involved in developing a ministry formation process for laity, in both English and Spanish.
[1] Titus Burckhardt, *Moorish Culture in Spain*, Alisa Jaffa, trans., (New York:

Nonetheless, a recent Spanish-language translation of this original German publication, has made the following point:

> ...the original text constantly employs the term *"moro,"* both in regard to its use as an adjective in reference to persons as well as to concepts or things. In the latter case this would be unacceptable in literary Spanish, and so "Hispanic-Arabic" or simply "Arabic" has been used [by this translator, Rosa Kuhne Brabant] instead [my translation].[2]

Also, many would question whether one can speak of a "homogenous cultural entity" when referring to the people of the *maghreb*. It would be more accurate to speak of the heterogeneity that is hidden by the homogeneity of both language, Arabic, and religion, Islam. Burckhardt further sees a link between the term *moro* and the Berbers, who were located in North Africa primarily in the region of the Riff and central Atlas mountains:

> The preponderance of Berbers [on the Iberian peninsula] can also be deduced from the fact that the Spaniards referred to all Muslims as *"moros,"* which comes from the Latin, *mauri* or *maurusci*, the term used for all Atlas Berbers and can be traced back indirectly to the late Greek *mauroi*, 'black', or the Phoenician *mauharin*, "Western."[3]

The earliest reference to *moros y cristianos* occurs in the middle of the twelfth century, in the year 1150.[4] During the wedding celebrations in Lleida honoring Queen Petronila's marriage with Don Ramón

---

McGraw-Hill,1972; Original work published Munich: Georg D.W. Calwey, 1970), 7.

[2] Titus Burckhardt, *La civilización hispano-árabe*, Rosa Kuhne Brabant, trans., (Madrid: Alianza Editorial, 1999; Original work published Munich: Georg D.W. Callwey, 1970), 11.

[3] Burckhardt, *Moorish Culture in Spain*, 29.

[4] Miguel-Angel González Hernández, *Moros y Cristianos, Del Alarde Medieval a las Fiestas Reales Barroca (ss. XV-XVIII)*, (Monforte del Cid, Alicante, Spain: Ayuntamiento de Monforte del Cid, 1999), 25.

Berenguer de Barcelona, along with some two thousand "jugglers," there is noted *"un combate de moros y cristianos."* Clearly it is a dramatization but no more details are given.

With regard to scholarly discussion as to whether this is, indeed, the earliest reference, Max Harris provides his analysis:

> The evidence for the Lleida dance of Moors and Christians is therefore rather shaky... This is not, however, quite the same as saying that the evidence has been proven false... In the end, however, the Lleida *moros y cristianos* may be nothing more than legend. Unless we can locate and verify Teixidor's sources or some independent account of the Lleida performance, we must remain, at best, agnostic.[5]

The roots of this dramatization have been traced by González Hernández to *fiestas de alardo*.[6] The term comes from the Arabic, "al-ard," and it is translated into Spanish as *alarde*. It was the review of the Arab-Islamic troops that was carried out to assure the preparedness of the local militia for the defense of the city. This review of the troops was carried out at the end of the tenth century, for example, by Almanzor, in preparation for summer military campaigns.

It is in the sixteenth and seventeenth centuries that there is a shift in meaning and terminology. The military troop and weapons muster (*alarde*) gives birth to a new but very closely linked term: *alardo*. This new term carries with it the characteristics of a festival. It refers to the parading of the city or townspeople, dressed up as soldiers, going through the streets, firing weapons known for their noise (the use of gunpowder), and also imitating and adopting for themselves the titles of "captain" (*capitán*) and "lieutenant" (*alférez*).

The *alardo* itself has two clear phases of evolution. There is at the beginning what could be described as the *alardo* in its simple form. A group of people of the city or town accompany the patron saint in the procession that takes place during the local festivities, without any other intention than the firing of loud weapons. But the second phase of development can describe the *alardo* as one that is more elegant, more

---

[5] Max Harris, *Aztecs, Moors, and Christians: festivals of reconquest in Mexico and Spain* (Austin, TX: University of Texas Press, 2000), 32-33.
[6] González Hernández, *Moros y Cristianos*, 265.

"dressy" (*alardo compuesto*). Here there is not only the use of gunpowder, but there is also much more order and organization which includes music and a parade in military fashion. The role of the "captain" is key in the festivities, and the lieutenant (*alférez*) is often entrusted with the standard or the banner which is waved or "danced" in artistry at very places in the course of the parade.

The outcome of all this is that this festival of *alardo* is indeed a mixture on the one hand of the festival of the nobility and on the other of the popular festival organized and carried out by the Guilds and their members. It is that which gives birth to the *fiesta de moros y cristianos*.

On the Spanish peninsula itself, González Hernández provides abundant documentation of the *fiesta de moros y cristianos* occurring in the coastal city of Alicante from at least 1599 to 1789.[7] The outline of the festivities begins with the disembarking of the Moorish troops at the port. There then follow subsequent street skirmishes, the 'conquest' followed by the 'reconquest' of a 'castle' [one made of wood] with appropriate 'delegations' playing their parts. It is clearly a festival organized and carried out by the Guilds and their members: with the role of the Moors normally being taken by those who are sailors and fishermen, and the role of the Christians often being filled by those who are carpenters.

There is a variation of the *fiesta de moros y cristianos* that takes place during the same time period in the city of Valencia. Here one finds a battle, described as a *naumaquia*, that takes place on the Turia River, followed by an assault staged at the river's bank, where there is a "festival" castle. These festivities are documented from as early as the year 1373, and continue up until 1769.[8] This variation of the festival may have some roots in the earlier Roman mock sea battles, that the Romans themselves inherited from the Greeks before them, where there is an explicit reference to this in the writings of the Roman author Suetonius.

During the nineteenth century, it was economic growth that was the principal factor in the expansion and growth of the *fiesta de moros y cristianos* in the two provinces of Alicante and Valencia.[9] For example one finds the celebration in the interior city of Alcoy and in coastal town of Denia. The structure of the festival also models itself on the structure of the earlier *fiestas reales*, or Royal Festivals, which lasted for three days: the first day consisted in the "entrances" or parades; the second day

---

[7] Ibid.., 155, 35.
[8] Ibid.., 34, 25.
[9] Ibid., 238, 270.

was dedicated to the city or town patron; and the third day saw the battles and eventual negotiations for peace by the various ambassadors. Over time the structure continued to develop into a more organized and complex one: more and more groups or *comparsas* were taking part, there was more music, greater variety with regard to the street routes for the parading, and much more importance given to creating the "scenes" for the battle and the subsequent negotiations.

A Sociological Perspective

Gema Martín Muñoz, notes that in:

> Western societies the Muslim world is frequently perceived and interpreted in terms of a "culturalist paradigm" in which the explanation of facts revolves around the principle of a *cultural difference* which recreates the East beyond its proper reality into what the West wants to see [my translation].[10]

This paradigm, she goes on to state, is rooted in an essentialist and comparative vision which corresponds above all else to the western need to constantly invent "the other," in this case, the Muslim, in order to complete the image of the one original, thus defining the boundaries of the supposed classical and universal subject of the Judeo-Christian tradition. Furthermore, such an essentialist interpretation looks at these cultures as a closed universe, incapable of being modified, so that what results is a vision of the other culture as inferior or backward, the bearer of unchanging traditionalism, irrationality, and aggressiveness. In this way those values that are considered to be western are presented as the only valid paradigm for humanity. All of this means that cultural diversity is not seen as a variety of options with equal importance, but in terms of an hierarchical scale of modernization versus backwardness. And this "ethnocentric cosmopolitanism," which lays claim exclusively to the paradigm of rationality and progress, tends to define the Muslim world as far from modernity. In fact this mental and social construct forms a part of the process of both the assimilation and the destruction of all those cultures which do not belong to the Western "nucleus," as well

---

[10] Gema Martín Muñoz, "Lo real y lo irreal en la representación del mundo musulmán," *Revista de Occidente* (Enero, 2000): 106.

as the necessary invention of "the other" in order to achieve this process.

The view of "the other" that results is one that is fully univocal, that both idealizes (the exotic and the beautiful) and demonizes (the 'morisco' [the baptized Muslim], the "Turk," and the "terrorist.") This "culturalist paradigm" is one that is filled with both prejudice and stereotypes. It proceeds from a legacy of historical misunderstandings, the result of a relationship that has been interpreted primarily as one of confrontation for many centuries. And in our own day this "culturalist paradigm" has been promoted by focusing almost exclusively on this paradigm with regard to the development of Islamic movements. Edward Said stresses a very similar perspective:

> Without significant exception the universalizing discourses of modern Europe and the United States assume the silence, willing or otherwise, of the non-European world. There is incorporation; there is inclusion; there is direct rule; there is coercion. But there is only infrequently an acknowledgment that the colonized people should be heard from, their ideas known.[11]

González-Casanovas compares "the Reconquest of Iberia from the Moors and the Spanish Conquest of America" and argues that they "present significant parallels as historical phenomena and subjects of historiography: They not only offer similar sociopolitical and ideological developments in eras of national formation but also give rise to hybrid types of historical writing in the vernacular."[12] And Harris offers a very interesting study of folk dance traditions by asking and answering the question: "In which direction did such folk dance traditions cross the Atlantic? We should not, because European ships first sailed westward, assume that subsequent cultural traffic always flowed in the same direction."[13] And Harris notes that Maria Soledad Carrasco Urgoiti is among the few scholars that have considered the mutual influence of culture be-

---

[11] Edward Said, *Culture and Imperialism* (New York: Knopf, distributed by Random House, 1993), 50.

[12] Roberto J. González-Casanovas, "Imperial Histories from Alfonso X to Inca Garcilasco: Revisionist Myths of Reconquest and Conquest," *Scripta Humanistica* 134 (Potomac, MD, 1997): x.

[13] Harris, *Aztecs, Moors, and Christians*, 169.

tween Europe and the Americas,[14] leading Harris to conclude that "traditional Spanish combat dances may have their roots not in Medieval Europe but in Native America."[15]

John Esposito, writing from a religious context, points to the roots of concern and misunderstanding that have marked Islamic-Christian relations.[16] "Ancient rivalries as well as modern-day conflicts have so accentuated differences as completely to obscure the shared monotheistic roots and vision of the Judaeo-Christian-Islamic tradition." Even though Christians and Muslims share many common beliefs and values, their relations with each other have been overshadowed by conflict. And he cites, as one example among many, the expulsion of the "Moors" from Spain. Tragically, "Islam's relationship with the West has often been marked less by understanding than by mutual ignorance and stereotyping, confrontation and conflict."

One cannot also not fail to recognize that the presence, the role and the relationship of Jews on the Peninsula with both Christians and Muslims is itself a significant reality.[17] For example, Burckhardt points to the "incredibly swift success of the Muslims" of its conquest of the Visigoths, dating from 711 and completed in less than three years, and that certainly one factor among many was "the assistance the Muslims received from the Jews, who had been oppressed by the Visigothic church."[18] And he goes on to add that "the greatest beneficiaries of Is-

---

[14] María Soledad Carrasco Urgoiti, "Aspectos folclóricos y literarios de la fiesta de moros y cristianos en España," (Originally published in P.M.L.A., LXXVII [1963]: 476-491), *El Moro Retador y El Moro Amigo (Estudios sobre fiestas y comedias de moros y cristianos)*, (Granada: Universidad de Granada, 1996), 39.

[15] Harris, *Aztecs, Moors, and Christians*, 178.

[16] John Esposito, "The Threat of Islam: Myth or Reality?," in Hans Küng, Jürgen Moltmann, Edit., *Islam: A Challenge for Christianity*, (Concilium June, 1994/3): 39.

[17] On this topic, see Vivian Mann, Thomas Fr. Click, Jerrilyn Dr. Dodds, eds., *Convivencia: Jews Muslims, and Christians in Medieval Spain* (New York: G. Braziller in association with the Jewish Museum, 1992); Norman Roth, *Jews, Visigoths and Muslims in Medieval Spain: Cooperation and Conflict* (Leiden / New York: E.J. Brill, 1994); Robert Ignatius Burns, *Muslims, Christians, and Jews in the Crusader Kingdom of Valencia: Societies in Symbiosis* (Cambridge / New York: Cambridge University Press, 1984); and Anita Novinsky, Diane Kuperman, Edit., *Ibéria judaica: roteiros da memória* (Rio de Janeiro: Edusp, 1996).

[18] Burckhardt, *Moorish Culture in Spain*, 24.

lamic rule were the Jews, for in Spain (*Seph_r_d* in Hebrew) they enjoyed their finest intellectual flowering since their dispersal from
Palestine to foreign lands." And Burckhardt stresses that:

> ...guaranteeing peaceful co-existence between the three
> religious communities was not nearly so difficult as
> overcoming the tensions between the different races, and
> it was this that constituted the severest problem for the
> Arab rulers of Spain. Besides the indigenous mixed
> population consisting of Iberians and Romans, there was
> also the Germanic minority of Visigoths, who, as the
> former nobility, expected certain priorities even under
> Arab rule. The Jewish population was unusually large in
> Spain. Then there were the Arabs and the Berbers, not to
> mention all the different elements that had been intro-
> duced as a result of the slave trade.[19]

Gerhard Böwering notes that from the modern period, the West
has seen itself in an even more emphatic way as the norm and standard.[20]
Through the Enlightenment, the West became almost obsessed with its
own "knowledge, freedom and happiness," and this view of superiority
was itself reinforced through the military colonial powers. The result was
one that made the West "the standard of culture and induced the church
to see no salvation beyond the confines of its own deposit of faith."
Böwering notes, however, that this situation is no longer the same. He
states that "in the changing world of today, the global religions are no
longer confined within geographical borders. A great migration of people
is in progress." This is certainly the case in Spain, and indeed in all of
Europe itself. For, according to the United Nations report, in an ironic
twist of fate, the lowering birth rates in Europe, and in Spain in a particularly pointed way, require the influx of approximately 250 million people
over the next fifty years if the current level of economic and social well-
being is to be maintained.[21]

---

[19] Ibid., 27-28.
[20] Gerhard Böwering, "Christianity – Challenged by Islam," in *Islam: A Challenge for Christianity*, Hans Küng, Jürgan Moltmann, Eds., *Concilium* 1994/3
(1994/3): 103-104.
[21] United Nations Population Division of the Department of Economic and Social Affairs, *Replacement Migration: Is it a Solution to Declining and Ageing*

Martín Muñoz documents that today there are more than fifteen million Muslims living in Europe,[22] with those in Spain, according to Bedoya numbering officially 500,000 (without counting those who are undocumented).[23] Martín Muñoz then outlines three different approaches as to how these individuals are seen relative to the larger society. The first approach is that of "assimilation," which is based on the acceptance of the Other through the denial of any difference. The Other is welcomed in as much as she or he renounces one's cultural personality in favor of the dominant culture of the country in which one is accepted. A second approach is that of "insertion," which stresses the importance of the community over that of the individual. In this approach, the minority group preserves its specific religious, familial and linguistic reality, but it does so at the risk of closing itself off from the dominant society, laying the basis for a ghetto mentality. The third approach is that of "integration," which is much more open and flexible. In this case one does not have to renounce one's culture of origin, but respects the fundamental laws of the country in which one is accepted. In the long run this promotes "mestizaje."[24]

Populations?,
< http://www.un.org/esa/population/unpop.html >, (March 17, 2000).

[22] Gema Martín Muñoz, "Lo real y lo irreal en la representación del mundo musulmán," *Revista de Occidente* (Enero, 2000): 114.

[23] J. Bedoya,. "50,000 niños musulmanes que viven en España estudiarán islamismo en colegios públicos," in *El Pais Digital,* Sociedad (Madrid, October 4, 1999), < http://www.elpais.es. > (October 6, 1999).

[24] Martín Muñoz, "Lo real y lo irreal en la representación del mundo musulmán," 114. On the topic of *mestizaje* in the Americas, see, especially p. 38, the writings of Virgilio Elizondo, "Popular Religion as Support of Identity; A Pastoral-Psychological Case-Study Based on the Mexican American Experience in the USA." in *Popular Religion*, Norbert Greinbacher, Norbert Mette, Eds., Concilium 186 (August 1986): 36-43. Elizondo speaks of a "second" *mestizaje*: "In the pre-Colombian / Iberian-Catholic *mestizo* based culture of Mexico it is the one who can endure all the opposing tensions of life and not lose his or her interior harmony who appears to be the upright and righteous one" in contrast to the "secular based culture of the United States" where "it is the one who succeeds materially who appears to be the upright and righteous person" And see, also, the critical analysis of Mexican statesman-philosopher José Vasconcelos' development of the concept of *mestizaje* by Roberto S. Goizueta, *Caminemos con Jesús, Toward a Hispanic/Latino Theology of Accompaniment* (Maryknoll, NY: Orbis, 1995), 77-131.

But Martín Muñoz makes the point that one of the most important factors to bear in mind with regard to those who are Muslims living
in Europe is that they have, in almost all cases, come from a country in
which Islam is the official State religion –or at least is the majority religion– to countries in which one will now find oneself in a minority
position. In fact, Bedoya stresses that in Spain the law has been in force
only since 1980 guaranteeing the fundamental right of Muslim children
to be taught Islam in the public schools.[25]

In an effort to promote an integration approach that is built upon
a true affirmation of the Other, Martín Muñoz looks to *al-Andalus*.[26] The
term itself, *al-Andalus*, has found many interpretations. These have been
summarized by Pedro Chalmeta in the Introduction of his work.[27] In the
end, he argues that the only explanation that seems worthy of truth is that
of Joaquín Vallvé: the North African Berber term has its roots in the
Greek deity Atlas, from which is derived the term Atlantic. (The oldest
inscription of the term *al-Andalus* is found on a coin, a *dinar*, minted in
the year 916.) But Chalmeta insists that it is important to recognize that
the term *al-Andalus* is one that designates, primarily and essentially, a
political-religious-cultural *community*, rather than a geographical territory. One always centers on the human person. In the Arabic context, one
describes and identifies oneself in relation to one ancestors, one's belonging to a particular clan or tribe. Thus, the fundamental meaning of
the term *al-Andalus*, must always be rooted in the human and not in the
territory itself.

Martín Muñoz argues that Arabic-Islamic culture must be seen
as a constituent element of both the Hispanic and European personality.[28]
For example, Overbye cites Historian of Science, King, in pointing out
that "from the 10th to the 13th century, Europeans, especially in Spain,
were translating Arabic works into Hebrew and Latin 'as fast as they
could,' The result was a rebirth of learning that ultimately transformed
Western civilization."[29] This, in fact, is something that needs to be "re-

---

[25] Bedoya, "50,000 niños musulmanes."

[26] Martín Muñoz, "Lo real y lo irreal en la representación del mundo
musulmán," 116-117.

[27] Pedro Chalmeta, *Invasión e islamización: La sumisión de Hispania y la for-
mación de al-Andalus* (Madrid: Mapfre, 1994), 22-26.

[28] Martín Muñoz, "Lo real y lo irreal en la representación del mundo
musulmán," 118-120.

[29] Dennis Overbye, "How Islam Won, and Lost, the Lead in Science," *The New*

captured" for the benefit today of both Spain and Europe. But the way in which *al-Andalus* is presented and taught in contemporary Spain consti-tutes, in Martín Muñoz's judgment, a clear example of the rejection of the Other. She points out how the terminology in both elementary and secondary school textbooks frequently refers to "the presence of Mus-lims in Spain," or that "the Muslims lived on the Peninsula for eight hundred years," marginalizing eight centuries of the history of Spain as provisional and not really "Spanish." Even the creation of the term, "Re-conquista," represents the objective of seeking to delegitimize the "Spanishness" of *al-Andalus,* and to present eight hundred years of Span-ish history from the point of view of Christian continuity. The result is that eight hundred years of Arabic culture in Spain is viewed instead as an eight-hundred year struggle of liberation. And this has produced an at-titude, not of one that promotes cultural integration, but of one that unjustly demeans both the Arab and the Muslim.

Theological Analysis and Reflections

The Second Vatican Council's *Declaration on the Relationship of the Church to Non-Christian Religions* officially promulgated October 28, 1965, voiced a fundamental change with regard to the relationship of Christians and Muslims. It stated:

> Although in the course of the centuries many quarrels and hostilities have arisen between Christians and Mus-lims, this most sacred Synod urges all to forget the past and to strive sincerely for mutual understanding. On be-half of all humankind, let them make common cause of safeguarding and fostering social justice, moral values, peace, and freedom [Paragraph 3].[30]

Demonstrating the difficulties in always achieving accuracy in a translation, in this same Paragraph 3, there is a serious mistranslation of

---

York Times (New York, October 30, 2001), < http://www.nytimes.com >, (Oc-tober 31, 2001). Cites David A. King, *Astronomy in the Service of Islam* (Aldershot, U.K.: Variorum,1993).

[30] *"Declaration on the Relationship of the Church to Non-Christian Religions"* in Walter M. Abbott, Edit., *The Documents of Vatican II* (New York: Guild Press, America Press, Association Press, 1966), 663.

an earlier section on the part of the Flannery text, [31] which states that "although not acknowledging him as God, they [Muslims] *worship* [sic] Jesus as a prophet." On the other hand, the Abbott text more accurately translates, "though they do not acknowledge Jesus as God, they *revere* him as a prophet." [my emphasis].

More recently, in March, 2000, the Vatican International Theological Commission published a document entitled, *Memory and Reconciliation: The Church and the Faults of the Past.*[32] Here there is a call, *not* to "forget the past," but to face it, to acknowledge "what was done in contradiction to the Gospel," and to strive for reconciliation. The task is not to eliminate these memories, but to "purify the memory of the past and generate a new one. The basis of this *new memory* cannot be other than mutual love or, better, the renewed commitment to live it." The document quotes the earlier words of Pope John Paul II himself:

> Another sad chapter of history to which the sons and
> daughters of the Church must return with a spirit of re-
> pentance is that of the acquiescence given, especially in
> certain centuries, to intolerance and even the use of force
> in the service of truth." And it stresses the wrong that
> was committed by not respecting "the consciences of the
> persons to whom the faith was presented, as well as all

---

[31] "Declaration on the Relationship of the Church to Non-Christian Religions," in Austin Flannery, Edit., *Vatican Council II, The Conciliar and Post Conciliar Documents*, (Collegeville, MN: Liturgical Press, 1975), 740.

[32] See especially paragraphs 4.0, 5.2, and 5.3. The "Preliminary Note" to the document provides its historical genesis: "The study of the topic 'The Church and the Faults of the Past' was proposed to the International Theological Commission by its President, Joseph Cardinal Ratzinger, in view of the celebration of the Jubilee Year 2000. A sub-commission was established to prepare this study; it was composed of Rev. Christopher Begg, Msgr. Bruno Forte (President), Rev. Sebastian Karotemprel, S.D.B., Msgr. Roland Minnerath, Rev. Thomas Norris, Rev. Rafael Salazar Cardenas, M.Sp.S., and Msgr. Anton Strukelj. The general discussion of this theme took place in numerous meetings of the sub-commission and during the plenary sessions of the International Theological Commission held in Rome from 1998 to 1999. The present text was approved in *forma specifica* by the International Theological Commission, by written vote, and was then submitted to the President, Cardinal Ratzinger, Prefect of the Congregation for the Doctrine of the Faith, who have his approval for its publication." The document was subsequently published March 7, 2000.

forms of force used in the repression and correction of errors.[33]

The document continues that acknowledging the faults of the past:

> ...tend(s) toward the *purification of memory*, which –as noted above– is a process aimed at a new evaluation of the past, capable of having a considerable effect on the present, because past sins frequently make their weight felt and remain temptations in the present as well. Above all, if the causes of possible resentment for evils suffered and the negative influences stemming from what was done in the past can be removed as a result of dialogue and the patient search for mutual understanding with those who feel injured by words and deeds of the past, such a removal may help the community of the Church grow in holiness through reconciliation and peace in obedience to the Truth.[34]

Kevin Lenehan has characterized the Pope's leadership for this *purification of memory*, as "an attempt at undoing the apocalyptic interpretation of history."[35] The resulting outcome is that by "linking 'the structure of memorial with that of celebration,' [one] opens up an alternative hermeneutical approach to history, one that is properly eschatological." Lenehan argues that "the notions of time, history and human autonomy that characterize the modern era lead inevitably to the cultivation of a secularized apocalyptic hermeneutic." And he further states that "when confronted with suffering, a worldview that is closed and self-realizing offers fertile soil for the cultivation of the apocalyptic imagination."

A challenge that one encounters with regard to the *Fiesta de moros y cristianos* is interpreting this event not from the context of a closed

---

[33] John Paul II, "Apostolic Letter, Tertio Millennio Adveniente," in *Origins* 24 (November, 1994), 401-416, n. 35.

[34] International Theological Commission, *Memory and Reconciliation: The Church and the Faults of the Past* (Vatican City, March, 2000), < http://www.vatican.va/roman_curia >, (March 25, 2001), Paragraph 6.1.

[35] Kevin Lenehan, "The Great Jubilee and the Purification of Memory," *Louvain Studies* 25 (2000): 299-301.

and self-realizing worldview from which apocalyptic proceeds, but from the context of a worldview that is open to the remembrance of the suffering of the victims, from which the eschatological proceeds. All too often in the past, it is this apocalyptic trajectory that has emerged, using the language of conflict and conquest. But an eschatological perspective can and does emerge when "dialogue and the patient search for mutual understanding" come to the forefront. The *Fiesta de moros y cristianos* allows for a recognition of the mutuality of these two partners in dialogue.

Max Harris unequivocally supports this same perspective and interpretation:

> It seems to me that the nature of the Spanish folk festival of Moors and Christians is not to reenact history but to *embody* a vision of what might have been and what might yet be. The performers do not believe that historical battles between Moors and Christians ended with conversion and fraternity, but they may well wish that it had been so. And they may wish, too, that human relationships now could be less conflicted and more able to encompass difference without hostility. I am persuaded that Spain's festivals of Moors and Christians, by rewriting the country's most prolonged ethnic conflict so that it ends not in exile but in reconciliation, express that yearning.... The fiestas deliberately revise history, not to deny its pain or to conceal its guilt, but to envision a better outcome.[36]

Harris goes on to highlight his thesis, placing the *fiesta de moros y cristianos* in a wider historical context:

> Thus even though they entertained no hidden transcript of resistance, the medieval *moros y cristianos* were still about the dynamics of power. Insofar as they were also about those they named, the *moros y cristianos* offered a vision of *convivencia* rather than bloodshed. Moors do not get killed in these battles. They survive to be con-

---

[36] Harris, *Aztecs, Moors, and Christians*, 211-212.

verted and to dance and feast with their former enemies. While such a resolution may require, as one modern scholar has put it, that the Moors lose "their very identity," it still compares favorably with the harsh treatment afforded Spanish *moriscos* in the sixteenth century and with the kind of ethnic cleansing we have seen in our own day . It is hard to imagine such a festive ending if Serbs were now to stage a mock battle between Christians and Muslims in the Balkans. Muslims, on the whole, are not demonized in the medieval festivals of the reconquest... They are honored as worthy opponents and as welcomed partners in feasting."[37]

The *Fiesta de moros y cristianos* is the face to face encounter of two Hispanic groups, of two Hispanic worlds, of two Hispanic religions which have interpenetrated one another. María Soledad Carrasco Urgoiti clearly recognizes that today the *fiesta* occurs in an altered form, due in part to Romantic Medievalism, but she nevertheless stresses that:

> "perhaps someday the lens of historical research will allow us to come to the point that connects the *fiesta de moros y cristianos* with the conscious rejection of a plural identity."[38]

And in a similar vein, Harris points to the presence of *los moros* in the festival as representing "the temporary resurgence of all that is suppressed but cannot finally be expelled by church and state.[39] 'The Moors are not just a symbol,' said one of my [Harris'] friends in Villena. 'They are something in us. Look at our faces. Many are Moorish.'"So that today in Spain, in town after town, and city after city, the celebration

---

[37] Ibid., 62.

[38] María Soledad Carrasco Urgoiti, "La fiesta de moros y cristianos y la cuestión morisca en la España de los Austrias," (Originally published in *Actas de la Jornadas sobre Teatro Popular en España*, Joaquín Álvarez Barrientos, Antonio Cea Gutiérreaz, Edit. [Madrid: Consejo Superior de Investigacion Científica, 1987], 65-84), in *El Moro Retador y El Moro Amigo (Estudios sobre fiestas y comedias de moros y cristianos)*, (Granada: Universidad de Granada, 1996), 89-90. Translation of quote by Jerry T. Farmer.

[39] Harris, *Aztecs, Moors, and Christians*, 221.

of the *Fiesta de moros y cristianos* welcomes, honors and accepts –with an acknowledgment of the pain and suffering that was endured– those who have been instrumental in the reality that is Spain today, and with this honesty, provides hope toward a new future. This is the opposite of the type of forgetfulness promoted by the entertainment industry.

In this regard, Lenehan cites from Moreira, Theodor Adorno's analysis of the category of *memory*:

> He [Adorno] argues that the culture of mass capitalism sustains itself by insulating its consumers from the content of their own (alienated) experiences. Such experiences no longer arise freely and involuntarily in the memory, but are replaced by a culturally and socially induced content. The same capitalistic mechanism which produces alienation and suffering also produces an "industry of oblivion," the entertainment industry, to mask and conceal the suffering of its victims. Knowledge and reason are also marked by this socially engineered forgetfulness. [Quoting Adorno] "It is of the essence of domination to prevent recognition of the suffering it produces of itself."[40]

Several months after the publication of *Memory and Reconciliation: The Church and the Faults of the Past*, the Declaration, *"Dominus Jesus,"* was published by the Vatican Congregation for the Doctrine of the Faith.[41] The Introduction of the Declaration provides the purpose of

---

[40] Lenehan, , "The Great Jubilee and the Purification of Memory," 295-296, where he cites Alberto Moreira, "The Dangerous Memory of Jesus Christ in a Post-Traditional Society," in *Faith in a Society of Instant Gratification,* Maureen Junker-Kennedy, Miklós Tomka, edit., *Concilium* (1999:4): 41, where Moreira himself cites Theodor Adorno, *Minima Moralia: Reflections from a Damaged Life* (London: New Left Books, 1974), no page cited.

[41] Congregation for the Doctrine of the Faith, *Declaration "Dominus Jesus" on the Unicity and Salvific Universality of Jesus Christ and the Church* (August 6, 2000), < http://www.vatican.va/roman_curia >, (March 25, 2001), Paragraph 2. The declaration is signed by Joseph Cardinal Ratzinger, with the concluding note that "the Sovereign Pontiff John Paul II, at the Audience of June 16, 2000, granted to the undersigned Cardinal Prefect of the Congregation for the Doctrine of the Faith, with sure knowledge and by his apostolic authority, ratified and confirmed this Declaration, adopted in Plenary Session and ordered its publica-

the document, namely "giving reasons for and supporting the evangelizing mission of the Church, above all in connection with the religious
traditions of the world." It affirms the importance of "inter-religious dialogue," which "requires an attitude of understanding and a relationship of
mutual knowledge and reciprocal enrichment."

The sixth and final major section of the Declaration is entitled
"The Church and the Other Religions in Relation to Salvation."[42] Within
this section it is stated that "if it is true that the followers of other religions can receive divine grace, it is also certain that *objectively speaking*
they are in a gravely deficient situation in comparison with those who, in
the Church, have the fullness of the means of salvation." The declaration
immediately continues by quoting from the Vatican II Document, *Lumen
gentium,* that "all the children of the Church should nevertheless remember that their exalted condition results, not from their own merits, but
from the grace of Christ."[43] While these two statements follow immediately upon each other in *"Dominus Jesus,"* they are really addressing two
very different realities.

Karl Rahner employs the distinction between "offered grace"
and "accepted grace."[44] My own study of this theme is done from an ec-
clesiological perspective.[45] This double aspect of Offer-Acceptance
recognizes the freedom of the human being as the addressee of God's
self communication. In an attempt to interpret how one ought to understand this statement in *"Dominus Jesus,"* I would argue that those in the
Church who "have the fullness of the means of salvation" *have it* [my
emphasis] with reference to offered grace. Rahner speaks of this offered
grace as "a grace which always surrounds the human being, even the sin-
ner and the unbeliever, as the inescapable setting of one's existence."[46]
One's "exalted condition" comes about in and through what the docu-

---

tion."

[42] Ibid., Paragraph 22.

[43] Ibid., Paragraph 22, n. 93.

[44] Karl Rahner, *The Trinity*, Joseph Donceel, Trans. (New York: Crossroad,
1997; Originally published in Einsiedeln, Switzerland: Benziger, 1967), 92-93.

[45] Jerry T. Farmer, *Ministry in Community, Karl Rahner's Vision of Ministry*,
Louvain Theological & Pastoral Monographs, Vol. 13 (Leuven, Belgium: Peeters Press / Grand Rapids, MI: W.B. Eerdmans, 1993).

[46] Karl Rahner, "Nature and Grace," in *Theological Investigations*, Vol. 4, Kevin
Smyth, Trans. (London: Darton, Longman & Todd, 1966; Originally published
in Einsiedeln, Switzerland: Benziger, 1960): 181.

ment *"Dominus Jesus"* calls the "grace of Christ," and which Rahner insists enables, but never forces, the acceptance of that grace. But one must also recognize that all who accept the one grace of Christ, both those in the Church as well as those from within other religious traditions and contexts, share in this "exalted condition."

And a very troubling issue with regard to *"Dominus Jesus"* is the apparent deliberateness of the declaration to eliminate any reference to an important emphasis in the incomplete and therefore misleading citation of paragraph 2 of the Vatican II text, *Nostra aetate*. There one finds the following exhortation addressed to all Christians, which has been "edited out" of the *"Dominus Jesus"* declaration:

> ...prudently and lovingly, through dialogue and collaboration with the followers of other religions, and in witness of Christian faith and life, acknowledge, preserve and promote the spiritual and moral goods found among these [men], as well as the values in their society and culture. [47]

Rahner's distinction between "offered grace" and "accepted grace," is particularly significant. His distinction is rooted in the one self-communication of God, which he insists takes place in "two and only two manners": the modality of history and the modality of spirit.[48] Within this context, one identifies four double aspects of God's self-communication, one of which is that of Offer-Acceptance. He identifies the other three double aspects as 1) Origin-Future; 2) History-Transcendence, and 3) Knowledge-Love; and this last pair actually follows that of Offer-Acceptance.[49] Rahner underscores the dimension of acceptance by affirming "that the very acceptance of a divine self-communication through the power and act of freedom is one more moment of the self-communication of God, who gives himself in such a way that his self-donation is accepted in freedom."[50] The double aspect of Offer-Acceptance recognizes the freedom of the human being as the addressee of God's self-communication. Rahner goes on to stress that this aspect of acceptance must be brought about by the self-

---

[47] Abbott, 662-663.
[48] Rahner, *The Trinity*, 94.
[49] Ibid., 88.
[50] Ibid., 92-93.

communicating God.[51] If the acceptance were realized on the part of the human being, then the self-communication of God would be done away with. But God "creates the possibility of its acceptance and this acceptance itself," so that God's self-communication can take place.

To link this more explicitly to the reality of non-Christian religions, one finds a key perspective on the part of Rahner: the Christological aspect is seen to be Offer, and the pneumatological aspect, that is, relating to the Holy Spirit, is Acceptance. It is clear that through this concept Rahner is seeking to recognize more explicitly and more clearly the trinitarian doctrine in both Christology and pneumatology. The Christological aspects are seen to be: Origin, History, Offer, and Knowledge. The pneumatological aspects, that is, those relating to the Holy Spirit, are: Future, Transcendence, Acceptance, and Love. For Rahner insists that between Jesus and the Spirit there is "both a unity and a difference, and a relationship of mutual conditioning."[52] The Holy Spirit, the "universal self communication of God to the world," has an "intrinsic relation to Jesus Christ," because God's self-communication and its acceptance can never take place in "mere abstract transcendentality," but takes place in "historical mediation." And Jesus Christ is this historical mediation toward which the Spirit is directed from the very beginning.

Jesus is seen simultaneously as the "high point" of historical mediation, but also as the only point. Here, one must refer to Rahner's reflections on the "Anonymous Christian." He summarizes his view by saying:

> There must be a Christian theory to account for the fact that every individual who does not in any absolute or ultimate sense act against one's own conscience can say and does say in faith, hope and love, Abba within one's own spirit, and is on these grounds in all truth a sister or brother to Christians in God's sight.[53]

---

[51] Ibid., 97-98.

[52] Karl Rahner, *Foundations of Christian Faith*, William V. Dych, Trans. (London: Seabury Press, 1978; Originally published in Freiberg im Breisgau, Germany: Herder, 1976), 334, 317-318.

[53] Karl Rahner, "Observations on the Problem of the 'Anonymous Christian'" in *Theological Investigations*, Vol. 14, David Bourke, Trans. (London: Darton, Longman & Todd, 1976; Originally published in Einsiedeln, Switzerland: Benziger, 1972): 291.

And Rahner further clarifies his position in a later work:

> The grace of God (which the history of the Crucified and
> Risen One made effective and irreversible in the history
> of humanity) is consequently the grace of Jesus Christ
> even when it is not explicitly and reflectively grasped
> and interpreted as such. This is not merely and opinion
> which a Christian may hold; it is part of his faith,
> which... forbids him to hold the opinion that this salvific
> will of God in Jesus Christ effects a person's salvation
> only when the latter has explicitly become a Christian.[54]

God's self communication always takes place in and through historical mediation. God's Spirit is clearly operative wherever there is, in the language of the Vatican document, *Memory and Reconciliation*, this "dialogue and the patient search for mutual understanding."[55]

The *fiesta de moros y cristianos* can be seen as a paradigm of God's self communication. In the dramatization that takes place, neither the *moros* nor the *cristianos* are presented as "the Other." They are seen and celebrated as equal subjects. Indeed, one celebrates their mutual encounter. And it is proclaiming, in a powerful symbolic manner, that out of this encounter has emerged the reality that is Spain, and, to a certain extent, the reality that is Europe itself.

Harris further reflects on this reality by referring to the foundational work of Martin Buber's dialogical principle:

> ...that the other be recognized not only as an object of
> which we may speak or whom I may address as a Thou
> but also as a subject, an I who speaks about me within
> his or her own circle and who in turn addresses me as a
> Thou... This realization that the other is not merely an
> object of my discourse and my gaze, but that he or she is
> also a subject observing me, leads to the startling insight
> that the other has a point of view that is not my own and
> which is no more a defective version of mine than mine

---

[54] Karl Rahner, "Experience of the Holy Spirit" in *Theological Investigations*, Vol. 18, Edward Quinn, Trans. (London: Darton, Longman & Todd, 1983; Originally published in Einsiedeln, Switzerland: Benziger, 1978): 205-206.

[55] International Theological Commission, 2000, Paragraph 6.1.

is a defective version of his or hers.[56]

Harris then goes on to further incorporate the perspective of Mikhail Bakhtin, for whom the other "was a source of joy... His 'other' signals the diversity of human experience, joyously challenging the totalitarian assumption that there can ever be a single point of view."

To acknowledge the sins and weaknesses of the past, stresses the document, *Memory and Reconciliation: The Church and the Faults of the Past,* "is an act of honesty and courage. It opens a new tomorrow for everyone."[57]

John Paul II repeats this emphasis "at the close of the Great Jubilee of the Year 2000":

> In the years of preparation for the Great Jubilee the Church has sought to build, not least through a series of highly symbolic meetings, *a relationship of openness and dialogue with the followers of other religions* [emphasis in text]. This dialogue must continue. In the climate of increased cultural and religious pluralism which is expected to mark the society of the new millennium, it is obvious that this dialogue will be especially important in establishing a sure basis for peace and warding off the dread spectre of those wars of religion which have so bloodied human history. The name of the one God must become increasingly what it is: *a name of peace and a summons to peace....*We know in fact that, in the presence of the mystery of grace, infinitely full of possibilities and implications for human life and history, the Church herself will never cease putting questions, trusting in the help of the Paraclete, the Spirit of truth (cf. *Jn* 14:17), whose task it is to guide her 'into all the truth' " (*Jn* 16:13).[58]

This continuing encounter that takes place in Spain between *mo-*

---

[56] Max Harris, *The Dialogical Theatre, Dramatizations of the Conquest of Mexico and the Question of the Other* (New York: St. Martin's Press, 1993), 157.

[57] International Theological Commission, Paragraph 6.4.

[58] John Paul II, *Novo millennio ineunte* (Vatican City, January, 2001), < http://www.vatican.va/holy_father > (March 25, 2001), Paragraphs 54-56.

ros and *cristianos* year after year can be seen as a paradigm of God's on-going self communication with humanity, deepening and developing the relational life that humanity is offered by God, and –even more remarkable– that life which God enables humans to accept.

THE *MARTYRDOM OF RAWH AL-QURAYSHI* AND THE DEVELOPMENT OF AN EARLY ARABIC CHRISTIAN COMMUNITY

David H. Vila[*]

Most scholars of early Christian-Muslim relations (7th -9th centuries CE) focus on texts that are either theological or historical in nature. A growing body of scholarship is beginning to demonstrate that Arabic and Greek Christian hagiography are a significant and neglected source for the study of early relations between Christians and Muslims.[1] In particular, the differences between how Greek Christians and Arab Christians interact with Islam in their respective hagiographies provide us with important insights into the nature of early Christian-Muslim relations and of the development of an early Arabic Christian community more broadly.

In contrast to the general demonization of Arabs and Muslims that is a common thread to most of the Greek hagiography of the period, Arab Christians often sought to emphasize the cultural, linguistic, and even religious affinities that they had with the Arab Muslims. Surprisingly enough, this is true even in the Arabic accounts of Arab Christians who were put to death by Muslims for their conversion from Islam to Christianity. As such, these texts provide significant and timely examples of how members of different religious communities sought out commonalities that enabled them to achieve a relatively peaceful co-existence and more specifically, how Arab Christians sought to define themselves vis-à-vis the Muslims among whom they lived.

My paper is a study of the Arabic account of the martyrdom of

[*] David Vila is Assistant Professor of Religion and Philosophy at John Brown University, a private, independent, liberal arts college in Siloam Springs, Arkansas. In 1999 he was awarded a Ph.D. in Historical Theology from Saint Louis University with a dissertation on early Christian-Muslim relations.
[1] See for instance, Ignace Dick, ed. and trans., "La Passion arabe de S. Antione Ruwah néo-martyr de Damas (+25 déc. 799)," *Le Museon,* 74 (1961): 109-33; Sidney Griffith, "The Arabic account of `Abd al-Masih an-Nagrani al-Ghassani," *Le Museon*, 98 (1985): 344-47; and David Vila, "The struggle over arabisation in medieval Arabic Christian hagiography," *Al-Masaq: Islam and the Medieval Mediterranean*, 15,1 (1985): 35-46.

Rawh al-Qurayshi, an Arab Christian who had converted from Islam and was eventually put to death. I will survey the socio-cultural elements in the text that provide an important window into the nature of early Christian-Muslim relations and then will look at how the story of the martyrdom was used for different purposes among Arab Christians of three to four centuries later.

Anthony al-Qurayshi

One of the more important hagiographical texts for reconstructing the development of an Arabic Christianity, on a popular level, is the account of the martyrdom of the Syrian saint named Rawh al-Qurayshi.[2] More properly, the account is a telling of the martyrdom of a man named simply "Anthony" who before his baptism was named Rawh al-Qurayshi. What is significant for the present is that before his baptism, Rawh was a Muslim and, according to the text a nephew of the Caliph Harun al-Rashid, of "One Thousand and One Nights" fame. He was put to death, according to the text because of his conversion to Christianity and his refusal to recant this conversion.

The memory of Anthony figures prominently in the history of Near Eastern Christianity. He finds notice in a number of liturgical calendars, including the tenth century Palestinian calendar found in *Sinai Georgien 34*.[3] Likewise, the Melkite *Vatican Syriac 243* mentions in the entry for December 24 "This same day, the commemoration of Saint Anthony the Qurayshite; he possesses *megalynaria* and *canon*."[4] He is also referred to in Theodore Abu Qurrah's *Treatise on the Icons*.[5]

---

[2] Al-Qurayshi's name has been variously spelled Rawh, Ruwah, Ruh, Ruhay, among others. For a definitive statement on the proper orthography see: Samir Khalil Samir, "Saint Ruwh al-Qurashi: Étude d'onomastique Arabe et authenticité de sa passion," *Le Museon* 105 3.4 (1992): 343-359. The most recent full-length study of the text is that of Emaneuela Braida & Chiara Pelissetti, *Storia de Rawh al-Qurashi: Un discendente de Maometto che scelse di divenire cristiano*, Silvio Zamorani, ed. (Turin: 2001).

[3] See for instance Gérard Garitte's *Le Calendrier Palestino-Géorgien du Sinaticus 34 (Xe Siècle)*, (Bruxelles: Société des Bollandistes, 1958), 135-36.

[4] Dick, 109. Dick mentions that the Manuscript is described in Assemani, *Bibliothecae Apostolicae Vaticanae codicum manuscriptorum catalogus*, III, 522-24.

[5] For this see Sidney Griffith's recent translation of the text, with introduction, *Theodore Abu Qurrah: A Treatise on the Veneration of the Holy Icons*. (Louvain: Peeters, 1997), 21.

In the Jacobite tradition, Anthony is mentioned in the 12th century *Chronicle* of Michael the Syrian. There Michael summarizes the story of the conversion and eventual martyrdom of Anthony, including many of the main events found in the full account.[6] The 13th century Bar Hebraeus also mentions Anthony, as does Rabban Sliba.[7] The memory of Anthony was therefore strong among Near Eastern Christians of various confessional allegiances for quite some time. Oddly, there is no mention of Anthony in any Byzantine source, a fact that I tend to attribute to racial prejudice and an almost complete failure of the Byzantine hagiographical tradition to distinguish between Arab and Muslim, much to the detriment of their Arab co-religionists.[8] One exception could be a possible mention of Anthony in the Greek *Passion* of the 20 Monks of Mar Saba. The events depicted in the *Passion* took place in the year 797, two years before the traditional date of Anthony's conversion, and so there are problems with the dates involved. Nonetheless, near the end of that text we read of a figure named Christopher who was converted out of unbelief (i.e., Islam) into the holy faith (i.e., Christianity) and was baptized to God.[9] According to the text these events took place "a few years ago" and the person is said to have converted "from the Persians," - a common misnomer for Arab Muslims - became a monk, was falsely accused of denying God and then was taken before the Caliph and his chief advisor, where after making a "good confession," was "presented to the Lord with the crown of martyrdom," having his head cut off with a sword.[10]

The details of the account are very similar to those found in the martyrdom of Anthony, but in many ways are the stereotypical elements found in the genre. Both were Muslims who converted to Christianity, were baptized, became monks, went before the Caliph, and both were beheaded by the sword. In the Byzantine text the figure is named Christopher, which could be a simple play on "one who bears Christ" in this

---

[6] Michael the Syrian, *Le Chronique de Michel le Syrien: Patriarche Jacobite d'Antioch*, J. B. Chabot, ed. and trans., Vol. 3 (Paris, 1905), 18-19.

[7] See his *Gregorii Barhebraei Chronicum Syriacum*, Paul Bedjan, ed. (Paris, 1890), 132.

[8] Vila, 35-46.

[9] Text found in A. Papadopoulos-Kerameus, ed. "The Account of the Twenty Martyrs of Mar Saba [in Greek]," *Pravoslvnyj Palestinskyi Sbornik*, v. 19 (St. Petersburg, 1907), 40-41.

[10] Ibid.

case, to the Muslims, or it could be a proper name. The text is somewhat unclear though. This Christopher is known in no other source except the tenth century Palestinian calendar of saints that is extant only in Georgian, in which a separate entry is found for Anthony.[11] The entry in the Georgian calendar is based on the text of the *Passion* of the monks of Mar Saba and so yields no new information beyond that found in the martyrdom text itself. It is possible therefore that the calendar reflects a tradition that was passed from the far reaches of Near Eastern Christianity back to the Greek speaking "west." It seems then that the Christopher of the *Passion* of the 20 monks of Mar Saba and the Arab figure Anthony are two separate individuals. It seems that a more likely candidate for this Christopher might be the Arab martyr, ʿAbd al-Masih, though more work needs to be done to substantiate such a claim.[12]

While it may never be possible to recover what exactly happened in the late eighth century regarding Anthony and his alleged martyrdom what is clear is that as early as within one decade of the date of the events described in the text the story of Anthony's conversion was already well known enough for Theodore Abu Qurrah (d.c. 830 C.E.), a prominent Arab Christian theologian to use elements of that story as evidence supporting his iconophile treatise.[13] It is thus clear that in a number of ways the story of the martyrdom of Anthony was important to Near Eastern Christians. The text is thus a significant window into the development of an early Arabic Christianity.

The account of the Martyrdom of Rawh al-Qurayshi is found in three manuscripts from the Monastery of St. Catherine on Mt. Sinai. Of these manuscripts, *Sinai Arabic 513* dates to the tenth century and the other two, *Sinai Arabic 445* and *Sinai Arabic 448* both date to the 13th century. The copy found in *British Library Oriental 5019* dates to the 11th century. The text is also found in an abbreviated form in *Vatican Arabic 175,* which is dated to the late 13th century, to which I will refer toward the end of this paper.

According to the story, Rawh al-Qurayshi was through the tribe of Quraysh related to both the Prophet Muhammad and also to the Caliph Harun al-Rashid (r. 786-809 C.E.). As a Muslim living in Damascus

---

[11] See Garitte, 198-99.

[12] See Griffiths reconstruction in "The Arabic Account of ʿAbd al-Masih an-Nagrani al-Ghassani," 344-47.

[13] For this see Sidney Griffith's *Theodore Abu Qurrah: A Treatise on the Veneration of the Holy Icons,* 21.

Rawh used to watch the goings on of the Church of Saint Theodore down the street from where he lived. From time to time he would sneak into the church after the priest had left and tear down the crosses, consume the consecrated bread and wine, and tear the altar cloth. One day, the Muslim entered the church and saw the icon of St. Theodore. Infuriated at the sight of the saint, Rawh shot an arrow at the icon. The arrow as it neared the icon turned in mid air and came back to pierce through the infidel's hand.

A number of days later during the feast of St. Theodore, as a procession of Christians passed down the street to the church, Rawh sat off to the side watching. Following the crowd into the church he watched as the priest performed the Mass. Much to his shock at the "moment of the Eucharist" he looked and saw the bread converted into a white lamb laying on the altar, which the priest then carved up and gave piece by piece to the parishioners. Afterwards, the unbelieving Muslim confronted the priest who insisted that there was no lamb and that nothing out of the ordinary had taken place. Rawh was amazed and exclaimed in a loud voice that the Christian religion was truly an amazing and very noble religion. The priest then returned to his parishioners and with them prayed that God would be made known to the Muslim.

That night St. Theodore mounted on horseback and in shining armor appeared to Rawh. The saint chided the Muslim for his impious acts and commanded him to repent and accept the "powerful Christ, to depart from error and accept the truth, the victory, and the proof." When Rawh arose that morning his heart was aflame with faith in Christ. He mounted his horse and as if by chance came upon a number of Christian pilgrims bound for Jerusalem. He went with them and in the holy city related his story to the patriarch Elias. Soon thereafter he was baptized in the Jordan River where his name was changed to Anthony. He then went to Damascus and informed his former co-religionists of his conversion. After several imprisonments and after speaking with the Caliph, Harun al-Rashid, he was beheaded and his body was crucified on the bank of the Euphrates River. The colophon notes that the martyrdom took place "in the year 1100 of the years of Alexander and 183 of the years of the Arabs," which corresponds to the year 799 C.E.

Throughout the text there are several elements which portray the Muslims as violent and capricious. The issue of allegations of Muslim violence against Christians in Greek Christian apologetic writings against Islam has been well known for some time, and has been exploited by some western and Byzantine scholars with an anti-Islamic agenda.[14] What is somewhat more curious is that also in many Arabic Christian writings there are examples of allegations of Muslim violence against Christians. With the element of racial prejudice removed in the Arabic Christian texts there is a very interesting nuancing of the allegations. Even so, that is a topic which is somewhat beyond the scope of the present discussion. For the moment I will focus on elements where the current text gives us clues about the formation and development of an early Arabic Christianity.

The first element in the text that is striking, and an element that is pervasive in early Arabic Christian hagiography, is the place of Arab ethnicity. As such the text offers an important window into Arab Christian self-identity in late eighth century Palestine as the surrounding culture was becoming increasingly arabized and islamized.

The text of the martyrdom of Anthony begins stating that the soon-to-be martyr is "a man from the nobility" which as becomes clear in the text is a reference to the caliphal house of Harun al-Rashid. Interestingly this is the reading of the two earliest manuscripts, *Sinai Arabic 513* and *British Museum Oriental 5019*, from the 10th and 11th centuries, respectively. The later copies of the text, as found in *Sinai Arabic 445* and *Sinai Arabic 448* - both 13th century - each add "a man from the nobility *of the Arabs*." The convert from Islam is thus not only from the nobility but from the *Arab* nobility. The text, and especially the later versions, thus attempts to make it perfectly clear to the reader that the protagonist was an Arab.

Later in the text various figures attempt to convince Anthony to recant telling him that in becoming a Christian he has abandoned his nobility and his family heritage and has turned to unbelief. The implication in the text is that in becoming a Christian, he has turned his back not only on his Muslim faith but also on his nobility and his very Arab identity. The text makes it clear that the Muslim claim was that for an Arab to be other than a Muslim was to be a less than noble Arab. Nowhere is this made more clear than from the mouth of Harun al-Rashid himself.

---

[14] Among the more egregious examples are: Bat Ye'or's *The Decline of Eastern Christianity under Islam* (Rutherford, New Jersey: Fairleigh Dickenson UP, 1996); Ibid., *The Dhimmi: Jews and Christians under Islam*, (Rutherford, New Jersey: Fairleigh Dickenson UP, 1985); and Demetrios Constantelos' "The Moslem Conquests of the Near East as Revealed in the Greek Sources of the 7th and 8th Centuries," *Byzantion* 42 (1972): 325-357.

Upon seeing his nephew in the clothes of a Christian monk the Caliph says to Anthony "Indeed O noble Rawh, what has induced you to make of yourself what was not made?"[15] The Caliph here attempts to convince Anthony - though al-Rashid refuses to call him by his Christian name - that in becoming a Christian he has become outwardly what he can never be inwardly! An Arab according to al-Rashid cannot be a Christian for to do so is to go contrary to the very nature of what it means to be an Arab, and that is to be a Muslim. The martyrdom text functions as an apology against such a claim attempting to prove the legitimacy of an Arab Christianity by highlighting the fact that this noble Christian convert was also from the nobility of the Arabs.

A second feature is the mention of specific tribal affiliation. Rawh al-Qurayshi is said to be a nephew of the ruling Caliph Harun al-Rashid, and as a member of the Quraysh tribe a direct descendent of Muhammad. Thus his name indicates that he is not only an Arab, but an Arab *par excelance*. The name Qurayshi would have been respected by Muslim and Christian Arabs alike, associated as it was with both the ruling Caliph and with the Prophet Muhammad. And indeed, in Muslim apologetic writings against Christianity of the same period, the nobility of the Quraysh was seen as one argument in favor of the truthfulness of Islam.[16] The fact that a Qurayshi Arab converted to and eventually died for his Christian faith would have played a significant role in legitimizing a nascent Arabic Christianity. The text thus implies that if a noble, Qurayshi Arab can be a Christian, then *a fortiori* Arabs of less noble stock can certainly also legitimately be Christians. There is a concerted effort in the text therefore to portray the protagonist not only as a Muslim who converted to Christianity but also as a noble, Arab Muslim *from the Quraysh* who converted to Christianity.

Another element that brings out cultural affinities can be seen in the transmission of the text of the present martyrdom account. At a number of places, the text of the martyrdom account was emended by later copyists. It is in fact not possible to know with any specificity at how much later a date the texts were emended. All that is known for certain is

---

[15] Dick, 125. Interestingly, the two later copies of this text add "and so part company with your noble heritage."

[16] For a reference to the Quraysh being "the most excellent of the Arabs" found in a Muslim apologetic text against Christianity see David Thomas' "Two Muslim-Christian Debates from the Early Shi'ite Tradition," *Journal of Semitic Studies* 33 (1988): 59.

that the two earliest copies that are extant date from the tenth and eleventh centuries. The two later copies both date from the thirteenth century. In both of these later manuscripts there are numbers of places where the text has been changed to strengthen the apologetic tone of the text against Islam.

One of the more significant cases occurs fairly early on in the text. When the Muslim Rawh sees the bread converted into a lamb on the altar, he says to himself *"Subhan Allah,"* which is "Praise be to God." Later, when the Muslim approaches those who were present at the mass he tells them "Truly your religion is very noble religion." When the priest and the Christian parishioners heard him they exclaimed together a slight variant of the same phrase that came from the mouth of the Muslim: "Praise be to God!" The particular phrase, *"Subhan Allah"* is a term that is found literally hundreds of times in the Hadith literature and numerous times in the Qur'an, though there, not as an exclamation.[17] In the later copies of the manuscript of the martyrdom text, the phrase spoken by the priest and the parishioners is emended to "Praise be to God, *Christ the Savior.*" It seems to me likely that the addition of the name of Christ as savior was done to make it perfectly clear that the Christians in the story were not using a Muslim phrase. Their exclamation is a praising of Christ, not to be confused with the referent of the Muslim's exclamation of praise. The earlier text though was less concerned with distinguishing the statements made by the Muslim and the Christians in the story and so felt free to use the same terminology for both. Thus it would appear that as Arab Christian communities developed over the intervening three centuries, they may have felt it necessary to make a more clear statement that distinguished Christianity from Islam, where that distinction was blurred by the use of a phrase that later came to be identified as Muslim

---

[17] Earlier I noted that the Muslim Rawh exclaimed "Praise be to God" when he saw the miracle of the lamb on the altar. The phrase "Praise be to God" as used there is one that is fairly common in early Islamic circles. It is found in this exact form in the Qur'an 9 times and in slight variation, of number or tense, 37 times. In the traditional "six" collections of Sunni Hadith literature the phrase occurs in this exact form 302 times and many times in variation. An interesting factor is that in the Qur'an it is never used as an exclamation of amazement, while in the Hadith literature it is often used in this way, as it was used by the Muslim Rawh in the present text. Muhammad ibn Isma'il Bukhari, *Sahih al-Bukhari: the translation of the meanings of Sahih al-Bukhari: Arabic- English.* Dar AHYA Us-Sunnah al Nabawiya, 1971.

terminology.

Another incident that bears mention as a textual variant in the later texts that appears to strengthen the distinction between Islam and Christianity is in the account of Rawh's baptism. The two priests who led the recently converted Rawh to the Jordan River asked him to remove his clothes and descend into the water. This he did "with great joy and gladness." The text then states that it was very cold that day and then simply "they baptized him." The emendation to the text in both of the later Sinai manuscripts – dating to the 13th century adds "in the name of the Father, and of the Son, and of the Holy Spirit."

I contend that the emendation was inserted in order to strengthen the force of the Christian nature of the rite that took place at the Jordan River. What in fact happened, according to the later texts was that this prominent Muslim became a Christian, and unmistakably so. The early text, I argue, was too vague for the later scribes and failed to make clear the distinctly Christian nature of what happened at the Baptism. Thus the Christian baptismal formula was added to the later texts, to clarify the religious nature of the rite.

While it is possible that this emendation is due merely to developments of an Arabic liturgy, such is not likely. Even at the earliest period of Arabic Christian texts, the baptismal type formula "In the name of the Father and the Son and the Holy Spirit" is present at the beginning of almost every text, parallel to the more commonly Muslim phrase "in the name of God the merciful the compassionate." So it seems to me likely that a more clear and forceful distinction between Christianity and Islam is made in the later manuscripts on socio-cultural and religious grounds, not on liturgical grounds. And in this way, the later manuscripts attempt to strengthen the Christian apologetic force of the account of the martyrdom of this prominent Arab Muslim, who converted to Christianity.

I will now deal briefly with the "autobiography" of Anthony as it is found in *Vatican Arabic 175* to show how the apologetic force of the conversion and martyrdom of Anthony developed as the text itself was shaped for another community.

The Autobiography of Anthony al-Qurayshi

Vatican Arabic 175 is one of a collection of nearly 200 Christian Arabic manuscripts found in the Vatican library which were catalogued by Angelo Mai in the early 1800s.[18] All of the Christian Arabic codices were microfilmed in 1970 and are available for study through various universities.[19] Information on the contents or condition of these materials is found only in sporadic essays published over the past century by scholars of Arabic Christianity. The first study of a text from Vatican Arabic 175 was by Paul Peeters in 1914, and passing mention is made to the manuscript in various essays since. But there is yet no complete description of the entire contents of the manuscript.[20]

The texts contained in Vatican Arabic 175 have a unified theme of what I describe as 'the man of God who overcomes under duress.' All of the protagonists are in fact male and all are examples of men who endured suffering and overcame adversity for the sake of their faith in God. The protagonists range from Job, the story of Joseph in Egypt, a handful of early Christian martyrs, a smattering of desert saints, a Christian named Abu Qaltiya who was martyred at the hands of the Muslims, and of course, the story of the conversion and eventual martyrdom of Rawh al-Qurayshi, which occupies folios 122v through 127v.

Folio 86r contains the only date present in the codex. There we read:

> Completed with the help of God and made expedient by
> his success in the city of Cairo the guarded on the 9th of
> the month of Hatur of the year one thousand and one of
> the righteous martyrs corresponding to the twenty-fourth

---

[18] See Angelo Mai, ed., *Scriptorum veterum nova collectio e vaticani codicibus* (Rome: Typis Vacticanis, 1825-1838), *ad. loc.*

[19] The cataloging of the Islamic Arabic manuscripts in the Vatican Library began in 1935 by Giorgio Levi Della Vida. See "Elenco dei manoscritti Arabi Islamici della Biblioteca Vaticana: Vaticani, Barberiniani, Borgiani, Rossiani," *Studi e Testi* 67 (1935). These manuscripts are available on mircofilm through the Knights of Columbus Vatican Film Library at Saint Louis University, St. Louis, Missouri.

[20] A comparison of the Georgian version of the "autobiography" with the Arabic version of Vatican Arabic 175 is found in Paul Peeters' "L'autobiographie de S. Antoine le néo-martyr," *Analecta Bollandiana* 33 (1914): 52-63. Mention of the codex is found in Dick, 111; Samir Khalil Samir, 345; and J. Nasrallah, *Histoire du movement litteraire dans l'église melchite du Ve au XXe Siècle* II, 2 (750=Xe S.), (Louvain et Paris: Peeters, 1988), 165-66. Regrettably, the most recent study of the story of Anthony does not include any discussion of the account as found in Vatican Arabic 175. See Emanuela Braida & Chiara Pelissetti.

of Sha'ban, six hundred and eighty-four. Oh Lord, have mercy on your servant Habakum b. Girgis.[21]

That date corresponds to 1285 C.E. and thus is removed in time significantly from the two early manuscripts of the Anthony text (from the 10th and 11th centuries) but is within a few decades of the two later Sinai manuscripts. Notice should also be made that the provenance of the text is Egypt. Thus we are able to get a good idea of how the use of this text developed over time and in differing circumstances.

The text has been called the "autobiography" of Rawh al-Qurayshi because it is told in the first person, and thus presumably ends before his death – it is not possible to tell because the last folio is missing (although in this genre one shouldn't be surprised if an "autobiography" continued *post mortem*!). The text then, is written from the pen of the martyred saint, himself. This adds significantly to the dramatic force of the text. Here we have, according to the text, the very speech of the martyr, who attested to the truth of his confession of Christ with his own blood and exhorts his fellow co-religionists to remain faithful to their own Christian confession, despite pressures that they might have to endure at the hands of Muslims.

As far as the use of the text goes, it seems clear that the text was intended for public reading. Peppered throughout the account is the phrase "*ya ikhwati*" [O my brothers!] a clear indication that the text had a performative dimension, surely to be read at least on the martyr's feast day. The use of this phrase is also common in Muslim sermons of the period. See for example the sermons of Ibn 'Abd Rabbihi (d. 940) where his use of "*ya, nas*" [O men!] parallels that in the present text.[22] The phrase "O my brothers" occurs 11 times throughout the Vatican text, increasing in frequency during and after Rawh's conversion up to the end

---

[21] This is the translation of Peeters. The matter is not quite so simple though. The text as found in the microfilm of Vatican Arabic 175 is quite unclear and mostly illegible.

[22] The use of this phrase is also common in Muslim sermons of the period. See for example the sermons of Ibn 'Abd Rabbihi (d.940) where his use of "Ya, Nas" [O men!] paralells that in the present text. Ahmad ibn Muhammad Ibn 'Abd Rabbihi, *Adab al-Minbar*, Arthur Wormhoudt, trans. (Oskaloosa, Iowa: William Penn College, 1988), see for example p.11. Also instructive is a work by Ibn al-Jawzi (d. 597 A.H.), *Kitab al-Qussas wa'l-Mudhakkirin*, Merlin L. Swartz, ed. and trans. (Beirut: Dar al-Mashreq, 1986). In this work al-Jawzi defends the homelitical use of pious stories.

of the extant text. An example is found at Rawh's baptism where our protagonist relates (in the first person, of course) "then I was baptized, *oh my brothers*, in the name of the Father and the Son and the Holy Spirit." Clearly then, the text was intended for public, and very likely monastic use. The narrow audience of the Vatican text then, might account for some of the hardening of tone that will be discussed shortly.

The text itself begins on folio 122v with a prayer of eight lines where the converted Rawh gives thanks to Christ who brought him to his new-found faith. Twice in this prayer Rawh refers to his former religion as "the pagan religion," a relatively harsh tone, and much more harsh than that found in the earlier Sinai manuscripts. The term "pagan" is used numerous times in other places throughout the text to refer to Islam. The contrast between Islam and Christianity is also heightened as Rawh describes his conversion experience as his having been "enlightened by the light of Christianity." After this prayer the protagonist states that before his baptism his name was Rawh and that he lived near the Church of St. Theodore.

With regard to other emendations to the manuscripts of this text that I discussed earlier we look down to see how the priest and the people respond to Rawh's profession of what he saw when the bread was converted into a lamb at the altar and we find that "they increased [their] praise to Christ," rather than the more Islamic "*Subhan Allah*" found in the earliest texts. Fairly clearly, this Christianizing of the text is done, again, to set a clear distinction between Christianity and Islam, a distinction that, for whatever reason, was not so necessary in the earlier texts.

Paul Peeters said that this text was of little value and was not even worth publishing, largely due to the embellishments found in the text and to the several lacunae, omitting details that were present in the earlier versions. Peeters was looking to the text for historical data and thus the text naturally fell short of his standard. I would argue though that Peeters' approach misses the point entirely. The text is hardly "*notablement abrégée*" as he said, and is missing only one page in the middle and not more than one folio at the end.[23]

First, all the main elements of the story of Rawh al-Qurayshi are present. Second, the hagiographical embellishments are an important witness into the development of the text as it came to express the beliefs

---

[23] So near to the martyrdom is the Vatican text at the point it is broken off that I imagine there could not be more than ten to fifteen lines at the most that is missing from the end.

and practices of later Arab Christian communities. And finally, and most significantly, Peeters never even mentioned the important fact that the text surely was intended for public reading, as the insertions of "O my brothers!" make clear. We have here then a hagiographical sermon that was formed by turning a 3rd person narrative account of the martyrdom of an Arab Christian into the first person "autobiographical" telling of the same events. And what is especially significant for my purposes, is that just as we saw a hardening of the apologetic tone against Islam in the later texts of the full account, we also see a more harsh tone against Islam taken in the version of the text as found in *Vatican Arabic 175.*

From the elements I mentioned at the beginning of the "autobiography" it is clear that the tone taken in this 13th century telling of the story of Anthony is a much more forceful attempt to make a distinction between Christianity and Islam than any of the full accounts of Anthony's martyrdom discussed earlier. Especially important to note is that in the initial prayer the text consistently refers to the religion from which Rawh was converted as "the pagan religion." The term "pagan" is used numerous times throughout the text to refer to Islam, clearly meant to disparage Islam in the light of Christianity and to assure readers that their Christian faith is superior to that of the Muslims among whom they live. This is heightened as Rawh describes his conversion as having been "enlightened by the light of Christianity." By extension, the "pagan" Muslims are living in darkness.

It is likely that this, being a sermon and thus intended exclusively for a monastic Christian readership, the author was less concerned that the text not be offensive to its hearers or readers. Thus as time passed, as can be seen both in the later Sinai manuscripts and in this Vatican manuscript it seems clear that Arab Christians felt less and less compelled to emphasize the affinities that they had with the Muslims among whom they lived and were much more likely to express the distinctiveness of their Arab Christian faith in a milieu that was increasingly becoming arabized and islamized. It would seem then that the type of harsh apologetic tone that can be seen in the later texts is not a necessary element in early Christian-Muslim relations. There was a time, as seen in the earlier texts, when even in an account of a Christian martyr under Islam, Christians sought to express their situation as a religious minority in terms that respected the faith of the Muslims among whom they lived and sought to bring out the cultural affinities that they had with their Arab Muslim neighbors.

INCULTURATION FOR EVANGELIZATION IN AFRICA: A CHALLENGE IN EMPOWERING THE LOCAL CHURCH

Darius Oliha Makuja[*]

The essay looks at the apparent ambivalence in the conciliar and post-conciliar recognition of the need for inculturation. It includes theological views of various scholars, including African theologians, showing that inculturation is more than translations of texts into native languages or incorporation of local songs and dance into liturgies. In its truest sense, it is a birth of Christ out of and into a given culture. There is a need for greater flexibility in inculturating faith into native African cultures.

Although the Second Vatican Council and other magisterial statements appear positive toward inculturation, caution remains the guide for authorizing new adaptations to rituals of worship. The absence of specifics has made some African Church leaders more and more hesitant to inculturate, and in practice they become more "Roman" than what Rome itself professes. It is important, first of all, to define the term *inculturation* as a theological construct in contemporary theological debate. In the context of this presentation:

> The inculturation of the Church is the integration of the Christian experience of a local Church into the culture of its people, in such a way that this experience not only expresses itself in elements of this culture, but becomes a force that animates, orients and innovates this culture so as to create a new unity and communion, not only within the culture in question but also as an enrichment

[*] Darius Oliha Makuja is a graduate of Saint Louis University, Missouri, USA. His work is in Historical Theology with a concentration in Medieval-Church History, with special research interests in Religion, Culture and Inculturation. Makuja is currently a Visiting Assistant Professor at the Relgious Studies Department, LeMoyne College, Syrcasue, New York where he is teaching African Traditional Religion and its encounter with Christianity since the 19th century colonial intrusion into Africa.

of the Church universal.[1]

Use of the term *decentralization* suggests, in a narrow sense, a dispersal of authority from the center of concentration in Rome to the local level for effective implementation of inculturation. It underscores the claims that while an inculturated faith maintains universality within the Catholic Church, its African context must reflect local pastoral concerns. This shift in mentality puts positive emphases on native cultures. Sound theology will avoid extremes and syncretism that evoke reactionary tendencies in the debate on inculturation. Scholars use the term "incarnation" in the sense of "immersing Christianity in African culture, so that, just as Jesus became man, so must Christianity become incarnated into African cultures and mentalities."[2]

This article focuses on the ramification of this "incarnation," the face of inculturation with the value of diversity, and the element of social justice in contemporary African situation. This is a delicate task because it challenges conformity with the Roman tradition. Diversity calls for liturgical creativity that must not merely adapt, but must also recognize and take into account the rich cultural values enshrined in African concepts of community and family life.

Incarnation and Inculturation in Africa

When the evangelization of Africa gained momentum in the nineteenth century, most people in the West regarded the continent's positive cultural values as savage, pagan, and thus incompatible with the Gospel. Historically, decisions about adaptations of liturgy for missions have come from Rome. But with Vatican II (1962-65), this perception has changed. African theologians have been challenged to break out of centralized Eurocentric normative forms of evangelization. As Aylward Shorter writes, "for centuries the Catholic Church espoused a philosophy of Eurocentric monoculturalsim."[3] This dominant view has shifted towards a pluralistic cultural diversity. The tendencies and shifts in

---

[1] A.R. Crollius and T. Nkeramihigo, *What Is So New About Inculturation?* (Rome: Gregorian Pontifical University, 1984), 15.

[2] A.J. Chupungco, Liturgies of the Future: The Processes and Methods of Inculturation (New York: Paulist Press, 1989), 28.

[3] Alyward Shorter, *Christianity and the African Imagination: After the African Synod Resources for Inculturation.* (Nairobi: Paulines Publications, Africa, 1996). 35.

theological inculturation have been radical, with emphasis more on "immersing Christianity in African culture, [so that] just as Jesus became man, so must Christianity become incarnated into African cultures and mentalities."[4]

In this sense inculturation becomes a concrete expression of an incarnated faith, enfleshed in African society. Inculturation has always dominated debates on mission and many agree on the urgent need for diversity in ritual and worship as essential in making the Church both truly Christian and truly African. For the first time in a detailed statement, the Second Vatican Council spelled out the relationship between the Church and native cultures:

> Nevertheless, the Church has been sent to all ages and nations and, therefore, is not tied exclusively and indissolubly to any race or nation, to any one particular way of life, or to any customary practices, ancient or modern. The Church is faithful to its traditions and is at the same time conscious of its universal mission; it can then, enter into communion with different forms of culture, thereby enriching both itself and the cultures themselves.[5]

A dominant concern among theologians in Africa today is a positive recognition of rich African values that should be integrated into the Christian message. To put this discussion into context, a brief historical review of the evolution of mission and of the magisterial teachings on adaptation is in order. The post-conciliar documents and Papal Apostolic Exhortations, especially *Ecclesia in Africa* (1995), and the Pontifical Council for Culture document, *Towards a Pastoral Approach to Culture* (1999), are probably the best sources for tracking the contemporary Catholic Church's shifts in attitude on cultural evangelization in Africa. Most scholars tend to view inculturation as a new term in theology, but the concept is rooted in the very nature of the Church's mission. Many historical instances demonstrate that the Church has been flexible in accepting unity within diversity in worship.

Toward the end of the sixth century Gregory the Great (590-604)

---

[4] Aylward Shorter, *African Theology: Adaptation or Inculturation?* (Maryknoll, NY: Orbis Books, 1977), 150.

[5] Austin Flannery , ed., "Unitatis Reditengratio," Vatican II: The Basic Sixteen Documents (Northport, NY: Costello Publishing, 1996), no. 21.

in his mission to the Anglo-Saxons, developed an approach that was prototypical of the modern missiological concept of inculturation. The elements of inculturation were evident in his adaptation of and flexibility in applying the Church's regulations. A letter to Mellitus (who was one of the second group of missionaries sent by Gregory in 601) is the first official statement by a Pope that endorses the possibility of the Church adapting to local culture.

In Gregory's mind, pagan idols of the English people were to be destroyed but the temples spared. The missionaries were to erect an altar and sprinkle it with holy water and continue to use the pagan temples, for once "people see that their shrines are not destroyed they will be able to banish error from their hearts and be more ready to come to places they are familiar with, but now recognizing and worshiping the true God."[6] As Irvin has pointed out, "the pope in effect was calling for a more open attitude toward the indigenous religiosity. Modified accommodation was to replace immediate eradication."[7]

Likewise, in the ninth century, St. Cyril and his brother Methodius (861-885), apostles to the Slavic nation, translated the Bible into the Slavic language, and developed the Cyrillic alphabet. They adapted the liturgy to their converts. Despite controversies over their decisions, Pope John VIII approved them in 880.

In the seventeenth century, Matteo Ricci (1552-1610), a missionary to China, was "a precursor of inculturation who justified his missionary strategies in China in terms of civil customs which did not affect Christian religion and morality."[8] Ricci was convinced that the supreme deity of the Confucian classics was personal and could be assimilated to Christian theism. This method drew criticism from other missionaries and the Vatican was not supportive as he developed unique Chinese rites. The conflict culminated in the famous Rites Controversy. Recently, John Paul II praised Ricci for "building between the Church and the Chinese culture a bridge that seems still solidly anchored and secured."[9]

---

[6] D. Norberg, ed., *S. Gregorii Magni: Registrum Epistolarum Libri*, 2 vols., *Ep.* xi. 56. Cf. (Turnholt: Brepolis Editores Pontificii, 1982).

[7] D.T. Irvin & S.W. Sunquist, *History of the Christian Movement, vol. 1: Earliest to 1453* (Maryknoll, NY: Orbis Books, 2001), 329.

[8] Shorter, *Christianity and the African Imagination*, 37.

[9] R.S. Pelton, "Inculturation," in *The HarperCollins Encyclopedia of Catholicism*, R.P. McBrien, ed. (San Francisco: Harper San Francisco, 1995): 660.

In providing a reasonable argument for inculturation, the Second Vatican Council's *The Pastoral Constitution on the Church in the Modern World* opened up a new look on mission:

> There are many links between the message of salvation and culture. In his self- revelation to his people culminating in the fullness of manifestation in his incarnate Son, God spoke according to the culture proper to each age. Similarly the Church has existed through the centuries in varying circumstances and has utilized the resources of different cultures in its preaching to spread and explain the message of Christ, to examine and understand it more deeply, and to express it more perfectly in the liturgy and in various aspects of the life of the faithful.[10]

In his message to the peoples of Africa, *Africae Terrarum*, of 1968, Paul VI "appraises the potential resources in African cultural heritage for promoting Christianity in Africa."[11] On July 31,1969, in his address to the *Symposium of the Bishops of Africa and Madagascar*, in Kampala, Uganda, Pope Paul VI said, "by now you are missionaries to yourselves. The Church of Christ is well and truly planted in this blessed soil.... You Africans must now continue, upon this continent, the building of the Church."[12] This was the first endorsement by a reigning Pontiff of the possibility of a truly African Christian Church. In 1975, Paul VI said:

> Nevertheless, the kingdom of God, which is proclaimed by the gospel, is put into practice by men who are imbued with their own particular culture, and in the building up of the kingdom it is inevitable that some elements of these human cultures must be introduced.[13]

During his pastoral visit to Uganda in 1993, responding to the is-

---

[10] Flannery, "Gaudium et Spes," no.58.

[11] Paul VI, "Africae Terrarum," in *African Ecclesial Review, 10*(1), (1968): 71.

[12] Paul VI, "Address at the Closing of the All African Bishops' Symposium.," in *Ecclesial Review, 11*(4), (1969): 403.

[13] Paul VI, *Apostolic exhortation: Evangelii Nuntiandi* (Vatican City: Liberia Editrice Vaticana, 1975), no. 20.

sue of incluturation, Pope John Paul II also sounded positive but warned of the difficulties. Regarding recommitment to continuing inculturation of the Christian faith, he was hopeful the work of the Special Assembly of the Synod of Bishops for Africa, that he announced that day, would throw light on this difficult and delicate task. He said:

> It follows that inculturation does not consist only in transforming the mentality of human beings or groups of people, but also implies approaching cultures in such ways that they are enabled, from within themselves, to be fertile. Christianity becomes itself enriched when through inculturation it enters into dialogue with peoples and with their cultures. An inculturated evangelization will help peoples give flesh to evangelical values in their language and symbols, their history, politics, business life and their own ways of developing.[14]

Two years later, John Paul II said, "every culture needs to be transformed by the Gospel values in the light of the Paschal Mystery."[15] The "ultimate transformation of authentic cultural values through their integration into Christianity, and the insertion of Christianity in the various cultures is a path towards full evangelization, and one of the greatest challenges for the Church on the continent on the eve of the third millennium."[16]

While the above statement appears positive, one does not find explicit direction on implementation. The question remains to be answered: How can we resolve the apparent ambivalence of the cautiously optimistic magisterial statements, which give hope, and further provide the main principles on how the process of inculturation could be done, but which lack specifics on how to concretely proceed in inculturating the faith into diverse cultures?

The challenge of finding means of integrating the major themes of our faith in view of inculturation was pushed further ahead in the African Synod of 1994, where the African bishops expressed unanimously

---

[14] John Paul II, Working Paper, "Evangelizing Mission of the Church in Africa," in *Origins, 22*(39), (1994): 664.
[15] John Paul II , *Post-Synodal Apostolic Exhortation: Ecclesia in Africa* (Nairobi: Pauline Publications, 1995), no. 61.
[16] Ibid. no. 59.

that this need was indeed urgent. In Africa as elsewhere, skeptics always tend to resist novelty. Yet the African Church must, "as it were, be born into African societies. This is not just a matter of adapting ourselves to what others do, but making the Christian message part of our very selves."[17]

Even among the hierarchy of the Africa Church, some religious leaders are probably more cautious than Rome itself in what it actually professes regarding inculturation. Of course, extremes must be avoided. However, unless Christianity learns to dialogue with native cultures, its very roots will lose impact and relevance to the African people. A decentralized form of inculturation of the Gospel may give some solution by accepting unity within diversity in the Church's worship without prejudice to the fundamental doctrinal issues. The Church should take seriously the positive elements in African culture and integrate them into Church liturgy. The concepts of community and family from the African perspective are good examples of elements that can be integrated into the Church's life and worship in Africa. The African Synod, as a way of building a truly African local Church, adopted the Small Christian Communities model.

In Africa, religious experiences pervade daily life. They are manifested in communal religious rituals and social institutions: birth, initiation, adulthood, and marriage. Sacred ritual-dances are performed to mark life transitions. Essential in this worldview is the aspect of the traditional African religious outlook. Religion and life form a unity. God is not distant. He is encountered and experienced daily. Africa's social structure is fundamentally holistic, sacred, and highly integrated in its world-view. Christianity, if it is to appeal, must take into account these cultural values. This face of inculturation calls for full recognition of diversity of expressions in worship, rooted in cultural values, within the universal Church.

In 1967, Joseph Cardinal Malula, a great African theologian, typified this vision of inculturation in Africa when he advocated a lively local Church in Zaire (now the Democratic Republic of Congo): "The European missionaries have Christianized Africa in the past, today the African Christians will Africanize Christianity."[18] He called the Afri-

---

[17] P.K. Sarpong, "Christianity Should Be Africanized, Not African Christianized," in *African Ecclesial Review, 17* (6), (1975): 325.
[18] K.F. Lumbala, *Alliances avec le Christ en Afrique: Inculturation des rites religieux au Zaire* (Athens: Les Editions Historiques S. D. Basilopulos, 1987), 14.

canization of the Church a matter of vital importance in establishing a local Church that is faithful to the values it received from its creator as
constituting the truth of its life.[19] This was the starting point of the "Living Christian Communities" as a pastoral priority for building the Zairian
local Church.

The Association of Members Episcopal Conferences of Eastern
Africa's (AMECEA) model, called the "Small Christian Communities,"
illustrates the face of inculturation as developed in Africa. In 1973, eight
years after the celebration of the Second Vatican Council (1962-65), the
AMECEA Plenary Study Session adopted as a priority "The Small Christian Communities" model of building the local Church. It put the ecclesiology of the Second Vatican Council into practice by developing a
pastoral pedagogy for establishing a truly local Church. The bishops envisioned this as a new way of being a Church, in which creative ways of
worship would be experienced at the grassroots. The following characteristics are central to The Small Christian Communities:

> (a) They are engaged in evangelizing themselves, and bring the
> Gospel to others,
> (b) They are communities sharing, and listening to Word of God,
> (c) They encourage members to take on responsibilities in the
> community,
> (d) The members in the community learn to live an ecclesial life,
> and
> (e) They reflect on different human problems in the light of the
> Gospel,
> (f) They are committed to living Christ's love for everybody, a
> love that transcends the limits of the national solidarity of clans,
> tribes or other interest groups.[20]

A crucial element in inculturating the Gospel is the Church's
openness to diverse expressions of worship in The Small Christian Communities. As the Pontifical Council stated: "what is most noticeable
about the world in which the Church carries out her mission of evangelization today is the diversity of cultural situations which have developed from the perspectives of different religions." [21]

---

[19] Ibid., 7.
[20] John Paul II, *Post-Synodal Apostolic Exhortation*, no. 89.
[21] Pontifical Council for Culture. *Towards a Pastoral Approach to Culture* (Cita

The Face of Inculturation: Decentralizing Power

In highlighting the tension at the heart of the theological debate on incul-turation, this article proposes a more "decentralized" devolution of au-thority that "resists views of faith and culture premised on mere adapta-tion or translations."[22] It is not sufficient to see translations of texts from English or Latin into local languages, or the introduction of drums and other cultural arts and dance that characterize the vibrant liturgies in Af-rica. On the contrary, an inculturated faith must evoke transformation in society, reflecting the socio-political and economic realities of the Afri-can continent and its people. The Church, in an African context, should be born into the culture of the African societies. Rome has shown hesi-tancy about specifics about how to exercise inculturation. For Rome, the difficulty is in having different rituals within the same jurisdiction. Nev-ertheless, indigenous cultures have a lot to offer the Christian mission and its concern for conversion.

Moreover, in the Decree on Ecumenism of 1964, the Second Vatican Council voiced a crucial element to any encounter with other re-ligions and liturgical rituals: "while preserving unity in essentials, let everyone in the Church, according to the office entrusted to him, pre-serve a proper freedom in the forms of spiritual life and discipline, in a variety of liturgical rites, and even in the theological elaborations of re-vealed truth. In all things let charity prevail."[23] This implies addressing human persons in their complex wholeness, spiritual and moral, eco-nomic, political, cultural and social. Thus, as John Paul II says "through inculturation the Church makes the Gospel incarnate in different cultures, into her own community"[24]

Positive African cultural elements based on a source of commu-nity are incorporated into the Church's experiences. Africans affirm and celebrate life in community, as attested to by the large numbers of rituals, festivals and ceremonies performed daily. Through ritual and ceremony, these mark many key moments in the life of the individual in commu-

---

del Vaticano: Liberia Editrice Vaticana, 1999), no.19.

[22] J. Coleman, "Inculturation and Evangelization in the North American Con-text," in *The Catholic Theological Society of America: Proceeding, 45,* (Louisville, KY: Catholic Theological Society of America, 1990), 17.

[23] Austin Flannery, ed., "Unitatis Reditengratio," Vatican II: The Basic Sixteen Documents (Northport, NY: Costello Publishing, 1996), no. 21.

[24] Austin Flannery, ed., "Redmptoris Missio," Vatican II: V. 2: More Conciliar Documents, New Rev. Ed. (Northport, NY: Costello Publishing, 1998), n.52.

nity, particularly, birth, initiation and puberty, marriage and death.[25] For example, initiation rituals like circumcision and jumping over the ritual fire among the Didinga are essential steps for incorporating members into the society. Baptismal ritual is similarly an essential Christian step into membership in the Church. Peter Schineller argues that "liturgy is the public celebration of the faith of a particular people, and unless that lived faith is *inculturated* into the customs and culture of that people, the liturgy will remain foreign or even imposed, rather than flowing from the lives of the people."[26] For liturgical inculturation to be "truly Christian and truly African,"[27] it has to be creative and make liturgy appealing to native cultural and religious experience.

Taking the Church as God's family as its guiding idea for the evangelization in Africa, the African bishops offered the image of the family as "an expression of the Church's nature particularly appropriate for Africa."[28] As a domestic Church, an African Church family is "a place where the value of the sacredness of life is protected, and nurtured. It is a place of belonging, where sharing and solidarity are at the heart of daily life, and where each person feels himself/herself to be truly at home."[29] The vitality of the Church as family is expressed in The Small Christian Communities. Without changing essentials, the liturgical celebration could be made to reflect local customs. The individual is, often, expected to promote the well being of the community by participating in Eucharistic celebrations in Small Christian Communities.

Also related to this are such values as hospitality, bonds of brotherhood and sisterhood, and caring and sharing in family life. Individuality has no place in African traditional society and culture. In most of these societies, religious worldview sees no dichotomy between the sacred and secular. There is unity of religion and life, which provides an experience of a God in their daily struggles. In other words, religion pervades daily life, and is explicitly manifested in communal religious

---

[25] S.A. Oware, "Inculturation: The Vision of CIWA Towards the New Millennium," in *African Christina Studies*, *14*(4), (1998): 47.

[26] P. Schineller, "Inculturation of the Liturgy," in *The New Dictionary of Sacramental Worship*, P.E. Fink, Ed. (Collegeville, MN: The Liturgical Press, 1985), 598.

[27] E.E. Uzukwu, *Liturgy: Truly Christian, truly African* (Eldoret, Kenya: Ggaba Publications, 1982), 29-36.

[28] John Paul II, *Post-Synodal Apostolic Exhortation*, no. 63.

[29] Ibid.

rituals and social institutions like initiation, marriage, and sacred ritual dances.

Efforts continue to be made in academic circles to have an incarnated and inculturated faith in Africa that responds to actual experiences of local communities and is rooted in their social and cultural settings. African theologians and Church leaders, debating on inculturation as an option for evangelization, generally agree on the necessity to adopt this model for the Church in Africa. But the apparent ambivalence, mentioned earlier in this paper, can be demonstrated by the hesitancy of Rome towards the first creative, alternative liturgical worship established in Zaire (now the Democratic Republic of Congo), in 1970. The Episcopal Conference there initiated a project for an alternative African liturgy for the Eucharist. The work, completed in 1973, was submitted to Rome for authorization to implement in Zaire, but it took fifteen years for Rome to officially give approval to *The Roman Missal for the Dioceses of Zaire*, or the *Zairian Rites*. This is popularly known as the *Missa Luba*. This delay underlines Rome's caution toward creativity in liturgical inculturation.

The need for liturgical creativity, however, found its official backing during the African Synod in 1994. The publication of the *Apostolic Exhortation* of John-Paul II, *Ecclesia in Africa* (1995), ratified these aspirations for an African Church that is vibrant and relevant to concrete local situations. Through inculturation, the Church makes the Gospel incarnate in different cultures and at the same time introduces peoples, together with their cultures, into her own community.[30]

It is, however, important to underline the necessity for openness to diversity in worship while affirming unity in essentials, namely, the doctrinal matters of faith. There is still much to be done in this regard so far as Church leadership is concerned. While many official and magisterial statements affirm inculturation as an urgent model for the Church, there are still skeptics in the Church's hierarchy who question the viability of inculturation. There are also cosmetic expressions of indigenous celebration that are merely shallow adaptations to local customs. There is a lot to do to fill the Vatican's call for an authentic inculturation. Current scholarship does not go far enough to place the evolution of the notion of inculturation in its historical context.

---

[30] Pontifical Council for Culture, *Towards a Pastoral Approach to Culture*, no.16.

The Social Impact of Inculturation

Justice and peace form an integral part of inculturation in the evangelizing mission of the Church. Its mandate is derived from the Lord himself, who declared that he came to liberate oppressed people. In Africa, this message remains as vivid as ever, and the Church is charged to be more proactive in issues affecting its people. Sarpong emphatically puts it: "A good understanding of inculturation exposes acts of exploitation and injustice as culturally condemnable, deplorable, and indefensible."[31] Africa has faced social and political difficulties in the past four decades since independence. The Church had to respond to poverty, hunger, and issues of human rights, justice and peace, economic inequality, and globalization of trade. Aware of these realities, the African Bishops have stated clearly: "if we desire peace, we should all work for justice, we should foster the rule of law. In many cases the people have turned to the church that she might accompany them as they set out on the journey of the democratic processes."[32] The situations in Sudan, Angola, Somalia, The Democratic Republic of Congo, Rwanda, and Burundi are a few examples today. In these nations, the Church is challenged to adequately respond and apply the Gospel to concrete situations by utilizing traditional African approaches for solving problems affecting their community.

The pursuit of justice and peace in conflict situations requires dialogue among the warring parties or groups leading to the ultimate transformation of society. This challenge is more apparent in Sudan, where Muslims and Christians are engaged in a long war that has pitted the Muslim North against the mainly Christian and Traditionalist religious followers in the Southern part of the country. Archbishop Zubeir of Khartoum pointed out that:

> In the Sudan, Islam is not only a religion, but also a socio-political system. The inculturation of our people envisage is often the superficialities we have introduced into the liturgy: the music, the dances and the colored vestments. What I think we need to inculturate are the ways to hand on the Gospel message: its expression in

---

[31] P. Sarpong, "Conclusion," in *The African Synod: Documents, Reflections, Perspectives*, M. Browne, Ed. (Marykoll, NY: Orbis Books, 1996), 222.
[32] Special Assembly of the Synod of Bishops for Africa, "Final Message of the Synod for Africa," in *Origins*, 24(1), (1994): no. 34.

our lives, its terminology...the structures of governance in the Church, the exercise of authority, the style of leadership, community involvement and the channels as well as methods of consultation.[33]

A theology of inculturation that appeals to the socio-economic systems, the struggle against racism, poverty, cultural oppression, and exploitation should propose specific ways for peace making in a proactive African Church.

Conclusion

Before concluding this article, it is good to mention that the challenge to propose how positive African values can be incorporated into the Church's sacred liturgy" remains real to scholars and local hierarchy today in Africa.[34] As a result of the collapse of colonialism and the rise of new nationalism in the 1960s, the Church looked more carefully at itself. To a great extent, the Church has now recognized and inculturated the religious cultural values of the people, and has promoted these in liturgy. There is a desire for a more decentralized approach to the specific implementation of inculturation in an African context, so that the Church can be born into the culture of the African societies.

Only some of the challenges to inculturation have been mentioned here. The African church faces pressing problems of polygamy and female circumcision, for example, and they have yet to be adequately addressed. Peter M. Kanyadogo's study on evangelizing polygamous families reflects this challenge for the African Church in its pastoral approaches to polygamous relationships.[35] But the African church must achieve its own genuine identity by incarnating and evangelizing African cultures. This involves not just one inculturation, or "incarnation," but several. John Paul II reinforced this idea of cultural incarnation where the Gospel becomes part and parcel of the people of Mozambique:

You have not been placed at the head of the Church in Africa in order to bring a culture to it, but to impregnate

---

[33] G.Z. Wako, "Dialogue," in *African Ecclesial Review, 36*(4), (1994): 201.

[34] Oware, 57.

[35] P.M. Kanyadago, *Evangelzing Polygamous Families: Canonical and African Approaches* (Eldoret, Kenya: Ggaba Publication, 1991).

African culture itself evangelical values. As you are already integrated into your natural culture, are aware of
the aspirations and the life of the flock that is entrusted
to you, and are at the same time profoundly imbued with
the Christian faith, you will understand how to find a
away to integrate these two vital poles: faith and culture.
For this important cultural incarnation, the Holy See
gives directions so that the unity of the universal Church
remains strong and the essential elements of the Catholic
faith are preserved.[36]

In his view cultural incarnation means the integration of two vital poles of faith and diverse cultures reflecting diversity of the African
people. The Eucharist might be celebrated in one way in one village and
in quite a different way in another. Members of one tribe might plan a
special liturgy for harvest; another might do so for planting. Still another
might celebrate a new workplace. The "Small Christian Communities"
should reflect its members: what issues do they face and how can their
church assist them? How can they assist the Church?

No one term describes Africa. Deserts, forests, mountains,
plains, seashores, urban and rural traditions all are part of its heritage.
And no one term should describe the African church. With sound theological principles that foster flexibility, inculturation becomes an appropriate way to integrate the church into the African milieu.

Regardless, what is needed are African theologians and local
Church leaders with unhindered empowerment to study, and to "propose
sound ways in which the liturgy of the Church in Africa will be more
meaningful, valid, relevant, participatory and salvific."[37] Leadership in
The Small Christian Communities must be inspiring, enabling and unifying the grassroots of the Church in each region. Through sharing the
Word of God, Christ becomes, as it were, "native" to the people of Africa. The role of lay ministries is significant in this regard and needs
more attention by the hierarchy. This implies decentralizing authority by
equipping local leadership with the necessary tools for their active participation in the evangelizing mission of the local Church. This will

---

[36] John Paul II, "Espérance pour l'église au Mozambique: Discours aux évêques
en visite 'Ad limina'," in *La Documention Catholique, 79,* (1982): 917 [Transla-
tion by D. Makuja].
[37] Kanyadago, 57.

further help lay people at the parish and community level appreciate their participation and responsibilities in the Church.

True inculturation implies not simply adaptation, but also an approach that radically incorporates the people's cultural values. There are still voices that look at this as straying too far from the center of Rome. With sound theological principles that foster flexibility, however, inculturation can become an urgent and appropriate way by which the Church is adequately integrated into the African milieu. It implies establishing ways of expressing faith that reflect on contemporary African issues affecting the Church and its mission in Africa, thus fostering genuine liturgical inculturation.

Following the nuances of the conciliar and post-conciliar documents, Church leaders should recognize the apparent ambivalences in the magisterial teachings on culture and inculturation. By and large, the positive attitude by Rome appears at the same time to be cautious in delegating powers of implementing inculturation at local levels. This attitude leaves a crippling indecision in many issues affecting the local Churches. The African Church must find appropriate new ways of evangelizing. Empowering laity by deepening their level of participation in leadership, and giving more responsibilities in decision-making can enhance efforts of achieving a truly local Church. Bishop Louis J. Lebulu's remarks at the African Synod shows how practically this can be achieved. He urged:

> That each diocese in Africa should be encouraged to invoke and carry out a diocesan synod in order to reach the Church at its kernel-the hearts and minds of people, the family and the Small Christian Communities in their socio-economic and political situations so as to allow the people at the grass-roots to evaluate, plan and follow-up the pastoral and development action and experience of the Church in Africa.[38]

In this context, an inculturated evangelization must evoke transformation in society, reflecting the socio-political and economic realities of the African continent and of its peoples. Under dynamic decentralized struc-

---

[38] Louis J. Lebulu, "The Principles of Inculturation," in *African Ecclesial Review*, *36*(4), (1994): 213.

tures of the local Church, inculturation can be a point of departure for pastoral policies in the African Church in fulfilling this necessity for evangelization. The small Christian Communities through their sharing of the Gospel and reflecting on their daily experience become a living and active force in the local Church. The future of the Church in Africa depends on getting the right balance in the encounter between Christianity and native cultures.

EARLY CATHOLIC LAY MINISTRY IN EASTERN AFRICA[*]

Paul Kollman[**]

The first Catholic lay catechist in eastern Africa was a former slave named Hilarion Maruammakoma, who assumed his duties in 1877 in what is today Tanzania. Hilarion served at the first Catholic mission founded inland from the coast, at a place called Mhonda. Twenty years later Hilarion still lived near Mhonda, but he was a Muslim and the arch-enemy of the local Catholic mission. This paper will describe and

[*] Research for this article has depended upon cooperation given by members of the Congregation of the Holy Ghost on three continents, cooperation for which I am most grateful. In Paris, the archives of the Congregation at Chevilly were made available to me by the generous assistance of the late Father Ghislain de Banville, CSSp, in 1996 and the more recent help of his successor, Father Gérard Vieira. I also thank the community at Chevilly for their welcome to me, despite my halting French. In Zanzibar and Tanzania, I wish to thank the clergy, staff, and people at St. Joseph Cathedral, Zanzibar, and the Catholic mission, Our Lady of Bagamoyo. I interviewed some of them, and they were most open and helpful. These included Mzee Barnabas Mkuku of Zanzibar, and from Bagamoyo, the following: Mzee Michael Misheli, Mzee Ferdinand Petro, Mzee Michael Joseph Kabelewa, Mzee Damas Francis, Bibi Leonia Richardi, Bibi Sofia State, Mzee Joseph Ignasio ("Mzee Fisi"), and Bibi Faustina Innocent. Spiritans who were supportive in Zanzibar and Bagamoyo included Bishop Augustine Shao and Fathers Daniel Bouju, Valentine Bayo, John Henschel, and Jason Ishengoma, all Spiritans. In Morogoro, Tanzania, Father Theodore Winkelmolen, CSSp, was helpful with food, wit, and wisdom, as well as his house for researching his carefully preserved documents, most of them now at the main congregational archives in Chevilly, Paris. Finally, the Holy Ghost archives in Bethel Park, Pennsylvania, have also opened themselves to me, thanks to the kindness of the late Father Henry Koren, CSSp, who was for years the able and courteous director there. I am grateful for him and his confreres for their open-hearted hospitality, and also to the Spiritan community at Duquesne University, where I stayed when I examined Spiritan materials on microfilm at the university library. I also thank Nicholas Creary, Troy Feay, Emily Osborn, and Shawn Colberg for their comments on this paper.

[**] Paul V. Kollman, CSC (PhD Chicago) is assistant professor in the Department of Theology, in the area of the history of Christianity, with special interests in African Christianity and mission history. A fellow of the Kellogg Institute for International Studies, the Kroc Institute for Peace Studies, the Nanovic Institute for European Studies, and moderator of the African Working Group at Notre Dame, he has received fellowships from the Erasmus Institute and the Lilly Endowment for Theological Education. He is currently preparing a manuscript on the evangelization of slaves in 19th-century eastern Africa.

attempt to explain Hilarion's transformation from valued assistant of the missionaries to their *bête noire*. Besides allowing his interesting evolution to reveal the complexities inherent in the emerging new identities of African Christians in the era prior to and during formal colonial overrule in eastern Africa, I will also use his story to show the limitations of usual conceptual terms in describing someone like Hilarion. Finally, I will make an argument for other concepts that place dynamics of personal identity within mobile social fields.

The use of lay catechists represents one type of innovation in forms of ministerial service in emerging African Christianity in the 1870s and 1880s in what is today Tanzania. These innovations arose in response to new circumstances in the missionary setting as the Catholic missionaries who founded the church beginning in 1860 pursued their goals with the help of Africans. The interesting thing in this case is that African lay people, neither ordained nor belonging to missionary religious orders, received a great deal of responsibility for the church's life and growth, a level of responsibility that at that time was almost unheard of elsewhere in the church. With this unprecedented responsibility came new forms of Christian identity, as delegated African Christians made the faith their own and challenged missionary preconceptions that placed limits on African responsibilities.

One remarkable example of what we would today call lay ministry in nineteenth-century eastern Africa took place in the 1880s at the coastal mission at Bagamoyo. There a group of women served as *baptiseuses,* or baptizers, surreptitiously consecrating Muslim children in the area around Bagamoyo, site of the first Catholic mission on the mainland in modern times.[1] These women, former slaves who grew up under the tutelage of the mission, assisted a Catholic priest whose similar ministrations had angered the local populace once they discovered what his "healing water" actually signified. In response to these efforts to end his

---

[1] During the Portuguese occupation of the eastern African coast, from the early sixteenth until the early eighteenth century, Catholic churches existed and missionaries attempted small-scale evangelization, but those efforts bore no fruit that persisted into the mid-nineteenth century, when Christian missionaries returned to the region. See John M. Gray, *Early Portuguese Missionaries in East Africa* (London: MacMillan and Co., Limited, 1958) and Paul Kollman, *Making Catholics: The Evangelization of Slaves and the Origins of the Church in Nineteenth-Century East Africa* (Ph.D. Dissertation, University of Chicago, 2001), 53ff.

baptizing, the priest instructed women of the mission to disguise themselves in local costume and offer their services as midwives and healers, all in the effort to baptize. This innovation reveals the contradictions inherent in the relationship between baptism and evangelization within the missionary ideology. A profoundly clerical and male-dominated church had recourse to non-clerics and women to achieve the goals it set for itself.[2]

Unfortunately, the experiences of these women have been lost. We know that they baptized hundreds of children in the years between 1884 and 1889, when the priest died and colonial war came to eastern Africa, because their names, and often their signatures, fill the baptismal register of the Bagamoyo Catholic mission. But little else about their activities and nothing of their perspectives on their ministry has been recovered. More promising for the historian than the *baptiseuses*, however, are a second group of lay ministers, the largely male catechists like Hilarion, whose roles took more formal shape in the missionary strategy of the time.

My contention will be that the experiences of African lay ministers like Hilarion—as far as we can recover them—shed light on the complexity at work in the appropriation of Christian identity by Africans in the pre-colonial and colonial periods. At the same time, his story will allow a reconsideration of the terms usually used to describe this sort of religious change. *Culture* and *conversion* are normally invoked to describe changes in religious identity like those that Hilarion and others underwent under the influence of missionary evangelization. I will argue that Hilarion's transformation from valued assistant of the missionaries to an object of their intense hatred illustrates the limitations of the terms culture and conversion. In the face of these limitations, I will suggest that Hilarion's evolving religious identity can be better understood by using the notion of the *moral economy*, originally developed by the late English historian E. P. Thompson.[3] I will argue that the moral economy allows for a more precise analytical grasp on Hilarion's changing alle-

---

[2] For a general discussion, see Kollman, 447-452. Primary documentation includes the following: Bagamoyo journal, 2vii83; BG 13:53-54, 1077; BG 14:619f; BG 15:135f; CSSp 196axiii: Courmont to Holy Childhood, 5x84; AA 1888: 86-93. *Note:* See Primary Sources, Abbreviated Sources and Archives Consulted at the end of the paper.

[3] E.P. Thompson, "The moral economy of the English crowd in the eighteenth century," in *Past and Present* 50, (1971).

giances than the typical invocations of culture and conversion.

The Early Catholic Mission in Eastern Africa[4]

Hilarion was one of the thousands of slaves who came to the Catholic mission founded in eastern Africa, a mission inaugurated on the island of Zanzibar in 1860. The evangelization of ransomed slaves stood at the center of the mission's strategy during its first three decades. After 1863 the Catholic presence was maintained by a French missionary order, the Congregation of the Holy Ghost, also known as the Spiritans. The Spiritans, like those who preceded them, opted to evangelize slaves because the Islamic regime in Zanzibar that dominated the region forbade public preaching. The mission bought slaves by the thousands at Zanzibar's slave market, gathered those abandoned by their masters, and later received large numbers from the British navy, which intercepted slave-bearing ships leaving the Indian Ocean coast for trade in the Americas, India, or the Middle East. Such slaves were trained, first at Zanzibar and later and more extensively at the coastal mission of Bagamoyo.

The Holy Ghost missionaries pursued the comprehensive evangelization of these former slaves. Their goal was the formation of new Catholics who, after being formed at the coast, would then settle in the interior at new mission stations. In the interior, the missionaries thought, the influence of Islam would be less and Christianity might grow. On account of these ambitions, the Spiritans preferred to receive or purchase slave children. Children, they reasoned, were more amenable to the mis-

---

[4] For a discussion of this mission, see Kollman as well as an outstanding earlier work by John A. Kieran, *The Holy Ghost Fathers in East Africa, 1863 to 1914* (Ph.D. dissertation, University of London, 1966). For further summaries see the following: Norman R. Bennett, "The Holy Ghost mission in East Africa: 1858-1890," *Studies in East African History* (Boston: Boston University Press, 1963), 54-75. Alois Engel, *Die Missionsmethode der Missionare v. heiligen Geist auf dem afrikanischen Festland*, (Knechsteden, Germany, 1932). Henry Gibson, "Mission of Zanguebar" in *The Month* (London, 1886): 58, 197-214 (part one) and 564-580 (part two). Henri de Maupeou, "Le R. P. Horner et la fondation de la mission du Zanguebar," in *Revue d'Histoire des Missions* IX, (1932): 506-533. Jacqueline O'Hare, *The Christian response: The work of the Church Missionary Society at Freretown and Congregation of the Holy Ghost at Bagamoyo for the slaves of East Africa, 1868-1904*, Unpublished manuscript (1969). F. Versteijnen, *The Catholic Mission of Bagamoyo* (1968), reprint by A.K. Zuber and COD Saarbrucken (1991). F. Versteijnen, "Pioneer days in East Africa," in *African Ecclesiastical Review* 10:4, (1968): 362-366.

sionary regime of education, liturgical worship, and physical labor, thus more easily formed into the kinds of Catholics the missionaries wanted, and the missionaries built dormitories, schools, and workshops to house and train these children. They established daily schedules of education, prayer, and work to shape these children into strong Catholics for the future. The missionaries also set apart some children for specialized training as possible priests, sisters, and brothers, in programs developed in the late 1860s and 1870s.

By the late 1860s several of the children reached marriageable ages, and families emerged who settled in villages run by the mission. Most settled at Bagamoyo, which by the mid-1870s had eclipsed Zanzibar as the main Catholic mission in eastern Africa. Bagamoyo housed some 400 children in its dorms, 60 or so families inhabited the nearby village, and ten sisters and seven Spiritan priests and brothers oversaw the entire operation, which sprawled over an extensive area dotted by large buildings and carefully laid out fields. Bagamoyo became a prominent stop for traders, explorers, and other visitors to eastern Africa, and it earned fame for agricultural innovation as well as the comprehensive formation of African Catholics.

Unfortunately for the mission's strategy, the attempts to form priests, brothers, and sisters from these former African slaves had, by the latter 1870s, borne little fruit.[5] This failure left the missionaries without the African assistants they anticipated. The Spiritans needed help to do the missionary work they wanted, work that expanded in the late 1870s when they launched a new mission away from the coast, pursuing their dream of evangelizing the interior of Africa. In 1877, two Spiritans and two married couples of ex-slaves left Bagamoyo to build and cultivate at Mhonda. Of the two couples, one husband, the aforementioned Hilarion, soon emerged as a forceful figure and quickly assumed the title of catechist at the new mission. He became what the missionaries called their "powerful auxiliary."

Hilarion's Evolution

Hilarion, his wife, and the other couple joined the missionaries and left for their new home a few weeks after their wedding, arriving at Mhonda on November 5, 1877. The mission journal, sporadically kept but none the less the best historical source on the life at the mission, describes the

---

[5] For details on these efforts, see Kollman, 314-317, 368-371, 375-384, 408-417.

early building and planting, and also shows that Hilarion quickly became a trusted emissary for the missionaries. He is frequently mentioned as accompanying them on errands and was often even sent alone on important mission business. He was sent to find one of their number whose return had been delayed;[6] accompanied the head of the mission at Mhonda, Father Machon, on a futile search for a preferable site for the new Christian colony;[7] went back to Bagamoyo to get wine for Mass when the mission ran short;[8] tried to make peace on the mission's behalf with a threatening local chieftain;[9] and even went with money to go ransom some children for the mission.[10]

At the same time, however, the journal also indicates that Hilarion began to act on his own, apart from the mission, that is, as his own independent agent. In May of 1879, for example, he ransomed a child from slavery on his own behalf, and in the next month he took two porters on a journey, probably for personal trade.[11] Meanwhile, Mhonda mission had grown, largely due to the arrival of other Christian couples from Bagamoyo. All such couples from the coast had control of their own houses and fields to a certain extent, part of the missionary strategy of encouraging both their loyalty to the mission and their self-sufficiency as Christian households. Hilarion's independence, however, soon moved beyond Spiritan expectations and became troublesome in the eyes of the missionaries.

Hilarion's first substantial conflict with the mission came in 1880 when he was implicated in a scheme to steal guns and gunpowder from the mission. Exactly what was planned for the guns and powder remained unclear, but a possible explanation emerged in light of the "war," as the missionaries called it, that occurred four months later. Hilarion was instrumental in this conflict with a local leader in February of 1881, in which several of the Christians were injured and neighboring villages were burnt in retaliation.

---

[6] Mhonda journal, Journals of Holy Ghost mission stations in eastern Africa (microfilm, Bethel Park, PA: Holy Ghost Archives), 26vii78. *Note:* See Primary Sources, Abbreviated Sources and Archives Consulted at the end of the paper.

[7] Ibid., 8ix78.

[8] Ibid., 10vii79.

[9] Ibid., 8ix79.

[10] Ibid., 29x80.

[11] Ibid., 11v79, 22vi79.

While the journal details the fighting itself,[12] a letter from a Spiritan to Paris written shortly after the events narrates the background to the conflict. Hilarion had apparently been robbed and was paid a slave in compensation, which he in turn traded for six sheep. Not having been paid the sheep, he complained and received a gun from the mission in order to strengthen his demand for payment. Rebuffed, Hilarion later took the gun again and seized a youth of the village from where the sheep were supposed to come. That village then attacked the village of the Christians at Mhonda, but the latter were prepared and fought off the assault. The next day the Christians (the missionary uses "we") went back with a friendly chief and burned the offending village, returning with cheers and congratulations at the courage of "the children of the whites." Another letter says that Hilarion had taken the young man as surety for a debt, which was customary in the region, but also blamed the missionary who had written the first report, whose liberality with the mission's "children" had only encouraged this independence of spirit, an opinion seconded by another missionary, who also singled out Hilarion for blame.[13]

This conflict did little at first to change Hilarion's relationship to the mission, and he continued to assist the missionaries as messenger, preparer of caravans, and catechist. But he also maintained the pursuit of his own interests—as a landowner, local trader, and purchaser of slaves for his own household. Such slaves he no doubt promptly "freed," though as the missionary example likely taught him, this did not mean that such people could leave his household.[14] In early 1884, however, he began to act independently of the mission in more obvious ways, and even began a plan to start his own village, apart from the mission. In February he left without permission to spend the night outside the Christian village, taking along with him one of the females whom he had ransomed from slavery. A missionary, commenting on this misbehavior in the mission journal, wrote, "Deliver us, Lord,"[15] apparently asking re-

---

[12] Ibid., 8ii81.
[13] The letters in question are, in order of reference, as follows: *CSSp* 197a: Foels to Schwindenhammer, 8ii81; Ibid., Machon to Schwindenhammer, 9ii81; Ibid., Baur to Superior [in Paris], 8iii81.
[14] The question of the freedom of those ransomed by the mission is a vexed one. The missionaries never described their charges as slaves, but neither did they call them free, and when some tried to escape they were forcibly returned to the mission. For a discussion, see Kollman, 168ff.
[15] Mhonda journal, 19ii84, 20ii84.

lease from Hilarion and such scandals.

A few months later a local non-Christian leader named Baraka visited the mission to ask about the onetime catechist, who was now living in Baraka's village and apart from the mission. Understanding Hilarion's state of mind at this point is difficult, but the missionaries say that Baraka, fearing retaliation for sheltering a runaway Christian like Hilarion, wanted assurances that his village would not be attacked by the mission. He also probably wanted to ascertain if he was dealing with a rascal, and he promised to bring Hilarion back, bound hand and foot, should the missionaries so desire. The journal-writer opines that Baraka might well have been in debt to Hilarion, who "is always in revolt against us." The journal adds that these two—Baraka and Hilarion—are "wolves who will devour each other."[16] Over the next months Hilarion remained away, leaving his wife and family behind at Mhonda. In December he returned, pleading his submission to Spiritan rule, but a few months later the missionaries felt his submission was not "pure and simple."[17]

The 1885 visit to Mhonda of the first bishop of eastern Africa, the Spiritan Raoul de Courmont, led to a reconsideration of the arrangement at the Christian village at the mission, where there was increasing dissatisfaction, even open resistance, among the local Christians. Hilarion met with Bishop Courmont to discuss the situation. As a consequence the catechist received permission to start his own village a day's journey or so from Mhonda and thus still connected with the mission, and later he even began to run his own catechumenate at the new village.[18] His wife Germaine joined him there,[19] and for the next year or so relations between the central mission station and the new Christian village remained cordial. Hilarion supported the mission when it was threatened and this support was reciprocated when he felt pressure;[20] Machon, the superior, visited Hilarion's village[21] and in response Hilarion sent the mission ivory;[22] Machon saw Hilarion again when he was

---

[16] Ibid., 11v84.
[17] Ibid., 29xii84, 9ii85.
[18] Ibid., 5vii85, 4ix85.
[19] Ibid., 21x85.
[20] Ibid., 14viii85, 22-29ix85, 13x85, 13vi86, 29vi86, 30xii86.
[21] Ibid., 7i86.
[22] Ibid., 22i86.

wounded, for Hilarion had medical skills.[23] In another "war" around Christmas of 1886, Hilarion joined the mission against its enemies.[24]

In early 1887, Courmont visited Mhonda again and wrote that Hilarion had been courted by the enemies of the mission but had remained faithful.[25] A few days later the bishop visited the catechist, however, only to find him living with a concubine and with his wife gone.[26] Courmont met with both the wife and husband, hoping for reconciliation. Then some months later again there was trouble again when Hilarion seized a woman from a local village which threatened retaliation.

By the early 1890s, after German control over what would become Tanganyika had been achieved, Hilarion and his village had become a thorn in the missionary side. As the decade progressed, tension in the area only increased as German colonial ambitions encroached on the mission's autonomy, and Hilarion's insubordination to the mission emerged ever more strongly as a result.[27] In their efforts to create local administrative order over their colonial possessions, the Germans appointed Africans as "headmen" (Swahili, *majumbe*, sing. *jumbe*) in charge of local villages, and Hilarion received this post in 1896. To the dismay of the missionaries, he and his entire village converted to Islam the following year. The Spiritans regarded this decision as intended not only to build his alliances with other local Muslim chieftains, but also to deepen his friendship with the Germans, who now held formal power over an area that had long been nominally under the control of the Sultan of Zanzibar while missionary authority had played a prominent role for nearly two decades. The missionaries recognized that the new colonizers tired of the strong personalities of the both the missionaries and mission-educated African Christians, who could, with missionary support, often resist demands for wage laborers and also dispute colonial land claims. If they could explain it, the Spiritans simultaneously lamented Hilarion's

---

[23] Ibid., 29vii86.

[24] Ibid., xii86.

[25] *CSSp*, 198b, Carnets, 24i87.

[26] Ibid., 30i87.

[27] For details on these events, see the discussion in Kieran, 317ff. Friction grew between the missionaries, German colonial authorities, and Hilarion, with open fighting between Hilarion's followers and those of the mission at the turn of the century. Eventually the Germans expelled one of the Spiritans who resented the colonial policy that supported local Muslim authority vested in Hilarion and others (Kieran, 319).

defection.

Understanding Hilarion

Missionaries have long been prodigious writers and careful compilers of their experiences in the mission field. Such accounts usually follow certain literary conventions appropriate to their genre—the report to a superior or mission-sponsoring body, a story designed to please or further encourage benefactors, a letter to a friend—but a series of missionary reports also charts missionary experiences which themselves have particular patterns. One quite common pattern reveals glowing initial missionary reports—for example, describing the simple virtues of the people in the mission field, the nobility of their culture, the quickness with which they are drawn to the gospel—only to find that, within a few years, the descriptions turn bitter: the people are stubborn, ignorant, materialistic, stupid, trapped in depravity, incapable of virtue, nearly hopeless as objects of missionary activity. One constant in this well-grooved rhetorical arc from an optimistic beginning to later frustration, an arc traced by Spiritan descriptions of Hilarion, is the complaint of *ingratitude*. In one form or another, missionaries grumble, "I/we have done so much and the people do not appreciate it. They are an ungrateful lot."

Missionary explanations for such ingratitude fall into at least four categories: 1.) demonic possession; 2.) racist explanations, such that "not much can be expected of such stock"; 3.) problems with conversion—it was inadequate or shallow, somehow Christianity failed to "take"; and 4.) or the determinative influences of culture. The first two of these categories have disappeared from serious studies of missionary activity, for recourse to demonic possession or racial shortcomings to explain recalcitrance to the missionary message is, thankfully, rare among contemporary students of African history and Christian mission.

Explanations dependent on the concepts of *conversion* and *culture* to describe experiences like Hilarion's with missionary Christianity, however, have enjoyed a longer shelf life. Culture tends to denote the ways in which the evangelized are (and remain) different from the missionary, while conversion names the desired result, from the missionary's point of view, which is rarely as complete as hoped. Recent missionary histories often invoke these terms in relation to each other, as cause to effect, so that a given people's culture becomes the reason for the success or failure of conversion attempted by a group of missionaries. Such analyses often presume that culture encourages or discourages conversion to Christianity.

In a broader sense, of course, culture and conversion appear in a variety of discursive situations, both popular and analytic. But their disciplinary homes are quite precise. Culture has been the prerogative and specialty of anthropologists, though it appears in other venues with varying degrees of sophistication. Conversion is primarily a term used by both sociologists and theologians to indicate change in religious identity. Sociologists tend to focus on changes of identity in an external, observable sense, whereas theologians note changes in an internal, spiritual, or psychological sense.

The terminological inadequacy of both culture[28] and conversion,[29] at least as commonly used to describe change in religious identity,

---

[28] For influential critiques of the notion of culture as traditionally used in anthropology and common parlance, especially its roots in colonial-era structural-functional anthropology, see the following: Aiden Southall, "The illusion of tribe," in *Journal of African and Asian Studies* 5,(1970): 28-50. Talal Asad, Ed., *Anthropology and the Colonial Encounter* (London: Ithaca Press, 1973). John Iliffe, *A Modern History of Tanganyika* (Cambridge: Cambridge University Press, 1979), 318-341. Leroy Vail, Ed., *The Creation of Tribalism is Southern Africa* (Berkeley and Los Angeles: University of California Press, 1989 and 1991). Jean Comaroff and John Comaroff, *Of Revelation and Revolution, vol.1: Christianity, Colonialism, and Consciousness in South Africa* (Chicago and London: University of Chicago Press, 1991), 49-67. Thomas Spear and Richard Waller, Eds., *Being Maasai* (London: James Currey, 1993). In a recent address to the American Historical Association, Joseph Miller, the distinguished African historian, referred to "the hoary colonial fallacy that Africans could usefully be understood as belonging to enduring, homogeneous ethnic aggregates..." Miller continues,

> "Tribes" usually lie concealed behind polite euphemisms—"cultures," "ethnic groups," and neo-logistical "ethnicities," even "communities"—but politesse does not eliminate the time-defying, history-denying static logic of the notion: stereotyped Africans confined within abiding structures, individuals submerged in depersonalized, abstracted aggregates, who act mostly by realizing social (or cultural) norms, that is, by preserving unchanged what colonial era-language reified as "tradition."

[Joseph Miller, "Presidential address: History and Africa/Africa and history," in *American Historical Review*, 104:1, (1999): 15-16].

[29] Conversion, in common language linked with Christianity, derives from the Greek notion of *metanoia*, and its model in the West has been St. Paul's conversion on the road to Damascus (Acts of the Apostles 9:1-19, 22:6-16, 26:12-18). Filtered through the analyses of William James, *The Varieties of Religious Ex-*

has become increasingly clear. Neither term is supple enough to describe the ways social or individual identities change. Cultures are never as bounded, uniform, or unchanging as certain anthropologists in the past have suggested, and conversion fails to grasp the intricacies of evolving personhood in changing times and places. Certainly neither culture nor conversion, as traditionally invoked, offers much explanation for Hilarion's estrangement from the mission.

Hilarion's culture, for example, is hard to describe. He was a ransomed slave, raised and socialized in the mission from a young age, and subject to the disciplinary, educative, and spiritual regime of the Spiritan missionary program. Before that he would have been socialized, but we know not how. Given the diversity of peoples in the region, his "culture" was probably shared more with the other Africans at the Mhonda mission who came with him from Bagamoyo than with the Africans in the area around it. The power of culture to explain his behavior, therefore, begs the question of why other mission Christians acted differently. Recourse to his conversion, too, explains little. In the first place, the missionaries themselves eschewed this term, which suggested a voluntaristic approach to religious adherence with Protestant overtones. Second, they no doubt believed that Hilarion had become a sincere Catholic, judging from their reliance upon him. He convinced them of his rectitude and abilities, so much so that they accorded him a great deal of responsibility in their new mission. Such trust was not misplaced; after all, even the independent village he established maintained its Christian identity and its ties with the mission for over a decade. He even conducted a catechumenate there for a time, preparing those who wanted to become Christian for baptism outside the supervision of the missionaries.

---

perience (New York: 1902) and A. D. Nock, *Conversion* (New York: Oxford University Press, 1933), conversion has been envisioned as individual, sudden, profound, irreversible, and centered in religious beliefs. As Jean and John Comaroff [*Of Revelation and Revolution,* vol I, 250-251; *Of Revelation and Revolution,* vol. 2: *The Dialectics of Modernity on a South African Frontier* (Chicago and London: University of Chicago Press,1997) 117-118.] have effectively argued, conversion understood in this fashion, in company with certain teleological assumptions about the inevitable advance of "world religions" like Islam and Christianity and intellectualist assumptions about the need for "macrocosmic" worldviews when previously "microcosmic" peoples get thrust into more "modern" and "historical" situations [Robin Horton, "African conversion," in *Africa* 41:2 (1971) and Robin Horton, "On the rationality of conversion," in *Africa* 45, (1975): 3-4.], tends to explain what it purports to describe, and substitutes theological opinion for sociological analysis.

If neither Hilarion's culture nor problems with his conversion explain his disillusion and separation from the mission, what does account for his estrangement and then new Islamic identity? I believe that a firmer grasp of the social history of the proto-colonial and then colonial frontier allows for a more revealing insight into the structural incongruities that led to the break between Hilarion and the mission. Joined to this better awareness of that history, I will invoke the notion of the moral economy, used first by historian E. P. Thompson, to make sense of the changes in Hilarion.

Thompson developed the idea of the moral economy in an effort to explain the basis for generalized outrage by clients against their patrons, in particular to make sense of the appearance of food riots in early modern England.[30] These occurred, Thompson argued, because expectations guiding the relations between social classes were not being met, so that the lower classes felt that obligations understood as traditional and customary went unobserved by those accorded social authority. Using this idea of the moral economy, I contend that missionary evangelization engendered in former slaves like Hilarion a moral economy of the mission, in which they internalized an implicit social contract. As new householders, Hilarion and the other colonists of the interior carried certain expectations about their relationship with the mission—they would receive food, education, and a chance to improve their land, while the labor required of them on the mission's own fields would not be so onerous that they could not till their own—and such expectations grounded the authority accorded the priests and brothers. It also generated their identity as African mission Christians as well as whatever sense of loyalty encouraged them to maintain that identity. They carried this view of authority and identity with them from the coast to the new mission at Mhonda.

Mhonda, however, was a frontier, quite unlike the Bagamoyo mission at the coast where the moral economy had been generated. Official European colonial control in eastern Africa was not to come until 1885, when German claims to the mainland spurred British claims to the island of Zanzibar, but the Sultan's grasp was weakening even earlier, and his direct control over eastern Africa's hinterland away from the coast had long been sporadic. In light of the distance between the Sul-

---

[30] Thompson, "The moral economy of the English crowd in the eighteenth century."

tan's stronghold at Zanzibar and the myriad of smaller political authorities in the regions near their missions, most of the Catholic missions became political authorities in their own right. Nowhere was this as clear as at Mhonda. Father Machon, the formidable head of the mission most of the years from 1877 until his death in 1898, created a militia from the Christians soon after his arrival, and they intervened in a number of local skirmishes over witchcraft accusations, the taking of slaves, and land disputes.[31] Local leaders sought refuge and counsel from Machon, who often settled disagreements and established terms of reparation in meetings called *massa* in the local idiom, or *baraza* in Swahili. Once, when he departed on medical leave, even the Spiritans' own publication called him "in effect, like the grand ruler of the Nguru [the ethnic designation for the people in the area]."[32] Hilarion's position allied him with this emerging political authority, but he was also an African, unlike the missionaries, thus uniquely poised at the colonial frontier.

As far as I am aware, there exists no direct evidence of Hilarion's state of mind as these circumstances changed, and thus any attempt to piece together his evolving self-awareness must remain conjectural. Nonetheless, it seems clear that the social field in which Hilarion acted changed rapidly after his arrival at Mhonda, and his resulting social identity mutated as the moral economy grounding that identity and sustaining his loyalty to the mission also mutated. To articulate this further, let me consider three aspects of Hilarion's social identity where his interests intersected with those of the missionaries. The incongruities between these three aspects shed light on the changing moral economy of the mission and help make sense of Hilarion's move away from the mission.

First, Hilarion was one of the mission "children," a term the missionaries used for their former slaves who had been formed at Zanzibar or Bagamoyo. With his wife and children he helped make up the Christian village the Spiritans established at Mhonda, something they did at all their interior missions for the next several decades. Such villages would, the missionaries thought, attract local peoples by their virtue, orderliness, and agriculture productivity. Predictably, many such villagers chafed at the missionaries' control over them as the 1880s progressed, Hilarion among them. The village Christians protested the burdens placed upon

---

[31] Kieran, 234ff.
[32] BG 16:720.

them to manage the mission's own fields and sometimes, like Hilarion, fled the mission's control. In 1883, several even complained to the French consul at Zanzibar about their treatment at the missionaries' hands, an event that created consternation and anxiety among the Spiritans.[33]

Along with his place as one of the Christian villagers, Hilarion was also a catechist at Mhonda, which provided a second role in which he interacted with the missionaries. He thus bore particular responsibility for the Christian education of the children born in the village and for catechizing any of the surrounding peoples who came to the mission. This role suggests that the missionaries trusted him at least in the beginning. He likely seemed clearer in his understanding of the faith than others and could organize classes and instruction. At Bagamoyo he no doubt received more thorough training and formation to prepare him for this role. Besides being a villager and a catechist at Mhonda, however, Hilarion also stepped into a third position as an ambitious patron-to-be, who quickly showed his desire to become a prominent local leader in the region around the mission. This third role was complicated because, as already noted, the mission itself, with its material wealth not to mention its connections to the Sultan and Europeans at the coast, represented potent authority in the local area. Hilarion attached himself to this potency, serving as a cultural and political broker between the mission and surrounding peoples.

One aspect of Hilarion's potency as a local power broker deserves particular mention. Because of their connection to the mission, Hilarion and the other Christians had access to weapons and gun powder, which they could use not only to defend the mission or advance its objectives, but also in pursuit of their own interests. With his access to this destructive technology, which was still rather scarce in the area of the mission and thus could be decisive in local conflicts, Hilarion was ably situated to serve as a cultural broker for all sorts of exchanges between the mission and the local populace, both under the mission's purview and increasingly outside of it. With the onset of formal German overrule in 1885, the value of such cultural brokers only increased, as did Hilarion's tendency to act independently of the mission.

Hilarion's evolving and overlapping roles demonstrate that he went from being a client of the mission before and just after arriving in

---

[33] Kollman, 393ff.

Mhonda to being simultaneously a client *and* a patron who established his own clients within the region around the mission. As client of the missionaries he was to be obedient to them. As a catechist, they gave him much responsibility, and as a fledgling patron he sought to expand his own wealth and power. Besides these personal changes, the previous expectations of the moral economy, forged in the closed environment of the large mission station at Bagamoyo, no longer obtained. Hilarion had been raised where the boundaries between himself and the world outside had been clear and where missionary authority was evident. At Mhonda, on the contrary, he entered a place where his roles and the mission's circumstances allowed him new opportunities for the assumption of authority and the expansion of his social capital. Clear and stable expectations of a moral economy had existed in the coastal mission but the new world of the proto-colonial and then colonial frontier destabilized the structure of duties and obligations so that the original moral economy of the mission no longer functioned. Inasmuch as Hilarion was now a patron as well as a client, the norms of the moral economy shifted, and missionary control over him was not as complete as before.

Hilarion, villager and catechist, never simply acted as a tool of the missionaries after arriving at Mhonda, but his disenchantment shows how the missionary strategy generated contradictions that could not be resolved within the previously existing expectations of missionary authority. He pursued his own interests as his identity as an African Christian evolved, culminating in his alienation from the mission. Living first as a monogamous Christian husband then polygamist, while simultaneously a father, landowner, slaveholder, trader, arbitrator, village chief, and, yes, catechist, he ended as a Muslim.

Recent studies of Christianity in Africa have emphasized how Africans themselves, and not missionaries, effected the lion's share of Christianization on the continent.[34] Whether as formal lay catechists, preachers, teachers, or unofficial bearers of the Christian message, women and men pushed the gospel beyond the boundaries of mission stations, where missionaries themselves often remained. At the same time, however, our understanding of how Africans took on a Christian identity remains limited. Here, instead of accounting for missionary frustration by recourse to notions of shallow conversion, cultural barriers, or

---

[34] David Maxwell, ed. with Ingrid Lawrie, *Christianity and the African Imagination: Essays in Honour of Adrian Hastings* (Leiden, Boston, Köln: Brill, 2002).

demonic possession, I have tried to present Hilarion as a reasonable, historically conditioned social actor whose identity evolved in a certain
place and time, and who responded in ways that made sense to him. He
was neither trapped in a pre-contact culture nor poorly converted to
Christianity, but he was like many of the earliest African Catholics in
eastern Africa, who also responded in ways that can make sense to us, if
we have the right tools to understand them.

I contend that there are thousands of stories like Hilarion's—
people connected to but not contained by missionary definitions of what
it meant to be a Christian. Their Christian identity emerged in relation to
shifting historical circumstances. Their conversions, therefore, look tran-
sitory not because of their spiritual shortcomings but because circumstances generated that sort of fluidity. This is how Christianity was made
local in Africa, through the assumption of Christian identity by Africans,
on terms not always set by missionaries. Unfortunately for the missionaries' plans, Christian identity as they understood it could melt away when
their missionary strategy, designed to forge such an identity, depended
on contexts that themselves changed.

Conclusion

As remarked above, missionary descriptions of new Christians follow a
standard pattern, moving from initial enthusiasm to almost inevitable
frustration. What does this rhetorical pattern demonstrate? It certainly reveals nothing inherent to "the indigenous," whatever that category might
mean, and it seems to me too simple to say that it represents *inevitable*
missionary frustration before local resistance. Missionaries themselves,
of course, have offered their reasons for their frustrations. Here I have
tried to show that even explanations based on culture and conversion,
though obvious improvements on earlier recourse, for example, to demonic possession, fail to account for the complex ways in which
Christian identity emerged in missionary and colonial contexts. The reasons for the relegation of these terms to a different role in the present
historical analysis emerge first from the nature of the evangelization carried out, which does not implicate culture and conversion in ways
congenial to the usual narrative canons of mission history, since Hilarion
had no obvious culture associated with an ethnic designation and the
missionaries eschewed conversion as a missionary goal.

Yet I also want to suggest that the notion of the moral economy
can yield insights into the ways evangelized peoples abide in or change

their new Christian identity in less obvious cases. In much of the evangelized and colonized world, Christian missionaries sought to forge what in retrospect looks like a moral economy according to which the mission generated loyalty in those evangelized, a loyalty rooted in the very pragmatic expectations that obtain in any circumstance in which relationships are organized around shared, though asymmetrical expectations. Hilarion's trajectory demonstrates that the changing circumstances that undermined the foundations of the moral economy that the missionaries sought to establish could also undo the loyalty that missionaries achieved with their new Christians. Conversion in this case, understood as loyalty to the mission, depended on a particular moral economy, which was itself dependent on certain expectations appropriate at a coastal mission but not operative at a new mission inland, especially as colonialism drew near.

Primary Sources, Abbreviated Sources and Archives Consulted

AA: *Annales Apostoliques de la Congrégation du Saint-Esprit et du Saint Coeur de Marie*

Bagamoyo Catholic mission - n.d. Baptismal Register.

BG: *Bullétin Général de la Congrégation du Saint-Esprit et du Saint Coeur de Marie*, Paris. Quarterly publication of the Holy Ghost Congregation, distributed to every community, begun in 1857. After the designnation of volume will follow the page number, e.g., BG 11: 335. Because the sources of the materials in this journal are often not identified, the date of the excerpt cited is difficult to ascertain. The dates of the issues, however, are as follows:

BG 1: 1857-1859	BG 11: 1877-1881
BG 2: 1860-1862	BG 12: 1881-1882
BG 3: 1862-1863	BG 13: 1883-1886
BG 4: 1863-1865	BG 14: 1887-1888
BG 5: 1866-1867	BG 15: 1889-1891
BG 6: 1867-1869	BG 16: 1891-1893
BG 7: 1869-1870	BG 17: 1893-1896
BG 8: 1871-1872	BG 18: 1896-1897
BG 9: 1872-1874	BG 19: 1898-1899
BG 10: 1874-1877	BG 20: 1899-1900

CSSp: Holy Ghost Archives, Chevilly, Paris. Letters and files will be cited with box number, then file number, then writer (and recipient of the letter) if relevant, page number (if relevant), and date, in European-dated format. E.g., CSSp 196bii, Horner to Schwindenhammer, 4ii65. *Note:* In the late 1990s the archives in Paris adopted another system of cataloguing. I have used the older system as it has been the practice in previous literature on the Holy Ghost missionaries in eastern Africa.

Bagamoyo journal
Mhonda journal
Journals of Holy Ghost mission stations in eastern Africa (microfilm, Holy Ghost Archives, Bethel Park, PA). Cited by date of the entry.

PART II

The State of Christian Inculturation with the Native Cultures of South Asia, The Far East, Polynesia, Melanesia and Australia

Edited by
Cyriac K. Pullapilly
Saint Mary's College

HINDU CUSTOMS AND PRACTICES IN CHRISTIAN CEREMONIES: THE CASE OF THE MALABAR CHURCH

Natalia Abraham[*]

There is something very fascinating about the way the ancient Syrian Christians interacted with Hindus in Kerala: they were active participants in Hindu society. The Christian community in Kerala came to hold a Malayalee identity – these Christians were integrated members of Hindu community, even enjoying a relatively high social status. Kerala Christians were not considered foreign; rather, their Indian identity prevailed over their type of worship. Although their liturgy displays little adaptation other than some additions to the marriage rite, there occurred many cultural adaptations in the social aspects of Christian life. Being a minority Eastern Church, Malabar Christianity was and is adamant in protecting its own religious traditions. It is Orthodox in title and attitude - yet traditionally, it has recognized the need for continued participation in their native culture. Certain of its customs and traditions can be directly linked to ancient Hindu practices in South India. The traditional marriage ceremony itself contains incorporated Hindu practices, as do the customs surrounding this event, and other festivals. This inter-religious borrowing became institutionalized, and the respect accorded to each religious community seems to have played a major part in the lack of tension between them. Perhaps the absence of clear distinctiveness contributes to the idyllic image of peace between the Christian and Hindu communities painted by surviving historical documents. In this essay, I shall investigate how this small Christian community has survived in a religiously pluralistic society while maintaining friendly relations with the dominant Hindu community.

A Confusing History

The Kerala Christians have been known to the ancient and modern world as Thomas Christians due to their tradition of apostolic succession from St. Thomas. They believe that in 52 C.E., St. Thomas the Apostle landed

[*] Natalia Abraham has an M.A. in Religious Studies from McGill University, Montreal, Canada.

in the port of Muziris in the island of Maliankara,[1] where he founded seven churches and an administrative system.[2] Although there are a number of feasible routes that would have made travel to India at the time possible, there is no evidence that proves St. Thomas traveled to India.[3] This absence of concrete proof did not put any damper on the strong tradition of the Kerala Christians that their Church was established by St. Thomas the Apostle. It is a religious tradition that survives on belief and fragmented remnants of history. The next 1500 years of the history of the Malabar Church is also vague; with the information available, one can only loosely estimate the origins and evolution of the community.[4] It is known that Kerala Christians became connected with Orthodox Churches in Persia within the first few hundred years of the Common Era. The liturgy, doctrines, and traditions that became dominant in Kerala were adopted from a Persian, Syriac speaking Church that was most probably Nestorian.[5] There were several migrations from Persia to the Malabar Coast[6] between the fourth and ninth centuries. Leslie Brown describes further evidence existing in the records of several travelers from the Western world who, from the 6th century onwards, gave mention of Indian Christians who were under the guidance of a Persian Church.[7] There is also belief that there was a Syrian Christian royal dynasty that died out before the 15th century. Apparently, it ruled over the kingdom of *Villiar-*

---

[1] Maliankara is an island close to the area of Cranganore, a famous trading port in Kerala (South India). In ancient times, it was a town important for commerce and culture. The fact that it was a Jewish centre as well could have attracted St. Thomas to the area.

[2] V.C. Samuel, "A Glance into the past and a peep into the future," in *New Life in an Old Church: A Symposium on the Syrian Orthodox Church of India*, Fr. Munduvel V George, Ed. (Calcutta: Orthodox Syrian Church, 1963), 2-7. An account of St. Thomas' works is outlined in the *Acts of St. Thomas*; however, it is an apocryphal text [David, Daniel, *The Orthodox Church of India* (New Delhi: Printaid, 1972), 4, 8-10]. In this text, we are told that he was able to attract people (Brahmins) to Christianity through the miracles he performed.

[3] Leslie Brown, *The Indian Christians of St. Thomas: An Account of the Ancient Syrian Church of Malabar* (Cambridge: University Press, 1982), 59.

[4] Samuel, 2. This is most probably because almost all evidence of connection with the Church in Persia were destroyed in the 16th and 17th centuries in a Portuguese attempt to rid Kerala of "heresy".

[5] Nestorians have the position that Christ is One person, of two hypostases, and of two natures [John Chapman, "Monophysites and Monophysitism," in *Catholic Encyclopedia*, X (1999),
http://www.newadvent.org/cathen/10489b.htm, Nov. 26, 2001].

[6] The Malabar Coast is in Kerala; Kerala is often referred to as Malabar.

[7] Brown, 65-85.

vattom (known to the Portuguese historians as the kingdom of Beliarte) from the 6th century. After the coming of the Portuguese, the Kerala Christians entered into alliance with the Orthodox Church of Syria, which has been labeled as "Monophysite" by Western theologians.[8] Thus, they are no longer affiliated with a Nestorian Church.[9]

Kerala boasts trading ports that have been engaged in trade with Eastern and Western countries since centuries before the birth of Christ.[10] To the Kerala Christians, no foreign presence was as monumental as the Portuguese in the 15th and 16th centuries C.E., save that of St. Thomas himself. Being Roman Catholics, the Portuguese sought with great fervor to bring the Syrian Christians under the authority of the Pope. Considering the commercial importance of Kerala in the fourteenth century, it was very likely that authorities in Rome were economically motivated in sending a bishop and forming a diocese there.[11] In a series of political moves that were often subversive, the Portuguese attained complete administrative control over the jurisdiction, where they brought the spirit of the Inquisition to bear.[12] They enforced the Latinization of the Church in India:

> The enforced celibacy of the clergy, the introduction of images into their church, and attempts to supersede the Syriac language by the Latin in their religious services were especially offensive to (the Syrian Christians), as also the pride, arrogance, and intolerance of the Jesuits towards all who could not conform to their injunctions.[13]

The Portuguese authorities sought to sever all connections between Kerala and Syria. Being masters of the sea at the time, the Portuguese were able to physically intercept any attempts at communication. They effec-

---

[8] Catholics hold a diophysite position (One person, one hypostasis, two natures), a monophysite would maintain: One person, one hypostasis, and one nature. [Chapman, http://www.newadvent.org/cathen/10489b.htm, Nov. 26, 2001].
[9] There remains a small community of Chaldean (Nestorian) Christians in Trissur that has survived the Portuguese era.
[10] Robin Jeffrey, *The Decline of Nayar Dominance: Society and Politics in Travancore, 1847 – 1908* (London: Sussex University Press, 1976), 32.
[11] Daniel, 42.
[12] The Portuguese made Goa their headquarters in India, and the Archbishop of Goa was given jurisdiction over all of India in 1557 [Daniel, 43].
[13] Daniel, 54.

tively controlled the Syrian Christians for over half a century,[14] and resentment towards their policies grew.

A rumor that a prelate sent to Cochin from Persia had been detained by the Portuguese and drowned[15] brought Indian resentment to a peak. In defiance, about twenty thousand Kerala Christians met in Cochin on January 16th, 1653. Holding a rope tied to a stone cross (the *Coonen* or bent Cross), they took a solemn "oath to expel the Jesuits and to submit to no ecclesiastical authority except that of the archdeacon, until they should get a bishop from the Eastern Church."[16] Soon after, the church was able to re-establish an alliance with the Syrian Orthodox church. However, the oath of the *Coonen* Cross split Syrians into two sects: Romo-Syrians, and those who again sought the tenuous links with the Jacobite Patriarchs in West Asia.[17] Since the sixteenth century, the ancient Christian community in Kerala has undergone various divisions, large and small. It may be described as a "history of splits and litigations."[18] Most churches ally themselves with the Catholic Church, the Protestant (or Protestant-based), or the Orthodox Church. Within these broad headings, further splits have occurred, and new churches have been founded due to the missionary works of Western Christians. For the purposes of this paper, I will use the terms Kerala, Malabar, and Syrian Christians to signify a general group of Christians in Kerala who follow the Syrian Orthodox Liturgy, and trace priestly ordination to the converts of St. Thomas the Apostle.[19]

Plurality and the Kerala Christians

For thousands of years, Kerala has engaged in significant trade with Eastern and Western countries, constantly interfacing with different cultures. As a result, a unique society evolved that was perpetually involved in trade with foreign countries. Strong Christian and Jewish communities

---

[14] Neill, 87. It was the Portuguese's strategy to control the Christians through the Church in order to gain control politically and economically over all of Kerala, and eventually make it a colony.

[15] The Portuguese authorities at the time claimed that this was an accident; however, Kerala Christians regarded the event as murder.

[16] Brown, 100.

[17] Jeffrey, 17.

[18] Samuel, 11.

[19] I will not distinguish between 'Jacobite' and 'Syrian Orthodox': I will refer to them interchangeably, as they have a shared history and culture as a cohesive community.

were established in Kerala before the rise of Islam in the seventh century.[20] Even now, religious pluralism is quite evident: the 1991 Census of India states that the population in Kerala consists of 57.3% Hindus, 23.3% Muslims, and 19.3% Christians[21].

Keralites often speculate that there existed a peaceful attitude between Hindus and Christians in the pre-colonial, pre-Portuguese era. This utopian scenario strongly contrasts with the tense interactions that currently prevail in India. Hindu-Christian hostilities often escalate into violence: extremist Hindu militant nationalists vie for a Hindu nation, while Christian missionaries proselytize. The reason that such tension does not exist in Kerala can be attributed to the fat that in ancient Kerala, Hindus and Christians lived as one cohesive community, sharing the social aspects of their lives and even their attitudes towards worship. Dr. Parackel K. Mathew, a Syrian Orthodox priest, comments on the Kerala Christian tradition of peaceful coexistence with Hindu neighbors:

> There was no Hindu opposition until recently... Maybe until about two centuries ago, in the same family there could be Hindus and Christians. A brother may be Hindu, while another brother may be Christian. They did not see a great distinction between Hinduism and Christianity. A Hindu could come and attend Christian church ... Because they coexisted and because there was no serious institution, Christians adopted many of the Hindu customs... to a Hindu festival, Christians may go; to a Christian festival, Hindus may also come. [Any] kind of festival that developed in India developed from the pattern of the Hindu festival. We have *palli perunal* (festival celebration remembering the patron saint of the church) with procession, flags, and musical accompaniment... developed from Hindu practices... The social life was virtually the same.[22]

In addition, Malabar society was characterized by a unique camaraderie and the participation in each others festivals that transcended religious boundaries of ritual exclusivity. The communities interacted with each

---

[20] Trade routes were often associated with Jewish communities [Brown, 65].
[21] Statistics taken from: http://www.censusindia.net/cendat/datatable24.html
[22] Dr. Parackel K. Mathew, personal communication, March 2001.

other, each borrowing from the other; traditions were shared as they emphasized their cultural identity, rather than their religious exclusivity. Malabar Christians and their Hindu brethren behaved in a manner that largely did not cause any apprehension for either the Hindu or the Christian traditions. The symbiotic relationship between these communities was largely supported by the Hindu customs incorporated into the community of the Malabar Church, and this symbiosis may have contributed to the survival of this minority church as an Indian Church. Based on the approaches to syncretism Droogers outlines,[23] I shall make a case for the syncretism of the St. Thomas Christians. It is my contention that the level of syncretism we find in the Malabar Church had exhibited positive influence to the extent that it enabled (or contributed to) the survival of a minority church without generating conflict, where the community in fact became socially accepted as indigenous. In this context, one issue needs to be discussed, as well: have the St. Thomas Christians in any way diminished their Christian identity in order to remain part of a largely Hindu community?

St. Thomas Christians have been both applauded and criticized for their "syncretic" practices. However, it is debatable whether the term syncretism may be applied to this community. Syncretism is a term that is widely used to describe the result or process of the meeting of two cultures, i.e. the mixing of religions. Unfortunately, there is a lack of consensus on its exact usage. Often, its transient meaning is determined by the context in which it is used and the attitude of its user. Droogers offers two basic usages of the term: the objective and subjective.[24] The objective usage is neutral and descriptive in nature, whereas the subjective is evaluative from the point of view of one of the religions involved. Although most authors seem to intend to be objective, syncretism has been used more often in the past subjectively, as a negative concept that necessitates the corruption of a religion and an alteration of its basic belief system. Usually, the alteration deviates from and contradicts doctrine in a fashion that is considered abnormal and inferior. Positive subjective definitions have occurred less often.

Droogers offers many more possible ways of approaching syn-

---

[23] André Droogers, "Syncretism: The Problem of Definition, the Definition of the Problem," in *Dialogue and Syncretism: An Interdisciplinary Approach*, Jerald Gort, Hendrik Vroom, Rein Fernhout, and Anton Wessels, Eds. (Grand Rapids: Wm. B. Eerdmans Publishing Co, 1989). 7-13.
[24] Ibid., 7.

cretism.[25] One characterization scheme deals with the way in which religious meaning can be changed with syncretism. Syncretism can be a temporary ambiguous coexistence of elements from diverse religious and other contexts within a coherent religious pattern, where a) one meaning is eliminated, b) a new meaning is attained, or c) the two meanings drift apart. This issue is possibly problematic in the case of the Syrian Christians and raises the questions of whether their belief system has been altered to the point where they can no longer be called Christian, or whether the separation of their social and liturgical life allows space for new social meanings that do not challenge Christian tenets. The definitions of both syncretism and religion would be pertinent to the issue. Droogers elucidates further usages of the term syncretism as occurring between religion and religion, religion and culture, religion and ideology, religion and science, and so on. Depending on one's definition of the term religion, the type of syncretism that occurred with the Thomas Christians can be labeled as between religion (Christianity) and religion-culture (Hinduism). Whether this syncretism is a corruption of the Christian belief is a subjective matter.

When the Portuguese came face to face with the Kerala Christianity, they could easily judge any custom alien to their own tradition and label it illegitimate syncretism in a subjective, negative fashion. However, if one looks at the liturgy of the Syrian Christians, their Bible, their calendar, etc., these components of Christian life have been taken directly from the West Asian, Oriental Orthodox Church. Historically, the Oriental Orthodox churches are regarded as schismatic, that is, they separated at the Council of Chalcedon in 451 C.E.[26] Because of this division, the Oriental Churches have been regarded as "Monophysites;" a term they adamantly contend is not representative of their actual Christology. There is much stigma associated with the Chalcedonian separation, and biases towards the Oriental Orthodox practices may have contributed to accusations of illegitimate Christianity in Kerala.

The Orthodox reputation of strict adherence to tradition and stagnancy in form come to the aid of the Malabar church in this case. Liturgical activities were kept uncorrupted. Whether "Nestorian" or "Mo-

---

[25] Ibid., 11-13.

[26] Daniel, vi - viii. Oriental Orthodoxy is distinct from Eastern Orthodoxy, the latter having separated from the Latin Church 1054 C.E., when Pope Benedict sanctioned the *Filioque* clause alteration in the creed. Orthodox Christianity thus has two wings, each self-governed and of equal status: Oriental Orthodox Churches and Byzantine Orthodox Churches.

nophysite," they held close communication with the West Asian patriarch by whom they were supported. Visiting Orthodox bishops oversaw Orthodox practices, and would guide the churches in Kerala[27]. Many clashes that Western Christianity had with the Syrian Christian's liturgy had little to do with syncretic Hindu practices, and were more related to differences between the Oriental Orthodox and Catholic / Protestant-stemmed traditions.

The Oriental Orthodox Churches maintained many practices that were unknown or had been lost to Western Christianity. In her book, *The Christians of Kerala: History, Belief and Ritual among the Yakoba*, Susan Visvanathan highlights narratives of 19th century Syrian Christians and Anglican influence.[28] When the first important British ecclesiastical contact with the Syrian Christians was initiated, a British Reverend, Dr. Claudius Buchanan, offered to send translations of the English Bible in Malayalam. A reaction of one Syrian priest illustrates the clash:

> "But how," said one old priest, "shall we know that your standard copy is a true translation of our Bible? We cannot depart from our Bible. It is the true book of God, without corruption, the book, which was first used by the Christians of Antioch. What translations you have got in the West we know not, but the true Bible of Antioch, we have had in the mountains of Malabar for fourteen hundred years or longer."[29]

Clearly, theology and ritual in liturgical life derives wholly from the Syrian church; it remains unaffected by Indian thought. A new translation of the Bible was not necessary to this Syrian priest: his own version was an ancient one, from an ancient Christian church. Differences in Christology between the Chalcedonian churches and the Syrian Orthodox were minimal: the liturgical manifestation of this is found in the Nicene-Constantinopolitan creed, the *Filioque* clause. Because of East-West dialogues that have been occurring in the 20th century, a new, more objective view is emerging. The Catholic Church has officially recog-

---

[27] See Daniel, 34-41, for information on the relations of the Kerala Christians and West Asian Patriarchs.

[28] Susan Visvanathan, The Christians of Kerala: History, Belief, and Ritual among the Yakoba (Madras: Oxford University Press, 1993), 18.

[29] A quote taken from Visvanathan, 19, quoted from C,M. Agur, *Church History of Travancore* (Madras: SPS Press, 1901), 82.

nized the Oriental Orthodox Churches as legitimate forms of Christianity, and has stated that conflicts in Christology have been due to language differences. The issue of syncretism with regard to the West Asian Orthodox practices in Kerala is thus only relevant from a subjective, colonial or missionary point of view, and not from an ecumenical or Oriental Orthodox point of view.

Most authors who deal with syncretism in the Malabar Church community tend to create a dichotomy between liturgical life and social life, probably because the liturgy shows little syncretism. Only a few identifiable Hindu elements have been incorporated into the wedding ceremony. Visvanathan similarly divides ritual life into ceremonies of the house and ceremonies of the church.[30] Hindu practices in the Christian community have included political affiliations to Hindu kings, compliance to Hindu standards of purity and pollution, auspiciousness and caste, and observance of cultural customs pertaining to food and language. On the other hand, the ritual and ecclesiastical life of Malabar Christians have dictated their world-views including conception of time and salvation through Christ. Religious worship perhaps was considered private. Boundaries separating Hindus and Christians also seem to have been made explicit through endogamy, although interbreeding may have been acceptable to an extent.

Much of the discourse on Kerala Christian history focuses on race and caste. Within these discussions, one can extrapolate from the Malabar Christian community's documented accomplished status (in traditional times) what their relations with Hindu communities entailed. Malabar Christians occupied a position roughly similar to that of the Nayars in terms of numbers and status;[31] caste structure in India varies regionally, and in Kerala, Nayars were the dominant caste, occupying roles accorded elsewhere to both Vaishyas and Kshatriyas.[32] Bayly as-

---

[30] Visvanathan, 102.

[31] Latin Catholics, converts of St. Francis Xavier in the 16th century, comprised perhaps 6% of the population; but because they were generally low-caste converts, they were treated as vastly inferior to Syrian Christians

[32] There are four major castes in the Hindu social order [Klaus K. Klostermaier, *A Survey of Hinduism* (Albany: State University of New York Press, 1994), 334-335]. From highest to lowest status, the order is as follows: *Brahmins* (custodians of ritual and sacred word, teachers and advisors of society, priests), *Kshatriyas* (warriors, nobility, kings, administrators), *Vaisyas* (farmers and merchants), and *Sudras* (labourers, servants). Untouchables exist outside of this caste system. In theory, the higher a caste was, the purer, and the lower castes

serts that the mediaeval chiefdoms of Kerala were highly militarized societies with large warrior populations and a distinctive martial culture.[33] As tradition indicates, Syrian Christians were believed to be the descendants of high-caste converts made by St. Thomas the Apostle in the 1st century C.E.[34] Another tradition traces Syrian origins to Thomas of Cana, a Canaanite merchant from West Asia, who settled in Kerala with his followers and converted a number of Hindus in the 4th century.[35] This community's arrival provides a strong example of the interaction between Hindu kings and favored Christian communities.[36] According to one narrative, Thomas Cana brought with him about 72 families consisting of about four hundred people, including a bishop and some priests in 345 C.E. The Malabar king invested this *Knanaya*[37] community with the rights enjoyed by Brahmins and royal honors, an event that was inscribed on copper plates. Over one thousand years later, these artifacts were given to the factor of the Portuguese factory in Cochin for safekeeping, but apparently, they were lost after some time.[38]

The honors described on the copper plates are very difficult to obtain in Hindu society; such rights are usually granted only by birth. Kerala Christians were bestowed rights in a non-normative fashion because of their successes as merchants and warriors; their accomplishments superseded caste boundaries. Their role was complex and it is difficult to ascertain their exact position within Kerala's caste

---

could incur pollution. However, the rules guiding this system vary regionally in India
[33] Susan Bayly, "Hindu Kingship and the Origin of Community: Religion, State and Society in Kerala, 1750-1850," in *Modern Asian Studies* (1984), 179.
[34] This tradition is sometimes regarded as a biased claim put forth by Syrian Christians to raise their social status; however, it is possible that St. Thomas could have encountered a Brahmin community and converted them upon arriving in Kerala. The geographical segregation of the castes prevalent in Kerala may have made possible the exclusive conversion of a community with a common caste. Although it is unlikely that St. Thomas was a supporter of segregation by caste, it would have been strategically beneficial for him to convert among Brahmins given their status as religious and philosophical leaders.
[35] Within the Syrian Christian community lays a further classification between Suddists and Nordists, two endogamous groups. The Suddists claimed to be direct descendants of the early west Asian missionaries and racially pure; and Nordists claimed to be descendants of early high-caste converts [Jeffrey, 17].
[36] Neill, 42.
[37] The Malayalam corruption of the term "Canaanite." Though a single community, they are now distributed from the Orthodox and Roman Catholic Church in Kerala.
[38] Brown, 85.

structure. According to Robin Jeffrey, "Caste Hindus not only accorded Syrians respectable status but endowed them with the power to cleanse polluted food and objects.[39] Whether this resulted from Syrians' position as petty traders and middlemen is open to question." Apparently, a Brahman could consult a passing Syrian Christian to remove pollution from tainted articles. Thus, the role of the Syrian Christians in Hindu society interweaved with Hindu norms of pollution and social structure. Christians were not regarded as outsiders of the community, as is often implied in modern discussion. Syrian Christians traditionally were given the same honorific titles accorded the accomplished Nayars, the same marks of distinction, and they even occasionally took wives from the Nayar community.[40] Bayly describes Syrian Christians as high-caste converts[41] who were a population of elite *Kalari* warriors, traders, and landholders. She also maintains that they were a highly mobile group that had risen to prominence before the coming of the Portuguese, and were treated by Hindu chiefs as members of a ritually superior caste group equivalent in status to the upper Nayar warrior groups.

Although socially, an Indian identity prevailed for the Syrian Christians, spiritually, differences existed. However, these differences mainly were realized on the part of members of the Christian church. Christians considered themselves unique among Hindus, whereas Hindus may well have regarded the Syrian Christians as Hindus who worshipped Christ, another *avatara* of God. In addition, one-god mechanisms in Hindu thought may be in part responsible for perceptions of differences: indeed, it is possible for many Hindus to declare, "I am a Christian, Muslim, Hindu..." and be consistent with modern Hindu philosophy. This outlook creates a broadly inclusive environment where conversion can be quite difficult. All-encompassing philosophical systems could possibly be an old tradition in Kerala, the home of Sankaracarya (the father of Advaitic – non-dual – philosophy, which views distinction as illusory). Nonetheless, Syrian Christians have kept their distinct tradition alive.

---

[39] Jeffrey, 33. This is a power only the Brahmin priests possess, being the purest caste. The caste system is riddled with ideas of pollution and purity, the higher castes being obliged to be pure. Lower castes could pollute a higher caste person simply by touching them; a Brahmin was considered polluted even if his eyes caught sight of an untouchable. Pollution could be cleansed by ritual.
[40] Brown, 171.
[41] Bayly, 179. There exists in Christian society a 'remembrance' of caste even today. Because of geographical segregation and patrilineal heritage, many Christians have a memory of what caste their ancestors belonged to.

Conversion was not their focus, and their community grew slowly through migrations and the small bursts of conversions that came with them. At the same time, they were able to maintain an identity as Indians; they maintained themselves as a functioning unit of Hindu society. Their Indian identity can sometimes be difficult to see today, given that modern political and religious movements have weakened the conception of the Syrian community as a caste.[42]

Hindu Customs in Ceremonies of the House

The Christian community attached great importance to the Church, which guided the people throughout the year and through rites of passage. Festivals and ceremonies were opportunities for social gatherings; the Church was the center of the community activities. Pothan describes the old tradition as being

> ...a way of life that is fast disappearing... The social life simple as it was, gravitated round the parish or family church, and drew its sustenance and strength from the importance attached to the church and its festivals, and the allegiance and attendance the church demanded for the observance of ceremonies connected with the domestic occurrences of birth, marriage and death. These events were the occasions for social intercourse and gatherings.... such a social pattern bred an innate conservatism that fostered the observance of old customs, which remained unaltered until the first two decades of this century. Thereafter, revolutionary changes were brought about by Western education, industrialization and quick transport, which exerted a powerful impact on the traditional way of life and customs, and compelled a modification, if not a radical change, among those who lived in cities which became industrialized, and more especially, among the large numbers who were forced to seek their livelihood elsewhere in India.[43]

Because of these changes in Malayalee society, the customs described

---

[42] Brown, 3.

[43] S.G. Pothan, *The Syrian Christians of Kerala* (Bombay: Asia Publishing House, 1963), 55-56.

hereafter are not in general use any longer; those communities who have retained some customs are found in rural areas.

Among the more known syncretic practices the Christians observed were faith in horoscopes, the tying of the *thali* or marriage locket, death pollution of ten to fifteen days, vegetarianism during mourning periods, ceremonial bathing to remove death pollution, funeral rites followed by feasting, the celebration of *Ōnam* and *Vishu* (harvest and new year festivals), the celebration of the first feeding of a child with rice, and the non-admission of low castes into the house.[44] Visvanathan observes that through these syncretic practices, Hindu and Christian communities were in dialogue. It was in these practices that food, rites for fertility or good health, and auspiciousness were shared.[45]

The ceremonies related to birth and child rearing shared many customs with South Indian Hindus.[46] The birth of a baby boy was heralded by a *kurava*, a shrill call produced by inserting the tips of the fingers in the mouth, and moving the fingers up and down against the lips so that they create vibration in the sound. Nambudiris (priestly Brahmins) and Nayars made a similar cry on such an occasion. As the birth of a son was considered auspicious, the occasion was celebrated with a feast. The child had a horoscope written – the exact time of the child's birth was carefully recorded for this purpose. As previously mentioned, these Kerala Christians relied on the horoscope's prediction of life events. Like Nambudiri newborns, Christian newborns were bathed and then given a few drops of honey in which some gold was mixed (the presiding lady rubbed her ring on a stone on which some drops of honey had been smeared). The Nambudiri belief was that this action ensured prosperity. An appreciation for the Hindu worldview was reflected in a ceremony marking the beginning of the child's education. This ceremony was similar in purpose to the thread ceremony initiating the Hindu child.[47] Although not as elaborate as its Hindu counterpart, its purpose and meaning were similar.

---

[44] Visvanathan, 3-4.

[45] Ibid., 132-148, outlines another rite of passage: death. Here, the Christians are ultimately exclusive of Hinduism in their concept of the after-life. She maintains that the 'Syrian Christians seem to assert that their faith underlines the separateness of their destiny after death'.

[46] Pothan, 61-63.

[47] *Upanayana*, the initiation, is a Hindu sacrament where a child officially enters the first of the four stages of life: studentship. The sacred thread is put on for the first time, to be worn at all times afterwards [Klostermaier, 186].

Even now, these types of ceremonial activities are acceptable in the eyes of most Syrian Catholic, Jacobite, some Protestants, and Orthodox Church leaders in Kerala, and they are often an anticipated part of Christian life in Kerala. Although Christians perform these rites in a way similar to that of the Hindus, subtle ritual or theological differences exist. Christians often have retained a distinctiveness when sharing practices that separates them from their Hindu neighbors.

St. George in Puthupalli

In her book, *Kerala Christian Sainthood: Collisions of Culture and Worldview in South India*, Corinne Dempsey frames her discussion of saint-cults in Kerala using sibling metaphors to describe Christian-Hindu relations.[48] Often the narratives in local communities dictate a sibling-type relationship between a local Hindu deity and a local Christian saint, explicitly in their myths and implicitly in the customs surrounding festivals and inter-religious communication. St.George's Church in Puthupalli exemplifies Dempsey's framework, as the depiction of St. George and Kali as having a kind of sibling relationship, a tradition that has survived into modern times. In this Church, there is a tradition called *kozhyvettu* where chickens are killed, boiled, and served to the congregation. It is claimed that this practice originated from the neighboring Kali temple, where a rooster is sacrificed to Kali. Dempsey asserts that *kozhyvettu* is sacrificial in nature, and that it is linked to the protection from snakes.

In a personal interview, Dr. Parackel Mathew, who has a family history with this particular church, expressed a slightly different view of *kozhyvettu*.[49] He stated that Kali of the neighboring temple and St. George were friends,[50] and that in Puthupalli, Hindus and Christians cooperated in each other's festivals. In the case of *kozhyvettu*, the killing of a chicken takes on a distinctive Christian character, i.e. it become "Christianized." Instead of seeing the practice as "sacrifice," Mathew viewed it as an offering prepared on the premises of the church. He asserted that this was done by Kerala Christians with the belief that such an offering

---

[48] Corinne Dempsey, Kerala Christian Sainthood, Collisions of Culture and Worldview in South India (New York: Oxford University Press, 2001).

[49] Mathew, Personal communication, 2001.

[50] It is customary for one to address cousins or friends using the endearing term for brother or sister in Malayalam, another application of Dempsey's sibling metaphor.

can protect homegrown chicken and even other animals. He reasoned that although the act of killing chickens is completed on church grounds, it is not done within the church itself (unlike the Hindu sacrifice of a chicken). A sacrificial interpretation of *kozhyvettu* was further problematic in Mathew's opinion because the only sacrifice within the Malabar Church worship is the Holy Qurbana (Eucharist). Mathew maintained that this tradition should be regarded as a variant of *nercha*, where Christians bring food to church, for example, *upam* and other treats, or candles and money. The chickens are considered part of the food offerings that are representative of gratitude for St. George. He emphasized that *nercha* is an ancient practice of the Malabar Christian tradition that has been accepted by the Syrian Orthodox Patriarch (in Syria) for generations. He did not see *nercha* as a practice taken directly from the neighboring Kali temple, but rather as a variation of an institutionalized Syrian Orthodox custom. Mathew did not associate any meaning with the blood of the chicken, and he did not associate this offering with protection from snakes. However, one cannot completely deny Hindu influence. With syncretism, meaning can be merged, changed or stay the same. In the case of *kozhyvettu*, new meaning is achieved, and Christian belief is blended with an aspect of a Hindu ritual. Both Christian and Hindu belief systems remain unchallenged by this activity, perhaps because of variation in the way it is carried out and the way it is viewed by each religious community.

When looking at Malabar Christian syncretism, it is important to question the extent to which such local traditions are necessarily due to Hindu influences as opposed to being intrinsic religious expression. It is also important to consider how syncretic practices in the Malabar Church gain a new identity, even meaning in the new context. Many Hindu inspired practices are changed and given a Christian character to accommodate for the Christian perspective. For example, the Orthodox Christians will use a cross in processions, replacing the idol of a Hindu procession. In some cases, a picture or painting of a saint may be used instead of a cross. Romo-Syrian Catholics generally use statues of saints in their processions, a remnant of Portuguese influence. In addition, although there are many characteristics the Syrian Christians have in common with South Indian Hinduism, the same religious phenomena occur within Christian traditions beyond South India. For example, processions and physical embodiments of sacred power occur in Christian traditions beyond South India (e.g. Italian, Spanish, Greek, Latin American Christian traditions).[51] Communal identification with a patron deity occurs often in South Indian Hindu communities; the deity often contributes to the expression of local identity. This type of deity-community relationship also occurs within patron saint cults, e.g. in Spain.[52]

The Catholic Church's approach to syncretism or "inculturation" allows for much intercultural borrowing. Robert de Nobili represents one of the first Catholic attempts at inculturation. He donned the robes of the *sannyasi*[53] and used Sanskrit to spread the word of Christ in the sixteenth century. Although he was criticized for his approach, he ultimately was not condemned for corrupting Christian belief with Indian influence.[54] Since the Second Vatican Council, there have been efforts to incorporate various Indian cultural and religious symbols into the liturgical life of Indian Catholicism. Although they do not appear to have met with much success in India recently, it may be inferred that to the Catholic Church, inculturation does not diminish one's belief in Salvation through Christ.

Conclusion

Has syncretism occurred in the Malabar Church? Syncretism has not occurred in the Malabar liturgy; however, Hindu customs have been incorporated into the social aspects of Malabar Christian religious life. Malabar Church worship and theology remain completely Orthodox, and social life and customs have allowed for institutionalized inter-religious borrowing where there are set boundaries of mutual respect. There have been many warnings against syncretism as "a constructed fusion of religions," as a threat to Christianity. However, this practice may have preserved Christianity in Kerala by making it adaptable and dynamic within the social sphere. Syrian Christians have retained their Christian identity and individuality, while being aware of the points of difference that separate them from the larger Hindu population. Their relationship with the Hindu community was symbiotic, and they made no attempts to evangelize. This fact may have been a major factor in the absence of religious tension even when their community was flourishing. Christians recognized and respected the existence of Hindu gods but did not worship

---

[51] Dempsey, 100.
[52] Ibid., 53.
[53] A person initiated into sannyasa has renounced the world, has no fixed place of residence, is devoid of attachments, and is devoted to realization of the absolute [Klosteraier, 345].
[54] Brown, 302.

them. In effect, they respected the faith and customs of their rulers. Their participation in and contributions to the Hindu community granted them tolerance from Hindu rulers, and special rights. This type of syncretism has exhibited positive influence to the extent that it enabled (or contributed to) the survival of a minority church in a relatively peaceful environment, one in which it came to hold an institutionalized niche. Kerala was a plural society in the true sense of the word. While Brown asserts that "the assimilation of the [West Asian] community to its environment is certainly one of the reasons for its survival through the centuries;"[55] perhaps they were not outsiders conforming to Hindu practice, but insiders adopting new forms of worship – as the apostolic tradition would have it. They were Christian in faith, but Indian in all else.

---

[55] Brown, 3.

INTERFACE BETWEEN HISTORY AND MUSIC IN THE CHRISTIAN CONTEXT OF SOUTH INDIA

Joseph J. Palackal[*]

Christianity in South India is a complex socio-religious phenomenon encompassing an array of sects and practices. The diversity of
the Christian experience in this geographical area that consists of five
states (Kerala, Tamil Nadu, Andhra Pradesh, Karnataka, and Goa) is the
result of multiple missionary enterprises, dating probably as far back as
the middle of the first century. According to the information available in
the *Indian Christian Directory*, published by Rashtra Deepika in 2000,
there are more than thirty-three Churches active in South India. These
Churches may be divided into seven broad categories: the Syrian Church,
whose members are also known as St. Thomas Christians; the Latin (Roman) rite Church; the Lutheran Church; the Anglican Church; the Methodist Church; the Baptist Church; and the Pentecostal Church. The membership varies from a few thousand up to several million. In the absence
of exact statistical data, we may estimate that out of the thirty million
Christians in India, about twenty million live in the South. They constitute a diverse set of communities shaped by language, culture, and even
caste.

Although the early history of these churches is inevitably linked
to the history of individuals and their places of origin (the Middle East,
Europe, and America), each Church has developed its own character in
India over the centuries.[1] The interaction between divergent religious and
theological perspectives, proselytization policies, and attitudes toward indigenous and foreign cultures are among the many factors that
contributed to the formation of their particular histories which, in turn,

---

[*] Joseph Palackal is a performer of Christian bhajans and Syriac (Aramaic)
chants from India, and is principal vocalist for over thirty releases in four languages. His scholarly interests are in the area of music and religion in South
Asia. He has contributed articles to leading publications, including The New
Grove Dictionary of Music and Musicians, and the Garland Encyclopedia of
World Music. He is the founder president of the Christian Musicological Society
of India. Currently, he is writing on the "Syriac Chant Traditions of South India."
[1] M. Mundadan, *History of Christianity in India, Vol. I, From the Beginning up
to the Middle of the Sixteenth Century (Up to 1542)*, (Bangalore: Church History
Association of India, 1970, 1989; First published in 1984).

are embedded in the larger history of South India.

Music has been an integral part of the Christian experience, and musicological discourse can be an effective tool in historiography. The music history of these churches can enhance our understanding of their general history and vice versa. The formation and transformation of musical styles in any given culture are often closely associated with events of historical significance mediated by individuals and communities. A community's awareness of its mission and identity can affect its musical choices regarding what is retained by one generation and what is transmitted to the next. Musical memories preserved and transmitted from generation to generation through oral tradition can be a valuable source of information, especially when there is a dearth of written documents.

My focus here is the musical history of the Syro-Malabar Church in Kerala to show how musical and historical inquiries can be interdependent. As we shall see later, sometimes a single chant can tell us the story of interactions at multiple levels between distant regions and diverse peoples within a span of several centuries.

The vast musical repertory of the Syro-Malabar Church consists of a wide variety of genres ranging from the ancient Syriac chants of St. Ephrem the Syrian (d. 373) to the most modern compositions intended for multimedia consumption. For practical purposes, I shall limit my inquiry to the liturgical music genre, and within the liturgical music genre to the history of the Syriac chant tradition from what may be called the Portuguese period, dating from the early sixteenth century.

The Syro-Malabar Church is one of the seven Syrian Churches, or more appropriately, 'Syriac Churches' of South India that use Syriac language and music in their liturgy. Syriac is a form of Aramaic, which developed as an independent dialect in the first century AD, and became the literary language of the Aramaic-speaking Christians. By the fifth century, Syriac differentiated itself into East Syriac and West Syriac on the basis of the method of writing and the manner of pronunciation. Edessa, which was outside the boundary of the Roman Empire, became the center for the East Syriac (also known as Chaldean) liturgical tradition, and Antioch, which was within the boundary of the Roman Empire, became the center for the West Syriac (also known as Antiochean) tradition. The Syro-Malabar Church follows the Chaldean liturgical tradition with a few elements adopted from the Latin liturgy. The name 'Syro-Malabar Church' is the official designation given by Rome in 1896 to the section of the St. Thomas Christians which is in communion with the

Roman Church. The term 'Syro-Malabar' denotes the use of Syriac language in what was known in the West as the Malabar region. Malabar is one of the old names for the region currently known as Kerala; the name, probably coined by early Arab traders, seems to be a combination of the Malayalam word, *mala* ('mountain') and the Persian, *bar* ('place').

Figure 1 Map of India showing the southern states of Kerala, Tamil Nadu, Andhra Pradesh, Karnataka, and Goa.

When the Portuguese missionaries arrived in Kerala at the dawn of the sixteenth century, they were pleasantly surprised to find a prosperous community of Christians, who traced the origin of their faith to the preaching of St. Thomas the Apostle (hence the name, 'St. Thomas Christians'). This community handed over from generation to generation their belief that the Apostle Thomas arrived in Kerala in 52 AD, preached the new faith (*mārggam*) and established seven 'churches' (*palli*).[2] However, disappointment set in when the missionaries found that the native Christians followed another liturgy in a language different from Latin, professed allegiance to the Chaldean Patriarch, and shared many customs and practices of their Hindu neighbors, including the caste system. The rift widened as the Portuguese gained military, mercantile, and missionary power in Kerala, and political power in Goa, on the western coast. The Portuguese missionaries failed, in the words of Stephen Neill, "to understand…the intensity of the attachment of the Thomas Christians to the ancient ways and in particular to Syriac their liturgical language."[3] To the St. Thomas Christians, the Syriac language, the liturgy, and other social and religious traditions were markers of their unique identity for which they even coined a term, *mārthommāyute mārggawum wazhipātum* (approximately, 'the way and lineage of St. Thomas').[4] The missionaries, on the other hand, wanted the local Christians to wean themselves from their dependence on the Chaldean Church and to adopt the Western form of Catholic religion, which they believed was the authentic form. The conflict of ideologies and allegiances finally led to what is known as the Synod of Diamper, a watershed moment in the history of Christianity in India. The Synod was called by Alexis De Menezes, the Archbishop of Goa, and was held at Udayamperoor, in Kerala, in June 1599. Archbishop Menezes persuaded the St. Thomas Christians to denounce the patriarch of the Chaldean Church and profess their allegiance to the pope. The Archbishop also asked the St. Thomas Christians to discard many indigenous social customs and rituals. The result was a gradual process of Latinisation of the St. Thomas Christians that succeeded to some extent.

One of the decrees of the Synod provides interesting information on the role of music in the celebration of the Syriac liturgy. In decree XIV of Session V, the Synod decried the local custom of inviting Hindu

---

[2] Both terms, *palli* and *mārggam*, belong to the Buddhist tradition. Buddhism was present in South India in the early Christian era.
[3] Stephen Neill, *A History of Christianity in India: the Beginnings to A.D. 1707* (New York: Cambridge University Press, 1984), 195.
[4] The scholars of Indian Christianity and specialists on Indian languages are yet to arrive at a full explanation of the term. The translation found in English writings,'Law of Thomas,' does not do justice to the original concept.

musicians to perform inside the church during the celebration of mass on festive occasions in the following words:

> Whereas up on several festivals of the church there are musicians called to the celebration thereof, according to the custom of the country, who are all heathens, small care being taken in what part of the church they are placed, or to hinder them from playing during the time of the holy sacrifice, at which no excommunicate person or infidel ought to be present, therefore the Synod doth command, that great care be taken not to suffer them to remain in the church after the creed is said, or the sermon, if there be one, is ended, that so they may not behold the holy sacrament; the vicar shall also be careful to drive all heathens who may come upon such occasion, from the doors and windows of the church.[5]

The decree poses several points for discussion, some of which require further research. For example, it is not clear what were the 'several festivals' for which Hindu musicians were invited to perform. The nature of the musical instruments that the 'heathens' played in the church is not clear either. Probably, they were playing instrumental ensembles such as *panchawādyam* or *chentamēlam* (see *Figures 2 & 3*) that are considered auspicious in India. *Panchawādyam* is a drumming ensemble consisting of five kinds of instruments, *timila*, *maddalam*, *itaykka*, *ilattālam*, and *kompu*. *Chentamēlam* is an ensemble of three or four *chenta* (a two-headed cylindrical stick drum) and an *ilattālam* (a pair of hand cymbals). These mostly percussive instrument ensembles were, and are still, the most popular in the region, and are essential to temple festivals and religious performing arts of the Hindus. The performers belong to a particular Hindu caste, called *mārār*. It is difficult to determine whether the musicians provided instrumental accompaniment to the Syriac chants or whether they played their own music at certain points in the celebration of the mass. Probably, they played before the beginning of the mass, following the indigenous practice of *kēlikottu* (literally, 'striking to hear') to announce the commencement of a solemn and auspicious event. It is also possible that they played an instrumental prelude or a coda to *trisagion*

---

[5] *The Acts and Decrees of the Synod of Diamper, A.D. 1599*, S. Zacharia, edit. (Kottayam, Kerala, India: Indian Institute of Christian Studies, 1994), 142.

and *lākumāra*, two hymns that used to be sung three times consecutively with great solemnity.

Figure 2 Chenta players leading the procession during the celebration of the feast of the Assumption of the Blessed Virgin Mary at St. Mary's Forane Church, Pallippuram, Kerala. August 15, 2000.

Figure 3 Panchawādyam ensemble performing in the middle of the procession.

The decree alludes to the presence of the musicians inside the church during the Anaphora (Eucharistic prayer), the central part of the mass. In those days, after the mass of the catechumens, the deacon asked all those who had not received baptism and those who were not prepared to receive the holy communion to leave the church, and the acolytes closed the main doors of the church for the rest of the mass.[6] Therefore, there must have been a significant reason for the community to allow the presence of Hindu musicians inside the church during such solemn parts of the liturgy. It may be presumed that the musicians were asked to play at the end of the mass to announce the conclusion of the ceremonies. Until further evidence appears, these ideas will remain as mere conjectures.

Musical practices of a society often reflect the social structure of the time. The Christians' invitation to Hindu musicians to perform inside the church, especially during mass, and the willingness of the Hindus to accept the invitation tell volumes about the social harmony that existed between Christians and their Hindu neighbors in Kerala. Such permeability of socio-religious boundaries deeply offended the missionaries, who sincerely believed in the superiority of the Catholic religion over all other faiths. Therefore, the Synod pressured the St. Thomas Christians to redraw the Christian cultural and ritual boundaries within a predominantly Hindu society. To cite a few other examples, the Synod forbade the Christians from giving Hindu names to their children (session IV, decree XVI), from participating in the local Hindu festival of *ōnam* (session IX, decree IV), and from piercing their ears to wear ornaments like the Hindus (session IX, decree XVII).

There is another aspect of the decree under discussion that deserves attention. Two versions of the decrees of the Synod came into existence some time before 1603, one in Malayalam, the local language, and the other in Portuguese.[7] The original decrees that were read at the end of the Synod for approval of the participants were written in Malayalam. However, the Portuguese version contains thirty-five more canons that are not found in the original text;[8] the decree on the presence of Hindu musicians inside the church is one of them. There are two possible

---

[6] Although rarely executed today for practical reasons, the instructions are still part of the printed text in the Malayalam translation of the Syriac missal.

[7] Zacharia, 9.

[8] Antonio de Gouvea prepared the Portuguese version, *Synodo Diocesano da Igreia e Bispado de ngamale dos antigos christaôs de Sam Thome das Serras do Malavar das partes da India Oriental* (Coimbra: Diogo Gomez Loureyro, 1606). Michael Geddes, the chaplain to the English factory in Lisbon (1678-88), prepared an English translation, *The History of the Church of Malabar, from the time of its being discover'd by the Portuguezes in the Year 1501* (London: Sam. Smith and Benj. Walford, 1694). A reprint of Geddes' translation with an introductory essay can be found in Zacharia.

reasons for the omission of the decree in the original text: either the issue was so sensitive to the St. Thomas Christians that Archbishop Menezes thought that an open discussion would have had a negative impact on the Synod,[9] or the Archbishop and his colleagues became aware of the issue only after the Synod. In any case, the Archbishop considered the issue so important as to include it in the Portuguese version. Whatever the case may be, the decree seems to have succeeded in achieving its goal, to some extent, because we do not hear about Hindu musicians playing instrumental ensembles inside the church in the subsequent period. However, their participation in church festivities has not ceased to exist. Either *panchawādyam* or *chentamēlam* or both are integral parts of the church processions during major feasts of the Syro-Malabar churches even today, and the performers of these ensembles are mostly Hindus. The photos in *Figures 2 & 3* were taken during the annual celebration of the feast of the Assumption of the Blessed Virgin Mary at St. Mary's Forane Church at Pallippuram, in Kerala. As is seen in *Figure 2*, it is the Hindu instrumental players who lead the procession, placing themselves in front of the processional cross.

The missionaries probably disliked not only the presence of Hindu musicians but also the use of indigenous musical instruments inside the church, because of their association with the 'heathens' and their festivals. In the churches of Syriac Christians, built or rebuilt under the supervision of the missionary bishops in the seventeenth century, we find a new phenomenon: music iconography. In the wooden reredos of the main altars of some of these churches there are carved figures of angels playing musical instruments (see *Figure 4*). This was quite new at that time and, in fact, even strange, because the pre-sixteenth century churches in Kerala had no statues or any carved figures inside the church, not even a crucifix, but only a cross. The instruments represented are mostly violin, harp, bugle, triangle, bass drum, and tambourine. None of these instruments is indigenous, although the tambourine might have been familiar to the area because of the presence of Muslims in the region. The exclusion of instruments familiar to the region seems to be a matter of deliberate choice. The specific location of the iconography, too, seems to be a matter of deliberate choice. The iconography appears invariably in the sanctuaries of churches, either on the reredos or inside the dome above the main altar, and not on the sides or outside the walls of

---

[9] The submission of the St. Thomas Christians to the inquisition of Goa (session III, decree XXII) is another example of the decrees added after the Synod.

the church. Those are crucial locations that represent heaven on earth, thus giving a heavenly status to the musical instruments. And, without exception, it is the angels, and not human figures, who play the instruments. This raises the prestige of the instruments and provides legitimacy to their use inside the church.

Figure 4 Six angels playing musical instruments on the wooden reredos of the main altar of St. Mary's Forane Church, Pallippuram.

The missionaries probably used music iconography as an ingenious means to influence the minds of the worshipers. At the time of their representation in Kerala, the iconography provided a semblance of the future rather than a reflection of the present. It also implied, to some extent, value judgments on the existing musical practices of the Syriac Christians, and an invitation to break away from the past and to redefine the future by adopting more 'respectable' musical and religious practices of the West. Indeed, the strong suggestive power of the visual medium did have an effect on the church musicians. Three of those instruments, violin, triangle, and bass drum, soon became part of the Syriac choirs of the churches under the control of the missionaries. Those musical instruments can be heard even today in some of the Syro-Malabar churches in Kerala (see *Figure 5*).

Figure 5. The Syriac choir of St. Mary's Forane Church, Pallippuram. From left to right: Jose Paul Vathappallil (drum), Joy Paul Vathappallil (triangle), Paily Vathappallil (harmonium, lead singer), Joseph Pathiamoola (vocal), Ouseph Vathappallil (violin). October 2, 2000.

The presence of music iconography in Syro-Malabar churches has to be analyzed in view of their absence in the churches of the other sections of the St. Thomas Christians, who established their separate identity after the revolt against the religious hegemony of the Portuguese missionaries in 1653.

The time of the introduction of music iconography in the churches of Kerala coincides with the adaptation of paraliturgical services from the Latin rite, such as Benediction of the Blessed Sacrament, novena to saints, and *ladīnj* (Malayalam adaptation of the Portuguese word, *ladainha*, meaning 'litany') by the Syro-Malabar Church. The missionaries, with the help of local Syriac scholars, translated the Latin chants into Syriac for use in the Syriac churches under their control. This gave rise to a new and unique category of Syriac chants in Kerala. Musically, these chants are different from the earlier repertory of Syriac chants for the mass, the liturgy of the Hours, and the services for the dead. We shall examine two music examples from a recent release, *Qambel Māran: Syriac Chants from South India*.[10] I organized the re-

---

[10] *Qambel Māran: Syriac Chants from South India*, CD with 16-page booklet by Joseph J. Palackal, PAN 2085 (PAN Records, Netherlands, 2002).

cording of this CD in Kerala in August 1999. The texts in both examples are free translations of the famous hymn *Pange Lingua* ('Sing My Tongue') that St. Thomas Aquinas (d. 1274) composed for the feast of Corpus Christi. In Kerala, as in the Latin rite, the chants were sung during Benediction of the Blessed Sacrament. The accompanying instruments are harmonium, bass drum (known by its Portuguese name, 'tambor'), and triangle (pronounced *tiryānkōl* in Malayalam). The violin player could not participate in the recording as he was sick on that day.

Music example 1, track # 21, *śanbah leśān* ('Praise My Tongue'): A distinctive feature of this melody is its range of a complete octave, in contrast to the older Syriac melodies which, in general, have a limited range of about four to five notes. The melody gradually ascends a full octave to its climactic point at the upper tonic and then descends slowly, forming something like a bell-shaped curve. A few other melodic gestures that may be considered characteristics of Western musical style are also present in this chant. For example, the use of the raised fourth in an otherwise major scale and the leap of a perfect fourth in both ascending and descending manner are features seldom found in Syriac chants, especially those of the pre-Portuguese period. It is not yet clear if this was an adaptation of a Western chant melody.

Music example 2, track # 22, *kollan daśnē* ('Let Us All Offer'): This is the second chant for Benediction and consists of the last two stanzas of *Pange Lingua*. In the Latin rite, the chant is known as 'Tantum Ergo,' the first two words of the penultimate stanza. The Syriac translator, however, interpolates a line, which is either borrowed from a Syriac or Latin source, or composed anew. The line appears as a trope on the word *fides* in the first stanza: "By it [faith] we sail as in a ship, in this sea which is turbulent." A unique feature of the melody is its metric structure, known in South Indian classical music theory as *miśra chāpu tālam*. It has a total of seven beats divided into two sections (3 + 4) with accents on the first and the fourth beats.

To conclude, the chants tell us stories of communication between distant peoples and diverse cultures. A good example is the course of the chant in music example 2. St. Thomas Aquinas composed the text in Latin, in the thirteenth century; the Portuguese missionaries brought the chant to South India, some time in the sixteenth century; local scholars, with the help of missionaries, translated the Latin text into Syriac, a Semitic language, in Kerala; the translator interpolated a verse either composed by himself or borrowed from another unknown source into the original Latin text; an anonymous local cleric or musician disregarded the original Western melody and decided to compose a new melody; in doing so, the composer adopted a metric structure that was popular in South India; the performers of the chant used musical instruments adopted or adapted from the West to accompany the melody; and the chant exists even today, at least in the treasured musical memory of a group of people in the Syro-Malabar Church.

This short survey of the history and music of the Syro-Malabar Christians of Kerala is a case in point for the mutuality of musical and historical inquiries in which musicological discourse assumes a significant role as a tool in historiography. Such an approach does not seem to have caught the attention of scholars who study Christianity in India. The survey is also intended as part of a larger project to reconstruct the history of Christian music in India. Considering the sheer variety and multiplicity of musical styles of Christians across the country, and the ongoing formation and transformation of those styles, such an endeavor might even lead to the development of a new field of study, which may be called Indian Christian musicology.

SERVICE TO GOD, SERVICE TO ENGLAND: CONVERSION, CIVILIZATION, AND HEALING IN BRITISH INDIA

D. George Joseph[*]

"It's terrible, doctor. Soon we'll have no lepers at all," laments a nun to Dr. Colin in Graham Greene's 1961 novel, *A Burnt-Out Case*; Greene describes the nun as "an old maid, without imagination, anxious to do good, to be of use.[1] There aren't many places in the world for people like that. And the practice of her vocation is being taken away from her by the weekly doses of D.D.S. [dapsone] tablets."[2] And in a sentence, Greene captures a critical tension in the historical relationship between the sufferers of leprosy and their caregivers. Historian Sheldon Watts

---

[*] D. George Joseph is a historian of medicine and public health at Yale University in New Haven, Connecticut, USA. His research has focused on the social history of American public health since 1800, with a particular interest in efforts to control leprosy between 1880 and 1920. This paper is part of a larger study comparing American and British missionary efforts to address leprosy in their late nineteenth century empires. A different version of this paper was first published as "'Essentially Christian, Eminently Philanthropic': The Mission to Lepers in British India," *História, Ciências, Saúde: Manguinhos 10*; Supplement 1 (2003): 246-275. Earlier versions of this paper were presented to the Section of the History of Medicine at the Yale School of Medicine (New Haven, February 2001) and at the meetings of the American Society of Church History (New Haven, March 2001), the Middle Atlantic Conference of British Studies (New York City, April 2002), and the "Christianity and Native Cultures" international conference, Saint Mary's College (Notre Dame, Indiana, September 2002). For their comments and suggestions, I am grateful to the participants in these meetings, and also to Dolores Liptak RSM, Rebecca Stoddart, and Jacqueline R. deVries.

[1] Since the International Leprosy Congress, Havana, 1948, and Madrid, 1953, the illness caused by *Mycobacterium leprae* has been called Hansen's disease. Because of the stigma associated with the disease and the term "leper," the common use of "leper" to describe those afflicted by the disease is discouraged and is regarded as pejorative, but because this was the only term used during the period examined in this study, I have retained it for solely historical accuracy.

[2] Graham Greene, *A Burnt-Out Case* (London: William Heinemann and Bodley Head, 1961), 18. For a discussion of this passage, see Janice Dickin McGinnis, " 'Unclean, Unclean': Canadian Reaction to Lepers and Leprosy," in *Health, Disease, and Medicine: Essays in Canadian History, Proceedings of the First Hannah Conference on the History of Medicine, McMaster University, June 3-5, 1982*, Charles G. Roland, ed., (Toronto: Hannah Institute for the History of Medicine, 1984), 250-251.

characterized this anxiety more bluntly: "missionaries needed their lepers more than the lepers needed them."[3] Greene introduced the idea that some people are attracted to leprosy and its sufferers in a 1959 essay written while traveling to the Yonda leper colony in West Africa, doing research for the novel that became *A Burnt-Out Case*.[4] Although Greene situates the novel in a small, obscure leprosarium in the Belgian Congo operated by the earnest Dr. Colin with the support of a Catholic clerical order, Greene is most interested in leprosy not as a physical condition, but as what the sixteenth-century English writer Samuel Rowlands described as the "defiled soul."[5] For Greene, leprosy is a moral and spiritual debilitation, as much as it is a physical one, and it is the dual nature of this enigmatic disease that attracted European and American missionaries to Africa, Southeast Asia, and the Indian sub-continent to care for those with leprosy beginning in the late nineteenth century.

In asking what it was that drew hundreds of largely middle-class, white Westerners to forfeit comfortable lives to become missionaries to leprosy sufferers, Greene's concept of "leprophilia" is useful for initiating a discussion of religious missions to those with leprosy in the late nineteenth and early twentieth centuries. A confluence of historical events marked the period: the expansion and the consolidation of the British Empire under the reign of Victoria; the opening of Japan to the West in 1853 and the end of the second Opium War between China and European powers in 1858, allowing for the official toleration of Christianity and the state protection of missionaries; the emergence of the Second Evangelical Awakening between 1858 and 1863 during when new missionary societies were founded and new missionaries dispersed throughout Europe's growing empire; and, the revival of evangelical interest in Africa after the 1857 publication of David Livingstone's *Missionary Travels and Researches in South Africa*. These larger forces coupled with two milestones in the history of leprosy during the 1870s: in 1873, the Norwegian leprologist Gerhard Armauer Hansen described the etiology of leprosy with *Mycobacterium leprae*, and in 1874, the Irish missionary, Wellesley Cosby Bailey, founded the Mission to Lepers, the first missionary society devoted solely to serving leprosy sufferers.

---

[3] Sheldon Watts, *Epidemics and History: Disease, Power, and Imperialism* (New Haven: Yale University Press, 1997), 73.
[4] Graham Greene, "Congo Journal," in *Search of a Character; Two African Journals* (London: Bodley Head, 1961).
[5] Samuel Rowlands, *The Betraying of Christ* (London: Adam Islip Printers, 1598), 24.

Hansen's scientific work and its consequences in the late 1860s and the early 1870s posed a crisis for Christian missionaries.[6] Until that point, as sociologist Zachary Gussow has suggested, the Christian tradition employed the concept of biblically defined lepers in a general and vague way because the biblical definitions themselves were unclear and vague.[7] In the late 1830s and the 1840s, the work of Daniel Cornelius Danielssen and C. Wilhelm Boeck in Norway employing extensive clinical data and postmortem findings marked what Rudolf Virchow described as "the beginning of the biologic knowledge of leprosy."[8] Danielssen and Boeck, particularly in their 1847 color atlas, provided a means to distinguish "true" leprosy from the many skin conditions that were commonly mistaken for the disease. In isolating *Mycobacterium leprae*, Hansen went further by providing a scientific basis to identify "true" leprosy, as his bacteriological findings provided the precision and the clarity that the biblical definitions lacked. Stripped of its cultural accretion, leprosy could be now defined as an infection by *Mycobacterium leprae*. This also meant that the Christian missionary community that had taken advantage of the biblical definitions' vagueness in their proselytizing had to recast their thinking of leprosy not as a moral condition, but as a physical one.

However, the missionary community saw advantages in the older, biblical conceptions of the disease, in part because they fitted more closely with the cultural and popular imagination of leprosy. Even as Hansen clarified leprosy's etiology, the Mission to Lepers promoted the erroneous but widely held biblical and medieval claims that associated leprosy with moral contamination, defilement of the physical body, and pollution of the environment.[9] Hansen's work showed a scientific basis for the contraction of leprosy, but the evangelical and relief efforts of

---

[6] On Hansen's findings, see Paul F. Mange, "Hansen and His Discovery of *Mycobacterium leprae*," *New Jersey Medicine 89* (1992): 118-21.
[7] Zachary Gussow, *Leprosy, Racism, and Public Health: Social Policy in Chronic Disease Control* (Boulder: Westview Press, 1989), 201-202.
[8] Quoted in Olaf K. Skinsnes, "Notes from the History of Leprosy," *International Journal of Leprosy 41* (1973): 224. Also, Daniel Cornelius Danielssen and C. Wilhelm Boeck, *Om Spedalskhed: Atlas / udgivet efter foranstaltning of den Kongelige Norske Regjerings Department for det Indre* (Bergen, 1847) and *Traité de la spédalskhed; ou, Eléphantiasis des Grecs* (Paris, 1848).
[9] These associations with leprosy have been examined by the anthropologist Mary Douglas in Mary Douglas, *Purity and Danger: An Analysis of Concepts of Pollution and Taboo* (Baltimore: Penguin Books, 1966); and, Mary Douglas, "Witchcraft and Leprosy: Two Strategies of Exclusion," *Man 26* (1991):723-36.

missionary groups were predicated on beliefs that the affliction of leprosy was caused by moral failings and by physical and racial inferiority. As leprologist Thomas A. Stringer later wrote, "it was in the interest of Christians to see modern leprosy sufferers as 'Biblical lepers.'"[10] Secular and religious missions to leprosy patients appealed to societal misunderstanding and traditions about leprosy and its sufferers to raise financial support and to promote their evangelical activities. Given the social and political circumstances of late Victorian England, it should be no surprise that it is difficult, if not altogether impossible, to disentangle and distinguish the rhetoric of political imperialism from medical imperialism from religious imperialism. Each fades into and serves the interests of the other.[11]

Although the practice of medicine, science, and public health under Western imperialism and, in particular, their practice in British India have been two of the most active areas of medical historical scholarship for more than a decade, this paper considers two still developing areas within this history: the place of leprosy and its sufferers in the British imperial imagination and the role and the motivations of medical missionaries in caring for them in India. Despite the fact that leprosy was a significant public health problem in nineteenth-century India, with nearly 150,000 documented cases and with some medical officials warning there were as many as a million cases, leprosy in India has not garnered significant attention from medical historians. The two leading historical studies of medicine and public health in British India together mention leprosy in passing fewer than ten times, and even fewer articles on the subject exist in the scholarly literature.[12] Even less histori-

---

[10] Thomas A. Stringer, "Leprosy and A Disease Called Leprosy," *Leprosy Review 44* (1973): 454.

[11] The most comprehensive history of the British empire reflecting current scholarship is Wm. Roger Louis, ed., *The Oxford History of the British Empire*, 5 volumes (Oxford and New York: Oxford University Press, 1999), of which Andrew Porter, "Religion, Missionary Enthusiasm, and Empire" (pp. 222-246); D. A. Washbrook, "India, 1818-1860: The Two Faces of Colonialism" (pp. 395-421); and, Robin J. Moore, "Imperial India, 1858-1914" (pp. 422-446), in Andrew Porter, ed., The Nineteenth Century, volume 3 are particularly germane to this discussion. A detailed monographic treatment of the place of religion in the British imperial program is Brian Stanley, *The Bible and the Flag: Protestant Missions and British Imperialism in the Nineteenth and Twentieth Centuries* (Leicester, 1990).

[12] David Arnold, *Colonizing the Body: State Medicine and Epidemic Disease in Nineteenth-Century India* (Berkeley: University of California Press, 1993) and Mark Harrison, *Public Health and British India: Anglo-Indian Preventive Medi-*

cal analysis has been done of the activities of medical missionaries generally, much less those caring specifically for leprosy in India. Standing true is David Arnold's observation in 1993 that "the extent to which missionaries were successful disseminators of Western medical ideas and practices in India remains, for the present, a matter of speculation as it has yet to receive serious scholarly attention."[13]

This paper then considers the interplay between religion, politics, and medicine in the context of British colonialism of India by examining the work of Wellesley Bailey and the Mission to Lepers, the missionary group Bailey founded in 1874 to aid leprosy sufferers, first in India and later throughout the British colonies. They pursued the dual but inseparable goals of *evangelization* and *civilization*, advancing not only a religious program but also a political and cultural one. In the process, the missionaries constructed for their metropolitan audience and supporters an image of the colonial leper that fulfilled their cultural imagination and expectations of leprosy and lepers and reinforced the wider need for British imperialism. The images of lepers underscored their racial and moral inferiority, and reiterated the burden that the British had assumed in India (and elsewhere) to civilize its colonial population. These activities and their consequences were multi-faceted because while the missionaries pursued their religious calling, they also provided medical care to people and in places that the colonial government was unable or unwilling, an activity that the historian Rosemary Fitzgerald has called "clinical Christianity."[14] Within the context of the British imperial program, the work of the missionaries was simultaneously political, religious, and medical, imparting Western social and cultural ideals on the colonial populations

---

cine (Cambridge and New York: Cambridge University Press, 1994). Among the few historical articles on leprosy in the Indian imperial context are: Sanjiv Kakar, "Leprosy in British India, 1860-1940: Colonial Politics and Missionary Medicine," *Medical History 40* (1996): 215-230; Michael Worboys, "The Colonial World as Mission and Mandate: Leprosy and Empire, 1900-1940," *Osiris 15* (2001); 207-218; Sanjiv Kakar, "Medical Developments and Patient Unrest in the Leprosy Asylum, 1860 to 1940," in *Health, Medicine, and Empire: Perspectives on Colonial India*, Biswamoy Pati and Mark Harrison, eds., (Hyderabad: Orient Longman, 2001), 188-216.
[13] Arnold, *Colonizing the Body*, 244.
[14] Rosemary Fitzgerald, " 'Clinical Christianity': The Emergence of Medical Work as a Missionary Strategy in Colonial India, 1800-1914," in *Health, Medicine, and Empire*, 88-136. Also useful is C. P. Williams, "Healing and Evangelism: The Place of Medicine in Later Victorian Protestant Missionary Thinking," in *The Church and Healing: Studies in Church History, volume 19*, W. J. Shiels, ed. (Oxford: Blackwell Publishers, 1982), 271-285.

they served, inculcating patients with Christian beliefs, and providing medical care to individuals who had been expelled from their own communities. Physical healing was intimately tied to religious salvation, spiritual healing, and the civilizing process.

Biblical Mandate Against the "Imperial Danger"
Late nineteenth-century missionaries to those afflicted by leprosy identified the biblical basis of their missions in two New Testament passages:

> And a leper came to Jesus, beseeching Him and falling on his knees before Him, and saying, 'If You are willing, You can make me clean.' Moved with compassion, Jesus stretched out His hand and touched him, and said to him, 'I am willing; be cleansed.' Immediately the leprosy left him and he was cleansed. (Mark 1: 40-42)

> Jesus summoned His twelve disciples and gave them authority over unclean spirits, to cast them out, and to heal every kind of disease and every kind of sickness.... 'And as you go, preach, saying, 'The kingdom of heaven is at hand.' 'Heal the sick, raise the dead, cleanse the lepers, cast out demons. Freely you received, freely give.' (Matthew 10: 1, 7-8)

Almost all missionaries regarded their work as imitating Jesus' actions, but also directly fulfilling his instructions to those who considered themselves his disciples. Wellesley Bailey and the Mission to Lepers, and other missionaries and societies explicitly reiterated that their work with leprosy sufferers was biblically prescribed. For instance, Reverend Edward Guilford, serving in Tarn Taran, India with the London-based Church Missionary Society, affirms in a May 1890 speech at Exeter Hall describing the efforts of the Mission to Lepers:

> To seek out men like this, burdened with sin, tortured by pain, and cast out from the society of men, and to bring them into the blessed fellowship of saints, and to alleviate their sad lot, is the work which the Mission to Lepers is doing in India. And can we, my friends, wonder that God has blessed their labours? Was it not the work

which our Saviour Himself came to do? And was it not
the work Jesus sent forth His disciples to do after His
resurrection?[15]

The administrators of the Mission to Lepers continued to be equally out-spoken about the spiritual origins of the mission. "A new day began for lepers," reads one later Mission to Lepers publication, "when one of them dared to approach our Divine Lord and was cleansed by Him. Later, Christ gave to His disciples the express command, 'cleanse the lepers.' The extensive work on behalf of the victims of leprosy to-day is largely due to Christian sympathy and effort which the Divine Command has inspired."[16]

It can not be overlooked that the arousal of missionary interest in leprosy and its sufferers coincided with the growth and the consolidation of European imperialism in Africa and Asia during the nineteenth century.[17] By the nineteenth century, leprosy was rarely seen in Europe outside of Norway, but colonialism brought Europeans into contact with peoples where leprosy was endemic, raising the specter in the eyes of some European observers of a resurgence of leprosy in the Western world. Many of these observers saw the solution to the problem as two-fold: the forcible isolation and containment of leprosy sufferers and the civilization of the peoples where leprosy persisted. And some even suggested that missionaries were in the best position to carry out these measures because they were consistent with the Christian commitment and biblical mandate to care for lepers. Henry Press Wright, archdeacon

---

[15] Quoted in Wellesley C. Bailey, *The Lepers of Our Indian Empire: A Visit to Them in 1890-91* (Edinburgh: The Darien Press, Bristo Place, 1899), 112.

[16] The Mission to Lepers, *Gateways of Hope: Being Glimpses of the Work of The Mission to Lepers* (London: The Mission to Lepers, 1932), 7.

[17] A thorough study of the relationship between imperialism and missionary activity is still lacking. The papers in the following volumes serve as an introduction: Wilfred Wagner, ed., *Kolonien und Missionen: Referate des 3. Internationalen Kolonialgeschichtlichen Symposiums 1993 in Bremen* (Münster; Hamburg: Lit Verlag, 1994) and Karl Hammer, ed., *Weltmission und Kolonialismus: Sendungsideen des 19. Jahrhunderts im Konflikt* (München: Kösel-Verlage, 1978). On the history of missions generally, see Stephen Neill, *A History of Christian Missions* (London: Penguin Books, 1964); J. Herbert Kane, *A Concise History of the Christian World Mission* (Grand Rapids, MI: Baker Book House, 1982); Angelyn Dries, *The Missionary Movement in American Catholic History* (Maryknoll, NY: Orbis Books, 1998); Edward M. Dodd, *The Gift of the Healer: The Story of Men and Women in the Overseas Mission of the Church* (New York: Friendship Press, 1964).

of the Church of England in Greatham, Hants, cautioned in 1885 that while the "loathsome" leprosy had disappeared in civilized societies, it persisted in colonial India, "eat[ing] into the nerve-tissues of [England's] people."[18] Wright envisioned a time when the land pressures of the island Great Britain would be relieved by its subjects living in its colonial possessions. The commercial and population exchange this development would entail required that the English address the "Imperial Danger" of leprosy immediately. To address these concerns, Wright advocated the creation of a "Society for the Segregation and Comfort of Lepers." As Sheldon Watts writes, "Wright pleaded for Christian commitment to the despised 'Lazar in his rags,' who like the lepers known to Jesus 'invites us to hasten and help him.'"[19] For Wright and others, ridding the empire of leprosy and preventing its spread to the West were Christian obligations which the British had assumed and which had to be realized.

The influence of the biblical definitions of and prescriptions for leprosy can be seen in Wright's writings. Wright and others saw the medieval zeal to the biblically-sanctioned isolation and expulsion of the infectious leper from the community as the reason leprosy was largely eliminated from the West after the sixteenth century. A return to such measures would again serve to eliminate leprosy from England's imperial lands. Wright's ideas received support from the medical community with the publication of George Thin's *Leprosy* in 1891. Thin argued that "modern nerve leprosy" was the same disease described in Leviticus and called for the same measures advocated three millennia earlier, pointing to the success of such measures during the Middle Ages.[20] The forcible isolation of patients with leprosy became medically sanctioned in 1897 when at the first World Leprosy Conference meeting in Berlin, delegates, including Gerhard Hansen and James Cantlie, endorsed a policy of strict isolation for lepers in the *non-Western* world. As a consequence, the British colonial government enacted the "Lepers Act of 1898" which mandated the medical and social segregation of leprosy sufferers in In-

---

[18] Henry Press Wright, *Leprosy and Segregation* (London: Parker and Company, 1885), 103-104, 106. See also, Henry Press Wright, *Leprosy an Imperial Danger* (London: Churchill, 1889).

[19] Watts, 40.

[20] George Thin, *Leprosy* (London: Percival and Co., 1891), 7. See Watts, 40-41. On medieval attitudes toward leprosy and lepers, see Saul Nathaniel Brody, *The Disease of the Soul: Leprosy in Medieval Literature* (Ithaca: Cornell University Press, 1974), and Peter Richards, *The Medieval Leper and His Northern Heirs* (Cambridge, UK: D. S. Brewer, 1977).

dia; the 1898 Lepers Act placed a double-bind on Indian lepers as it required the isolation of any leper "who publicly solicits alms or exposes or exhibits any sores, wounds, bodily ailment or deformity with the object of exciting charity or of obtaining alms," but at the same time left no option for lepers to earn a livelihood by prohibiting them from nearly all trades and occupations.[21]

The mass isolation policy advocated by the Berlin conference posed two problems for Europe's colonial administration. First, the maneuver of a foreign government incarcerating members of the local population would only further antagonize and weaken the already strained relationship between the colonial administrators and the native population. Second, and more importantly in the minds of administrators sensitive to the costs of the colonial enterprise, the expenses and the logistics of a widespread isolation policy would be prohibitive. In India alone, some conservative estimates in the 1890s placed the number of lepers at 250,000 in a total population of approximately two hundred million people.[22] Watts has suggested that confronted with the enormity of the task, "colonial administrators resorted to face-saving tokenism."[23]

It was into this situation that Christian missionaries stepped at the end of the nineteenth century, and both the colonial government and the missionaries stood to gain from the symbiotic relationship. The missionaries gained the opportunity to pursue their biblical mandate to aid the sick, and in particular, "to cleanse the lepers." The missionaries received the protection and the sanction of the colonial administration for their proselytizing. Missionary efforts provided an avenue for administrators to pursue their "tokenism" without having to bear the expenses, as the missionaries raised private funds to support their causes. And though not fully articulated, missions extended the imperialist agenda, all the more important in the non-Christian, non-Western empire.[24] The ques-

---

[21] The Lepers Act, 1898 [Act Number 3 of 1898] as assented by His Excellency the Governor-General, February 4, 1898.

[22] Executive Committee of the National Leprosy Fund, *Leprosy in India : Report of the Leprosy Commission in India, 1890-1891* (London: William Clowes and Sons, 1893), 49.

[23] Watts, 41.

[24] There is obviously a very deep and vibrant literature on the relationship between medicine, science, and imperialism that I can only allude to in this brief paper. As an introduction to the literature, I would suggest David Arnold, "Medicine and Colonialism," in *Companion Encyclopedia of the History of Medicine*, William F. Bynum and Roy Porter, eds. (London: Routledge, 1993), 1393-1416; Andrew Cunningham and Bridie Andrews, "Western Medicine as

tion must be asked to what degree missionary groups were aware of the use to which they were being put in the colonial program? Or were they aware, but accepted the situation as a liability in pursuing their own program of Christian Good Works?

Founding of the Mission to Lepers

A dramatic rise in missionary activity marked the period from 1858 to 1914, largely because of political events in the 1850s and 1860s that contributed to the opening of Asian and African countries to Western missionaries. For instance, Christianity was prohibited in Japan (to the point of being punishable by death), but following the establishment of formal ties between the United States and Japan in 1858, four missionary groups—the Episcopalians, the Presbyterians, the Reformed, and the Free Baptists—entered Japan between 1859 and 1869. Similarly in China, the largest mission in the world, the China Inland Mission, began operations in 1865, following the 1858 resolution of the Second Opium War, which included provisions for the toleration of Christianity and missionary work (albeit with some restrictions). Missionary and historian Stephen Neill estimates that about 1,500 missionaries went to China after 1858 and established about 500 missions throughout all of the provinces.[25] 1858 was also a watershed year for what was the most desired posting for nineteenth-century missionaries, India, as British control over India was transferred from the East India Company to the crown on 2 August 1858 in response to the military mutiny and revolt of 1857-1859.

Wellesley Cosby Bailey arrived in India a decade after the establishment of the British Raj. Born in 1846 in Abbeyleix, Queen's County, Ireland, Bailey enjoyed a comfortable childhood provided by his father's position as an agent for the Stradbally Estate. Unsure of what he wanted to do with his life, Bailey left Ireland for New Zealand and then on to New Caledonia where he worked as a gold prospector and ranch hand. Neither line of work interested him very much, so he left in 1869 to join the oldest of his three brothers, Christopher, who was an officer in the British Army at Faizabad in north central India (now the state of Uttar

---

Contested Knowledge," in *Western Medicine as Contested Knowledge*, Andrew Cunningham and Bridie Andrews, eds. (Manchester, UK: Manchester University Press, 1997); Shula Marks, "What is Colonial about Colonial Medicine? And What has Happened to Imperialism and Health?," *Social History of Medicine 10* (1997): 205-220.
[25] Neill, *A History of Christian Missions*, 286.

Pradesh). His hope was to receive a commission in the North West Police, but the position required that he know Hindi, which he received instruction in while staying with his brother in Faizabad. Shortly after Bailey arrived in Faizabad, the Eleventh Infantry to which Christopher Bailey belonged was transferred and Bailey was placed in the care of a Reverend Reuther, a German missionary posted by the Anglican Church Missionary Society. Reuther's example shaped Bailey's own future. Of Bailey's time with Reuther, Bailey's biographer Donald Miller has written that "as [Bailey] watched the work of his German host and saw the great need of the people to possess a dynamic Christian faith to replace a too ready acceptance of conditions as they are, he found that there was a better vocation than that of a police officer beckoning him."[26] After completing his studies in Hindi, Bailey volunteered to be a teacher at a school in Ambala, operated by the Ludhiana Mission and headed by Reverend J. H. Morrison of the American Presbyterian Mission in India.

At this point, it is instructive to comment on the course of Bailey's career from being a ranch hand in New Zealand to becoming a missionary in north India. Sheldon Watts has pointed out that in the hierarchy of British colonial administration, "Administrators, military officers, medical doctors, missionaries, and other professional sorts whom home authority considered first rate went out to India; the rest went 'somewhere else,' which is to say to Africa."[27] In deciding to pursue a missionary career while already in India, Bailey had bypassed the authority of a mission's home office in deciding where to post him. Bailey, however, could not avoid the kind of criticism that Sir John Willoughby leveled against the Church Missionary Society missionaries who he encountered in East Africa while hunting big game:

> [They] were manufactured out of traders, clerks, and mechanics. The process is not a difficult one: a man, thinking he can improve his position by missionary work, has only to go to school for a year or two and learn a certain amount of medicine and carpentry, fla-

[26] A. Donald Miller, *An Inn Called Welcome: The Story of the Mission to Lepers, 1874-1917* (London: The Mission to Lepers, 1965), 10

[27] Watts, 74. On colonial medicine in India, in addition to Arnold, *Colonizing the Body and Harrison, Public Health and British India*, see also Poonam Bala, *Imperialism and Medicine in Bengal: A Socio-historical Perspective* (New Delhi: Sage Publications, 1991) and Anil Kumar, *Medicine and the Raj: British Medical Policy in India, 1835-1911* (Walnut Creek: Altamira Press, 1998).

voured with a little theology, and he is turned out a full-blown missionary.[28]

Although it is unlikely that Bailey's financial station improved by becoming a missionary, it is not a stretch that his new position gave him social mobility and social security that he previously lacked. Leading figures and leading institutions in tropical medicine, including Ronald Ross and the *Journal of Tropical Medicine*, appealed to young people in England to consider a career as a medical missionary in the growing empire. Ross, for instance, romanticized the medical missionary's role in healing:

> During the beginning of civilization in Egypt, Greece, and Rome, the priests were also the physicians...In my opinion, the missionary of today may still hold a similar position among the barbarous peoples he is called upon to educate...Often called upon to live in the remotest districts, far from hospitals, municipalities, health departments and officials, he is now exactly in the position of the priest of old, and to him still belongs the double duty of caring both mind and body."[29]

Bailey, however, was not prepared for where his career would lead him next. Shortly after reaching Ambala in late 1869, Bailey and Morrison visited a small leper asylum attached to Morrison's mission. The asylum was an example of the relationship forged between the missionary community and the British colonial administration that was discussed earlier. Although operated as a missionary institution, a monthly stipend from the municipality and private contributions from British officers and civilians helped to maintain the asylum. As in Faizabad when he was influenced by the example of Reuther, his work at the Ambala leper asylum profoundly affected Bailey. Describing the experience in his 1924 autobiography, Bailey wrote:

---

[28] Quoted in Watts, 74. Originally quoted in Robert Strayer, *The Making of Mission Communities in East Africa: Anglicans and Africans in Colonial Kenya, 1875-1935* (London: Heinemann, 1978), 5.

[29] Ronald Ross, "Missionaries and the Campaign against Malaria," *Journal of Tropical Medicine and Hygenie 13* (15 June 1910): 183.

I became more and more interested and received great encouragement in my efforts for their spiritual welfare, several were baptized and became very earnest Christians. I was convinced that their first and greatest need was the Gospel, and that it would indeed prove to them 'the power of God unto salvation,' completely changing their lives and their outlook on life, and giving them something to look forward to even in this life, but especially in that which is to come; and that it brought to them very real comfort in the midst of their dreadful sufferings. Thus was born the germ of what has ever since been the watchword of our beloved Mission, *viz*: The Gospel for the lepers.[30]

Bailey soon realized that "taking them the Gospel" would also require providing lepers with housing, food, clothing, medical care, and other basic needs, but he was unable to convince other missionary groups or government officials to increase their commitment to the cause of leprosy.[31]

By 1870, Bailey was engaged to be married to Alice Grahame of Blackrock, Dublin, and in his letters to her, he would describe his work among the lepers. Grahame traveled to India in 1871 and Bailey and Grahame were married in Bombay in the same year. Before leaving Ireland, Grahame had told of Bailey's efforts to the three Pim sisters of Monkstown, Dublin; Isabella, Charlotte, and Jane Pim were long-time family friends of Grahame and were enthusiastic about Bailey's work. Bailey and his new wife returned to Ambala to continue the work he had begun among the lepers under Morrison's direction. Morrison left India not long after Bailey reached Ambala, leaving Bailey to run the entire mission. By the end of 1873, the Baileys, due to Alice Bailey's failing health, would also leave Ambala and return to England and then on to Ireland in 1874.

Upon returning to Dublin, the Pim sisters invited the Baileys to meet privately with their friends and discuss his work in India, all in the hopes of raising support and funds for the leprosy cause. These private

---

[30] Wellesley C. Bailey, *Fifty Years' Work for Lepers, 1874-1924; An Account of the Founding and Growth of the Mission to Lepers* (London: The Mission to Lepers, 1924), 8.
[31] Ibid., 8-10.

meetings were followed by an invitation to give a public lecture at the Friends Meeting House in Monkstown at which Bailey "told them simply of the terrible conditions of India's lepers, physically, mentally, and spiritually, and of what we were trying to do, for just a few of them..."[32] After the public meeting, Bailey with the Pims' encouragement printed and distributed two thousand copies of a pamphlet titled "Lepers in India." The charitable pursuits of the Pims were not usual for women of the late Victorian period as F. K. Prochaska and Anne Summers have suggested. Drawing on their work, Maneesha Lal in examining the Lady Dufferin's Fund has written, "This type of charity had strong roots in Victorian society, and for leisured women, especially philanthropy was seen as the most obvious outlet for self-expression. Philanthropic work enabled wealthy women to venture outside of the home and perform tasks which, precisely because of their voluntaristic, unpaid nature, and because they drew on an ideology of friendship, sympathy, were deemed acceptable."[33]

The Baileys returned to India in 1875 having joined the Foreign Missions of the Church of Scotland and received a post at Chamba in the Himalayas, where they built their first leper asylum. Bailey, later wrote, that the asylum was "wonderfully blessed of God, in the comfort and help it has brought to many lepers, and better still, in the leading of many of them to the feet of the Saviour."[34] Meanwhile, the appeals and the efforts of the Pims in Dublin were resulting in growing financial contributions to Bailey's work in India. By 1878, the total contributions were sufficient to support leper asylums at Ambala, Chamba, Sabathu, and Almora, and a fledgling society, the Mission to Lepers in India and the East, was formed to administer and to distribute the funds. Bailey instituted a "grants in aid" program whereby he would distribute contributions among leper asylums in India that needed the Mission's support. The Baileys remained in India until 1882 when the increasing bureaucracy of collecting and distributing donations required their return to

---

[32] Ibid., 10.

[33] Maneesha Lal, "The Role of Gender and Medicine in Colonial India: The Countess of Dufferin's Fund, 1885-1888," *Bulletin of the History of Medicine* 68 (1994): 29-66. For background, see F. K. Prochaska, *Women and Philanthropy in Nineteenth Century England* (Oxford: Clarendon Press, 1980), and Anne Summers, "A Home Away from Home—Women's Philanthropic Work in the Nineteenth Century," in *Fit Work for Women*, Sandra Burman, ed. (London: Croom Helm, 1979), 33-63.

[34] Bailey, *Fifty Years' Work for Lepers*, 12.

Ireland. After his return to Dublin, Wellesley Bailey served as secretary of the Mission from 1886 to 1917, traveling, speaking, and writing extensively on behalf of the Mission's cause.[35] By the time of his retirement, the Mission had an annual income of nearly £45,000 (approximately £1,375,000/$1,990,000 in 2001 terms) that was used to help nearly 15,000 patients in eighty-seven asylums in twelve countries, and in cooperation with thirty-seven missionary societies.[36]

Operations of the Mission

When founded in 1874, the Mission's charter stated its purpose as "to provide for the spiritual instruction of temporal relief of lepers and the children of lepers in India and such other countries to which its operations have been or may be extended from time to time, and in so far as lies in its power, to assist in bringing about the extinction of leprosy."[37] By 1910, there were approximately 4,500 European missionaries serving in India, representing approximately 130 missionary societies. The Mission to Lepers was the only one with a stated objective of serving lepers. The Mission, however, did not have its own missionaries or directly engage in evangelization. Rather, it provided funds to missionaries and to institutions from other missionary societies that requested support of their work among lepers. This financial support was interdenominational, and in India alone by 1910, it provided funds to nineteen British, sixteen

---

[35] The Mission to Lepers in India and the East was the first modern missionary society devoted solely to the care of leprosy sufferers. There are, however, older Roman Catholic orders—the Military and Hospitaller Order of Saint Lazarus of Jerusalem (founded 1098) and Daughters of Charity of St. Vincent de Paul (founded 1850)—that pre-date the Mission to Lepers. For the earlier history, see Robert Needham Cust, "Leprosy and Lepers, 1890," in *Orientation of Early Christian Missionaries in Africa and Asia* (Delhi: Daya Press, 1988; reprint of 1891 first edition).

[36] John Goodwin, "Leprosy Missions" and "Bailey, Wellesley Cosby," in *Concise Dictionary of the Christian World Mission*, Stephen Neill, Gerald H. Anderson, and John Goodwin, eds. (Nashville: Abingdon Press, 1987), 49-50, 343-44. See also, Christoffer H. Grundmann, "Bailey, Wellesley Cosby," in *Biographical Dictionary of Christian Missions*, Gerald H. Anderson, ed. (Grand Rapids, MI: William B. Eerdmans Publishing Company, 1976), 39-40; Walter Fancutt, "The Leprosy Mission," in *The Encylopedia of Modern Christian Missions: The Agencies,* Burton L. Goddard, ed. (Camden, NJ: Thomas Nelson and Sons, 1975), 364-365; [n.a.], "Lepers; Special Labors for," in *The Encyclopedia of Missions: Descriptive, Historical, Biographical, Statistical*, Henry Otis Dwight, H. Allen Tupper, and Edwin Munsell Bliss, eds. (New York and London: Funk and Wagnalls Co., 1904), 391-393.

[37] *The Mission to Lepers charter.*

American, and three European Protestant missionary societies. As will be discussed later, Roman Catholic efforts among lepers were not supported and were often regarded with displeasure by Bailey and other Mission officials. As the finances and prominence of the Mission grew, it also began to establish and to build asylums in India and elsewhere, but continued to hire medical staff and workers from other missionary societies.

The Mission did not provide funds to all missionary groups that asked for its support. Rather, the asylums seeking support generally had to be aligned with the moral agenda and evangelical goals of the Mission. The asylums had to be segregated by sex, preferably on separate campuses; the untainted children of lepers admitted to the asylums had to be removed from their parents and send to a separate institution to receive Christian teaching; the asylums had to engage in a program of evangelization and Christian instruction; and, the Mission preferred that the administration of the asylum be largely Westerners rather than native Indians. The final component of the Mission-funded asylums was an expectation that the residents contribute to the asylum's operations as much as their health condition allowed. Erving Goffman would later call such an operation a total institution, which he defined as "a place of residence and work where a large number of like-situated individuals, cuts off from their wider society for an appreciable period of time, together lead an enclosed, formally administered round of life."[38] The Mission, however, believed that the contribution of the lepers served another function, that of inculcating the residents with a sense of discipleship, Christian good works, and service. As one Mission publication describing the lepers' service asked, "Do they not, indeed, in a real sense follow the example of service our Divine Lord gave to His disciples."

Evangelization was directly tied to the disbursement of medical care. While the Mission to Lepers has always maintained that it was not necessary for a non-Christian leper to convert to Christianity to receive medical care, it has also made clear that being receptive to Christian teaching was a pre-requisite to care. This is made clear in a report that Bailey receives in November 1890 from a Dr. Hutchinson, the medical superintendent of the asylum at Sailkot. Hutchinson writes that:

> The evangelistic side of our work has been very interest-
> ing and encouraging. The work in the Dispensary every

---

[38] Erving Goffman, *Asylums* (Garden City: Doubleday Anchor Books, 1961), 11.

morning was commenced with a short address, which
was always listened to with attention. Not once was
there any unpleasantness. The audiences were often
large, though it is not possible to have the whole of the
patients present at one time, owing to the great distances
many of them had to come. In the villages we often have
very large audiences throughout; and in addition to the
ordinary address a catechist went on preaching while we
were engaged in distributing medicines. Nothing but
kindness was experienced everywhere; and even bigoted
Mohammedans became pleasant and friendly in sight of
the medicine-chest.[39]

The missionaries valued the time that the lepers were under their care
and sought ways to extend that time because the patients were effectively
a captive audience to their proselytization. The residential facilities of the
asylums were constantly at capacity, as the medical staff when possible
encouraged the patients to remain for extended care, promising medicines, food, and activities. And discreetly, medical missionaries in the
"leper fields" saw both medical and practical advantages to the use of
chaulmoogra oil and its derivatives for the treatment of leprosy not only
because it was a seemingly effective treatment but because to receive the
regimen, lepers had to return to the asylum frequently and regularly over
many months, affording missionaries more opportunities to preach.[40]
Bailey emphasized the importance of reinforcing the relationship between Christian teaching and physical healing, reminding Mission
workers that "if it is the same hand which gives the medical relief that
breaks to them the 'Bread of life,' the patients will be quick to discern
the connection between the two, and they will gladly receive both at the
same hand, while at the same time their hearts will be more open to accept the teaching."[41]

The Mission to Lepers sought to extend their reach over India's
lepers in other ways, particularly by broadening the definition of leprosy
and by encouraging the colonial government to enforce the 1898 Lepers

---

[39] Wellesley C. Bailey, *The Lepers of Our Indian Empire: A Visit to Them in
1890-91* (Edinburgh: The Darien Press, Bristo Place, 1899), 33.
[40] Sir Leonard Rogers, "The Treatment of Leprosy," in *Report of a Conference
of Leper Asylum Superintendents and Others on The Leper Problem in India*
(Cuttack: Orissa Mission Press, 1920), 23-38.
[41] Bailey, *Lepers of Our Indian Empire*, 19-20.

Act, requiring that lepers be isolated (forcibly if necessary) in asylums. By 1910, particularly in light of the passage of the 1898 Lepers Act, the Mission was the most significant influence in the care of lepers in the British administration of India. Mission officials, however, were generally dissatisfied with the Lepers Act because the colonial government lacked the funds and the resources to fully enforce the Act, which meant in turn that the full potential of lepers did not come under the care of the Mission's asylums. Frank Oldrieve, the Mission's Secretary for India, pointed to several problems with the Act enacted in 1898 and amended in 1903.[42] Its enforcement was left to the individual states, and in the confusion of the British Raj with its combination of princely states and British-appointed governors, some states failed to implement the law. Enforcing the law meant local police were required to apprehend lepers and bring them to the asylums, a task which the police avoided as much as possible. Finally, the Mission felt that the definition of "leper" employed in the law was not sweeping enough. The 1898 Act defined a leper as a person in whom "the process of ulceration has commenced"; the Mission wanted the Act amended to define a leper more generally as "any person suffering from any variety of leprosy."[43] In meetings of asylum superintendents at Purulia in 1908, at Chandkuri in 1911, and at Raniganj in 1913, Mission officials pressed for the expansion and amendment of the Lepers Act. The network of asylums either directed or funded by the Mission meant that its resources and personnel exceeded those of the colonial government's modest leprosy control programs. Nevertheless, to point to the enormity of the task of isolating all Indian lepers, by 1910, only about 10,000 of an estimated 150,000 documented lepers in India were in the Mission's asylums.[44]

Competition for Souls

By the late 1880s, as the activities of the Mission to Lepers increased in India, it faced growing competition from the dozens of other foreign missionary societies also engaged in evangelization. In 1886, when Bailey

---

[42] Frank Oldrieve, "Legislation Providing for the Care and Control of Lepers," in *Report of a Conference of Leper Asylum Superintendents and Others on The Leper Problem in India*, 60-79.

[43] Section 2, Sub-section (1), The Lepers Act, 1898 [Act Number 3 of 1898] as assented by His Excellency the Governor-General, February 4, 1898; Oldrieve, "Legislation Providing for the Care and Control of Lepers," 62.

[44] Sir Leonard Rogers, "The Treatment of Leprosy," in *Report of a Conference of Leper Asylum Superintendents and Others on The Leper Problem in India*, 26.

traveled to India for the first time after returning to Ireland to oversee the Mission's administration, he wrote of being pleased to see the "earnest work" of the Church Missionary Society, the Free, and Established Churches of Scotland, the London Missionary Society, the Wesleyan Mission, and the American Episcopal Methodist.[45] Ecstatic at the possibilities held by evangelization (and conversion) in a country with nearly two hundred million non-Christians, Bailey, however, had to express frustration at the lack of funds and the lack of missionaries for the enormous task. Writing from Lahore in March 1887, Bailey is:

> ...convinced that, were the Church of Scotland but to realise the true state of matters—the glorious harvest of precious souls that is waving on all sides in the Panjab at present, and that is *not* being reaped, and *cannot* be reaped, just because of the paucity of labourers, they would never as a Church allow this state of matters to remain.[46]

Addressing the crisis Bailey believed "require[d] now for India men and women of means and position—the very best, the very flower of our land, educationally and spiritually—who will give themselves and their all to Christ for the evangelization of India."[47] By recruiting to the mission field individuals who had wealth, Bailey's hope was to increase the number of missionaries who did not have to rely on Mission funds for income and support.

Bailey's call for more missionaries for India, by which he meant Protestant missionaries, reflected what he saw as another problem: the growing influence of Roman Catholic interests in India. Arriving in Lohardugga on New Year's Day 1887, Bailey is dismayed to learn that missionaries supported by the Mission to Lepers are having:

> ...their troubles from without, too; their field has been entered by the Jesuits, who, we are told, do not hesitate 'to steal the sheep of the flock.' And they know what it is to see converts, upon whom they had expended great

---

[45] Wellesley C. Bailey, *A Glimpse at the Indian Mission-Field and Leper Asylums in 1886-87* (London: John F. Shaw and Co., 1888), 21, 30
[46] Ibid., 161.
[47] Ibid., 179-180.

labour, and in whom they had placed the utmost confidence, suddenly turn aside, and return as the 'dog to his vomit,' or as 'the sow that was washed to her wallowing in the mire.'[48]

The threat of Catholic missionaries appropriating Protestant converts had diminished by the time of Bailey's next trip to India in late 1890-early 1891, but he could not overlook that the "plague of Popery is not extinct."[49] From Sailkot in November 1890, Bailey reported that the Papists working in the area had not influenced any more Protestant converts, and he relished telling that "several have returned to us, confessing that they have been thoroughly deceived in both worldly and spiritual matters, and some express contempt for Romish idolatry."[50] Bailey insinuated that the Catholic "mode of work" was to bribe coverts with money and goods. Hence while the Mission was "trying *to teach the people* liberality," Catholic missionaries were "being liberal with their money."[51] Bailey and the Mission to Lepers were concerned about the Catholics' "underhanded way" because their efforts were directed at those *already* converted to Christianity by Protestant missionaries, conversions that required a considerable expenditure of Protestant funds, resources, and manpower. Missionaries of the Church of Scotland posted at Sailkot wrote Bailey that the problem occurred because too many Indian workers had been given the power to baptize converts. The result they wrote Bailey was that "Having offered schools and other worldly inducements, they found no trouble in baptizing as many they wished. The consequence is, that we have on hands a lot of *baptized heathen*, who reproach us on account of our unfulfilled promises. They are ten times harder to reach than they would otherwise have been."[52] Dissatisfied by the Protestants, many of the Protestant converts were drawn to the Catholic missionary appeals, although the Catholic groups themselves were not necessarily in any better position to offer the converts what the Protestant could not.

The pressure and competition between missionary societies to attract converts might have contributed to actions that could be regarded as

---

[48] Ibid., 59.
[49] Bailey, *Lepers of Our Indian Empire*, 26-27.
[50] Ibid., 27.
[51] Ibid., 27.
[52] Quoted in Ibid., 26.

duplicitous, such as in conflating the biblical stories of Lazarus. Christian missionaries to lepers often referred to the New Testament story of Lazarus in their proselytizing work, as testimony to the power of a belief in Christian teachings, and Lazarus has long been associated as the patron saint of leprosy sufferers. But it must remembered that there are two stories of two different Lazaruses in the New Testament. And although the details, the meanings, and the power of each story differ, Bailey's workers used the stories interchangeably to appeal to his audience. The Book of Luke, chapter 16, tells the parable of the rich man and the poor man:

> There was a rich man, who was clothed in purple and fine linen and who feasted sumptuously every day. And at his gate lay a poor man named Laz'arus, full of sores, who desired to be fed with what fell from the rich man's table; moreover the dogs came and licked his sores. The poor man died and was carried by the angels to Abraham's bosom. The rich man also died and was buried; and in Hades, being in torment, he lifted up his eyes, and saw Abraham far off and Laz'arus in his bosom... [To the rich man,] Abraham said, 'Child, remember that you in your lifetime received your good things, and Lazarus in like manner bad things; but now he is comforted here, and you are in anguish (John 16: 19-23, 26)

Beyond the reference to "sores," there is little else in the story to suggest that Lazarus might have leprosy; missionaries, in their use of the parable, almost always ascribe Lazarus with leprosy.

The Book of John, chapter 11, meanwhile tells the story of Lazarus of Bethany and his sisters, Mary and Martha; Lazarus falls ill, dies, and is buried. Four days after Lazarus' death, Jesus and his disciples arrive in Bethany, where he performs the miracle of resurrecting Lazarus from the dead. To see how these stories are put to use in the leprosy mission field, one can turn to the instance of Wellesley Bailey's sermon to the lepers of Tarn Taran in Ambala on 29 November 1890. Bailey wrote that all of the lepers at the Tarn Taran asylum were assembled in the prayer-room for his sermon, and he found it:

> ...a great privilege to tell 'the old, old story' to such an audience. What a majesty there is in those words, 'I am

the resurrection and the life,' at all times; what a peculiar power they must have when first spoken in view of the raising of Lazarus, and what tremendous force they seem to have as one repeats them before these poor decaying frames of humanity, these 'living corpses'...[53]

It must be asked if Bailey's audience was aware or informed that there were two stories—one promising a peaceful after-life to those living in anguish in this world and the other promising a resurrection from death for those professing a Christian faith—both of which would have been appealing for Bailey's asylum audience.

Travel Narratives in Making Imaginary Anatomies Real

Janice Dickin McGinnis has noted that John Jackson's *In Leper Land: A Record of 7,000 Miles among Indian Lepers, with a Glimpse of Hawaii, Japan, and China*, published in 1901 by the Mission to Lepers, reads like "an inviting travelogue."[54] Unfortunately, McGinnis fails to ask the obvious question: why would a book about leprosy and lepers be written like "an inviting travelogue"? Jackson was a successful London businessman who joined the Mission as its Honorary Secretary for London in 1894 and entered the Mission in full-time service beginning in 1898, serving as the editor of *Without the Camp*, the Mission's quarterly magazine until his death in 1917. Jackson's *In Leper Land* details his visit to India during 1900 and 1901 "to ascertain by personal observation the real condition of the lepers of India, and to obtain a direct insight into the work of ministering to their physical and spiritual needs."[55] Jackson's *In Leper Land* (1901) and his *Lepers: Thirty-Six Years' Work Among Them* (1911) were not the first of their kind. Wellesley Bailey had published two books, *A Glimpse at the Indian Mission-Field* (1888) and *The Lepers of Our Indian Empire* (1899), chronicling his visits to Indian lepers and leper asylums during 1886-1887 and 1890-1891, respectively. Together, these four books detail the activities of the Mission to Lepers in India for its first quarter-century, and as McGinnis noted in the instance of Jack-

---

[53] Ibid., 65-66.
[54] McGinnis, "'Unclean, Unclean': Canadian Reaction to Lepers and Leprosy," 251.
[55] John Jackson, *In Leper Land: A Record of 7,000 Miles among Indian Lepers, with a Glimpse of Hawaii, Japan, and China* (London: The Mission to Lepers, 1901), 15. See also, Jackson, *Lepers: Thirty-Six Years' Work Among Them* (London and Edinburgh: Marshall Brothers, 1911).

son's book, they read like travel literature. The frontispiece of *The Lepers of Our Indian Empire* is an inspiring mountain scene in the Himalayas. Bailey writes of the indignities a British traveler must endure in colonial India: while traveling from Dalhousie to Dharmsala, he finds himself abandoned at the roadside unable to find four natives willing to carry him in his doolie; he complains that "Natives have the most wonderful power of putting themselves to sleep at all hours, and under the most adverse and uncomfortable circumstances..."; and most critically, on numerous occasions, he is unable to find a servant willing to prepare him a cup of tea.[56] And Jackson, in landing in Bombay, writes that "the absolute novelty of the whole was almost paralysing to one enjoying his first sight of the mysterious East, whose myths and fables fall far short of its living facts in real and even romantic interest."[57] What McGinnis hints at can be pushed further. Bailey and Jackson introduced to a mass English audience the work of the Mission to Lepers by adopting a literary genre that was widely popular in late nineteenth-century Europe and America—the travel narrative. Christopher Mulvey, for instance, have written of the broad readership travel narratives enjoyed in the late nineteenth century.[58]

Bailey and Jackson's travel narratives in India served another rhetorical function for the Mission to Lepers. It must be remembered that by the late nineteenth century, few people in the United Kingdom would know what a person suffering from leprosy looked like. By the late sixteenth century, leprosy was rarely seen in Europe, and certainly by the nineteenth century, outside of Norway, cases of leprosy were even more rarely encountered. What late nineteenth-century British men and women would have known of leprosy was largely the product of cultural accretion, myth, and imagination. The imagination of leprosy strongly influenced Europeans' perception of the disease as "An Imperial Danger," and Bailey, Jackson, and the Mission to Lepers took advantage of these perceptions in describing their missionary efforts. Their often vivid descriptions, and accompanying photographs, made real what Europeans had only long imagined of leprosy. Their descriptions of limb-less lepers

---

[56] Bailey, *Lepers of Our Indian Empire*, 52-54.
[57] Jackson, *In Leper Land*, 15-16.
[58] Christopher Mulvey, *Anglo-American Landscapes: A Study of Nineteenth-Century Anglo-American Travel Literature* (Cambridge and New York: Cambridge University Press, 1983), and, Mulvey, *Transatlantic Manners: Social Patterns in Nineteenth-Century Anglo-American Travel Literature* (Cambridge and New York: Cambridge University Press, 1990).

who must be carried to receive communion, who lacked hands to receive the communion wafer, and who lacked lips to receive communion wine appealed to all emotional and spiritual sensibilities of their readers.

What Bailey and Jackson made real for their British readers was what the theorist Jacques Lacan coined as "imaginary anatomies." Catherine Waldby, Georges Canguilhem, and Sander Gilman have extended Lacan's ideas to show that "imaginary anatomies" that are ascribed to those who are sick, or mentally ill, or simply different, are a basis in medical discourse to demarcate those deemed normal from those considered the undesirable, the pathological, and the deviant. Waldby, in her study of sexual differences and AIDS, has defined "imaginary anatomies" as "the products of the biomedical imagination, arrived at through processes of selectivity, idealization, utopian speculation, and analogy."[59]

Ultimately, the Mission to Lepers needed to arouse the sympathy, compassion, and indignation of its supporters in the United Kingdom to raise funds to support its evangelical activities in the British empire. The most powerful medium available to the Mission in their fund-raising were the photographs in the promotional literature that they distributed to their donors. The caption of one photograph of a leper in Bombay read: "This typical picture shows us the homeless leper in all of his misery, and in his unspeakable need. Diseased and destitute, cast out by his friends, regarded as accursed by his gods, afflicted with a loathsome and incurable disease, he is surely of all men the most in need of our pity and help. It is to give home, shelter, and Christian teaching, together with medical relief, to such as he is that the Mission to Lepers exist." Appearing on the opposite page is an idyllic, tranquil scene of the Leper Asylum in Ambala operated by the Mission, reminding readers what their donations to the Mission will provide for the lepers. Another photograph depicts the Mission-funded asylum at Tarn Taran, with some of the patients having been placed in front of the building's dedication stone which reads, "This stone was laid to the Glory of God and the Help of Suffering Humanity." The photographs of patients with leprosy constitute a process by which the disease's sufferers were ascribed with more

---

[59] Catherine Waldby, *AIDS and the Body Politic: Biomedicine and Sexual Difference* (New York: Routledge, 1996), 26-27. See also, Georges Canguilhem, *The Normal and the Pathological* (New York: Zone Books, 1991); Sander Gilman, *Difference and Pathology: Stereotypes of Sexuality, Race, and Madness* (Ithaca: Cornell University Press, 1985); and, Sander Gilman, *Disease and Representation: Images of Illness from Madness to AIDS* (Ithaca: Cornell University Press, 1988).

than "imaginary anatomies." They, in fact, describe the process by which lepers were defined to be deviant, pathological, different, or simply not normal. The photographs made real what the Mission's European audience had only imagined or assumed, and the photographs fulfilled their imagination and assumptions.

The photographs, however, have to be regarded carefully because they present an inaccurate version of reality in India's nineteenth-century leprosaria. Bailey, in "Lepers in India," the tract that he distributed with the Pims in 1874, wrote:

> In India the lepers are often turned adrift by their friends, and cast out of house and home, to wander about the country in the most pitiable condition imaginable. Their hands and feet drop bit by bit, joint by joint, until they have nothing but the bare stumps left. As they are unable to work for themselves, they have to eke out their living by begging from door to door, and take whatever is thrown to them—and *thrown* to them it often is, as if they were dogs. When too ill to totter along on their poor stumps, they sometimes lie down and die from exhaustion. The disease attacks them generally in the hands and feet, and often in the nose and face. The bridge of the nose falls in, and gives them a most forbidding appearance.[60]

The pre-dominant image of the leper that medical missionaries perpetuated, with severe facial deformities, auto-amputated limbs, and other features of advanced leprosy, was only the most uncommon sights in the field. Medical missionaries overlooked less conspicuous, less debilitating, and more common forms of leprosy (the tuberculoid form), in favor, of rare and advanced cases (the lepromatous form), leaving their English audience with an indelible conclusion that all lepers appeared this way. In the process, the most abnormal forms of leprosy became in the minds of readers, the normal. Portraying lepers and leprosy in this way served multiple ends. The images of lepers reiterated the inferiority and the backwardness of the native populations and underscored the need for British colonization. And for missionaries, the images served the practi-

---

[60] Wellesley C. Bailey, *Lepers in India* (Dublin: The Mission to Lepers, 1874).

cal issue of raising charity funds for evangelization and justifying their evangelical efforts among those whom "all but God had abandoned," making real only what had been learned from biblical parables and from medieval stories of the banishment of lepers. Like the travel narratives that were a popular genre of literature in late Victorian society, the Mission's photographs of lepers would have served their audience's fascination and desire to "picture" their empire as the historian James Ryan has claimed.[61]

Religious Conversion as the Civilizing Process

A reader of the Mission's publications is immediately struck by the statistics it contains. In Bailey's and Jackson's books, as well as in the society's annual reports, there are careful records of the operations of each of the asylums which the Mission funded, including the number of inmates, the number converted in any year, and the number of converts baptized. Of particular importance to the Mission was the counting of "happy lepers," those lepers who have been converted and who exhibited the Christian characteristics that the Mission sought. In his 1924 autobiography, Bailey writes of visiting an asylum in Naini near Allahabad and the superintendent tells Bailey, "We have had a great many distinguished visitors recently, all of whom commented on the happy looks where they expected to see people hopeless and dejected. The happiness, I believe, comes from the fact that so many of them have learnt to know and love and serve the Lord Jesus."[62] Or similarly in 1886, Bailey points to the study of Drs. Lewis and Cunningham, appointed by the Colonial Office to investigate the asylums' operations in India:

> ...which mentioned that what had struck them most was the happy, cheerful, and contented spirit of all the inmates. It is the well-known effect of the malady to produce the exactly opposite temper of mind; and though it may be thought that this difference apparent in the inmates of the asylum may be accounted for by their more comfortable outward circumstances, it is a fact that this did not show itself until after they had become Christians, and had in some measure learned by experience

---

[61] James R. Ryan, *Picturing Empire: Photography and the Visualization of the British Empire* (London: Reaktion Books, 1997).
[62] Bailey, *Fifty Years' Work for Lepers*, 55.

'the peace which passeth all understanding,' which
keeps their hearts and minds in Christ Jesus.[63]

And Bailey concludes, "the Christians to-day all seemed bright and
happy, and this is no mere fancy of mine. I always do see the greatest
difference between Christians and heathen in these asylums; the one
seems borne up in his sorrow, the other utterly cast down and dejected."[64]

 The Mission to Lepers saw the act of conversion to Christianity
as also the act of civilization, and here in particular, it is difficult to divorce the sentiments of religion from the political and social objectives
of imperialism. In March 1887, Bailey visits the leper settlement at Tarn
Taran and writes of:

> ...the difference between the Christians and the heathen
> ...The Christians keep themselves and their houses clean,
> and in general health are much better than the others,
> while they always look more cheerful; many of them,
> too, have learned to read, and so have the grand resource
> and consolation of studying the pages of the blessed
> Book: while the heathen and the Mahommedans are
> dirty in their persons, and their homes are nothing like as
> clean or so well kept as those of the Christians, and one
> rarely gets a smile or bright look from their poor
> woe-begone faces, nor is it to be expected that you
> should, for a *leper* without Christ and the consolations of
> His gospel is, I think, the very personification of hope-
> lessness—he is one in whose poor breast the last spark
> of hope has for ever gone out.[65]

Or similarly writing in January 1891 from Assam, Bailey reiterates the
connections between the Christian conversion of Indians with their contributions to civilization:

> The boys and girls are all taught to work as they would
> have to do, and as they *will* have to do, in their own vil-

---

[63] Bailey, *A Glimpse at the Indian Mission-Field*, 113.
[64] Ibid., 155.
[65] Ibid., 155-156.

lages. They work in the fields, sow and reap, etc.; and the girls are taught to do the most menial work, such as they will have to do in their own village homes. I saw Christian carpenters, Christian servants, Christians making bricks, Christians binding books, Christians at all sorts of employments. Gradually the whole place is becoming Christian. At first heathen had to be employed, but now they are all giving way to Christians. The whole face of the country is becoming changed, the heathen now, for very shame sake, giving up many of their heathenish customs. Heathen women are often ashamed to be seen wearing the extravagant ornaments on their feet and legs which they used to wear. Some of these anklets weigh as much as three pounds each. Heathen men are ashamed to be seen drunk, whereas they used to glory in it. They even ask pardon of the Christians for such conduct. The great heathenish drinking festivals, which used to be the most terrible orgies, and would last for weeks at a time, are now comparatively tame affairs, and do not last so many days. Owing to the strenuous efforts of the missionaries, the great majority of the licensed liquor shops, which were fast ruining these simple-minded aborigines, have been done away with.[66]

In short, Bailey acknowledges the larger goal of the Mission's work not only as to provide medical care, shelter and food, and religious instruction, but to realize the long-term consequences of "civilizing" Indian society with Western values and inculcating them with the Christian ideals and behavior that the British missionaries held as suitable.

Legacy of Medical Missions to Lepers

In the closing days of January 1999, newspapers across India and around the world carried the story of the murder of Graham Staines and his two young sons in the north Indian state of Orissa, survived by his wife and daughter.[67] Staines had lived in the remote village of Baripada since

---

[66] Ibid., 198.

[67] Christopher Kremmer, "Missionary And Sons Die In A Blaze Of Hatred," *Sydney Morning Herald*, 25 January 25 1999, p. 1; Celia W. Dugger, "47 Suspected Militants in India Charged in Missionary's Death," *The New York Times*,

1965 serving as a missionary under the Evangelical Missionary Society based in Queensland, Australia and operating a small leprosy hospital funded by the Leprosy Mission (the name assumed by the Mission to Lepers in 1965). On 23 January 1999, returning from an annual religious retreat outside the village of Manohapur, India, unable to find housing in the late night, Staines and his sons decided to sleep in their Jeep. A crowd of villagers surrounded the vehicle, poured gasoline on it, and set it ablaze with the Staines family inside. Some in the crowd blocked the doors of nearby houses so that other villagers could not help the Staines. A subsequent Commission of Inquiry lead by Justice D. P. Wadhwa, a sitting judge of the Indian Supreme Court, recommended the arrest of forty-nine villagers involved in the murders. The murders, which were the most violent of a series of attacks against Christian missionaries in northern India, prompted a national outcry, and Prime Minister Atal Bi-hari Vajpayee of the nationalist Bharatiya Janata Party (BJP) faced intense criticism from within and outside of India to quell the violence stirred by Hindu nationalists. Many of the arrested villagers were members of Barang Dal, the youth wing of the Vishwa Hindu Parishad (the World Hindu Council), which had close ties to the BJP. The villagers would argue that Staines was killed because he was engaging in the conversion of Hindus to Christianity, under the aegis of the medical care and instruction his family provided at the leprosy hospital in Baripada.[68]

The political controversy ignited by the murders of the Staines and other Christian missionaries in India came near the end of decade during when nationalist political parties assumed greater power in India. A component of this transition was a renewed, intense criticism of the work of Western missionaries in India throughout its history, highlighted by the publication of two books—Arun Shourie's *Missionaries in India: Continuities, Changes, Dilemmas* and *Harvesting Our Souls: Missionaries, Their Design, Their Claims*—that have served as the Hindu nationalist response to Christian evangelization.[69] Already a widely known writer and political commentator, Shourie would go on to be elected to the Indian parliament and be appointed a minister in the BJP-controlled gov-

---

25 January 1999, p. A3; Peter Popham, "Hindu mob burns missionary and two young sons to death," *The Independent* (London), 25 January 1999, p. 11.
[68] "Social Work a 'Cover Up' for Conversions, Says VHP," *The Hindu*, 28 January 1999.
[69] Arun Shourie, *Missionaries in India: Continuities, Changes, Dilemmas* (New Delhi: ASA Publications, 1994) and *Harvesting Our Souls: Missionaries, Their Design, Their Claims* (New Delhi: ASA Publications, 2000).

ernment. Shourie maintains that the work of medical missionaries in colonial India was part of a coordinated effort by missionaries and colonial
administrators to extend British rule by converting and civilizing the native population. Medical missionaries to leprosy sufferers again entered
the debate when during a 1997 interview, Shourie, in remarking on the
missionaries' intentions, claimed:

> Every organization does some good—in this case estab-
> lishing educational institutions and hospitals and setting
> examples in leprosy work. But to me, missionaries in In-
> dia are what Gandhiji called "vendors of goods." They
> are in the business of body counts, numerical conver-
> sions. This has no relation to an individual's conviction.
> Gandhiji warned them that by pursuing numbers they
> were debasing the great example of Jesus, by using
> schools and hospitals to do so, they were robbing service
> of its nobility.[70]

Shourie's reference to leprosy missions—on the one hand praising it as
an example of good work, but quickly dismissing it as an example of the
failings of missionary work—underscores the enormous difficulty in
evaluating the legacy of Bailey and the Mission to Lepers. In describing
the Mission's efforts, John Jackson wrote in 1911 that, "a many-sided
work reveals itself...it is essentially *Christian*...eminently *philanthropic*
...*preventive*...and to a large extent *medical*."[71]

The murder of Graham Staines and his sons and the long history
of medical missionaries to lepers in India raises questions that are difficult for the historian to answer, but critical to understanding the encounter between Westerners and Indians in the colonial (and post-colonial)
context. Historians have to resist the temptation to tease apart the religious, political, and medical aspects of the missionary's work in nineteenth-century India. Rather their activities have to be regarded as one of
a myriad of cultural encounters that constituted Western imperialism. To
ask simply what was political or religious or medical about their work
overlooks the power and the consequences of the work as a whole. And
only in regarding the work of medical missionaries as a multi-faceted en-

---

[70] Interview of Arun Shourie by Sanghamitra Chakraborty, "They are only in the
business of body counts," *The Times of India*, 21 December 1997, editorial.
[71] Jackson, *Lepers*, 39.

terprise in which the religious, political, and medical were inextricably linked can the historian began to understand totality of the imperial agenda, but also the colonial response and post-colonial legacy that persists.

FRENCH MISSION WORK IN JAPAN: CULTURE AND RELIGION IN THE NINETEENTH CENTURY

Ann M. Harrington[*]

The story of Christianity in Japan remains one of the most fascinating in the history of religion. Introduced first in 1549 through the efforts of the Jesuits, Francis Xavier and his companions, Christianity made some inroads until Japanese officials banned it in 1618 and drove Westerners out of Japan in1639. The subject of Japanese Christianity piqued my interest in a graduate seminar on Japanese history. In one particular class we were discussing the influence of Christianity in Japan and someone made the comment was that it would be interesting to know what happened to Catholicism when it was forced underground for 250 years. The question caught my imagination and I set out to discover an answer.[1]

So began what has become a life-long interest. In an attempt to broaden the story of Roman Catholicism in Japan, this paper discusses the work of French missionary priests and women religious who worked in nineteenth-century Japan. I explore three questions: first, how French culture affected their life and work in Japan; second, what part Roman Catholic culture played in the lives of the priests and the sisters; and finally, how being male or female affected their work. I argue that the culture that most influenced the relative lack of success in proselytizing in Japan was the culture of the Roman Catholic Church, and show how that resulted in the fact that the women religious experienced more long-lasting success than the priests.

After Commodore Matthew C. Perry from the United States forced Japan to open its ports again to the West in 1853-54, other countries followed suit immediately. France, in the persons of the Paris Foreign Mission Society priests, won the right from the Pope to be the

---

[*] Ann M. Harrington, Associate Professor of History at Loyola University Chicago, teaches Japanese history and Asian Women's history. Her publications include a book, *Japan's Hidden Christians* (Chicago:Loyola University Press, 1993), and numerous articles. Her current research focuses on the work of the first Roman Catholic sisters to go to Japan as missionaries. They represented three religious orders, all from France, and went to Japan in 1872, 1877, 1878.
[1] For some answers to the question see Harrington, *Japan's Hidden Christians*.

only clergy allowed to proselytize in Japan. The origins of the group date to 1660, and the men who joined were priest who wanted to dedicate their lives to mission work. They wanted exclusive rights to proselytize because they did not want a repeat of the bickering that had occurred during the first Christian period among the various religious groups regarding methods of conversion. The Jesuits had arrived first in 1549, then Franciscans in 1593, and the Dominicans and Augustinians in 1602. Eventually, all foreign priests were forced out of Japan on pain of death.

The Rites Controversy which had erupted in China in the late seventeenth and early eighteenth century revolved around whether it was a compromise of Roman Catholicism to use Chinese words to express Christian concepts, to relate Catholicism to Confucianism, and to allow Chinese converts to perform rites in honor of Confucius and their ancestors, according to Chinese custom. Just as Francis Xavier and his followers in Japan, the Jesuits in China believed that these practices in no way compromised the Catholic faith. Franciscan and Dominican missionaries were highly critical of what the Jesuits were doing and brought their criticisms to the attention of Rome.

The final solution to the rift among the missionaries came through a series of statements from the pope in 1704, 1715, and 1742, which forbade the missionaries to continue what today we might call enculturation. It was a sad chapter in Church history and its effects have yet to be fully eradicated. That this is the case is evidenced in the letter the Japanese bishops sent to the Vatican in 1997 protesting the advance directives for the Asian Synod to be held in 1998. Their main argument centered on the fact that one must win converts to Christianity in a different way from methods used in countries that are predominantly Christian. For example, one cannot begin with the message that Jesus Christ is the one, true savior. This immediately cuts off dialogue. One must live in such a way that Japanese will be attracted to Christianity and move from there. Rome's response showed clearly that the Vatican had not even begun to understand the challenges of the Roman Catholic priests and sisters in Japan, or in Asia for that matter.[2] It was into the post-Rites Controversy Church that Catholicism returned to nineteenth-century Japan.

Once the Paris Foreign Mission Society priests established themselves in Japan in the nineteenth century, some of the descendants of the

---

[2] See Thomas Fox, *Pentecost in Asia: A New Way of Being Church* (Maryknoll, New York: Orbis Press, 2002).

first Christians revealed themselves to a Paris Foreign Mission priest, Bernard Petitjean, in Nagasaki in 1865. From this point on, the priests tried to find other Christian descendants and they attempted to win them back to an orthodox practice of Catholicism. Of the group that had passed the faith along underground, about 30,000 wanted to practice their faith as their ancestors had taught them, and they remain today "hidden Christians." The remaining Christians regularized their baptisms and their marriages as taught by the French priests, and they became the link to Japan's Catholic past and the hope for a revival of Roman Catholicism in Japan. At this point the second century of Catholicism takes root.

Because of changes in spreading the faith after the Rites Controversy, the religion reintroduced into Japan in the second half of the nineteenth century carried all the trappings of the Western church. When one asks why Roman Catholicism was not more successful in winning converts during these days, several reasons can be given. First, Christianity was a foreign import and no attempt was made to seek ways to make it fit Japanese culture. Second, it came in with Westerners who quite literally forced their way into Japan, bringing missionaries and a foreign religion with them. So it has long carried the burden of being part of Western imperialism. In addition, the Japanese religious tradition, able to accommodate several religious beliefs at once, found no flexibility in the claims of Roman Catholicism presented as the one, true faith. This obviously would prevent any significant dialog with other religious beliefs so integral a part of Japanese cultural life. And, finally, the plurality of Christian beliefs introduced into Japan during these days by Episcopalians, Presbyterians, Roman Catholics, and others, in seeming and actual competition with each other, confused the Japanese. The nineteenth century missionaries, on the other hand, saw Japan as especially attractive because of the aborted efforts toward conversion in the sixteenth and seventeenth centuries. In addition, because so many Japanese died for the faith, they saw Japan as a fertile field for the return of Catholicism.

As the Paris Foreign Mission priests began their proselytizing they realized they needed assistance. Three French congregations of women religious responded to the requests of the priests for help and sent sisters to Japan. The first to arrive, in 1872, were five Sisters of the Infant Jesus, also known as the Sisters of St. Maur, from Paris.[3] Founded in 1662 to teach the young, they retained that goal when they reestablished

---

[3] The official name of the order is Congrégation des Soeurs de l'Instruction Charitable du Saint Enfant-Jésus.

themselves after the French Revolution.[4] The Sisters of the Infant Jesus of Chauffailles, a new congregation that had its beginnings in 1859, followed them five years later; they were dedicated to education and social work.[5] And finally, in 1878, the Sisters of St. Paul of Chartres, a congregation dating back to the last years of the seventeenth century, took up residence in Hakodate on the northern most Japanese island of Hokkaido. This group was known especially in the area of health care and social work, but they were also involved in education.

One does not find in the letters of the priests or the sisters any indication that they felt themselves to be representatives of France, or that they were in anyway working in Japan for the glory of France. Rather, one finds French or Western influences arising in the very situations of their lives, such as the architecture of their churches and residences, the food they chose to eat, and, most obviously, the religion they practiced. During the first years of their life in Japan, all foreigners were required to live in the newly opened treaty port towns in areas designated for foreigners. This resulted in the development of foreign settlements in Yokohama, Tokyo, Kobe, Hakodate, Niigata, and Nagasaki.

As early as 1859, the Japanese government allowed the priests to provide religious services, but these were to be exclusively for the French residents in Japan. The priests immediately built Western style churches in Yokohama (1861) and in Nagasaki (1865). One might argue that these were Western style because they were for Westerners, but the sole reason for the priests' presence in Japan was to convert Japanese to Catholicism; they tolerated the existing condition only as a means of taking up residence in Japan. There was no doubt in the minds of the priests that these buildings were for the Japanese ultimately. Thus, gothic, Romanesque and baroque architecture signaled Roman Catholic and other Christian places of worship.

The letters of the first sisters indicate that soon after arrival they constructed residences that complied with their French and religious lifestyle. For example, the house the priests had obtained for the sisters is described as "too small for us to dream of establishing ourselves here permanently." Further, the document mentions that the sisters found a

---

[4] For more information on the work of the women religious see Ann M. Harrington, "The First Women Religious in Japan: Mother Saint Mathilde Raclot and the French Connection," *The Catholic Historical Review*, Vol. LXXXVII, N. 4 (October, 2001), 603-623.
[5] The founder of this order broke away from the Congrégation des Dames de l'Instruction du Puy, founded in the seventeenth century.

piece of land on the bluff in Yokohama where they built a place big enough to accommodate classes and an oratory for the sisters.[6] Not impressed with the Japanese wood and paper style buildings, Mother Saint Mathilde Raclot, one of the first sisters in Japan, took it upon herself to show the Japanese workmen how to make good mortar.[7] According to the "Journal" of Sister Saint Martha Aginel, not dated but written between 1873 and 1877, the sisters had beds as in Europe; the children slept on the tatami mats, undoubtedly on futon.[8]

When one reads the treaty-port newspapers of the time, for example *L'Echo du Japon*, published in Yokohama from 1870 to 1885, it is clear that every conceivable item of want or need was available in the treaty ports, from French wine to French pastry. The talk of food in their letters demonstrates that the sisters continued to eat French food, and found the Japanese cuisine less than adequate. For example, one of the early women religious says, "I do not know of a people who eat more poorly than the Japanese. Never meat, never fat or oil, or butter in the preparation of their fish or vegetables. Their fruits are without taste, and they don't ripen."[9] Sister Saint Martha remarks, "[T]he vegetables all have a taste and an odor that is unbearable."[10] Michel Sauret, one of the priests who had accustomed himself to Japanese food describes his diet: white rice cooked in water, flavored with tea or soy sauce, boiled or salted vegetables, and sometimes a little fish. "This is my ordinary meal morning, noon and night."[11] It appears that many of the French priests lived in Japanese style houses, probably because many lived alone in remote areas of Japan, while the sisters, in greater numbers, lived in larger groups connected to their schools, clinics or orphanages.

In terms of Japanese customs, Mother Mathilde tells her mother

---

[6] "Rélation sur Yokohama," unpublished manuscript written by Mother Saint Mathilde Raclot, Archives, *Soeurs de l'Enfant-Jésus*, Paris, 18. These archives hereafter cited as ASEJ. Note that in referring to Mother Saint Mathilde the French sources often leave out the "saint," so I have followed that practice in the remainder of the paper.

[7] ASEJ, "Vie de la Reverende Mère Sainte Mathilde," unpublished handwritten account in French by a contemporary, Marie-Louise Flachaire de Roustan, 528. Hereafter cited as "Vie."

[8] ASEJ, Sister Saint Martha Aginel, "Journal de Sr Ste Marthe Aginel," (unpublished manuscript, 1873-1877). Hereafter cited as "Journal."

[9] ASEJ, letter written by Mother Mathilde Raclot, August 27, 1872.

[10] ASEJ, letter written by Sister St. Martha, Jan. 4, 1974.

[11] Letter of M. Sauret, November 18, 1880 in *Annales de laPropagation de la Foi* Vol. 53, 1881, 243.

superior in Paris, in somewhat self-congratulatory prose, about her effort to "conform to all the Japanese demands [of etiquette]" during a visit of three dignitaries from a nearby village to their Yokohama establishment. She describes her accommodation. "I sat on the tatami mats on the floor with them, I took tea with them, holding the tiny cup to my lips with both hands, ate with them the bread and cake, as they would offer in similar circumstances. They laughed at my clumsiness and seemed happy to see me follow their customs." She goes on to show her continued attempts to follow Japanese custom, "I inhaled and exhaled forcefully after each swallow of tea in order to savor the scent with more show of feeling, and I would sniff again every ten or twelve minutes in order never to be behind the good gentlemen." In explaining her reasons for her actions, she says that one "must sacrifice one's self and one's times for the good of souls."[12] Clearly, this proves that this was not the ordinary lifestyle of the sisters.

These elements of material culture seem relatively unimportant today and how these early priests and sisters accommodated themselves to Japanese mores is the subject of another paper. A much more telling lack of understanding, given their reasons for being in Japan, is their attitude toward Japanese religions. And this comes from the culture of the Roman Catholic Church, which I argue was the most influential culture determining their life in Japan.

France has long borne the title of the eldest daughter of the Catholic Church. The French Revolution and its resultant chaos profoundly shook the foundations of French Catholicism. Under Napoleon, peace with the church was again established but with severe restrictions. Those persons who chose to live their lives as priests or religious sisters clung to the faith in the pre-revolutionary way that allowed no distinction between being French and being Roman Catholic. And in the nineteenth century they embraced a Catholic faith that rejected the world as a vale of tears and a place of evil; a faith that emphasized moral behavior (especially in regard to sexual matters); and a faith that sought to bring about proper behavior by the preaching of punishments here and hereafter if one sinned.[13]

On a societal level, the writings of the institutional Church of the

---

[12] ASEJ, Letter of Mother Mathilde Raclot to the Mother Superior, March 1, 1880.
[13] Ralph Gibson, *A Social History of French Catholicism 1789-1914* (London and New York: Rutledge, 1989), 54; 241-248.

time emerge as equally stringent. For example, Pope Pius IX's encyclical *Quanta Cura* (September 1864) attacks the major intellectual trends of the time, such as rationalism, salvation outside the Catholic Church, separation of church and state, political liberalism, and the idea of progress.[14] The *Syllabus of Errors* published along with that encyclical attacked current trends such as naturalism, pantheism, indifferentism, utilitarianism and it ends with the biting statement, "If anyone thinks that the Roman Pontiff can and should reconcile himself and come to terms with progress, liberalism, and with modern civilization, let him be anathema."[15]

The Japan of the 1870s and 1880s was in a serious struggle to become equal to the West, which had forced Japan into trade relations. To the frustration of the priests and sisters, the only way the Japanese could compete was by injecting some elements of progress, liberalism and modern civilization into Japanese politics and society. In fact, Japan in those years was in the heyday of a movement called Bummei Kaika -- Civilization and Enlightenment -- which looked to eradicate all in Japan's past institutions and learning that hindered Japan's ability to compete with the West. One Japanese intellectual went so far as to say "all Japan has to be proud of ...is its scenery."[16]

The Japanese in the last third of the nineteenth century sought answers in the civilization and enlightenment that came from the West. For a brief period of time, Christianity held some favor as a potential key to Western wealth and power, but here Protestantism, much more at home in the modern world, proved more popular to the Japanese. By the mid-to-late 1880s, preoccupation with things Western began to fade, and with it the passing interest even in Protestant Christianity. What the Japanese embraced were the very concepts and practices that the Roman Catholic Church rejected, namely, progress, science and technology, and utilitarian knowledge. Monsignor Bernard Petitjean laments in his 1875 account to the Paris headquarters, that an obstacle to preaching Christian-

---

[14] See Gordon Craig, *Europe Since 1815* (Hinsdale, IL: The Dryden Press, 1974), 106. For an English translation of the encyclical, see the *Dublin Review* Vol. 4: 500-513.

[15] See *Henri Daniel-Rops, The Church in an Age of Revolution 1789-1870,* trans. by John Warrington (New York: E.P. Dutton & Inc., 1965), 283-284. For a translation of the Syllabus, see *Dublin Review* Vol. 4: 513-529.

[16] See Albert Craig, "Fukuzawa Yukichi: The Philosophical Foundations of Meiji Nationalism," in *Political Development in Modern Japan*, Robert Ward, ed. (Princeton: Princeton U. Press, 1968), 120-121.

ity is the bad influence of the "'pretended' progress, as one understands it today. The government schools, as well as certain private schools opened by Japanese who studied in Europe, promise only the fruits of materialism, of atheism and of immorality."[17] And Mother Mathilde Raclot makes a similar point when she complains about the bad example of Western Christians in Japan involved in commerce. She writes they are able to go anywhere, even to the palace of the princes, "in order to fool them and steal their gold." And she goes on to say that the representatives of France and England lack faith. "They have a lot of prudence, of worldly wisdom, and do not aim for anything higher than those virtues."[18]

The certainty of truth embedded in the Catholic teachings made compromise with the indigenous beliefs of Japanese unacceptable, and appreciation of them or sensitivity to them by both the priests and the sisters impossible. One finds numerous instances in the letters of both the priests and the sisters lamenting that the followers of the Japanese beliefs are living in darkness; that they are in error and are missing out on living the true faith. Some of the sisters were not below indulging in deception, so convinced were they that only conversion to the faith would save a child. For example, a sister of St. Paul de Chartres, Sister Marie Auguste, writes from Hakodate to her mother superior in France that, just when she was feeling her efforts in vain as she tried to bring light to "the pagans made obstinate by their blindness," she encountered a baby with no more than a cold. The child's mother says to her that there is nothing that can be done for the child. "He is lost." Marie Auguste replies, "He is indeed ill...but I have a medication which will perhaps do him some good; one simply applies it on his forehead. Would you permit me to try it?" The mother answers, "Yes, of course." Marie Auguste ends her story with, "And the baby is baptized; one more angel."[19]

A second instance of a surreptitious baptism proves more unsettling to all concerned. Again a sister of St. Paul de Chartres was stopped on the street by a three or four year old boy in Hakodate. He asked the sister to visit his house because his sister was ill. When the sister arrived, the parents, visibly annoyed, said no, they had not sent for her. She asked

---

[17] Société des Missions-Étrangères de Paris, *Compte Rendu des Travaux*, 1875.
[18] ASEJ, letters from Mother Mathilde Raclot to the mother house in Paris, Jan. 14, 1877 and July 17, 1872. Grace Fox expresses this same idea in *Britain and Japan 1858-1883* (Oxford: Clarendon Press, 1969), 517.
[19] *Annales de l'Oeuvre de la Sainte-Enfance*, N. 291 (August 1896), 235.

if she might see the sick child. Explaining that to refuse would go against the Japanese sense of civility, she says that the parents let her in. After examining the child, she asked the mother if she might try her remedy. The hesitant mother finally consented while the father quietly grumbled. Suddenly, the sister experienced an inexplicable discomfort along with great fear. Hurrying so she could leave the house, she took her flask of blessed water and in a low voice pronounced the words of baptism over the dying child. At that moment, an inhuman cry was heard. Frozen with fear, the sister turned her head. The father, who had become very tense, and whose face showed his rage, gave her looks filled with fury and appeared to her filled with hate, a satanic hate. Terrified, she quickly fled. The sisters learned that the father had given the child to the devil. They concluded that at the instant of baptism, the bad spirit, seeing his prey rise up, let out the desperate cry heard by the sister, which the father understood.[20] These two stories show the lengths some of the sisters went to save souls they deemed lost without baptism. The added supernatural elements in the second story speak to the importance of their work and the power of evil.

Mother Mathilde Raclot, after describing a religious exercise performed by a follower of Amida Buddha, says, "My God, when then will the divine light illumine with its sweet rays the hearts of these foolish (*insensés*) people. Why can we bring the light to such a small number? Why so few fathers of families?"[21] Sister Saint Martha Aginel, in her "Journal" asks "prayers for all these poor Japanese who do not know the good God: most adore the sun, others the abominable idols called *kami*."[22] In yet another letter that same year, Sister Saint Martha writes of a child of African descent who was brought to the sisters. A young Japanese man who was taking instructions to become Christian was shocked to see a black child. "I responded to him, 'Your soul is blacker than her skin because you are not Christian.'"[23] Finally, Sister Mary Justine of the Sisters of the Infant Jesus of Chauffailles records the following on April 21, 1881. "How sad to it is to see the blindness of this people, otherwise so intelligent and so full of talent." She goes on to say that the very fact

---

[20] Jean Vaudon, *Les filles de St. Paul au Japon* (Chartres, France: Procure des Soeurs de St-Paul, 1931), 12-13.
[21] ASEJ, letter, January 14, 1877.
[22] ASEJ, "Journal." *Kami* refers to the gods of the Shinto religion, Japan's indigenous religion.
[23] ASEJ, July 8, 1874.

of the sisters' presence in Japan reveals to the Japanese the true God.[24] The rigidity of Catholicism carried to extremes by one sister, however, proved, at least to Mother Mathilde, that the sister in question was no longer able to serve the mission satisfactorily. She writes to the mother superior in Paris that the sister says she "is unable to believe it is God's will that she care for the children, most of whom are illegitimate, nor is she able to love them."[25] The sister was promptly sent home.

Protestants come in for some rather severe criticism from the priests and the sisters. However, in all fairness, it should be noted that Mother Mathilde Raclot goes out of her way to speak of some Protestants who aided the work of the sisters. In a letter written in December of 1879, she mentions that there were some Protestants who donated money to help the sisters care for the children at Christmas time, including an upper class Protestant women and a banker.[26] Interestingly enough, Protestantism is blamed for some of the failures of the Catholic mission as Mother Mathilde bemoans the seemingly enormous sums that the Protestant missionaries had to further their work. In a letter to the Saint-Enfance, a fund raising group in Paris, she wrote in 1875:

> The Protestants are profiting from our poverty, from our powerlessness, to establish themselves throughout Japan. They already have more than 50 ministers with their wives and children, in the capital, where they spend considerable sums of money building churches, opening schools in all the big centers; almost every trunk from England and America brings them aid. To counterbalance all that, the missionaries and the sisters have only weeping (*gemissements*) and tears.[27]

She remarked, "The Japanese feel the absurdity of their religion and desire to know the truth. It is painful to see here apostles of lies and errors [the Protestant missionaries] more numerous than the envoys of the Holy Church. It is true that the former make more noise than work, but they are not the less an obstacle to good."[28] Sister Saint Martha adds

---

[24] Letter to the Sainte Enfance, *Annales de l'Oeuvre de la Sainte-Enfance,* Vol. 17, N. 202 (1881), 323
[25] ASEJ, July, 1878.
[26] ASEJ, December 27, 1879.
[27] ASEJ, Letter from Singapore to the Sainte-Enfance, September 9, 1875.
[28] ASEJ, Letter, March 19, 1876.

that the "Protestants do a lot of harm, and they are in great numbers."[29]

Michel Sauret, a Paris Foreign Mission priest, commenting on the same theme, throws in a judgment on the Japanese.

> If we Catholics were alone in Japan our position would be beautiful, however, the Japanese, seeing the divisions which exist between Catholics, Protestants and Russians, figure that the Christian religion is the same thing as Buddhism, which is to say it is divided into a number of sects and it is impossible to discover which is the true one. As they are superficial in all they do, they do not take the trouble to discover the difference.[30]

Since both the priests and sisters held these rigid views toward Japanese non-believers and European and American Protestant missionaries, did being male or female make any difference in their work? The priests commenced their preaching illegally as they sought out the descendants of Japan's first Christians who had kept the faith alive underground for 250 years. For the most part, these folks were farmers and fishermen, living in areas outside the mainstream, which was the only way they could continue the practice of their secret religion. Once restrictions were lifted, the priests expanded to urban areas, but their message, couched in the rigid stance of the Catholic Church, was not exactly what the Japanese, aspiring to improve their lot, wanted to hear. The work of the French priests consisted primarily of proselytizing; they were not trained as educators or in health care. They engaged Japanese Christians to carry out some of these works for them until they could bring in resources from France.[31]

Only when it became clear that the Japanese government was no longer going to persecute those who practiced and preached Christianity did the priests invite French women religious to join them in Japan. The women religious provide an interesting contrast to the priests. Though they embraced the same dogmatic Catholicism, they belonged to religious orders that had broken from the formerly more prevalent cloistered way of life, which demanded a life lived as much as possible out of contact with the world. Perhaps for this very reason, the numbers of women

---

[29] ASEJ, Letter, 1874.
[30] *Les Missions Catholiques,* XIX, 1887, 101.
[31] See Harrington, *Japan's Hidden Christians.*

entering these active congregations mushroomed in nineteenth century France, growing from 12,300 in 1808 to 135, 000 by 1878.[32] Because the Napoleonic Code of 1804 greatly restricted women's rights, religious orders of women provided the only place where women could exercise their considerable talents outside of marriage and motherhood.[33]

These women arrived with virtually no knowledge of Japanese language, little knowledge of the culture, but with the requisite skills to open orphanages, schools, and medical clinics. Their first work in all cases was with orphans. Japan was in the throes of a major political and economic change. Just four years earlier, 1868, the Japanese overthrew their feudal government in the Meiji Restoration, and they were in the process of creating a new government and reforming their social structure. The Charter Oath proclaimed, "Knowledge will be sought from all over the world."

The country had begun serious efforts toward modernization and industrialization. As in the West, this resulted in major dislocation for many, with evidence of poverty and inability to care for children on the rise. The sisters located themselves in the treaty port towns of Yokohama, Tokyo, Kobe, Hakodate, Niigata, and Nagasaki and were able to care for orphans without knowing the Japanese language. For example, as early as 1873, one of the priests reports that the girls' school in Yokohama had 15 European boarders and 36 orphans.[34] The sisters in Kobe had an infant delivered to them the day after their arrival. The child had no blanket, so they took clothes from their suitcases to wrap the baby. Because they were initially without furniture, they used their suitcases as beds for the orphans.[35] According to a report dated December 21, 1877, the sisters already had turned away children because of the lack of resources.[36]

Almost immediately, the sisters opened medical clinics and had numerous clients. The sisters in Hakodate reported that one month after

---

[32] Claude Langlois, *Le catholicisme au féminism: Les congrégations françaises a supérieure générale au XIXe siècle* (Paris: Editions du Cerf, 1984), 321.

[33] Ralph Gibson, *A Social History of French Catholicism, 1789-1914* (New York: Rutledge, 1989), 118-119.

[34] ASEJ, from "Vie," 517, taken from note from the Paris Foreign Mission Society *Compte Rendu de la Mission*, 1873.

[35] Soeurs de l'Enfant-Jésus de Chauffailles, *Cheminement avec le Seigneur 1877-1977*, p 21; Georges Goyau, *La France Missionnaire Dans les Cinq Parties du Monde*, vol. 2, (Paris: Société de l'Histoire Nationale, 1948), 255.

[36] *Les Missions Catholiques*, n. 446, 618.

their arrival, they were already serving an average of 25 persons a day in the medical clinic they had set up.[37] For the most part during these early years, they dealt with foreign residents in Japan and the disadvantaged. The work that has endured and been most effective is education. Once the sisters sufficiently established themselves and were able to hire Japanese teachers, they developed schools, which eventually won recognition from the Japanese government. Some of these schools were designed to serve the poor while others eventually catered to the elite in Japanese society.

For example, the Sisters of St. Maur established schools for Japanese and Europeans in Yokohama. The primary school originated for orphans, but soon began admitting day students from the area. By 1875, the sisters opened similar establishments in Tokyo. In 1898, a secondary school was added. That same year, in order to reach some members of the upper class, the sisters began a course in foreign languages and arts for girls. It began with three students; by 1903 there were 48; 120 in 1913; and by 1923, more than 400. And thus began what has been the most enduring contribution of women religious: the teaching of the culture and languages of the West. In addition they offered first-rate education for women and girls in compliance with the Japanese government guidelines, once these became binding on all schools in Japan. While their care of orphans and the sick certainly provided a service to nineteenth-century Japan, more long-lasting have been the educational institutions founded by members of all three of the first religious orders of women to go to Japan.

We have already mentioned the status of women in France; the position of women in the Church was no better. For example, because women could not become priests they could not, strictly speaking, be called missionaries. That term, according to the Roman Catholic Church's Code of Canon Law, referred exclusively to clerics subject to the jurisdiction of the Propagation of the Faith. The sisters were in Japan as assistants to the priests. In the letters written by these early sisters to their foundation houses in France, they refer to themselves as the "sisters" and the priests as the "missionaries."[38]

---

[37] Francisque Marnas, *La Religion de Jésus réssuscité au Japon dans la seconde moitié du XIXe siècle,* vol. 2 (Paris: Delhomme et Briquet, 1896-97), 371-372.

[38] For example, recall the March 19, 1876 letter of Mother Mathilde cited above where she writes: "the missionaries and the sisters have only weeping..." This is common practice in the sisters' and priests' letters at this time.

The priests obviously spent their days trying to win souls to Catholicism. The sisters, too, had this as their ultimate aim, but they had to do this through their works, namely, schools, orphanages, medical clinics, workshops for women. However, a Japanese could partake of and benefit from these endeavors, and not become Catholic. Whereas in dealing with the priests, once a Japanese had rejected the faith, the conversation was over.

Thus, it appears that, because the sisters were relegated to this "assistant" status, they were able to exercise their talents in a way that was impossible for the priests. Many of the schools that they began in the 1870s, 1880s and 1890s continue to exist today; they serve a predominantly non-Catholic population, and are fully accredited by the Japanese government. All three religious congregations of women still have sisters in Japan and most if not all are Japanese. Their influence has been primarily through their educational institutions.

The priests, on the other hand, certainly succeeded in ordaining Japanese men to the priesthood, but their numbers pale in comparison to the numbers of Japanese sisters. Because their work was confined to proselytizing, and their message was unbending due to the stance of the Church at that time, their fruits were limited. For example, in 1951, there were 195 Japanese priests and 1,874 women religious. The latest statistics indicate that there are 6,024 Japanese sisters and 970 Japanese priests.[39] This may also be a strong comment on the status of women in Japanese society, where Japanese women may see religious life as an outlet for their talents, just as Gibson argues was the case in nineteenth-century France.[40]

In conclusion, the priests obviously saw themselves as French and as Roman Catholic, but were able to separate themselves from the commercial aspects of nineteenth century France, those elements that embodied the modern, progressive, liberal side of the society. They held on to the old cultural ties that were acceptable to nineteenth century Catholicism. For example, Petitjean at one point taught French for the sole purpose of making himself known as a priest, "whose character is completely misrepresented or distorted (*denaturé*) by the Japanese government."[41]

---

[39] Catholic Population in Japan,
<http://www.cbcj.catholic.jp/jpn/data/00data.htm>
[40] See Gibson, *A Social History of French Catholicism 1789-1914*, 54; 241-248.
[41] *Annales de la Propagation de la Foi*, vol. 37, n. 222, 409.

The sisters, likewise, maintained those elements of being French that coincided with their faith. However, because of the nature of their work – conducting schools that offered good general education, along with instruction in French language, literature, music and needlework – their services became popular among those seeking to advance themselves in the new Japan. In addition, the sisters served the poor through their medical services, and their care and education of children who would not otherwise have had access to either. The Japanese, in turn, were able to take from the sisters in particular those elements of French culture that they felt would serve them in nineteenth-century Japan, while at the same time they could separate out the Catholic religion. Protestant Christianity, while it was more in tune with the modern world at that time, was not all that much more successful by the late nineteenth century. What may be the case is that Japanese religious beliefs are so deeply embedded in the culture and of such a different nature from Western religious beliefs that an easy conversation has yet to emerge. What is evident is that the Japanese were able to do what they had done so successfully in their past history, that is, borrow and adapt what was practical for their needs, and discard or reject what did not fit.

CHRISTIAN ETHICS AND NATIVE CONCEPTS OF MORALITY IN WESTERN POLYNESIA

Jack A. Hill[*]

The South Pacific represents the last major region of the world to encounter Christianity. But when this contact occurred in the nineteenth century, first in Polynesia and later in Micronesia and Melanesia, it appeared to take hold with a vengeance.[1] According to historians, entire populations "converted" to the new faith, often at the behest of local political leaders, who found it advantageous for a variety of reasons to become Christians.[2] Polynesian islands such as Samoa, Tonga, Tuvalu and Tokelau quickly became some of the most monolithic Christian enclaves in the modern world. At one time there were a "greater number of pastors in the Pacific on a per capita basis than in any other part of the world, except for Japan."[3] Today, if one drives through any village in Samoa on a Sunday morning, one still finds young and old, dressed in white suits

---

[*] Dr. Jack A. Hill is Associate Professor of Social Ethics in the Religion Department at Texas Christian University. Dr. Hill is the author of *I-Sight: The World of Rastafari* (Scarecrow, 1995); *Seeds of Transformation: Discerning the Ethics of a New Generation* (Cluster Publications, 1998), and *Making Ethical Decisions* (Pacific Theological College Publications, 2002) in addition to numerous articles in journals and periodicals. His main research interests have focused on understanding the ethics of marginalized persons—the Rastafarians of Jamaica, freedom fighters in South Africa, and indigenous islanders in Fiji and Western Polynesia. Dr. Hill received his Ph.D. in Religion from Vanderbilt University, a Masters of Theological Studies from Harvard University, and a B.A. in Philosophy from Occidental College, Los Angeles.
[1] The South Pacific has been traditionally subdivided into the broad culture regions of Polynesia, Melanesia and Micronesia, although these categorizations are somewhat arbitrary. Geographically speaking, Polynesia includes islands within a triangle ranging from New Zealand eastward to Easter Island, and then north to the Hawaii group, including Tonga, Samoa, Tahiti, Tokelau and the Cook Islands. Melanesia refers to the islands west of Polynesia, including Fiji, New Caledonia, Vanuatu, the Solomon Islands and Papua New Guinea. Micronesia encompasses the smaller islands north of Melanesia and west of Polynesia, including Kiribati, the Federated States of Micronesia, the Marshall Islands, the Marianas and Guam.
[2] John Garrett, *To live among the stars: Christian origins in oceania* (Suva, Fiji: Institute of Pacific Studies, University of the South Pacific,1982), 5-6.
[3] D. Munro and A. Thornley, eds., "Editorial introduction - retrieving the pastors: Questions of representation and voice," in *The covenant makers: Island missionaries in the South Pacific* (Suva, Fiji: Pacific Theological College & the Institute of Pacific Studies, University of the South Pacific, 1996), 2-3.

and dresses, streaming to and fro from morning church services.

But as in nearly all cases of culture contact, the introduction of Christianity to the South Pacific was not a smooth, uniform or simple process.[4] The new faith was necessarily filtered through the pre-existing cultural lenses of Pacific island indigenous religious experience. In Polynesia, islanders who had been recently converted also frequently transmitted the faith, although the early European missionaries tended to use the term "teacher" for indigenous islander missionaries and reserve the term "pastor" for European missionaries.[5] In some instances, there were affinities between Christian beliefs and practices and indigenous traditions, but in many cases there were points of difference. Although missionaries often ran roughshod over valuable indigenous traditions, sometimes they challenged oppressive dimensions of indigenous authority structures.[6] As shall be argued below, occasionally the new faith was initially resisted with a passion, but then later gradually accepted and incorporated into the prevailing way of life.

Introduction: Tokelau as a Subject of Research

This paper explores the relationship between indigenous moral experience and the values introduced by Christian missionaries in some of the most remote islands in the South Pacific—the Tokelau Islands. The Tokelau Islands are three Western Polynesian[7] atolls (Fakaoho, Nukunonu and Atafu) located approximately three hundred miles north of Samoa. Focusing on these tiny islands as locales for comparative research is useful for several reasons. First of all, thanks to the extraordinary rich fieldwork of the anthropologists, Judith Huntsman and Antony Hooper, we have detailed transcripts of traditional Tokelauan oral narratives, recorded in Tokelauan and carefully translated into English just

---

[4] Daryl Whiteman has outlined the complex character of culture contact between Christianity and indigenous religions in the Melanesian context in *Melanesians and missionaries: An ethnohistorical study of social and religious change in the southwest Pacific* (Pasadena: William Carey Library, 1983), 3-29.
[5] R. Crocombe & M. Crocombe, eds., *The works of Ta-unga: Records of a Polynesian traveler in the South Seas, 1833-1876* (Canberra: Australian National University Press, 1968), xv.
[6] Jack Johnson-Hill makes this argument in "The missionary-islander encounter in Hawaii as an ethical resource for cross-cultural ministry today," *Missiology: An International Review*, 23(3), (1995): 309-330.
[7] Western Polynesia is a distinct culture area within Polynesia, in which different island groups share striking material, social, linguistic and historical similarities.

prior to major modern developments in the late 1970s.[8] Although there is probably no such thing as a purely "traditional" extant version of a Pacific Island oral narrative in the sense of a tale that is "pre-Christian" in all respects,[9] these narratives reference beliefs, figures, objects and events that point to the pre-Christian past. Some of these narratives are quite lengthy and none refer explicitly to Christian beliefs, figures or practices. This does not mean that Christian teaching did not influence them though. In fact, one of Huntsman's major informants, the renowned storyteller Palehau, once attended a Catholic school in Samoa. But, subtle Christian influences can, in part, be separated out from a text with careful attention to the conventions of narrative analysis.

Secondly, Tokelau represents a particularly rich context for cross-cultural analysis because of its extreme remoteness, even within the larger remote sub-culture area of Western Polynesia. In the first instance, atolls were unattractive destinations due to reefs and precipitous drop offs that made it impossible for large ships to enter a safe harbor or drop anchor nearby. For example, the three coral atolls of Tokelau rise steeply from the ocean floor. Moreover, atolls are small in size, low in elevation, have poor soil and have a very limited terrestrial biota. For passing whalers, they offered little more than coconuts for barter offshore.[10]

Moreover, Europeans did not exert substantial influence on Tokelau until the LMS and Catholic missionaries arrived in the mid-nineteenth century.[11] In fact, even though there were sporadic contacts with Europeans in the first half of the twentieth century, the Tokelau Islands were arguably "the least visited group of inhabited atolls in the

---

[8] Excellent texts of these narratives, in Tokelauan and English, can be found in Judith Huntsman, *Ten Tokelau tales*, Working Papers No. 47 (Auckland, New Zealand: University of Auckland, Department of Anthropology, 1977) and in her *Tokelau tales told by Manuele Palehau*, Working Papers No. 58 (Auckland, New Zealand: University of Auckland, Department of Anthropology, 1980).

[9] Basil Kirtley's research illustrates this point. See his "Some extraneous oceanic affinities of Polynesian narrative," in *Directions in Pacific traditional literature*, A. L. Kaeppler & H. A. Nimmo, eds. (Honolulu: Museum Press, 1976), 217-239.

[10] J. Huntsman & A. Hooper, *Tokelau: A historical ethnography* (Honolulu: University of Hawaii Press, 1996), 181.

[11] A. W. Whistler, "Ethnobotany of Tokelau: The plants, their Tokelau names and their uses," *Economic Botany* 42(2), (1988): 156.

South-west Pacific."[12] When Huntsman arrived in the late 1960s, she found islands where a subsistence economy was the norm, most homes were constructed of thatch, and oral performance and traditional arts were still central to cultural life. In Huntsman's words, it was still possible to identify an "ethnographic present" (the period between 1967 and 1971) that preceded the rapid onset of modern western development.[13] In fact, it was only after this period that Tokelauans began to distinguish between *pototudi* (the old understandings) and *poto fou* (the new understandings) in their language.[14] Consequently, the tales that Huntsman recorded were still narratives of older times. It is interesting to note that Tokelau remained the very last nation to establish satellite communications with the rest of the world in 1997.

Third, the legends Huntsman recorded were primarily drawn from the Tokelauan atoll of Nukunonu, where Christian influences had somewhat of a limited impact on indigenous traditions or oral performance. Huntsman notes that on Nukunonu, traditions of story telling were much better preserved than on Fakaoho or Atafu.[15] She argues that this was due in large measure to the fact that Nukunonu was a Catholic mission field, whereas Atafu and Fakaoho were evangelized by LMS missionaries (although there was a minority Catholic presence on Fakaoho as well). Huntsman states that the Catholic priests tended to leave the cultural practices alone, whereas the Protestants sought to convert Tokelauans to a whole new way of life and actively undermined certain indigenous practices which were viewed as in any way in competition with Christian faith and practice.

Furthermore, there was a degree of resistance to British cultural influence on Nukunonu that was not present on the other two atolls. Nukunonians tended to align with the loyalties of the French Marist missionaries who introduced Catholicism in their atoll.[16] After Tokelau became a British Protectorate in 1889, the Union Jack was graciously accepted and flown in Fakaoho and Atafu. But in Nukunonu, the chiefs and elders did not want the flag flown. A visiting priest reported that one of

---

[12] J. Thornton, "Notes and queries: Field notes and three legends recorded in the Tokelau Islands," *Journal of the Polynesian Society,* 64(2), (1955): 246.

[13] Huntsman & Hooper, *Tokelau: A historical ethnography,* 8.

[14] Ibid., 9.

[15] Huntsman, *Tokelau tales told by Manuele Palehau,* x-xiv.

[16] T.B. Cusack-Smith, *Report of a visit to Manua and the Union Islands,* Unpublished manuscript, Western Pacific High Commission, Inwards Correspondence 230/96, (1896).

the local Nukunonu *aliki* (chiefs) once said:

> Tell the *aliki vaka* (captain) that we do not know *Vikatoria*
> (Queen Victoria); she is in *Papalagi* (Europe) and I am here;
> she should stay there and not come here and bother me…We
> do not want anything to do with her flag; can you not see
> that our's is flying above our heads…take your's away…we
> will never agree to what you have brought to our island;
> your flag will never replace ours.[17]

Although British authorities subsequently raised the British flag, it was
done over the objections of Nukunonu leaders. Moreover, the nature of
the early missionary enterprise in Nukunonu was such that reading was
not emphasized to the extent that it was in the other two Protestant-
dominated atolls.

These historical notes illustrate the fact that the nature of the first
contacts between the indigenous cultures of Tokelau and Missionary
Christianity varied considerably among the atolls. Accordingly, in this
analysis I seek to examine the nature of the transformations of moral experience in Tokelau with due regard to these variations. At the same
time, it is also the case that certain generalizations can be articulated with
reference to the group as a whole. In this paper, I will first outline a few
of the core indigenous moral values in the atolls and then describe the
moral values of one of the two major missionary groups which established churches in Tokelau—the London Missionary Society.[18] I will
then conclude by noting three ways in which Tokelauans have interrelated these contrasting sets of moral values in their Christian ethics

---

[17] J. Huntsman & A. Hooper, "Structures of Tokelau history," in *Transformations of Polynesian culture,* Huntsman & Hooper, eds. (Auckland: Polynesian
Society, 1985), 135. Huntsman and Hooper note that the reference to "our flag"
is to the "flag of Mary" given to the Nukunonians by the French Marist Mission.
[18] There is not space here to develop an account of the other group, the Societe
de Marie (Society of Mary), known as the Marists. The Marists established their
primary Tokelau mission on Nukunonu, where virtually the entire population
was converted to Catholicism. For historical references to the Marist mission in
Polynesia, see Ralph M. Wiltgen, *The founding of the Roman Catholic Church
in Oceania: 1825 – 1850* (Canberra: Australia National University Press, 1979).
For a fascinating account of the earliest mission forays in Tokelau, see A. Mon-
fat, *Les Samoa du Archipel des Navigateurs* (Lyon: Emmanuel Vitte, 1890).
These manuscripts are housed in the Marist Archives, 78 Hobson St., Wellington, N.Z.

today. I will argue that Tokelauans were not simply passive victims dominated by European colonizers, but that they creatively and pragmatically appropriated and transformed Missionary Christian teachings in the light of their own cultural heritage. Although I am cognizant of many of the abuses and imperialistic practices of the missionary movements in question, the point of this paper is to explicate the senses in which Tokelauans played constructive roles in re-framing their moral universe, often in spite of external assaults on their very existence.

The *Faka Tokelau* (Tokelau Way)

The task of delineating what is distinctly "Tokelauan" is fraught with difficulty because, as with atolls in general, "everything has come from somewhere else."[19] The very material substance of the inhabited atolls consists of wave deposited coralline sand and gravel derived from the adjacent reef and lagoon.[20] Aboriginals introduced the two most important trees (*niu* [coconut palm] and *pandanus*), and Samoans probably introduced banana and papaya trees.[21] While local storytellers claim that the original inhabitants of Tokelau were there from the very beginning, scholars argue that the ancient ancestors migrated from distant islands. One indication that there may have been early migrations within Western Polynesia is that the Tokelau language is a member of the Samoic-Outlier subgroup of nuclear Polynesian languages,[22] and Tokelauan songs include borrowings from Samoa and Tuvalu.[23] Consequently, to speak of an "indigenous tradition" with regard to Tokelau, is to speak of recollections and ways of life that reflect multi-cultural influences.

Nevertheless, Tokelauans speak a distinctive language and have

---

[19] Peniamina Ieremina, interview aboard the *M.V.Tokelau*, 22 May 2002. Rev. Ieremina is a native of Atafu who who pastors a congregation in N.S.W., Australia.

[20] R. McLean & A. M. d'Aubert, *Implications of climate changes and sea level rise for Tokelau: Report of a preparatory mission*, SPREP Reports and Studies Series No. 61 (Apia: South Pacific Regional Environmental Programme, 1993), 6.

[21] W.A. Whistler, "Ethnobotany of Tokelau: The plants, their Tokelau names and their uses," *Economic Botany* 42/2 (April-June, 1988): 158.

[22] Arnfina M. Vonen, "The noun phrase in Samoan and Tokelauan," Thesis, University of Oslo, 1988, 1. Vonen cites as his source, B. Biggs, "The languages of Polynesia," in *Current Trends in Linguistics*: Vol. 8, T.A. Sebeak, ed. (The Hague: Mouton & Co., 1971), 466-505.

[23] A. Thomas, I. Tuia, & J. Huntsman, eds., *Songs and stories of Tokelau: An introduction to the cultural heritage* (Wellington: Victoria University Press, 1990), 9.

a distinctive folklore tradition. Although pronunciations are similar to other Polynesian languages, in established orthography there are peculiar differences exist. For example, the 'f' is spoken with a soft 'wh' sound and if the 'h' is preceded by 'a,' 'o,' or 'u,' it is sounded as if in combination with a 'y.' And although many Tokelau stories have affinities with those of other Polynesian peoples, Tokelau tales also have their own unique nuances, character portrayals and plot developments. One way to begin to explore the *Faka Tokelau* is to focus on the sense in which it is "grounded" in the sea.

When one first sees any one of the Tokelau atolls, one is struck by the sense in which each atoll is made up of many small *motu* (islets). These *motu* are contained within an encircling reef surrounding a large lagoon. The reef rims are continuous and there are no natural passages through them, such that they act as boundaries that block large vessels from gaining access to the islets. Most *motu* rise barely five to eight feet above sea level and many partially disappear at high tide. McLean and d'Aubert counted a total of 127 *motu* that together constituted only about 12 square kilometers.[24] By contrast, the total area of the three lagoons is 187 square kilometers.[25] The sea is the primary means of subsistence, and without fishing, the people would perish.[26] In interviews conducted a decade ago, residents remarked that the beauty of the lagoon, reefs and ocean was also a central element of the *Faka Tokelau*.[27] Fish feature prominently in *kakai* (fictional tales), *pehe* (songs) and dance themes. For example, in the Tale of the Tavake, fish are portrayed with human characteristics and meet to avenge the abduction of the heroine, Hina.[28] When the European missionaries first visited the islands, they learned that certain fish, such as '*a a*' and "*komotuio-utu*" were once regarded as sacred to the god, *Tui Tokelau*.[29]

The centrality of the sea and the mobility of islanders within it, suggest a key element of what might be called, a 'Tokelau way of think-

---

[24] McLean & d'Aubert, 6.
[25] Huntsman & Hooper, *Tokelau: A historical ethnography*, 2.
[26] Pio Tuia, interview, Nukunonu, 25 May 2002. Mr. Tuia was the *faipule* of Nukunonu at the date of the interview.
[27] McLean & d'Aubert, 31.
[28] Huntsman, *Tokelau tales told by Manuele Palehau*, 54-62.
[29] W.W. Gill & P.G. Bird, "Third missionary voyage of the *John Williams* to the Tokelau (or Union) group of islands, January 8-February 4, 1863," in *LMS South Sea Journals 1844-1871* (Wellington: Archives of New Zealand and the Pacific, Turnbull Library, National Library of New Zealand), Reel 8, 3.

ing.' There is a dialectical tendency—a continual movement outward, coupled with a return to a shared point of origination, traversed in a circular fashion. Survival in atolls necessitates leaving one's islet and venturing into the sea. And sea voyaging, in turn, is rarely a matter of taking the most direct linear route between two points, especially given changing directions of winds and currents. The circularity of this outward and inward movement is reflected in the circularity of the islets themselves, the lagoons, the demography of Fakaoho and alternations in wind currents.[30] Although marked by straight paths, Fakaoho is actually a village of concentric circles. While Atafu village is more open and diffuse and Nukunonu village is laid out in a grid-like pattern, one always has a sense of being encircled by the surrounding sea. A degree of circularity is also seen in the plots of tales, in which discord arises, action is taken in response to the discord and there is a return to the harmonious state that preceded the discord. It is reflected in the way in which the elders seat themselves in circles or semi-circles for traditional meetings and rituals.

As a basic feature of the Tokelau way of thinking, the to-and-fro dialectic of circularity represents a capacity for entertaining a number of options while deliberating on courses of action. It is often confounding and appears illogical to Europeans, who are used to thinking in more linear ways. Just as the circularity of islet, reef and lagoon influence Tokelauan senses of space, daily rhythmic alterations of life in the atolls shape the sense of time as well. The rising and falling of tides, large gatherings of birds in certain places, full moons, the sudden presence of a northeasterly wind—all of these types of phenomena influence decisions about when it is appropriate to fish or sail. And these decisions in turn influence other courses of action, such as eating meals, bathing or embarking upon a journey.

The ever-changing *M.V.Tokelau* boat schedule is a case in point.[31] On a recent voyage to Tokelau in May 2002, I was informed of five different schedule changes, entailing ongoing conversations between various parties—the ship's captain, administration officials in Samoa, government advisers in Tokelau and New Zealand, and traditional leaders in the islands, who are themselves responding to desires of present

---

[30] The author made the following observations during a visit to the atolls in May 2002.

[31] For a recent account of on-again off-again fluctuations regarding departure and arrival times, see Peter Methven, *Tokelau News*, 1/1 (Oct-Dec, 2001). This 32 page newsletter is located in the Manuscripts and Archives section of the Turnbull Library, National Library of New Zealand, Wellington.

and future passengers—all of whom lobby for changes to accommodate specific needs and events. After an extensive process of working through different informal proposals, one time is eventually agreed upon and the voyage ensues. In other words, time is "events-driven." It is much more a question of when conditions are right or of when people are ready to begin a certain activity, than it is of adherence to a preset, quantitatively measured chronology.

To sum up the points developed thus far, the *Faka Tokelau* is rooted in the sea and the livelihood, which the sea makes possible. Spatially, the circularity of islet, reef and lagoon in the atoll ecology, and the movement of persons in and among these circular spheres, is conducive to a Tokelau way of thinking—dialectic of venturing forth, entertaining various possibilities, and returning to a point of origin. Temporally, the natural rhythm of tides, the flights of birds and shifts in wind patterns give form and shape to a Tokelauan time sense.

Like the concepts of space and time, Tokelauan notions of sociality are also rooted in the atoll ecology. Although fish are plentiful, life is precarious. Until recently, there was often a shortage of water and severe drought was a life-threatening experience.[32] Due to the coral soil, the planting, nurturing and harvesting of crops often yields limited foodstuffs. Moreover, there was always a relatively small working-age population base in each of the villages. Consequently, in order to survive, let along develop recreational, educational and religious institutions, Tokelauans were forced to work together.

This need to cooperate—to pool and share available resources—especially in the procurement and distribution of food, lies at the core of Tokelauan social life. It is expressed in the terms *fakatahi* (to be as one together) and *fakamua* (communal, of the village).[33] "Everything is morally better done together than alone."[34] To actively join in group discussions and activities is to be *maopoopo* (to contribute to a sense of harmony or unity of spirit).[35] *Fakamua* can be contrasted with *fakamuli* (to

---

[32] In the past quarter century, as a result of New Zealand government development projects, there has been a widespread construction of concrete houses with permanent roofing material that allows for the catching and storage of rain water in tanks which are attached to most homes.

[33] Office of Tokelau Affairs, *Tokelau Dictionary* (Apia, Samoa: Office of Tokelau Affairs, 1986).

[34] Huntsman & Hooper, *Tokelau: A historical ethnography*, 9.

[35] Tuia, interview, Nukunonu, 25 May 2002.

remain at home, stay behind).[36] To *Fakamuli* is to act in solitary ways or to refrain from participating in a village activity.

In Tokelauan moral experience, *fakatahi* (communal solidarity) and *maopoopo* (unity) are linked to the concept of *pule* (authority). There is not enough space here to delineate the complex nature of the Tokelau polis, but suffice it to say that in formal settings persons still speak from *tulaga* (positions) or certain roles. These roles pertain to one's status as a child, married adult or elder. Gender roles are also clearly delineated and reflected in the Tokelauan saying, "*E nofo te fafine i loto, ka ko te tagata e fano i te auala*" (the woman stays inside while the man goes in the path).[37] For example, although gender roles are changing, the work lives of men traditionally took them outside the home while women tended to stay at home in the village.

Moreover, each village is governed by a *taupulega* or *fono toeaina* (council of elders), a *fai pule* (an administrative officer) and a *pulenuku* (mayor). Each of the three islands has its own *taupulega*, which is made up of representatives of the toeaina and may include the heads of all family units. The *pulenuku* directs the village work program and organizes daily local, routine activities, while the *fai pule* is the local representative of the New Zealand administration and magistrate. He oversees larger policies and represents the island at international gatherings. The pastor or priest also has a key status, especially because he is the mediator regarding knowledge of God's directives.[38]

These leaders have senior status in part because of age. To be an elder in the canoe's stern is metaphorically to be the person who is responsible for the safety of those in the village, in a way analogous to how the person who occupied the canoe's stern could be crucial to the survival of the crew. Similarly, the leadership of *toeaina* (elders/old men) is considered essential to the well being of the land-based canoe—the village. Younger, less experienced persons are to obey the commands of the *toeaina*, and younger women, children and youth are also to pay difference to *lomatutua* (older women). For instance, last year when six youth went fishing without prior sanction from the elders, they were summoned to appear before the *taupulega* (village council) and were chastised. Their punishment included doing two weeks of collecting rubbish and

---

[36] Office of Tolelau Affairs, *Tokelau Dictionary*.

[37] Huntsman & Hooper, *Tokelau: A historical ethnography*, 49.

[38] The use of the male pronoun is intentional in this instance because, as of the time of this writing, all of the pastors and priests in Tokelau have been male.

cleaning out septic tanks.[39] In another case, Methven noted that youth were sternly admonished for drinking and smoking.[40]

Huntsman and Hooper observe that an elder who occupies the stern of the canoe should not only be mature in age, but also wise due to his experience and penchant for "far-seeing," including "the ability to weigh all the implications of any decision rather than seeing only its immediate effects."[41] This capacity for perspicacity is another aspect of the Tokelau way of thinking discussed above. As a *toeaina* sifts through various scenarios for action, he not only entertains different ideas, but he also considers how unusual perspectives can be reconciled with the interests of the community as a whole. For instance, in some Tokelau tales, the voice of those on the margins is sometimes given special consideration, depending on the merits of the proposal (e.g., in the meeting of the fish in the Tale of the Tavake). And while decisions are ultimately made by the *toeaina*, they are "good" decisions only to the extent that they represent the consensus of the village. Actions will be *tolo* (postponed) if there is not unanimity of opinion.[42]

Along with seeking consensus, Tokelauans practice *inati* (sharing). Up to the present day, fish caught by a group of men in the village are equally distributed among all the families on the island. The *fai pule's* family receives no more than the family with the least social standing.[43] Early missionaries commented on how a well found in Fakaoho was "evidently intended for the use of all."[44] On formal occasions there are no prescribed seating arrangements according to age or status, as there are for example in Samoa or Fiji.[45] And, as Huntsman and Hooper state, even age and gender hierarchies reflected in the composi-

---

[39] Methven, 11.

[40] Ibid., 15.

[41] Huntsman & Hooper, *Tokelau: A historical ethnography*, 46.

[42] Huntsman & Hooper, Tokelau: A historical ethnography, 43.

[43] Tuia, interview, Nukunonu, 25 May 2002.

[44] Gill & Bird, Reel 8, 11.

[45] This observation is based on a first-hand experience of seating arrangements in the *falepa* (meeting house) during a welcome ceremony I attended in Atafu, which was later confirmed by interviews with Tokelauans. It should be noted in this connection that there is a degree of egalitarian sharing among Samoans and Fijians, within particular categories and groups. As early as 1858, George Stallworthy and George Gill observed that the cocoa nut and breadfruit trees were "all equally divided among the residential students" at the fledgling theological college in Samoa (1858). This was the first LMS missionary voyage to Tokelau where the aim was to establish a new missionary field at Fakaoho.

tion of the *taupulega* have an egalitarian dimension in that everyone can "look forward to having a greater say as the years go by."[46] Perhaps the most striking values of the *Faka Tokelau*, which are found throughout Polynesia, are generosity and gratitude. This spirit of beneficence is expressed in the Tokelauan word, *fealofani* (mutual compassion). The earliest missionaries noted numerous cases in which islanders willingly gave of their produce. For example, Gill observed that Fakaohoians gave them "a considerable number of coconuts" when they were departing and that these were "unasked for."[47]

This brief description of Tokelauan moral values—harmony, communal solidarity, authority and obedience, perspicacity in discerning the implications of actions, consensus, sharing, egalitarianism and mutual compassion—is only a general gloss of their moral universe. A careful analysis of oral narratives discloses a host of subtle moral nuances, including having *fakamita* (kind thoughts) for fauna, the special regard of brothers and sisters for each other, the loyalty and steadfastness of a devoted spouse, kind treatment of children, and disapproval of jealousy.[48] But for the sake of comparative inquiry regarding cross-cultural encounter, I shall now move to a parallel sketch of values associated with London Missionary Society (LMS) missionaries.

Missionary Christian Values

The vast majority of Protestant missionaries in the Pacific Islands were not Europeans, but Pacific Islanders.[49] In Tokelau, Faivalua, a Tokelauan originally from Fakaoho, was the first missionary to "bring the gospel."[50] At some point, Faivalua left Tokelau and became an LMS convert in Samoa. In the late 1850s he returned to Fakaoho, but his missionary endeavors were rejected there. He then traveled to Atafu where he is

---

[46] Huntsman & Hooper, *Tokelau: A historical ethnography*, 46.

[47] Gill & Bird, Reel 8, 12.

[48] For an explication of some of these themes, see Jack Hill, "A Postmodern interpretation of oral narrative: Interpreting indigenous moral knowledge of the Tokelau Islands into the discourse of comparative religious ethics." Paper presented at the meeting of the Southwest Commission on Religious Studies, Irving, Texas, March 9, 2002.

[49] D. Munro & A. Thornley, "Pacific Islander pastors and missionaries: Some historiographical and analytical issues," *Pacific Studies*, 23(3 & 4), (2000): 2.

[50] The ensuing historical sketch draws on my own archival research of missionary letters and archives in New Zealand (2001-2002), but also parallels the account provided by Huntsman & Hooper, *Tokelau: A historical ethnography*, 181-215.

credited with having been the original evangelist on the island. In 1861, Faivalu requested that the Samoan LMS mission send a "teacher," and then died shortly thereafter. Maka, a Rarotongan LMS teacher, then established the first church and school in Atafu.[51]

Mafala was a Samoan who became a teacher in Fakaoho in early 1863.[52] Although he departed soon after slavers ravaged the islands in the mid 1860s, he later returned to Fakaoho and became their first pastor in 1868. The third atoll, Nukunonu, was evangelized by Takua, who was the son of a high-ranking *aliki* (chief) in Nukunonu. In 1861, Takua initiated the conversion of the entire atoll to Catholicism, and had responsibility for the mission until the early 1900s.

In each of these cases, the Missionary Christian moral ethos was filtered through islander converts who themselves had been influenced and in many cases taught be either Protestant missionaries in Samoa and Rarotonga, or Catholic missionaries in Samoa, Uvea and Australia. One consequence of this early history of missionaries was that both Protestant churches in Atafu and Fakaoho, as well as the Catholic Church in Nukunonu, used the Samoan translation of the Bible. This is significant for several reasons. First, it meant that from the very beginning, Christian converts in Tokelau heard, and apparently soon began to read, the gospel in a Pacific language that had similarities with Tokelauan. Gill and Bird noted that twelve of the sixteen Atafuans on board the *John Williams* in 1863 could "read fluently" the Samoan scriptures.[53] It was consequently less "foreign" then it might otherwise have been, and it was preached and taught by fellow Polynesian islanders.

Second, unlike Tokelauans, Samoans developed two languages, one for common use in everyday life and another for formal use on special occasions, especially by chiefs and high-ranking persons when addressing important religious and moral concerns. The Bible was translated in this chiefly language.[54] Hence, the understanding and portrayal of Jesus was couched in chiefly terms such that the same word that was used for "chief" in Samoa was also used with reference to Jesus. Third, to study and develop expertise in using the Samoan Bible gener-

---

[51] Rarotonga is an island in the Cook Island group, south and east of Tokelau, where the LMS had established an early missionary outpost in Polynesia.
[52] Huntsman & Hooper, *Tokelau: A historical ethnology*, 195-196.
[53] Gill & Bird, Reel 8, 7.
[54] I am indebted to Dr. Jacques Nicole, formerly Lecturer in Biblical Studies, Pacific Theological College, Fiji, for this and other insights regarding the use and translation of the Samoan Bible.

ally meant studying it in the context of Samoan culture, if not directly under a Samoan teacher. This is significant because Samoan culture is generally much more hierarchical in practice than Tokelauan culture.[55] For example, the pastor has a pre-imminent status in Samoan society that he does not usually have in Tokelauan society, where he has been considered an outsider.

Thus, to inquire into the nature of Missionary Christian values in the Tokelauan context, is already to engage in a complex investigation of Polynesian (especially Samoan) as well as European (especially British Protestant and French Catholic) moral worlds. At the risk of grossly oversimplifying the task at hand, I would like to simply sketch out a few of the moral values that were expressed by early Protestant missionaries, primarily by Europeans, since the bulk of the nineteenth century historical documents were penned by Europeans. This way of proceeding can be helpful, because the early Polynesian missionaries were themselves ardent students of European instructors. They learned at the feet of the westerners and because their own cultural traditions placed such a high value on deference to authority and, at least in the case of many Samoans, passionate obedience to authorities, we can trust that they inculcated much of what the missionaries taught almost more intensely and thoroughly than European students on the continent might have done. Gill notes, "The islanders shame many who have long enjoyed higher privileges in their faithful devotion."[56]

As a case in point, Maka expressed moral sentiments about dress and literacy that are strikingly western.[57] Commenting on Atafuans, in contrast to Fakaohoians, Maka states that the former are "neatly and modestly attired to the best of their ability" and that "most of them can read."[58] Maka also states that there is scarcely a New Testament on Atafu and asks whether or not Samoans might be willing to donate one hundred copies when they have completed their publications of it. Maka thus af-

---

[55] Pat O'Connor, phone interview, Auckland, N.Z., 8 June 2002. Father O'Connor was Monsignor, Catholic Mission in Tokelau, at the date of the interview.

[56] Gill & Bird, Reel 8, 18.

[57] Nevertheless, British missionaries, who were clearly prepared to "hear" comments with reference to their own moral framework, recorded these sentiments. One should not underestimate the senses in which Maka was also perhaps telling the missionaries what he intuited that they wanted to hear. This said, it is also important to acknowledge that, as later developments in Tokelau validate, these moral sentiments did take root in Tokelauan church life.

[58] Gill & Bird, Reel 8, 17

firms the sense in which the new *loto* (religion) will entail a valuing of literacy, as well as "neatness" and "modesty." He also reported that "polygamy" had been essentially abolished, thus affirming the value of monogamy. Commenting on both Maka and Mafala's homes, Gill observes that they were plastered, as opposed to being made of pandanus leaf.[59] Further, Maka's home was furnished with a bedstead, table and chairs of his own making. The assumed superiority of western development regarding housing construction and household furnishings is thus implicit at the earliest stage of missionary activity in Tokelau.

Indeed, the missionaries were not only concerned about saving souls, but in transforming entire civilizations.[60] Material prosperity was not only equated with good living in terms of worldly success, but also viewed as evidence of spiritual progress.[61] Most of the LMS missionaries belonged to the lower middle classes of their societies and espoused Victorian English values. They saw their mission as both this-worldly and other-worldly—to bring the light of day upon far away "savages" not only by introducing them to the gospel, but by transforming their customary ways of life to conform to European standards of attire, education, governance, religion and family life.

Other western Christian values are explicitly and implicitly expressed by the early missionaries, including a stress on belief in "the True God," divine providence and denominational orthodoxy. Several reports relate seemingly miraculous stories of being led by the Christian God through storms at sea, epidemics and hostile encounters. From the very beginning, however, Protestants were virulently anti-Catholic and the Catholics were anti-Protestant. LMS missionaries characterized Catholic Nukunonu as a "dark island" bewitched by "popery."[62] The Catholic Fathers viewed the LMS dominated Fakaoho as an enclave of tyranny and intolerance. Thus, western European denominational and sectarian biases were transplanted to the Tokelauan context.

The missionaries also valued what they believed to be voluntarism. They praised the decision of a Nukunonian priest, Pou, because he decided to leave his home island so that he could freely practice his faith

---

[59] Ibid., 16

[60] For a discussion of this theme with regard to the early American Congregationalist missionaries in Hawaii, see Johnson-Hill, "The missionary-islander encounter in Hawaii as an ethical resource for cross-cultural ministry today."

[61] N. Gunson, Messengers of grace: Evangelical missionaries in the South Seas: 1797-1860 (Melbourne: Oxford University Press, 1978), 33.

[62] Gill & Bird, Reel 8, 2.

in Fakaoho. Indeed, European missionaries tended to "elevate individual experience at the expense of social context..."[63] In this connection, the missionaries encouraged an egalitarian impulse. A commoner might deviate from the wishes of his or her chief in the interests of individual personal salvation. All creatures were fundamentally equal in the eyes of God.

The missionaries also valued what they perceived as "order." Commenting on the LMS Society's Malua Seminary, one of the earliest visitors to Fakaoho noted that the cottages and dwellings, as well as the overall curriculum, were in "good order and arrangement."[64] When Captain John Williams received his commission as consul, it was viewed as a fitting appointment because there was an expectation that Williams would establish "order, peace, morality and religion."[65] The importance of the Protestant work ethic, which produces such order, is also stressed in the missionary journals. For instance, Rev. George Turner is viewed as "diligent and indefatigable" in his pedagogical role at Malua Seminary.[66] Self-discipline and abstinence, the dignity of labor and the rightness of trade were all assumed.[67] Idleness was one of the greatest moral evils. In addition, like their New England counterparts, the LMS missionaries brought a sense of eschatological urgency to the Tokelau atolls. The Gospel was now being spread to the four corners of the earth and the dawn of the millennial age was believed to be just around the corner. Therefore, time was of the essence.

In summation, the Protestant missionaries brought a gospel to Tokelau, which was only part European because many if not most of the early missionaries were Pacific Islanders themselves. Christian ethics were mediated through a Samoan Bible which utilized chiefly language and reflected hierarchical cultural norms. Nevertheless, western European values regarding literacy, monogamous marriage, social transformation (including housing construction, education and models of government), family life, radical monotheism, divine providence, sectarian

---

[63] Munro & Thornley, 6.

[64] G. Stallworthy & G. Gill, "Deputation in the *John Williams* to New Hebrides, Loyalty Islands, Niue, Savage Island and Fakaoho group," in *LMS South Sea Journals, May 21-August 22, 1858* (Wellington: Archives of New Zealand and the Pacific, Turnbull Library, National Library of New Zealand, 1858), Reel 8, 3 June.

[65] Ibid.

[66] Ibid.

[67] Gunson, 33.

divisions, individualistic voluntarism, order, the Protestant work ethic and eschatological urgency were inculcated in the early Pacific Island missionaries as well. Let us now indicate how these values have been integrated with indigenous Tokelauan values in three general ways.

Toward a Contemporary Christian *Tokelauan* Ethics

In certain respects, the *Faka Tokelau* of 2002 represents a creative blending of hierarchical and more egalitarian traditions. On the one hand, there is still a strong sense of deference to local leaders as well as pastors and priests. Young men are still not permitted to go fishing in certain areas without the permission of elders. Trees cannot be cut without the prior approval of village councils. Parishioners are reluctant to take independent initiatives to change church life.[68] And even in the urbane New Zealand context, officers of the Pahina Tokelau are reluctant to make decisions in the absence of the pastor.[69]

At the same time, the Tokelau way is not necessarily as hierarchical as the *Fa'a Samoa* (Samoan Way). As noted above, the seating arrangements at formal gatherings are not strictly correlated with social status and rank. While men and women may tend to sit together in different areas for Sunday morning worship, separation by gender and age is not hard and fast, and women may be seated near the rear of what is ostensibly the "men's" section.[70] Above all else, the practice of *inati*, where the all-important commodity—fish—is shared among households in equal portions, underscores an essential equality. Further, certain oral narratives reflect a long-standing egalitarian predisposition. In the Tale of the Tavake it is the small marginal fish who carries the day. An egalitarian ethos is implicit in the way in which everyone in the village may anticipate having a say in the future when they come of age.

Clearly, the mediation of Christianity via the Samoan Bible and the Samoan missionary reinforced hierarchical predispositions in traditional Tokelauan life. But perhaps because the pastor and priest remained

---

[68] Pat O'Connor, phone interview, Auckland, N.Z., 8 June 2002.

[69] Afa Lotoasa, interview, Porirua, N.Z., 8 June 2002. Mr. Lotoasa was Treasurer of the Pahina Tokelau at the date of this interview. However, the current pastor of the church, Rev. Tui Soopoaga, may be somewhat atypical in that he called the congregation together, rather than being invited to lead it by parishioners [Judith Huntsman, phone interview, Auckland, N.Z., 20 June 2002].

[70] Personal observation, Pahina Tokelau, June 9, 2002. Members of the church, questioned during a focus group interview, confirmed this observation, June 16, 2002.

essentially outsiders, their influence on Tokelau moral experience was somewhat limited. It did not overwhelm egalitarian proclivities, which may have also been subtlety reinforced by the European emphasis on voluntarism and individual autonomy over and against social context. What has resulted is a social order that retains both deference to authority and a sense of one's essential equality with everyone else in the village.

This emphasis on conforming one's personal life to community life, suggests a second moral orientation; namely, a tension between conserving traditional values and being open to change and development. Pio Tuia, *de facto* head of Tokelau in 2002, laments that one of the main problems of addressing recent environmental concerns is that while the *toeaina* (elders) are willing to entertain unfamiliar ideas, they are only predisposed to act within certain traditional parameters. One of these parameters has been a dependence on aid and expertise provided by the New Zealand government. The recent shift toward modernizing housing in Tokelau is a case in point.

Depending on who one speaks with, the dramatic introduction of concrete houses with metal roofing by New Zealand engineers has subtly, or significantly, altered life in the atolls. Traditionally, houses were constructed with pandanus leaf. These houses "breathed" in the sense that air was not trapped inside. They also did not block the flow of air currents across the lagoon through the villages, at least in the way that concrete walls interrupt wind currents.[71] This resulted in cooler homes, less mosquitoes and less accumulation of mold.[72] On a positive note, the concrete houses are more durable in storms, last longer and require less maintenance. Villagers are no longer saddled with the laborious job of continually constructing and repairing thatched homes, which deteriorate rapidly. But the crucial argument in favor of the concrete homes is that they support roofing that is designed to catch rainwater and drain it into storage tanks. Whereas, in the past, Tokelauans were frequently threatened with water shortages, now—thanks to the tanks—most families have a year-round supply of water.

Despite such innovations, the question still arises as to whether or not it might be possible to have a water catchments system without the concrete walls on individual houses. Might it be possible to develop more ecologically relevant alternative housing that utilizes concrete sup-

---

[71] Huntsman, phone interview, Auckland, N.Z., 20 June 2002.
[72] John Ineleo, interview, Lower Hutt, N.Z., 21 June 2002. Mr. Ineleo, a storehouse of Tokelauan indigenous knowledge, is a brother of Pio Tuia.

ports, but retains large areas of pandanus leafing? This or a similar type of innovation may yet become a reality, but since the concrete housing scheme was implemented as an outgrowth of New Zealand development aid, the *toeaina* appear reluctant to act in terms of alternative housing proposals. At the same time, there are a number of Tokelauan officials who are advocating various development initiatives, from pearl farming to waste management. Some of these initiatives represent a form of transformation with conservation. Pearl farming in the lagoons would represent a significant, new economic development, but it would also constitute something very traditional—a utilization of the sea for enhancing the quality of life.

Contemporary church life reflects this value polarity. In the 1980s, a Tokelauan missal at the Catholic Mission in Nukunonu replaced a Samoan liturgical guide. An indigenous carving of the crucifix, depicting Jesus beneath pandanus leaves, was placed in the sanctuary, along with traditional mats and shells. When the Bible was carried forward and then placed on the altar, it was now encircled in an island *lei*—a wreath of flowers. Similarly, in the Protestant churches, *leis* are frequently brought forward and placed around the pastor's neck during the service. Women wear traditional straw hats and the entire service is punctuated with intermittent singing, just as in traditional story telling, performances of tales were interspersed with verses of song. In a Tokelauan community mass recently held in Petone, New Zealand, the ushers who brought the tithes and offerings forward, did so by re-enacting the arrival of a canoe from a voyage. Each elder, holding a wooden oar, pantomimed the rowing movements associated with bringing the fishing catches to shore.

Thus, today, Christian ethics in Tokelau and in Tokelauan communities in New Zealand and Australia entails change and innovation, but the changes frequently incorporate and conserve traditional values. In the above examples, the singular importance of the sea as a source of livelihood (re: pearl farming) and as source of offerings of thanksgiving (re: liturgical dramatization) is reaffirmed. Western models of development are appreciated on one level, but it is interesting to note that Tokelauans express serious reservations about changes, like the concrete houses, which are detrimental to the traditional quality of life in the atolls.

This point leads to a third dimension of today's Tokelau ethics. As well as being hierarchical-egalitarian and transformative-conservative in nature, Christian ethics in Tokelau is radically eco-sensitive. During my recent travel to the atolls on the *M.V.Tokelau*, I was struck by the moral outrage Tokelauans expressed when two fellow travelers tossed coconuts overboard without breaking them open beforehand. The moral problem was that while these passengers were satisfying their thirst with these "drinking nuts" (green coconuts which retain an abundance of water), they were neglecting their responsibility to feed the fish in the sea. Even the greenest of drinking coconuts has a layer of "white meat" inside the outer shell, and therefore to simply throw a coconut into the sea without cracking it open is to deprive fish of food they would otherwise receive.

This episode illustrates a fundamental interdependency between humans and the natural world that is very much a part of traditional Tokelauan moral life. This theme is stressed in traditional oral narratives, such as the Tale of the Tavake, where the heroine is portrayed as having *fakamiti* (kind thoughts) for the birds, and where the birds in turn are attracted to her. It is reflected in the way Tokelauans rely upon observations of flights of birds in order to determine where to fish. It is evoked in Tokelauan songs that focus on calls to spirits of the wind in cases where boats are stranded at sea during periods of dead calm.

This indigenous environmental ethic has been challenged by modern inventions, such as the gas powered outboard motor, which both facilitates fishing and also drives fish away. But it still represents a major element in Tokelau moral reasoning. For example, there is now talk of not renewing a fishing lease previously granted to the U.S. government because of fear of over-fishing by U.S. ships in Tokelau waters. This aspect of indigenous Tokelauan ethics would appear to represent an enlargement or extension of western Missionary Christian ethics to include, not just the human community, but also the animal and biotic community as a whole. This may well be a case where Tokelauans have not so much blended western and indigenous elements as much as they have transformed Christian teaching in such a way that it applies to all of creation. Notwithstanding the eco-friendly currents in western Christian thought, this level of interdependency with the environment is unfathomable to westerners who are so alienated from other species that they do not perceive their moral interdependency with them.

Conclusion
In conclusion, I have tried to show that Tokelauan Christians have creatively blended aspects of both indigenous and Missionary Christian

moral values into their own unique Christian ethic. It is an ethic that both affirms the unity and authority of the village community, while simultaneously valuing and honoring each individual as a person of integrity and worth. It is a moral perspective that is open to, and welcomes, change, but is particularly receptive to change which also conserves indigenous values. It is a Christian ethic that highlights our corporate responsibility not just for the human community, but also for the entire created world.

MISSIONARY INTERVENTION AND MELANESIAN VALUES IN PAPUA NEW GUINEA*

Philip Gibbs**

According to archaeological sources, Papua New Guinea (PNG) has been inhabited for over 40,000 years.[1] There have been various migrations from South East Asia, resulting in a cultural complexity evidenced in the 800+ languages in PNG alone. Today PNG is an independent nation with a population of some 5,100,000 people, 96% of whom identify as Christian. Thus, there has been a long period for the development of values in traditional societies, and also the recent influence of modern Western and Christian values.

What is the impact of modern Western values on traditional Melanesian values in PNG? To what degree has this been a result of missionary interaction? A single paper cannot deal in depth with such questions applied to the whole of PNG, particularly since values do differ especially between the Highlands and Coastal/Islands regions.[2] After some general comments, I will focus on one particular culture group, the

---

* A condensed version of this paper by Philip Gibbs was previously published as "Moral Muddle? The Missions and Traditional Enga Values" in *Catalyst: Social Pastoral Journal for Melanesia,* Volume 33, No. 1 (Papua, New Guinea: Melanesia Institute, 2003): 61-91.
** Philip Gibbs is a Divine Word Missionary priest. He studied at Canterbury University in New Zealand, Sydney University, Catholic Theological Union in Chicago, and the Gregorian University in Rome. He did pastoral ministry in the Enga Province in Papua New Guinea. More recently he has been teaching at Catholic Theological Institute, Port Moresby, and is now a faculty member of the Melanesian Institute, Goroka, Papua New Guinea.
[1] Geoffrey Irwin, *The Prehistoric Exploration and Colonisation of the Pacific* (Cambridge: Cambridge University Press, 1992), 30.
[2] J.T.C. Joyce, "A Preliminary Study of Cultural Differences in Values Influencing Western Education in the Enga District," (Parts 1 and 2) *New Guinea Psychologist* 6 (1974): 9-16, 63-77. One of many examples given by Joyce is a simple test for aggression. Joyce unexpectedly tossed a lemon to Enga boys [PNG Highlands]. In 80% of the cases (n = 20) the Enga warded the object away to the ground. The same experiment performed in Rabaul [PNG Islands] resulted in 100% attempts either to catch the lemon or to ignore it. Joyce concludes: "Aggression appears as a well conditioned response to possible threats among the Enga. There seems to be a predisposition to regard an unknown situation primarily as threatening" (p. 12).

Enga of the Central Highlands.[3] Many of the findings from this culture group could apply to other groups, especially those from the PNG Highlands region.

I have tried to discover traditional values by two principal methods: firstly, asking old people what they were taught by their parents and grandparents, and secondly, asking the first missionaries who are still living today, about their experience with the people in their early years of contact. The study then looks at the values of young people in contemporary PNG, using findings from a 1992 study by the Melanesian Institute in Goroka, and recent responses from high school students, seminarians and university students.

Mission Presence in PNG

Marist Missionaries (French) first landed on Woodlark (Murua) Island in 1847. However, the effects of malaria on the missionaries and influenza on the indigenes, soon brought an end to the project and the surviving missionaries left in 1855. With hundreds of languages, competing tribes and malarious climate the next groups of missionaries, the (British) Anglicans and the London Missionary Society, tried a different approach on the South Papua Coast in 1871, using evangelists from Polynesia (Samoa and the Cook Islands in particular). Shortly after, the Catholic effort began again with German and French Missionaries of the Sacred Heart (MSC) in the islands of New Britain (1882) and of Papua (1884), the (German) Society of the Divine Word (SVD) along the New Guinea North Coast in 1896, and the (French) Marist Missionaries again in Bougainville in 1901.

After 1899 the British and German governments assumed responsibility for their respective colonies in Papua and New Guinea. During this time the (Australian) Seventh Day Adventists came to Papua in 1908, and the (German) Liebenzell Evangelical Mission (LzMS) entered the Admiralty Islands in 1914. After the defeat of Germany in the First World War, much of the Lutheran missionary work was continued by the American and Australian Lutheran Churches. Also, between the two world wars, the (Australian) Unevangelised Fields Mission (UFM)

---

[3] I wish to thank the PNG students and Enga people who helped by willingly, responding to my endless questions, and those who assisted me, particularly, Regina Tanda, Joseph Lakane and Philip Maso. I also wish to thank Dr. Willard Burce, Fr. Gerard Bus, Fr. Tony Krol, Fr. Bernard Fisher, and Rev. Otto Hintze for the information the historical information they provided

entered Papua.

The fratricidal war of the so-called "civilised" nations in the Second World War had shocking effects on the missionary enterprise. The Catholic SVD missionaries lost 122 (over half) of its pre-war missionaries, particularly in two instances where 102 missionary prisoners died on the Japanese ships Akikaze and Yorishime Maru.

In the pre-World War period there had been just seven denominational groups working in PNG: Anglicans, Congregationalists (LMS), Evangelicals (LzMS, UFM), Lutherans, Methodists, Catholics, and Seventh Day Adventists. However, servicemen returning home from the Pacific Island campaigns were instrumental in stimulating an interest in the world's "last great unknown" and many other denominations and interdenominational missionary groups began to arrive, such as the Baptists, Assemblies of God (AOG), South Seas Evangelical Mission (SSEM), Christian Brethren (CMML), the Australian Church of Christ (ACCM), the Swiss Evangelical Brotherhood Mission (SEBM), the Nazarene Mission, the Apostolic Church Mission (APC) and the New Tribes Mission. Prominent among the Pentecostal-type missions were the Four Square Gospel Church, the Christian Revival Crusade, and the Swedish Pentecostal "Philadelphia" Church. Whereas in 1927 there were 531 missionaries in the area comprising Papua and New Guinea. By 1971 there were 3411 missionaries present.[4] By 2002, with localisation of the churches the number has been reduced to 2832 non-citizen church workers in PNG (including the 50 non-citizen staff in the two church-run universities. However, the churches continue to multiply. There were six major denominations at work in 1927, by 1971 there were over thirty, and currently that number has almost trebled. In 2002 there are 88 different church organisations requiring work permits from the PNG Department of Labour and Employment.

Mission to the Enga
The Enga-speaking area of the Central Highlands was first opened to missionaries in 1947. The area comprises some 7,000 sq. km of rugged mountainous valleys. The Enga Province now has a population of 295,000 people. The four initial missionary groups to enter the area were the Lutheran (Missouri Synod), Catholic (Society of the Divine Word

---

[4] Rufus Pech, "The Acts of the Apostles in Papua new Guinea and Solomon Islands," in *An Introduction to Ministry in Melanesia*, ed. Brian Schwarz, *Point Series*, no. 7. The Melanesian Institute, 58.

and Sister Servants of the Holy Spirit), Apostolic, and Seventh Day Adventist missionaries. There was some competition between the four missionary groups seeking adherents as areas were "derestricted." (The main parts of the Kandep region, the Eastern Lagaip, Maramuni and Wale Tarua areas of Enga were "opened" at derestriction as late as 1961.)

Traditional Values

How does one discover a people's traditional values after they have been exposed in one form or other to Western culture for over fifty years? Anthropologists and missiologists have tried various means to deal with this issue.

Anthropologist Kenneth Read looked at the concept of the "person" in traditional Highlands society.[5] The Western concept of person results in a pronounced sense of individuality. Read points out how in PNG people are viewed more as social individuals. This social dimension does not imply any weakening of the sense of self. Particularly in the Highlands, modesty (in terms of being unassuming or retiring) is not a virtue. Often the respected and successful are those who are most loud in their own praise and most positive in their expressions of self importance. The closely knit fabric of traditional Melanesian society does not hinder independence of character. Rather it fosters it – but it is a character that is fundamentally socio-centric rather than individualistic. People are seen as social individuals so that the individual and their social role are not clearly separable. As a consequence the value of the human person lies not in some theory of the spiritual component of the person, but rather in the nature of the ties which link people socially with each other, through kinship and descent, through marriage ties, trading links, and other ways of relating.

Missiologist Ennio Mantovani has pointed to four principal values in traditional PNG society: community, relationships, exchange, and the ultimate value of "life." Taking community as an example he points out that for traditional Melanesian society:

> What is good for the community is ethically good.
> What is bad for the community is ethically bad.
> What is indifferent for the community is ethically indifferent.

---

[5] Kenneth E. Read, "Morality and the Concept of the Person among the Gahuku-Gama," *Oceania* 25.4 (1955): 233-282.

A healthy community ensured *gutpela sindaun,* or security, health, wealth, growth, prestige, good relationships, meaning, and the absence of sickness, barrenness and death.[6]

Solomon Islander Henry Paroi has written and lectured about concepts of "time" and "work" in Melanesia and how they differ from the modern Western concepts. He points out how traditionally Melanesians did not calculate time in terms of figures or instruments. Time was marked by socio-cultural events and occasions. Paroi gives the example of a village feast.

The actual occasion will take place only when all members are present, and they have no set time to finish. Although a feast finished very late in the evening the most important thing is that people are there, and that they have shared their food, joy, laughter and so on. Human relationship therefore becomes most [sic] important than the actual period that is spent in that particular gathering. People do not care how many hours they spend on that spot, but one thing they know is that they participate so that the notion of wasting of time does not really apply, it does not mean anything.[7]

While I agree substantially with the three writers cited above, my approach is somewhat different. I prefer to discover traditional values by asking old people what they were taught by their parents and grandparents. This approach is possible among the Enga, as one can still meet and talk with people who experienced the pre-Western-contact times.

Traditional Values Taught to Enga Children
In Melanesia, values and ethics tend to be more practical than theoretical. Values are estimates of the importance or worth of things. They are the foundation for decision-making, directing people's choices and decisions about how to live. Thus they are often associated with "wisdom." Values

---

[6] Ennio Mantovani, "Traditional and Present Day Melanesian Values and Ethics," *Occasional Papers of the Melanesian Institute,* no. 7, Goroka, Papua New Guinea, 1998.
[7] Henry Paroi, "Concepts of Time and Work in Melanesia," n.d., TMs, Melanesian Institute, Papua New Guinea.

may be personal or shared. Moral values, such as treating people with re-spect, carry an obligation. They tell us what we ought to do (even when, at times, we'd rather not). Nonmoral values carry no such obligation and express what we want or like.

Andrew, an elderly man from the Tsak Valley in the Enga Prov-ince recalls the wisdom and values passed on to him by his father. Some of these are the following:

1. Stay well away from menstruating women.
2. Be strong. Even though it is cold outside, leave the house early in the morning. *Kana pipilyu dee andala naenge.* The stones around the fireplace do not grow and neither will you if you sit around the fire.
3. Don't kill anyone. *Akali taiyoko ongo kunao napenge.* "It is very hard to wash off a man's blood."
4. Don't go around aimlessly. *Kangapupi kaita paenge ongo kumapae singi.* "Insects that travel all the time die on the road."
5. Work unless you don't mind being hungry. *Nee nanalamo kumalamo lenge.* "If you don't eat you die."
6. Don't steal because if you do, eventually you will pay for it one way or another.
7. Listen to what your parents tell you. It doesn't matter if you are blind, deaf or lame – they are the ones that bore you. *Embanya ongome mona nenge.* If you don't respect them while they are alive, they will "eat your heart" when they are dead.
8. Share food with others, whether they need it or not. *Sapos you no givim long ol, orait ol bai i no inap long wanbel long yu na bai yu dai.* "If you don't share, they will feel badly towards you and you will die." *Endakali ongome pyapenge.* "Give to others."
9. Plant trees wherever you go, especially pandanus trees. You reap what you sow. *Yuu ae latamo lao katengepe.* "You don't want the earth to cry out from neglect."
10. Look after your sisters. When you die, others will pretend to cry, but your sisters will shed real tears. *Lindi waku tenge.* They are the ones who will put on clay and mourning beads.
11. Keep up good relations with your sisters because when you are in trouble they will surely help you. *Wanakunya nuu ongo ly-ini pingi.* A girl's net bag is full of concerns. In other words, she will bring something in her net bag to help you.
12. Don't hit your wife. You are stronger than she is, so when she is angry, listen to her and then go outside until she has cooled down.
13. Stop trouble before it gets out of hand. *Tata telya ongo yapa*

konjingi. Extinguish a "bushfire" quickly.

14. When there is trouble, be careful with what you say. *Piimi lao endaki tokopi uanga pingi.* "Words can bend bridges." Words are powerful and can ruin relationships.

15. You must like your brothers and sisters and aunties and uncles. If you do, they will say good things about you and you will live a long life. *Apa kaiminipi ongo kalipi nalenge.* Don't play tricks with your relatives.

16. Observe a woman carefully before you marry her, otherwise later you will have trouble. *Tupaita imbupi andaka singi ongo lyii lenge.* "Bean skins may be soft at first, but when you leave them in the house they become brittle and hard."

17. Don't seduce another man's wife, otherwise you will start a fight. *Enda yanda ongo isa asale mende napenge.* Fights over women erupt quickly and we don't want any fights over women around here.

18. Take care of your land. Don't risk losing it in a fight. *Nee nanoapi embanya yuu ongonya katao auu pingi.* "Whether it provides you with food or not, it is always better to be on your own land." *Yuu ongo mena maitakai.* "Your land is like a mother pig." It will feed you.

19. Don't travel alone. *Mailaepi lakeo nepenge ongo pao kumingi.* "The bird that gets separated from the group dies."

20. *Akali kamongopi lyangapi ongonya pii ongo singi.* "Your destiny lies in listening to your leaders and your elders."

21. Don't say things you don't mean. If you say you will do something, then do it. *Lyaa buyoko yumi luu pia.* Your words should bear fruit.

22. *Akali ongo akali yangonya lao mandenge.* It is true that "men are destined to be killed by men" (in fights), however it is equally true that men are not like trees that you can cut and they grow again. So be careful. Take care of your life. You only live once.

23. If you promise to give a man a pig, then honour that promise and don't give it to someone else. *Mena duna lakala naenge.* "Don't break a pig's end!"

The practical wisdom here is obvious and the ethical values are apparent if one looks carefully at these words of a father to his son in pre-contact, pre-Christian days. They concern values like the following:

> *Firstly* -- respect: for the land, and for others, like spirits, one's elders, one's sisters. Also, respect for life,

whether your own or that of another.

Secondly -- work and industriousness.

Thirdly -- proscriptive values such as: not stealing, not being untruthful, guard one's words, not causing trouble with one's own wife or another's wife.

Fourthly -- communal values such as: "Share with others," or "Don't be a loner."

Such values typically recur in discussions with other mature men. In the isolated Kandep region men shared many examples of *mana pii* or traditional wisdom that they had learned from their fathers. Typical *mana pii* would be the following:

1. If you obey your parents by breaking firewood, fetching water, you will live a good life. But if you disobey your parents' words, you would wish a long enjoyable life but it will never happen because your parents will have cursed you. You will die after a short life.

2. You are just like the *auwa* (spinach) seedling. If you have sex with another person's wife, it is like planting *auwa* seeds in another person's garden because the child the woman would bear will not be yours.

3. Always be present at the *akalyanda* (men's house). When there is no one in the men's house, the centre post of the house will teach you some wisdom to make you an upright person. So never leave the men's house for a long period of time.

4. If you are coming from a feast carrying food, and you happen to meet an old man, woman or a child, give him or her the food. Their love and thankfulness or appreciation will make you live longer.

5. When you hear that two tribes are at war, do not go to fight because they might kill you. It is better for you to remain back and look after your pigs, wife and children. If you see tribal wars as fun and go there to help, the other side will look for a man to kill and you might be the victim.

The values of family and communal loyalty, discipline, and respect for one's elders come through clearly. One point to note is the underlying sanction of fear, that if one would engage in behaviour that disregards such values, then the price would be a shorter life.

Values for Enga Women

So far the focus has been male-oriented. In traditional society with its clear separation of men and women symbolised in separate houses, what were the values passed on from mother to daughter? Much could be said, but ten examples follow.

1. The first thing a girl was taught was that she was born to become a wife and mother. *Wanaku akalinya lao mandenge.* "The girl is born for a man." Thus a lot of the values instilled in the young girls were to prepare them for marriage and all that it involved. *Wanaku kuli nakandenge.* "One does not see girls' bones." In other words, in the Enga patrilocal society she will move to live in her husband's land and will be buried there, not where she grew up. She will maintain links with her family of origin, but she should remember that, *londati ongo londati, tengesa ongo tengesa.* "Far is far and near is near". If she will have difficulties with her husband, her family may be far away and not close at hand.

2. She would be told: *Akalimi itange ongo sambala naenge. Akalimi kingi ongo sambenge.* "A man doesn't pay a brideprice for your skin/body, but for your hands." Again, she would be told, *Akalinya yuu kenda pingi.* "You will work hard in the land of your husband." *Maita ongo enesa lakenge.* "You must bend your back working." If you do that, they will say that you are a woman who works hard and you will live a long life. Enga women are proud of their ability to work hard and old women lament that they can no longer carry heavy loads.

3. The value of work will benefit both herself and her husband. *Endame mena minatala akali kenge lenge.* "A woman who is good at looking after pigs will give her husband a good name." At a deeper level the way a woman cared for herself particularly during the time of her monthly period would have consequences for both

her and her husband. She was taught not to touch food to be given to men, and to conceal the blood. If she did this: *wanaku yonge lake singi.* Her skin would have a good appearance. It is believed that this would also affect the appearance of her husband.

4. Hospitality was another important value taught to girls. *Endaki mate nee nanyingi.* "You can't stop the public from coming to the water source." The same applied to a man coming to the house. A girl should always welcome men to the house. *Endakali ongo ane lao lanyingi. Nee nanalanyapi enomba ongo titi lenge.* She should welcome them with a smile, even if there is no food available to offer them.

5. Men can go around but the virtuous woman stays at home. *Wakamanya andaka tilyame napae ongo anda embanya ongonya auu pyuu napalenge.* (Literally this means, "If a flea bites you in another house, you will not sit well in your own house.") *Wanaku ongo wanakuna latala petenge.* She should sit in the house as a woman (not like a man).

6. A girl was taught the value of patience and discipline in responding to others, particularly her husband. *Itamai kaa pilyamopa yapa lao nao goe lenge.* Literally this means, "Just as you swallow ginger quickly because it is bitter if it remains in your mouth, so, swallow the bitter words of your husband."

7. A girl was also taught the value of having children. *Wane lapyali lapyali lao nee nenge.* Literally, because of the noise of her children she can eat, implying that if she didn't have children, her husband would ask why she was eating. *Muumi olya pyao pyandele pingi.* "A woman without a child is like an owl that eats mosquitoes in the night." A child gives a woman strength and a place in society. *Kana patapatanya omonalya.* "A woman without children is like a plant growing on a stone unable to put down roots."

8. A girl was taught the value of housekeeping. *Enda ongo anda matapu,* Literally: a woman is like a belt that holds a house together. If she didn't keep her house

clean then people would say, *Yui neenya kolao paenge.* "She is going around like a rat looking for something to eat." A woman noted how her mother used to say, *Enda ongo andaka ita.* "A woman supports the house as a house post." When you are home the fire must be alight so that people will see smoke seeping through the thatched roof of the house and they will know that you are home and the house is warm.

9. A woman was taught the value not only of having a good food garden and a warm house, but also the importance of raising pigs. *Endame mena minatala akali kenge lasingi.* If she looked after the pigs well then both she and particularly her husband would have a good "name," if not, the pig would go and look for food in other people's gardens and she would be branded as, *enda litiyoko mende* -- "a lazy, useless woman."

10. A girl was taught to be industrious, symbolised in the net bag. *Aiyumba nuu lapipae mandenge.* At an early age she should learn to weave net bags so that she would not be carrying old ones made by someone else. Even as a child she was taught to wear a net bag on her head. *Wanaku ongo wanakuna latala nuu mandenge.* Boys don't wear net bags, but a girl should always wear one. An elderly woman said, "I would complain as we returned from the garden with vegetables and tell my mother that the net bag was too heavy, and my mother would reply that we women have to carry heavy net bags until we die -- *Nuu kende ongo pitalamo lao epea, Maka ongo etala naenge.* "The tired feeling is here to stay and there is no getting away from heavy loads, so you might as well get used to it."

One could sum up the ten points above by saying that the principal values instilled in young women were values associated with garden, hearth and home. She should be hospitable, disciplined, fertile, hardworking. She should delay her own gratification in favour of her husband and children and in this way she would achieve good standing in the community. If a woman would follow values such as these, then she would live a long life and *wanenya kingi napala kumate* -- literally, you die eating the hand of your children. What this means is that her children would look after her in her old age and she would die satisfied that she had performed her task as a wife and mother.

Values Observed by the First Missionaries

With the Christian church being relatively young in Enga, many of the first missionaries are still living. So, thinking that those early missionaries might provide insights into traditional values in their "first contact" situation, the writer contacted some of the first Catholic and Lutheran missionaries to seek their views on the values they encountered in their initial contact with the indigenous people, and how these values were in harmony or conflict with the missionary message they had brought. From their replies it is apparent that there were some practices that missionaries condemned or discouraged, such as polygamy, tribal fighting, and the physical abuse of woman, such as cutting off a woman's nose or other body parts. Yet they also discovered values that harmonised with the Christian message.

One of the earliest Lutheran missionaries to Enga, Rev. Dr. Willard Burce writes:

> I'm sure that all of us who lived among the Enga as missionaries in those times were often surprised at the extent to which they exemplified St Paul's comment in Romans 2: "The Gentiles do not have the Law, but... their conduct shows that what the Law commends is written in their hearts. Their consciences also show that this is true, since their thoughts sometimes accuse them and sometimes defend them" (TEV). "Honour your father and your mother... . You shall not kill... . You shall not commit adultery... .You shall not steal... . You shall not bear false witness... . You shall not covet." These were not new 'values' to the Enga, nor did they have to create new words in order to talk about them. They were in their hearts; they were in their culture. Which is not to say that they were not violated continually, *post lapsum* human beings being what they are.[8]

---

[8] Willard Burse, personal communication, June 15, 2002.

At the time of first contact with missionaries, what did people value or have a high regard for? Willard Burce responds with reference to political election times today when one notices "a high pitched fever." He notes that a half a century ago you would have seen a like fever and crescendo during the *tee* pig exchange. "Out in public, with all the pigs lined up to be witnessed, counted, and distributed. And with everyone there to see and with the same questions: who is who; who is trying to be who; who is for whom; who is winning, who is losing?" The whole point, at least for the men, was to be a *kamongo* – a Big Man or a man with a name. Burce continues, "becoming one was something every boy could aspire to; that to be a *kamongo* was to be one across the board – in energy, in knowledge, in food production, in pigs, in building, in pragmatic wisdom, in courage and generosity, in all human relations, in persuasive rhetoric, in political leadership: all this was important."

Burce sees this aspiring to be a Big Man as a possible area of conflict with values witnessed by Jesus, who taught that, "Anyone who wants to become great among you must be your servant, and anyone who wants to be first among you must be a slave to all" (Mk 10:43-45).

The first resident expatriate Catholic missionary to the Enga was Fr. Gerard Bus. Writing now from Europe, he says that the values he first noted were: courage, bravery, fighting ability and virility in men; gardening skills, pig husbandry and fecundity in women. Other areas of value included possession of pigs, especially with the *tee* pig exchange, a good name, respect, ability to contribute to support of clan both in personnel and material goods, skills like house building, manufacture of tools, decorations, string bags, etc.[9]

Gerard Bus adds:

> The survival of the clan was their uppermost concern. There was a readiness to give one's life for the well being of the clan. There is a story, recorded by a Lutheran pastor, of a clan leader who was a convinced Christian, a close friend of this pastor. He insisted on going into battle, although the pastor was telling him he shouldn't do it, as he was surely going to be the first to be targeted, and it was not Christian to fight. This leader answered that he knew all this very well, but he had to lead the

---

[9] Gerard Bus, personal communication, February 12, 2002.

battle, it was his duty as clan leader. He was indeed the
first to be killed."

The example above shows how difficult it is to judge to what degree and when, being a Big Man, conflicted with the Christian value of
being ready to lay down one's life for another. The writer knows of one
Christian Big Man near Yampu in the Enga Province who asks his
friends not to address him as "*kamongo*," since that is the term now attributed to Jesus Christ as "Lord."

Did the early missionaries sometimes confuse Christian and
Western values? Gerard Bus admits, "I'm sure we do (did)." Consider
the position of women. Willard Burce recalls domestic arguments and,
for example, a woman asserting that her husband was so poor that he had
to use a pig rope for a belt. "The man would hear that and go verbally
ballistic!" However, the confrontation often did not remain on the verbal
level. Bus notes how men might torture women in cases of unfaithful-
ness, for instance, burning female genitals by applying hot stones to them
or cutting a woman's hamstring so that she would be crippled. In the face
of this, "I sometimes took action when I saw women attacked." Bus sees
the value he was defending as "genuinely Christian and based on the respect we owe to any and every human person." He admits though that in
the case of marriage, he is inclined to think that missionaries imposed
Western Church law which has been absolutised.

Another early Catholic missionary, Fr. Tony Krol, says that in
traditional Enga society people with advanced illnesses such as leprosy
might be killed (by drowning) and some old people and unwanted babies
might die of neglect (not given anything to drink).[10] Missionaries sometimes intervened in such situations, and in fact set up Yampu hospital to
care for people with leprosy.

Early Lutheran missionary, Rev. Otto Hintze, notes how:

> Try as hard as we did [to be aware of the difference be-
> tween "Christian" and "cultural" values], cultural values
> crept in not only from the Western missionaries but also
> from the surrounding PNG Christian communities and
> were taken to be Christian values.... Clothes – Chris-
> tians had to wear clothes. Baptismal garb and new name

---

[10] Tony Krol, personal communication, February 3, 2002.

– one had to buy and dress in a white t-shirt and laplap and accept a new name which had a Christian connotation. Some may have thought that kind of dress and name change to be essential to Christian baptism, although we baptized a few dressed in native dress and did not change the name of others.[11]

Willard Burce gives the example of the rational empiricism of the West:

> Can anyone today see the unseen, dream the future, break the trammels of nature, perhaps make a dead child or a dead engine, come to life again by prayer with faith? I have known Enga who would instantly answer Yes, and give examples. And I have known missionaries who, spellbound by the Enlightenment, would be uncomfortable saying anything but No.

With their Western scientific worldview, missionaries, whether they were aware of it or not, became agents of secularisation.

Traditional, Secular, and Christian Values

Fifty years later, what is the situation? In a challenging paper, published fifteen years ago, Garry Trompf claims that there are three sets of values affecting the destiny of PNG: traditional, Christian and secular values. He points out how traditional societies survived through the development of "military" values: revenge on the foe was a virtue. He claims that pacification through colonial and missionary interventions has radically affected those military values.

> And whoever they have been, I should remind you — whether kiaps, missionaries, users and abusers of labour — they have been, in concentrating on the removal of warrior elements and violence, responsible for ripping 'half the guts' out of traditional cultures or religions or group ethics. To put away the spears completely is to shed and repress much of the most important raisons

---

[11] Otto Hintze, personal communication, July 21, 2002.

d'etre for traditional societies.[12]

He adds that now people use neo-traditional ways of sorcery to protect and to harm.

Trompf notes that most traditional values are influenced by Christian values in Melanesia today. He points out that perhaps the "noble traditions" referred to in the Preamble to the PNG Constitution are really only "noble" because they have already become indistinguishable from Christianity as Melanesians express it. He also notes there is a whole spectrum of approaches in "Christian" attitudes to Melanesian traditional values, from condemning everything as evil, to a broad acceptance.

Secular values are those supposedly self-evident to any rational person, but not tied to religious beliefs, traditional or otherwise. In PNG the introduction of a money economy has provided new opportunities for people to choose and has had a radical effect on the traditional value system. Trompf comments, "Money makes for moral muddle, especially in the dazzling pluralism of the city."[13] He concludes:

> Some of us perceive that in the values of traditions (especially the noble or ennobled ones), and of Christianity (left unbastardised), and even of apparently secular universal humanistic principles enshrined in United Nations charters (too often unimplemented), lie the sources of inspiration to forestall the creeping, sneaking, debasing propensities of massive world changes which service the greedy and the cunning few at the expense of the needy and the naive many.[14]

Contemporary Urban Life

A recent study of the effects of urbanisation on Engans in Port Moresby, confirms Trompf's claims.[15] A "city" like the capital Port Moresby is fascinating for the newcomer. There is TV, and there are dance halls, and

---

[12] Garry Trompf, "Competing Value-Orientations in PNG" in Ethics and Development in Papua New Guinea, ed. Gernot. Fugmann, 17-34. *Point Series* no. 9, The Melanesian Institute (1986), 19.

[13] Trompf, 31.

[14] Trompf, 32.

[15] Philip Gibbs, "Finding Faith in the City: Inculturation and the Urban Experience of Engan Catholics," *Catalyst* 32.2 (2002) 165-196.

beer clubs with poker machines. However, after the initial fascination, the bright lights begin to fade when one begins to feel their social consequences. There is little industrial development in the cities to absorb the migrants, leading to mounting unemployment and unrest as living standards decline with the struggling national economy. Because of the high costs and security problems, Port Moresby is not a place favoured by transnational corporations (There are no McDonald's in PNG!), and mining companies usually prefer a "fly-in-fly-out" (to Australia) arrangement for their skilled workers. A city Business Seminar was told recently that the unemployment rate in Port Moresby is estimated at 60%![16] Long term unemployment is dehumanising, with serious implications for the value system.

In order to earn K10 or K20 (US$2 or $4) a day to buy food, many Engan women sell betel nut, loose cigarettes, second-hand clothing and cool drinks. Most do this illegally since they are not in assigned market areas. So they have to contend with police or "city rangers" who appear on the scene to disrupt their trade and steal their goods.[17] When this happens, they go home empty handed and "go to bed worrying." As one woman said, "After the police have kicked and broken my "eski" (cooling container) and taken all my drinks and ice blocks, I am totally taken up with finding food for my family, and I have no time to think about church matters." Nothing is free in the city. One has to think of how to get enough money each day, so it is difficult to take time off to attend Mass on Sunday let alone attend church functions, meetings or courses at other times. A father of a family noted bitterly, "At home [Enga] I don't get a power bill. Here power is money, water is money, *olgeta samting i stap antap long moni* (everything depends on money). Another added, "*Long hia moni em i laip bilong ol*" (Here money is their life).

Attitudes of Young People in Melanesia
Over a number of years, beginning in 1992, the Melanesian Institute (MI) in Goroka, PNG, conducted a study on the attitudes and aspirations of young Melanesian people in PNG.[18] One of the principal findings of

---

[16] *Post Courier*, September 12, 2001, p. 5.
[17] *Post Courier*, February 17, 2000, pp. 19-20. *The National*, November 28, 2000, p. 12.
[18] Franco Zocca and Nick de Groot, eds. *Young Melanesians Project: Data Analysis. Point Series* 21, The Melanesian Institute, 1977.

the study was the great variation in attitudes of young people found in the four main regions of PNG: The north coastal region, the South coastal region, the Islands, and the Highlands. The regional variable appeared as a major factor, making it difficult to generalise about the attitudes and aspirations of youth over the nation as a whole.

The MI study focused on attitudes towards eighteen items: Families of origin, marriage and divorce, parents, spouses and children, school education, social problems, Christian churches, religious practice, some traditional beliefs and practices, work, urbanisation, youth association, leisure time and sport, women in charge of business, criminality, police force, judicial system, politicians, and "wantokism" (preference given to family ties).

Some relevant points from their findings are the following:

1. The majority of youth think that the main cause of trouble in PNG communities are excessive drinking of alcohol and smoking marijuana (p.97). This is particularly a problem in the Highlands (p.210).
2. The majority of PNG youth does not believe in traditional healing practices and consider them opposed to Christianity (p.126).
3. The great majority of PNG youth deny that ancestors can help them in their life. "They are dead" (pp.122, 126).
4. The main reasons for young people moving to town are the "hard life" in the villages (particularly working in gardens and lack of modern facilities) and the attractions of life in the town (entertainment) p.163.
5. Western education is valued, but it appears that only a minority of youth (14.4 %) would like to learn more about village customs. This desire is stronger in the Islands and Southern Regions and the researchers wonder if this is a consequence of their having much longer exposure to missionaries and the modern world thus feeling more estranged from their ancestor's traditions (p.204). Likewise the researchers notice a stronger desire for literacy and reading and writing in local languages amongst Southern youth and question whether this is a sign that they have already lost their own languages

more than young people elsewhere in PNG.

Mission Impact Viewed Today

As noted above, the MI study showed a variation in attitudes in the four main regions of PNG. Partly because of this factor, the writer of this paper is taking examples from just one Highlands region, and it must be stressed that a careful study would need to be done to compare the attitudes and values expressed in that region with those of the other three regions of PNG.

The Melanesian Institute study did not ask explicit questions about young people's view of missionaries and mission impact. Therefore the writer conducted a study among Secondary and Tertiary students from the Enga Province (See Appendix A). The study was conducted with 63 students from the two Secondary Schools in the Province, and 11 Enga students at Divine Word University. Males outnumbered females 52 to 22. The majority of the students who participated were Catholic, with five Lutherans and one each from the Assemblies of God, Jehovah's Witnesses, Seventh Day Adventist and Four Square Pentecostal church.

Table 1: Attitudes of Modern-Day Enga Students to the Early Missionaries

Question	Response Choices	Wabag Secondary N = 42 M = 32 F = 10	Kopen Secondary N = 21 M = 17 F = 4	Divine Word University N = 11 M = 3 F = 8
1. What expression best describes your feeling about the early missionaries who came to Enga?	I have good and thankful feelings towards them	37	21	11
	I have angry negative feelings towards them.	2	0	0
	I have no feelings either way	3	0	0
2. Many of the early missionaries tried to learn and use the local Enga language. How do you feel about that?	They were wasting their time.	0	0	0
	I respect them for trying to learn the language	40	21	11
	I have no feelings either way.	2	0	0
3. Some people today say that "The missionaries destroyed our culture". Do you agree or disagree with this statement?	I agree that they did destroy our culture	17	1	4
	I disagree with the statement	24	19	6
	I don't know.	1	1	1
4. Do you think the early missionaries had a positive approach to Enga culture or a negative approach?	Positive	17	8	4
	Negative	2	2	1
	Both positive and negative	21	8	5
	I don't know	2	3	1

As may be seen from *Table 1*, the majority of modern-day students have "good and thankful" feelings towards the early missionaries. They respect them for trying to learn the language (and culture) of the people. Only 9 of the 74 students could not name one of the early missionaries, but the rest could. Opinions are more diverse when it comes to questions of whether missionaries "destroyed" their culture, and whether the early missionaries had a positive or negative approach towards Enga culture. However the trend is still positive.[19]

---

[19] In feedback from seminary students in the second year Anthropology Course at Catholic Theological Institute in Port Moresby, it appears that, in contrast to the Highlands, students from the Islands region, which received missionaries

There are various reasons why the students generally have positive attitudes towards the early missionaries. The most common reasons given are that they brought the Good News and development in terms of education and health services. Several noted that the missionaries did not use weapons and approached people in a more friendly manner than the earlier explorers. Enga student comments included the following:

> When the first missionaries came, the Engans did not know them so they felt afraid. But the missionaries tried their best to attract them by giving the natives some modern items like salt, clothes, etc. As a result the Engans went close to the whites and worked together. Finally they became Christian.

> Missionaries came to Enga not to destroy our culture but to add some more things (e.g., in our culture people are not allowed to steal and also the missionaries said that stealing is not a good habit.) Missionaries came to fulfil Enga with some good laws which are existing today.

> The missionaries have come to Enga for our material, spiritual and physical benefit and to know what is really true from what is not true. According to the approach of the missionaries we know many things which are right

---

more than fifty years before the Highlands, tend to be more critical of early missionaries. For example, one student from East New Britain writes, "Missionaries came and introduced a foreign culture–Christianity–that, to some extent has some things in common with the traditional Melanesian religion. But without prior and proper assessment of the new environment and culture in which they found themselves, they tried to eradicate the people's cultures and to replace it with the culture of Christianity, by regarding the traditional Melanesian practices as evil and satanic, the result of which is a culture clash and thus confusion."

Another seminary student from West New Britain writes, "It is very saddening to see today that our cultures and traditions have changed dramatically. Some of its values have been lost. It is due to the fact that many missionary fanatics in the past emphasised so much on their exotic Christian teachings that were so contradicting and suppressing toward the Melanesian cultures. ... Because many cultures have been destroyed, it is a formidable task for one (as a Melanesian) to today revive and revitalise them for the good of Christianity and the people– meaning we are losing some of our valued cultures–a gift from God Himself. What a sad thing."

from our traditional beliefs and the Christian life, etc.

When asked what the missionaries opposed, the frequency of responses from the 74 students is as follows: Polygamy (32), Tribal warfare (32), Magic and sorcery (26) Worshiping (evil) spirits (19), Stealing (8), Traditional healing (6), "Worshiping" spirits of the dead (6).

What traditional customs do the modern students feel fit well with Christian life today?

The most popular custom is the male initiation mentioned in 20 responses. In fact, male initiation is for the most part abandoned today. Other customs include: Compensation (13) ("It means reconciliation and bringing clans together"), Sharing (11), Brideprice (10), Traditional dress and dancing on special occasions (8), Showing respect for others (4). (One added the traditional dictum, "and you will live a long life.")

What traditional customs do the modern students feel conflict with Christian life today? Tribal fighting (24), Polygamy (21), "Worshiping" evil spirits (12), Paying compensation (9), Mourning for a long time after the death of a family member (4).

What aspects of modern Western culture do the students feel fit well with Christian life today? The most popular response to this questions was "clothes" or "dressing up" (7). Education and literacy came equal with seven responses, then health services and hygiene (3). Notably, 5 students could not think of anything to respond to this question. Other responses included, equality for men and women, peace and law and order, and getting to know people from different cultural groups.

What aspects of modern Western culture do students feel conflict with Christian life? Responses to this question included: Alcohol (14), Marijuana and other drugs (10), Discos and dances (12), Watching "bad" movies and videos (4). Other responses included: girls wearing short skirts "which encourages boys to rape them," people being too busy to greet others properly, modern forms of the "wantok" system (nepotism), not sharing food, and modern (corrupt) political activities.

Comments made by some of the female Enga students at Divine Word University are revealing:

> Today I feel that my ideas and values are totally different because most of the good values that my parents and my grandparents practiced were dropped on the line or forgotten by me. For example, raising pigs, making gar-

dens, going for initiation and so on. I think I drop most of our good cultural values which I should try to fit in with parts of Western culture which I think are good and helpful and which fit my Christian life. But I do note the problem of totally different ideas and values from my parents and grandparents because they are able to fit themselves into both traditional and modern cultures.

Before the men were the superior beings. They taught that the women's place was in the house and garden. Today, men and women are equal. In this changing world woman can do anything that men can do and even better.

Before girls were only "used" by the relatives to get bride-price. It was as though she was just good at getting married. Today ladies have better things to do than just to getting married, for example, being educated, have a job and looking after their own family members.

In sum, the students today generally feel a real gulf between the lives of their parents and grandparents and their own lives. This is particularly apparent with educated young women. The findings from this study of Enga students complements the study conducted earlier by the Melanesian Institute, particularly in their perception of what aspects of modern culture conflict with Christian life today. Focusing more on missionary efforts, it appears that the students themselves concur with what they understand were the customs opposed by the early missionaries.

Initiation rites, based on a pre-Christian cosmology, have been largely abandoned in the Enga province, yet it is notable that many students still see value in the rites. Although the initiation was only for males, female students also mentioned this custom in their responses. Traditionally the *sangai/sandalu* initiation rite was the most significant moment for young men to learn customs and values, and no doubt both young men and women today experience a moral vacuum and see initiation rites as a possible solution to this.

Modern Values and Young People Today

Having identified some of the areas in which modern-day students in the Enga Province in PNG perceive how traditional and modern Western values fit or are in conflict with Christian life, I now try to assess the extent to which young Papua New Guineans are moving from the traditional value system of their parents to the value system typical of modern

Western cultures.

　　　Norman T. Feather has used an instrument with a list of 36 values taken from a cross-cultural study by M. Rokeach to assess how different nationalities rank in what he calls instrumental and terminal values.[20] Terminal values are connected with "end states of existence" such as freedom, equality, salvation. Instrumental values are "modes of conduct" such as being obedient, loving, responsible (See Appendix B). Included in Feather's study (from 1971) was a group of 1128 tertiary students from the University of PNG, Unitech, five Teachers' Colleges, an Agricultural College, and the Administration College in Port Moresby. In the study, males outnumbered females four to one. *Table 2* presents the results of the same study conducted with male students at the Catholic seminary at Bomana in 2000, and also surveys conducted at one High School and two Secondary Schools in the Enga Province in 2002. In Enga, 97 students responded, 78 males and 19 females. The male and female responses are shown separately for comparison.

Table 2a: Comparison of Rank Order of Median Scores on Instrumental Values (The lower the median the higher the relative importance of the value)

Instrumental Values	High and Secondary Schools, in Enga Province, PNG. 2002 Male N= 78	High and Secondary Schools, in Enga Province, PNG. 2002 Female N = 19	Bomana Seminarians PNG (2000) N = 35	PNG Tertiary Students (M/F 1971) N = 1128	Male Students, Flinders University, Australia (1971)	Male Students Michigan State University, USA (1971)
Ambitious	15	10.5	14	5	6	3
Broad-minded	11	15	6	13	2	4
Capable	9	13	13	12	8	5
Cheerful	12	14	15	11	9	15
Clean	16	16	16	15	17	17
Courageous	13	10.5	12	8	10	8
Forgiving	5	1	8	7	11	12
Helpful	7	3	10	2	13	14
Honest	3	5	3	1	1	1
Imaginative	18	17	17	18	15	13
Independent	17	18	18	16	7	6
Intellectual	14	10	4	14	14	9
Logical	10	9	11	17	12	7
Loving	6	2	5	9	4	11
Obedient	8	6	7	4	18	18
Polite	4	4	9	6	16	16
Responsible	2	7	1	3	3	2
Self-control	1	8	2	10	5	10

---

[20] Norman T. Feather, *Values in Education and Society* (NY: The Free Press, 1975).

Table 2b, Comparison of Rank Order of Median Scores on Terminal Values (The lower the median the higher the relative importance of the value)

Terminal Values	High and Secondary Schools, Enga Province, PNG. 2002 Male N = 77	High and Secondary Schools, Enga Province, PNG. 2002 Female N = 19	Bomana Seminarians PNG (2000) N = 35	PNG Tertiary Students (M?F 1971) N = 1128	Male Students, Flinders University, Australia (1971)	Male Students Michigan State University, USA (1971)
Comfortable life	4	6	17	11	13	11
An exciting life	16	17	14	13	11	12
Sense of accomplishment	13	12	13	15	4	5
A world at peace	7	4	9	1	9	10
World of beauty	18	18	16	18	15	18
Equality	3	8	5	2	10	13
Family security	11	16	12	5.5	12	7
Freedom	6	9	6	3	3	1
Happiness	5	3	8	9	7	2
Inner harmony	9	5	4	12	8	9
Mature love	10	15	3	17	5	6
National security	17	11	15	5.5	17	17
Pleasure	15	14	18	16	14	15
Salvation	12	10	10	8	18	16
Self-respect	2	2	2	14	6	4
Social recognition	14	13	11	10	16	14
True friendship	8	7	7	4	2	8
Wisdom	1	1	1	7	1	3

The PNG students generally rate ambition, a sense of accomplishment and independence far lower than their counterparts overseas. Moreover, the PNG students place a higher value on "social" values such as forgiving, being helpful, and particularly being obedient and polite. Equality also rates higher with the Enga students. On the other hand, honesty, which received the highest rating in Australia and the USA (and in the PNG Tertiary Students study) ranks lower with the Enga students, possibly due to social pressures which have to be balanced with a value such as being honest. Values receiving a high rating elsewhere, such as being broad-minded, freedom, and mature love do not rate so high with the Enga students.[21]

How might the Enga students rate against the values observed

---

[21] The high ranking of "mature love" by celibate seminarians at Bomana merits comment as does the lowest rating for "a world of beauty" by both male and female Enga students

previously in the wisdom passed on to their parents and grandparents: values such as respect, industriousness, proscriptive and community oriented values for men, and values such as strength and hard work, delayed gratification, fertility and "garden, home and hearth" values for women? Obviously the list from Norman Feather does not bear direct comparison with those values. Nevertheless, one sees a reflection of such values in the responses of the Enga students.

The male students rank self-control as the most important value. Self-discipline and self-control are important virtues for a social individual in support of his community. Boys were to be taught the discipline of leaving the warm house to go out into the cold early in the morning lest they become soft and lazy. The three highest values given by the male students: self-control, responsibility and honesty, are all virtues much appreciated in traditional society. Other values given a high rating such as being polite, helpful and forgiving fit well with the high value given to respect in traditional culture. The low rating for "ambition" is an anomaly given the observations of the early missionaries of the common desire to become a "Big Man."

The female students rate forgiveness as the highest value and rank equality far lower than their male counterparts. The example was given in a previous section of this paper of a girl being taught to "swallow" the bitter words of her husband as she would swallow ginger. Enga women are by no means docile or passive, but they are seldom if ever in favour of warfare, and at times offer themselves in marriage to someone from an enemy clan in order to facilitate the peace-making process. One may also see the high rating given to "loving" "helpful" and "polite"–all values that are important in domestic life.

Thus, while the students observe that they live in a different world with different ideas and values, yet their values according to the perceived ranking of instrumental and terminal values indicates that they are still social individuals with a high regard for the values and virtues required for living a communal rather than an individualistic lifestyle. The high value given to "self-respect" "comfort" and "happiness" sometimes leads to conflict in the lives of young people having to juggle traditional discipline and modern self- expression, the personal and the social, in their lives.

Missionary Intervention and Change

To what extent has missionary intervention been part of these developments? The mission enterprise has had both a transformational and a conservative effect in terms of people's values.

Historically the Churches have provided the bulk of educational and medical services in PNG. Commenting on education prior to World War II, John Kadiba says, "What little education the Colonial Administration achieved was through the mission agencies, which were solely responsible for educational work until 1941.[22] It was not until 1985 that government school enrolments rose higher than those in mission schools.[23] Even today the Churches provide 45 % of PNG health services (49 % in rural areas), 60 % of general nurse training, and 100 % of community health worker training.

No matter how much one might try to avoid it, education and health work erode traditional values. Children come to school and for many this means living away from their families. Boys and girls sit together and relate in ways that would be unimaginable in the village setting. With new-found ways to wisdom, the traditional structures for transmitting the wisdom of the ancestors in initiation rites and other rituals have gradually fallen into disuse. Modern medicine was the greatest challenge to traditional religious practices. It did not take people long to notice that often an injection of Penicillin was more effective (and "cheaper") than killing a pig to placate an angry spirit. So, intentionally or inadvertently, the missions' involvement in education and health contributed to undermining traditional values and to promoting values associated with a modern scientific worldview including the undisputed primacy of reason and the concept of the emancipated, autonomous individual.[24]

The missions also had a conservative effect in that they tried to promote human, religious and communal values in the face of secular influences. Many Papua New Guineans have noted that almost all the Ten Commandments of the Judeo-Christian tradition can be found in their own Melanesian traditions. In promoting teachings such as the Commandments, the missions may well have been helping to preserve traditional values.

---

[22] John Kadiba, "Murray and Education," in *Papua New Guinea: A Century of Colonial Impact 1884-1984*, ed. S. Latukefu (The National Research Institute, 1989), 279.
[23] R.D. Fergie, "Church state partnership in PNG – and the folly of reinventing the wheel." Position Paper 2. The Second consultation between NGOs and the Government. Port Moresby, March 30-31, 1993, p. 15.
[24] David Bosch, *Transforming Mission* (NY: Orbis Books, 1991), 342.

However, there are two significant areas in which the Christian and Traditional Melanesian traditions differ. Firstly, the Christian tradition proposes a "love" ethic whereby "love of God and one's neighbour" is the primary motivation for Christian behaviour. By contrast, as may be seen in some of the examples given already in this paper, the motivation for action in traditional society was often one of fear. One helped one's parents while they were alive for fear of their ghostly revenge. One tried to live a virtuous life lest one's life be shortened. Christian "God-fearing"– an expression one hears often these days in reference to politicians – is more "respect" and is considered one of the seven gifts of the Holy Spirit by the Church. Of course ideal and reality never match and one could debate to what degree Christian love has become accepted as a supreme value in peoples' lives.

The second significant area is the status of women. As may be seen from the comments of the female students in the section above on "Mission Impact Viewed Today," women no longer see themselves as having been "bought" by their husband's clan to serve and obey their husbands. Fr. Gerard Bus noted how he would intervene if he felt a woman was being mistreated. People also observed the lives of married missionary couples. Church-run institutions like Divine Word University have a policy of gender equality in the selection of students. This is one area where missionary intervention has, and still is, having an effect on values in PNG society.

Conclusion

This study has obvious limitations, particularly in its bias towards responses from members of the Catholic Church. It would be interesting to broaden the study to include Pentecostals, and Seventh Day Adventists. Responses from a more diverse group might differ in some ways from those given in this paper.

Nevertheless, as we have seen, the "moral muddle" pointed out by Garry Trompf, has resulted in various responses: continuity, conflict, change and confusion. Many young people feel a sense of conflict and confusion. One of the Enga women students from Divine Word University comments:

> One very shameful thing from this generation is we
> don't know our own customs and traditions. Even some
> do not speak their mother language. We let this modern

culture influence so much that we get out of hand. Instead of practising good things the young people do the
most disgusting things…, not respecting elders and parents, learning how to handle dangerous weapons, and
rarely thinking about God. We should follow only the
good values of both the new and the old.

How to follow the "good" values of both new and old? Sr. Stella
Kambis, AD, in a talk to Papua New Guinean sisters at Xavier Institute,
Port Moresby, comments as follows:

By nature and culture we are happy, friendly and care-
free people. Our energy and vitality come from our relationships with people and nature. This is how we derive
our Melanesianness and identity. This is where we encounter God who gifted us with the values of sharing,
loving, compassion, community, celebration, song and
dance and so on, as well as our sense of respect for ancestry and nature that express the values of the kingdom
of God…. We come to these stages in our life, and it
looks like we are on a crossroad. Which way to go?
Tumbuna [ancestral] ways are in question, certain structures in culture are being shifted, changes have come,
and I believe it is good that they come. We have to find
new directions, new ways, new ideas to suit us at this
point in our life.

"Mission" has now become "Church" and it is the local church
that has the task of accompanying people as they seek to discover values
to guide their lives in a rapidly changing world. We must avoid funda-
mentalistic approaches that perceive the world simply in black and white
or good and evil. Part of the mission of the local church must be to draw
on both the Gospel and cultural traditions so as help the new generation
discover positive values that guide their actions as respectful and responsible members of our increasingly globalised society.

Appendix A

Questionnaire   (No…

Name: (optional)	*Gender*: (a) male (b) female
Age:	*Place/Clan*:
Grade: 9 10 11 12	*Church*:

Today the Christian Churches in Enga are for the most part led by Papua New Guineans. However most of these churches were started / planted by expatriate missionaries. This questionnaire is intended to find out more about the attitude of young people from Enga (in High School or Secondary School) towards the early missionaries and their cultural values.

The information will be used in a paper being prepared by Fr. Philip Gibbs on the topic of "Melanesian and Western values and how they impact as a result of missionary interaction." Fr Philip will be happy to forward a copy of the paper to the school, once it is finished.

1. What expression best describes your feeling about the early missionaries who came to Enga? (mark one box)
☐ I have good and thankful feelings towards them
☐ I have angry negative feelings towards them.
☐ I have no feelings either way.

2. Many of the early missionaries tried to learn and use the local Enga language. How do you feel about that? (mark one box)
☐ They were wasting their time
☐ I respect them for trying to learn the language
☐ I have no feelings either way

3. Your parents and grandparents may have told you stories about some of the early missionaries. Can you write down the names of some of the very early missionaries from your church (the first ones that were here in the 1940's and 1950's)

☐ I don't know any of their names
☐ I know some names. They are _____

_____   _____

4. Some people today say that "the missionaries destroyed our culture."
Do you agree or disagree with this statement? (mark one box)
☐ I agree that they did destroy our culture
☐ I disagree with the statement
☐ I don't know

5. Do you think that the early missionaries had a positive approach to
Enga culture or a negative approach?
☐ positive   ☐ negative   ☐ both positive and negative ☐ don't know

If you marked any of the first three boxes above, please explain why you
gave that response. Try to give some practical examples.

_____

_____

6. Did the early missionaries forbid (tambu) people to do certain things
or to follow certain customs?
☐ Yes, they did forbid some things   ☐ No, they did not forbid anything
If you answered "yes" then list some of the things that they forbade.

_____

_____

7. In your opinion, are there some traditional Enga values and customs
that fit well with Christian life today?   If so, what are they?

_____

_____

8. In your opinion, are there some traditional Enga values and customs
that conflict or do not fit well with Christian life today. If so, what are
they?

_____

_____

9. In your opinion, are there some aspects of "modern Western" culture that fit well with Christian life today? If so, what are they?

_____

_____

10. In your opinion, are there some aspects of "modern Western" culture that conflict or do not fit well with Christian life today. If so, what are they?

_____

_____

11. Do you feel that your values and ideas are different from those of your parents and grandparents?

☐ Different   ☐ No Difference

If you answered that your values and ideas are different please explain giving examples.

Appendix B
Instrumental and Terminal Values Questionnaire

Below are two lists of values. Please rank the two lists by putting a number behind each of the values, putting the number 1 for the value you feel is most important for you, and 2 for the next, 3 for the next in importance, and so on until you get to 18.

Instrumental Values	Rank here 1-18	Terminal Values	Rank here 1-18
Ambitious		A comfortable life	
Broad-minded		An exciting life	
Capable		A sense of accomplishment	
Cheerful		A world at peace	
Clean		A world of beauty	
Courageous		Equality	
Forgiving		Family security	
Helpful		Freedom	
Honest		Happiness	
Imaginative		Inner harmony	
Independent		Mature love	
Intellectual		National security	
Logical		Pleasure	
Loving		Salvation	
Obedient		Self-respect	
Polite		Social recognition	
Responsible		True friendship	
Self-controlled		Wisdom	

Year (circle one): 1 2 3 4 5 6
Home (circle one): Papua   Highlands   Momase   Islands   Solomons

Appendix C

Papua New Guinea and the Eastern Pacific

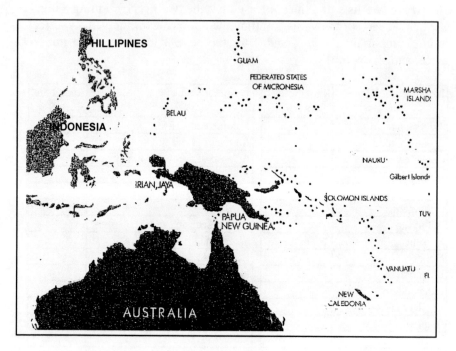

MACKAY AND THE ABORIGINALS: REFLECTIONS UPON THE AMBIGUITIES OF TAIWANESE ABORIGINAL CHRISTIAN HISTORY

James R. Rohrer[*]

Although barely three percent of the total population of Taiwan adheres to Christianity, between sixty to seventy percent of Taiwan's indigenous tribal people are Christians. In the largest Christian denomination, the Presbyterian Church in Taiwan (PCT), aboriginals account for some forty percent of the total communicants. A hypothetical first-time visitor to Taiwan who bypassed the island's populous west coast and landed in one of the central mountain or east coast towns, where a majority of the aboriginal people resides, might conclude that she had come to a predominantly Christian society. Churches, which are highly visible in virtually every mountain village and all along the east coast, serve a wide variety of social functions. In the past half century the church has become a key integrative institution around which embattled Taiwanese aboriginal cultures have organized.[1]

Aboriginal people have been a focus of Christian missionary efforts in Taiwan from the beginning. Since the early 17th century, when the first missionaries from Holland arrived in Formosa (as the island was known to Europeans), aboriginals have been heavily targeted for conversion. Dutch Calvinist and Spanish Catholic missionaries both worked among the indigenous people of Taiwan in the period from 1624 to1662,

[*] James R. Rohrer is associate professor of religion and history at Northwestern College, where he specializes in American Religious Culture as well as World Christianity. Dr. Rohrer served in Taiwan as a missionary educator before coming to Northwestern in 1998. His book, *Keepers of the Covenant*, about the decline in Congregationalism after the American Revolution, was published by Oxford University Press in 1995. He is now working on a second book about the origins and growth of Christianity in Taiwan.
[1] Scholars have yet to write a detailed history of aboriginal churches in the modern era. Ralph Covell, *Pentecost of the Hills in Taiwan: the Christian Faith among the Original Inhabitants* (Pasadena: Hope, 1998) provides a helpful survey. Two older but still very useful sociological studies are George Vicedom, *Faith That Moves Mountains: A Study Report on the Amazing Growth and Present Life of the Church Among the Mountain Tribes of Taiwan* (Taipei, 1967); and Justus Freytag, *A New Day in the Mountains: Problems of Social Integration and Modernization Confronting the Tribal People in Taiwan* (Tainan, 1968).

baptizing more than 10,000 converts before an army of Chinese Ming loyalists under the leadership of Cheng Ch'eng-kung expelled all foreigners from the island.[2] When Protestant and Roman Catholic missionary efforts resumed in the mid-19th century, both parties found that the heavily acculturated lowland aboriginals—the so-called "Pepohoan" or "plains barbarians"[3]—responded far more readily to missionary appeals than did the dominant Chinese population. By the close of the Chinese era in 1895, well over half of all baptized Christians in Taiwan were lowland aboriginals.

Although the Japanese who colonized Taiwan from 1895 to 1945 carefully regulated missionary efforts and attempted to frustrate Christian access to the unacculturated tribal people in the central mountains, the gospel had infiltrated the "high mountain" villages by the late Japanese era. Largely through the efforts of small bands of aboriginal converts, such as the elderly Sediq woman named Chi Oang, thousands of Sediq, Tayal, and Bunun people embraced Christianity during the years of World War II, a time when foreign missionaries were absent from the island. When Western missionaries returned after the War, they were startled to find thousands of new converts in the mountains of Taiwan awaiting baptism, many of whom had never seen a foreign evangelist. During the following decade the mountains of Taiwan witnessed a mass people movement as one tribal group after another turned *en masse* toward Christianity. Especially after mainland China expelled foreign missionaries, numerous western mission agencies diverted personnel and

---

[2] See William Campbell, *Formosa under the Dutch* (London, 1903; SMC reprint, 1992) and William Campbell, *An Account of Missionary Success in the Island of Formosa* (London, 1887; SMC reprint, 1996) for primary accounts of the Dutch mission. Useful secondary accounts are John Jyigiokk Tin, "Christianity in Taiwan," in *Christianity in Asia*, T. K. Thomas ed. (Singapore, 1979); J. J. A. M. Kuepers, *The Dutch Reformed Church in Formosa, 1627-1662: Mission in a Colonial Context*, Reprint from *Nouvelle Revue de science missionnaire* 33 (1977), 247-267, 34 (1978), 48-67; Leonard Blusse, "Dutch Protestant Missionaries as Protagonists of the Territorial Expansion of the VOC on Formosa," in *Conversion, Competition and Conflict: Essays on the Role of Religion in Asia*, Dick Kooiman, et. al., eds. (Amsterdam, 1985); Henry Rowald, "Seventeenth Century Roman Catholic Missions in Taiwan," *The South East Asia Journal of Theology* 15:2 (1974), 68-79; John Robert Shepherd, *Statecraft and Political Economy on the Taiwan Frontier, 1600-1800* (Stanford, 1993), 47-90.
[3] This common term is an English corruption of the Chinese *p'ing -p'u- fan* or "plains barbarians." The lowland aboriginals were also commonly called *shu-fan* or "cooked barbarians" as opposed to the high mountain *sheng-fan* or "raw barbarians."

resources to these groups, making the aboriginal people of Taiwan one of the most intensively evangelized populations in the world.[4]

Unfortunately, despite the lengthy history of Christianity among Taiwan's indigenous peoples, to date almost all Taiwanese aboriginal Christians are members of denominations controlled largely by non-aboriginal leadership. This reality has served to frustrate-- in sometimes subtle but sometimes painfully obvious ways—efforts to forge an authentically indigenous expression of Christian faith for the aboriginal people. Although the Presbyterian Church in Taiwan has in recent decades placed great emphasis upon the need to indigenize the gospel, the strong identification of the PCT with the dominant Taiwanese population has made it difficult for aboriginal Christians to achieve equality within established ecclesiastical structures.

Earlier mission efforts among the lowland aboriginals offered even less opportunity for the integration of aboriginal culture and Christianity. In both the Dutch period and the 19th century significant numbers of aboriginal people turned toward Christianity seeking some sort of protection against external threats, only to find the church itself a primary instrument for their more rapid acculturation to, or even assimilation into, the dominant population. The following paragraphs will briefly examine one illustrative case study, the mission established by George Leslie Mackay, a Canadian Presbyterian who planted Protestantism in North Taiwan in the late Ch'ing and early Japanese eras (1872-1901).

During the nearly thirty years of his ministry Mackay gained fame in Canada as an ardent exponent of a native church. He planted sixty churches, each with a Taiwanese preacher, and steadfastly resisted the introduction of additional foreign missionaries, hoping that the Taiwanese Christians would become independent after his death. Moreover, of all the hundreds of missionaries who labored in the Chinese empire in the 19th century, Mackay is one of only two who married a native spouse. Throughout his career he shared every dimension of his ministry with his wife, Tiu Chhang-mia, the adopted granddaughter of his first female convert. The Mackays lived in Taiwanese fashion, spoke only Taiwanese within the family, and reared three children who identified themselves as

---

[4] In addition to Covell and Vicedom, cited above, see James Dickson, *Stranger Than Fiction: A Thrilling Story of the Modern Mission Movement Among the Aborigines of Formosa* (Toronto, 1948); and Margaret L. Copland, *Chi-Oang: Mother of the Taiwan Tribes Church* (Taipei, 1962). Grace McGill, *The Path of Life: Memoirs of Clare and Grace McGill* (Belleville, Ontario, 2001) highlights the work of one influential missionary couple.

Taiwanese. Mackay's two daughters both married Taiwanese preachers, who served as influential leaders in the Taiwanese Presbyterian Church after his death in 1901.[5]

In striking contrast to most Victorian missionaries, Mackay has never yet been deconstructed. He remains a potent icon among Taiwanese Christians, and has been elevated to folk hero status in the broader society. Indeed, in their efforts to secure close relations with western democracies, Taiwanese leaders have found in Mackay a useful political symbol. During the centennial anniversary of Mackay's death, the Taiwanese Ministry of Cultural Affairs joined with the Canadian Trade Office in Taipei and the Presbyterian Church in Taiwan in hosting an amazing weeklong tribute to his missionary career. The centennial was capped by the release of a commemorative postage stamp by the government of Taiwan, in recognition of his "unselfish devotion to Taiwan, and so to strengthen the bonds of friendship between Taiwan and Canada."[6]

Advocates of Taiwanese aboriginal rights played a conspicuous role in the centennial observances. News releases widely reported (erroneously) that Mackay's wife was a lowland aboriginal woman.[7] Taipei's Shung Ye Museum of Formosan Aborigines mounted a major exhibition of aboriginal artifacts collected by Mackay and now housed at Toronto's Royal Ontario Museum. The exhibition opening, which was covered by national television, featured an address by former ROC President Lee

---

[5] The author is currently writing the first full scholarly analysis of Mackay and the North Formosa mission. See Alvyn Austin, "Mackay, George Leslie," in *Dictionary of Canadian Biography* XIII (Toronto: 1994); Graeme McDonald, "George Leslie Mackay: Missionary Success in Nineteenth Century Taiwan," *Papers on China* 21 (Cambridge, MA, 1968); and James R. Rohrer, "The Development of Mission Theory and Principles in the Field: George Leslie Mackay of Taiwan, 1872-1901," University of Cambridge, North Atlantic Missiology Project Consultation Paper, March 19, 1998. Available on-line at: www.divinity.cam.ac.uk/carts/namp

[6] Quoted from the first day cache issued by the Directorate General of Posts, Republic of China, June 1, 2001. The stamp is also featured on the cover of the Directorate General's philatelic magazine *Postal Service Today*, no. 521, May 20, 2001.

[7] This is a widespread folk story among Taiwanese aboriginals, and asserted as fact by the Alvyn Austin biography cited above. Family history materials given to the author by the descendents of Mackay indicate that his wife came from a Chinese family. Because many Chinese migrants to Taiwan took aboriginal wives, it is common for Taiwanese to have mixed ancestry. If this was true in the case of Mackay's wife, however, there is no evidence that her family had any awareness of the fact.

Teng-hui, who suggested that Mackay was an early exponent of aboriginal rights. Yohani Isqaqavut, Chairman of the cabinet-level Council of Aboriginal Affairs, likewise cited Mackay as a lifelong champion of the aboriginal people. According to the Shung Ye Museum, the Mackay exhibition was intended to "encourage everyone to consider how harmonious relationships might be constructed between Taiwan's ethnic groups, and how a pluralist outlook may be developed for the new century."[8]

Significantly, not all aboriginal leaders share this enthusiasm for Mackay. At an international symposium, sponsored by the Canadian Trade Office in Taipei and Taiwan's Ministry of Cultural Affairs as part of the centenary, a few advocates of aboriginal rights voiced their strong belief that the missionary was guilty of cultural genocide. The artifacts exhibited at the Shung Ye Museum, they pointed out, were all that remained from the bonfires that supposedly destroyed most of the material culture of Mackay's aboriginal converts. The entire Mackay centennial, these critics charged, represented an effort by the ROC government and the Canadian Trade Office to whitewash past sins committed against the aboriginal people of Taiwan.[9]

What is the truth about Mackay and the aboriginals? An analysis of the available sources suggests that his harshest critics have greatly overstated their case. George Leslie Mackay was probably less inclined toward the destruction of aboriginal culture than most other missionaries of his age. On the other hand, it is equally an exaggeration to represent Mackay as a champion of the aboriginal people. It is bizarre to characterize him as an effective symbol for a "pluralist outlook," or a model for interracial relationships. The historical record clearly reveals a deep ambiguity in his relationship to aboriginal culture.

Unlike many of the English Presbyterian and Roman Catholic missionaries who worked in the South of the island, Mackay did not focus his energies upon aboriginal groups. He was certain that he had been

---

[8] The author was present at the opening ceremony. There is a brief English account of the ceremony by journalist Jason Pan, "Dr. Mackay collection of aboriginal artifacts goes on local display," *Taiwan News*, June 3, 2001. The stated purposes of the exhibition are printed on a pamphlet, "The Dr. Mackay Collection of Formosan Aboriginal Artifacts: Treasures Preserved Abroad," printed by the Shung Ye Museum for the exhibition.

[9] The author was a panelist in the symposium and engaged in an open discussion of this issue during the question and answer segment of the presentation. Mark Munsterhjelm, a western human rights activist, expressed similar views in the *Taipei Times*, February 26, 2001.

called specifically to plant the gospel among the dominant Hokkien populace whose roots lay in China's Fukien Province. Having acquired a high level of proficiency in Taiwanese *(Fukien-hua)* during his initial year on the island, he soon gathered around him a cadre of dedicated Taiwanese converts who served as his close lieutenants and the vital leadership of the movement throughout his remaining years of ministry. Identifying himself with the Taiwanese populace, Mackay adamantly resisted suggestions that he ought to expand his labors to the unacculturated mountain groups. Missionaries devoted exclusively to the goal of converting tribal people, he insisted, should necessarily launch any such mission.[10]

Nonetheless, there is no doubt that lowland aboriginals constituted a very significant portion of Mackay's converts from the beginning of his ministry in 1872, although available sources make it impossible to pinpoint with any precision what percentage of the total Canadian mission community was drawn from this group. Numerous villages of highly acculturated aboriginals existed in the hill country of northwest Taiwan in the late nineteenth century, as well as on the Ilan Plain on the northeast coast.[11] As Mackay and his Taiwanese students itinerated throughout the northern end of the island between 1872 and 1901, they routinely passed through these villages, whose inhabitants readily understood Taiwanese and were easily gathered into an audience.

Mackay's journals indicate that these lowland aboriginal villagers were more ready to embrace Christianity than the Chinese populace whom he regarded as his primary target. During his first year in the island, although he gained numerous dedicated Taiwanese converts and opened his first chapel in the Taiwanese village of Go-kho-ki, the most receptive audience he encountered was in the Pepohoan village of Sinkang. Barely one month after his initial visit in October 1872, a delegation from the village visited Mackay at his home in Tamsui, carrying the names of many villagers who wished to receive Christian instruction. By April 1873 he had opened his second chapel among these acculturated aboriginals, and the church there grew much faster than those he planted

---

[10] Mackay stated this viewpoint many times. See, for example, George Leslie Mackay, *From Far Formosa* (New York, 1895), 265-66.

[11] The best treatment in English of these lowland groups is the Shepherd monograph cited above. See also a very useful essay by I-Shou Wang, "Cultural Contact and the Migration of Taiwan's Aborigines: A Historical Perspective," in Ronald G. Knapp, ed. *China's Island Frontier: Studies in the Historical Geography of Taiwan* (Honolulu, 1980), 31-54.

in predominantly Taiwanese towns. Mackay reflected that these Pepohoan villagers were "more emotional, approachable, and responsive than the Chinese."[12]

Despite this success Mackay believed that his primary focus should remain with the more resistant Hokkien people. After Sinkang he would open no new chapels among the Pepohoan for nearly a decade. "Our work is chiefly amongst the Chinese," he explained to the mission board in 1875, "and I thank God for that because they are the advancing race."[13] Mackay, who rejected Darwinian natural selection on biblical grounds, nevertheless proved to be a thoroughgoing social Darwinist. He was certain that the aboriginals were racially inferior to the Chinese, "less solid and stable," more prone to dissipation and laziness, and less intelligent. "The longer my experience among them the plainer appears to me the inferiority" of the aboriginal, Mackay asserted. "For downright cruelty and cut-throat baseness the Pepohoan far outdistance the Chinese," he wrote, "they manifest the revengeful spirit of the race to which they belong."[14] These biological tendencies, coupled with their minority status, made it inevitable that they would soon be altogether absorbed by the superior race. In his letters and journals he repeatedly refers to the aboriginals as "poor," "pitiful" and "doomed" to disappear.

Accompanied by Pepohoan guides, Mackay often took foreign visitors on tours into the central mountains to visit the "untamed savage" aboriginals, the notorious headhunters of Formosa who featured prominently in virtually all western publications about the island. He relished these trips because they gave him an opportunity to collect specimens for the natural history museum he kept in his home, but also because he enjoyed impressing dignitaries with his knowledge of the exotic tribal people. On one such excursion in 1889, a British engineer named John Wilkinson recorded that Mackay "exhibited his savages much as he might an inanimate curio, they taking the necessary pullings and tappings with the utmost good humour and gravity."[15]

---

[12] See Mackay's manuscript Diary, Vol. 1 (1871-1872), 150, Taiwan Theological College Archives, Taipei, Taiwan.

[13] Mackay to William Mclaren, June 28, 1875, Formosa Mission Correspondence, Records of the Board of Foreign Missions of the Presbyterian Church in Canada, United Church Archives, Victoria University, Toronto. Hereafter cited as *FMC*.

[14] Mackay, *From Far Formosa*, 207, 215.

[15] W. H. Wilkenson to Sir John Walsham , March 27, 1889, FO 228/881, Public Record Office, London.

In light of Mackay's attitudes about Taiwan's indigenous cultures, the recent efforts to cast him as an early champion of aboriginal rights seem misplaced. Much of his reputation as a friend to the aboriginal people rests upon his work among the Kavulan group of the Ilan Plain, who turned *en masse* to Christianity during the 1880s. As had been the case with Sin-kang a decade earlier, lowland aboriginals in Ilan approached Mackay in late 1881 requesting Christian instruction. Over the next two decades he crossed the mountains to visit the aboriginal villages in the Ilan district at least twice yearly, carrying western medicine, performing dentistry and surgery, and establishing churches. He found this latter task easy, for the aboriginals were eager to attach themselves to his movement. Within four years he established eighteen aboriginal churches in Ilan, and baptized over 1100 converts, nearly doubling the total number of communicants in the Canadian Presbyterian mission.[16]

In his reports to Canada Mackay portrayed the conversion of the Kavulans as a miraculous work of God. He was, however, well aware of the economic and political factors sparking the movement. Taiwan at the time was entering the global market as a major supplier of tea, sugar and camphor, and the population of the island steadily swelled with migrants from across the Formosa Straits, generating increasing conflicts between Chinese and aboriginals over land tenure. Many lowland aboriginal people, long shielded by government policies designed to protect their property rights, now found themselves confronting mounting efforts by Chinese neighbors to dispossess them of their lands. Mackay acknowledged that many aboriginals looked to the missionaries as a source of protection against Chinese incursions, a reality that disturbed him. "I was not altogether satisfied with the people," he noted of one group of Pepohoan, "They seemed to me too much concerned about the... missionaries coming as their protectors."[17]

By the 1880s Mackay had become famous throughout North Taiwan for his diplomatic handling of conflicts between Christian converts and their enemies. In a series of cases during the 1870s involving the destruction of chapels by Chinese mobs, Mackay ingratiated himself with local Chinese authorities by scrupulously following Chinese law and refusing to support converts in instances when they did not clearly have law on their side. He had a knack for knowing how to address local gentry and court officials, when to compromise, and when it was neces-

---

[16] Mackay to Thomas Wardrope, March 27, 1886, *FMC*.
[17] Mackay Diary, Vol. 1, 54-55.

sary to appeal to British consular authorities. His sensitivity to local custom and social etiquette earned him the respect of both British and Chinese administrators, and eventually gained the favor of Taiwan's first provincial governor, the reformist Liu Ming-chuan.

In one particularly dramatic case Mackay faced down the powerful Lin family of Bangkah, the largest landowners in North Taiwan and one of the wealthiest gentry families in the island. When the Lins sought to prevent the establishment of a church among their renters, resorting to violence to intimidate both Mackay and the local Christians, Mackay's patient and carefully measured response earned the full support of the British consular staff and brought the provincial governor to act against the Lins.[18]

It is not surprising that embattled aboriginals in Ilan, seeking security against land-hungry Chinese neighbors, eagerly sought Mackay's favor. In turning towards the church they hoped to find a protected space in which to maintain at least something of their independence from the Chinese. Mackay described the aboriginals of Ilan as being highly acculturated, and yet retaining many of their traditional beliefs and rituals. Most of them could speak the dominant language of the Hokkien populace, and most had adopted Chinese garb and nominally accepted Chinese folk religion. Yet, Mackay observed, their hatred of the Chinese burned strong, and their practice of Chinese religion was more a matter of political necessity than conviction. "Whenever a tribe submits," he wrote, "the first thing is to shave their head in a token of allegiance, and then temples, idols, and tablets are introduced." Although a few younger aboriginals embraced Chinese religion and customs wholeheartedly and sought to distance themselves from their cultural past, Mackay observed that most "hate the new order of things. Idolatry does not suit the average Pepohoan, and it is only of necessity that he submits to even the formal observance of its rites and ceremonies. It is political rather than religious, and to the large majority is meaningless except as a reminder of their enslavement to an alien race."[19]

It is against this background that we need to interpret Mackay's tour of Ilan in 1882 and 1883, when hundreds of lowland aboriginal vil-

---

[18] Mackay's highly romanticized account of the case can be found in his book, *From Far Formosa*, 164-171. Detailed records of the case can be found in the British Foreign Office papers at the Public Record Office in London. See FO 228/596, 616, 635.

[19] Mackay, *From Far Formosa*, 208.

lagers on their own initiative built bonfires, and threw their Chinese idols and ancestor tablets into the flames. It is to these bonfires that Mackay's modern critics point when making the charge of cultural genocide, an accusation that fails to appreciate the agency of the aboriginal people themselves. Mackay, in fact, did not employ the burning of indigenous religious artifacts as a bridge-burning ritual, which was a standard practice followed by other missionaries in Taiwan. Instead it was his policy to ask converts to "surrender" their gods and tablets to him, as one would surrender to a conquering military leader. He then preserved these "trophies" intact in his own house, where one entire room was filled with shelf upon shelf of vanquished deities and surrendered tablets. By preserving these artifacts intact, Mackay symbolically demonstrated that he had power to keep them locked away without suffering harm, a gesture that reinforced his own spiritual authority over the converts.

In the case of the Ilan aboriginals, Mackay carefully preserved any artifacts that had significance within traditional aboriginal culture, but allowed the people to destroy the hated symbols of Chinese rule. In short, the bonfires were not a crime against aboriginal culture, but rather a sort of Kavulan declaration of independence from Chinese control. Or so the aboriginal converts undoubtedly assumed at the time they embraced Christianity.[20]

Mackay realized that the aboriginals in Ilan had little understanding of Christian doctrine and that their motivation for seeking Christian instruction was more pragmatic than spiritual. Under normal circumstances he would have required a lengthy period of instruction before organizing them into churches, or admitting them to baptism. Yet within four years he baptized more than one thousand and gathered them into eighteen churches. His eagerness to establish churches among the Kavulan was sparked not by any new found commitment to aboriginal ministry but rather by his hatred of the Dominican priests from the Philippines who in 1886 made an appearance in Ilan. According to his missionary colleague John Jamieson, Mackay, who like most Victorian Canadian Presbyterians was virulently anti-Catholic, feared that these priests would "lead away the simple-minded Pepohoan." In an effort to prevent the "papists" from "possessing" the "long-waiting" ground, he rushed to establish a chapel with a native preacher in every significant town in the Plain, admitting that had it not been "for the plotting design

---

[20] Ibid, 231.

of the priests, these new stations would not have been opened for some time."[21]

During the next two decades some aboriginals undoubtedly acquired a sincere commitment to Christianity. But the Christianity that they embraced left little room for traditional aboriginal customs. With all but a handful of exceptions the Pepohoan churches had Taiwanese preachers trained by Mackay. Throughout the 1880s and 1890s a steady stream of aboriginal youth—especially young girls—left Ilan annually and traveled to Tamsui to attend either the boarding school for girls or the theological college established by Mackay. Here they spoke only in Taiwanese, learned to read and write both in Chinese characters and also the romanized colloquial Taiwanese script. Here they learned English hymnody (sung in Taiwanese translation), and here they studied Western science and the rudiments of Western medicine. Here too they studied the Confucian classics, as well as geography, botany, astronomy, church history, the Bible and Reformed Theology. There is also evidence that some of the aboriginal girls schooled in Tamsui became wives for Taiwanese preachers. For such women, the church was the door to complete assimilation.[22]

Given the degree of acculturation already prevalent among the lowland aboriginals at the time of their conversion, coupled with Mackay's assumption that the tribal people must inevitably be absorbed by the superior Taiwanese, it is not surprising that the Presbyterian Mission made no effort to indigenize the gospel for the Kavulan. Rather, lowland aboriginal Christians were expected to fit into a church that identified itself as Taiwanese, and were as a matter of course expected to utilize the same language, conform to the same rules of conduct, and learn the same theology as Christians from the dominant culture. While this theology made some room for Chinese tradition, for Confucius *was* a part of the curriculum at Oxford College, aboriginal tradition played no discernible role in the mission biculture. Missionaries frequently complained about

---

[21] John Jamieson to Thomas Wardrope, 11 May 1887, *FMC*. The Dominican view of the Protestants was equally jaundiced. Their own efforts to establish posts in North Formosa were motivated at least partly by their stated desire to "neutralize" Mackay's work. See the letters translated and reproduced in Fr. Pablo Fernandez, *One Hundred Years of Dominican Apostolate in Formosa, 1859-1958* (Manila, 1959; SMC reprint, 1994), 156-174.

[22] These generalizations are based upon my careful reading of the Mackay letters in *FMC* and Mackay's unpublished diaries. See also *From Far Formosa*, 285-307.

the tendency of aboriginal Christians to "backslide" into traditional life-styles of dissipation—meaning bouts of group drunkenness—and they placed a heavy emphasis upon temperance as a sign of authentic conversion. But when, in the early 20th century, a group of visiting Japanese dignitaries asked a congregation of Pepohoan Christians to perform some of their ancestral dances, the request was refused as inappropriate behavior for Christians. [23]

Within a few years of the death of George Leslie Mackay, all but a few of the aboriginal churches established in Ilan had ceased to exist.[24] Nominalism had always been a problem. With the coming of the Japanese and the creation of a new colonial system, the legal status of Christian missions in Taiwan changed dramatically; the missionaries no longer constituted effective sources of protection for aboriginal people. Many lowland aboriginals simply drifted away from the churches, while those that remained became increasingly indistinguishable from the Taiwanese Christians among whom they had cast their lot. Today, most of the Christian descendants of these Plains aboriginal converts have fully assimilated into the dominant society.[25]

There are hopeful signs that the mountain aboriginals who embraced Christianity in the mid-20th century are more successfully resisting assimilation. Certainly the Presbyterian Church in Taiwan is today far more strongly committed to the preservation of aboriginal culture than was true half a century ago. The Bible has been translated into most of the remaining tribal languages, and the PCT has taken a strong stands in support of aboriginal land rights and government programs to preserve aboriginal cultural identity. The PCT has also for more than half a century maintained a theological institution --Yushan College and Seminary--specifically to train leaders for the aboriginal churches. In recent years aboriginal presbyteries have been established, in recognition of the unique needs of the aboriginal churches and the communities that they serve. These institutions have served to launch some discussion of the need for a more indigenous expression of Christian faith for Taiwan's aboriginal people.

Nonetheless, aboriginal Christians still experience frustrations

---

[23] Duncan McLeod to John Armstrong, October 15, 1913, *FMC.*
[24] Mackay's successor William Gauld did not follow up on the work among the Ilan Pepohoan, believing that they were "pests" who cost more time and energy than they were worth. See Thurlow Fraser to R.P. Mackay, May 19, 1904, *FMC.*
[25] Covell, *Pentecost of the Hills*, 144-146 discusses the failure of the early Pepohoan movement.

within the PCT, an organization which is patterned after western denominational bureaucracies and which pursues a model of theological education heavily influenced by western models despite much talk of indigenization during the past several decades. As a former professor at Yushan College and Seminary, I have had personal conversations with aboriginal leaders who feel marginalized within the PCT, and who question whether a more indigenous church for aboriginal people can emerge within the existing ecclesiastical structure. I have also had personal conversations with Taiwanese Christians who feel that too much attention is paid to aboriginal issues and that the aboriginal leadership places unrealistic demands upon the denomination. In short, despite much progress in recognizing that aboriginal Christians are not the same as Taiwanese Christians, the two groups have still not come to a point where they fully trust one another and are able to work together effectively within a common organization toward meeting the unique needs of the aboriginal people of Taiwan.

INCULTURATING THE EASTER FEAST IN SOUTHEAST AUSTRALIA

Clare V. Johnson[*]

The connection between the Christian Easter Feast and the Northern Hemispheric season of spring can be traced back to the very origins of Christianity. The date on which Easter is celebrated each year, determined according to the occurrence of the vernal equinox, along with traditional theological interpretations of Easter and its overall liturgical theme, have all been closely linked to the season of spring. However, as Christianity has spread throughout the world, the celebration of Easter has been transposed into various different climatic and cultural circumstances. For reasons of ecclesial unity and ritual uniformity, the Northern Hemisphere dating and ritual pattern for this feast has been maintained wherever the church has taken root. But, when the Easter Feast is celebrated in the Southern Hemisphere, both the lunar dating and natural season are reversed, leaving Southern Hemisphere Christians with an often incongruous symbolic, ritual and linguistic dilemma when celebrating this feast according to the universal anniversary date.

In *Sacrosanctum Concilium* #38, the Second Vatican Council called for provisions to be made "for legitimate variations and adaptations (of the liturgy) to different groups, regions, and peoples, especially in mission lands, provided the substantial unity of the Roman Rite is preserved."[1] The Council, proposed that adaptations of the liturgy be made in order to bring it closer to the cultural experience of the local church, within the limits set by the *editiones typicae* of the liturgical books.

Inculturation of the liturgy involves the process of inserting the texts and rites of the liturgy into the framework of the local culture, resulting in the assimilation into those texts and rites, of the people's

---

[*] Clare V. Johnson is a Ph.D. Candidate in Liturgical Studies at the University of Notre Dame. She holds a B.Mus. (Hons) from the University of Melbourne, an A.Mus.A., a B.Theol. (Hons) from the Melbourne College of Divinity, and an M.A. (Theol) from Catholic Theological Union at Chicago. She is the editor of *Ars Liturgiae: Worship, Aesthetics and Praxis*, (Chicago: Liturgy Training Publications, 2003), and has published articles in *Worship, Pastoral Music*, and *The Summit*.
[1] *The Liturgy Documents: A Parish Resource*, Elizabeth Hoffman, ed., (Chicago, IL: Liturgy Training Publications, 1991), 17.

thought, language, value, ritual, symbolic and artistic pattern.[2] *Contextualization* of the liturgy means taking into account not only the verbal and cognitive elements of a cultural setting but also the physical and environmental circumstances in which the local church operates when placing the liturgy in dialogue with a local culture.

Universal celebration of the Easter Feast fulfills the principle of time concurrence for the anniversary of Christ's death and resurrection. However, the simultaneous, but vastly different, environmental seasons in the Southern Hemisphere and Equatorial regions of the world provide different interpretations of the primary natural symbols used in the ritual of the Easter Feast, from those used in the Northern Hemisphere.

This essay investigates the dilemma facing Christians in southeast Australia as they attempt to make sense of the universal ritual mandated for the celebration of Easter, in a climatic pattern that is diametrically opposed to that in which the Easter Feast originally was conceived and developed. Various solutions have been proposed to address the dilemma facing Christians in southeast Australia as they try to deal with discrepancies between designated universal rituals and commonsense local knowledge. However these solutions challenge the recently promoted ecclesial principle of liturgical uniformity for the sake of universal unity.[3] In many ways challenges to the principle of liturgical uniformity tend to result in deep divisions between those who are proponents of maintaining the 'substantial unity of the Roman Rite' and those who recognize the need to make legitimate adaptations of the liturgy to the needs and circumstances of local cultures.

A theological revisioning of the major natural symbols of the Easter Feast, consonant with the experience of these symbols in the local context of southeast Australia, can aid in the process of revivifying and inculturating the liturgy in this context, while maintaining the universal dating of Easter.

I. The Easter-Spring Connection

The Christian liturgical year is arranged around two major poles:

---

[2] Anscar J. Chupungco, *Liturgical Inculturation: Sacramentals, Religiosity and Catechesis* (Collegeville, MN: The Liturgical Press/Pueblo, 1992), 30.
[3] See for example, the documents from the Vatican Congregation for Divine Worship and the Discipline of the Sacraments, *Varietates Legitimae*, 23:43 (1994): 745,747-756, and *Liturgiam Authenticam*, 31:2 (2001): 17, 19-32.

the feast of the Nativity of Christ (observed annually in the Western church on December 25) and the feast of Easter, the Resurrection of Christ, which has a moveable date. The dating of the Easter Feast (for the Western church) is determined annually, according to the occurrence of the Vernal (or spring) Equinox, with Easter being celebrated on the Sunday after the full moon which follows the equinox. The equinox is the time when the sun crosses the equator of the earth making night and day of equal length in all parts of the world.

The dating of Easter Sunday determines the dating of the ritual celebrations which immediately precede it: Holy Week, and the forty days of Lent and the three Sundays preceding Lent, as well as the ritual celebrations which immediately follow it: the Ascension (forty days after Easter) and Pentecost, (fifty days after Easter).[4] Christianity has always stressed the importance of times and places in its history, theology and scripture. There is no escaping the fact that Christianity is a profoundly historical religion, and that, historically, Jesus Christ died and rose in the Northern Hemisphere season of spring.

According to Talley, the Gospel of John situates the crucifixion of Jesus on the Preparation of the Jewish Passover, 14 Nisan:

> ...at the time of the slaying of lambs for the feast that would begin at nightfall.... The synoptic gospels identify Jesus' Last Supper with his disciples as the Passover, eaten at the beginning of 15 Nisan, but it is the Johannine tradition of his death on 14 Nisan that has been most significant in shaping the liturgical year.[5]

In Old Testament biblical tradition, the first day of Nisan is considered to be the first day of a New Year, "thanks to the influence of the Babylonian calendar and the prescription of Exodus 12:2 which ordains that 'this month shall stand at the head of your calendar; you shall reckon it the first month of the year.'"[6] In many religions, with Judaism being no exception, the beginning of a New Year has long been associated with cosmogony, or the creation of the world or origin of the universe, which

---

[4] Thomas J. Talley, "Calendar, Liturgical," *The New Dictionary of Sacramental Worship*, Peter E. Fink, ed., (Collegeville, MN: The Liturgical Press, 1990), 150.
[5] Ibid., 154.
[6] Anscar J. Chupungco, *Shaping the Easter Feast* (Washington, D.C.: The Pastoral Press, 1992), 23.

is thought to have taken place in springtime. For the Jewish people, the night of the full moon in the month of Nisan (between the 14th and 15th) is a crucial ritual time, during which the feast of the Passover is celebrated with a sacred meal. Nisan took on special significance as it was not only the month in which the Jewish people escaped from Egypt in the Exodus, which followed the Passover event, but also because it was traditionally believed to be the time when God created the universe, at the precise moment which we call the vernal equinox. Anscar J. Chupungco suggests that the season of spring:

> ...brings to mind everything that Passover signifies: creation, new birth, renewal of life. The traits of springtime enable Passover to depict in a graphic way the event of the Exodus, the creation of Israel as God's chosen people, and allegorically the passage of souls from vices to virtue.[7]

The formation of Christianity from within the midst of first century Judaism also meant that the month of Nisan took on special significance for Christians, as it was the month in which Jesus Christ was crucified and rose from the dead.

The connection of the Easter Feast with the season of spring dates back, therefore, to the very origins of Christianity, both in biblical tradition and according to extra-ecclesial sources. Chupungco notes that:

> The Christian tradition of cosmogony in spring is the direct legacy of Philo of Alexandria's work which carries the title *Special Laws*... [This work] shaped the patristic thinking on the date of Easter, especially with respect to the allegorical and spiritual interpretation of its cosmic elements. According to Philo, God created the world in springtime, in the month of Nisan... As Philo puts it, 'every year God reminds us of the creation of the world by setting before our eyes the season of spring when everything blooms and flowers.'[8]

Philo was a first-century philosopher, writer and political leader

---

[7] Ibid., 26.
[8] Ibid., 25.

who was the leading exponent of Alexandrian-Jewish culture, and a significant figure in Jewish-Greek literature, whose works had a formative influence on Christian theology from the first century forward.

Chupungco informs us that "the association of spring with the Christian feast of Easter surfaced for the first time in Origen's *Commentary on the Song of Songs*."[9] Origen (d. 253) does not connect spring with cosmogony in his commentary, but rather links spring (or the end of winter) with the time of Christ's passion. As the influence of Philo's writings spread, so too did the connection of the Christian Easter Feast with springtime imagery. Evidence from the writings of Eusebius of Caesarea, Cyril of Jerusalem, Gregory of Nanzianus, Ambrose of Milan and Pseudo-Ambrose attests to the widespread and increasingly popular connection of spring with the Easter Feast.[10] This connection made obvious sense, as spring was the time of nature's passage from death to new life, as well as the time of Christ's *transitus* from death to resurrected life. Spring was the season in which God created the world and also the season when Christ died and rose from the dead, creating the world anew in the Easter event. The development of the doctrine that God the creator of the world and Jesus the savior of the world are one and the same led eventually to the understanding that the feast of Christ's Passover could not be celebrated outside the time frame of spring.[11] Hence, spring has two important roles: as an element in the dating of Easter and as a useful allegorical tool for extrapolating theological interpretations of the Easter event.

Chupungco theorizes that the concept of anniversary is crucial in the continued connection of the Easter Feast with spring. Anniversaries are designed to be annual commemorations of significant events. "Christian tradition is constant in affirming that Christ died and rose from the dead in spring; hence the church commemorates the event in spring."[12] He notes further that:

> The feast is kept in spring in order to satisfy the requirement for an anniversary celebration: the feast should coincide with the date of Christ's passover. However, time is relative. When Christ died, it was spring in Pales-

---

[9] Ibid., 27.
[10] Ibid., 27-30.
[11] Ibid., 33.
[12] Ibid., 37.

tine, but simultaneously autumn and summer in the southern and equatorial regions. Churches in these parts of the world comply with the principle of time concurrence when they celebrate Easter in autumn and summer.[13]

The theological interpretation of Christ's death and resurrection through the lens of springtime does not function so well when the concurrent local environmental season in a particular culture is other than that in which the theological concept was formed originally.

One might ask, why should it matter what environmental season it is when the Church celebrates the Easter Feast? Should not this feast transcend time and place in order to enable Christians the world over to celebrate the paschal mystery uniformly and concurrently?

I suggest that the impact of local climatic conditions on the culture of native peoples leads to consequent problems for local churches as they attempt to celebrate rituals conceived and developed in diametrically opposite climatic circumstances.

II. The Impact of Environment and Climate on Culture

Ecology or the study of the relationship between living beings and their environment is a well-established branch of the natural sciences. Ecological anthropology studies the specifically human aspects of ecology, i.e. the ways and forms by which culture and society are influenced by the environment.[14] It is widely accepted that the natural environment deeply affects human life and must be considered to be one of the fundamental factors of and influences on culture.

The native environment forms what is perhaps the one undeniably common denominator between the people living in a particular culture, especially if that culture has been largely constituted of and by migrants, as is the case in modern multicultural Australia.

Research in ecological anthropology demonstrates that there is even a physiological impact made by particular environments on the people living in them. Emilio F. Moran notes that:

---

[13] Ibid., 38-39.
[14] See Bernardo Bernardi, "The Concept of Culture: A New Presentation," in *The Concept and Dynamics of Culture*, Bernardo Bernardi, ed. (Chicago, IL: Aldine, 1977), 80-81.

Human physiological functioning is, to an extent, regulated by the pattern of light and darkness in a twenty-
four hour period. Numerous physiological functions in
human beings are known to vary according to a circadian
rhythm synchronized to a twenty-four hour scheme.
Body temperature, blood pressure, pulse, respiration,
blood sugar, hemoglobin levels, amino acid levels, levels
of adrenal hormones, and levels of minerals excreted in
the urine all follow a daily rhythm.[15]

In experiments in which animals are placed consistently in the
light or dark, it has been shown that circadian rhythms (the functioning
of the biological clock) are innate and repetitive, adapting to the changing properties of the environment. Moran writes that the circadian path of
body temperature is higher at midday (when there is the most sunlight)
and lower in the morning and at nighttime. "Blood sugar, liver glycogen,
white corpuscle counts, adrenal activity, RNA and DNA synthesis, cell
division and drug-specific sensitivities have also been shown to follow
circadian rhythm."[16] Light, temperature and social interaction are three
synchronizers that have been identified as important in setting (or destabilizing) biological clocks. A logical and seemingly obvious conclusion
to be drawn from this data is that the nature of the environment in which
human beings live shapes their lives and their cultures to a certain degree. Any comprehensive program of cultural study cannot ignore the
influence of the physical environment on a people's physiology, mentality, psychology and overall cultural milieu.

So, how does the physical environment of southeast Australia
contribute to the development of local culture there?

Australians and Their Land

Australia is the smallest of the world's continents, an island nation surrounded by a huge expanse of water in the Southern Hemisphere. The
oceans surrounding Australia prevent any great extremes of temperature
on the continent, and while the summers can be very hot, the winters are
never really cold, except in the southeastern highlands. Often the cold
clear nights of July are followed by warm days, and while frosts are

---

[15] Emilio F. Moran, *Human Adaptability: An Introduction to Ecological Anthropology*, (Boulder, CO: Westview, 1979), 124.
[16] Ibid., 92.

common in winter, they are never extreme or prolonged.[17] The vast majority of the Australian people are congregated in an urban society, perched on the fringe of a fragile yet often harsh environment, living where there is sufficient water to sustain life. Thorne and Hall write: "Apart from a strip of land 200 to 300 miles wide stretching around the eastern half of the continent's perimeter and a small area in the southwestern corner, the remaining 90% of the continent is arid or semi-arid."[18]

Within Australia, large distances separate the major cities from one another. The vast stretches of intimidating desert-land spread across much of the interior of the country, coupled with the lack of neighboring border countries can engender a feeling of living in an empty, isolated environment.

In southeast Australia, the seasons are inverted by northern European standards, which leads to a very different rhythm in both the climatic and liturgical year from that in Europe or North America. David Ranson asserts that rather than the traditional northern European four-season climate, what can be observed in the natural environment in southeast Australia more closely resembles five seasonal periods. Ranson suggests the following structure:[19]

From mid-August to mid-November: we observe an intensification of the light, native plants flower, bursts of growth occur on already established plants, there is a rescinding of grayness and dampness, but the potential for springtime rains to result in flooding is ever present.

From mid-November to mid-January: the sun reaches its zenith, growth tails off, grasses go to seed, the role of the sun changes from one of nurturance to one of purification, we burn off excess undergrowth and we harvest our crops.

---

[17] See J. Gentilli, "Climate," in *Australia: A Geography*, D.N. Jeans, ed., (Sydney: Sydney University Press, 1977), p. 22

[18] Ross Thorne and Rob Hall, "Environmental Psychology in Australia," in *Handbook of Environmental Psychology: Volume 2*, Daniel Stokols and Irwin Altman, eds., (New York, NY: John Wiley and Sons, 1987), 1140.

[19] David Ranson, "Fire in Water: The Liturgical Cycle in the Experience of South-East Australian Seasonal Patterns." *Compass: A Review of Topical Theology* 26 (1992): 10.

From mid-January to mid-March: there is an aching heat and glaring light that bleaches timber, cloth and countryside; life is only conscious in the early morning and the evening. This is summer, the dominant season of the Australian year, a blazing core when the landscape begins to die from the heat and aridity. There is a consciousness of the destructive power of bushfire, coupled with its capacity to regenerate many native species. The signs of death and lifelessness confront us - the charcoal of fire and the landscape bleached of color by the incessant heat of the sun. We begin to yearn for a cool breeze, and rain to rejuvenate the parched land.

From mid-March to mid-May: as the rains are welcomed, the grasses change color from silver and brown to green. Change sweeps over the land, temperatures cool and we return from the beach no longer needing the proximity of water as a psychological defense against the immanence of death. It is the season of rejuvenation, of restoration to harmony.

From mid-May to mid-August: this is the time of gray solemnity, the 'twilight' of the annual cycle. The rains of winter dominate, and we await the return of the sunshine and blue skies to come.

Temperate regions of the world (as opposed to extreme geographic locales such as the Arctic or the desert) have measurably different seasons, that is, of changing climatic conditions over two, four or five distinct time-periods and climatic differentials. The number of seasonal variants depends on whether the region is tropical and hence has only a 'wet' and a 'dry' season, or whether the region has a measurable four season pattern (spring, summer, autumn, winter). Other regions demonstrate less easily defined seasonal patterns, such as that in southeast Australia (e.g. the five seasonal periods described by Ranson).

People in temperate regions adapt themselves to the seasonal variations of the geography by changing their clothing, lifestyle and activities depending on the operative weather matrix. As mentioned above, differing levels of light and darkness in a 24-hour period have an effect on the circadian rhythms of the human body during the different 'seasons' exhibited by the climatic circumstances. The human biorhythmic cycle is different in spring than it is in summer, in autumn or in winter. For example, Antarctic psychological researchers have noted that insomnia, disrupted sleep, anxiety, depression and irritability are common among people in winter, as people living for long periods without light experience disturbed physiological functioning, which in turn can disturb psychological well-being.[20]

Beyond the outer trappings of seasonal change (e.g. clothing, time spent outside, dietary differences due to available foods, etc.,) there are also differences to be noted in one's level of mental activity, psychological outlook, and, it can be argued, spiritual disposition according to the different seasons of a local climate. As a result, the type of *ritual activity* a people is involved in during springtime varies in theme, focus and style from the type of ritual activity a people is involved in during autumn.

With the coming of springtime one notices a reawakening of the earth after a period of inactivity during the barren winter months. Signs of new growth, the planting of seeds and birthing of young animals are witnessed in the lengthening daylight hours as general activity levels increase. The type of ritual pattern often seen during a Northern springtime focuses on celebrating the triumph of light over darkness, the reawakening of the earth after its winter slumber, and the evident fertility and rapid plant growth that comes with spring. There is an overall sense of anticipation in the rituals of springtime, whereas in autumn with its cooler temperatures and shorter daylight hours, people begin to spend less time outside and general levels of activity decline. The type of ritual pattern often encountered during this season focuses on sentiments of thankfulness for a bountiful harvest and preparation for the coming of winter. There is an overall sense of completion or culmination in the rituals of autumn.

When the ritual pattern of Easter, originating from the Northern Hemisphere and filled with springtime imagery and theology is imported without change to the Southern Hemisphere, where a chronologically simultaneous season of autumn is in progress, there are bound to be some incongruities and problems in 'translation.' These problems stem not only from the fact that the seasonal pattern is opposite and the concurrent

---

[20] Moran, 124.

climatic conditions are different, but also because people coming off a summer pattern of behavior are operating with a different set of bio-rhythms and a different psychological mind-frame than a people exiting a winter pattern of behavior.

Naturally a culture cannot celebrate a harvest festival during springtime when the seeds have just been planted. Neither can a culture logically celebrate fertility rituals during autumn when the earth is pre-paring itself for winter. To do so makes no sense.

So, what are some of the factors contributing to the feeling of in-congruence and the problem of logical coherence which is present when the Easter Feast is celebrated in southeast Australia in autumn rather than spring?

III. Problems with Ritual Translation in Southeast Australia

While it is difficult to point to many examples of specifically 'springtime' terminology within the post-Vatican II liturgy prescribed for the Easter Feast, there remains an overarching impression that this is in-deed a vernal feast. In referring to the 'Easter Feast' here, only the Easter Vigil liturgy of the Roman Catholic Church is considered, though it must be understood that this celebration cannot be divorced conceptually or ritually from the rest of the Triduum, and indeed the whole seven weeks of the Easter Season.

The prayers of the Easter Feast abound with metaphorical lan-guage of 'new birth,' Christ leading us 'out of darkness into eternal light,' movement from death to life, Christ the Passover Lamb, etc. Many of the natural ritual elements employed in the Easter Vigil (e.g., fire, light, water, natural elements used in a unique way in the Easter Feast) are either used in a way that stems directly from northern hemispheric springtime understandings, or have been made so generic for the sake of 'universal' ritual usage, that they convey only a fraction of their latent symbolic potency.

It may seem that such basic natural elements as fire, light and water, which are found in every cultural circumstance and should be eas-ily translatable into local languages and understandings, can indeed act as 'universal' symbols for the theological code they convey. However, the primary messages the official church understands them to convey (e.g., the Easter Candle as a symbol of Christ the light of the world, dis-pelling the darkness of death, sin, night and winter), are still theologically charged with the context from which they were born. When the Easter Feast, viewed through the interpretive lens of 'spring,' is celebrated in autumn the ritual experience often can be dissonant, because the natural symbols convey different meanings when they are used in altered cultural and climatic circumstances.

Southern or equatorial Christians sometimes feel the need to make a mental leap into the Northern Hemisphere in order to make sense of parts of this ritual. In order to enable such peoples to enter into the realms of meaning codified by the official church as 'authentic' for these natural symbols, translation and reinterpretation of them (back into the northern context from which they came) is often necessary, in order to avoid the potential for misinterpretation, thus weakening the local impact of these symbols. Some examples may elucidate the problem further.

Fire
The rubric for the Easter Vigil instructs that a large fire is to be lit outside the church and blessed as a 'new fire.' In the Northern Hemisphere, this action constitutes a defiant statement against the darkness of the night and the darkness of the winter just ending. Adolf Adam notes that:

> The old Roman liturgy did not have such a blessing of fire; the blessing is rather of Frankish origin and seems intended from the beginning as a sacramental of the Church that would replace the fires lit in spring by the pagans in honor of Wotan or some other heathen divinity, in order to assure good crops.[21]

The historical linkage of springtime and the Easter Fire clearly is apparent. However, in southeast Australia, the use of fire in the ritual can convey an entirely different meaning, as lighting a large fire outside during autumn is generally regarded by locals as a very foolhardy act, possibly placing communities and property in danger. Considering the sometimes tinder-dry condition of the land at that time of year, and the potential to spark a much larger conflagration than was intended by the rubric, lighting *any* kind of fire outdoors is culturally discouraged in southeast Australia in autumn. The 'universal' ritual fails to address ade-

---

[21] Adolf Adam, *The Liturgical Year: Its History and Its Meaning after the Reform of the Liturgy*, (Collegeville, MN: The Liturgical Press/ Pueblo, 1981), 77-78.

quately the power of the natural symbol of fire as it conveys meaning according to the local circumstances. While the rubrics of the Blessing of Fire do acknowledge that it may not always be possible to light a fire outside the church, the 'norm' of the ritual is to do just this.

Praying that the morning star which never sets may "find this flame still burning,"[22] can carry a bittersweet poignancy, conveying a quite unintended but powerful subtext, when the threat of bushfires lighting the southeast Australian sky throughout the night, and the smell of smoke drifting into the cities from the burning countryside nearby remains so real. The fire Australian Christians light at the Easter Vigil may in itself be a 'new fire' when compared with all the others that are still burning or have recently been systematically extinguished with great purpose, but this meaning is not quite what the church of 'the North' intends. Rather than incorporating the richly expressive local understandings of the natural symbol of fire in the ritual prayers, the anemic Blessing of Fire prayer in the typical edition robs a rich symbol of its potential theological power by 'universalizing' it to the point where its possible impact at the local level is well and truly muted or simply ignored.

Light

The request voiced in the Exultet prayer that the Easter candle "might bravely burn to dispel the darkness of this night,"[23] may be a request that is literally true in terms of the darkness of that particular Easter Vigil night in southeast Australia. However, in the local context such a request loses a tremendous amount of the metaphoric weight it holds in the Northern Hemisphere where the image of the light of Christ shining forth in the springtime, raised up from the night of death, dispelling the lingering darkness of winter, makes eminently more sense. In southeast Australia, when the darkness of winter is still to come and when the experience of the light of the sun at its zenith throughout the summer months is freshly imprinted in the memory, the impact of this symbol once again is mitigated by the climatic circumstances in which it is being employed ritually.

Water

The Blessing of Water prior to the baptismal ritual at Easter contains the

---

[22] Catholic Church, *The Sacramentary* (New York, NY: Catholic Book Publishing Company, 1985), 184.
[23] Ibid.

sentence: "Bless this water: it makes the seed to grow, it refreshes us and makes us clean."[24] When southeastern Australians hear this prayer we can only relate to certain parts of it (i.e., refreshing and washing), which lessens its overall impact, especially if one's mind gets stuck on the 'growing of seeds' image which does not fit with what is going on in the local environment. The prayer over water fails to make room for the inclusion of a local understanding of the powerful symbol that water is in a climate such as that of southeast Australia, starved of water during the hot summer. In many ways the 'universal' ritual misses the mark in terms of speaking to and making use of the natural symbol of water as it operates in a land where droughts can last up to seven years at a stretch.

These are just a few examples of the problems in ritual translation which can be pointed out in the liturgical celebration of the Easter Feast in southeast Australia. A more closely detailed analysis of the entire Easter Feast would be impossible in this context, but undoubtedly would yield some additional ritual translation issues in need of further consideration at the local level.

Anscar Chupungco reminds us that:

> When a local church is vividly conscious of its cultural pattern, it will react negatively to a liturgy that employs a foreign cultural pattern.... A liturgy whose cultural pattern differs radically from that of the local church has to adapt or be pushed to irrelevance.[25]

It is time for Australian Christians to accept no longer the discrepancies between designated 'universal' ritual patterns and common-sense local knowledge. How is such a dilemma to be overcome?

IV. Possible Solutions

Christians in southeast Australia are faced with a sort of "ritualistic imperialism,"[26] which alienates us from the natural seasons of the year, so that we are forced into a conflict between the official liturgical

---

[24] Ibid., 203.
[25] Chupungco, *Liturgical Inculturation*, 35.
[26] Anthony Kain, "'My Son's Bread.': About Culture, Language and Liturgy," in *The Promise of Presence*, Michael Downey and Richard Fragomeni, eds., (Washington, D.C.: The Pastoral Press, 1992), 254.

year (imported from the northern European context) and the natural seasons of our local environment. Robert Schreiter (describes the dilemma faced by 'young churches' as they struggle to wed the universal aspects of the church with those of their local situation. He writes:

> Given the fact that colonialism has often been part of their national history, they are keenly sensitive to what amounts to a paternalism in church relationships. They feel that the tradition is enacted in a paternalist fashion in their situations. This means, basically, that it is assumed that the younger churches are not in a position to understand their own questions or that their questions are really not as they might believe. The older churches impose a solution to their questions, knowing much better what the younger church needs or would ask for it if could properly speak. Often this is done in a cavalier fashion, with the older churches not bothering to learn many of the details surrounding the younger church's question. The abrupt character of the answer often given doubles the sense of offense. [27]

In theory, the process of liturgical inculturation should enable resolution of the conflict between the universal church's requirement for ritual uniformity and the local church's desire for logical coherence in its ritual practice and local environment.

Ideally, an inculturated liturgy "is one whose shape, language, rites, symbols and artistic expressions reflect the cultural pattern of the local church,"[28] which in this context ought to include reference to the inverted environmental conditions in southeast Australia.

Various possible solutions to the problem of ritual incongruence clouding the celebration of the Easter Feast in southeast Australia have been proposed, such as moving the celebration of the Easter Feast from its present home in the autumnal months of March and April, to the springtime months of September and October. As the exact date of the celebration of the Easter Feast is reckoned according to the occurrence of the Vernal Equinox, it falls somewhere within the period of March/April

---

[27] Robert Schreiter, *Constructing Local Theologies*, (New York, NY: Orbis Books, 1985), 99.
[28] Chupungco, *Liturgical Inculturation*, 37.

in the Northern Hemisphere. If the feast were shifted in order to be cele-
brated in spring in southeast Australia, the date of the Easter Feast would
be reckoned according to the Vernal Equinox in the Southern Hemisphere, and hence would fall somewhere in the months of September and
October. This suggestion is highly problematic for a number of reasons.
If the concept of 'anniversary' is to be respected, and the importance the
Catholic Church has placed historically on universal celebration of the
Easter Feast throughout the world is to be reflected locally, the option of
changing the date of the celebration in southeast Australia to the local
springtime is not preferred. Changing the date of Easter in Australia logically would entail changing the dates of all the other feasts whose dates
are dependent on Easter, and ultimately would mean a chronological divorce of Christian unity between the northern and southern hemispheres.
However, continuing to celebrate a universally mandated ritual when it
houses so many incongruities simply for the sake of uniformity is equally
problematic to the Catholic Christians of southeast Australia.

A second option for dealing with the problem of ritual incongruence facing Australian Christians as they celebrate Easter entails
reinterpreting the natural symbols used in the liturgy. Such a reinterpretation may seem to be approaching a dangerous line between maintaining
the theological code embedded in the symbols, and changing that code
for the sake of logical coherence. However, I am not proposing major
changes to the typical editions for use in southeast Australia, simply
some nuancing of various prayers which harbor associations with spring,
to rid these prayers of such associations and allow them to reflect local
theological understandings of the natural symbols used in the ritual.
David Ranson suggests that:

> To celebrate the liturgical cycle in a way that is mean-
> ingful to those who participate means that they are
> seeing and hearing their experience, even though they
> themselves may not be able to bring that experience into
> articulation. This can principally occur through sensitive
> and intelligent analogous imagery in prayers which open
> and conclude, and in our hymns. It is the challenge of re-
> reading our liturgical experience in the light of our Aus-
> tralian experience of season.[29]

---

[29] Ranson, 12.

In his description of the process of liturgical inculturation, Chupungco stresses the importance of carefully delineating those elements of the liturgy which are replaceable (i.e., the outer liturgical form of the rite), and those which must stay untouched (i.e., the inner theological content of the rite).[30] Chupungco suggests that the 'theological content' of the rite is different from the liturgical form of the rite, writing that:

> ...the meaning of the liturgical text or rite (basically is) the paschal mystery present in various degrees and under different aspects in the celebration.... However, this same mystery is expressed in different outward forms according to the meaning and purpose of each liturgical rite. The liturgical form, which consists of ritual acts and formularies, gives visible expression to the theological content.[31]

A reinterpretation of the natural symbols of the Easter Feast aims to change only the liturgical form not the entire theological content of these prayers. However, emphasizing *different* aspects of the theology inherent in the natural symbol may be necessary in service of making sense of the natural symbols in the local setting. If the church truly believes that "seeds of the word"[32] are planted in every culture, enabling such seeds to germinate and bloom into locally inculturated liturgies and theological expressions should not constitute a threat to the overall unity of the Church. However, whether the relevant ecclesial authorities actually intend to allow inculturation to occur at this level remains an open question. Aylward Shorter expresses doubt that this will occur, writing:

> It *is* true that the structures of ecclesial communion are culturally biased in favor of Europe, and it *is* true that the authority of the Church is in no hurry to put the theology of inculturation into pastoral practice.[33]

---

[30] Chapungco, *Liturgical Inculturation*, 42.

[31] Ibid., 42.

[32] See Justin Martyr, *Second Apology* 8:1-2, 10:1-3, 13:3-6. For Full text see Justin Martyr, *Apologie*, Guiseppe Girgenti, trans., and ed., (Milano: Rusconi, 1995).

[33] Aylward Shorter, *Toward a Theology of Inculturation*, (Maryknoll, NY: Orbis Books, 1988), 247.

The underlying theological message does not need to be compromised if the vocabulary used to describe elements such as fire, light and water in the prayers of the ritual is allowed to reflect the natural symbols as they occur in the local setting.

The Easter Fire we light in southeast Australia can be interpreted in terms of the regeneration wrought by fire in the natural environment, as occurs in many native species of plants such as the Acacia and the Banksia, which can only germinate when their seed-pods are burned open by high intensity fire. The destructive death-dealing power of fire as it makes its dramatic passage through the countryside is tempered by the knowledge that from the death it brings, new life is born in the native plants. Fire can symbolize the *necessary* death, which brings new life, as Christ's death was necessary in order to bring new life to the world. Interestingly, in Australia there are also species of native eucalypts which will re-grow from buds under the bark (epicormic buds) and in swollen tuberous areas at the base of the trunk (lignotubers), after being burned black by bushfires. The trees may appear dead on the outside, but in fact they harbor new life within. Species of the Proteacea family (Hakeas, Grevillias, Banksias) rely on the ashes of bushfires for essential nutrients, while various shrubs such as the dianella and the stylidium thrive when exposed to the smoke of bushfires.

The light of the Easter Candle or the light of Christ, can be for southeast Australians a beacon to guide us through the darkness and grayness of the winter months into which we are heading. In this way, the underlying theology of the symbol remains intact: Jesus, the risen Christ, is the light of the world, shining ever brightly to lead us through the dark times to come.

The waters into which a baptismal candidate is plunged at Easter bring them 'new life' in Christ. The new life wrought by the baptismal waters is mirrored in nature in southeast Australia, as the rains of autumn and winter, absent over the long hot summer bring new life to the parched earth, greening and refreshing the land. These waters are a tangible natural theological symbol, powerful and accessible to all local people regardless of ethnic background.

A great difference could be made to the celebration of the Easter Feast in southeast Australia by the simple addition of some carefully worded and poetic phrases to the blessing prayers and collects of this feast which situate it in *our* time and in *our* place, i.e., southeast Australia. The addition of such phrases would not have to come at the expense of expressions in the prayers that are genuinely universal, such as those which are scripturally based and seasonally neutral. Such minor attempts at inculturation would not separate the southeast Australian church from the Easter celebration of the universal church, but would enable us to embrace the universal ritual as our own, rather than perpetuating an incongruent ritual pattern for the sake of universal uniformity.

The Church in southeast Australia is faced with the dilemma of being a part of a universal church originating and administered in the Northern Hemisphere, but also being a branch of that church located in the Southern Hemisphere. The incongruence experienced by the church in southeast Australia as it celebrates universally mandated ritual patterns in an environment diametrically opposed to that in which the rituals were developed can be overcome. But in order for that to happen, true liturgical inculturation must be undertaken - allowing the symbols and texts of the typical editions to be reinterpreted in light of the local circumstances in which the church finds itself in southeast Australia.

I have not attempted to explore in more than a general way here how this complex task ultimately may be accomplished. Naming the incongruence and pointing out firstly that it *can* be resolved, and secondly, suggesting the manner by which such a resolution may come to birth will have to suffice for now.

Anscar Chupungco expresses well the ongoing challenge facing the church in southern and equatorial regions today, writing:

> Easter symbols need not, should not, be drawn from spring.... Had Christ died in autumn, the early Christian writers would have discovered in it such unsurpassable qualities as would win for it the title of *epidemia*, the sojourn of God among us.... We should not go on pretending that it is spring when it is actually fall or summer. We should not allow the paschal mystery to be indissolubly bound up with one season of the year. For indeed, every season of the year is the season of Christ's death and resurrection.[34]

---

[34] Chapungco, *Shaping*, 39.

PART III

Seeing Eye to Eye:
The Struggle of Inculturation Between
European Christian Views and the Native
American Cultures of North America

Edited by
Bernard J. Donahoe, C.S.C.
Saint Mary's College

"IMPURITY," "UNCHASTITY," "INCONTINENCE," "LUST," AND "FORNICATION": MARRIAGE, SEXUALITY, AND NINETEENTH CENTURY CALIFORNIA MISSION HISTORY*

Quincy D. Newell**

"Fornication" ranked "first" among "the most dominant vices of [the] Indians" at Mission Santa Clara according to its two resident missionaries in 1814.[1] Fathers Magín Catalá and José Viader wrote in response to a questionnaire sent from Spain and forwarded to every mission in Alta California in 1812. It took some two years for all of the missions to respond. In this essay, I focus on the responses from the three northernmost missions–Missions San Francisco de Asís, Santa Clara, and San José. The missionaries at all three of these missions signed their responses within a week of each other in November of 1814.[2] The ques-

* I would like to thank Jill DeTemple and Professors Michael Green and Laurie Maffly-Kipp for their helpful comments on this manuscript, and Professor Kathryn Burns for pointing me to the work of James Lockhart and Karen Viera Powers. I am also grateful to Father Virgilio Biasiol, O.F.M., the archivist at the Santa Barbara Mission Archive Library, for sending me reproductions of the original responses to the 1812 questionnaire from Missions San Francisco, Santa Clara, and San José.

** Quincy D. Newell is a graduate student in Religious Studies at the University of North Carolina at Chapel Hill. She specializes in the religious history of the American West. Her dissertation explores the creation of familial, social, political and economic interpersonal networks at Mission San Francisco during the Spanish colonial period.

[1] M. Catalá & J. Viader, "Response to 1812 questionnaire," 4 November 1814, *Preguntas y Respuestas* collection, Santa Barbara Mission Archive Library, Santa Barbara, California. This and all subsequent translations are my own, unless otherwise noted.

[2] Fathers Magín Catalá and José Viader signed Santa Clara's response on November 4, 1814; Fathers Narciso Durán and Buenaventura Fortuny signed San José's response on November 7, 1814; and Fathers Ramón Abella and Juan Sainz de Lucio signed San Francisco's response on November 11, 1814. By that time, all of the missions had been in existence for quite some time: San Francisco was founded in 1776; Santa Clara in 1777; and San José in 1797. Though missionaries came and went in California, all of the missionaries at these three missions had been there for a significant amount of time by the time they penned their responses. Fathers Durán, Fortuny, and Sainz de Lucio arrived in Alta California together in 1806; Father Abella arrived in 1798; Father Viader in 1796; and Father Catalá in 1793 [M. Geiger, *Franciscan missionaries in Hispanic California, 1769-1848: A biographical dictionary* (San Marino, California: The Huntington Library, 1969), 282-293]. Missions San Rafael and San Francisco Solano, both further north than these three missions, had not been

tionnaire covered everything from demographics and social organization to arts, literature, religion, and industry. This remark about fornication answered a question about which vices were most prevalent among the California Indians. Catalá and Viader were not alone in their assessment; other missionaries agreed. "The dominant vices of the Indians," wrote Fathers Narciso Durán and Buenaventura Fortuny from Mission San José, "are those that are prohibited in the fifth, sixth, seventh and first part of the eighth commandments of the Holy law of God."[3] These commandments enjoined believers to refrain from murder, fornication, theft, and lying. In fact, of the sixteen California missions whose responses to the question survive, thirteen mentioned "impurity," or more specifically, "unchastity," "incontinence," "lust," or "fornication."[4] Clearly, in the missionaries' eyes, sexual immorality was a major problem.

Yet the term *fornication* only has meaning within a doctrinal framework that stigmatizes sex outside of certain norms. The Spanish missionaries defined those norms based on Catholic teachings about human sexuality and marriage. Ideally, according to the priests, all unmarried persons were chaste and all married persons—each married to only one person—had sex only with his or her spouse. Within the mission walls, as the missionaries saw it, all of the Indians' sexual activity outside the bounds of a marriage performed in the Church was fornication—and therefore a sin.

As a category, fornication covered a broad range of sexual "sins." It applied not only to sex outside of marriage, but also to "improper" sexual relations within marriage and to individual sexual activity.[5] This included immoral thoughts, *coitus interruptus*, masturbation, anal sex, homosexual sex, and heterosexual sex in unorthodox positions.[6]

---

founded when the questionnaire was distributed.
[3] N. Duran & B. Fortuny, "Response to 1812 questionnaire," 4 November 1814, *Preguntas y Respuestas* collection, Santa Barbara Mission Archive Library, Santa Barbara, California.
[4] M. Geiger & C.W. Meighan, trans. & eds., *As the Padres saw them: California Indian life and customs as reported by the Franciscan missionaries, 1813-1815* (Santa Barbara, California: Santa Barbara Mission Archive Library, 1976), 105-106.
[5] See, for example, A. Lavrin, "Sexuality in colonial Mexico: A Church dilemma," in *Sexuality and marriage in colonial Latin America*, A. Lavrin, ed. (Lincoln: University of Nebraska Press, 1989), 53. She notes that "Under such strict regulations [in marriage] sexual activity was the opposite of the sin of 'fornication,' which consisted in engaging in any of the sexual practices forbidden by the church."
[6] The missionaries in California used confessional manuals containing translations of questions and phrases designed to help them root out all sorts of sexual sins among the Indians. See, for example, H. Kelsey, trans. & ed., *The doctrina and confesionario of Juan Cortés* (Altadena, California: Howling Coyote Press, 1979), 113, ("How many times have you spilled your semen?"), 115 ("Have you

According to Catholic doctrine, marriage was "a preventative of or a cure for concupiscence."[7] It was a key element in the regulation of human sexuality, providing a legitimate way of satisfying sexual urges that might otherwise lead one to sin.

Central Californians also used marriage as a means of regulating sexuality, but the traditional California Indian understanding of marriage differed sharply from that of the Catholics. Many practices forbidden by the Catholic Church–divorce and remarriage, polygamy, homosexual sex, and a variety of heterosexual positions and practices–were commonly accepted by natives of Central California. The priests' complaints about "fornication" reflected the continuing acceptance of these practices among the Indians who entered the missions.

Something Old, Something New. . .

At first glance, it might appear that the Indians who entered the missions checked their traditional practices at the gate. Certainly, the missionaries seem to have been under this impression. The missionaries at Santa Clara, for example, explicitly contrasted the traditional Indian process of marriage to the new practices introduced in the missions: "The Indians in their Gentile [unconverted] state do not celebrate formal contracts, pacts, or conditions," they wrote. "Once the consent of the bride and her parents is obtained by the suitor, he gives them some little gift, and from that moment they are considered married." In the missions, Fathers Catalá and Viader assured their readers, things were different. They continued: "In the Mission they marry with all the solemnities of the Holy Church, without other pacts nor services on the part of the married people beside some gifts before the celebration, to the Bride, or her Parents, or closest Relatives."[8]

These two ways of marrying, however, are less distinct than Catalá and Viader made them out to be. Despite their assertion that Indians outside the missions did not make any "formal contracts," Catalá and Viader described precisely the means by which anthropologists believe California Indians entered into a formal marriage contract–by obtaining the consent of the parties involved (including the parents of the man and woman to be married) and giving gifts, usually to the bride's family and

---

sometimes thought about doing bad things for pleasure with a Woman, with Women, with a man, with men?"), 116 ("Did you couple [with your wife / husband] in the right way?"), 121 ("When you coupled with your Husband or with another man, did you spill the semen so as not to become pregnant?" and "Have you sinned with a homosexual?"), and 123 (which has no questions, but just the phrases "to do something bad with a man;" "through the buttocks;" "with the hand;" and "alone.").

[7] Lavrin, "Sexuality in colonial Mexico: A Church dilemma," 53.

[8] Catalá & Viader, "Response to 1812 questionnaire."

sometimes also to the groom's.[9]

Catalá and Viader's mention of gift-giving within the mission clearly suggests that traditional marriage rituals persisted in the mission, alongside the newly adopted "solemnities" of the Church. Other missionaries were even more explicit, though they also failed to recognize the giving of gifts as a continuation of traditional practices. From Mission San Francisco, for example, Fathers Ramón Abella and Juan Sainz de Lucio wrote that "the most generous [suitor] might give the bride some abalones, which are perforated shells, or some small marble stones, also carved."[10] Though they sound modest in the priests' description, these gifts were likely valuable trade goods. Shell beads like those Abella and Sainz de Lucio mention had long been a standard form of currency for intertribal trade in California.[11] The continued use of these goods in the missions confirms the enduring strength of traditional marriage practices within the mission walls.

Why did the missionaries not recognize the persistence of traditional marriage practices? This appears to be a classic case of what scholar James Lockhart has called "Double Mistaken Identity," a phenomenon of cultural contact "in which," Lockhart writes, "each side of the cultural exchange presumes that a given form or concept is functioning in the way familiar within its own tradition and is unaware of or unimpressed by the other side's interpretation."[12] Gift exchange in conjunction with marriage, after all, occurred among the Spanish as well. Writing about eighteenth- and nineteenth-century New Mexico, Ramón Gutiérrez notes that Spanish Catholic families routinely exchanged gifts upon the betrothal of their children. "To contemplate marriage without being able to present the bride with an appropriate trousseau," he writes, "was considered inappropriate and shameless."[13] Though the missionaries were celibate, other Hispanic families who lived near the missions–in

---

[9] L.J. Bean, "Social organization," in *Handbook of North American Indians: Vol. 8. California*, W.C. Sturtevant, general ed., R.F. Heizer, vol. ed. (Washington, D.C.: Smithsonian Institution, 1978), 677; E. Wallace, "Sexual status and role differences," in *Handbook of North American Indians: Vol. 8, California*, 684-87.

[10] Ramón Abella and Juan Sainz de Lucio, "Response to 1812 questionnaire," 11 November 1814, *Preguntas y Respuestas* collection, Santa Barbara Mission Archive Library, Santa Barbara, California.

[11] R.F. Heizer, "Trade and trails," in *Handbook of North American Indians: Vol. 8, California*, W.C. Sturtevant, general ed., R.F. Heizer, vol. ed. (Washington, D.C.: Smithsonian Institution, 1978), 690-91.

[12] J. Lockhart, "Double mistaken identity," in *Of things of the Indies: Essays old and new in early Latin American history*, J. Lockhart, ed. (Stanford, California: Stanford University Press, 1999), 99.

[13] R.A. Gutiérrez, *When Jesus came, the corn mothers went away: Marriage, sexuality, and power in New Mexico, 1500-1846* (Stanford, California: Stanford University Press, 1991), 261-62.

pueblos or presidios–demonstrated Spanish marriage practices. Apart from other Indians, these settlers were the only models of Catholic marriage available in Central California. Yet while the Indian practice of gift exchange between families may have been reinforced by the examples of Hispanic settlers, its roots remained in traditional Central Californian practice and emphasized the importance of marriage in Central California Indian societies as a means of creating a bond between families.[14]

Then again, perhaps the priests *did* recognize the gift exchange as a continuation of traditional practices but simply did not care. After all, Indians who married in the mission also went through the Catholic wedding ceremony, and it was the completion of "all the solemnities of the Holy Church" that legitimated the union in the priests' eyes.[15] Whether gifts were exchanged or not may have mattered little.

Policing Polygamy, Denying Divorce

Once the Catholic ceremony was in place, the priests were far less concerned with *how* the Indians married, and far more concerned with *whom* they married. One of the greatest complaints voiced by the priests in relation to the Indians' marriage practices concerned polygamy, particularly because it might also lead to unions defined as incestuous under the Catholic system of reckoning kinship. In addition to biological kin, each person also had spiritual and affinal kin.[16] Both of these kinship relationships created a danger of incest, but affinal relationships were particularly problematic. "[The Indians] recognize in their marriages no relationship of affinity," wrote Father Francisco Palóu in 1786. Whereas

---

[14] For an extended discussion of the use of marriage to create bonds between families in Central California, see Q.D. Newell, *Indian marriage in the California missions: An ethnohistorical study of Missions San Francisco, San José, and Santa Clara*, Unpublished master's thesis, University of North Carolina, Chapel Hill, 2001, 35-44.
[15] The Council of Trent marked a turning point in ecclesiastical control over marriage. After 1563, the Roman Catholic Church required that the ceremony be celebrated by a clergyman in the presence of witnesses. Asunción Lavrin points out that by redefining clandestinity as an impediment to marriage, the church gave itself "a theoretical tool to curb covert attempts to escape its surveillance." See A. Lavrin, "Introduction: The scenario, the actors, and the issues," in *Sexuality and marriage in colonial Latin America*, A. Lavrin, ed. (Lincoln: University of Nebraska Press, 1989), 5-6.
[16] Spiritual kin included godparents and godchildren; affinal kin were people related through sexual activity, licit or illicit. A woman who has sex with a man, for instance, gains an affinal relationship with everyone in that man's family. Likewise, he becomes an affinal kinsman to everyone in the woman's family. P. Seed, *To love, honor and obey in colonial Mexico: Conflicts over marriage choice, 1574-1821* (Stanford, California: Stanford University Press, 1988), 273-274, n. 35.

Catholic doctrine prohibited marriage between affinal kin, he complained, "on the contrary, this [relationship] incites them to take as wives
their sisters-in-law, and even the mothers-in-law. The custom they observe is that he who takes a wife takes also as wives all her sisters."[17]
Palóu exaggerated: most Central Californians did not practice polygamy.
Generally, the practice was reserved for wealthy, high-status men like
village headmen and shamans, who were able to support multiple wives
and who required the additional help an extra wife could provide.[18] Nor
was sororal polygyny, in which one man marries two or more sisters, the
general rule. In many tribes, wealthy men married women from several
different villages in order to multiply their political connections.[19]

When a polygynous man entered the missions, he was forced to
choose one wife with whom to solemnize his marriage. Though the
priests expected him to remain with his first wife, many men opted instead to solemnize a more recent union with a younger woman. This
choice may have been based partly on sexual desire, but there were also
more pragmatic considerations: a younger woman would bear more children and be better able to care for her husband in his old age.[20] Randall
Milliken has written that "many women were left without spouses...
when their husbands were forced to marry only one cowife.[21]" While it is
true that many women were left without *ecclesiastically sanctioned*
spouses, ethnohistorian James Sandos, writing on the Chumash Indians
of Southern California, cautions scholars against too easily assuming correspondence between what the Church sanctioned and what the Indians
did. "If concurrent marriage for chiefs prevailed outside the mission,"
Sandos asks, "why should we think that *ipso facto* it disappeared when
chiefs were baptized?" Sandos' point is that unless there is specific evi-

---

[17] M. Geiger, trans. & ed., *Palóu's life of Fray Junípero Serra* (Washington,
D.C.: Academy of American Franciscan History, 1955), 194.
[18] Bean, 677.
[19] The Yokuts are an example of a tribe known to have practiced the latter type
of polygyny. Anthropologist Alfred L. Kroeber writes that "A man with several
wives seems normally to have been married in as many villages, dividing his
time between his various households." [A.L. Kroeber, *Handbook of the Indians
of California* (Washington, D.C.: Government Printing Office, 1925), 493]. For
a fuller discussion of marriage as a means of creating political connections in the
Central California missions, see Newell, 45-58.
[20] In some cases, first wives formally ceded their right to have their marriage
solemnized, thus leaving the way open for a polygynous man to solemnize his
marriage with a more junior wife. See, for example, Mission San Francisco de
Ass, *Libros de misión*: Tomo 1, Libro de bautismos, 10 Agosto 1776-20 Enero
1810 [Mission books: Vol. 1, Book of baptisms, 10 August 1776-20 January
1810], (San Francisco, California: 1776-1870), microfilm.
[21] R. Milliken, *A time of little choice: The disintegration of tribal culture in the
San Francisco Bay area, 1769-1810* (Menlo Park, CA: Ballena Press. 1995),
135.

dence to the contrary, the most logical assumption is that deeply ingrained cultural practices such as polygyny persisted.[22]

When he analyzed the baptismal and marriage records from the
Santa Clara mission, Milliken found that "some of the individuals in the
large baptismal blocks [from 1794 and 1795] never remarried at the mission. This most commonly occurred," he writes, "among women aged
forty and older and men aged sixty and older."[23] While the persistence of
polygyny would not explain any reluctance to remarry on the part of
older men, the women's failure to remarry might indicate that they continued to consider themselves cowives of their original husbands. The
missionaries simply failed to recognize the existence–and persistence–of
these marriages.

Some cowives may well have chosen to remain outside the mission altogether. Indians frequently left the missions to gather food or
simply for a "vacation."[24] While these furloughs benefitted the mission
economy by reducing the amount of food required for each mission resident, the missionaries worried that the Indians' spiritual progress suffered when they were away from the missions and "mixed up with the
Gentiles such as their Parents."[25] It is likely that these times were occasions for conjugal visits between polygynous male mission residents and
their "former" wives.

Because only the wealthiest men were able to support multiple
wives, polygyny alone does not explain the apparently high rate of "fornication" that the missionaries observed. In traditional California Indian
societies, even the poorest men and women were able to divorce their
spouses.[26] There does not appear to have existed any formal procedure
for obtaining a divorce; one partner or the other simply left, usually returning to his or her family.[27] Among some tribes, a divorce required that
the gifts given to the bride's family be returned.[28]

The missionaries were aware of the ease with which the Indians
divorced one another. As early as 1786, Francisco Palóu remarked that

---

[22] J.A. Sandos, "Christianization among the Chumash: An ethnohistoric perspective," *American Indian Quarterly,* 15, (1991): 75.

[23] Milliken, 135.

[24] Luis Arguello mentions these trips in a letter to Governor Diego de Borica. [L.
Arguello, "Letter to Governor Diego de Borica," Unpublished manuscript in
California Mission Documents collection at the Santa Barbara Mission Archive
Library, Santa Barbara, California, 1798]. Milliken also documents several of
these trips, which he terms *paseos.* See Milliken, 88, 95, 180, 203, 209, 300.

[25] Ramón Abella and Juan Sainz de Lucio, "Response to 1812 questionnaire."

[26] Anthropologists agree that it was easier for men to initiate a divorce than for
women, due at least in part to the patriarchal nature of Californian societies
[Bean, 677; Wallace, 686].

[27] Geiger, *Palóu's life of Fray Junípero Serra,* 445, n. 46.

[28] Wallace, 686.

the marriages of unconverted Indians "last until there is a quarrel, when they separate. Then they marry another man or woman.... The only expression they use concerning the dissolution of the marriage is: 'I threw her over,' or 'I threw him over.'"[29] What is not clear is whether Palóu or his fellow Franciscans understood that separation fully dissolved the marriage bond, freeing each partner to remarry without stigma. Such a concept was unknown in Catholic doctrine, in which, Asunción Lavrin explains, "'divorce' meant physical separation of the couple. Remarriage after 'divorce' could take place only after the death of one of the spouses."[30] Because these restrictions did not apply in the Indian understanding of marriage, missionaries may have interpreted legitimate sexual activity in a second marriage as "fornication."

Re-reading the Missionaries, Re-thinking the Missions

By reinterpreting the missionaries' comments about Indian marriage and sexual practices, we see that, in all likelihood, Indians in the missions behaved much as they had outside the mission gates. The only difference inside the mission was the imposition of a Catholic doctrinal framework that privileged Church ceremony as a symbol of marriage and stigmatized any sexual activity outside a narrow range of "acceptable" behavior. Because the missionaries classified all of the Indians in the mission as "neophytes"–implying that they either had converted to Catholicism or were about to convert–the priests believed that their imposition of that doctrinal framework was justified. This understanding of the mission residents led the priests to view the space inside the mission as homogeneously Catholic, in contrast to the area outside the mission, which was populated by unconverted "Gentile" Indians.

For the most part, historians who deal with the missions have adopted the missionaries' assumptions uncritically. Throughout the scholarly literature on the California missions, Indians who enter the missions are referred to as *neophytes*. In part, I suspect, scholars employ this term for the sake of convenience: *mission residents* and other such terms sound clunky and take longer to type. But even when used by modern scholars, the term *neophytes* still carries the hidden assumptions of the missionaries: it implies that the Indians to which it refers had converted, or were about to convert, to Catholicism and thus naturalizes the imposition of a Catholic doctrinal framework on the behavior of the Indians in question. In addition, by highlighting the distinction between mission residents and Indians who lived outside the mission, scholarly use of the term *neophyte* creates a stronger divide between the mission and non-mission populations than may have actually existed.[31]

---

[29] Geiger, *Palóu's life of Fray Junípero Serra*, 194.

[30] Lavrin, "Introduction: The scenario, the actors, and the issues," 43, n. 55.

[31] Karen Vieira Powers points out that historians have adopted Spanish terms

More troubling than scholars' use of the missionaries' terminology, however, is their uncritical adoption of the missionaries' underlying assumption that most of California could be divided geographically between Catholic territory (inside the missions) and Gentile territory (the surrounding countryside). This geographical dichotomy forces scholars into another interpretive dichotomy–that of accomodation versus resistance. Indians who leave the "Gentile" countryside and enter the Catholic missions appear, in this interpretive paradigm, to be accomodating Catholicism, whereas Indians who stay outside the missions seem to be resisting it. Among those who enter the mission, there are Indians who resist Catholicism by retaining traditional practices, and there are Indians who accomodate Catholicism by adopting Catholic practices. But this tried-and-true interpretive framework leaves no space for those Indians in the missions who both retained traditional practices–gift-giving at marriage, for example–and adopted Catholic practices, such as the Catholic wedding ceremony. Nor is there a way to make sense of those Indians who remained outside the missions, but received baptism and other Catholic sacraments. These in-between cases – examples of behavior that is not clearly accomodation *or* resistance–suggest that perhaps the framework itself needs re-thinking.

That re-thinking begins with a fresh examination of the assumptions underlying the framework, such as the presumption that the missions themselves were thoroughly Catholic. If we recognize that the Indians did not simply check their traditional beliefs and practices at the mission gates, we begin to see that the missions were not simply islands of Catholicism in a sea of traditional Indian practices, but rather centers of intense interaction between people from differing cultures, places where Catholicism and traditional beliefs and practices coexisted and interacted.

---

such as "conquest" in a similarly uncritical fashion. Use of this terminology, especially in relation to the "sexual conquest" of Latin America, she argues, perpetuates "a historiography that continues to glorify male sexual domination and ascribes to women the constricted role of passive sexual objects." [K.V. Powers, "Conquering discourses of "sexual conquest": Of women, language, and mestizaje," *Colonial Latin American Review*, 11, (2002): 7-32].

"THEY SHOULD BE ASHAMED TO EAT
WHO ARE RELUCTANT TO WORK:"
THE JESUIT AGRICULTURALIST ETHIC ON THE
FRONTIERS OF EIGHTEENTH-CENTURY NEW SPAIN

Emma Anderson[*]

An examination of the public and private correspondence of a number of Jesuit missionaries writing from what were then the north-western fringes of New Spain reveals a number of intriguing patterns which suggest that Jesuit cultural assumptions were arguably as important as their theological convictions in decisively influencing their perception of the Amerindian groups they encountered. In particular, native patterns of settlement and methods of production (i.e. - sedentary agriculture and migratory hunting and gathering) were evaluated by European Jesuits in moral terms, decisively effecting which tribes were seen as appropriate targets for Christianization and enculturation.

These moral assumptions were informed by an implicit theory of cultural hierarchy which placed European civilization at the top, and evaluated indigenous cultures by their approximation of it. Thus sedentary aboriginal tribes employing agricultural production were perceived as culturally superior, even when the adaptive advantages of a migratory lifestyle were recognized and conceded. Their demonstrable preference for sedentary-agricultural societies meant that Jesuit missionaries often reinforced rather than challenged the entrenched indigenous military antagonisms which existed between such cultures and their migratory hunting-gathering rivals, and in so doing inadvertently circumscribed the scope of their own missionary agenda. The classic pattern of Jesuit alliances with and missionization of sedentary tribes, and simultaneous antagonistic relationships with these tribes' traditional nomadic enemies in Sinaloa, Sonora, and Pimeria Alta had other important effects. Specifically, the proximity of a "hostile" group gave the missionary and missionized Amerindians a common enemy and shared defensive priorities, and fulfilled the psychological function, for the missionary, of 'externalizing' threats present within the mission community itself. When such externalizing conditions existed, in the form of a proximate 'enemy' tribe, Jesuits tended to derive their primary sense of community affilia-

---

[*] Emma Anderson is a doctoral candidate in the Study of Religion at Harvard University.

tion from their mission, and to use relatively optimistic and inclusive language when describing missionized Amerindians, identifying them as (comparatively) 'civilized' and (relatively) 'Christian,' in contrast to the external, enemy tribe. Jesuits' derivation of a sense of identification with their mission community through this process of contrastive externalization was successful in large part because its inner logic utilized, rather than challenged, their preexisting moral assumptions about each mode of production.

However, where such 'externalizing' conditions were not present, in Baja California, for example, the Jesuit missionary was more likely to derive his primary sense of identity from the Jesuit community itself, and to use psychologically distancing language in describing missionized Amerindians. For lack of a contrastive or 'externalizing' mechanism, Jesuit missionaries in this situation were significantly more likely to denigrate the level of cultural sophistication of those they were attempting to convert, and to question the sincerity of native conversions by applying more rigorous 'internal' or psychological evaluative criteria than did those Jesuits under 'externalist' conditions, who tended to utilize behavioral criteria, especially performance of ritual obligations, to adjudge Christianization. These psychologically distancing tendencies were all the more pronounced where local environmental conditions thwarted missionary attempts to render missionized Amerindians fully sedentary, because their concession to the utility of a migratory way of life did not mitigate their intense disapproval of it.

Appreciation of the moral categories through which missionaries apprehended various indigenous means of production, then, can help us to better understand how Jesuit relationships with given tribes were almost predetermined, as categorization and moral evaluation of each tribes' customary means of production decidedly influenced which of them would be targeted for Christianization. It can also help us to appreciate the specific psychological and sociological effects upon Jesuit missionaries of having two supposedly contrasting indigenous groups existing proximally, explaining differences in missionary identification, self perception, and external vs. internal threat perception, as well as the limits that these patterns of perception and affiliation often imposed upon overall missionary success in a given region. Moreover, the thesis that Jesuit moral evaluation of the means of production played an important role in the initial selection of particular tribes for missionization, and that the presence of mutual enemies was paramount in strengthening community cohesion and fostering missionary identification with their mission communities provide at least partial answers to the most pressing questions arising out of the primary materials: why would missionaries who had narrowly avoided death in an internal mission insurrection still frame the primary danger to the missions in external terms, as threats from marauding non-Christian tribes? Moreover, why would the determination to counter such perceived threats through military means, or mass deportation, not be perceived by such missionaries as being in direct contradiction to their own cherished goal of the Christianization of all indigenous peoples?

Aspects of the Jesuit Agriculturalist Ethic

The strong Jesuit preference for sedentary agriculturist tribes over nomadic hunter-gatherers is apparent in their great enthusiasm for undertaking missionary activity among such indigenous groups, the highly approving terms in which they discuss them, and in their policy of attempting to render nomadic tribes sedentary through 'reduction.' Such a strong partiality for a given type of social organization and means of food production, I would suggest, merits very close examination. Some might object that Jesuit enthusiasm for sedentary forms of social organization stems, not from its supposed moral associations with Christianity, but from *purely pragmatic* issues of social control: that unilocal settlement aided the hegemonic control of native behavior by removing geographic and seasonal barriers to missionary influence, thus resulting in more complete indoctrination and acculturation of aboriginals under the continuous gaze of the missionary. Such pragmatic considerations were, indeed, a factor. Joseph Och, a Jesuit from Wurtzburg who worked primarily among the sedentary agriculturalist Pima and Opata tribes of Northwestern New Spain in the 1750's and '60's, writes: "...we influenced them to construct their villages in a complete square, one house next to the other. Thus, in my mission I could see every doorway in the entire place from my window...."[1] To suggest, however, that this strongly

---

[1] Joseph Och, *Missionary in Sonora: The Travel Reports of Joseph Och, S.J. 1755-1767*, Theodore E Treutlein, tran. (San Francisco: California Historical Society, 1965), 151. Joseph Och was born in Wurtzburg in 1725 and died there in 1773, after having spent much of his career in New Spain. He was admitted to the Jesuit order in 1743, and came to Mexico in 1755. He was sent to Sonora in 1756, and resided at the Mission of San Ignacio from 1756 to 1758, Mission Cumuripa, until 1761, Mission Baseraca until 1764, and Guasavas until 1766, when he was recalled to Mexico City due to ill health. Throughout his career,

articulated preference for aboriginal agriculturalists was due to purely pragmatic concerns, one would have to believe that the Jesuits made a clear distinction between means and ends, a distinction which is not apparent in their writings. Eighteenth-century Jesuit missionaries very clearly saw adaptation to a sedentary agricultural way of life, not as a means to an end, or even as a necessary precursor to the adoption of Christianity, but rather, in some sense, as indispensably coincident with it, as its materialist expression. The supposedly pragmatic concerns of establishing unilocal residence and an agricultural form of subsistence, then, far from repudiating the proposed underlying conceptual apparatus, are themselves expressions of it: they illustrate the propensity of predominantly Northern European Jesuit missionaries in northwestern New Spain to conflate Christianity 'itself' with prevailing models of European social organization and food production. Thus missionary evaluation of native means of production considered those closer to European models more civilized, morally superior, and incipiently Christian, as is evident in these passages penned by Johann Nentwich of Schleswig,[2] a Jesuit working in mid-century Sonora:

> "...thanks to incessant labor, the bad seed is being eradicated, and a commonwealth may be formed, not only political as far as their disposition will allow, but even Christian. This - God be thanked, we have obtained, principally among the Opata and Eudebe nations, which being more devoted to the tilling of the land and the breeding of cattle, are more faithful to their villages, and consequently better instructed in the mysteries of the holy Faith..."[3]

Och worked primarily among the Pima and Opata tribes, who were sedentary agriculturists.

[2] Johann Nentwich, who signs himself Juan Nentwig, was the author of the formerly unattributed Rudo Ensayo [as explained in Jacobo Sedelmayr, *Jacobo Sedelmayr: Missionary, Frontiersman, Explorer in Arizona and Sonora, Four Original Manuscript Narratives, 1744-1751*, Peter Dunne, tran. (Arizona Pioneers' Historical Society, 1955), 82, and at rather more length in Och, 185]. A native of Schleswig, Nentwich was the Rector for the Rectorate of the Holy Martyrs of Japan in Sonora. He worked among the Opata, lowland Pima, and Eudebe tribes, who practiced sedentary agriculture.

[3] Johann Nentwich (unattributed by translator), *Rudo Ensayo: By an Unknown Jesuit Padre*, Eusebio Guiteras, tran. (Tucson: Arizona Silhouettes, 1951), 57.

> "The Opatas and some of the Eudebes, though in a lim-
> ited degree, are, in comparison to the other Indians, as
> the people of the towns are in comparison to the country
> people; for, although they do not cease to be Indians, yet
> in the end, reason prevails with them; among all of these
> they are the best Christians; they are the most loyal vas-
> sals of our Lord the King, having never rebelled against
> him...they are the most inclined to work, to till their
> lands and to raise cattle..."[4]

As is immediately apparent, Jesuit missionaries associated agricultural means of production with a concomitant set of values which they
presumed native sedentary agriculturalists shared with them, if only in
embryonic form: community organization and centralization, stability,
order, predictability, obedience to authority, responsibility, discipline,
delayed gratification, provision for the future, and the work ethic. Indeed,
the Jesuits had long believed the existence of such presumably shared
values to be good 'soil' in which to plant the 'seed' of the Gospel. The
writings of Andres Perez de Ribas, a Spanish Jesuit assigned to the Sinaloa missions in 1604,[5] indicate that the association between agriculturalism and Christian propensities was not peculiar to the eighteenth-
century:

> "...These Upper Nebomes are generally tractable and
> good natured, and much domesticated in their manner of
> living. They are little disturbed by wars, generally being
> left in peace to cultivate their lands...They have mas-
> tered the art of irrigation by the use of little canals taken
> at angles from the rivers, as successfully as have the
> farmers of Spain. They have acquired by this time chick-
> ens of the same kind as in Castile, and these they raise
> commonly about their houses. Their pueblos are well or-
> dered. Their houses are made of blocks of earth, packed
> together in the manner of adobes. In the building of

---

[4] Ibid., 71.
[5] Andres Perez de Ribas was born in Cordoba, Spain, in 1575, and entered the
Jesuit order at a young age. He came to Mexico in 1603, and was assigned to the
Sinaloa missions in 1604, where he resided for sixteen years, before returning to
Mexico City to become the Padre Provincial. He died in 1655.

these houses they are much advanced over the Indians of the plains westward, who are apt to be satisfied with houses made of mats of bamboo. Altogether the Nebomes are a very civilized people, even though they are not yet Christians."[6]

Such values all speak to the ordering and disciplining of the human person and community, through the marshaling of their resources and effort, and through their alignment with the great organizing structure of time, understood as a religious category.

Agriculture as fostering 'proto-Christian' notions of time

Jesuit missionaries may have believed that the aboriginal practice of agriculture itself helped to inculcate 'proto-Christian' views of time: views that somewhat paradoxically insisted that time was at once cyclical, an endlessly unrolling sequence of generally predictable, repetitious natural and ritual cycles, and linear, always pointing on to its own eventual, climactic cessation: in personal terms, death, and in collective terms, the end of the world and the last judgment. The practice of agriculture, by necessitating the performance of repetitive sequences of actions at different points in the seasonal cycle, and by requiring the deferment of present gratification in the service of future gains provided a sort of lived prototype of Christian time, in both its cyclical and linear aspects. The Jesuits may thus have expected that sedentary agriculturist Amerindians would more readily embrace, as a community, the ritual marking of the cycle of events of the Christian calendar (itself modeled, to some degree, upon the European agricultural cycle), and would understand the necessity of carefully utilizing present time with an eye to future good by pursuing a program of self-denial and behavior modification to secure future salvation. During the lengthy process of re-educating 'reduced' hunter-gatherers, Jesuits despaired over what they perceived as their overwhelming concern with present pleasure at the expense of anticipating and planning for their future, in both the material and spiritual senses. That is, they appear to see a present rather than future orientation as the underlying problem in their difficult adaptation to agricultural life and as the prime obstacle to their grasping of spiritual truths. Joseph Och dramatizes what he sees as both the spiritual and material peril of Amer-

---

[6] Andres Perez de Ribas, *My Life Among the Savage Nations of New Spain* (Los Angeles: The Ward Ritchie Press, 1968), 91.

indians, lamenting that "they are very wasteful in that they do not provide for the day to come" before elaborating:

> "Whatever they have harvested is all used up in a short
> time. Often they do not even await the maturing or rip-
> ening time...they tear off the maize cobs when they are
> still green and milky and boil them in large kettles...as
> long as the food lasts, they sing and dance for many
> nights until they have consumed it...Then they rely upon
> the missionary who must feed them for at least three-
> quarters of the year, and must also provide the seeds for
> the harvest..."[7]

His complaints are seconded by fellow Jesuit Ignaz Pfefferkorn,[8] who
laments the tendency of mid-century Papago to literally consume their
own future:

> "...he (the missionary) had to keep a watchful eye on the
> work of the Indians if he wished to prevent their con-
> suming not only their meals but also the seeds with
> which they had been supplied and which they had not
> yet planted. Such a trick I met with more than once..."[9]

linking such present-oriented behavior with an equally insalubrious spiritual present-mindedness:

> "The Sonorans could be considered as blessed were the
> indifference which they display in everything the effect
> of reason and of a well-considered philosophy...Would
> that the indifference with which they view everything
> transitory did not extend to the eternal and to the care of

---

[7] Och, 176.

[8] Ignaz Pfefferkorn was born in Mannheim in the Archbishopric of Cologne in
1725, entering the Jesuit order in 1742, at the age of seventeen. In 1755 he jour-
neyed to Mexico (on the same voyage as Och), and was sent, in 1756, to set up a
mission at Ati in Sonora, among the Pima and Papago. He remained there until
1762, when his health began to fail and he was reassigned to Cucurpe, among
the Eudebes, where he remained until the Jesuit Expulsion in 1767.

[9] Ignaz Pfefferkorn, *Sonora: A Description of the Province*, Theodore Treutlien,
translator. (Albuquerque: University of New Mexico Press, 1949), 274.

their souls!"[10]

His desire to adjust Amerindian material and spiritual focus from the present to the future was shared by the Alsatian Jesuit, Johann Jakob Baegert,[11] who writes, of the Guaicura:

> "...if only the California natives, who really enjoy this temporal happiness, would also give a thought (now that the light of the faith shines upon them) to the bliss of the other world and the future life, and try to gain it by a more Christian conduct..."[12]

The accustomed aboriginal means of production, with its characteristic time-orientation, was thus seen as a key factor in facilitating or thwarting Amerindian Christianization.

Agriculture as inculcating a salutary work ethic

Agriculture was seen as valuable by the Jesuits not simply because of its induction of a sense of time amenable to that of Christianity, but because it was felt to inculcate a salutary work ethic wholly lacking in other forms of indigenous cultural organization. By far the most common accusation missionaries made against both missionized Amerindians and hostile tribes was that of a stunted work ethic. Agriculturist tribes, however, were generally judged far less harshly than non-agriculturists, because agrarian work was recognized as such, whereas hunting and gathering activities were not. To Jesuit observers unfamiliar with such economies, their activities appeared spontaneous and ill-organized, which made their success appear accidental, rather than the result of inherited knowledge and meticulous planning. Laziness and lack of purposeful employment were thought by missionaries to be the root of all other aboriginal sins. Baegert's caustic evaluation of the Guaicura hunter-gatherer peoples is seconded by Pfefferkorn's denunciation of

---

[10] Ibid., 172.
[11] Johann Jakob Baegert was born in Schlettstadt, Alsace, in 1717 and died in 1772 in the Rhenish Palatinate. He was admitted to the Jesuit order in 1747. He came to Mexico in 1750, and was sent to the Baja California missions. He resided at the mission of San Luis Gonzaga from 1751 to 1768, among the Guaicura tribe, who were migratory hunter-gatherers.
[12] Johann Jakob Baegert, *Observations in Lower California*, Brandenburg and Carl L. Baumann, trans. (Berkeley: University of California Press, 1952), 50.

Sonoran 'idleness':

> "Laziness, lying, and stealing are their three hereditary
> vices, their three original sins...They never work, never
> bother about anything except when it is absolutely nec-
> essary to still the pangs of hunger as it overtakes
> them...They could easily improve their living conditions
> at least a little if they were more industrious and more
> willing to work. Here and there they could sow a handful
> of corn, plant pumpkins, and cotton....but nothing of this
> kind must be expected of them. They do not care to eat
> pigeons unless they fly roasted into their mouths..."[13]

> "...the pursuit of idleness is the favorite occupation of
> the Sonorans. They would not move for the whole world
> from the position where they sit, lie or stand, were they
> not brought to it by some sport, by some pleasurable
> thing, by some necessary labor..."[14]

Manual, and particularly agricultural labor, on the other hand, was presented by missionaries in almost salvific terms, as a great civilizing and
Christianizing force, as Pfefferkorn puts it, as a necessary "means of educating the unconverted to become people of worth and gradually drawing
them away from shameful excesses to which their idleness contributed."[15] Nentwich uses parable in his presentation of the wholesome
necessity of labor:

> "(there is) a worm, similar to the silk-worm...like the
> silkworm, it does not live after its work has been accom-
> plished, for when this is finished it makes its exit and
> dies. This creature teaches a wholesome lesson to many
> idle people; that they should live to work, recalling the
> words of the Sacred Scriptures that we were born to
> work, and that, as the Apostle says, they should be
> ashamed to eat who are reluctant to work..."[16]

---

[13] Ibid., 83-84.
[14] Pfefferkorn, 201.
[15] Ibid., 274.
[16] Nentwich, 51-52.

Indeed, the sheer repetitiveness of missionary discussions of an aboriginal work ethic, or the lack thereof, can blind us to a more subtle and interesting appreciation of the meaning of work and material success to Jesuits. Why would an order committed to the abandonment, for religious reasons, of material gains, be so concerned with fostering a sense of worldly ambition, and a desire to substantially improve living standards, in their native charges?[17]

Agriculturalism as a necessary underpinning to Christian volitional fasting cycles

I would suggest that Jesuit attempts to secure at least a minimal level of dependable year-round provisions for their missions, and to champion a 'work ethic' in missionized Amerindians, which would make this goal possible, have theological roots independent of and in addition to their obvious strategic and practical advantages.[18] Such goals can be seen as a

---

[17] Johann Baegert is the only Jesuit writer in our period who ponders at length the potential clash between the Jesuit urge to improve material conditions of life among aboriginal groups, and Biblical mandates of God's provision, though his evaluation of the benefits of what he sees as the utter privation of aboriginal life depends almost entirely upon the audience for which he is writing. Addressing a European public, Baegert uses aboriginal happiness in poverty of the Guaicura people to attack the materialism and greed of his readers: "These are the riches and pleasures of the California natives, with which, however, they spend the days of their lives in health and in greater peace of mind, serenity, and joyfulness than thousands upon thousands of human beings in Europe, who know no end to their possessions and are hardly able to count their old and new coins. To be sure, California has thorns, but they do not hurt and wound the feet of the Indians as often or as deeply as do those which are stored up in the money chests of Europe, stingingly worrying the hearts of their owners...the extreme poverty of the Indians and their total lack of those goods which seem indispensable is a fair proof that nature is not complicated and that life can be maintained with very little" [Baegert, *Observations in Lower California*, 64]. However, such lyric descriptions of the noble poverty of Amerindians are notably lacking in his private correspondence [Johann Jakob Baegert, *The Letters of Jacob Baegert, 1749-1761: Jesuit Missionary in Baja California*, Elsbeth Schulz-Bischof, tran. (Los Angeles: Dawson's Book Shop, 1982)], where he links the harsh environment of Baja California and the difficulty of finding adequate food and water to native resistance to his own attempts to "civilize" and "Christianize" them.

[18] Some, for instance, would characterize the goal of a largely self-sufficient food supply as an attempt to inculcate Amerindian dependency upon the mission system. My own sense is that such dependency was an unfortunate side effect of missionary policy rather than its intentional result. By instructing already sedentary agriculturalist tribes in new farming techniques, and introducing reduced nomadic tribes to their rudiments, the Jesuits deliberately and irrevocably modi-

Jesuit attempt to salvage and justify the idea of *voluntary* poverty and self-denial in a New World context which threatened to render such concepts wholly irrelevant: both as an aspect of community ritual expression, in the form of weekly and seasonal restrictions upon both the amount and type of food consumed, and the source of a traditional sense of clerical identity and self-definition. What I am suggesting is that the sheer material poverty of some frontier missions posed a serious conceptual problem for the Jesuits on several levels: it threatened to subvert their concept of stylized, ritual self-denial and sacrificial or voluntary poverty. This, in turn, had implications for both community observation and cohesion, and for the Jesuit sense of self. Let us, then, examine each of these implications in more detail.

Native borderline-subsistence, or fluctuating patterns of minimal ingestion followed by periods of luxuriant abundance, were often seen by Jesuit missionaries in the eighteenth-century as an affront to their ethos of discipline and order. They also saw aboriginal concerns with meeting immediate needs rather than planning for the future as having theological as well as material ramifications, as we have already explored. But, arguably, such fluctuations in the amount and nature of food consumed were objectionable to the Jesuits only because they were the result of environmental conditions: that is, they were involuntarily imposed rather than voluntarily assumed. It is apparent from the writings of both Pfef-

---

fied aboriginal means of production, with often disastrous results. If Jesuits had sought to inculcate aboriginal dependency, however, it is unlikely that they would repeatedly express bafflement as to why Amerindians generally returned to them for personal assistance rather than simply applying the medical or agricultural techniques they had been taught. This native desire for the Jesuits' personal intervention, however, may demonstrate less a sense of dependency than a respect for the priest's status as a powerful ritual actor. Missionized Amerindians may have, logically, extended the priest's role as a ritual specialist, regarding his personal attention to agricultural tasks as being essential to their efficacy as was his presence in the administration of the sacraments. Moreover, Jesuit missionaries appear to have desired to give aboriginal peoples skills they could *ultimately* use independently: upon their transfer to a parish system, Amerindians were expected to control their own economic destinies using the agricultural techniques they had been taught. But while the fostering of aboriginal dependency many not have been the conscious goal, missionary practices do appear to have both initiated and reinforced it by offering material inducements, in the form of food or tobacco, to encourage Amerindians to perform religious duties. Moreover, while the Jesuit missionary may have taught agricultural techniques that were intended to be applied independently, he was still the primary source for the equipment and materials upon which missionized Amerindians had been taught to depend.

ferkorn and Och that traditional aboriginal periods of lean and fat seasons mimicked those of the Christian ritual pattern of alternate feasting and fasting:

> "If the Sonorans have consumed their food supply, it is not difficult for them to go without nourishment for two or three days. But if they are then able to get a bite, they make up in doubled gluttony for the hunger they have suffered..."[19]

> "Even my already domesticated, gentle Indians looked forward with pleasure during the whole year to the two months' feasting time of June and July when they could gorge themselves like swine on pitahya...gorging and sleeping without being concerned or troubled about anything was their only thought, happiness, and goal, although in three or four days they could again suffer the pangs of hunger..."[20]

But while such dietary vagaries certainly displayed the contrast of Christian feasting and fasting, they lacked their essential element of *volition*. *Volitional* abstention expressed the defining ethos of individual and collective self-control which was at the heart of Jesuit 'agriculturalist' values, in a way that merely *circumstantial* abstention decidedly did not. A dependable food supply was thus necessary for the mission community to be able to exhibit ritually this essential element of volitional abstention: simply put, you can't give something up if you don't have to begin with!

Evidence suggests that Jesuit attempts to keep such distinctions absolute ultimately failed. In particular, those Jesuits stationed in the most environmentally forbidding areas tended to increasingly blur volitional and circumstantial forms of fasting. Forced to adjust to a wholly unfamiliar dietary repertoire while stationed in Baja California, Johann Baegert's fasting practices seem more motivated by distaste for the scanty food available than by the desire to renounce something pleasurable. His sense of having limited options for demarcating *voluntary* food abstention is pronounced, even as he adopts the traditional period of forty

---

[19] Pfefferkorn, 195.
[20] Och, 180.

days to attempt to give a modicum of Christian structure to practices adopted by dint of environmental necessity:

> "...I often found myself forced to give up the evening meal entirely because I had nothing I cared to eat. For several years I fasted for forty days on dry vegetables and salted fish five or six times within twelve months."[21]

To address such difficulties, some Jesuits creatively adapted the language of fasting and renunciation to describe whole periods of their own lives: presenting their time in the mission field, for example, as a "one continuous fast,"[22] thus reinstating the essential element of volition by setting it in the wider frame of their missionary call.

As well as being undercut in its communal, ritual aspects by problems of unreliable food sources and entrenched patterns of aboriginal food consumption, the prestige of volitional abstention as a marker of superior religiosity, distinguishing liberal lay observance from more rigorous clerical asceticism, was directly challenged by the difficulty of subsistence in the arid terrain of northwestern New Spain and the subsequent refusal of aboriginal people to accord European standards of privation much respect. Both Och and Baegert ruefully relate how their attempts to inculcate aboriginal awe for the voluntary abstention of European saints go woefully awry:

> "What to us seems the greatest punishment, yea, what would seem for us impossible to ensure, that is, to get along only with bread and water, would be the best fare for the Indians, and if they had enough of it, they would for the rest of their lives be satisfied. For this reason they have only seven fast days to observe during the entire year; namely, the Fridays during Lent, and the days preceding this Feast of the Trinity and that of Saints Peter and Paul. It is useless to set before them the example of St. Francis: of that of a hermit living a stern life of fasting on bread, water, or herbs. They laugh a great deal at this and say that he was better off than they. And his crude garments they envy for themselves as a protection

---

[21] Baegert, *Observations in Lower California*, 143.
[22] Perez de Ribas, 208.

against heat and cold..."[23]

"Now let anyone try to...deliver a beautiful sermon in praise of the saints, explaining how they crushed all vanity under their feet, forsook princely domains and entire kingdoms, distributed all their belongings and possession among the poor, voluntarily chose poverty, subjected themselves for years to the severest penances, conquered their inclinations, subdued their passions, spent eight and more hours daily in prayer and divine meditation, hated the world and their own lives, how they were chaste and humble, slept on the bare ground, ate no meat, drank no wine, and so on... a California Indian will tell him that he never slept in a bed in all his life, that he does not even know what bread is, much less how beer and wine would taste, that he hardly ever ate meat, except that of rats and mice..."[24]

Aboriginal perceptions of Christian ascetic practices, then, called into question the severity of such behavior by suggesting that such supposed ascetics were actually enjoying a comparatively *higher* standard of living, even in their asceticism, than did aboriginal people in the normal course of life. This perception effectively thwarted the usage of such practices as a means of establishing clerical superiority, particularly when the issue of voluntarism is occluded: as Baegert admits, "they can fast much longer than I."[25]

Arguably, then, Jesuit missionaries in eighteenth-century northwestern New Spain lost one of the ways that they had traditionally dramatized their difference from the lay communities that they served: because the deprivation of the aboriginal community made their own sac-

---

[23] Och, 180.

[24] Baegert, *Observations in Lower California*, 97. Ironically, much the same type of lively, competitive contempt is visible in Baegert's own comparison of his ordeals as a Californian missionary with those of the Desert Fathers: "...I would have to cheat myself immensely to compare the California desert with its unfertile sandy soil...with the Egyptian fields and forests through which Saint Anthony...made his way, not even to mention those crystal-clear wells at which they enjoyed the bread sent to them by heaven, while we often have warm, partly stinking water always taken out of not very clean ditches." [Baegert, *The Letters of Jacob Baegert*, 212].

[25] Ibid., The Letters of Jacob Baegert, 203.

rifices seem unimportant, and their preoccupation with their own prestige merely selfish. Jesuit attempts to foster a dependable food supply through the engendering of European standards of 'daily work for daily bread' as well as being pragmatic attempts to address perceived aboriginal poverty, were also a way of attempting to rectify the theological conundrums that such poverty posed to traditional religious values of *voluntary* self-denial.

Jesuit Perceptions of Migratory Aboriginal Hunting and Gathering

While aboriginal sedentary agriculturism, then, was subject to this passionate 'Euro-identification,' and seen as being the font of a 'proto-Christian' conceptualization of time, and as the nursery of the work ethic, migratory hunting and gathering was perceived as its moral and cultural opposite. Just as the agricultural means of production, with its associated values of order, work, and delayed gratification was seen as ideally receptive to Christian precepts, migratory ways of life, with their associated 'idleness' were felt to occlude perception of these sacred truths. Johann Baegert, writing of the Guaicura in the 1750's, notes: "It is difficult and unusual to find many good Christians in a country which offers no opportunities for work or community life...,"[26] adding:

> "The aridity of California and the consequent lack of agriculture, trades, and work bring with them the constant idleness, the continuous roving about of the native Californians, and their lack of clothing and housing. This idleness and roving is the cause of innumerable misdeeds and much wickedness, even among the very young..."[27]

Other Jesuits also pair migration's 'restlessness' or 'shiftlessness' with the twin sins of inattention to agriculture, and a lack of diligence regarding religious duties. Johann Nentwich observes:

> "...the people are restless; sometimes they do some work, and sometimes they rove around the towns of the

---

[26] Baegert, *Observations from Lower California*, 86.
[27] Ibid, 48.

vicinity, caring nothing about the cultivation of the land, and less of going to confession even on their deathbed..."[28]

Freed from the gentle tyranny of the agricultural cycle, with its sowing and reapings, and the anchor of a settled home, nomadic Amerindians were thought to live a life of total antinomianism, devoid of the authority structures missionaries felt necessary for civilization and religion:

"Here would be the time and place to tell about the California form of government and religion before the natives were converted to Christianity. Yet there is nothing to say about these two subjects except that not a trace of either can be found. Consequently, they had no magistrates, no police, no laws, no idols, no temples, no religious worship, no rites. They neither prayed to the true and only God, not did they believe in false deities. What kind of magistrate, what kind of government could there be in a country where all are equal, where no one owns nor would be able to own more than another...Where a child, as soon as he is able to walk, refuses to obey his parents and does not consider it a duty to obey? Each native did as he pleased, asking nobody, caring for nobody...The different tribes did not represent communities or a commonwealth; they rather resembled a herd of wild pigs, each one going his own way and grunting wherever he pleased, together today, scattered tomorrow, without order or leadership, without any head or obedience... It seems that where there is no authority religion cannot exist, for the latter requires laws and their enforcement..."[29]

In contrast to their analysis of agriculturist tribes, in which they emphasize community and a strong internal cohesion, and a 'natural' tendency toward order and authority, Jesuit missionaries portray the life of migra-

---

[28] Nentwich, 117.
[29] Baegert, *Observations from Lower California*, 91; for similar remarks see Pfefferkorn, 174.

tory tribes as an anarchic, individualistic frenzy, with each against the other in a struggle to survive. Their way of life was thus thought to constitute in and of itself a disturbing sin against the Jesuit ideals of discipline, order, and hierarchy. Ignaz Pfefferkorn relates with horror that:

> "...The Sonoran does not deliberate about the management of his affairs, and he observes no order whatever in his daily business. He does things and drops them when, how, and where his pleasure dictates. He eats at any hour of the day or night, whenever he feels hungry and has something to eat. When his belly has been well filled, he lies down on the ground and goes to sleep."[30]

Such negative perceptions of the nomadic life persisted even when the missionary was forced by dint of his own experience to concede the advantages of such a social organization. Johann Baegert acknowledges that Guaicura mobility was a highly effective adaptive response to harsh environmental conditions, chiefly a lack of water and fertile soil, which made agriculture impossible:

> "...They spend all their lives wandering about unendingly, driven to it by the necessity of collecting food. They cannot start every morning from the same place and return to it in the evening, because a small stretch of land is not sufficient to provide them with provisions for the whole year. This is true in spite of the small size of the tribes..."[31]

The Jesuits also recognized that a migratory way of life was ideally adapted to conditions of intermittent warfare, whether with aboriginal or European antagonists, as a mobile existence leaves no homes to be burned or food sources to be plundered. Habitual mobility, moreover, ensured that the regular means of production would be unaffected by war time conditions. Pfefferkorn contrasts the speed and efficacy of aboriginal antagonists with the clumsy slowness of Spanish soldiers:

---

[30] Pfefferkorn, 173; for a nearly identical passage see Baegert, *Observations from Lower California*, 70.
[31] Baegert, Ibid., 59.

"They are amply supplied with food as well as with war equipment from their storehouse, the forest. There they find animals, wild fruits, and roots for their sustenance, as well as all the materials for making new weapons. Beds are at all times ready for them, for they require only a place on the bare earth for the night's rest....they have no field equipment to delay them in moving hastily from one place to another...The Spaniards, on the other hand, find the difficulties of warring with these Indians almost insuperable, for they must carry all supplies and necessaries with them. This circumstance slows up their campaigns by depriving them of the mobility which is required against such a fast-moving foe...when the supplies which have been brought along are exhausted, the Spaniard can no longer continue the battle."[32]

Jesuit recognition of the adaptive advantages of a migratory lifestyle, however, did not result in a wholesale reevaluation of its moral status: missionaries persisted in characterizing migratory hunter-gathering tribes as culturally inferior, unstable, anti-authoritarian, and oriented towards the immediate gratification of present needs, in short, they saw migratory life as the root cause of much sin and sorrow in aboriginal culture: "So the most pitiable people never live together, neither in their own place nor at the mission, and that causes all the misery."[33]

During the process of reduction and enforced sedentary settlement, then, missionaries sought to fundamentally reground the established patterns of subsistence of migratory tribes by forcibly imposing upon them the agriculturist model. Juan Antonio Balthasar, a Swiss Jesuit who served throughout the frontier areas of northwestern New Spain for over forty years,[34] couples aboriginal baptism with the explicit expectation that such new Christians will adopt a life of agricultural cultivation and communal residence: "This mission requires the assistance of soldiers who will force these Indians to live in the pueblo, since they are

---

[32] Pfefferkorn, 209; for an identical point, see Nentwich, 150.

[33] Baegert, *The Letters of Jacob Baegert*, 154.

[34] Juan Antonio Balthasar was born in Lucerne, Switzerland in 1697, and died in Mexico City in 1763. He entered the Jesuit order at age fifteen, in 1712. He came to Mexico in 1720, and served for some years as, successively, a rector, an official visitor to Sonora and Baja California, a provincial, and a procurator.

baptized, to labor in the fields which are fertile...,"[35] and argues for the long term use of an armed force to 'gently assist' the Jesuits in their project of reduction:

> "In order to reduce these Series and the Pimas of Santa Rosa, the royal aid of soldiers will be necessary, who with gentleness and without irritating them could lead them back to the pueblos were they have land for raising crops. So, it is necessary that we have the continued assistance of a corps of ten or fifteen soldiers for two or three years, so that after being gathered into a pueblo the Indians do not return immediately to their old haunts; that they give themselves constructively to the cultivation of the land, sow their corn, and develop some love for the pueblo."[36]

The Jesuit agriculturalist ethic decreed that migratory Amerindians be made to confront agricultural Christianity: taught the inadvisability of living in and for the present, and the necessity of anticipating future needs, materially by food over-production and storage, and spiritually by preparation for inevitable death and judgment. They, like their agriculturist neighbors, must be made to appreciate the practical advantages as well as the moral necessity of the delayed or thwarted gratification of needs. By introducing them to both a highly structured set of daily, weekly, and extraordinary ritual observances and a similar, seasonal pattern of agricultural labor, Jesuit missionaries on the frontiers of northwestern New Spain thought that their native charges would be "kept from evil, guided toward goodness, weaned from idleness, roused to work" and, finally, "brought into a human course of life."[37]

The internalization of such standards can be seen in vignettes such as the following, related by Baegert:

> "One of them requested a number of goats from his missionary in order to live, as he put it, like a human being,

---

[35] Juan Antonio Balthasar, *Juan Antonio Balthasar: Padre Visitador to the Sonora Frontier, 1744-1745, Two Original Reports*, Peter Dunne, translator. (Arizona Pioneer Historical Society, 1957), 78.

[36] Ibid., 76.

[37] Pfefferkorn, 175; see also Baegert, *Observations from Lower California*, 121.

that is, to keep house, to pasture the goats, and partly to support himself and his family with the goat's milk and the flesh of the kids... ."[38]

Eighteenth-century Jesuit missionaries, then, perceived aboriginal modes of production as a significant determiner of the success of their Christianization efforts: and clearly saw those populations with extant sedentary agricultural practices as being, because of their lifestyle, more amenable to Christianity than those employing a non-sedentary, non-agricultural means of production. At times the language used approaches a sort of geographic determinism. Jacobo Sedelmayr, a Bavarian Jesuit who worked in the Pimeria Alta and Sonora regions from the 1730's through the 1760's,[39] in a wide-ranging discussion of the factors necessary for aboriginal Christianization, frankly links missionary success with the climactic and environmental features of the target tribe's geographical location. Success or failure of the mission is seen as largely the product of whether the site in question is suitable for supporting extant aboriginal agriculturalism, or nurturing its introduction:

> "Although the Society does not refuse to labor in harsh and sterile regions such as Topia, California, part of Tepehuana and such like, in order to gain souls for God, yet it cannot be denied that for the more efficient reduction, instruction, and taming of Indians those regions are preferable which can better support the padres."[40]

Johann Baegert blames the harshness of the environment in Baja California, where he was stationed, for thwarting the development of even rudimentary sedentary agriculture in his mission, for the consequent 'moral depravity' of aboriginal culture, and ultimately for his own paltry 'harvest' of souls:

---

[38] Baegert, Ibid., 71.
[39] Jacobo Sedelmayr was born in Inhausen, Bavaria, in 1703, and died in Aldea de Avila in Spain, in 1779. He entered the Society of Jesus in 1722. He came to Mexico in 1735, and was sent to the Pimeria Alta, where he resided at the mission of Tubutama from 1736 until 1752, after which he was assigned to Tecoripa in mid-Sonora until 1762. From thence he went to the mission at Matape and was there until 1767 and the Expulsion.
[40] Sedelmayr, *Jacobo Sedelmayr: Missionary, Frontiersman, Explorer in Arizona and Sonora*, 31.

> "...they live without household, law or order, without any economy, and I almost could say, without reason. A lot this has to be blamed on the country - the part I saw - in which ordinary civilized life, as I thought and hoped for, cannot be introduced to them...it is not possible to live a human life in California..."[41]

> "...nothing very edifying can be told about the Californians because the results of our work among them, in terms of the applied toil and diligence, are very poor indeed, though the reason for that must in part by attributed to the inferior quality of the land..."[42]

These reflections demonstrate once again the strong link many eighteenth-century Jesuit missionaries perceived as existing between the physical environment, the consequent means of aboriginal production, and the overall success of their attempts at religious enculturation.

As already suggested, patterns of Christianization among Amerindian groups often occurred along lines of established indigenous political antagonisms. Eighteenth-century Jesuit missionaries entered a complex arena of tribal politics and entrenched rivalries in many parts of Sonora, Sinaloa, and Pimeria Alta. Animosity between migratory hunter-gatherer and sedentary agriculturist tribes tended to be reinforced rather than challenged by the arrival of European missionaries. By a coincidence of native political realities and the missionary preconceptions we have just examined, strong alliances tended to form between sedentary agriculturist tribes and the Jesuits: missionaries perceived in the 'ethos' of such groups the shared values discussed earlier, whereas indigenous agriculturists often saw alliance with the missionaries as affording them access to new military resources and agricultural techniques. Moreover, both groups appear to have shared a sense of the moral superiority of this way of life, as is demonstrated by Johann Nentwich's account of this

---

[41] Baegert, *The Letters of Jacob Baegert*, 123. Baegert's comments about the meager possibilities of living "a human life in California" are strikingly similar to his purported attribution of a very similar phrase to an aboriginal informant, who is quoted as expressing a desire to "to live...like a human being" (quoted in the text, above). It is unclear, however, whether this quote truly demonstrates his informant's internalization of Baegert's own way of viewing the world, or merely illustrates Baegert's own interpretive 'spin' on the man's request.
[42] Baegert, *Observations in Lower California*, 7.

Opata victory ceremony:

> "when a victory has been obtained and they bring a scalp
> or some plunder, the entrance is made in day time, and
> notice is sent of their happy arrival. An old woman arms
> herself with bow and arrow and comes out to meet
> them...the scalp is told with much bragging by the old
> woman and her companions in a singsong manner...all
> the miseries, hardships, etc. that the enemies have to en-
> dure when they come to steal and kill, adding that the
> cause of all these misfortunes is their laziness, for it they
> would till the land, as is done by them, the victors, they
> might stop doing mischief and live in safety..."[43]

Nomadic tribes, on the other hand, often resisted missionaries because of
their emphasis on orderly settlement, and their erstwhile alliance with
their traditional foes. Thus, Jesuit assumptions about which cultural con-
figurations were most suitable for Christianization were only reinforced
by the reactions of both groups. Despite Sedelmayr's unintentionally
ironic presentation of Christianity as a pacific force, capable of preventing war: "By the introduction of the Faith among these people, civil wars
could easily be abolished, as we have seen in our Pimeria...."[44] Jesuits'
preconceived notions about culture only deepened and reinforced pre-
existing tribal antagonisms, when it did not openly and consciously exploit them:

> "Those tribes are well adapted to the reception of our
> Holy Faith. In the first place they are gentle, affable, af-
> fectionate, and laborious. They are enemies of our ene-
> mies, friends of the Spaniards, given to trade and barter
> with the Christians, and now for fifty years they have
> peacefully admitted the fathers into their country...[45] If
> the regions of those rivers could be organized into a mis-
> sion district and a presidio could be located on the upper
> Gila, where it issues forth from Apache country...then

---

[43] Nentwich, 68.
[44] Sedelmayr, *Jacobo Sedelmayr: Missionary, Frontiersman, Explorer in Ari-zona and Sonora*, 26.
[45] Ibid., 41.

those tribes could be held together and, as it were, conquered through our dedication to them and the aid we
give them against the common foe...”[46]

Such intrigues helped to cement the common Jesuit view that some tribes
were wholly unameanable to Christianity, as these patterns of affiliation
and rejection tended to deepen with time. In their solicited musings upon
conditions in their particular regions, missionaries often stressed the need
for large scale military operations against these renegade tribes, or their
large scale deportation, if Christianity was to prevail in the province.[47]
Such analysis betrays the fact that this mutual antipathy had become so
entrenched that the irony of advising the mass deportation of the very
people they had come to convert is completely unacknowledged in these
documents, nor is this failure ever bewailed. It is simply accepted as impossible.

In Sinaloa, Sonora, and Pimeria Alta, then, mission communities
were often composed of sedentary agriculturist peoples, such as Opadas,
Eudebes, Papagos and (‘lower’) Pimas, existing alongside unconverted
hunter-gatherer and raider cultures such as the (‘upper’) Seris and
Apaches. It is my contention that the proximity of unconverted hunter-
gatherer/raider cultures to agricultural mission communities created a
specific set of psychological circumstances for the missionaries living in
them: decisively affecting everything from how they evaluated possible
threats to themselves; to how they perceived missionized Amerindians
and adjudged their adaptation to Christianity; to how they experienced
and expressed their primary sense of community affiliation; to how they
characterized the overall success of missionizing efforts. Specifically, I
want to argue that missionaries in such contexts tended 1) to see what
were often internal threats in external terms; 2) to apply the ‘negative’
poles of ‘Christian-heathen’ and ‘civilized-barbarian’ dyads to this external tribe, and the ‘positive’ poles to the mission community itself, and to
adjudge missionized Amerindian conversion on the ‘orthopraxic’ basis of
ritual observance rather than the ‘orthodoxic’ basis of theological understanding; 3) to derive their primary sense of identity and community
from the mission itself; and 4) to express general optimism for the future
of their missions, particularly if steps could be taken to curtail the power
of adjacent, unconverted Amerindian tribes.

---

[46] Ibid., 35.
[47] See Nentwich, 147 and Pfefferkorn, 153-154.

In regions such as Baja California, on the other hand, where there was a more uniform cultural pattern of migratory hunting and gathering and less inter-tribal warfare, the 'externalizing' mechanism enabled by the presence of a proximate 'enemy' tribe could not function. In its absence, particularly when environmental factors made the 'reduction' of migratory Amerindian groups impossible, the strong sense of Jesuit identification with the mission community and optimism regarding its future tends to be discernibly eroded. Specifically, missionaries in this context appear 1) to recognize rather than externalize the reality of internal threats; 2) to apply to missionized Amerindians the 'negative' poles of 'Christian-heathen' and 'civilized-barbarian' dyads, reserving exclusively for the Jesuit order the 'positive' poles, and to evaluate the Christianization of missionized Amerindians in individual and 'orthodoxic' rather than collective, 'orthopraxic' terms; 3) to derive their primary sense of community and identity from the Jesuit order, rather than the mission community; and 4) to express pessimism for the future of mission activities. Simply put, Jesuit classification of threats to missionary security in either internal or external terms leads to different usages of conceptual polarities, and contrasting standards for evaluating the Christianization of missionized Amerindians, which in turn leads to differences in the articulation and experience of primary community affiliation, which, finally, leads to dissimilar evaluations of the success of the missionary enterprise. Let us examine each of these claims in greater detail.

...the classification of threats to missionary security in either internal or external terms...

At the heart of my theory is the contention that the presence of hostile, non-Christianized Amerindian groups on the periphery of the mission often allowed its missionaries to psychologically externalize the dangers to both their authority and their safety that were always present within it. This in turn allowed them to both perceive missionized Amerindians as comparatively 'Christian' and 'civilized' in contrast with other aboriginal groups, and to look to the mission as the primary source of their own community and identity. The presence of a "common enemy," then, permitted the individual Jesuit missionary to think of 'his' mission community as united in a way which he was arguably unable to do in the absence of such a threat. The existence of this enemy, and the necessary practicalities of defense against it in many cases obscured the fact that the Jesuits and their missionized Amerindian allies were not enemies with this external group for the same reasons, and that missionized Amerindians undoubtedly had more in common culturally with even their implacable aboriginal foes than they did with missionary Europeans. The tendency of Jesuit missionaries in these 'externalizing' situations to deny the reality of internal threats to their safety can be seen in Och's defensive characterizations of the loyalty and Christian submissiveness of 'his' missionized Amerindians:

> "In such a manner all live in proper submissiveness and obedience, constitute a peaceful republic, and serve faithfully God and the King. They show no anger against the father or against their superiors, rather after having endured a punishment they approach the missionary quite humbly, kiss his hand, and say; "Father, you do not punish me, my offense punishes me..."[48]

Such characterizations of the mildness and submissiveness of missionized Amerindians persist even following aboriginal insurrections which resulted in the deaths of their fellow Jesuits. Ignaz Pfefferkorn, in this remarkable passage, portrays the Pima revolt of 1751 as an unimportant, childish fit of pique, rather than as a deadly expression of aboriginal dissatisfaction with missionary incursion and Spanish colonial domination:

> "After the deed was done the Pimas repented and soon showed that their revolt had originated more from thoughtlessness, imprudence, and the foolish fear of their wicked general, than from their own ill will. For the following year they voluntarily returned to their deserted villages, without compulsion delivered their ringleaders to the Spaniards for merited punishments, and welcomed their returning spiritual fathers lovingly and penitently. Thereafter, to the time of the expulsion of the Jesuits from Sonora, they showed not the least sign of unrest."[49]

Even those missionaries who themselves had escaped death by only the

---

[48] Och, 168.
[49] Pfefferkorn, 35.

narrowest of margins, such as Johann Nentwich, who was besieged for three days within a neighboring mission church by his own native charges,[50] nevertheless identify the main impediment to the progress of Christianity in Sonora as the *external* aggression of the Seris and the Apaches. He presents such groups as the ultimate threat to Christianity and civilization, and pleads for concerted military campaigns against them:

> "In regard to the Seris, although they live within the limits of this Province, it seems unreasonable to me to count them among its inhabitants; they should rather be considered (like the Apaches, notwithstanding that they hold as their own all the mountains) as its most cruel enemies and ravagers."[51]

> "At this very moment, while writing these lines, I pray God that He may give victory to the soldiers sent upon them (the Seris) so that we may obtain the desired peace so necessary to prevent the complete ruin of the Province of Sonora, and so that we may turn the scanty forces we can command against another and more fearful enemy, the Apache..."[52]

Those who lived in missions relatively less affected by internecine aboriginal animosities, and characterized by more uniform means of production among tribes, being unable to exercise this 'externalizing' technique, are noticeably more frank and unsentimental about the existence of threats to missionary security from within the mission itself. Johann Baegert, stationed among the Guaicura of Baja California, displays a more diffuse sense of potential danger by presenting the differences between Christianized and non-Christianized Amerindians as relative, rather than absolute:

> "It would be foolhardy to go and preach the Gospel to these half-human Americans without taking along a

---

[50] See Sedelmayr, *Before the Rebellion*, xii, and Balthasar, *Juan Antonio Balthasar: Padre Visitador to the Sonora Frontier*, 47.
[51] Nentwich, 54.
[52] Ibid., 83, my note.

bodyguard. It would even be daring to live without protection among those already baptized, because of their
vacillating and changeable character. The only thing a
missionary without protection could expect to find
among these people is an untimely death and the loss of
the expense for such a long journey."[53]

...leads to different usages of conceptual polarities, and contrasting standards for evaluating the Christianization of missionized Amerindians...

Jesuit missionaries who perceived themselves as being allied with missionized Amerindians against a common foe tended to identify with their mission community by projecting out of it not only its threats of violence and disorder, but also what they perceived as its 'barbaric' and 'idolatrous' elements, by explicitly and implicitly comparing missionized Amerindians, in terms of their cultural characteristics, and amenability to Christianity, with this outside group. Such statements excuse the 'problematic' cultural tendencies of those within the mission by comparing them with the yet more barbaric habits of those beyond its walls. Thus Joseph Och contrasts the primitive, but adequate dwellings of' 'his' missionized Amerindians, the Pimas, with the "holes in the ground" of the "stupid and wild" Papagos,[54] and contrasts the "civilized" stability of Pima cultivation with the brash disorder of Papago hunting and gathering. Moreover, he suggests that, when expressed, Papago willingness to aid in the harvest must be interpreted as a disguised reassertion of their hunting ethos, in the service of their 'uncivilized' dietary preferences:
...the Indians are so greedy for these rats that all wish to cut wheat (i.e. -
to reveal the rats)...though they are more interested in the rats than the

---

[53] Baegert, *Observations in Lower California*, 146. Occasionally, someone with a view of the 'bigger picture,' such as a Padre Visitor, will discuss both internal and external threats to mission security with relative even-handedness: "...the new mission would require the protection of some fifteen soldiers since, as we have said, these people live on the edge of Apache land, indeed they are practically in it. So the missionary who will be resident there, even when he will not have to be on his guard against the Pimas themselves, who are still rather rude and rough, will have much to fear from the Apaches, and without a guard of soldiers the pueblo cannot be formed, nor a church built." [Balthasar, *Juan Antonio Balthasar: Padre Visitador to the Sonora Frontier*, 80-81]
[54] Och, 152-153.

grain... ."[55] Similarly, Johann Nentwich contrasts the relative sobriety of 'his' Opatas and Eudebes with the drunkenness of neighboring apostate Pimas,[56] and approvingly describes their gender roles, which are closer to European norms than are the practices of other tribes:

> "Men and women till the land together, but there is not the barbarity which observed among the Indians of other Provinces, and even here among the Apaches and the Pimas of the highlands, where the women bear all the burden of the labor. Among these, women do the lightest work; and if one of them is pregnant she does not come out, but stays in the house to cook pozole for the laborers...and spin the cotton and weave...while the Pimas of the mountains make their women work in the fields, and they themselves spin and weave, although this is a woman's trade."[57]

By continuously contrasting the social organization and means of production of 'insider' and 'outsider' groups, the Jesuits soon came to perceive those within the pale of the mission community as (comparatively) civilized and (relatively) Christian.[58] This process of projection

---

[55] Ibid., 153, my note.

[56] Nentwich, 61-62.

[57] Ibid., 71.

[58] This Jesuit habit of either implicitly or explicitly contrasting religious and cultural behavior among groups was not just exercised with regard to aboriginal groups. Missionaries also compared the spiritual and material 'production' of 'their' missionized Amerindians with that of their European readers, as an object lesson for the latter. Many of the statements betray a sort of nostalgia for pre-Enlightenment European collective religious expression, as we see in this statement by Ignaz Pfefferkorn: "There was always a large assemblage at the daily prayers of the rosary, at the festive processions, and at the other customary devotional exercises of the Church. These Indians displayed at such functions an admirable piety, a fear of God, and a virtue which could put to shame many European hypocrites, who, instead of humiliating themselves before their creator...mock religion and shamefully give the most horrible offense by their indecent behavior" [Pfefferkorn, 240]. Jesuits also utilized the example of Amerindians to question both the work ethic and skills of Europeans. Och states: "...I taught the boys who worked with me how to read and write, which they did more avidly from natural zeal than would a European child with blows or coaxing...in the missions they were eager for learning...I had Indians who made for themselves violins, harps, and even zithers, and this they did with little more than an old knife and a sharp flint...the womenfolk...are also very skillful...they

was greatly aided by the fact that Jesuit patterns of military alliance, as we have already explored, were often made along lines conditioned by their cultural presuppositions, which perceived aboriginal sedentary agriculturalists in valorized, 'Europeanized' terms. Thus the process of community maintenance, through the projection of problematic elements out of the mission, drew extensively on the very same cultural prejudices which had helped to engender the mission community in the first place.

Another feature of this attempt to create community through a process of continuous contrast and projection involves the criteria of judgment used in evaluating the conversion of missionized Amerindians. I want to suggest that those Jesuits engaged in the process of comparing 'their' internal aboriginal community with a hostile outside group or groups tended to use more 'orthopraxic,' collective standards of evaluation than those who were not so engaged. That is to say, the conversion of missionized Amerindians in such contexts was often judged by the quality of their *ritual adherence:* their observance of the Angelus, attendance at daily mass, morning catechism, evening prayers, and weekly high Mass; their completion of the annual obligations of confession and communion; their observance of such life-cycle rituals as baptism and marriage within the church, and their expressed desire for extreme unction and Christian burial. Pfefferkorn's presentation of the admirable devotion of 'his' missionized Amerindians, while doubtless intended as a prod to his European readers, stresses ritual adherence almost exclusively:

> "The Opatas and Eudebes not only attended Mass very assiduously and devoutly on Sundays and feast days, but also throughout the week. They appeared gladly and eagerly as often as the dogma was presented, and their attention and indefatigability were admirable. At Easter it was not necessary to press them to do confession, they

---

made such durable fabrics for tablecloths that it would have been difficult for a German weaver to imitate them...with astonishing care and patience they made their dishes and pots..." [Och, 120]. This process of contrasting pious and hardworking Amerindian Christians with their dissipated European counterparts, however, was an intentional rhetorical strategy, rather than a largely unconscious defensive mechanism. Not surprisingly, given our earlier discussion of missionary 'perceived shared values' with sedentary agriculturist tribes, whether the comparisons are of material or spiritual productivity, it is nevertheless diligence and industriousness that are praised in each case.

went voluntarily without compulsion at the hour set for them by the spiritual guide to fulfill his Christian duty. There were almost none among them who did not at this time partake of Holy Communion. Those who were particularly distinguished in their understanding of the truths of the faith were also permitted the more frequent partaking of the holy sacrament..."[59]

Johann Nentwich also stresses collective conformity, rather than individual exceptionalism, in his description of Eudebe and Opata piety:

"It is a comfort to the Missionary Fathers to see among these people, particularly among the women, some who come to confession and Holy Communion at other seasons, such as the great festivals of Christmas, Pentecost, and those of the Blessed Virgin. In some Missions, particularly where our most holy Lady of Loreto is venerated, as at Matape, Bacaquatzi and Popsura, they recite every evening the Rosary with the Litany of the Blessed Virgin...At all the Missions, on Saturday evening, the Rosary is recited with the Litany and Salve Regina, the two last being sung in most of them. The Indians consider it a great act of devotion to hear Mass on Saturday, and not withstanding the assertion of the ministering father that no sin is committed by omitting that Mass many of them never fully believe so."[60]

Jesuit commentators evaluating aboriginal conversion in this context, then, tend to stress the proficiency and piety of missionized Amerindians in moments of collective ritual engagement, whether official or impromptu. The willingness of missionized aboriginals to participate enthusiastically in Catholic rituals is felt to be direct evidence of their genuine conversion by these missionaries, indeed, they are often held up as laudatory examples that European readers would do well to follow:

"During the procession were witnessed many very mov-

---

[59] Pfefferkorn, 239-240; See also Perez de Ribas, 121.
[60] Nentwich, 121.

ing examples of penitence and heartfelt participation in the bitter sufferings. Some pressed thorn crowns on their heads, other scrounged themselves with ropes which were stuck full of sharp thorns, one dragged a heavy stone, another carried a heavy cross or castigated his body in some other way fitting to his devotion and penitence."[61]

This propensity to present ritual engagement as a marker of aboriginal conversion would only have been strengthened by the apparent belief of many Jesuits that the magnificent tangibility of Catholic ritual was ideally suited to aboriginal sensibilities: "Everything that pertained to external ceremonies, processions, and singing was most agreeable to them."[62]

It is my contention that Jesuit evaluation of missionized Amerindian conversion in collective, 'orthopraxic' terms under 'externalizing' conditions occurs not simply because such criteria represent a relatively less stringent standard of judgment, but because such collective standards of evaluation are the logical result of the sense of identity being shaped and the underlying comparison being made. If we are correct in assuming that the individual Jesuit, under externalizing conditions, is influenced in his assessment of the conversion of missionized Amerindians by his sense of community identity or affiliation with them, then it is only natural that he would stress ritual moments of engagement and incorporation, making the *collective* observance of Catholic ritual, rather than *individual* understanding and acceptance of doctrine, his focus. Moreover, the comparison being made, we must not forget, is a comparison of two *communities*: that of the mission and that of the outside or enemy tribe: thus, the inception of Christianity within the mission is conceived of and celebrated as a collective event, rather than as an individual engagement.

Where the 'externalizing mechanism' of a proximate enemy tribe is absent, however, patterns of identification and standards of evaluation both change dramatically. We may illustrate these differences by utilizing the writings of Johann Baegert, an Alsatian Jesuit who, we will recall, was a mid-century missionary to the migratory Guaicura tribe in environmentally forbidding Baja California. Though Baegert's dour ethnocentrism and often stunning lack of empathic imagination point to the

---

[61] Pfefferkorn, 241.
[62] Och, 134.

possible difficulties of using him as a test case of our hypothesis, the fact remains that his extreme, almost unalloyed pessimism about the missionary enterprise was forged in an situation devoid of many of what I have put forward as possible community-building mechanisms, inviting us to interpret his outlook as having been forged by experience rather than being the product of his unique personality. Because the Guaicura had no significant aboriginal enemies, Baegert, unlike his fellow missionaries in Sonora, Sinaloa, and the Pimeria Alta, was unable to cement community cohesion by playing on mutual antipathy to an external group, or to valorize his mission community by means of tacit comparison with them. Therefore, he was unable to evaluate missionized Amerindians as 'Christian' and 'civilized' in comparison to a proximate, non-missionized aboriginal group. Moreover, the entrenched Jesuit perception of sedentary agriculture as culturally superior to hunting and gathering only reinforced Baegert's estrangement from his native charges, as local conditions (chiefly a lack of water and arable land) necessitated that traditional nomadic gathering continue even after the establishment of the mission community: "It is not possible for them to live together, for California is not a land, but in comparison to Alsace, a veritable purgatory, if not even a hell, as I sometimes used to say."[63] As a result, Baegert was able to realistically demand mission residency only one week out of every four, staggering this tenancy period in order to constantly maintain the maximum number of Amerindians that he could supply with food.[64] Baegert's private musings, in which he contrasts his naïve expectations of mission life with its harsh realities, illustrate the depth of his alienation, an alienation which appears to stem from his inability to reconcile himself to the continued necessity of traditional aboriginal means of production. In this passage we see his longing for a community which more closely approximates a familiar, European, pastoral way of life:

> "...all missionaries who come to the Indies, and certainly those who come to North America lamentably feel cheated twofold, including me...one imagines one could with so much space have more cows and consequently more cheese and butter than in the entire canton of Bern. One also could sow and harvest in abundance. And one

---

[63] Baegert, *The Letters of Jacob Baegert*, 137.
[64] Baegert, *Observations in Lower California*, 121; Baegert, *The Letters of Jacob Baegert*, 153-154.

imagines if one comes to mission, one would meet there
well-dressed people living together in huts, living on agriculture the way people do in Europe. And so you can
say Mass in a nice way, can hear a lot of confessions on
Sundays and holidays, and give communion, can sing
vespers and the Salve and could have a lot of enjoyment
with them, and so on. Or if one would receive an order
to found a new mission, after some years, one would be
able to establish a little market town. However, with
these ideas one is again cruelly cheated, but again it is
not your fault. For who in Europe would look at a globe
for such countries as California...or for the people in
such countries?"[65]

As a result of this marked estrangement from his native charges,
Baegert comes to utilize the dualities of 'civilized' and 'barbarian,'
'Christian' and 'heathen,' not to distinguish his mission community from
a competing or antagonistic native group, but, in effect, to distinguish between himself, as a European Jesuit, and the members of his own mission
community: he exemplifies 'Christianity' and 'civilization': they, emphatically, do not. The lay/clerical divide, which under 'externalizing'
conditions acted to preserve for other Jesuits a simple sense of their own
authority, superiority, and loyal membership in the Jesuit community becomes, in Baegert's circumstances, the source of his primary community
identity, and a mantra of complete difference.

Baegert manipulates the categories of 'civilized-barbarian' and
'Christian-heathen' in ways which are noticeably different in tone and
emphasis from other Jesuit commentators (though these distinctions are,
of course, relative rather than absolute). Baegert, far more frequently
than his colleagues, highlights the continuing 'barbarity' of 'his' missionized Amerindians, to at once demonstrate his own psychological
distance from them, and to create the same sense of distance in his European reader through explicit descriptions of activities calculated to shock,
horrify, or disgust:

"At this point I ask permission of the patient reader to
mention something of an exceedingly inhuman and re-

---

[65] Baegert, *The Letters of Jacob Baegert*, 157.

pulsive nature, the like of which has probably never been told of any other people in the world. It discloses better than anything else the poverty of the California Indians, their voracity and uncleanliness...Pitahayas contain a great many small seeds, resembling grains of powder, which for reasons unknown to me are not consumed in the stomach but passed in an undigested state. In order to use these small grains, the Indians collect all excrement during the season of the pitahayas, pick out these seeds from it, roast, grind, and eat them with much joking. This procedure is called by the Spaniards the after or second harvest! Whether all this happens because of want, voracity, or out of love for the pitahayas, I leave undecided...It is useless to try to persuade them to abandon this old practice..."[66]

Many of these related episodes, as well as both demonstrating and inculcating psychological distance, also project Baegert's feelings of alienation into the community he is describing by dramatizing a perceived lack of indigenous community cohesion. Baegert portrays native society as atomistic, selfish, and individualistic, with each independent of and estranged from the other, even within the family group:

"As soon as the (wedding) ceremony is over, the husband will go in one direction, the wife in another, each for himself, in search of something to eat...Husband and wife will wander where ever it pleases the one or the other. As far as food for their support is concerned, the husband does not provide for his wife, not the wife for her husband, nor either for their children beyond infancy. Both parents eat whatever they have or find, each one for himself, without being concerned about the other or about their offspring..."[67]

The differences between Baegert and his colleagues, while considerable, should not be overstated. Baegert, like his fellow Jesuits,[68]

---

[66] Baegert, *Observations in Lower California*, 68.
[67] Ibid., 73.
[68] See Och, 119-120; Pfefferkorn, 18, 169.

clearly and explicitly defends Amerindians from charges that they are subhuman and congenitally lacking in rationality, charges which would, if accepted as correct, vitiate the Jesuit program of enculturation and Christianization. Like them, he emphasizes the role of the physical environment, the modeled behavior of parents, and insufficient education in propagating such 'barbarism:'

> "As a general rule, it may be said that the California Indians are stupid, awkward, rude, unclean, insolent, ungrateful, mendacious, thievish, abominably lazy, great talkers to their end, and naive and childlike so far as intelligence and actions are concerned. They are an unreflecting people...a people who possess no self control, but follow, like animals in every respect, their natural instincts. Nonetheless, the California Indians and all other American natives are human beings, true children of Adam, as we are...they are endowed with reason and understanding like other people, and I think that, if in their early childhood they were sent to Europe, the boys to seminaries and colleges and the girls to convents, they would go as far as any European in mores, virtues, in all arts and sciences...Their animal-like stupidity is not inborn but grows slowly, just as intelligence does with others, and becomes more pronounced with the years..."[69]

adding that Europeans would act in precisely the same manner if born under similar brutalizing conditions:

> "...This idleness and roving is the cause of innumerable misdeeds and much wickedness...from which the European, according to my guess, would not have been able to protect himself either had it been his lot to be born in such a land... ."[70]

However, what Baegert gives with one hand, he often takes away

---

[69] Baegert, *Observations in Lower California*, 81.
[70] Ibid., 48.

with another, by himself labeling the Guaicura primitive or sub-human,[71] or by making extended analogies between their cultural practices and animal behavior:

> "...Miserable nation, they are like the animals, except without horns," for they go around absolutely naked; live under the open sky; go daily to the pasture; do not wash, except, if you will excuse the expression, with urine; hang their heads into the water, lay down on their bellies and drink like cows; work only if one stands behind them with a stick...throw themselves down and sleep wherever the night overtakes them; and finally, have a language of which I used to say it has only three dozen words. If foxes were able to speak, they would have a variety of necessary words of which the Californians would not know a thing...."[72]

> "...concerning honor, interest, satisfaction, or taste, one seeks in vain conversations with pigs, if you will excuse the expression, who do not even have such words in their language. They do not even know what it is to say thank you or to be thankful. If one gives them half an oxen, they spit on the newly whitened wall and leave as if bitten by a dog. So polite are the Guaicuras."[73]

As important as Baegert's psychologically distancing descriptions of 'his' missionized Amerindians are his standards for evaluating their conversion to Christianity. Whereas his Jesuit colleagues engender and reflect their sense of community identification by systematically externalizing problems internal to the mission, and adjudge the Christianization of missionized Amerindians positively on the collective, 'orthopraxic' basis of ritual engagement, Baegert utilizes individualistic, 'orthodoxic' criteria, emphasizing native understanding and acceptance of Christian theology, to formulate an overwhelmingly negative picture of both the quality and quantity of native conversions:

> "...out of self interest they pretend as if they are com-

---

[71] Baegert, *Observations in Lower California*, 87; Baegert, *The Letters of Jacob Baegert*, 144.
[72] Baegert, *The Letters of Jacob Baegert*, 138.
[73] Ibid., 158.

pletely convinced, in favor of, and touched by the truth
of Christianity upon which they do not show the least reflection or which they did not even understand and
grasp."[74]

"It must be regretted that they are just as careless in trying to understand and know about their spiritual salvation. Nobody will ever ask anything and they never have
any doubts; and as they know nothing, they will learn
nothing. I am quite sure that out of a hundred local Indians, when they come for confession there are not four
who have any idea about God or Hell...when I ask one of
them...what his thoughts are...he answers very dryly,
'nothing'...many of them commit adultery immediately
after they went to confession the evening before..."[75]

Perhaps because of his emphasis upon orthodoxic understanding
rather than orthopraxic participation, Baegert is the only one of the missionary authors under consideration here[76] to focus upon the difficulties
of communicating theological ideas to native tribes in their own language, addressing the problem of a lack of analogous terms in the
Guaicura tongue, as well as the ever-present dangers of cultural misunderstanding and over concretization. In discussing one of his translations,
he states his reasons for changing familiar creedal formulas:

"I could not use 'He shall come to judge the living and
the dead' for an Indian would not understand the ethical
or theological meaning of these and similar words. Neither was it permissible to say 'the flesh will live again'
for 'flesh' is to them the meat of cattle or deer, they
would laugh if they were told that a human being was
also 'flesh' or has 'flesh.' Consequently, they would
come to believe that deer and cows would rise of judgment day if they were told of the resurrection of the
'flesh.'"[77]

---

[74] Ibid., 204.

[75] Ibid., 217.

[76] Ignaz Pfefferkorn does touch on matters of translation, but only briefly [see
Pfefferkorn, 231-235].

[77] Baegert, *Observations in Lower California*, 102-103; See also Baegert, *The
Letters of Jacob Baegert*, 146-148.

Baegert's translations make us aware of the considerable diffi-culties of conveying even the basics of Christian theology in an utterly foreign cultural context and language, as well as allowing us a glimpse of what must have been the utter bemusement of those on the receiving end of Baegert's efforts to translate the Lord's Prayer: "Our father arched earth thou art thee o, that acknowledge all will praise all will people and, etc."[78]

As I have already suggested, standards for evaluating native Christianization do not appear in a vacuum, but themselves reflect the individual missionary's sense of identity and community affiliation. In this case, Baegert's adoption of individualistic, 'internal' criteria proba-bly stems from his determination to use the polarities of 'civilized-barbarian' and 'Christian-heathen' to *dissolve* rather than to build a sense of affiliation with his mission community: his aim is to continually rhet-orically sharpen the distinction between himself and 'them.' Just as the comparison of two communities necessitated the use of collective crite-ria, such as ritual engagement, so Baegert's manipulation of the concep-tual polarities to inculcate distance between himself and 'his' mission-ized Amerindians necessitates the recasting of the evaluative genre into more individualistic terms. The question becomes not the relative status of missionized Amerindians in comparison to another community, through the use of collective referents, but their individual comparison with the missionary himself as a representative of the Jesuit order. In this passage, Baegert differentiates himself from his mission community by suggesting that they never practice celibacy, the 'clerical' virtue *par excellence*:

> "in the fifty-six years since Catholic priests landed in California, one does not hear of one California man or woman whom has lived to a specially edifying life; for instance one who took the vows of celibacy or intended to do so, or one who radiated this or that virtue and so on. On the contrary, I am pretty sure that no one, regard-less of sex, reaches the sixteenth year of life without overstepping many times the sixth commandment before and after his marriage, and they steal wherever they can. Consequently local missions are deprived by the Indians

---

[78] Baegert, *Observations in Lower California*, 97-103.

of not only their temporal comforts but also their spiritual consolation."[79]

Moreover, in contrast to his Jesuit colleagues, who link Christianization with displays of ritual participation and the assumption of ritual leadership, Baegert appears almost to enjoy severing the connection between ritual status and moral and religious excellence, at least in his private correspondence:

> "One lad, the age of seventeen, who had just married, the most skillful of all in the neighborhood, who was page, sacristan, and gardener, is now in prison because of a well-premeditated murder, during broad daylight on the feast of the Ascension, only a stone's throw away from the mission."[80]

Even in Baegert's discussion of ritual adherence, his analysis is qualitative rather than quantitative: the focus shifts from the simple issue of *whether* such duties were fulfilled (and by how many) to *how* they were fulfilled. Attention is focused on individual performance, rather than community participation:

> "To hear confession was in every respect a very disconsolate, highly annoying, and melancholic task (particularly after I came to know the natives very well and learned to see behind their trickiness, hypocrisy, and their wicked way of life). This was not only because of the coercion or the fictitious devotion which was for many the only reason to go to confession...most annoying was the lack of preparation for confession and the continuous return to sin of all or most of them. I once asked a native woman...why she had not done the penance imposed on her after previous confession...In good Spanish she replied, "Because I was eating." I asked another woman, a rather intelligent person, what she had done or thought before my arrival at the church. The blunt answer was 'nothing.'...My experience of many

---

[79] Baegert, *The Letters of Jacob Baegert*, 165.
[80] Ibid., 195.

years...proved to me only too well that nothing is less
important to them than to prepare for confession. One
reason among others is that preparation for confession is
an exertion engaging head, heart, and soul. Such efforts
a California Indian dislikes even more than manual labor....,"[81]

The fact that such a discussion of ritual encounter here serves to sever
rather than foster emotional identification with missionized Amerindians
suits Baegert's purpose of differentiating himself from them, rather than
identifying with them. Baegert's compulsive rearticulation of his own
identity as a European Jesuit is perhaps the result of his fear of cultural
capitulation: he appears to regard his deteriorating German and Latin as
evidence of an incipient lapse into 'barbarism.'[82]

...which in turn leads to differences in the articulation and ex-
perience of primary community affiliation...

To suggest that eighteenth-century frontier Jesuits had divergent perceptions of what constituted their primary community, resulting from the
presence or absence of an enemy tribe on the mission periphery, is not to
suggest that either view diverged from the normative model of community formulated by the Jesuit order, but merely that Jesuits in contrasting
circumstances emphasized different aspects of this normative vision.
There were, in fact, two discernible prescriptive models of community
articulated in the Jesuit Rule and precepts: one such locus of community
being the Jesuit order itself, and the other, the individual Jesuit's own
mission community. A sense of Jesuit community was induced by an insistence upon the uniform conduct, diet, and dress of its members,[83] an
emphasis upon the necessity of strict obedience to superiors, and the encouragement of reliance upon fellow Jesuits in times of crisis and
emergency. More informally, Jesuit community identity and cohesion

---

[81] Baegert, *Observations in Lower California*, 124.
[82] Ibid., 8; Baegert, *The Letters of Jacob Baegert*, 190.
[83] The effect of these codes caused Fontana to remark that missionaries Jesuits in
the eighteenth century led "lives almost unbelievably inhibited by proscription,"
[in his introduction to Sedelmayr, *Before the Rebellion*, xxxvi]. Similarly, Polzer
suggests that "the rules and precepts by which the missions of Northwestern
New Spain were governed show the minuscule concern of superiors for exact
observance" [Charles W. Polzer, *Rules and Precepts of the Jesuit Missions of
Northwestern New Spain* (Tucson: University of Arizona Press, 1976), 14].

was fostered by contrastive self-comparison with secular priests and members of other religious orders, who are often portrayed in Jesuit writings as avaricious, incompetent, lazy, or corrupt.[84] These factors, along with the mandatory, biannual meetings specifically implemented to nurture a sense of Jesuit community in the mission field, fostered a strong sense of Jesuit corporate identity in individual missionaries.[85]

But the Jesuit missionary is also urged, in these official documents, to take the mission itself as his community, his family: to see himself as a beneficent father to his "spiritual children."[86] Perhaps with the aim of fostering this sense of spiritual fatherhood, Jesuit precepts emphasize the primacy of the missionary aim, and the necessity of ministering to Amerindians in their own native languages. The precepts thus preclude Jesuit ministry to other Europeans, except in cases of dire need and the absence of any other priest to perform them.[87] Jesuits in New Spain were not permitted to take their final vows until linguistic training in native languages was satisfactorily completed.[88] Linguistic competency continued to be a central component in the evaluation of an individual missionary's performance: often the first sentence in the visi-

---

[84] See Och, 41; Nentwich, 145-147; Juan Antonio Balthasar, *Father Balthasar Visits the Sinaloa Missions, 1744-1745* (printed for Frederick W. Beinecke, 1959), 11; Sedelmayr, *Jacobo Sedelmayr: Missionary, Frontierman, Explorer in Arizona and Sonora*, 33.

[85] To suggest that Jesuits self-consciously attempted to foster a strong sense of identification with the order does not preclude the observation that considerable tensions existed within this articulation of identity. Discernible in many Jesuit documents is a tension between what we may term 'center' and 'periphery' or 'college' and 'field' Jesuits. The official Rule states that the precepts of the order should be kept by missionary Jesuits as perfectly as if they were within the colleges, leading us to speculate that there may have been some resentment on the part of 'college' Jesuits who feared that the distance of 'field' Jesuits from central authority may lead to a laxity in their observance. On the other hand, colleges were perceived by 'field' Jesuits, not as paragons of perfect practice, but rather as dumping grounds for incompetent, scandalous, ill, or otherwise unfit missionaries. In his short visitation record, Juan Antonio Balthasar, the Padre Visitor, recommends reassignment of three errant missionaries to colleges: one because of a suspected sexual liaison [Balthasar, *Father Balthasar Visits the Sinaloa Missions*, 7], another for alleged financial indiscretions [Ibid., 11], and a third for unspecified reasons [Ibid., 8].

[86] Balthasar, *Juan Antonio Balthasar: Padre Visitador to the Sonora Frontier*, 87.

[87] Polzer, 62.

[88] Balthasar, *Juan Antonio Balthasar: Padre Visitador to the Sonora Frontier*, 28.

tation records concerns a missionary's ability to effectively communicate.[89] But it was not enough to take the Christianization of native groups in their own languages as one's top priority: one needed to do so in the correct spirit of beneficent gentleness. Missionaries who failed to live up to this ideal were often roundly criticized by their colleagues: Johann Nentwich even seems to blame a fellow Jesuit for provoking his own death at the hands of 'his' missionized Amerindians by utilizing excessively harsh punishments.[90]

Thus, though the missionary Jesuit is urged in the Rule and precepts of his order to derive his sense of identity and community from these models, their very duality, as well as their often contradictory demands and expectations, allowed considerable scope for the individual missionary to emphasize the aspect of community identity he found most congenial, based on his individual circumstances. I have suggested that Jesuits were more likely to see their primary community as being the mission when circumstances allowed them to recast internal threats in external terms, and to contrast the incipient Christianity and civility of those Amerindians within the mission to the 'heathen barbarity' of those outside it. Where this constellation of circumstances did not occur, there was a greater likelihood that the missionary would not feel himself to be in any way a part of the native community he is charged with presiding over, and would be more likely to derive his primary sense of identity and community affiliation from the Jesuit order itself. In both cases, the creation of missionary identity and community affiliation – a sense of 'us' - appears to demand the existence of an oppositional 'them.' When a convenient antagonist can be located outside the mission gates, the mission community itself becomes the 'us,' when it cannot, the mission itself is perceived as an oppositional 'them,' and the 'us' becomes the Jesuit order.

...which, finally, leads to dissimilar evaluations of the success of the missionary enterprise.

Given the tremendous differences in interpretation and affiliation which, I have attempted to demonstrate, resulted from missionary immersion in these alternate political and environmental contexts, it is not surprising that their perceptions of the past success of missions, and expectations

---

[89] Balthasar, *Father Balthasar Visits the Sinaloa Missions*, 5-13.
[90] Ibid., 38.

for their future prospects should also differ markedly. Generally, Jesuit missionaries under what we have termed 'externalizing' circumstances tend to be the more optimistic: perhaps because the projection of internal tensions onto an outside group, and the attribution of potential failure to their presence, lead to a less diffuse sense of danger, and, consequently, to a simpler plan of action. Though Jesuit recommendations for securing the future success of the Northwestern missions of New Spain generally stress the urgent necessity of taking immediate, often extreme measures against the intransigent tribes whom they perceive as the primary threat, they appear to assume that their successful containment is all that is necessary to ensure Christianity's triumph in Sonora, Sinaloa, and the Pimeria Alta. Johann Nentwich, after first considering the possible theological meaning of such an entrenched enemy, and acknowledging the necessity of reliance upon God:

> "I do not gainsay that the enemies that lay waste and destroy this Province are a punishment from God, and a scourge from his merciful hand; for such is the teaching of innumerable instances in the Sacred Scripture... Consequently our first and principal remedy is to have recourse to God our Lord with true repentance and fervent prayers and supplications."[91]

proceeds to justify in both theological and historical terms the necessity and piety of human action:

> "However, I am of the opinion that besides these means we are to employ those which prudence, experience, and the military art dictate...our plan should be to pray to God and move our hands...This was done by those immortal heroes, our great ancestors, when they undertook to throw off the ignominious yoke of the Moorish domination, and when they went to conquer for their Catholic Monarchs the vast empires of both Indies, which, for the good of millions of souls, our great Spanish sovereign, Charles III, has under his rule. May God save him and increase his dominions even unto the confines of this

---

[91] Nentwich, 149.

New World; and may he lavish on his august head tri-
umphal wreaths for the glory and victory of the Holy
Catholic Faith..."[92]

With these layers of justification in place, Nentwich proposes
strategies to neutralize each of the main threats to peace and 'Christian
civilization' in Sonora, through a radical change in military and missionary strategy, recommending, in the case of the Seris, their outright
removal.[93] With regard to the Apaches, Nentwich recommends enhancing security by systematizing extant indigenous alliances into a tight
defensive frontier, and relying upon continuous, defensive monitoring of
enemy activity rather than intermittent offensive attack. Nentwich's emphasis on utter removal or decisive military defeat (as opposed to, say,
conversion) makes it abundantly clear that he no longer thinks of either
group as targets for missionary activity, but only as thwarters of it. That
they are seen in such terms, however, may be necessary to preclude his
perception of the whole missionary enterprise as a failure. Indeed, Baegert, who, as we have seen, is unable by dint of political and environmental circumstances to utilize an 'externalizing' attributional style,
summarizes his conclusions about his own missionary efforts in starkly
pessimistic terms. Only with children was his mission an unequivocal
success, Baegert implies:

"One also does not regret the work for the sake of the
children who die in first innocence: even less one regrets
having left Europe and simply everything... [94] This is the
cause of my joy when little children die. It is also my
strong fear, if it is true what Saint Xavier wrote...that
only a few Indians who life longer than fourteen years
go to heaven....those who are baptized in their childhood
are at once directly drawn down into the depth of all evil
from tender youth on through the flood of vicious examples. The adult Indians who at their baptism lied so infa-
mously to the missionary...and to the Holy Ghost, may
see where they get. But meanwhile many little children

---

[92] Ibid., 149-150.
[93] Ibid., 150-151.
[94] Baegert, *The Letters of Jacob Baegert*, 205.

are sent to heaven by the sacrament of rebirth."[95]

Baegert, unlike his colleagues, is unable to attribute the problems within his mission to a single causal factor, which, when decisively addressed, would dramatically improve the chances of future success. Rather, Baegert's writings suggest that the reasons for his meager harvest of souls are due to a complex mélange of environmental factors, aboriginal cultural and religious tenacity, linguistic barriers, and, perhaps most tellingly, his own fundamental failure of rapport and empathy, which necessarily limited both the scope of his accomplishments and his expectations for the future:

> "So it is and so it will remain until the people finally die out or the Final Judgment begins. Rather will the Indian become white, rather California cease to be California before they will start another way of life concerning their food, clothes, and dwelling habits. It is a harsh judgment about these things, but we can only labor in hope that we can be able to enlarge their fortunes in some small ways."[96]

The foregoing analysis seems to suggest that, far from being incidental, the moral and religious presuppositions of eighteenth-century Jesuits in northwestern New Spain regarding the means of production were of decisive importance in determining preferred aboriginal targets for missionization; strengthening extant indigenous military and political antagonisms; conditioning patterns of Jesuit identification and perceived community; and influencing their overall perceptions of past success and future prospects. The presence of a proximate, non-agriculturalist 'enemy' tribe seems to have, in many cases, provided the right set of psychological circumstances for Jesuits to positively identify with the target, agriculturalist tribe: adjudging their Christianization in 'orthopraxic,' ritual terms; perceiving the mission as their primary locus of community, and harboring triumphalist expectations regarding the missions' future, through a process of externalizing the internal tensions of the mission community onto this outside group. Where such externalizing circumstances were lacking, however, Jesuits tended to use more

---

[95] Ibid., 217-220.
[96] Ibid., 195.

'orthodoxic,' individualistic terms to adjudge native Christianization; to rely on the Jesuit order to provide them with a sense of community and identity; and to have a strikingly pessimistic assessment of the missions' past accomplishments and future aspirations.

FATAL AMBIVALENCE:
THE RELIGIOUS JOURNEY OF PIERRE-ANTHOINE PASTEDECHOUAN, SEVENTEENTH-CENTURY MONTAGNAIS AMERINDIAN

Emma Anderson[*]

Pierre-Anthoine Pastedechouan[1] was a Montagnais Amerindian of early seventeenth century Canada. Taken to France at the age of eleven or twelve to be educated by the Franciscan Recollet fathers, Pastedechouan underwent five years of theological indoctrination and extensive instruction in both French and Latin, which transformed him culturally, linguistically, and religiously. Returned against his will to act as a missionary to his people, Pastedechouan began a prolonged, agonizing struggle to reestablish his native cultural and religious identity, gain the acceptance of his society, and negotiate a new kind of relationship with the various European groups, both civic and religious, who vied to exploit his unique linguistic gifts. His encounter in 1632 with the Jesuits once again upset his fragile sense of self by reopening the question of his ultimate identity and allegiance. The last four years of his life were characterized by their reawakened ambivalence regarding the Catholic aspects of his identity: Pastedechouan ricocheted between a sometimes passive, sometimes vehement opposition to Jesuit missionary efforts and

---

[*] Emma Anderson is a doctoral candidate in the Study of Religion at Harvard University.
[1] I have used the spelling of Pastedechouan's name given by Jesuit Superior Paul Le Jeune in the Jesuit Relations, Rueben Thwaites, ed., *The Jesuit Relations and Allied Documents: Travels and Explorations of the Jesuit Missionaries in New France, 1610-1791* (Cleveland: The Burrows Brothers, 1897-1900), Vol. V, 107, and adopted by the Canadian Dictionary of Biography. Contemporary accounts vary the spelling of his name somewhat: his baptismal notice [reproduced in N.E. Dionne, "Le Sauvage Pastedechouan en France," *Recherches Historiques, Vol. 30* (1907), 120, and F. Uzureau, "Baptême d'un Montagnais a la Cathédrale d'Angers, le 27 Avril 1621." *Le Canada Français, Vol. 4* (1922), 390] refers to him as "Pastre-Chouen," recounting that his name means "passé-riviere"; Sagard calls him "Patetchounon" [Gabriel Sagard, *Histoire du Canada et Voyages que les Freres Mineurs Récollets y ont faicts pour la conversion des infidels depuis l'an 1615* (Paris: Librarie Tross, 1866), 850 new pagination / 936 old pagination]. Le Clercq mistakenly refers to him as "Ahinsistan," but it is clear from the details of his account that he is referring to Pastedechouan [Christian Le Clercq, *First Establishment of the Faith in New France* (New York: John G. Shea, 1881), 235].

an apparently sincere desire to become reconciled with the church. Following the death of the only remaining members of his family, Pastedechouan made a final, unheeded plea to live with the Jesuits. Thwarted, he died of starvation, alone in the woods, rejected by both the tribe whose approval he had so assiduously sought, and the church he had recurrently embraced and scorned.

Though he never reached the age of thirty, Pastedechouan's short, eventful life provides us with an unequalled glimpse into the mentality of a young Amerindian convert subject to the extraordinary demands of the prevailing missionization models of his time, both Recollet and Jesuit, which emphasized the extraction and isolation of the vulnerable child from his home environment, and coupled Frenchification with conversion. Pastedechouan's subjection to this model of Christianization seems to have imbued him with characteristically absolutist, 'either/or' ways of thinking which both underlay and withstood the two seismic shifts in religious and cultural identity which he underwent during the course of his life: broadly speaking, from 'Montagnais' to 'French,' and from 'French' back to 'Montagnais.' His enduring tendency to think of 'Montagnais' and 'French/Catholic' as competing rather than compatible categories precluded Pastedechouan from combining European and Amerindian modes of behavior and belief in any religiously meaningful or psychologically helpful way, as was done by other members of both his immediate and extended family.

Pastedechouan, and those Amerindians who, like him, defy easy cultural or religious characterization are chronically understudied. The propensity of scholars to focus either upon exemplary converts, who embraced and retained Christianity, or adamant traditionalists who unambiguously rejected it, as well as ingrained assumptions about the finality of religious conversion, have served to retard study of the significant group of Amerindians who had a far more equivocal relationship with Catholicism: those often labeled 'apostates' in the European sources. Amerindian conversion to Christianity, whether accepted as 'genuine,' or dismissed as impossible, given the linguistic, cultural, and conceptual barriers between the societies; whether understood as a divisive choice which divided and weakened Amerindian cultures, or adjudged an adaptive move that allowed aboriginals to retain and imaginatively reshape aspects of their own religious and cultural traditions, has rarely been cast as anything other than a final, unequivocal, and one-way movement. While Pastedechouan's particular life experiences and linguistic competencies made him, in one sense, a somewhat unusual aboriginal figure, his ambivalent religious identity was actually typical of a widespread pattern of Amerindian reactions to Christianity in early seventeenth century Canada, a cyclical pattern of 'conversion,' 'de-conversion,' and 're-conversion' which researchers have been slow to recognize despite its rich documentation in the primary sources. Failure to pay adequate attention to what European missionary sources generally term Amerindian 'apostasy,' despite the fact that fear of this very outcome shaped virtually every aspect of both Recollet and Jesuit missionary strategy, has resulted in a falsely dichotomized picture which represents Amerindian religious affiliation as a zero-sum proposition instead of what Pastedechouan's story reveals it to be: a shifting, ambiguous, and often highly ambivalent association. It is as if modern scholars, like Pastedechouan himself, are conditioned by the conceptual assumptions of the seventeenth-century Recollets and Jesuits that they study: preferring to see matters of confessional and cultural identity in starkly absolutist terms.

Though Pastedechouan's experiences are emblematic of an understudied Amerindian response to Christianity, they are, at the same time, virtually unique. Pastedechouan was one of only a handful of aboriginal youths in the seventeenth century be educated in France, and one of the even smaller number who actually survived the experience.[2] Though the number of children who underwent this process of extraction, isolation, and indoctrination is miniscule, it is nevertheless important to study both their experiences and the assumptions and desires of their European hosts, as the dramatic cultural and religious re-education of Pastedechouan and others like him represented the preferred missionization approach of both Recollets and Jesuits in the early part of the seventeenth century.[3] Though only a few aboriginal children made it

---

[2] See Le Clercq, 127; Sagard, 57 new pagination / 45, old pagination; Thwaites, Vol. VI, 85, 155, Vol. VII, 287; Olive Dickason, "Campaigns to Capture Young Minds: A Look at Early Attempts in Colonial Mexico and New France to Remold Amerindians," *Historical Papers* (1987), 64-65; Cornelius Jaenen, "Education for Francization: The Case of New France in the Seventeenth Century," *Indian Education in Canada: Volume One, The Legacy*, Barman, Hebert, and McCaskill, eds. (Vancouver: University of British Columbia Press, 1986), 50-52; Guy La Fleche, *Relation de 1634 de Paul Le Jeune: Le Missionaire, l'Apostat, le Sorcier* (Montreal: Les Presses de l'Universite de Montreal, 1973), 259-260; Marcel Trudel, *Histoire de la Nouvelle-France, Volume II: Le Comptoir, 1604-1627* (Ottawa: Editions Fides, 1966), 323-330.
[3] James Axtell, *The Invasion within: the Contest of Cultures in Colonial North America* (New York: Oxford University Press, 1985), 49-58, 77, 111.

as far as France, the basic strategy of utilizing young people as 'shock troops' in the conversion of their tribes, and the belief in the necessity of their isolation from family and familiar cultural surroundings shaped both Recollet and Jesuit domestic pedagogy until the mid-seventeenth century: decisively influencing how both groups conceived of and ran their native seminaries.

Pastedechouan's experiences with both the Recollets and Jesuits thus force us to question a number of lingering assumptions regarding the key ideological, theological, and methodological differences between early modern European missionary groups, especially the presentation of Jesuits as accomodationists willing to adapt themselves to their target cultures, and Franciscans as social and theological conservatives who demanded the cultural as well as religious capitulation of their converts. While this stereotype may be substantially true for some geographical venues and historical periods, such as early seventeenth century China, it does not hold for the same time period in Canada. Jesuit and Recollet policies regarding the Christianization of children in early seventeenth-century Canada were more similar than different. Both groups operated under the assumption that the removal of promising youth from 'unwholesome' influences and their immersion in a totally Catholic context would facilitate their conversion. Isolation from their families and communities was felt to be essential to their Christianization, as it meant that coercive techniques, including corporal punishment, could be employed without risking the outrage of the parents. The conversion of such children was expected to eventually benefit their entire society, as graduates of this course of religious and cultural indoctrination, whether it was received in makeshift 'seminaries' in New France, or in the mother country, were expected to aid the missionary cause by becoming influential apostles to their own people. Their shared expectation that children held the cultural key to the Christianization of their tribes, combined with their strong fears of adult apostasy, blinded both Recollets and Jesuits, during Pastedechouan's lifetime, to the potential for a very different missionary model that would harness the often lively interest of influential adults in Christianity, and utilize volition rather than coercion, and theological argumentation rather than indoctrination.

Pastedechouan was born in 1607 or 1608[4] into a Montagnais

---

[4] Our estimates of Pastedechouan's birth date are based on the impressions of Europeans who encountered him. Jean Dolbeau, the Recollet father who brought Pastedechouan to France describes him, in 1620, as "un petit sauvage de douze

family, probably at Tadoussac, on the banks of the St. Lawrence River east of Quebec, and appears to have been the youngest son in a family of four boys.[5] The Tadoussac of Pastedechouan's childhood was a place where the persistence of pre-contact ways of life, such as traditional patterns of migratory hunting and fishing, existed uneasily beside a growing reliance on European trade goods in an area heavily influenced by European presence. It was a place marked by intermittent guerilla war with the Iroquois, and troubled by famine and epidemic. It was, moreover, a bustling, religiously heterogeneous community, one in which the Recollet program of inculcating a rigorous post-Tridentine Catholicism was challenged both by the continuing strength of Montagnais traditional religious beliefs, and the presence of a significant Huguenot contingent among the merchants. Nevertheless, there was apparently a sizable Montagnais Catholic community at Tadoussac, numbering perhaps as many

---

ou treize ans..." [Abrégé de la vie du Reverend Pere Dolbeau, par Dom Gilles Jamin (Bibliothèque Municipal d'Orléans, Mss 509, fol. 171), reproduced in Odoric Jouve et al, *Dictionnaire Biographique des Récollets Missionnaires en Nouvelle-France, 1615-1645, 1670-1849* (Montreal: Bellarmin, 1996), 371-372], giving us a birth date of 1607 or 1608. La Fleche [259] uses the younger estimate, as does Uzureau [390]. Others like Lucien Campeau [*Monumenta Novae Franciae*, Vol. II (Quebec and Rome: Monumenta Historica Societatis Jesu and Laval University Press, 1987), 847; and Dionne, 120] paraphrase Le Jeune who simply states that he was "conduit en Frâce en son bas âge par les RR. Peres Recolets..." [Thwaites, Vol. V, 108-109]. Even if we take Dolbeau's estimate of Pastedechouan's age in 1620 as accurate, it is possible that he looked younger than his years. Jean Louvet, an eyewitness to his baptism at Angers in 1621, who, unlike Dolbeau, did not know Pastedechouan personally, describes him as "ung (sic) jeune garçon aagé (sic) de 10 à 11 ans, cathécumène de Canada, appellé la Nouvelle-France" [Bibliothèque d'Angers, MSS # 862, reproduced in Uzureau, 1922, p. 391] which would put his birthday around 1609 or 1610. This youthful appearance might also explain why the Recollet brother Gabriel Sagard refers to him as a "garçon" [Sagard, 851 new pagination / 937 old pagination] in describing his interactions with the English in 1628, when, using the Dolbeau estimate, he would have been twenty-one or twenty-two years old, or why Le Jeune uses a similar term ["pauure (sic) garçon," Thwaites, Vol. V, 110] to describe Pastedechouan in 1632, when he may have been as old as twenty-five.
[5] See Thwaites, Vol. IX, 69. His three older brothers, in descending birth order, are Carigonan, Mestigoit, and Sasousmat. According to Le Jeune [Thwaites, Vol. VI, 109], Sasousmat was 25-30 years old in 1633, giving him a birth date of 1603-1608, thus making him the closest in age to Pastedechouan. He describes Mestigoit as being between thirty-five and forty years old in 1633 [Thwaites, Vol. VII, 69; See also Campeau, Vol. II, 70], making him older than both Sasousmat and Pastedechouan. Le Jeune refers to Carigonan as the eldest brother [Thwaites, Vol. IX, 69].

as one hundred and forty neophytes.[6] Joseph Le Caron, the Recollect missionary who wintered there in 1617-1618, attempted to teach young Montagnais children to speak and write French, and acquaint them with the basics of Catholic doctrine, in order to "attract the Indians and render them sociable with us, to accustom them to our ways of living."[7] Young Pastedechouan, then nine or ten years of age, may well have been one of his pupils. Le Caron's desire to acquaint the children with French language, culture, and religious beliefs, and his longing for a seminary in which he could shelter his students from what he perceived as the dangerous religious heterogeneity which surrounded them were typical of the sentiments which would lead, in 1620, to the Recollets' construction of St. Charles, the first native seminary in New France, and inform the decision to send Pastedechouan to France later the same year.

We don't know why it was Pastedechouan who was selected to go to France,[8] or how the young adolescent and his family felt about this life-altering course of events. We do know that Pastedechouan left Canada with the Recollet father Jean Dolbeau in the summer or fall of 1620,

---

[6] Le Clercq, 133.

[7] Ibid., 135.

[8] Aboriginal children were sometimes given to French civic or religious officials to cement alliances: thus Champlain received three young girls whom he called Faith, Hope, and Charity. They could also be demanded by the French as both reparation and as a means of ensuring native docility. In 1618, Recollet father Joseph Le Caron, stationed at Tadoussac, writes that the Recollets had been presented with two young Montagnais boys, Nigamon and Tebachi, to serve as 'replacements' for two Frenchmen murdered by Montagnais, and as indicators of their future good will. One of these children, Nigamon, was taken by the Recollets to France to be educated, preceding Pastedechouan there by only two years [See Le Clercq, 127, and Sagard, 57 new pagination / 45 old pagination, who both describe Nigamon and Tebachi explicitly as "hostages." See also La Fleche, 259-260, and Trudel, 259, 324-327, 351]. That the Jesuits also thought of their students as guarantors of good behavior on the part of their parents and tribes is evident from Jesuit Superior Paul Le Jeune's comment: "…if the little Hurons, or the children of more distant tribes, are kept here, a great many advantages will result, for we would not be annoyed and distracted by the fathers while instructing the children; it will also compel these people to show good treatment to the French who are in their country, or at least not to do them any injury. And, lastly, we shall obtain, by the grace of God our Lord, the object for which we came into this distant country; namely, the conversion of these nations" [Thwaites, Vol. VI, 155, my emphasis]. For a more general overview of the fate of Amerindian children sent to France for education in the early seventeenth century, see Trudel, 323-330; Jaenen, "Education for Francization," 50-52; Dickason, 64-65.

at the age of eleven or twelve.[9] The purpose of Dolbeau's trip was to attract new financial and moral support for the Recollet missions, which were at the point of utter insolvency.[10] It is in this context that the decision to take Pastedechouan to France must be appreciated: his presence would aid the Recollet fundraising campaign by effectively serving as a living testament to the efficacy of their missionary work.

Dolbeau took Pastedechouan to his home convent of Basmettee-lez-Angers[11] and began in earnest his theological education, with the goal of preparing him for baptism. During the winter of 1620-1621 Pastedechouan was introduced to his powerful godfather Pierre de Rohan, the Prince of Guimenée, who was to finance his education for the next five years, even arranging for it to continue after his death. Rohan was apparently greatly taken with Pastedechouan and personally instructed him "to know and love God and to know his paternosters in French and in Latin."[12] On April 25th, 1621,[13] Pastedechouan's baptism was celebrated

---

[9] Abrégé de la vie du Reverend Pere Dolbeau, par Dom Gilles Jamin, 371-372. See also Dionne, 1907, 120; Uzureau, 1922, 390; La Fleche, 259; Trudel, 319, 324-325.

[10] See Dionne, 120. For a detailed recounting of the Recollet's various fundraising trips and building program, see Trudel, 318-320.

[11] The sources are unanimous that Basmette-lez-Angers was Dolbeau's home convent, where he first entered the novitiate in 1605 at the age of 19 [Odoric Jouve, *Dictionnaire Biographique des Récollets Missionaires en Nouvelle-France, 1645-1645, 1670-1849* (Montreal: Bellarmin, 1996), 368] and that it was where Pastedechouan was taken [Uzureau, 390-391, and Dionne, 120-124]. There is some variation in the spelling. Pastedechouan's baptismal notice, reproduced in both Uzureau and Dionne, describes Dolbeau as a "récollet de la Basmette, près ceste (sic) ville d'Angers…" [Dionne, 120; Uzureau, 391]. Louvet, the seventeenth-century eyewitness to Pastedechouan's baptism whose description of the event is reprinted in Uzureau, refers to the convent as: "couvent de la Basmette-lez-Angers" [Uzureau, 391]. Uzureau himself, in his introduction, uses "Baumette" [Uzureau, 390]. Dionne describes it as "(le) couvent de la Beaumette, dans la ville d'Angers" [Dionne, 120]. The Dictionnaire Biographique des Récollets has it as "La Balmette proche d'Anger" [Jouve, 368]. I have used Louvet's spelling.

[12] Uzureau, 391, my translation. Pastedechouan's baptismal record [reprinted in Dionne and Uzereau] identifies Pierre de Rohan, Prince of Guimenée, and his wife, Anthoynette of Bretagne, as Pastedechouan's godparents and namesakes (see also Thwaites, Vol. V, 109; Le Clercq, 235; Sagard, 865 old pagination / 785 new pagination). Sagard [865 old pagination / 785 new pagination] refers to Rohan's arrangements for the continuation of Pastedechouan's education after his own death.

[13] Uzureau gives conflicting dates for Pastedechouan's baptism. On page 390, in his introduction, he says the date is April 25th. In his title he gives it as April 27th. Louvet, the eyewitness that Uzureau quotes at length, gives it as the 25th,

at the Cathedral of St. Maurice in Angers. Following an exhortation on the holy work of the Recollets in New France, and an elaborate procession featuring a rich cross, many silver vessels of holy oil, candles and flowers, and other holy objects borne by the Prince's pages and servants,[14] the principal players gathered on the outside threshold of the church to play Pygmalion: to celebrate the civic sequence of Pastedechouan's public transformation from savage to Frenchman, pagan to Christian. In front of a crowd "so numerous that you couldn't turn around,"[15] Pastedechouan was "draped in the color of the green of the sea, in the French manner"[16] and effectively remade in the image of his godparents, being given both their names: Pierre after Pierre de Rohan, the Prince of Guimenée, and Antoyne after Anthoynette of Bretagne, his wife. Having stamped him with a new French name and identity, the architects of the ceremony then sought to demonstrate the rehabilitation of his barbaric soul. Stripped and anointed with holy oil at the base of the bell tower inside the church, Pastedechouan was taken to the altar of St. Cencle, where:

> they threw holy water on his head, and put on it the *cresmeau*, rich and precious, and the catechumen *margajat* held a candle of white wax in his hand and was dressed all in white and, this done, took him in front of the great altar of the said church where the said prince and princess had also gone, where the archdeacon Garende gave a beautiful exhortation, just the way they usually do for children's baptisms, after which he was taken ceremoniously to the choir and the nave to show him to the people who wanted to see him and they were in such great numbers everywhere in the church, in the choir, and they had even climbed up to the altar, near the shrine of St. Maurice. And so that he could be seen, they lifted him up onto the pulpit, where he was for a long time with the *cresmeau* on his head and a lit candle in his hand, where he appeared completely relaxed. And

so this is the date I have used. Oddly, neither Dionne nor Uzureau, both of whom reproduce the baptismal notice, give the date.

[14] Uzureau, 392. Uzureau reproduces in full the brief memoir of Jean Louvet, a law clerk who attended Pastedechouan's baptism and recorded his impressions.

[15] Ibid., 391, my translation.

[16] Ibid.

he was very black, his nose was flat, with a big mouth."[17]

This eyewitness description of the ceremony reveals the tension between its official purpose: to render the exotic, dangerous 'other' familiar and comprehensible, and the obvious interest of the crowd in just these suppressed elements: Pastedechouan's baptismal ceremony was thus a striking blend of publicity stunt, religious rite, and freak show. For the Pygmalion Recollets and their noble benefactors, this ceremony re-made Pastedechouan into their own European image, and celebrated their power in being able to effect this change: it was a triumphant demonstration of their piety, authority, and altruism. For them, Pastedechouan represented the challenge of Christianizing and civilizing New France: his baptism represented in miniature their aspirations for the conversion of a continent. For the spectators, by contrast, Pastedechouan was intriguing because of rather than in spite of his differences from them, differences which they appear to have perceived as being essentially unaltered by the ceremony. This is evident in our informant's designation of Pastedechouan as a '*cathécumène margajat:*' a 'second class' or 'marginal' catechumen,[18] and his fascination with his exotic appearance. Of Pastedechouan's reaction to the elaborate ceremony and gaping crowds, we unfortunately know nothing.

Following his baptism Pastedechouan resumed his studies, under Recollet supervision, for another four years. He learned to read, write, and speak Latin and French. He received further religious instruction, and training in other "natural and civil acquirements."[19] Though Pastedechouan was only one of several Montagnais children being "trained to piety and the service of the altar"[20] in France during this period, their separation and education in widely dispersed convents, perhaps to encourage their complete immersion into French culture, makes it unlikely that he had any contact with them. He did, however, have other opportunities to speak his native tongue. Pastedechouan instructed Gabriel Sagard, the famous Recollet laybrother and author of *Histoire du Canada* and *Long Voyage into the Country of the Hurons*, in the Montagnais language; upon his departure for Canada in March 1623, two years before

---

[17] Ibid, 372, my translation. A 'cresmeau' appears to have been a small crown.
[18] Ibid.
[19] Le Clercq, 235.
[20] Ibid., 236.

Pastedechouan's own return journey, Sagard took with him a "small dictionary, composed and written in the clear hand of Pierre Anthoine our Canadian."[21] He does not appear to have been called upon to use his aboriginal linguistic competencies after 1623; indeed, the sources are unanimous in suggesting that Pastedechouan "learned French so well he had forgot the Canadian language."[22] Likely, Pastedechouan's reported ignorance of his own native tongue says more about his strong identification with the linguistic and religious culture with which he was surrounded and his simultaneous, and encouraged, estrangement from the Montagnais milieu than with any actual deterioration of his language skills. This suspicion is confirmed by Pastedechouan's strong reluctance to return home in 1625: "as Peter Anthony was more advanced, having made five years stay in France, which he did not wish to leave, Father George and Father Joseph thought it proper to persuade him to make a journey home."[23]

Pastedechouan left Dieppe on April 24th, 1625 under the supervision of Recollet father Joseph de la Roche Daillon, and in the company of the Jesuits Charles Lallemant, Ennemond Massé and Jean de Brébeuf, and arrived at Quebec in June.[24] The intervening months of the journey do not appear to have quickened his interest in seeing his family at Tadoussac. Even following his repatriation at the age of seventeen or eighteen, Pastedechouan wished to remain in the safe confines of the Recollet seminary in Quebec, where he spent the first winter after his return. Le Clercq says "he had lost all idea of his natural language and the Indian mode of life, he was a naturalized Frenchman and very devout. He avoided intercourse with the few Indians who came."[25] When Joseph Le Caron, now the Recollet Superior of the missions, insisted that he return as a missionary to the Montagnais at Tadoussac, Pastedechouan allegedly

---

[21] Sagard, 359 old pagination / 334 new pagination, my translation. See also Ibid, 358-360 old pagination / 333-334 new pagination; La Fleche, 259; Jouve, 839; and Trudel, 328.
[22] Le Clercq, 235. See also Thwaites, Vol. V, 109; Thwaites, Vol. VI, 85; Dionne, 121; Trudel, 328.
[23] Le Clercq, 236.
[24] Jouve, 260. See also Le Clercq, 273; and Sagard, 865 old pagination / 785 new pagination). Though Grassmann, in his biographical sketch of Pastedechouan (Brown et al., *Canadian Dictionary of Biography*, 533-534), states that he arrives back in Canada in August 1626, this is clearly an error: Pastedechouan accompanied Daillon, who returned from France in 1625, and did not go back until 1629 (Campeau, Vol. II, 847; Brown et al., 420; Jouve, 259-265).
[25] Ibid., 273.

wept and, addressing the man who may have been his childhood teacher, apparently said: "My Father, how could your Reverence want to send me back to the beasts who know not God?"[26]

Pastedechouan's reported fear of return can be seen as a response to the dominant missionary model utilized by both Recollets and Jesuits in this period, in which children's removal from a their 'contaminated' culture was seen as the best way they could become and remain Christians. His fear was eminently logical given the central premise of this model: that one's individual identity is largely predicated on the nature of one's surrounding environment. Having labored for five years to transform himself culturally, linguistically, and religiously from a Montagnais to a Frenchman, he is concerned that this fragile new identity would be lost once its enabling environment was removed. His apparent characterization of his own family as "beasts who know not God" illustrates the way in which he has been taught to think of French and

---

[26] Ibid, 274; see also Sagard, old pagination 865 / new pagination 785-786. Trigger [Bruce G. Trigger, *The Children of Aataentsic: A History of the Huron People to 1660*, 2 vols (Montreal: McGill-Queen's University Press, 1976),17] Blackburn [Carole Blackburn, *Harvest of Souls: The Jesuit Missions and Colonialism in North America, 1632-1650* (Montreal: McGill-Queen's University Press, 2000), 6-7], and Jaenen (Cornelius Jaenen, "Amerindian Views of French Culture in the Seventeenth Century," *Canadian Historical Review, Vol. 55, #3*, (1974): 285] have suggested that the purported speeches of Amerindians in the missionary writings of Europeans should be taken simply as the rhetorical flourishes of their European authors rather than accurate restatements of actual Amerindian sentiments, pointing out that aboriginals in such texts often conveniently restate missionary ideology. My own view is that the purported words of Amerindians are far from flat and one-dimensional: they often challenge European perspectives as much, or more, than they affirm them. Particularly in their reported responses to Christianity, Amerindians brought forth a variety of novel and sophisticated challenges which attacked Tridentine theology at its most vulnerable points. Such reported challenges certainly taxed the theological imaginations of Jesuits who had the unenviable duty of responding to them: it stretches credulity that they would have been able to invent challenges which so effectively undermined their entire theological apparatus. In this case, as in many others where Pastedechouan apparently speaks to us out of the text, his words do not simply echo the party line: indeed, his putative reluctance to begin the missionary stage of his Recollet-sponsored career could be read as signaling the inadequacy of his theological and practical preparation. While, unfortunately, we will never be able to say with absolute certainty that Amerindians said something approximating what they are reported to have said (to do so would be to enter Bradley's "historian's heaven" where we can "truly, utterly, absolutely, completely, finally know" what occurred in the past) I believe we are justified in viewing them as reliable approximations, unless there is convincing evidence to the contrary.

Montagnais identity in deeply antithetical, either/or terms. In their insistence that true Christianity could best be nurtured in a totalistic environment, the Recollets appear to have infected Pastedechouan with their own fears regarding purity, pollution, and contamination. This sense of danger would only have been intensified by the elaborate rules of conduct given him by the Recollets to ensure his salvation was not threatened by contact with the unconverted. The set of assumptions Pastedechouan learned in France, then, demonstrably influenced how he thought about religion, culture, and identity even after his formal training with the Recollets was long over.

Nevertheless, Pastedechouan did eventually begin the long figurative journey back from France to the culture of his birth. His recalled words to the Recollets at the time of his forced return to Tadoussac were prophetic: "They are forcing me: but, if I once go there, they will not get me back as they wish."[27] Pastedechouan's actions demonstrate how he attempted to redefine his identity in Montagnais terms: he distanced himself from the French, reestablished close ties with his older brothers, married successive wives, and searched for the elusive respect of his community. Though Pastedechouan for the remainder of his life would periodically utilize his linguistic gifts in the service of Europeans, he always did so on his own terms, with marked concern for how such encounters would affect his reemerging Montagnais identity.

Pastedechouan's interactions with competing European military and political factions, from the invasion of the English Kirke brothers in 1628 to the restoration of the French civic authorities in 1632, illustrate how he was able to employ his European linguistic skills in the service of consistent Montagnais objectives. The English Kirke brothers, who would defeat Champlain at Quebec on July 29, 1629, and force the repatriation of the colony's civic elite and missionary personnel, gained the easterly Montagnais stronghold of Tadoussac, Pastedechouan's 'hometown,' a full year earlier. Pastedechouan's encounter with this invading English force, recounted at length by Gabriel Sagard, occurred sometime in the late spring or early summer of 1628. Walking along the banks of the St. Lawrence, Pastedechouan was spotted by Jacques Michel, a French deserter aboard the Kirke's ship and taken hostage. The English interest in Pastedechouan was, like that of the Recollets, and later, the Jesuits, primarily for his linguistic abilities, but for political and mercan-

---

[27] Thwaites, Vol. VI, 87.

tile rather than missionary motives. When Pastedechouan's attempts to deny his identity and linguistic abilities failed, he proposed heading a trading mission to Trois Rivieres, asking for canoes stocked with clothing, foodstuffs, and alcohol, to be manned by himself and his brothers. Having gained his freedom and the valuable supplies, he fled with his brothers to Isle Rouge, where they "fed well and mocked the English." The latter, according to Sagard, "vowed to their God to never forgive Pierre Antoine and to hang him if they could catch him..."[28]

Seventeenth-century Recollet historians interpret this incident as illustrating Pastedechouan's continued loyalty to France. Modern interpreters have emphasized its crassly self-interested motives. But Pastedechouan's actions might be better explained with reference to his regained Montagnais values. The foundation of Montagnais life was reciprocal social exchange: the holding of a feast was as essential to the social prestige of its host as it was to the survival of the group. Pastedechouan's underdeveloped hunting skills, stunted by the five critical years he spent away from his culture, denied him the ability to be a 'giver' in this reciprocal cycle: he was perpetually assigned to the less prestigious place of the receiver. His trickery of the English offered an irresistible chance for him to repay his older brothers' ongoing provision in spectacular fashion, with a huge and memorable feast that he had procured through the use of his unique skills.

Pastedechouan's eagerness to serve French colonial officials upon their return in 1632 initially seems to provide an intriguing contrast to his reluctance to serve the English. But if we again read the situation through the lens of Pastedechouan's re-emergent Montagnais priorities, his decisions seem more consistent. Pastedechouan's solicitation of employment from the returning French probably indicates the degree of deprivation he had endured over the four year English interlude, coupled, perhaps, with a desire to save a disintegrating marriage in which the main complaint may have been inadequate provision.[29] Pastedechouan's

---

[28] Sagard, old pagination 936-938 / new pagination 850-852.

[29] Thwaites, Vol. V, 111. This is not explicitly stated. Le Jeune merely notes: "He had married the daughter of Manitougatche; she, having become somewhat dissatisfied with him, left him." It is nonetheless probable. Pastedechouan married again in the summer of 1633 [Thwaites, Vol. VII, 69], but his next wife confided to Le Jeune in the winter of 1634 her intentions to leave him come the spring [Ibid., 173]. Her various complaints to Le Jeune all centered on a single theme: Pastedechouan's incompetence as a hunter and provider [Ibid., 89, 175].

status as a wanted man probably forced him to rely even more heavily than usual upon the goodwill of his brothers, provision which he perhaps sought to repay by seeking employment that would exploit his linguistic knowledge.

Pastedechouan secured employment as an interpreter for the newly arrived Commandant, Émery De Cäen, who welcomed him to the Quebec fort, and 'brought him to table' as his honored guest. Pastedechouan's apparently uncouth and erratic behavior, however, soon proved intolerable to De Cäen, who fired him[30]. When Pastedechouan approached his lieutenant, Duplessis-Bochart, for a similar job, he declined to employ him, and proposed that Pastedechouan's temporal difficulties were symptomatic of an underlying spiritual malaise, suggesting that both the supernatural cause and its worldly effects could be alleviated by his employment as the newly arrived Superior Paul Le Jeune's Montagnais language teacher.[31] Pastedechouan, however, was reportedly vehemently opposed to this course of action.

Why was Pastedechouan so reluctant to work for the Jesuits, given his willingness to work for French colonial officials? The answer centers, once again, around Pastedechouan's conceptualizations of cultural and religious identity.

Very likely, Pastedechouan's objections were grounded in the totalism that, as we speculated earlier, he may have learned from Recollet missionary models. Given his absorption of the Recollet assumption that one's individual spiritual destiny is intertwined with the collective environment in which one is placed, the invitation to join the Jesuits must have seemed, to Pastedechouan, nothing less than a call to yet another momentous identity shift. While working with the colonial authorities would allow him to at once retain his hard-won Montagnais identity while at the same time exploiting his unique linguistic gifts, the same could not necessarily be said for living and working with the Jesuits. Just as he feared, in 1626, that return to Tadoussac would erode his identity as a naturalized Frenchman, Pastedechouan now may have worried that entering the Jesuit milieu would dissipate his regained identity as a Montagnais. Working for the Jesuits entailed the abandonment of his migra-

---

In all, Pastedechouan had four or five unsuccessful marriages in ten years [Ibid., 173].

[30] François Du Creux, *The History of Canada or New France* (Toronto: The Champlain Society, 1951), Vol. I, 141; see also Thwaites, Vol. V, 109).

[31] Du Creux, Vol. I, 141-142; Thwaites, Vol. V, 107-113.

tory lifestyle, the severe disruption, if not abandonment, of married life, re-emersion into a disciplined religious observance, and obedience to his religious superiors. As the Jesuit Superior Paul Le Jeune astutely observed, joining the Jesuits meant a considerable loss of freedom for Pastedechouan, noting that "while breathing only liberty he rather abhorred our house than loved it."[32] To the beleaguered Pastedechouan, the decision implied the loss of more his freedom: it must have seemed nothing less than another assault upon his sense of self. Nor were Pastedechouan's fears wholly baseless: Le Jeune clearly saw Pastedechouan's arrival in November of 1632 as providential, and as the beginning of his reclamation for Christ, and his rehabilitation from savagery: for, like the Pygmalion Recollets, he saw the two things as virtually synonymous. His initial gift to Pastedechouan was a suit of French clothes donated by the pious Duplessis-Bochart, who imparted them to Le Jeune with the fervent wish that Pastedechouan could be induced to "lay aside the inner savage with the outer..."[33]

Perhaps because of these fears of identity dissolution, Pastedechouan's five month tenure at the Jesuit seminary of Notre Dame des Anges is a study in boundary setting. Pastedechouan dictated the degree of his religious involvement, participating in confession but repeatedly refusing communion, which he had taken in France, on the grounds that he was "more disposed to it there than here."[34] He established some power in his relationship with Le Jeune by dictating the pace and quality of his linguistic instruction. He maintained close contact with other Montagnais, repeatedly asserting his independence by unexpectedly leaving the seminary to hunt with his relative Manitougatche.

Pastedechouan's seemingly free participation in several Catholic rituals, notably confession, may indicate that he considered them in some sense meaningful: if not he probably would have refused them outright, as he generally did with communion. But what we may be tempted to interpret as lingering traces of interest in or commitment to Catholicism can equally well be attributed to Le Jeune's zealous interference. Le Jeune relates he was able to thwart Pastedechouan's plans to leave for a hunting trip in the middle of Holy Week, 1633, until Pastedechouan fulfilled his Easter obligations, including communion. While participation in this ritual marked an important high mark in Pastedechouan's life as a

---

[32] Thwaites, Vol. V, p. 109
[33] Du Creux, Vol. I, 141.
[34] Thwaites, Vol. V, 173.

Catholic during the four year period preceding his death, Le Jeune's unmistakable coercion precludes our interpretation of Pastedechouan's participation as indicating his genuine re-engagement with Catholicism. Significantly, it was also the last ritual he partook of under the seminary's roof – though he left for a supposedly short hunting trip, he did not return, but rejoined his brothers at a Tadoussac, which had once again fallen to English forces. In short, Pastedechouan's behavior while at Notre Dame des Anges seems to reveal his determination not to allow his decision to join the Jesuits to inaugurate another seismic shift in allegiance or identity; rather he seems to have approached it as a short-term necessity motivated by a concern for continued survival.

Pastedechouan's defensive attempts to preserve his Montagnais identity while living in a predominantly Catholic environment represented a significant step away from his earlier acceptance of the presupposition that one's character is derived almost automatically from the nature of one's immediate cultural milieu. However, his defiant guarding of his Montagnais identity from what he perceived to be Jesuit threats to it is a clear indication that he still perceived religious and cultural identity in either/or terms. This tendency was in marked contrast to the attitudes of other family members, notably his older brother, Sasousmat, and his father-in-law, Manitougatche, who, in their encounters with Catholic Christianity, balanced and intertwined French Catholic and Montagnais cultural and religious elements.

Asked the following fall to return and continue Le Jeune's language instruction, Pastedechouan, who had remarried during the summer, replied that he would not abandon his wife. This decision necessitated Le Jeune giving up his position as Superior to follow Pastedechouan and his brothers on their annual winter hunt, which commenced in October of 1633.

Pastedechouan's determination to cling to his hard-fought identity as a Montagnais continued throughout his second prolonged encounter with Le Jeune, if anything becoming more overt. Pastedechouan often turned a deaf ear to Le Jeune's pleas for linguistic instruction or aid in translation. He demonstrated his chosen allegiances by professing his belief in elements of Montagnais traditional religion[35] and taking part in Montagnais religious ceremonies, often aiding his eldest brother Carigo-

---

[35] Thwaites, Vol. VI, 169.

nan, a respected shaman,[36] participating in Christian rituals only when faced with the specter of terrible privation. This basic pattern of adherence to traditional religious norms, and experimentation with Christianity in times of dire peril was similar to the religious behavior of his nonconverted tribesmen. Pastedechouan's greater propensity to participate in Catholic ritual and prayer in the absence of his eldest brother Carigonan was also typical of the larger group: there is clearly a direct relationship between collective upsurges of interest in Christianity and the absence of the influential medicine man.[37]

Only rarely do we glimpse Pastedechouan's distinctive identity as a theologically literate, baptized Catholic, or discern any potential uncertainty he may have felt about his religious direction and ultimate fate. His ambiguous feelings are revealed only intermittently throughout the winter, most vividly in a late night conversation he had with Le Jeune. When Le Jeune tries to persuade Pastedechouan that, by forsaking the convent for the woods, he is rushing headlong into hell, Pastedechouan is reported to have replied:

> "I see clearly that I am not doing right; but my misfortune is that I have not a mind strong enough to remain firm in my determination; I believe all they tell me. When I was with the English, I allowed myself to be influenced by their talk; when I am with the Savages, I do as they do; when I am with you, it seems to me your belief is the true one. Would to God I had died when I was

---

[36] Le Jeune describes Pastedechouan's involvement in a ceremony intended by his eldest brother to kill a rival medicine man in February of 1644 [Thwaites, Vol. VI, 199], noting that Pastedechouan assisted Carigonan in many his ceremonies [Ibid., 203].

[37] Prior to the arrival of Carigonan on November 1st [Thwaites, Vol. VII, 93], Le Jeune had had some modest success in inculcating some rudimentary Christian practices. He had managed to impress the group with his fearlessness of a troublesome Manitou [Ibid., 87], to establish the practice of saying prayers before and after each meal [Ibid., 87-89; Thwaites, Vol. VI, 251], and to teach something of Catholic dogma, using Pastedechouan as a translator. When Carigonan joins the group, however, this all changes almost immediately. Though dialogue between members of the group and Le Jeune does continue in Carigonan's occasional absences, when Mestigoit and others often question and debate him [see Thwaites, Vol. VII, 187]. When Carigonan backs Pastedechouan's vociferous attacks on Le Jeune in December of 1633, this initial surge of interest in Christianity among the small group is effectively checked [Thwaites, Vol. VII, 159].

sick in France, and I would now be saved. As long as I
have any relations, I will never do anything of any account; for when I want to stay with you, my brothers tell
me I will rot, always staying in one place, and that is the
reason I leave you to follow them."[38]

This statement has several important implications. First, it indicates the evident porosity of Pastedechouan's identity, revealing the
lingering influence of his Recollect education, which continued to undermine his sense of self long after he left their care in 1626. The
Recollets predicated their missionization strategy upon the chameleon-
like ability of young children to adapt to a novel environment in the interests of survival, choosing to see this adaptability as signaling deep,
long lasting changes to the self that had religious as well as cultural significance. Pastedechouan's dependence upon the surrounding environment to tell him who he is may originate in that childhood experience of
defensive camouflage. His experiences in France may have thwarted his
development of a healthy sense of self and undermined his ability to
critically evaluate the competing claims of other cultural actors, each of
whom wished to define him, and have him define himself, in a particular
way.

Secondly, Pastedechouan's outpouring seems to indicate some
level of continued intellectual and emotional engagement with Catholic
theology: in purportedly expressing the wish that he had died in France,
so that his salvation would have been assured, Pastedechouan seems to
be indicating that he still finds the concept of salvation in some way relevant.

Thirdly, this statement demonstrates Pastedechouan's tendency
to perceive salvation as the product of external circumstances, such as
one's surrounding geographic and cultural environment, rather than internal, intellectual assent to theological propositions, or emotional
engagement with a deity. He associates France and being French unambiguously with salvation, and Canada, and being Montagnais, with
uncertainty, and possible damnation. We sense, in this statement, a sort
of longing for finality, for resolution: as much in his prolonged search for
cultural and religious identity as in the matter of his ultimate fate.

Fourthly, the quote highlights Montagnais perceptions of seden-

---

[38] Thwaites, Vol.VII, 89-91.

tary life,[39] and signals their resistance to sedentification, a proposal
backed by many Jesuits, including Le Jeune,[40] which called for migratory
tribes be settled and taught European-style agriculture as a necessary
precursor to their Christianization. It is interesting that Pastedechouan's
brothers' objections to his involvement with the Jesuits seem, in this instance, to focus on cultural rather than theological issues (as well as
demonstrating the intertwined nature of cultural and theological assumptions on both sides).

Despite Pastedechouan's demonstrable and lingering ambivalence regarding Catholicism, his actions over a ten year period lead us to
conclude that he had become as passionate in his pursuit of a Montagnais
cultural and religious identity as he had once been in his rejection of it.
Despite this desire to belong, his cultural reintegration was far from
complete: he was relegated to the status of a pariah by the contempt of
the group, and tolerated only because of the status of his esteemed older
brothers. Pastedechouan's status as an embittered outsider is well illustrated by an incident which occurs only several days into the winter hunt,
before the arrival of Carigonan, when Pastedechouan broke into the cask
of wine that Le Jeune has brought and flew into a drunken rage: "scream-
ing and howling like a demon, he snatched away the poles and beat upon
the bark of the cabin to break everything to pieces. The women, seeing
him in this frenzy, fled into the woods, some here, some there."[41]   He
then overturned the large cooking kettle, which Mestigoit calmly refilled.
Women fled to hide the bark covers of the shelters from certain destruction, as Pastedechouan "foaming like one possessed...completely infuriated, and not knowing upon what to vent his fury...was running here and

---

[39] Mockery of Pastedechouan because of his sedentary, European lifestyle was
not confined to his brothers but widespread, Le Jeune relates: "I must here speak
of the little esteem the Savages have for him. He has fallen into great embarrassment, in trying to avoid a slight reproach. He gave up Christians and
Christianity, because he could not suffer the taunts of the Savages, who jeered at
him occasionally because he was Sedentary and not wandering, as they were; he
their butt and their laughingstock..." [Thwaites, Vol. VII, 173].

[40] Le Jeune explicitly states his expectations that tribes already stationary, such
as the Huron, will more easily be Christianized that their migratory counterparts
[Thwaites, Vol. VII, 267; see also Thwaites, Vol. VI, 83]. He assumes that for
the Christianization of the Montagnais to be successful, they would have to be
settled and "made stationary" [Thwaites, Vol. VI, 83, 145-153]. He also expresses his own preference for working with sedentary people, though he sees
his mission to the migratory Montagnais as God-given [Thwaites, Vol. V, 193].

[41] Thwaites, Vol. VII, 73.

there on the shores of the Island..."[42] Pastedechouan was once again in the process of overturning the large cooking pot when Mestigoit threw its boiling contents over his face and chest. His behavior, Le Jeune reports, culminated with an apparent threat:

> my host has told me since that he asked for an ax with which to kill me; I do not know whether he really asked for one, as I did not understand his language; but I know very well that, when I went up to him and tried to stop him, he said to me in French, "Go away, it is not you I am after; let me alone;" then, pulling my gown, "Come, said he, let us embark in a canoe, let us return to your house; you do not know these people here; all they do is for the belly, they do not care for you, but for your food." To this I answered in an undertone and to myself, *in vino veritas.* [43]

The incident is revealing on a number of levels: most immediately for the depth of the anger and despair Pastedechouan seems to be experiencing, and the aggression he seems to feel toward his immediate family and tribespeople, as well as Le Jeune. The second point of interest is the mitigated nature of the attacks: for all the contradictory reports of threatened violence against individuals, the only person hurt in the one-man melee is Pastedechouan himself. Despite Le Jeune's language of foaming madness Pastedechouan's violence is notable for its carefulness – it is targeted, not at people, but toward the Montagnais apparatus of survival. The attack on these survival objects is a profoundly self-destructive as well as outwardly aggressive act: it hurts Pastedechouan himself as much as his intended victims. This curious blending of aggressive and self-destructive impulses repeats itself again a few days later: roused by his brother to join in the attempt to save boats that were being pounded against the rocks by a fierce storm, Pastedechouan refuses outright [44] The third point of interest is the profoundly un-Montagnais nature of these attacks – one of the most central codes of Montagnais communal life was the avoidance of displays of anger or pique even in

---

[42] Ibid., 75.
[43] Ibid., 75-77.
[44] Ibid., 81-83.

the face of serious provocation.[45] Emotions perceived by the Montagnais as negative, such as anger or sadness, were thought to lead not only to social disharmony but to the illness of the person experiencing them, as Mestigoit repeatedly explains to his guest Le Jeune, when he can see that he is frustrated by Pastedechouan's behavior. Indeed, Le Jeune records, with some amazement, the uniformly stoic reaction to Pastedechouan's outrageous behavior: "no one seemed to get angry at all this, but then is it foolish to fight with a madman…" [46]

What are we to make of Pastedechouan's rage? We could interpret it as the product of his intense frustration and shame regarding his inability to provide the very elements he is so bent on destroying: his fury at being unable to take his place within the circle of reciprocity which characterized Montagnais interaction. It could reveal his deep hurt that despite his passionate longing for acceptance, he is still regarded as something of an outsider, an oddity. Indeed, much of the often scathing criticism of Pastedechouan by his peers targeted his poor hunting skills. Le Jeune relates a conversation which he overheard during the six-month winter hunt: a conversation so scathing that Le Jeune half-sympathetically relates "they spoke aloud and freely, tearing this poor Apostate to pieces."[47] The women lambasted his incompetence as a hunter and his inability to sufficiently provide for his wife: "if only he could kill something!" one lamented.[48] When Pastedechouan unexpectedly entered the cabin, the excoriation ceased, and he was even offered tobacco by one of the women. But the teasing was far from being covert. Often the women humiliated Pastedechouan by coaching their hungry children to beg him for food as he returned to camp from yet another unsuccessful hunt.[49]

---

[45] Le Jeune relates in detail the Montagnais cultural taboo upon anger directed against members of one's own family and tribe: "They make a pretense of never getting angry, not because of the beauty of this virtue, for which they have not even a name, but for their own contentment and happiness, I mean, to avoid the bitterness caused by anger…I have heard one Savage pronounce this word, *Ninichcatihin*, "I am angry," and he only said it once." (Thwaites, Vol. VI, 231). The exception to the rule is shamanistic behavior, in which aggressive, crazed actions were thought to indicate contact with spiritual entities (see Thwaites, Vol. VII, 117, in which Le Jeune relates an episode of Carigonan's shamanistic possession, which greatly resembles Pastedechouan's fit, especially as it includes verbal threats and the destruction of property).
[46] Thwaites, Vol. VII, 75.
[47] Ibid., 175.
[48] Ibid.
[49] Ibid., 173.

Pastedechouan's lack of hunting competence, and the social derision that this brought, clearly had the effect of eroding each of his successive marriages. At several points throughout the winter, Pastedechouan's wife confided in Le Jeune her impatience and embarrassment with his inadequate provision and her determination to leave Pastedechouan come spring, if not sooner.[50] Such constant provocation shows that even the protection and support afforded Pastedechouan by his influential eldest brothers failed to fully facilitate his acceptance by the group. Indeed, far from countering such attitudes, Mestigoit and Carigonan seemed to have shared them. Though they faithfully provided for him, such provision was invariably tinged with contemptuous condescension: while they protected him from the rest of the group, they mirrored its general assessment of his weaknesses. In seeking to apologize to Le Jeune for his brother's drunken outburst, Mestigoit did not hesitate to insult Pastedechouan: "Don't you see that Petrichtich (it is thus they call the Renegade in derision) does not know anything, that he is a dog?"[51] His words after the incident with the boats were similar: "Petrichtich does not know anything; if he had tried to help me, this misfortune would not have happened."[52] Consistently, Pastedechouan is described by his two oldest brothers as an 'idiot,' a 'blockhead:' their characterizations stress his ignorance: "this stubborn fellow who has no sense and in whom we have no faith," his incompetence: "he would die of hunger if they did not feed him, that he gets lost in the woods like a European," his general contemptibility, dishonor, and lack of authority: "he has no sense, he is a buzzard, he resembles a dog…"[53]

It is in the context of Pastedechouan's poor hunting skills, and his endurance of the cruel taunts of his tribesmen that one of the key events of the winter must be understood. It is an incident which takes Pastedechouan from being the largely passive thwarter of Le Jeune's evangelism to being an active, outspoken critic of Christianity.

It is Christmas Day, 1633. The depleted band is starving, exhausted, and near desperation. Christmas dinner, Le Jeune reports, consisted of "the little ends of the trees"[54] and some bits of hide. Sensing an opportunity to press his message, Le Jeune once again appeals to the

---

[50] Ibid.
[51] Ibid., 171.
[52] Ibid., 183.
[53] Ibid, 105, 173
[54] Ibid., 147.

group, arguing that his God has the power to save them from want, if they will only believe in him. He assembles the whole encampment in a makeshift chapel which he has decorated with a Crucifix, a reliquary, and a picture from his breviary. With Pastedechouan's help, he explains that if they sincerely believe in the Christian God, they will be rescued from their dire predicament. The assembly of twenty nine men, women and children, including Pastedechouan, and eventually even Carigonan, kneel at the makeshift altar and repeat aloud a prayer which pledges their belief in God, and begs for his deliverance from starvation:

> Great Lord, you who have made heaven and earth, you know all, you can do all. I promise you with all my heart, I promise you wholly that, if it pleases you to give us food, I will obey you cheerfully, that I will surely be-lieve in you...Help us, for you can do it, I will certainly do what they shall teach me ought to be done for your sake. I promise it without pretence, I am not lying, I could not lie to you, help us to believe in you perfectly, for you have died for us. Amen.[55]

Following this simple prayer, Le Jeune assures them their hunt will be successful.

And so it is! Le Jeune reports "everyone took something, except the Apostate, who returned empty handed.[56]" As Le Jeune was hoping, this outcome generated greater receptivity to Christianity, even within Pastedechouan's immediate family. He relates that Mestigoit, Past-edechouan's older brother: "...approached me joyfully, recognizing the help of God, and asked what he should do. I said to him, "Nicanis, my well beloved, we must thank God who has helped us."[57] Pastedechouan at this point interjected: "What for indeed? We could not have failed to find them (the animals) without the aid of God."[58] This outburst was only the first of Pastedechouan's determined challenges of Christian interpre-tations of the hunt's success. Backed by Carigonan, he prevents Le Jeune from offering a prayer of thanksgiving at the celebratory feast, telling him to sit down and shut up, and interprets Le Jeune's reservations about

---

[55] Ibid., 153.
[56] Ibid., 159, my note.
[57] Ibid.
[58] Ibid, my note.

the 'gluttony' of Montagnais feasting practices to mean that "God was angry because they had something to eat."[59]

To be sure, Pastedechouan's message was consistent only in its negative evaluation of Christianity. Some of his remarks appear to largely accept many Christian claims, while simultaneously inverting them: thus it is not God's existence, but merely his nature, that is called into question. Pastedechouan contrasts Le Jeune's emphasis on the mercy of God by suggesting that he is punishing, miserly, or simply distant: rebuking Le Jeune for praying to "him who neither sees nor hears anything."[60] Some of his remarks, however, are more radical, obliquely suggesting that the Christian God is irrelevant in the Montagnais cultural context by discounting both God's willingness to help the Montagnais, and the effectiveness of divine intervention on Montagnais hunting outcomes: "That's all very well for you others whom God helps: but he has no interest in us, for, whatever he may do, we still die of hunger unless we find game."[61] Pastedechouan's repeated assertions about the punishing nature of the Christian God, and his attacks on Le Jeune's interpretation of the hunt's outcome, when backed by his influential eldest brother, appear to have eroded the Jesuit's modest gains in winning the confidence of the group.

Why did this incident turn Pastedechouan from an inconsistent and generally passive thwarter of Le Jeune's evangelism into an active theological agent with a consistently anti-Christian message? I believe it is because the equation which Le Jeune so neatly sets up in his original prayers, that the believing Christian will be a successful hunter, so thoroughly and brutally contradicts Pastedechouan's own experience. Arguably, Pastedechouan's failure to resume a respected place in his society is due to the fact that he spent five crucial years away from it learning to be

---

[59] Ibid., 163.

[60] Ibid., 185.

[61] Ibid., 167. Pastedechouan's skepticism of the Christian God's ability to affect Montagnais hunting outcomes was not uncommon: his charges are echoed by another Montagnais, Matchonon: "You say that it is through the guidance of your God that we find something to eat; tell him that he may oppose, with all his power, my taking Beavers and Elks; and you will see that I shall not fail to take them, in spite of him" [Thwaites, Vol. VII, 277]. Matchonon's biography parallels Pastedechouan's own final years: Le Jeune states that, following this 'blasphemous' statement, Matchonon fell ill and was unable to hunt. Abandoned by his own people, he was succored by the Jesuits. He subsequently converts to Christianity, but when he leaves the Jesuits to return to his people, he once again sickens, is abandoned, and finally killed [Ibid., 277-285].

Christian. But Le Jeune's well-intentioned formula makes Pastedechouan doubly inadequate: his empty handed return to camp brands him a failure in Christian as well as Montagnais terms. Moreover, any secret sense of residual pride or distinctiveness that Pastedechouan may have felt as the sole Montagnais Catholic of the group is dashed, as others, successful in the hunt, now have the visible blessing of the God to whom he alone is officially consecrated.

In April, 1634, Pastedechouan accompanied his brother Mestigoit on a harrowing journey along the icy St. Lawrence to deliver the ill Le Jeune back to Quebec. Following its safe conclusion, Le Jeune and Pastedechouan appear to have been out of contact for until the end of the following year, when Le Jeune reports the deaths of his two elder brothers, Carigonan and Mestigoit, whom he adjudged to have suffered the wrath of God for their ingratitude and apostasy following the successful conclusion of the Christmas hunt. He also recorded Pastedechouan's apparent renewed interest in living with the Jesuits.[62] This request to Le Jeune may have been prompted by Pastedechouan's recognition of the fact that, without the support of his influential brothers, his presence would no longer be welcome among his people – in effect, the death of his brothers cut the remaining sinews that bound him to his tribe. Alternatively, with their deaths, one of his primary motivations for his re-embracing Montagnais traditionalism, his desire to please his two eldest brothers, was rendered moot. His reflections on his religious life in his late night conversation with Le Jeune, quoted above, suggested that while they were alive he would not have been able to resume a sedentary way of life without suffering their ridicule and rejection: but perhaps, with their death, working for the Jesuits once again became an attractive option for Pastedechouan. Le Jeune, who suspected that his motives were dictated more by the stomach than the soul, coolly rebuffed him, telling him to return during a time of plenty so his sincerity would be more evident.[63] Though Le Jeune came to regret this decision, and repeatedly wrote to Pastedechouan at Tadoussac, his letters went unanswered and he never saw Pastedechouan alive again. Just as his brothers had predicted, that "he would die of hunger if they did not feed him,"[64] Pastedechouan succumbed to starvation and exposure alone in the woods, during the

---

[62] Ibid., 299-303.
[63] Ibid., 303.
[64] Ibid., 173.

winter of 1636, a year of unequalled plenty.[65] He died rejected by both the tribe whose approval he had so assiduously sought, and the church which had provoked in him a fatal ambivalence.

In his epitaph for Pastedechouan, Le Jeune reflects the uncertainty of his religious identity, questioning his own customary, offhand designation of Pastedechouan as 'L'Apostat,' even as he continues to utilize it:

> In a word, the Apostate is dead. Whether he died an Apostate or not, I do not know, at least he died without any earthly help; I do not know whether he received any from Heaven; I would be very glad if it were so....if it were in my power to free him from the irons and chains in which perhaps he now is, I would release him, that I might procure for him, in exchange for the wrongs he has done me, the greatest blessing that can be obtained for a reasonable creature, eternal salvation. Alas! Is it then so small a thing that a soul be damned? All the great affairs of Conclaves, of the Courts of sovereigns, of Palaces, and of Cabinets, are only child's play, in comparison with saving or losing a soul.[66]

This ultimate assessment is quite different from Le Jeune's typically terse and confident summaries of Pastedechouan's spiritual status, epitomized in his customary nickname for him. This apparent contrast is only underlined by Le Jeune's equivocal behavior in the months preceding Pastedechouan's death: his initial suspicious rejection of Pastedechouan's last request to come and live with the Jesuits, and his subsequent, urgent desire to find and spiritually rehabilitate Pastedechouan. His actions, as well as his analysis, then, beg the question: how did Le Jeune define apostasy, and would Pastedechouan have agreed with, or differed from, his often derisive assessments of Pastedechouan's spiritual status?

Upon examination of Le Jeune's writings, it quickly becomes

---

[65] Le Jeune relates: "That wretch died this year of hunger, abandoned in the woods like a dog. It is very remarkable that he did not have anything to eat, in their abundance; for perhaps not since ten years have the Savages killed so many Elk as they have this winter, the snow being in exactly the condition they desired for hunting them...." [Thwaites, Vol. IX, 71].

[66] Ibid.

apparent that he utilizes not one, but two functional definitions of apostasy, which exist in considerable tension with one another. Most often, Le Jeune speaks as if he understands apostasy to be a discrete, easily identifiable, and above all, a final act in which a soul, formerly obedient to God and his laws, willfully and knowingly spurns Him and them, in the process putting himself beyond the pale of the church and hope of salvation. This somewhat static definition of apostasy is based upon the premise that external behavior corresponds reliably with inner spiritual states, and that the nature of the alleged apostate's relationship to God can successfully be discerned from his analogical relationship with God's representatives on earth.[67] Le Jeune thus coins his customary tag for Pastedechouan, 'The Apostate,' upon hearing of his drunken association with English 'heretics' at Tadoussac following his desertion of the Jesuit convent in the spring of 1633. In so labeling him, he presumes that Pastedechouan's carousing with the English represents a deliberate religious and political statement and signals a clear renunciation of the Jesuits' teachings and defiance of their authority. Le Jeune is comfortable judging the state of Pastedechouan's soul purely on the basis of his external behavior and associations, without much apparent concern for his own motivations.

The unambiguous finality of this understanding of apostasy, however, is contradicted by how Le Jeune actually responds to Pastedechouan over the course of their four-year relationship, a response

---

[67] Under this functional definition the 'apostate' need not have even been baptized: thus Le Jeune interpreted the sudden and violent deaths of Pastedechouan's elder brothers, Carigonan and Mestigoit, as divine punishment for their failure to properly fulfill their promise to recognize the Christian God following the success of their Christmas hunt, and to render God their thanks and loyalty: "God has let his thunderbolts fall, so to speak, upon the three brothers with whom I passed the winter, for having wickedly violated the promise they had made to acknowledge him as Lord. They had had recourse to his goodness in their extreme famine; he had succored them, giving them food in abundance...They had not yet swallowed the morsel when God took them by the throat" [Ibid., 69]. He thus envisioned their apostasy as being on a par with Pastedechouan's, the only difference in their ultimate fate being one of timing. Le Jeune sees God's hand as having been stayed, if only temporarily, by the seal of baptism on Pastedechouan's brow: "I believe that the stamp of the Christian for a little while arrested divine justice. But, as he would not acknowledge it, the same thunderbolt, that struck his brothers, reduced him to ashes" [Ibid., 69-71]. Thus, for Le Jeune, baptism, even one supposedly renounced, could effectively protect its bearer from God's justified wrath, rather than itself being the necessary precondition for apostasy to occur.

which seems characterized more by absolution than absolutism. Despite his constant references to Pastedechouan as an 'apostate' or 'renegade,' Le Jeune's actions seem to imply that he was informed by a second, more fluid functional definition of apostasy which allows for the possibility of his being salvaged. Twice between 1632 and 1636 Le Jeune engages Pastedechouan as a language teacher despite, or perhaps because of his questionable spiritual status, and in each of their prolonged winter encounters he utilizes every weapon in his arsenal, including coercion, to bring Pastedechouan back into the fold, actions which would be nonsensical if apostasy was an irredeemable state.

Le Jeune's most extended and thoughtful consideration of Pastedechouan's ultimate fate, presented in the epitaph just quoted, precludes our dismissal of this second and more fluid definition of apostasy as simply a pragmatic, or even cynical redefinition in the interest of the mission's ultimate priorities. For, in it, Le Jeune questions not simply the finality of apostasy, but more fundamentally, the basis upon which he judged apostasy to have occurred. In his epitaph, Le Jeune eschews his typical confidence in his ability to adjudge internal spiritual states on the basis of Pastedechouan's outward behavior, or his attitude toward missionaries, recognizing that Pastdechouan's ultimate fate cannot, without arrogance, be presented as anything other than uncertain. The epitaph is predicated on the acknowledgment that Pastedechouan has a full, inner, and secret spiritual relationship with God on par with the missionary's own, and does not make Pastedechouan's salvation contingent upon his re-adoption of European ways, or his submission to missionary authority. In the final moments of life, at least, the definitive relationship is envisioned as being that which exists between the soul and God, rather than the social actor and the missionary. In his definitive analysis of Pastedechouan's religious life, then, Le Jeune was reaching for an understanding which transcended his usual insistence upon a conscious and final choice between aboriginal and European religious and cultural practices. Le Jeune's perception of Pastedechouan's spiritual state is thus far more nuanced, both in theory and practice, than his consistent use of nicknames such as 'The Apostate' and 'The Renegade' would lead us to believe.

These two contradictory definitions of apostasy also appear to animate Pastedechouan's motivations and behaviors. His putative exclamation: "Would to God that I had died in France, and I would now be saved!"[68] seems to place his hopes for salvation squarely in the distant past, before his reintegration into Montagnais society. Such an understanding reveals that Pastedechouan retained throughout his life the core of what he was taught in childhood by the Recollets, who presented Montagnais and French Christian identity as essentially inimical. His decision to attenuate his involvement with European forms of religious life and attempt cultural reintegration thus serves, ironically, only to illustrate the effectiveness of his indoctrination.

There are also indications, however, that Pastedechouan may have been influenced by the second, more fluid definition of apostasy, in that he often acts as if he is still part of the church, or can be reconciled to it. According to the admittedly flawed accounts we have of the last four years of his life, he apparently expressed such sentiments on at least four occasions.[69] Though it is difficult to untangle and critically weigh the welter of different motivations that led to Pastedechouan's ongoing relationship with European missionary orders (just as it is difficult to discern how much Le Jeune's own shifting definition of apostasy was based on Pastedechouan's utility for the mission), it can safely be said that there was nothing final or unambiguous in his relationship with them. One looks in vain for any incident that can claim to be the definitive statement of his religious philosophy that is uncontradicted by subsequent developments. Even his clearest and most passionate abjuration of Christianity, following the Christmas hunt in 1634, is apparently abrogated by his desire to rejoin the Jesuits following the death of his eldest brothers the following year.

But while the pattern of Pastedechouan's actions, like Le Jeune's, appears to be informed by two quite different functional definitions of apostasy: as, alternately, a deliberate, unambiguous, and above all, final act, and as one pole in the dance between human sin and divine forgiveness, it does not appear that Pastedechouan, like Le Jeune, ultimately recognized that his salvation rested upon a transcendent relationship with a divine other, rather than submission to missionary authority and European norms. While Le Jeune, in his epitaph for Pastedechouan, belatedly and almost reluctantly recognizes his status as an sovereign religious actor with a private relationship with God akin to his own, nowhere in the extant European record does Pastedechouan make any such claim to religious independence from or equality with his mis-

---

[68] Thwaites, Vol. VII, 89-91.
[69] Ibid., 71, 89-91, 303. See also Du Creux, Vol. I, 140.

sionary teachers: nowhere does he claim a relationship to the Christian God which is not predicated on European norms and rules or exempt from missionary interference. Both the static definition of apostasy, in which he envisions himself as eternally condemned because of his desire to reintegrate back into the Montagnais community, and the more dynamic definition, in which he sees himself as savable if he once again joins the Jesuits, involve an acknowledgement of missionary authority rather than a recognition of the primacy of his own relationship with God.

This aspect of Pastedechouan's religious behavior is in marked contrast with the other Christians in his family, Sasousmat, the brother closest to him in age, and Manitougatche, his one-time father in law, neither of whom were subjected to childhood removal and reeducation, but who both converted as adults. The curious flatness, resignation, and lack of intellectual curiosity so characteristic of Pastedechouan's religious mentality is in striking contrast to the theological imagination, confidence and playfulness of other members of his family. Both 'converts' and 'traditionalists' display is a sense of equality to and engagement with their missionary interlocutors, and see themselves as theological agents who are able to discern, define, and articulate the ontological and moral differences between Montagnais and Catholic conceptualizations and practices. In contrast to the rest of his family's demonstrated religious independence, Pastedechouan appears to see religion, whether Montagnais or French Catholic, as involving fear of, capitulation to, and obedience of religious authorities. In contrast to the propensity of his family members for active debate, Pastedechouan characteristically displays his dissent by silence, withdrawal, and refusal rather than engaged articulation. When he does formulate theological arguments, they are both less imaginative and less incisive than those of other family members, and tend to reflexively draw upon, and superficially counter, rather than drastically undermine, Christian ideas.

Pastedechouan's experiences exemplified and his lifespan circumscribed an influential, child-focused model of envisioning and effecting conversion, even as the contrasting experiences of the adult converts in his family presaged a new direction in missionary methodology. In the years following his death there was a gradual but decisive reimagination of what aboriginal conversion meant and how it should be effected: from the earlier model which envisioned conversion as the impress of Christianity onto the still pliable clay of childhood, and emphasized obedience, formal education, and memorization of doctrine, to an adult-focused model which accepted the necessity of theological disputation between adult equals. The inauguration of this shift is discernable in the qualitative differences in religious consciousness between Pastedechouan, a child convert who was subjected to cultural and religious dislocation, reeducation, and reintroduction, and that of the other, adult converts in his family. Le Jeune's reluctant acquiesce to Pastedechouan's religious independence in his epitaph, though presaging a wholesale shift in Jesuit missionary strategy, came too late to have any impact upon Pastedechouan's own spiritual sensibilities. While obliquely condemning Pastedechouan's Recollet education as having engendered in him "a faith born of fear and slavishness."[70] Le Jeune does nothing to correct this; indeed, his own dealings with Pastedechouan show a similar pattern of attempted indoctrination and coercion.

Our review of Pastedechouan's life and tragic death exposes the effects of a missionary model shared by both Recollets and Jesuits stationed in Canada during Pastedechouan's lifespan – roughly the first four decades of the seventeenth century. Pastedechouan, and the rest of his small cohort of compatriots taken from their tribal societies and immersed in the daily lives of these French missionary orders, were supposed to be the 'shock troops' of widespread aboriginal religious, political and cultural change. This cherished dream did not materialize: indeed, to the despairing eyes of their tutors, the children failed to retain the religious and cultural priorities that had been so assiduously drummed into them, and their attempts to reintegrate back into their native societies were often condemned as 'apostasy.' While fully aware of Pastedechouan's apparent turning from the faith, both Recollets and Jesuits during his lifetime continued to defend the viability of the missionary model that they had used to indoctrinate him. In Richard White's terms, the reluctance of both Jesuits and Recollets during this period to abandon a missionary model which advocated the detachment of children from their native environment, their complete reeducation, and their reintroduction into their communities as missionaries clearly represents their early resistance to the cultural imperative of finding a "middle ground"[71] with Amerindians by attempting to artificially create a situation in which

---

[70] Thwaites, Vol. V, 177.
[71] Richard White, *The Middle Ground: Indians, Empires, and Republics in the Great Lakes Region, 1650-1815* (Cambridge: Cambridge University Press, 1991), x.

they could maintain a spurious hegemony. Their isolation and control of a laughably small number of Amerindian children did little to help them understand their immersion in a shared cultural world in which accommodation and compromise were essential. Moreover, their indoctrination of similar views in the children under their care taught them to see native cultural practices and Christianity as antithetical. By teaching these children that the two worlds they inhabited simultaneously were fundamentally incompatible, these early modern missionaries created a whole class of people like Pastedechouan, who were culturally and religiously homeless, with often tragic results.

BLACK ELK *WRITES*:
SOME IMPLICATIONS OF HIS LITERACY

Ivan M. Timonin[*]

"Black Elk is illiterate; but thoughtful readers will allow that he is none the less an educated man in the fine sense of a term that sometimes seems to have lost its vital meaning for us in this excessively progressive age."[1]

Nicholas Black Elk (ca. 1863-1950) is best known as the source of two major works: *Black Elk Speaks: as told through John G. Neihardt (Flaming Rainbow) by Nicholas Black Elk*[2] and *The Sacred Pipe:Black Elk's Account of the Seven Rites of the Oglala Sioux,Recorded and Edited by Joseph Epes Brown*.[3] John Neihardt made a point of Black Elk's illiteracy. He claimed in addition that Black Elk spoke no English.[4] Joseph Brown also claimed that Black Elk spoke no English,[5] though he did not repeat the "illiteracy" claim. The notion of Black Elk's unilingualism has continued in, for example, Hertha Dawn Wong's 1992 work on Native American autobiography.[6]

Why the claim? And why has the claim persisted? It is important to understand that, far from being illiterate, Black Elk, who had gone to Europe in 1886 with the Buffalo Bill Wild West Show, was writing let-

---

[*] Born in Ottawa in 1938, Ivan Timonin has lived there and in Mobile, Alabama, Stockholm Sweden, Edmonton, Alberta, Chicago, and Vancouver. He worked in the fields of human resource development and immigration for thirty years, at progressively senior levels of the Canadian federal government. Ivan Timonin resumed theological studies in 1996. He received the MA(Th) degree from Saint Paul University in Ottawa, Canada, in 2000. He is currently completing a doctoral dissertation on Black Elk's *The Sacred Pipe* and is also teaching at Saint Paul University. Ivan Timonin is a Lay Reader in the Anglican Diocese of Ottawa and a Deputy Warden of Christ Church Cathedral.
[1] John G. Neihardt, *Black Elk Speaks: Being the Life Story of a Holy Man of the Oglala Sioux as told through John G. Neihardt (Flaming Rainbow) by Nicholas Black Elk* (New York: Morrow, 1932; reprint Lincoln: University of Nebraska Press, 2000 [Twenty-First-Century Edition]): Preface to the 1932 edition, xxi.
[2] Ibid.
[3] Joseph Epes Brown, *The Sacred Pipe* (Norman OK: University of Oklahoma Press, 1953; reprint 1989).
[4] Neihardt, "Preface to the 1961 Edition," in *Black Elk Speaks*, xxv.
[5] Joseph Epes Brown, "Editor's Preface" in *The Sacred Pipe*, xiv.
[6] Hertha Dawn Wong, *Sending My Heart Back Across the Years: Tradition and Innovation in Native American Autobiography* (New York: Oxford University Press, 1992): 118.

ters as early as 1888 and quoting Saint Paul in a second letter in 1889.[7] As well, Black Elk noted, in the 1888 letter, that he was "able to speak some of the white men's language."[8] On his return to South Dakota, Black Elk was employed as a store clerk. After his conversion, in 1904, to Catholicism, and after becoming a catechist for the Jesuit Mission on the Pine Ridge Reservation, Nicholas William Black Elk composed a number of reports which appeared in the Catholic mission monthly *Sinasapa Wocekiye Taeyanpaha* [*Catholic Herald*], published by the Benedictine Mission at Fort Totten, North Dakota.[9] In a 1920 article: "What is a Catechist?" Fr. J. Golden, O.S.B., Supervisor of the Cheyenne River Indian Mission indicated a number of tasks requiring literacy to be performed by catechists, including the writing of reports and reading the Gospel on Sundays.[10]

The importance of Black Elk's "literacy" is threefold. First, it contradicts the image of the illiterate aboriginal sage with a background largely or only in an oral culture. Second, Black Elk's evident familiarity with the Bible and necessary familiarity with prayer books, catechisms, hymn books, and other related texts indicates a basis for theological reflection in Euro-Christian terms, as well as in the terms of the oral tradition of the Lakota. This, in turn, together with an understanding of the sort of training and experience acquired by catechists like Black Elk, may provide a basis for proposing that he was actually a 'theologian' in the Euro-Christian sense. And, in that sense, literacy and writing are what make Black Elk a 'theologian.'[11] To the extent that he was dealing

---

[7] Black Elk, letter in *Iapi Oaye* 18, No.12, December, 1889, 1. *Iapi Oaye* was published on the Santee Agency in Nebraska by A. L. Riggs, a Congregationalist missionary. A translation of this and an earlier letter are in Raymond J. DeMallie, ed., *The Sixth Grandfather: Black Elk's Teachings Given to John G. Neihardt* (Lincoln NE: University of Nebraska Press, 1984): 8-10. In the 1889 letter, Black Elk quotes 1 Cor. 13: "Though I speak with the tongues of men and of angels...." He urges his readers to "Trust in God."

[8] DeMallie, *Sixth Grandfather*, 9.

[9] Reports signed variously N. W. Black Elk, Nick N. Black Elk, Nicholas Black Elk, and Nick W. Black Elk appeared in the issues of January 15, 1907, 4; March 15, 1907, 2; June 15, 1907, 2; December 15, 1907, 4; February 15, 1908; July 15, 1908, n.p.; July 15, 1909, 3; November 15, 1909; January 15, 1912, 4; April 15, 1913, 4; February 15, 1914, n.p.; May 15, 1915, 4; and April 15, 1916, 4. Issues containing these reports are in Marquette University Archive (MUA) Bureau of Catholic Indian Missions (BCIM), Series 14/1, Box 26, Folders 1, 2, and 3.

[10] Rev, J, Golden, "What is a Catechist," in *Sinasapa Wocekiye Taeyanpaha*, February 15, 1920, 4. MUA BCIM Series 14/1, Box 26, Folder 3.

[11] This follows the principal thesis of Walter J. Ong, S.J., in his *Orality and Literacy: The Technologizing of the Word* (London, New York: Methuen, 1982; reprint New York: Routledge, 1988; new ed. New York: Routledge, 2002). See, for example, pp. 8-9:

with the understanding of written texts, he was engaged in a hermeneutical exercise that he could apply, in turn, to the oral tradition in which he had his earliest formation.[12]

Black Elk's literacy raises two sorts of questions, one peripheral and one central, to this study. One might ask, peripherally, why Black Elk has remained "illiterate" in the general consciousness; and though there is no convincing evidence of a determination, on anyone's part, to keep him there, one can speculate about it. The central questions, as suggested above, relate to the consequences of Black Elk's literacy, consequences which speak also to the differences between oral and literate cultures.

"The Sioux were unique among Plains tribes for the development of widespread native-language literacy."[13] Ella Cara Deloria, her-

---

All thought, including that in primary oral cultures, is to some degree analytic: it breaks its materials into various components. But abstractly sequential, classificatory, explanatory examination of phenomena or of stated truths is impossible without writing and reading. Human beings in primary oral cultures, those untouched by writing in any form, learn a great deal and possess and practice great wisdom, but they do not 'study.'

[12] The point may be made clear by reference to Paul B. Steinmetz, S.J. having noted that eleven versions of the myth of the bringing of the sacred pipe "are the source of widely different meanings." See Steinmetz, *The Sacred Pipe: An Archetypal Theology* (Syracuse: Syracuse University Press, 1998): 111. The interpretive or hermeneutic function relates, as Paul Ricoeur notes, to written texts. Indeed: "To the extent that hermeneutics is text-oriented interpretation, and inasmuch as texts are, among other things, instances of written language, no interpretation theory is possible that does not come to grips with the problem of writing." Paul Ricoeur, *Interpretation Theory: Discourse and the Surplus of Meaning* (Fort Worth TX: Texas Christian University Press, 1976): 25.

[13] Raymond J. DeMallie and Douglas R. Parks, "Tribal Traditions and Records," in *Plains*, ed. Raymond J. DeMallie: 1072, Vol. 13 of *Handbook of North American Indians*, ed. William C. Sturtevant (Washington, DC: Smithsonian Institution, 2001). Parks and Rankin, "Siouan Languages," have summarized the earlier attempts at printed vocabularies and texts. These date to the 1778 vocabulary of the explorer Jonathan Carver. "Samuel W. Pond and Gideon H. Pond [Congregational missionaries] recorded the first collection of Santee texts (1840), and in 1842 Samuel Pond compiled a Hebrew-Dakota dictionary intended to facilitate translation of the scriptures from Hebrew into Santee...." In *Plains*, 97. More importantly, for our purposes, is DeMallie, "Sioux Until 1850:"

The work of missionaries among the Sioux ... had long-term significance. In addition to introducing the Sioux to Christianity, the missionaries focussed on education. In 1834 the Congregational missionaries Samuel W. Pond and Gideon H. Pond devised orthography for writing the Sioux language that was adopted as an integral part of mission work. Utilized first in the schools and churches, the foundations for native-language literacy were established in the 1840s. Newspapers, Bible translations, and other printed material spread liter-

self the sister and daughter of Siouan Episcopal priests, tells of the creation of the Riggs-Williamson translation of the Bible. Based on the Dakota phonetics of the Pond brothers, Dr Stephen Return Riggs and Dr Thomas S. Williamson made a mediated translation from the original Hebrew and Greek, via Joseph Renville, a trader of French-Canadian and Siouan parentage. Although Renville spoke both French and the Dakota dialect, he apparently spoke little or no English. Deloria describes the process:

> It is a blessing incalculable for all Dakota missions that Drs. Williamson and Riggs are scholars. One of them reads a verse—in Hebrew, if it is from the Old Testament, or in Greek, if from the New. He ponders its essence, stripped of idiom, and then he gives it in French. Renville, receiving it thus in his father's civilized (*sic*) language, now thinks it through very carefully and at length turns it out again, this time in his mother's primitive (*sic*) tongue.[14]

Because the dialects of the Teton and related members of the Siouan language group are mutually understandable, the Riggs-Williamson translation became a standard for the rest of the nineteenth century.

The fact that the early Bible translation went via French raises the interesting point that the Plains Indians were exposed to the French language for nearly two centuries before the advent of English. To confuse the issue further, the first generation of Jesuit priests on the Pine Ridge and Rosebud Reservations were German speakers and wrote some of their letters, reports and memoirs in that language. There is even a legend to the effect that the Lakota of the late nineteenth century spoke English with a German accent.

The Riggs-Williamson translation of the Bible was by no means the first book in the language of the Sioux. As early as 1833 the brothers Samuel W. and Gideon H. Pond, both Congregational lay missionaries, began work on an orthography for a written form of the Dakota dialect. The alphabet was arranged in 1834 and the first Dakota to learn it was Mazardhamani: "he soon learned to read lessons prepared for him and also to write letters which his teachers could understand. He was, of course, the first Dakota who learned to read and write."[15] Stephen Return

acy rapidly among the Sioux, making it a major force in the second half of the nineteenth century.
In *Plains*, 734.
[14] Ella Cara Deloria, *Speaking of Indians* (New York: Friendship Press, 1944; reprint Lincoln NE: University of Nebraska Press, 1998): 103.
[15] S. W. Pond, Jr., *Two Volunteer Missionaries Among the Dakotas or the Story of the Labors of Samuel W. and Gideon H. Pond* (Boston and Chicago: Congregational Sunday-School and Publishing Society, 1893): 53.

Riggs and his wife arrived at the Lake Harriet Mission in 1837 and began immediately to learn Dakota. According to Samuel Pond, Jr., who may be giving his father and uncle too much credit:

> Mr [Samuel] Pond translated the story of Joseph, and Mr Riggs took the manuscript with him when he went on to Lac Qui Parle, where it was revised by G. H. Pond and afterwards published with the following title, 'Joseph Oyakapi Kin,' and was one of the first books placed in the hands of the Dakotas. Translations of some other portions of the Bible were made in this year, 1837.[16]

That Black Elk, born nearly thirty years later, was himself literate should therefore come as no surprise. His ability to read and to write in the Lakota dialect did, however, surprise the Jesuit missionaries with whom he became associated after his baptism on the feast of Saint Nicholas, 1904. In a fund-raising pamphlet written about a decade later, Fr Henry Westropp, S.J., Black Elk's closest Jesuit associate, wrote: "Though half blind he has by some hook or crook learned how to read and he knows his religion thoroughly."[17] Black Elk's daughter, Lucy Looks Twice, made a similar statement to Michael F. Steltenkamp, S.J.: "He had poor eyesight, but he learned to read Scripture and prayer books written in the Indian language."[18]

As already indicated, Black Elk's literacy leaves its first known traces in the late 1880s. By the middle of that decade he was already a practising *wicasa wakan* or holy man among the Oglala Lakota,[19] and he had been settled on the Pine Ridge Reservation since 1882.[20] Along with many others, he decided in 1886 to join Buffalo Bill Cody's Wild West Show, with two principal consequences. First, he was baptized, along with the other Indians, in a Christian denomination, probably Episcopal since the Episcopal Church had a mission on the reservation, and it is probable that an Episcopal "minister" accompanied the troupe, perhaps a Lakota or Dakota Lay Reader or Deacon. Second, he traveled across the United States, spending time in Chicago and New York; and he so-

---

[16] Ibid., 112-113.

[17] Henry Ignatius Westropp, S. J., *In the Land of the Wigwam: Few Missionary Notes from the Pine Ridge Reservation Printed Entirely by Sioux Indian Boys* (Pine Ridge SD: The Oglala Light Press, The United States Indian Training School): 12. Located at Marquette University Archives, Holy Rosary Mission Series 7/1, Box 23, Folder 12.

[18] Michael F. Steltenkamp, S.J., *Black Elk: Holy Man of the Oglala* (Norman OK: University of Oklahoma Press, 1993): 56. In a footnote Steltenkamp makes reference to the work of Stephen R. Riggs.

[19] DeMallie, *Sixth Grandfather*, 7.

[20] Ibid.

journed, for the better part of three years in England, France, Italy, and Germany, his last six month being spent with a girl friend and her family in Paris. Apart from English, he therefore had exposure to German, Italian, and, needless to say, French.

Raymond J. DeMallie has provided translations of the two letters by Black Elk, which appeared in *Iapi Oaye* [The Word Carrier] in 1888 and 1889. Because they are the earliest indication of Black Elk's interest in European culture and religion, they are worth reproducing in full.

> Buffalo Bill's Wild West Show,
> Manchester, England,
> Feb. 15, 1888.
>
> Now I will tell about how I am doing with the wild west show. Always in my mind I hold to the law and all along I live remembering God. But the show runs day and night too, so at two o'clock we quit. But all along I live remembering God so He enables me to do it all.
>
> So my relatives, the Lakota people, now I know the white men's customs well. One custom is very good. Whoever believes in God will find good ways—that is what I mean. And many of the ways the white men follow are hard to endure. Whoever has no country will die in the wilderness. And although the country is large it is always full of white men. That which makes me happy is always land. Now I have stayed here three [two] years. And I am able to speak some of the white men's language. And a little while ago my friend gave me a translated paper [the *Iapi Oaye*] and I rejoiced greatly. Thus the Lakotas will be able to translate English.
>
> Here the country is different; the days are all dark. It is always smoky so we never see the sun clearly. A little while ago this month, Feb. 7, 1888, a woman [one of the Indian women of the show] gave birth. This woman is called "Imim" and her father is called Little Chief. Now today they will baptize it, then February 15 at six o'clock their baby will have the law [be baptized]. So it is. With kindness I cause you to hear.[21]

The second of the *Iapi Oaye* letters, though dated "Manchester, England, appears to have been written after Black Elk's return from Europe in the autumn of 1889; it was published in the December issue that year:

---

[21] *Iapi Oaye* 17(3), March 1888: 9. Translation in DeMallie, *Sixth Grandfather*, 8-9.

BLACK ELK'S STORY

From Red Cloud [Pine Ridge Agency], my relatives the Lakota people, I am writing this letter in the language you understand. My relatives, I am Lakota. Back in about the year 1885 [1886] I stayed in New York; all along I remembered God. Across the ocean I came to what they call England. I stayed there one year, then again after crossing an ocean four days I came to what they call Germany. I stayed there one year. So thus all along, of the white man's many customs, only his faith, the white man's beliefs about God's will, and how they act according to it, I wanted to understand. I traveled to one city after another, and there were many customs around God's will. "Though I speak with the tongues of men and of angels, and have not charity, I am become as sounding brass, or a tinkling cymbal. And though I have the gift of prophecy, and understand all mysteries, and all knowledge; and though I have all faith, so that I could remove mountains, and have not charity, I am nothing. And though I bestow all my goods to feed the poor, and though I give my body to be burned, and have not charity, it profiteth me nothing" [1 Cor. 13].

So Lakota people, trust in God! Now all along I trust in God. I work honestly and it is good; I hope the people will do likewise. Then my relatives I will tell about something funny [ironic]. My friend called Mexican Joe had a show that Lakotas joined—one called High Bear, the other called Two Elk. We stayed in a place called Manchester, England. I saw them in the show tent; they came there and then I arrived. Then the tent burned and six horses died and I also saw many other things burned.

Across the big ocean is where they killed Jesus; again I wished to see it but it was four days on the ocean and there was no railroad. If horses go there they die of thirst. Only those long-necks [camels] are able to go there. [It would require] much money for me to be able to go over there to tell about it myself.

Black Elk.
Manchester, England.[22]

---

[22] *Iapi Oaye* 18(12), December 1889: 1. Translation in DeMallie, *Sixth Grandfather*, 9-10.

DeMallie notes that Black Elk cited the Dakota translation of the Bible by Williamson and Riggs, transposing Dakota to Lakota. He notes, with regard to Black Elk's "wrestling with Christian concepts," that "Such personal investigation lies at the heart of all Lakota attempts to understand the spiritual realm."[23]

After his return to Pine Ridge, Black Elk worked as a store clerk; but the Ghost Dance religion, whose growing influence coincided with his return, immediately attracted him. As a messianic and eschatological movement, the Ghost Dance had strongly Christian, as well as Native-American sources, which, in light of Black Elk's recent experiences, may have been a part of its appeal to him. The Wounded Knee massacre of December 29, 1890 effectively ended the Ghost Dance as a major force; and it was, in fact, in the Wounded Knee district that Black Elk shortly thereafter made what would become his permanent home. He married Katie War Bonnet in 1892, and three children were baptized as Roman Catholics.[24] His own re-baptism as a Roman Catholic in 1904 followed his first wife's death,[25] and he was remarried, to Anna Brings White, in 1905.[26]

Nicholas Black Elk seems to have become a Catholic catechist soon after his baptism, perhaps following his Confirmation on July 2 1905.[27] Black Elk reports, in a letter dated January 9, 1912: "Last nineteen hundred & four I became a catechist...."[28] What appears to have been Black Elk's most active period as a catechist coincided with his close association with Henry Westropp, S.J., a missionary responsible for sending Black Elk and other Lakota catechists to reservations as far as Wyoming and Montana. Black Elk reported these sojourns, as well as his activity closer to home in the series of articles and reports, published be-

---

[23] DeMallie, *Sixth Grandfather*, 11. The Williamson-Riggs translation is *Dakota Wowapi Wakan: The Holy Bible in the Language of the Dakotas, Translated out of the Original Tongues* (New York: American Bible Society, 1880).

[24] Ibid., 13. He cites the Pine Ridge census rolls for 1983, 1896, and 1901.

[25] Katie War Bonnet died in 1901 or 1903. The earlier date is reported by Black Elk's daughter, Lucy Looks Twice, in Michael Steltenkamp, S.J., *Black Elk: Holy Man of the Oglala* (Norman OK: University of Oklahoma Press, 1993): 18. The later date is reported by DeMallie, *Sixth Grandfather*, 14.

[26] Steltenkamp, *Holy Man*, 18. Black Elk's Catholic baptism occurred on the feast of Saint Nicholas, December 6, 1904.

[27] William K. Powers, "When Black Elk Speaks, Everybody Listens," in *Religion in Native North America*: 141, Christopher Vecsey ed. (Moscow ID: University of Idaho press, 1990).

[28] Black Elk to Fr. William H. Ketcham, Director, Bureau of Catholic Indian Missions; in Marquette University Archives, BCIM records, Series 1, Box 78, Folder 13. Black Elk's earlier reporting of dates seems to be off by about a year. See DeMallie's corrections to the two *Iapi Oaye* letters, *supra*. A year was frequently dated from the onset of winter.

tween 1907 and 1916.[29] These appeared, as already mentioned, in *Si-nasapa Wocekiye Taeyanpaha* [*Catholic Herald*] a monthly newspaper, mainly in the Lakota dialect, which was published by the Benedictine mission at Fort Totten, ND.[30] They contain local news of the sort which enables people to see in print their names and the amount of their financial contributions: "Louis Bordeaux... $10.00; Mrs. Bordeaux... $1.00; Thomas Bordeaux... $1.00; Alex Bordeaux... $10.00."[31] They also contain words of encouragement,[32] catechesis and moral teaching:

> My friends and relatives: may the Holy Spirit be with you all and watch over you. Always look towards heaven and prepare yourselves. God has promised the Kingdom of heaven for us. When we die, if we have faith in God, the place that we go is the Kingdom of Heaven.
>
> Remember your commandments, and when you receive your sacraments, believe in them. God is our Father. Believe in Him. We will join Him someday [*sic*]. Remember, God has always loved us; not me, because I am old, but all of you younger people. He died for us.
>
> God did not come to the rich, but he came to the poor people. Not only Indians, but all of the poor people. When you feel bad, if you know how to say a Rosary, say your Rosary. And the prayer book that we have given you, use that because all the prayers are in there. And when you pray, always remember your priests, and your catechists—because we need prayers very much.[33]

This early letter is important. It is dated April 27 1907, two years and four months after Black Elk's baptism as a Catholic. In it, Black Elk

---

[29] In the latter year, Henry Westropp was moved to a Jesuit mission in India, possibly as a consequence of World War I, since many Jesuits in India were German. See Mary Claudia Duratschek, O.S.B., *Cruising Along Sioux Trails: A History of the Catholic Indian Missions of South Dakota* (Saint Meinrad IN: The Grail, 1947): 145-146, n. 79.

[30] Not all of the series had been translated prior to July, 2002. Paul Manhart, S.J., has reviewed earlier translations and has translated missing portions.

[31] Black Elk, Article in *Sinasapa Wocekiye Taeyanpaha*, March 15, 1907: 2.

[32] Ibid., translated by Michael F. Steltenkamp, S.J.: "I will encourage you people that you donate at least a penny to these catechists, so that they can continue on their work in the name of God. While we're still living on earth, we should be thankful to God for putting us here on this earth. And God has promised us a place when we die, and I'm pretty sure he'll never forget us."

[33] Black Elk, Article in *Sinasapa Wocekiye Taeyanpaha*, June 15 1907: 2. Translated by Steltenkamp..

speaks authoritatively; he speaks pastorally; and he speaks, one might even argue, theologically.

Translations of other letters indicate that Black Elk also reported on Catholic events of note: the annual Catholic Congresses[34] and Black Elk's missions to the Arapahos and the Cheyenne on behalf of the Jesuits.[35] What appears to be the last letter in the series was published in the April 15 1916 issue of *Sinasapa Wocekiye Taeyanpaha*. After that, there appears to be silence until the appearance, in 1932, of *Black Elk Speaks*. Then there is a further silence, apart from the letters of retraction of *Black Elk Speaks*, which were composed in 1934,[36] until the composition of *The Sacred Pipe*, mainly in the winter of 1947-48.

Black Elk wrote one last letter, dated Manderson SD, March 4, 1948.[37] "The letter was written[38] to a Trappist monk [in Rome] who had taught himself to write Lakota and corresponded with Nick. Nick came to regard him as a son...."[39] The printed version of the letter has been set up in short lines and strophes, much like English editions of the Psalms. Since Charlotte A. Black Elk claims to have reserved copyright, the letter cannot be cited *in extenso* at this time.[40] In brief, the letter appears to

---

[34] Black Elk, Article in *Sinasapa Wocekiye Taeyanpaha*, December 15 1907: 4.

[35] Black Elk, Article in *Sinasapa Wocekiye Taeyanpaha*, July 15 1908: reverse of Supplement page.

[36] There are three letters (MUA HRM Series 1/1, Box 1, Folder 5). The first pair, one in Lakota and one in English are in typescript, dated Holy Rosary Mission, Pine Ridge South Dakota, January 26, 1934, and signed by "Nick Black Elk," "Lucy Looks Twice" (his daughter), and "Joseph A Zimmerman, S.J." The third is an autograph, in English, with text and signature in a single hand, quite clearly not the hand of Black Elk, whose signature on the first pair of letters is very shaky: he would have been about seventy years of age at the time and is reported to have been nearly blind. Interestingly enough, the first pair of letters coincided with two executive orders of the Roosevelt administration: the first was entitled "Indian Religious Freedom...," while the second restricted missionary activity. See Kenneth R. Philip, *John Collier's Crusade for Indian Reform, 1920-1954* Tucson AZ: University of Arizona Press, 1077): 131-132. DeMallie reports ["Introduction to the New Edition" in John G. Neihardt, *When the Tree Flowered: The Story of Eagle Voice, A Sioux Indian (New Edition)* (Lincoln NE: University of Nebraska Press, 1991): viii.] that several months later, during the summer of 1934, the Neihardt family actually returned to Pine Ridge and camped on Black Elk's land. The third "retraction letter" is dated September 20, 1934

[37] Wednesday, November 2, 1983, written by Charlotte A. Black Elk, who identifies herself as the great-granddaughter of Nicholas Black Elk. The English version of the letter is Charlotte Black Elk's translation.

[38] This was just after Joseph Epes Brown had spent several months with Black Elk's family, transcribing what would become *The Sacred Pipe*.

[39] Charlotte A. Black Elk, Letter to *Lakota times*, Wednesday, November 2, 1983.

[40] Copyright is asserted by Charlotte A. Black Elk as follows: "All rights re-

stand as a summing up of Black Elk's life and the conclusion of his thought. Black Elk notes that Joseph Brown has been living with his family and that they are writing a book together. He professes belief in Catholic doctrine as, he claims, do all his baptized children and grandchildren. But he relates the Catholic God directly to Wakan Tanka, about whom the Lakota have known all along. Though the Lakota do not "worship adore" Wakan Tanka, they recognize all of Wakan Tanka's creation as sacred, belonging to Wakan Tanka because he has touched it. Black Elk asks for the prayers of the Trappist and offers prayer to Wakan Tanka on the Trappist's behalf.

It is unfortunate that the letter cannot be cited, because it stands as an extended poem of great beauty. It is also a relating of Christian and Lakota traditions most nearly approached, perhaps, in Black Elk's "Foreword" to *The Sacred Pipe*. He writes there that:

> We have been told that Jesus the Christ was crucified, but that he shall come again at the Last Judgment, the end of this world or cycle. This I understand and know that it is true, but the white men should know that for the red people too, it was the will of *Wakan-Tanka*, the Great Spirit, that an animal turn itself into a two-legged person in order to bring the most holy pipe to His people....[41]

Black Elk was literate. He was dealing with texts, both reading them and writing them. He was, as an apologist, engaged in the interpretation and explanation of texts. The interpretation of sacred texts and the work of homiletics are theological acts. Black Elk was a theologian.[42] Walter Ong, S.J., in his already-mentioned *Orality and Literacy*, has made two points that are central to this assertion. First: "Literacy ... is absolutely necessary for the development not only of science but also of history, philosophy, explicative understanding of literature and of any art...."[43] And second: "Literacy can be used to reconstruct for ourselves

---

served. No part of this letter may be reproduced in any form or by any electronic or mechanical means without permission in writing from Charlotte A. Black Elk."

[41] *The Sacred Pipe*, xix.

[42] I have depended in part, for this argument on Paul Ricoeur's *Interpretation Theory*, already mentioned in footnote 12, supra. Other relevant essays include "What is a Text? Explanation and Understanding" and "The Model of the Text: Meaningful Action Considered as a Text," In *Idem, Hermeneutics and the Human Sciences*, ed. and trans. John B. Thompson (Cambridge: Cambridge University Press, 1981): 145-164, 197-221.

[43] Ong, *Orality and Literacy*, 15.

the pristine human consciousness which was not literate at all."[44] This is to say, then, that Black Elk could reflect upon an oral tradition, his own, from a literate perspective and that he could recover that oral tradition with the tools of literacy.

As already indicated, Black Elk had access to a number of texts in the Dakota and Lakota dialects. The Williamson-Riggs translation of the Bible was cited in Black Elk's 1889 letter to *Iapi Oaye*. The complete Dakota translation had appeared in 1880, though individual books had appeared much earlier. As well, in the earlier letter of 1888, Black Elk had "rejoiced greatly" to have received copies of *Iapi Oaye*, a periodical in the Siouan dialects, in Europe.[45]

As a catechist, Black Elk would have used the various editions of the Ravoux-Marty prayer book and subsequent catechisms. The earliest of these had been prepared by Rev., later Monsignor, Augustin Ravoux, a French missionary priest, and printed by him by hand at Prairie-du-Chien Wisconsin in 1843.[46] The Ravoux catechism was the basis for the later work by Jerome Hunt, O.S.B., and for Hunt's prayer and hymn book.[47]

---

[44] Ibid.

[45] In *Iapi Oaye* (March 1888): 9. Translation in DeMallie, *Sixth Grandfather*, 8.

[46] Mgr. Augustin Ravoux, *Wakantanka Tiki Chanku, or The Path to the House of God*. The first part of the book, "The History of our Holy Religion" would greatly influence later methods of catechesis. Ravoux outlined it as follows: Subjects: 1, God manifests himself to men by his works; 2, The creation; 3, The fall of our first parents into sin; 4, The deluge; 5, Moses and his great works; 6, The Son of God made man for our redemption and salvation; 7, His doctrines; 8, His miracles; 9, His passion and death on the cross; 10, The manifestations of his power, even at the moment of his death; 11, His resurrection; 12, He appears and speaks to his apostles; 13, The descent of the Holy Ghost upon the apostles; 14, The first Christians, their sufferings and their victory; 15, All men shall die; 16, The end of the world, the resurrection and the last judgment, followed by an eternity of happiness or sorrow, etc.
In Augustin Ravoux, *The Labors of Mgr. A. Ravoux among the Sioux or Dakota Indians, From the Fall of the Year 1841 to the Spring of 1844* (Saint Paul MN: Pioneer Press Company, 1897): 4. The remaining three parts of the book consisted of a catechism in questions and answers, the principal daily prayers, and a collection of canticles translated from French. Salvation history would become a principal instrument of catechesis among the Native Americans.

[47] Hunt taught Dakota/Lakota to the initial Jesuit missionaries in South Dakota, using the Ravoux catechism as a text. See Mary Claudia Duratschek, O.S.B., *Crusading Along Sioux Trails*, 133. See also Ross Enochs, S.J., *The Jesuit Mission to the Lakota Sioux: A Study of Pastoral Ministry, 1886-1945* (Kansas City MO: Sheed and Ward, 1996): 30. Hunt's initial version appeared some time around 1900: *Catechism, Prayers and Instructions in the Sioux Indian Language* [Translated under the Direction of Rev. Fr. Jerome Hunt, O.S.B.] (Cincinnati OH: Joseph Berning Printing Company, n.d.). The Imprimatur was given by Rt. Rev. John Shanley, Bishop of Fargo. Bishop Shanley had also given Imprimatur

Roy Rappaport has proposed a difference between the relative invariance of rituals in oral and literate cultures, given "the six or so generations since creation constituted by living memory in... illiterate societies."[48] An example of the problem might be found in the existence according to Paul B. Steinmetz, S.J., as already noted, of eleven versions of the story of the bringing of the sacred pipe to the Sioux. Commitment of all eleven to writing creates an obvious "synoptic problem." In an oral tradition, the Lakota could accept that they had emerged from beneath the Black Hills, rather than as migrants from the area of present-day Minnesota. As well, though the essentials of the Sun Dance ritual were more or less similar, according to various accounts, the meaning of the symbolism and the reasons for pledging the dance varied widely. Black Elk's later interpretation, in *The Sacred Pipe* reflected a reading of the ritual as a parallel to the crucifixion of Jesus, as a substitutionary sacrifice.[49]

Pursuit of the theological implications of Black Elk's literacy gives rise, *inter alia*, to three sorts of questions. First, does literacy make possible a theological approach that is not available to a pre-literate culture? In short, can systematics be done in the absence of written texts? Walter Ong's answer to this question would be categorically positive. Second, in Black Elk's case, can one discern a Euro-literate theology? Do the texts reflect a Christian apologetics, based on Christian theology? Third, is there then a possible theological approach to the Black Elk material from the standpoint of Christian theology?

Black Elk has left us two major bodies of text: The *Black Elk Speaks* transcriptions edited by DeMallie, and *The Sacred Pipe*. Though there is debate about how much of Neihardt went into *Black Elk Speaks*, *The Sacred Pipe* stands to Black Elk much as would a modern English

---

to Hunt's initial prayer book, entitled *Katholik Wocekiye Wowapi* [entitled on the cover as *Prayers, Instructions, and Hymns in the Sioux Indian Language*] (published by Rev Jerome Hunt, O.S.B., Fort Totten, N. Dak., 1899; "printed at the Catholic Indian Mission, Fort Totten, N. Dak."). A later edition, 1907, was advertised in *Sinasapa Wocekiye Taeyanpaha*, March 15, 1908: Supplement page, as containing: "Morning Prayers, Evening Prayers, Salve Regina, Prayer to St. Joseph, Memorare to St. Joseph, Short Prayers, Prayers during Mass, Ten Commandments, Prayers for Confession, Prayers for Holy Communion, Rosary, Short Prayers with Indulgences, Prayers for the sick and dying, Stations of the Cross, Gospels for Sundays, and 33 Hymns, old and new ones." MUA BCIM Series 14/1 Box 25, Folder 19.

[48] Roy A. Rappaport, *Ritual and Religion in the Making of Society* (Cambridge: Cambridge University Press, 1999): 444. Rappaport refers, in turn, to E.E. Evans-Pritchard, *The Nuer: A Description of the Modes of Livelihood and Political Institutions of a Nilotic People* (Oxford: Oxford University Press, 1940).

[49] *The Sacred Pipe*, 82: "I shall suffer and endure great pain ... in behalf of my people. In tears and suffering I shall .... offer up my body and soul that my people may live."

translation of the *Summa* to Saint Thomas, who dictated much of his compositions, or as would a modern translation to one of the Greek recensions of Mark. Though Joseph Brown, as *amanuensis* and editor, could not forbear to intrude examples drawn from his study of comparative religion, he made a point of parking them in footnotes.

Black Elk drew upon his extensive knowledge of Lakota tradition, knowledge which, as presented extensively in the Neihardt transcriptions edited by DeMallie, he would have gained in the process of becoming a *wicasa wakan* or Lakota holy man. As well as this oral tradition, he had also the European, propositional basis for regarding his work 'theologically.' Vine Deloria Jr. has claimed *Black Elk Speaks* as a work of theology; but the attribution is improbable, since *Black Elk Speaks* is less an interpretation than a narrative. Storytelling of this type is integral to an oral tradition. But it is *The Sacred Pipe* that stands, together with Black Elk's interpretive and theological asides in the text, as a work of liturgical theology. It is this interpretive bent that comes from Black Elk's familiarity with text-based apologetic, as in the case of the catechisms he used, or even the Ignatian exercises conducted with catechists by Placidus Sialm, S.J., at summer retreats. An example attributed to Black Elk follows:

> On one occasion a preacher asked him if he thought it right to honor the Blessed Virgin. The following dialogue took place. Black Elk asked him:
>
> > "Are the angels good people?"
> > "Yes."
> > "And St. Elizabeth, is she good?"
> > "Yes."
> > "And the Holy Ghost?"
> > "Yes.
> > "Well then if all these honored her, why should not I?"[50]

As early as the 1888 letter to *Iapi Oaye*, Black Elk, then in his twenties, indicated his interest in the white men's religion and in the moral distinction in practice between its tenets of belief and the behaviour of its adherents.[51] The 1889 letter, containing the citation of Saint Paul's 1 Corinthians and the application of the citation to the situation in which Black Elk found himself in Europe, suggests that he was able to

---

[50] Henry Ignatius Westropp, S. J., *In The Land of the Wigwam* (Pine Ridge SD: The Oglala Light Press, n.d.: 12. MUA HRM Series 7/1, Box 23, Folder 12. The pamphlet was written as a fundraising device, some time before 1916, when Fr. Westropp was posted to India.

[51] Black Elk, Letter to *Iapi Oaye* 17/3 (March, 1888): 9.

relate one culture to the other even at that early stage.[52] It also indicates that he not only had access to the Dakota translation of the Bible, but he could read it and quote it accurately, and that he could use it apologetically.

The articles which Black Elk wrote for the *Sinasapa Wocekiye Taeyanpaha* give evidence of a literate approach to the metaphorical and contextual relationships between the two religious traditions, Lakota and Catholic, though how much of this was Black Elk and how much was the adoption of Lakota terms by the missionaries may be uncertain. The fact that "God" was generally translated as "Wakan Tanka" suggests a mixing of concepts, however unintentional, since the former is the "creator" God while the latter is more like a "creative force." Nonetheless, his *Taeyanpaha* articles indicate that Black Elk was composing texts in which he applied Christian teachings to the situation of his addressees.

Black Elk's last known letter—there is no available manuscript—is set up as already mentioned, in Charlotte Black Elk's translation, in psalmodic or rhapsodic format. Parts of the text read like a series of psalms, even to the concluding ejaculations which were later included as standard affirmations in John Neihardt's *When the Tree Flowered*.[53] Black Elk was one of three principal informants on whose narratives Neihardt's later text was based. The interviews were conducted toward the end of 1944.

In the 1948 letter, Black Elk is careful to distinguish, for his "son" the difference between the Christian concept of "worship adore," which may be something written in response to a letter from his addressee, and the relationship of the Lakota to the sacredness of all creation. Yet he is clear that while one "speak[s] to what Wakan Tanka made in ceremony," this does not imply pantheism. Rather the sacredness of the created world lies in the fact that the creator [*Wakan Tanka*] made it, though it may be incorrect to see Wakan Tanka as creator God. This is reminiscent of the Catholic refutation of Protestant charges of "statue worship," charges that were part of the occasional, vitriolic slanging matches between Protestant and Catholic missionaries and communities during Black Elk's most active period as a catechist.

The two *Iapi Oaye* letters and the numerous articles in *Sinasapa Wocekiye Taeyanpaha* give evidence of Black Elk's familiarity with Euro-Christian concepts. The articles in the *Taeyanpaha*, after his conversion to Roman Catholicism give evidence of an understanding of Trinitarian concepts and a gift for apologetics, not to mention the style of logical argumentation noted above. Could he have done this without the stability of texts? It seems doubtful.

---

[52] Black Elk, Letter to *Iapi Oaye* 18/12 (December, 1889): 1
[53] John G. Neihardt, *When the Tree Flowered: The Story of Eagle Voice, a Sioux Indian* (new edition Lincoln NE: University of Nebraska Press, 1991): *passim*.

As to an appropriate theological approach to the Black Elk texts, it appears that, from the letters and reports to *The Sacred Pipe*, they reflect a contextual theology, much as described by Stephen B. Bevans and Robert J. Schreiter.[54] But in Black Elk's case, there appear to be two contexts—Lakota traditional and Euro-Christian. The first context is an oral tradition; the second is based on the interpretation of written texts. This intercontextuality results in an intertextuality within Black Elk's writings.

The case is, in conclusion, well established that Nicholas Black Elk is supremely undeserving of the "illiteracy" label. His literacy and his familiarity with Euro-American, as well as Native-American, tradition qualified Black Elk to undertake a form of apologetics involving an "intertextual" approach to the thought underlying what he wrote. A detailed examination of his major theological work, *The Sacred Pipe*, is beyond the scope of this study; but the letters and reports should provide sufficient indication of Black Elk's hermeneutic. Black Elk is an apologist: his works are in the theological realm of 'apologetics' or *propaganda fidei*. Black Elk's letters and articles represent a "crossover."[55]

The "peripheral" question initially posed remains: Why proclaim that Black Elk was unilingual and illiterate? One possible answer is that the legend arose accidentally. Black Elk spoke in Lakota to Neihardt and Brown through his son, Benjamin, who acted as translator. By 1931, in his late sixties and suffering from tuberculosis and partial blindness, Black Elk may have merely *seemed* unilingual and illiterate. The evidence for that inference was, however, purely circumstantial. Another possible answer is that the image of the illiterate country sage may have corresponded to a rather romantic image of their interlocutor which developed spontaneously in the minds of Neihardt and Brown.[56] Finally, it is worth noting again that Black Elk's Catholic defenders, chief among them Henry Westropp, S.J., and Black Elk's daughter, Lucy Looks Twice, both expressed some amazement that the old fellow had actually

---

[54] See Stephen B. Bevans, *Models of Contextual Theology* (Maryknoll NY: Orbis Books, 1992); Robert J. Schreiter, *Constructing Local Theologies* (Maryknoll NY: Orbis Books, 1985); and *Idem, The New Catholicity: Theology Between the Global and the Local* (Maryknoll NY: Orbis Books, 1997).

[55] See Rt. Rev. Steven Charleston, "From Medicine Man to Marx: The Coming Shift in Native Theology," in *Native American Religious Identity: Unforgotten Gods*: 157-172, ed. Jayce Weaver (Maryknoll NY: Orbis Books, 1998).

[56] Steltenkamp reports a personal communication from Brown, with regard to the absence of mention of Black Elk the catechist: "I have felt it improper that this phase of his life was never presented either by Neihardt or indeed by myself. I suppose somehow it was thought this Christian participation compromised his 'Indianness,' but I do not see it this way and think it time that the record was set straight." In Steltenkamp, *Black Elk, Holy Man of the Oglala*, xx.

learned to read somewhere along the way.[57]

Black Elk wrote, he read, and he dictated; and his *The Sacred Pipe* has become "the most widely read work on Plains Indian religion."[58]

---

[57] See again Henry Westropp, *In the Land of the Wigwam: Few Missionary Notes from the Pine Ridge reservation Printed Entirely by Sioux Indian Boys* (Pine Ridge SD: The Oglala Light Press, n.d., but composed prior to Westropp's departure in late winter, 1916): 12, "Though half blind he has by some hook or crook learned how to read and he knows his religion thoroughly." See also Michael F. Steltenkamp, S, J., *Black Elk, Holy Man of the Oglala* (Norman OK: University of Oklahoma Press, 1993): 56, "He had poor eyesight, but he learned to read Scripture and prayer books written in the Indian language."
[58] Åke Hultkranz, cited in Walter Holden Capps, ed., *Seeing with a Native Eye: Essays on Native American Religion* (New York: Harper Forum Books, 1976): 91.

CHRISTIAN AND NATIVE SPIRITUALITIES IN BRITISH COLUMBIA: THE HISTORIC STRUGGLE TO RESPECT DIVERSITY AND AMBIGUITY

Vincent J. McNally[*]

"Native...[spirituality is] looked at as pagan [by the Roman Catholic church]....The church gives lip service [to the great value of Native spirituality and] then goes back to the old ways. It's 'do it my way or no way at all.'" The words of Ralph Partida, a Native person and a member of the Native Spirituality Council of the diocese of San Bernardino, California express well the inability that Christianity has had, almost from its inception, of respecting spiritual diversity and ambiguity. Initially this occurred between Jewish Nazarenes, the first Christians, and their fellow Jews; next between Nazarenes and Gentile Christians; then between Christians and non-Jews or pagans; and finally, given this foundational history and its inability to deal with "the other," even among other Christians, since, as Augustine of Hippo noted, "heresy [read pluralism] has no rights." Thus in refusing to truly value, by usually paying no more than "lip service" to Native spirituality, most Christian churches, including the Roman Catholic church, are guilty of continuing a long and very sad tradition of rejecting spiritual ambiguity and diversity.[1]

The Christian Shadow and the Native People

Examining the institutional shadow of the Roman Catholic Church was one of the aims of the Second Vatican Council (1962-1965). "*The Declaration on the Relationship of the Church to Non-Christian Religions*," also known under the Latin title of "*Nostra Aetate*," though the shortest, was also one of the Council's most revolutionary documents. For the first time in its long history, the Roman Catholic church officially recognised

[*] The author has taught in the University of Dublin, Trinity College where he completed his Ph.D. as well as Birkbeck College, University of London and Simon Fraser University, British Columbia. He is presently professor of church history at Sacred Heart School of Theology in Wisconsin. He has published numerous articles and three books mainly in Canadian and Irish social and church history; his latest book, *The Lord's Distant Vineyard* (Edmonton: University of Alberta Press, 2000), is the first survey history of the Catholic church in British Columbia.
[1] *National Catholic Reporter*, February 2, 2001, 38.

not only the existence of, but far more importantly, the inherent value of other, non-Christian religions. While still maintaining the church's claim to contain the fullness of revealed truth through the revelation of Jesus Christ, *"Nostra Aetate"* at least declared that other religions "nevertheless often reflect a ray of that Truth which enlightens all...[people]."[2]

"Nostra Aetate" does not mention North American Native religion or spirituality by name, but it declared that from ancient times a "certain perception" of God has instilled in the lives of all people "a profound religious sense." In an historic precedent, it defended religious freedom, insisting that the Catholic church rejected "any discrimination against...[people] or harassment of them because of their race, color, condition of life, or religion." Yet, after admitting that the Catholic church had made mistakes in its relationship with other religions, sadly *"Nostra Aetate"* then urged "all to *forget the past* and to strive sincerely for mutual understanding." But how can such understanding be achieved if the past, and especially its shadow parts, are forgotten? For, as the philosopher, George Santayana noted, "progress, far from consisting in change, depends on retentiveness," and that "those who cannot remember the past are condemned to fulfill it."[3]

The First Immigrants and Their Spirituality

Crossing an ice shelf that then covered the Bering Strait, the first immigrants to the Americas apparently arrived from Siberia between 50,000 to 20,000 BCE, gradually moving south and southeast. During much of this period, most of far-western Canada (including British Columbia) was covered by the great Wisconsinian glaciation. This enormous glacier only began to recede about 9,000 BCE, allowing the first explorers to enter from what is now Alaska and the Yukon which ironically, due to its "milder" climate, had been inhabited as early as 20,000 BCE. By about 8,000 BCE, as the ice continued to disappear, human settlers moved into the region in greater numbers. Because of continuing glacial melting, the region which now comprises far-western Canada reached its present geographical configuration by 3,000 BCE.[4]

---

[2] Walter M. Abbot, Gen. Ed., *The Documents of Vatican II, With Notes and Comments by Catholic, Protestant and Orthodox Authorities* (New York: The American Press, 1966), 662.
[3] Ibid., pp. 661, 668, 663. Italics added; R.T.B., ed, *The Oxford Dictionary of Quotations*, Third Edition (Oxford: Oxford University Press, 1980), 414.
[4] R. Cole Harris, ed. *Historical Atlas of Canada*, (Toronto: University of Toronto Press, 1987), vol. 1, plates 1-2.

Over many millennia the first immigrants to the Americas developed as profound a sense of the spiritual as any other inhabitants on this planet, then or now. Certainly early French Oblate missionary ethnologists such as Émile Petitot and Adrien-Gabriel Morice attested to this fact, as well as to their great diversity. Both men remained inextricably tied to their western European and Christian prejudices; still, in their groundbreaking studies, which saw the myths of the Native people of Canada as proof that they were the "lost remnants of Israel now [finally] converted to Catholicism," both at least admitted a spiritual integrity in Native beliefs *almost* equal to their European Christian counterparts.[5]

After many years of dismissing Native culture as irrelevant, if not evil, today there is awareness, even among Christian leaders, that the Native people of North America already possessed a powerful spirituality long before any European contacts. Through it, they had as profound a sense of what was wise and good that was equal, if not sometimes superior to, the Europeans who would not only steal their land, but who would also try to destroy their culture.[6]

Such wisdom is evident in the advice of Chief Seattle to European immigrants recorded in the 1880s: "The white man must treat the beasts of this land as...[their] brothers and sisters....Every shining pine needle,...every mist in the dark woods,...every humming insect...is sacred. The sap which courses through the trees carries the memories of the red [people]....This shining water that moves in the streams and rivers is not just water but the very blood of our ancestors."[7] Perhaps in time the Europeans, among the latest immigrants to North America, will see more clearly the profound insight and contemporary wisdom in such words, somewhat ironically reflecting the spirituality of St. Francis of Assisi, as

---

[5] Ralph Maud, *A Guide to B.C. Indian Myth and Legend*, (Vancouver: Talonbooks 1982), 10-15.

[6] "The Aboriginal Peoples have developed over the centuries rich traditions founded on experiences relating to ecology, education, economics, political structures, as well as expressing different social and spiritual values. The wisdom contained in them could enrich our own culture. Their loss would mean our own impoverishment. Why go searching abroad for that which Native citizens are willing to share with us here at home?" *Island Catholic News*, April 1991, "Church Leaders' Statement of Pastoral Concern." Signed by Bishop Ronald Shephard of the Anglican Diocese of British Columbia, The Rev. William Howie, Moderator of the United Church of Canada and Bishop Remi J. De Roo of the Roman Catholic Diocese of Victoria.

[7] Matthew Fox, *A Spirituality Named Compassion* (Minneapolis: Winston Press, 1979), 164-165.

well as the importance of the culture of the peoples who first settled in far western Canada.

The spirituality or religious worldview of the Native people who formed the initial inhabitants of the area that would become British Columbia contained innumerable variations. The Coast Salish religious legends and myths differ significantly from those of the interior Kutenai. Even so, there were also basic similarities which demonstrated a definite regional syncretism as well as the apparent collective unconscious unity of all human spirituality. The Native people believed that the powers of all living things differed in degree, and that except for this fact, they were identical, sharing consciousness, culture, spirits and even physical forms. Native spirituality held that non-humans were capable both of assuming human form and of preying upon humans for food and for the spirits necessary for their continued existence. While residues of these beliefs continued, gradually (particularly through contact with other Native cultures, reflecting the Native ability to deal with ambiguity and diversity) new insights and patterns arose that recognised the strengths and weaknesses of all things and beings, human and non-human, and so developed the basic principle of reciprocity or mutual dependence with its cyclic view of history. Therefore, the Native peoples of the region, through their rich variety of myths and legends, did not consider humans as the dominant species. They believed that they shared their powers with other creature-spirits upon whom, through the performance of sacred rites of initiation and blessing, they likewise depended for their mutual well-being, ultimate survival and happiness, both here and hereafter. This view was not dissimilar from many mystery religions of the Hellenistic world which had a significant influence on the early development of Christian spirituality.[8]

The shamans or holy persons were the central figures in Native spirituality throughout the region. They could be a man or a woman, who, through a personal and triumphant experience with non-humans which was recognised by their community, had gained important power in the spirit world, and who represented the central human-divine force behind all Native spirituality. Though they could employ their power for evil as well as good, shamans were generally considered "helpers," and their power was usually employed to assist other humans. This would mainly consist of driving out evil forces, especially a physical or psycho-

---

[8] Maud, *A Guide*, passim.

logical illness that had inhabited the body and/or spirit of their client.

Shamanic power died with the individual, but certain powers could be passed on from one generation to the next and could be possessed by anyone. Among the coastal peoples these hereditary "gifts" from the spirit world were often embodied in crests, as on totem poles, in regalia or on longhouse facades. The crests explained how an ancestor acquired such powers and represented hereditary "deeds" to certain territories.

A major cultural activity among the coastal Natives that reinforced important communal events was the potlatch which had a profoundly spiritual character. Reflecting the bounty of nature, it was during the potlatch that hosts gave away much of their wealth to their guests and thus gained social and political prestige. Such celebrations were an extremely important means of maintaining tribal relations and marking important events such as puberty, marriage, and especially death. Belief in an after-life was universal among the Native people of far western Canada. Funeral rites were crucial in separating the dead from the realm of the living. Because the death of a principal elder was especially critical, his successor was expected to hold an elaborate series of potlatches before assuming his new authority. Marriage was also accompanied by such feasts and was contracted only by persons from a different clan or extended family group, since marriage within the clan was considered incestuous. Though polygamy was practised, it was a sign of high rank and was only permissible for those who were financially capable of supporting more than one wife. The potlatch also, by encouraging those who wished to lead to dispose of their wealth, set a standard and ideal that Christianity has espoused as well, but which it has very rarely realized throughout most of its history since it has been so tied to western culture that almost always rewards the acquisition and retention of wealth.

Spiritual powers, whether Shamanic or not, were always believed to be vulnerable to human error and injustice. The social order was reflected in the cosmic. The stability of both depended upon the protection of the moral order and the recognition that all life was sacred and interconnected.

Myth narratives, as in all cultures and religions, reflected on the problems, solutions and reasons of existence that then, as now, perplex humans everywhere. Raven, wolf, beaver, mosquito, frog, eagle, whale: the narratives employed the non-human as well as the human to teach the profound wisdom of past ages. Creation was a central story, and in every version stressed the integrity of all life.

All Native people borrowed and adapted the spiritual insights of their neighbours, enriching and developing their own spiritual under-standing. In fact, such borrowing continued among Native people of the region when they had their first contacts with Europeans in the late eighteenth and early nineteenth centuries, most notably with French Ca-nadian trappers, most of whom were Roman Catholic and provided them with their first contacts with Christian spirituality. This was reflected in their adaptation of such Christian ceremonies as baptism, confession, and even monogamous marriages. When faced with such realities, some of the early Christian missionaries reached the absurd conclusion that the only explanation for such similarities was that the Native people either constituted the lost tribe of Israel, or, like the Mormons, that Christ had actually visited the Americas and preached the gospels, but that the Na-tive people, due to their "sinful and wicked" spirituality, had "forgotten" that "event." Of course, the actual reason was the Native ability to adapt to spiritual ambiguity and diversity. However, Christians had long for-gotten their own early borrowing and adapting of non-Christian ideas from the Hellenistic world to enrich their spirituality. Thus missionaries could only explain such discoveries by fantasizing "miraculous" past events. Certainly, given their deep prejudices against all non-Christian spirituality, the missionaries could never even contemplate the fact that, in their inability to accept "the other" and their spirituality, they were violating the very gospel they preached; neither could they accept that Native spirituality, in being far more open to ambiguity and diversity in their respect for "the other's" spirituality, including Christianity, was ac-tually "more Christian," as reflected in the parable of the Good Samari-tan. Rather, many, if not most missionaries, believed that Native spiri-tuality was undoubtedly from the devil, since for them it could never contain "truth."[9]

North America: The "Promised Land" for Europeans

G.K. Chesterton's observation that Christian ideals have not been tried

---

[9] Ibid., *9-28*; John J. Cove & George F. MacDonald, eds. *Tsimshian Narratives I collected by Marius Barbeau & William Beynon* (Ottawa: Canadian Museum of Civilization, 1987), vi-xii; Mircea Eliade, *A History of Religious Ideas* (Chi-cago: University of Chicago, 1982), vol. 2, 277-281; George Clutesi, *Son of Raven, Son of Deer,*(Sidney, B.C.: Gray's Publishing Ltd., 1967), 9-14, 113-124; Marius Barbeau, *Totem Poles* 11.*According to Crests and Topics,* (Ottawa: National Museum of Canada, 1950), 1-12.

and found wanting, but rather that they have been "found difficult; and left untried" would certainly be one reason for the failure of relations between the Native and European peoples of Canada.[10] A central reason for this failure was that most Christian European settlers in North America believed that "truth" and God were on their side, and thus the Native people and their culture, especially their spirituality, were of little or no value, and certainly contained no "truth." In short, most Euro-Canadians and Euro-Americans, including the Oblates (who are here explored as major clerical exemplars of this attitude in British Columbia) viewed Native culture as essentially "meaningless," if not "evil."

Another important element in explaining this prejudice, including its accompanying racism, was, as noted, the European inability to live with either cultural ambiguity or diversity. Historically, the cultural foundation for this tragedy began no later than the early second century, for by then Christianity had created a long list of "out" groups, including Jews and pagans, as well as their fellow Christians or "heretics." This attitude was given state sanction to spread in the fourth century when, by the edict of Milan of 313, the Emperor Constantine I legally recognised the Christian church's right to exist. And within a century, the church had successfully "convinced" the Roman state, who by then already viewed religious uniformity as a vital foundation for its survival, that Christianity must become the sole imperial religion. By the sixth century, Christianity's status became a legal fact under the Justinian Code, which outlawed all other non-Christian religions in the empire, thus finally abandoning a religious pluralism that, until then, had been one of the great strengths of Roman civilisation. So in the interest of supposed social "harmony," state Christianity long ago destroyed the healthy religious diversity and ambiguity that for many centuries had been a major part of the cultural vigour of the ancient Hellenistic world. In fact, it was into such a religiously pluralistic world that Christianity had been born, and which its gospels, as in the parable of the Good Samaritan, appeared to both support and defend.

However, by the time of Constantine I (d. 337), Christian spirituality had long held that, under the "great law of divine right," it was the only "true religion." Therefore, they believed, that before the world could experience the long expected second-coming of Christ, all of its peoples must be converted to Christianity, even, if necessary, by force.

---

[10] *Oxford Dictionary of Quotations,* 148.

During its first five centuries of existence, the Fathers of the church, its earliest and most formative theologians, used as proof texts for Christianity's supposed superiority the Jewish scriptures that the Fathers now claimed as their own. Thus, Jewish scripture was now interpreted by the Fathers to prove that, through Jesus' coming, God had disinherited the Jews, since they had not only rejected their "true" Messiah, but had even "killed" God. Subsequently, they further theorized that God had thus elected Christians to be his "new chosen people." In so doing, Christianity laid the cultural foundation of western anti-Semitism, making the Jews the first in a long list of Christian-inspired "out" groups. When, centuries later, such a theory was applied to the Native peoples of the Americas, it concluded that "in fact," like ancient Israel's view of the Canaanites, the first immigrants to the Americas were actually in "wrongful possession" of these "new promised lands." And so the "Christian God" now demanded that, like the ancient Israelites, his "truly chosen Christian people," the European Canadians and Americans, should take, by whatever means necessary, "their promised land." As justification for the use of force, many, if not most, Europeans theorised that such was "required by the superior right of the white man...founded in the wisdom of God." In the secular realm, the father of Social Darwinism, Herbert Spencer's "law of progress," (commonly known as the "survival of the fittest") was cited as the central reason, and meant that "all opposition" must ultimately be "hushed in the perfect reign of the superior aggressive principle." In effect, a "manifest destiny," whether it was viewed as divine or human, had preordained that North America now, as *always,* belonged to the Europeans.[11]

The Oblates and Their Spirituality

The founder of the Oblates of Mary Immaculate, a French nobleman, Eugene de Mazenod (d. 1861) revealed very early and gave his stamp of approval to his Congregation's spirituality and philosophy of life, both of which were greatly influenced by an Augustinian theology of suffering, fatalism and original sin; that view was dominated by the image of a

---

[11] Jennifer Reid, *Myth, Symbol and Colonial Encounter,* (Ottawa: University of Ottawa Press, 1995), passim; Jaroslav Pelikan, *The Christian Tradition: A History of the Development of Doctrine: The Emergence of the Catholic Tradition (100-600),* (Chicago: University of Chicago Press, 1971), passim; Charles S. Bryant & Abel Much, *A History of the Great Massacre by the Sioux Indians in Minnesota,* (Cincinnati: Rickey and Carroll, 1864), 134.

vengeful God and which, in its extreme, viewed human free will as hopelessly destroyed by original sin and thus dependent upon grace-alone for its salvation, or in a word, Jansenism. In 1713 Rome officially (*Unigenitus*) condemned Jansenism as a serious heresy, along with its central theology of predestination. However, given the church's neo-Platonist inspired theology of an immutable-impassible God, who knows all and whose will controls all, though condemned in theory, in practice predestination (as reflected in Jansenism) remained a major, though unofficial explanation for all that was inexplicable. For example, Eugene convinced himself that his call to be a priest was divinely fated, and thus must be followed "under pain of damnation." Again, when his little community of former secular clergy was expelled from the diocese of Aix, probably due to their success in preaching parish missions, and thus stealing "souls" from other clergy, Mazenod's assistant and ultimate successor, Father François de Paule Henry Tempier, reflected his own Jansenistic view of the hopelessly fallen state of human nature and free will, and thus the absolute need for a divine grace which could only come through much suffering. Referring to the expulsion, he wrote: "Would that God would always treat us so!" But without doubt, the most extraordinary expression of this type of spirituality was occasioned by Eugene's nobleman uncle's insistence that he would only accept the bishopric of Marseilles on condition that his nephew and Tempier were willing to become his vicars general. In convincing his uncle to accept Marseilles, Eugene's central reason was to provide his young congregation with a "safe" base in France that would be free from the interference of other bishops. However, this development prompted the other members of the congregation to come to the obvious conclusion that Mazenod had used them to gain high church preferment, for, in fact, he would succeed his uncle as bishop of Marseilles in 1837. In reaction, Eugene called for a general meeting at which, after stripping to the waist, he proceeded to inflict "a bloody flagellation upon himself in the midst of the tears and sobs of all his sons." Immediately Eugene's "spiritual sons" swore to him that they would never again challenge their "spiritual father" who, like a latter-day messiah, had saved them and his congregation by the shedding of his own blood![12]

---

[12] Louis Dupré & Don E. Saliers, eds. *Christian Spirituality: Post Reformation and Modern* (New York: Crossroad, 1991), 126-130; Jean Leflon, *Eugene de Mazenod, Bishop of Marseilles and Founder of the Oblates of Mary Immaculate*, (New York: Fordham University Press, 1961) vol. I, 288-289; T. Rambert,

Some Oblate Methods for Converting the Native People

From the outset, the first superior of the Oblate Vicariate of British Columbia, Louis D'Herbomez (reflecting the usual dismissal of Native
spirituality as "unimportant" and/or even "evil") coupled a form of Jansenistic theology to his determination to separate their first Native "converts" on the mainland of British Columbia, the Stó:lô, members of the
coast Salish, from the local Euro-Canadian population, and turn their villages into reductions. The classic and most extreme examples of Mission
reductions were those operated by the Jesuits, especially in sixteenth and
seventeenth century Paraguay, where well over fifty such self-sup-
porting, church-centered and missionary-controlled villages were
founded. The governing principle of such reductions was that the Natives
could be converted to both Christianity and western civilization only if
they were isolated from their own former culture and such evil influences
of western civilization as drinking and gambling, or any contacts with
bad, immoral Europeans. Instead, they were subjected only to what the
missionary judged was "good" in western civilization. In short, in what
was a very paternalistic system, their Native "children" were expected to
learn what was ultimately "best" for them from their missionary "fathers."

　　　　Central to such a system was the destruction of the entire Native
culture, which almost all missionaries had generally always believed
promoted laziness and moral corruption. As such, heading the list of
those things that had to be destroyed was the "idolatrous" system of Native spirituality. Therefore, the Jesuits sought to turn the essentially nomadic Natives of Paraguay into model "western" Christian peasant
farmers who would be under the care of their "feudal" missionary priest
overlords. This strict, top-down constitution of absolute control, very
similar to that which would be practiced by the Oblates, is reflected in
the fact that no Native ever become a priest. As such, when in 1767 the
Jesuits were finally expelled from Latin America by the governments of
Portugal and Spain, lacking Native leaders, the reductions quickly disintegrated.[13]

OMI, *Vie de Monseigneur Charles-Joseph-Eugene de Mazenod, éveque de Mar-
seilles, fondateur de la Congrégation de Oblats de Marie Immaculée*, (Tours:
Romber, 1883.) vol. I, 250; Achille Rey, OMI, *Histoire de Monseigneur
Charles-Joseph-Eugene de Mazenod, éveque de Marseilles, fondateur de la
Congregation des Oblats de Marie Immaculée*. (Rome: General Postulation,
1928.) Vol. I, 319.

[13] Hubert Jedin ed., *History of the Church*, (New York: Crossroad, 1989), vol.

The Oblates in British Columbia adopted and adapted such methods, but they never achieved such extreme levels of control due mainly to Stó:lô proximity to European settlers as well as Stó:lô resistance, both direct and indirect, to such programs. On the other hand, the general concept of the reduction, especially its central element of total clerical control, formed more or less the basis of all Oblate Missions. Among the many tools that the Oblates employed to achieve such control were the public celebrations of feast days, especially Marian ones, as well as Eucharistic processions and other pageants.

Reflecting their Jansenistic spirituality which emphasized the "virtue" of suffering, the Oblates placed special stress upon Stó:lô participation in passion plays. By means of a series of tableaux that represented various stages in Christ's passion, a Native person portrayed Jesus "from Bethlehem to Calvary." According to one Euro-Canadian eyewitness account, rather than reflecting a morally strong Jesus who challenged the status quo, especially social injustice, a milquetoast portrayal of Christ seemed the norm, for all the Native persons selected for these roles were reported to be "strangely alike in face and figure; less sturdy than their companions,...with a plaintive, loving sweetness so well suited to the character they represented." Also in the final tableau, when the figure was naked except for a loin cloth, Christ was not played by a Native, but by a large crucifix on which was affixed a "white" European-featured statue. As such, it reflected what was true of most attempts by Europeans to acculturate Natives, namely, that "God" was "white." Thus, no matter how hard a non-European might try, a major implication of such an approach was that "non-whites" could never be truly equal to their new "masters." The Oblates, whether consciously or not, promoted racism.[14]

Each hoped-for reduction would also have a residential school which would become a major means of gaining cultural control, especially among the next generation of Stó:lô. Unlike day schools, which were never very successful because of very sporadic attendance, students at a residential school were ideally to be isolated from both Stó:lô and secular European influences. Besides Oblate spirituality, they were to learn manual skills and basic education. Nonetheless, while the Oblates

---

V, pp. 585-587; Ibid., vol. VI, 570.
[14] Frances Herring, *Among the People of British Columbia: Red, White, Yellow and Brown* (London: T. Fisher Unwin, 1903), 184-89; Keith Thor Carlson, ed., *You Are Asked to Witness: The Stó:lô in Canada's Pacific Coast History.* (Winnipeg: Hignell Printing Limited, 1997), 100.

would have liked nothing better than to duplicate such schools through-out the region, they could not afford to do so until the federal government began to finance them in the 1890s. While other denominations would participate as well, the Catholic church and the Oblates would become the major partners with Ottawa in making such institutions a reality throughout Canada, and British Columbia would have a major share of such institutions. Yet almost every method of acculturation, and especially the residential school, had its roots in the concept of the reduction which the Oblates tried to firmly establish on the local Stó:lô reserves.

In attempting to put the reduction into operation, one of the Oblate's most important teaching tools was the Catholic Ladder. Its inventor appears to have been Norbert Blanchet who, along with Modeste Demers, were the first Catholic missionaries in the region, and who saw its major potential as a Native catechetical instrument. The Ladder consisted of a chart painted or printed on cloth or paper, or carved into a Sahale stick (Chinook for "a stick from above"). At one end of the chart or stick were forty marks representing the forty centuries before Christ when, until Charles Darwin, it was believed that the world had been created or in 4004 BCE; then there were thirty-three marks standing for Christ's life, followed by eighteen marks each representing a century, plus marks for each year of the nineteenth century to the present. This simple and ingenious device was essentially a time line beginning with creation and continuing with the fall of the angels, Adam and Eve, the coming of Christ, and his death and resurrection. Completing the Ladder were the major events since the beginning of Catholic church history. The Ladder became an important instructional device, particularly during missions, and afterwards it would usually be taught to Native leaders, such as the Stó:lô shaman or *siam*, with the expectation that they would continue to impart its message.

The Ladder also intensified local sectarianism, dragging centuries-old European religious conflicts into the far west. For instance, printed versions of the Catholic Ladder referred to the Reformation by depicting Protestants, such as Luther and Calvin, being literally dragged down to hell. Protestants responded with an equally bigoted brand of the Ladder which, not surprisingly, reflecting their own spirituality, showed Roman Catholics, especially popes, being consigned to eternal flames. No doubt, when Native people compared both versions, this element of the Ladder must have seemed at least a strange, if not a humorous one, as well as a very graphic contradiction of the supposed Christian "love" for one another.[15]

The Ladder had played an important role in the earliest visits of Catholic missionaries to the Stó:lô. Norbert Blanchet first used it in 1839 in preaching a mission to the Whidby Island Salish, and in the following year he employed it in his only contacts with the Stó:lô. At that time he described several elements of Stó:lô culture, and, as usual among most missionaries, Blanchet judged the practice of polygamy, in Native culture considered a sign of social standing and added responsibility, as an "abomination." Of course such prejudices revealed more about Blanchet and his fellow missionaries, including the Oblates, than it did about the Stó:lô, exposing the strong dualistic and Gnostic elements in Christian spirituality, especially the frequent European obsession with "pelvic morality."

This incident was also important in that it was the first time that Catholic missionaries visited the mainland, prompted essentially by their fear that Protestants had already arrived. This was the central purpose of Blanchet's visit to the Stó:lô in 1840. In the following year, fearful that Presbyterians from the Walla Walla area intended to convert the Stó:lô to "heresy," Blanchet's missionary colleague, Modeste Demers again traveled there, though he discovered no "heretics." However, Demers reported that he preached in Chinook to about fifteen hundred Stó:lô at their summer camp near Fort Langley, presented them with the Catholic Ladder, sang several hymns in Chinook, baptized about four hundred infants, and finally taught them to make the sign of the cross. In 1842, in the face of similar rumors that the "heretics" were again on the march into New Caledonia, (the first name given to the mainland of what would become British Columbia) the Jesuit missionary, Peter DeSmet, visited the Stó:lô, though the Protestants were still nowhere to be seen.[16]

The Oblates, like Blanchet, Demers and DeSmet before them, believed that the Stó:lô, like all Native people, were essentially "hea-

---

[15] Philip M. Hanley, *History of the Catholic Ladder* (Fairfield, WA: Ye Galleon Press, 1993), passim; Karachi, *Blanchet Historical Sketches*, 83; Nellie B. Pipes, "The Protestant Ladder," *Oregon Historical Review*, XXXVII (1936): 237-240; Margaret Whitehead, "Christianity, a Matter of Choice: The Historic Role of Indian Catechists in Oregon and British Columbia," *Pacific Northwest Quarterly*, July 1981, volume 72, Number 3, 98-106.
[16] Edward J. Kowrach, *Historical Sketches of the Catholic Church in Oregon by Most Rev. Francis Norbert Blanchet*, (Fairfield, WA: Ye Galleon Press, 1983), 31-32, 41-42, 49; Denys Nelson, *Fort Langley 1827-1927* (Vancouver: Vancouver Art Historical and Scientific Association, 1927), 19-20.

then" because they did not believe in a Supreme Being, which, as noted, was not true, nor since they did not accept such western, Hellenistic concepts as the soul, "mortal" sin, or salvation through Christ. Demonstrating his culture prejudice, D'Herbomez was also convinced that, before he could convert them, he had to first civilise the Stó:lô, whom he initially described as "savage hordes whose many vices degraded human nature." To do this, he hoped to establish among the Stó:lô a "model reduction" that would include both schools and a hospital, so that they might ultimately become both "good" Catholics and "good" Canadians.[17]

In achieving their aim, which by implication meant the ultimate destruction of Stó:lô culture, including their spirituality, the Oblates definitely had at least some understanding of that culture. For instance, in preaching early missions, the Oblates apparently hoped to enhance their position and gain respect and spiritual power among the Stó:lô. Thus, they tried to convince their listeners that they too were shamans or *siams* whose Christian God, or "the great one from on high" in Chinook, had far greater power than the Stó:lô spirits, whom the Oblates tried to convince their Native audience were all "demons," objectives which the priests also attempted to accomplish through the use of Oblate hymns and other Catholic rites. To communicate these ideas to their audience, the Oblates used Chinook and French, which was then "translated" by Saanich interpreters, another member of the Coast Salish. Since these interpreters spoke a dialect quite different than the Stó:lô, much of the meaning of what the Oblates were trying to teach was undoubtedly lost on their hearers. As they had and would do in all their Native Missions in Canada and the United States, in the interval between missionary contacts, the Oblates appointed Stó:lô men as catechists and/or watchmen who were expected to lead regular prayer services and teach their tribe by using such tools as the Catholic Ladder. They were also expected to report any lapsed participants to the priest whenever they were able to visit. Such reporting was especially important for those who wished to be baptised.[18]

---

[17] Missions de la Congrégation Des Missionaires Oblats De Marie Immaculée (hereafter *Missions*), 1, (1862), 93-111, D'Herbomez Report, 1861, 101, 183-84.
[18] Archives (OMI) Deschâtelets, Ottawa, Canada (hereafter AD) , PB 179. P47 R. 1, Regulations for the operation of Missions (1864), no place indicated, but probably New Westminster; Margaret Whitehead, "Now Your Are My Brother: Missionaries in British Columbia," *Sound Heritage Series*, Number 34 (Victoria: Provincial Archives of British Columbia, 1981), 34. Jacqueline Gresko, "Missionary Acculturation Programs in British Columbia," *Études Oblates,* vol.

Like other Christian missionaries, the Oblates baptised Native infants immediately, since they frequently died soon afterwards, mainly through contracting European diseases such as smallpox, often from the very missionaries who had baptised them. However, this was not true of Stó:lô adults. Like Saanich adults, the only Stó:lô who could receive baptism were those who, for at least a year, had kept their temperance pledges, were clearly following the directives of the Oblate appointed Native watchmen and/or catechists, and who were giving good example by publicly performing daily prayers. This was not an Oblate innovation, but had been considered prudent Catholic missionary practice for centuries in order to avoid the "superficial" Christianization of the Native people. However, given the propaganda value of the "numbers game," it was often practiced more as the exception than the rule. Nevertheless their founder, Mazenod, took such a practice very seriously, and it was certainly the recommendation of the Oblate Canonical Visitor to the region, François-Xavier Bermond, who, in 1858, suggested that "the longer the wait the better." Bermond believed that a year should be the absolute minimum preparation for the baptism of Native adults, and at least a second year should pass before their reception of first communion.[19]

A key element in the early Oblate ministry to the Stó:lô, as it had been to the Saanich and other Natives in British Columbia, was the establishment and maintenance of temperance societies. At the large annual reunions, or whenever the opportunity presented itself, there were meetings at which a missionary preached and Natives made bold public declarations of abstinence and equally open admissions of failure. Most Europeans, including the Oblates, believed that Natives, because of "their childlike nature," were more "easily led astray by unprincipled [white] men;" thus, it was assumed that they possessed a weaker moral character, reflected in their supposed "heathen spirituality" which led them to "more naturally" succumb to the "vile drink" than would "whites." While "public shaming" was a traditional method of moral control and betterment in Stó:lô as well as other local Native cultures, it was based on individual responsibility and was never intended to deliberately patronize and humiliate, a central element of the Oblate tem-

---

32, (1973), 145-158.
[19] Jedin, *History of the Church*, vol. V, 577-78; Paul Drouin, ed. *Les Oblats de Marie Immaculée en Oregon 1847-1860.*(Ottawa: Archives Deschâtelets, 1992) vol. III, 796-802. (Hereafter *Les Oblats*) François-Xavier Bermond, Report on Missions, 17 September 1858.

perance agenda. Like a parent punishing their disobedient child, the idea
of public confession and public penance represented a major means of
shaming those who had fallen, and of teaching those who had not the
consequences of failure. Again, as Jansenist spirituality insisted, all suffering was not only a sign of God's love, but an essential to true spiritual
growth. The Oblates, Demers and Blanchet had all used such methods,
including the appointment of a watchman, often a shaman or *siam*, to
maintain surveillance over everyone between meetings and to report any
lapses to the priest. Those "converted" to temperance after a communal
pledge were given a "ticket" that symbolized their commitment and
which, in a public shaming, would be ceremoniously taken from them if
they failed to keep their promise.[20]

The task of the watchman, who often doubled as a catechist, was
essential to the maintenance of a temperance society. Not only did they
report to the priest regarding those who had "fallen," but, even more importantly, they were expected to conduct daily morning and evening
prayer services and special services on Sunday. If they were *siams*, the
watchmen already held a superior position; but the major task of whom-
ever filled the role was to represent the priest and report to him all "sins"
upon his next visit, so they would provide the Oblate missionary with a
method of control of a Stó:lô group between visits. Besides drinking, a
vigilant watchman might also report adultery, failure to repay debts,
gambling and especially resorting to *siams*, which the Oblates saw as a
"very serious" sin, since it meant that Native spirituality had not yet been
crushed. As well as public humiliations, sinners were also fined money
or some other penalty at special "trials" presided over by the *siam* and/or
watchman, but, reflecting the paternalistic nature of the traditional reduction, whose "verdicts" were under the final control of the priest.[21]

---

[20] *Les Oblats,* vol. III, 796-802. Bermond, Report on the Missions, 17 September 1858; Herring, *Among the People of British Columbia,* p. 163; *Rapport sur
les Missions de Diocese du Quebec quo sont secourues par l'association de la
Propagation de la foi* (Quebec: Diocese du Quebec, 1820-72) (hereafter *Rapport*), no. 6, (July 1845): 34. Speaks of the first temperance society founded by
Blanchet and Demers in the Willamette River Mission in a letter: Blanchet to
Signay, 4 March 1843.

[21] *Les Oblats,* vol. III, 796-802, Bermond, Report on the Missions, 17 September
1858. Spells out the need to appoint "chiefs" to be the watchmen so as to keep
up "religious living" during a priest's absence as well as the use of trial, public
confession and payment of fines which could then be used to help support the
mission. ; *Missions,* 1 (1862): 121-129. Durieu to Mazenod, 1 September 1860.
Reports on his use of watchmen to also guard against "sorcerers."

Clearly, good behaviour for the reception of baptism went well beyond only temperance and required a whole new life style similar to the Jesuit-inspired reductions of Latin America, which were now to be replicated in British Columbia. This was to mirror both western and "Catholic" ways, including the renunciation of polygamy, refusing marriages with Europeans that had not been blessed by the Catholic church, and, apparently the most serious of all, calling upon a *siam* in time of illness. All were part of a continually growing Oblate list of requirements of what it meant to be a "good" Canadian, and, far more importantly, a "good" Native Catholic. In fact, even consulting with elders as teachers of traditional Native ways was viewed as practicing superstition, and so the Oblates considered such behaviour to be serious and sinful. Over time, farming as the Oblates did, "proper" Sunday dress, and even living in European-style homes were added to the list of acculturation to "white" ways. [22]

The Oblates constantly struggled to expand upon the ways western "Catholic" culture and its spirituality could be imposed upon or translated into Stó:lô culture. For instance, as with other tribes, the Oblates tried to "translate" Stó:lô into a combination of Chinook Jargon combined with either French or English prayers and hymns that were then printed in Roman-lettered transliterations. Easter and Christmas celebrations, as well as summer reunions, reflecting the times of traditional Stó:lô gatherings, usually twice a year in the late spring and early summer, were celebrated with great festivity at the central Mission of St. Mary's near New Westminster; reportedly such celebrations brought out large numbers of Native peoples. At this time catechism lessons were given, and those Stó:lô who had been judged faithful by the Oblates for at least a year were baptised. This was also considered "good example," so that others present would ultimately want to follow the example of these new Christians. In addition, these gatherings were used to administer the smallpox vaccine, especially to the children. [23]

In 1869, a Sister of St. Ann, Mary Lumena Brasseur, described one of these large meetings. The Stó:lô *siams* along with their entourage

---

[22] *Les Oblats*, Vol. III, 796-802. François-Xavier Bermond, Report on Missions, 17 September 1858; *Missions* 1, (1862): 101; *Missions*, 3 (1864): 207; *Missions* 9 (1870): 133; *Missions*, 12 (1874): 318; *Missions* 28 (1890); *Missions*, 50 (1912): 168, 173.

[23] *Missions* 4 (1865): 265-269, 326-330; John Webster Grant, *Moon of Wintertime: Missionaries and the Indians of Canada in Encounter since 1534* (Toronto: University of Toronto Press, 1984), 119-142.

arrived at St. Mary's Mission by boat, each group being greeted with salutes of gunfire, and then proceeding in a more or less formal procession towards the church. When they reached the front of the church, they first shook hands with each other and then entered the building for a brief time, where D'Herbomez and other Oblates welcomed them with more handshaking. After the opening ceremony, sufficient tents were erected on the grounds to hold upwards of two thousand people. In pre-contact times, such gatherings would have been major reflections of Native spirituality and would have been devoted to commemorating important natural or community events, such as the inauguration of a new *siam*, and which, like other tribes of the northwest coast, would have centered on potlatching. Under the Oblates, such "superstitions" had now given way to Catholic celebrations such as Corpus Christi processions and passion plays.[24]

In trying to achieve their objectives, the Oblates also demonstrated the effects upon themselves of their own, largely negative spirituality that placed such great emphasis on the "virtue" of suffering. As the years passed, the Oblates, then the overwhelmingly dominant clergy on the mainland of British Columbia, were continuously challenged to spread themselves more and more thinly among their growing and complex ministry: serving the Native peoples, the growing European population, attending to diocesan responsibilities, managing the needs of their farms, and fulfilling their individual spiritual duties. As their voluminous correspondence demonstrates, wherever they chose to concentrate their energies, they would regret the time taken from other activities. The need for more Oblate clergy in British Columbia also coincided with the Franco-Prussian war (1870-71), which in France had increased the demand for military chaplains and promoted nationalism, thus lessening the desire of many French Oblates to serve in the foreign missions. Given their very strained resources, especially in personnel, which was further compounded by their spirituality of Jansenistic perfectionism and "silent suffering" which encouraged denial and lack of communication, the Oblates discovered that there was no truly satisfactory solution to any of these problems.[25]

---

[24] Archives of the Sisters of St Ann, Victoria, BC (Hereafter ASSA), Mary Lumena MS: "A Sketch of Mission City" (c.1869-72) Ff. 20-26.
[25] AD, P 1497-1498, D'Herbomez to Fabre, 17 October 1870; Ibid., P 2437-2440, Fabre to D'Herbomez, 6 November 1870; Ibid., P 2441-2444, Fabre to D'Herbomez, 10 December 1870; Ibid., P 2445-2447, Fabre to Herbomez, 2 March 1871.

As in other missions, the frequent change in staff often reflected disagreements and resulting stresses, and thus a transfer was the only solution; it was a fact that highlighted an inherent instability in the Oblate method of assignments, encouraged greatly by their spirituality. Part of the problem lay in the fact that it was an extremely paternalistic system, grounded in a form of blind obedience and the willingness to suffer in silence. Therefore, superiors such as D'Herbomez frequently referred to priests under them as "my child" or "my son," while Oblate subordinates, whether priests or brothers, often addressed him as "your most obedient child." Superiors expected and usually received instant compliance from subordinates who were expected to "sacrifice themselves" and their needs to the will of their "spiritual father." Such a dysfunctional system was not designed to address interpersonal problems, which were further compounded by the fact, that, being men, Oblates were very unlikely to share in any intimate way with each other. Thus, personnel and personal problems were most often allowed to fester, increasingly undermining morale; these either led to yet another reassignment or, worse, through suppression, further poisoned staff relations. And while a handful of Oblates did leave the Congregation, again, their Jansenistic spirituality constituted a major barrier, for Jansenism demanded that one must always follow the will of the superior and not one's own will, corrupted, as it was assumed, by original sin. Since a good Oblate was supposed to believe that the will of his superior was indeed the will of God, to question it was to question God, and even possibly to endanger one's personal salvation. Consequently, such distorted spirituality which practically celebrated the need for suffering tended to encourage a terrible shame in anyone who would "abandon" their vocation, especially for such a "minor" reason as personal happiness. The Native people, however, were not as docile in their own compliance with Oblate demands.[26]

---

[26] AD, P 3745-3748, Jayol to D'Herbomez, 10 March 1865. Complains of problems with staff and Europeans; Ibid., P 3772-3779. Jayol to D'Herbomez, 3 November 1865. Senses that he is unable to cope with problems, and asks to be discharged; Ibid., P 17-18, Boudre to D'Herbomez, 7 September 2866. Asks to be able to stay in his room and say Mass; Ibid. P 3029-3034. Gendre to D'Herbomez, 5 February 1867. Troubled with lay brothers and terrible alcoholism among Europeans and Natives; Ibid., P 3041-3044, Gendre to D'Herbomez, 26 May 1867. Speaks of problems with others; Ibid., P 6828-6835, Richard to D'Herbomez, 16 March 1868. Asks for advice on how to resolve differences; Ibid., P 6836-6839, Richard to D'Herbomez, 25 May 1868. Pain from resulting differences and divisions in community; Ibid., PP 3094-3097, Gendre to D'Herbomez, 17 September 1868. Difficulties, trying to take responsibility;

Despite Oblate insistence that the Native people actually welcomed such interference and even oppression, Natives did fight back, though until very recently, their opposition was largely ignored by most Oblates and other Euro-Canadians as a case of not knowing what was truly best for them, namely, the forced imposition of western civilization, which always included Christianity. By the 1890s, when the federal government began to fund the residential schools, thus greatly increasing their numbers, this also meant that both church and state now insisted that "for their own good," Native children must be educated there, even if this resulted in the forcible removal from their families. The aboriginals of British Columbia had lost their land, their traditional government, their dependence on nature, or, in short, their entire culture, including their spirituality; now they were being told that they must also lose their children. It was too much for most. One result was that, initially, the schools only attracted a very small number of students. Certainly the Native people resented the strict atmosphere and the often brutal discipline which the Oblates and religious sisters, who educated Native girls, judged as only "necessary suffering" on the way to becoming "good Catholic" and "good Canadian" adults. Again, such a policy reflected a repressively Jansenistic spirituality which, as noted, had an obsession with pelvic morality. Based on the constant fear of and supposed terribly inherent "evil" in "sexual misbehavior," it also insisted upon the total separation of boys and girls, which usually only heightened the very problem it was intended to resolve.

While some graduates would later express positive feelings regarding their time at residential schools, most felt otherwise. Frustrated, lonely and even angry, students expressed their opposition in the only way they could: they ran away. By 1900, the problem had reached epidemic proportions in most schools, especially during the summer months when they were forced to remain at the school; the result was that over fifty percent would leave and not return. And reflecting their own frustration over such repressive state-financed systems, Native parents supported, and even encouraged, such behaviour, for they were rarely

---

Ibid., P 574-575,Brother Joseph Buchman to D'Herbomez, 11 October 1868. Complains of Gendre; Ibid., D'Herbomez to Pandosy, 11 October 1868. Stresses need for harmony with Gendre; Ibid. P 572-573, Buchman and Brother Guilllet to D'Herbomez, 24 March 1869. "Your most obedient child," instead of "servant," was a frequent usage among the Oblates when addressing superiors, especially bishops.

prepared to return runaways.[27]

Conclusion

Why did the Oblates and other Christians have such a difficult time respecting Native culture and spirituality? Much of the problem seems to center upon essential worldview, personality and spirituality differences between most of the clergy and the Native people. About seventy per cent of all clergy, Catholic or otherwise, "fall within...authoritarian personality types": that is, they tend to see reality in "black and white categories," which also reflects a largely negative mentality that "my way of thinking and doing is the only right way." Instead of looking "within" to the unconscious, which has so much to teach the conscience mind in the formation of a healthy conscience, this personality type puts most "trust in externalised and dogmatised formulas" espoused by church authorities. However, largely because of their spirituality and its openness to ambiguity and diversity, Native people tend to operate out of an "egalitarian personality" type which is "highly intuitive" and thinks in "both abstract and realistic ways." Thus, Native spirituality is grounded in service, particularly in looking at, listening to and learning from the other instead of trying to dominate and control them. Yet, the authoritarian personality type that influences mainly negative, uncritical thinking, and is so evident among most clergy, prefers to "play God" rather than allow "God to be God." In the end, however, as expressed in the Native shaman tradition, the only hope for the "white" missionary who wishes to "succeed" must be their willingness to be chosen and accepted by the Native people to whom they must be "present." They must then allow the Spirit and the Native people to determine what form that "presence" will take. As such, if it is ever to be realized, any Native Roman Catholic church will depend upon the ability of its clergy to abandon an "assimilationist framework" and move into one of "effective interaction" with those who see the gospel, as did Jesus, not as a weapon to control and subjugate other cultures and their spirituality, but "as a source of liberation and fulfillment." Instead, under the control of the "authoritarian personality type," most Oblates and other clergy in their ministry to the Native people did not, nor do they now, spread the gospel-- the "good news"--but rather, a form of denominational triumphalism for which

---

[27] Margaret Whitehead, *The Cariboo Mission: A History of the Oblates.* (Victoria: Sono Nis Press, 1981), 114, 122-125.

there is no real future in Canadian society. [28]

In August 1994, the Archbishop of Milwaukee, Rembert Weakland, OSB spoke to the Catholic bishops of Canada regarding the future of religious life in the church. He noted that the increasing disappearance of both men and women religious is a "weather vane" indicating that "the old order is passing away for the [Catholic] church and for how the church relates to the world." Like nationalism, especially as it is presently evolving in the European Union, rigid denominationalism is also "passing away," just as Catholicism and the Oblates in their *"present triumphalistic form"* have "no future." Nevertheless, perhaps nowhere is the path towards that future better expressed than in the hoped-for Oblate relationship with the Native people. Particularly as it was enunciated in their public *Apology* of 1991 to the Native people of Canada (in which the Oblates stated their genuine desire to form "a renewed covenant of solidarity" with the Native people) if realized, could become a model for them and the Catholic church in their service, not only to the Native people, but ultimately to all Canadians. [29]

Most Euro-Canadians, as well as Euro-Americans, still believe that they have little or nothing to learn from Native culture; however, many are beginning to realize that this is not true. For example, everyone has much to gain by abandoning a Judeo-Christian inspired linear and usually greed and consumption-driven view of history which, especially over the last fifty years, has had much to do with leading us all towards an increasingly likely global ecological catastrophe. Instead, there is a great need to move in the direction of a cyclical worldview which is still part of Native tradition, and which sees an integrity, wholeness and interdependency in all life; as such, it is an essential concept for ecological survival. Through mutual respect, and by looking, listening and learning, we all have much to gain from each other, for no culture has all the answers.

---

[28] Jerry A. Prazma, OMI, "The North American Indians and the Missionaries: From the Lessons of the Past, a Hope for the Future," (Master of Spirituality Thesis: Gonzaga University, 1989), 24-33; Achiel Peelman, "A Native Church for Today and Tomorrow," *Native Ministry Seminar – St Peter's Province, Galilee Community, Arnprior, Ontario* (Ottawa: Saint Paul's University, 1988), 5.
[29] Wayne Holst, "Revisiting Our Past: Revisioning Our Future, Reflections on the Next 150 Years of Missionary Activity in Canada," *Western Canadian Oblate Studies 4/Ètudes Oblates de l'Ouest* 4 (1994): 194-201; Doug Crosby, "Canadian Oblates' Statement: An Apology to Native People," *Origins* 15 (August 1991), 183-84.

Despite the long efforts of Euro-Canadians to destroy it, aboriginal spirituality never completely died. Though damaged by many years of European prejudice, which then prompted Native neglect and conscious and unconscious repression, Native religious rites and ceremonies of the far west have survived. In fact, in the last few decades Native spirituality has made a remarkable recovery and has attracted a reasonably large number of Native participants. Whether or not Christian spirituality benefits from an honest and open dialogue with Native spirituality, probably Native spirituality's greatest contemporary role is in helping to safeguard Native cultural identity and with it, individual Native self-respect.[30]

Franz Boas, the father of North American cultural anthropology, did some of his earliest fieldwork studying the Native cultures on the west coast of Vancouver Island. Boas believed that, with the gradual "increase in knowledge," all peoples would free themselves from their "traditional fetters" and experience an "emancipation from...[their] own culture," developing a greater appreciation of and respect for other cultures and their spiritualities, while enhancing their knowledge and appreciation of their own culture. In the ever-increasing globalisation of the planet, both Western European civilisation and Christianity have much to learn and gain from other cultures and religions, and this would certainly include Native spirituality, especially as reflected in its inherent respect for diversity and ambiguity. Certainly no culture or spirituality can continue to insist that it contains the only truth. [31]

---

[30] Ibid., *9-28*; John J. Cove & George F. MacDonald, eds. *Tsimshian Narratives I collected by Marius Barbeau & William Beynon* (Ottawa: Canadian Museum of Civilization, 1987), vi-xii; Mircea Eliade, *A History of Religious Ideas* (Chicago: University of Chicago, 1982), vol. 2, 277-281; George Clutesi, *Son of Raven, Son of Deer,*(Sidney, B.C.: Gray's Publishing Ltd., 1967), 9-14, 113-124; Marius Barbeau, *Totem Poles* 11.*According to Crests and Topics,* (Ottawa: National Museum of Canada, 1950), 1-12.

[31] Franz Boas, *Material for the Study of the Inheritance in Man.* (New York: Columbia University Press, 1928), 202, 235.

J.J. ENMEGAHBOWH AND THE CHRISTIAN ANISHINAABEG OF WHITE EARTH

Lawrence T. Martin[*]

In a recent issue of *Oshkaabewis*, an Ojibwe studies journal, Anton Treuer, an Anishinaabe scholar from Leech Lake, discussed the various proposed meanings of the word Ojibwe. Probably the most widely-held view connects the name to the notion of "puckering," whether of the lips, the style of moccasins, or something else. Without dismissing that possibility, Treuer finds also "highly plausible" Helen Tanner's alternative explanation, which derives the word Ojibwe from the Ojibwe practice of writing with pictographs on birchbark.[1] In support of this view, Treuer points to the word *ozhibii'ige* which means "he writes."[2]

If this explanation is correct, there is certainly a fittingness about the name, not only because of the traditional Ojibwe use of pictographs on birchbark scrolls, but also because the Ojibwe have excelled as writers, making use of cultural borrowings like the alphabet and the printing press. In the introduction to an anthology of work by Ojibwe writers, Gerald Vizenor was able to say that "the Ojibwe claim more published writers than any other tribe on this continent."[3]

In the first half of the nineteenth century, there was a group of Christianized Anishinaabeg in what is now Eastern Ontario. They had been converted by Methodist missionaries, and several of these Ojibwe converts themselves became missionaries to their fellow Anishinaabeg. Some of them also wrote and published a significant body of literature,

---

[*] An enrolled member of the Lac Courte Oreilles Band of the Lake Superior Chippewa, Dr. Martin is Director of American Indian Studies at UW Eau Claire and an English Professor who teaches American Indian Studies courses in literature and language. His major research interests are Ojibwe oral tradition and missionary linguistics. His special focus as a linguist (Ph.D., University of Wisconsin, 1977) and as a tribal member is to preserve American Indian languages by creating American Indian language courses at UW-Eau Claire and offering seminars on language teaching in the Wisconsin Indian communities.
[1] Helen H. Tanner, *Atlas of Great Lakes Indian History* (Norman, Oklahoma: University of Oklahoma Press, 1987), 4.
[2] Anton Treuer, "What's in a Name: The Meaning of Ojibwe," in *Oshkaabewis Native Journal*, Vol. 2, no. 1, (1995): 40.
[3] Gerald Vizenor, *Touchwood: A Collection of Ojibway Prose*, (Minneapolis: New Rivers Press, 1987), v.

mostly in English, but some in Ojibwe. The most well-known members of this Christianized Ojibwe literary movement were Peter Jones and George Copway, though the group included several more native writers as well.[4]

A relatively unknown member of the same group of Christianized Ojibwe from eastern Ontario was John Johnson Enmegahbowh, who signs his letters "J.J. Enmegahbowh." He differs from people like Peter Jones and George Copway in several ways. First, he spent his adult life far away from eastern Ontario, in what would become the state of Minnesota. Second, he left the Methodists and became an Episcopal missionary (or, more accurately, the Methodists abandoned him, a point to which I will return). Third, although he shared the literary aspirations of Jones and Copway, he actually published only a couple of short pieces, and these had a fairly limited circulation. The body of Enmegahbowh's unpublished work is, however, quite large. It is chiefly in the form of letters, though some of them are memoirs in epistolary form. His letters are mostly to be found in the collections in the Minnesota History Center library. They have been mined for historical information by a few historians,[5] but to my knowledge no one has approached Enmegahbowh's writings for their own sake. The present essay will provide an introduction to Enmegahbowh as a literary figure and a religious leader of the Christianized Anishinaabeg of nineteenth-century Minnesota.

Enmegahbowh was born around 1812, and he spent his early years among the Rice Lake band of Mississauga Ojibwe, north of Lake Ontario. In 1826-1827, Peter Jones, who had only recently been converted himself to the Methodist faith, as well as several other Ojibwe converts, visited the Rice Lake community to share the gospel with their fellow Anishinabeg.[6] Within a few years, most of the Rice Lake band

---

[4] Penny Petrone, *Native Literatures in Canada from the Oral Tradition to the Present* (Toronto: Oxford University Press, 1990), 35.

[5] Rebecca Kugel, *To Be the Main Leaders of our People: A History of Minnesota Ojibwe Politics, 1825-1898* (East Lansing: Michigan State University Press, 1998); Michael D. McNally, *Ojibwe Singers: Hymns, Grief, and a Native Culture in Motion* (New York: Oxford University Press, 2000); Melissa L. Meyer, *The White Earth Tragedy: Ethnicity and Dispossession at a Minnesota Anishinaabe Reservation* (Lincoln: University of Nebraska Press, 1994).

[6] Peter Jones, *Life and Journals of Kah-ke-wa-quo-na-by (Rev. Peter Jones), Wesleyan Missionary* (Toronto: Anson Green, 1860), 76-78; George Copway, *Life, Letters and Speeches*, A. LaVonne Brown Ruoff and Donald B. Smith, eds. (Lincoln: University of Nebraska Press, 1997), 93-99. Originally published in 1850 as *The Life, Letters and Speeches of Kah-ge-ga-gah-bowh, or G. Copway,*

had become Christians, and a school was established under the supervision of Rev. James Evans.[7] In one of his published works, Enmegahbowh tells how his father and mother were persuaded by Mr. Evans to allow young Enmegahbowh to make the long journey to Sault Ste. Marie to serve as interpreter for a missionary there and at other locations in upper Michigan, including the mission established by John Sunday at L'Anse on Keweenaw Bay.[8] From there he was sent, in the company of his cousin George Copway and Peter Markman, another Ojibwe convert, to establish a Methodist mission among those Enmegahbowh refers to as "still wilder Indians" at Lac Courte Oreilles in what is now northern Wisconsin.[9] The mission at Lac Courte Oreilles was not successful, and, after one winter, Copway, Markman, and Enmegahbowh were sent for further education to Ebenezer Manual Labor School in Illinois. They spent two years there, and then each of them was assigned to a different mission station in the Anishinaabe country of the western Great Lakes.[10]

Enmegahbowh was sent to establish a mission at Sandy Lake on the upper Mississippi River. An important fur trading post was located there, and the Presbyterians had attempted to start a mission, but it had been abandoned. Enmegahbowh arrived at Sandy Lake in 1840, and he spent most of the next decade there or in the vicinity. During this time he was ordained a Methodist deacon under the name John Johnson.[11] During this time he married a niece of the famous Ojibwe chief Bugonogezhig (Hole-in-the-day). She was baptized with the name Charlotte.[12] In 1849, Enmegahbowh's wife was in some way insulted or perhaps assaulted by a white man. Enmegahbowh "knocked the scoundrel down and held him while his wife gave the worthless scoundrel a sound threshing."[13] This resulted in the expulsion of Enmegabowh and his wife from the Method-

---

Chief Ojibway Nation (New York: S.W. Benedict); Donald B. Smith, *Sacred Feathers: The Reverend Peter Jones (Kahkewaquonaby) and the Mississauga Indians* (Toronto: University of Toronto Press, 1987), 95-96.

[7] Leroy Jackson, "Enmegahbowh—A Chippewa Missionary," in *Collections of the North Dakota Historical Society* (1908), 4.

[8] J.J. Enmegahbowh, "The Story of Enmegahbowh's Life," published as an appendix to Henry Benjamin Whipple's *Light and Shadows of a Long Episcopate* (New York: MacMillan, 1900; first printing 1899), 498-500.

[9] Ibid., 500.

[10] Jackson, 5-7.

[11] Owanah Anderson, *400 Years: Anglican/Episcopal Missions among American Indians* (Cincinatti: Forward Movement Publications, 1997), 47.

[12] Enmegahbowh, "The Story of Enmegahbowh's Life," 502-503.

[13] Anderson, 47.

ist church, even though Samuel Spates, Enmegahbowh's non-Indian associate at the Sandy Lake mission, supported Enmegahbowh in the case.[14]

The Methodists' loss was the Episcopalians' gain. After his expulsion, Enmegahbowh joined Hole-in-the-Day's band at Gull Lake, but sometime in 1850 or 1851 he happened to visit Fort Snelling, at the conjunction of the Minnesota and Mississippi Rivers, the present location of St. Paul. There he met an Episcopal army chaplain, who told him about an Episcopal mission and school established at St. Paul by Rev. Lloyd Breck. Enmegahbowh brought his young son to Breck to be educated, a meeting which "would change forever the course of Episcopal ministry among American Indians."[15] A year later, in 1852, Breck and Enmegahbowh together established at Gull Lake the mission of St. John's-in-the-Wilderness, later renamed St. Columba's, "the mother mission of Episcopal Indian work west of the Mississippi River."[16] In 1858 Breck founded Seabury Divinity School in Fairibault, Minnesota, and Enmegahbowh was left to run the Gull Lake mission by himself, being ordained an Episcopal deacon in 1859.[17]

Later the same year, Henry Benjamin Whipple was consecrated the first Episcopal bishop of Minnesota. Whipple "awakened the Episcopal Church to a social consciousness about Indian affairs,"[18] and he advocated on behalf of Indians against a corrupt Office of Indian Affairs. Today some of Whipple's views on Indian issues seem condescending, paternalistic, and assimilationist, but at his time he was unusual among churchmen for his untiring zeal on behalf of justice for Indian people. He also strongly favored the idea of native clergy, and in 1867 he ordained Enmegahbowh, the first American Indian to become an Episcopal priest.[19] Whipple and Enmegahbowh remained close friends for the rest of their lives—Whipple died in 1901 and Enmegahbowh a year later. A large percentage of Enmegahbowh's surviving writings are letters to the bishop which are now in the Whipple papers at the Minnesota History Center. Whipple also seems to have encouraged Enmegahbowh to write epistolary memoirs with the intention of having them published.

Enmegahbowh's fifty-year ministry to his fellow Indians in

---

[14] Jackson, 10.
[15] Anderson, 46.
[16] Ibid., 48.
[17] Ibid., 50.
[18] Ibid.
[19] Ibid., 62-63.

northern Minnesota is documented in his letters to Bishop Whipple as well as assorted other letters. It is not possible in the limited space available here to offer even a sketchy summary of that long ministry. Instead I will merely describe a pair of significant events in which Enmegahbowh played an important role which he describes in his letters.

1862 is an extremely important date in Minnesota Indian history, because it is the year of the "Great Sioux Uprising." Disgusted by the U.S. government's failure to carry out its treaty promises, a group of Dakota warriors in southern Minnesota, led by Little Crow, attacked the Redwood Agency and several other white settlements. The Indian warriors achieved some initial victories, but ultimately the uprising was put down with a vengeance by a large army under the command of Colonel Henry Sibley, and a military tribunal sentenced 307 Indians to be hanged. Bishop Whipple, facing violent white hostility, intervened with President Abraham Lincoln, who ruled that those Indian warriors who had merely fought in battle should be treated as prisoners of war. Nevertheless, on December 26, 1862, thirty-eight Indian warriors were hanged at Mankato, the largest mass hanging ever in the United States.

Although the Sioux Uprising was confined to the Dakota people of southern Minnesota, according to Enmegahbow the Ojibwe chief Hole-in-the-Day (the Younger) planned to join the uprising and massacre white settlers near Gull Lake.[20] In one of his letters to Bishop Whipple, Enmegahbowh tells how he thwarted Hole-in-the-Day's plans:

> The war spirit had been growing for a long time. Little Crow, a Sioux Chief and warrior, had sent secret messages to Hole-in-the-Day, urging him to take up arms against the whites and commence a general warfare, for there never was a better time, he said, as nearly all the soldiers from the interior forts had been taken away to fight the South [in the Civil War]. He took up the cause and was preparing to enter into it with full determination. He had summoned warriors from the interior Chippeways. When I heard that he was first to attack the little settlement of whites at the Agency, I prepared my family to start to Crow Wing secretly. At midnight we were ready and started with an ox-team. The Indians soon

---

[20] Kugel, 77.

missed us, and followed us. They overtook us between Crow Wing and Gull Lake and made us turn back. We had to do it. When the genuine war-whoop was heard resounding through these borders, what did the white deacons and priests do? Why, when a second war whoop was heard echoing through the borders, they took to their heels in disguise and left for country for the safety congenial to their cowardly spirits. Poor Enmegahbowh was left alone to do the best he could by himself. Hot times came, and when he with his poor family took flight to a place of safety, he was overtaken and compelled to return home and await his destiny. When the warriors unfurled their weapons of war to go upon the journey of massacre, I had already sent word to the settlers to make ready for an attack, and taking another flight I made good my escape to Fort Ripley.[21]

The hostility of white settlers in Minnesota sparked by the events of 1862 resulted in federal legislation that abrogated all Dakota treaties in Minnesota and expelled the Dakota from the state. A proposal was made to deport all Minnesota Indians, but the Ojibwe escaped deportation partly through Whipple's pleas to powers in Washington, and partly perhaps because of the gratitude of some white settlers to Enmegahbowh for foiling Hole-in-the-Day's plans.[22]

The second "Indian uprising" in which Enmegahbowh had a hand was of a very different sort. In 1867 a treaty was made that was designed to move all the Mississippi bands of the Ojibwe to a newly-created reservation at White Earth. Many Indian people opposed the move, and Hole-in-the-Day was particularly opposed, saying that he would shoot the first Indian who left his village for White Earth. Hole-in-the-Day was particularly determined that Enmegahbowh not move to White Earth. However, some of the sub-leaders of the Gull Lake band defied Hole-in-the-Day and made the move. Enmegahbowh was also able to move to White Earth after Hole-in-the-Day was assassinated in 1868. Four years later, Bishop Whipple sent Joseph Gilfillan to supervise the White Earth mission and to open new Indian missions in other loca-

---

[21] J.J. Enmegahbowh, "Letter to Rt. Rev. H.B. Whipple," undated, Minnesota History Center, Whipple Papers, Box 33.
[22] Anderson, 62.

tions. Later, Gilfillan was named the first Archdeacon for the Indians. Enmegahbowh and Gilfillan perhaps got along at first, and Enmegahbowh is said to have taught his superior the Ojibwe language.[23] Eventually, however, Enmegahbowh came to resent Gilfillan's paternalistic and authoritarian style, and the letters of both men to Bishop Whipple reveal growing tension over the years.

Enmegahbowh was not the only one who had a problem with Gilfillan. Whipple ordained a cadre of Ojibwe deacons, who were instructed by Gilfillan and Enmegahbowh. Each of the deacons was assigned to lead one of the satellite congregations of the White Earth mission. The native deacons developed a distinctively Anishinaabe orientation that came into conflict with Gilfillan's assimilationist aims, and the tensions came to a head in 1882, when the deacons went on strike for better wages, equal treatment with white missionaries, and the ouster of Gilfillan. Enmegahbowh sided with the deacons and gathered the native clergy in a closed session. Whipple did not agree to fire Gilfillan, but he did triple the deacons' salaries. Gilfillan's authoritarian style continued to grate, however, and three years later Enmegahbowh and the native deacons issued a call "to throw overboard all white people connected with the mission."[24]

I have not found many of Enmegahbowh's letters from this difficult period, and the letters I have found make no reference to the troubles. However, in a long epistolary memoir sent to Bishop Whipple in 1900, shortly before both Whipple and Enmehahbowh died, Enmegahbowh makes no secret of the fact that he found Gilfillan very high-handed and hard to take. In addition, there is one interesting letter from the time of the deacons' strike that may be indirectly related to the strike. It is a letter from Enmegahbowh to David Knickerbacker, an Episcopal rector in Minneapolis, concerning a proposed stained-glass window picturing Samuel Madison, an Indian deacon who died at Red Lake three years before. One cannot help but wonder whether displaying a cooperative dead Indian deacon was not a way for some church authorities to comment on the rebellious living Indian deacons of the time. Enmegahbowh makes no direct reference to the deacons' strike, but in characteristically Anishinaabe manner, he tells a story that calls into question the wisdom of the proposed portrait. The story is a sort of ghost story about moving Samuel Madison's body from Red Lake to White Earth for

---

[23] Ibid., 69.
[24] McNally, 100, quoting a letter of Gilfillan to Bishop Whipple.

burial:

> Mr. Beaulieu when bringing down the corpse to White
> Earth, Beaulieu said every night [he] heard noise[s] and
> rap[s from] inside of the coffin and the third and fourth
> nights [he] had to take the corpse some distance [away ,]
> that he was afraid to have it lay near his camp.....The
> Indians are naturally too superstitious for everything.
> Hence they do not want it [i.e., a picture of Samuel
> Madison] before them....Had you proposed a memorial
> window for our noblest chief Washburn, the chiefs and
> the whole settlement would have been pleased.[25]

Many of Enmegahbowh's letters are purely practical in content,
concerned with various aspects of missionary life. However, some of his
letters, particularly those I have referred to as epistolary memoirs, reveal
a literary impulse that perhaps originated with his youthful conversion by
the native Methodists of eastern Ontario like Peter Jones and others for
whom the Christian religion went hand in hand with writing and publishing. Perhaps the years that Enmegahbowh spent with his cousin George
Copway in northern Wisconsin and then at school in Illinois further inspired him to emulate his literary cousin. Finally, his friend Bishop
Whipple seems to have encouraged Enmegahbowh to write about his
life.

As far as I know, only two of Enmegahbowh's literary efforts
were published. In 1874, *The Church and the Indians*, a publication of
the office of the Indian Commission of the Episcopal church, included a
seven-page account by Enmegahbowh of the death of Chief Na-bun-a-
skong (Isaac Tuttle), who first led the Gull Lake band of Ojibwe to
White Earth in defiance of Hole-in-the-Day's opposition. Enmegahbowh's account is in the form of a letter, dated White Earth Reservation, Minnesota, January 13, 1874. It is addressed to an unidentified
clergyman, "Rev. and Dear Sir," and it begins with an interesting statement that seems to reflect Enmegahbowh's roots in Ojibwe oral tradition:

---

[25] J.J. Enmegahbowh, "Letter to David B. Knickerbacker, Jan. 17, 1883," Minnesota History Center, Whipple Papers, Box 16.

"Permit me to have a little talk with you in the way of writing."[26] The letter is concerned with Tuttle's initial resistance to conversion, then his acceptance of Christianity, and finally with his pious death. Much of the letter is in the form of dialogue between Tuttle and Enmegahbowh. For example: "But, my friend," I said, "there is a far better and more efficient way to defend your people, without your war-club and scalping knife. It is to have Missionary to tell you about the GREAT SPIRIT, to teach you how to worship Him, and, when you die, go to *ish pe ming*."[27] Tuttle responds to this by telling a story about a Christianized Indian who, upon his death, is allowed to enter neither the Christian's heaven or the traditional Indian's great Hunting Ground,[28] a story which is still part of the oral tradition of the Midewiwin.

Enmegahbowh's other published work is a fourteen-page memoir titled "The Story of Enmegahbowh's Life," printed as an appendix in Bishop Whipple's autobiography, *Light and Shadows of a Long Episcopate,* which was published in 1899, three years before Enmegahbowh's death. This memoir also has a vestige of epistolary form. It does not begin as a letter, but near the end we find a passage of direct address to Bishop Whipple, as well as the closing "Yours truly, J.J. Enmegahbowh." The first part of this memoir deals with the early events of Enmegahbowh's life, up to the time of his arrival in Minnesota. The second part tells about his marriage to Hole-in-the-Day's niece and his promise to her family that he would not take her back to Canada. Feelings of inadequacy and discouragement with his early efforts at missionizing the Minnesota Ojibwe led him, however, to go back on this promise, and he and his wife set off to journey back to Enmegahbowh's home in Canada. He tells this story by relating his experience to that of the prophet Jonah, drawing many parallels to the biblical story. Jonah in fact appears to Enmegahbowh speaking to him about the parallel course of their lives. It is at this point that Enmegahbowh reminds us that we are reading a letter:

> Dear Bishop, I know you will not understand me to say
> that I saw Jonah with my natural eyesight. Oh, no, I saw

---

[26] J.J. Enmegahbowh, "Letter from Rev. J.J. Enmegahbowh: The Death of Chief I.H. Tuttle," in *The Church and the Indians,* Office of the Indian Commission, Protestant Episcopal Church, New York (1874): 1.
[27] Ibid., 2.
[28] Ibid., 2-3.

him with my imagination. What is your great Milton's fiery lake, what the exquisite scenes of his paradise save the products of imagination?

I am persuaded that the pale faces would say that the Indian races have no imagination. If there were time, I would give you instances of the power of imagination among the most noted chiefs, warriors, and Grand Medicine-men.[29]

Among Bishop Whipple's papers there is a collection of four lengthy epistolary memoirs by Enmegahbowh, done in the same style as "The Story of Enmegahbowh's Life" printed in Whipple's book, but these four memoirs concern other phases of Enmegahbowh's life. Especially interesting is a portion of one of the letters which chronicles Enmegahbowh's troubles with his over-bearing white supervisor, Rev. Joseph Gilfillan.

All four of these epistolary memoirs are addressed to Bishop Whipple, and all but one are signed "J.J. Enmegahbowh." Two are dated, both in 1900 (one in July and the other in October). Despite the signatures, the handwriting does not seem to be that of Enmegahbowh. However, the rather flowery style is similar to that of a long letter written by Enmegahbowh to Whipple shortly before this time, in which he apologizes for his bad handwriting, which he attributes to his rheumatism.[30] Therefore it seems likely that, because of his difficulty with handwriting in his old age, Enmegahbowh dictated the four epistolary memoirs to an amanuensis. However, both the ideas and the language in these memoirs are essentially his own, and they are extremely interesting because they provide an unusual example of a nineteenth-century Christian Ojibwe writing reflectively, and also with a good deal of charm and humor, about his long life in the service of the gospel in the woods of northern Minnesota.

---

[29] Enmegahbowh, "The Story of Enmegahbowh's Life," 509.
[30] J.J. Enmegahbowh, "Letter to H. B. Whipple, Dec. 1, 1898," Minnesota History Center, Whipple Papers, Box 25.

TRUE CONFESSIONS: THE OJIBWA, BISHOP BARAGA AND THE SACRAMENT OF PENANCE

Michael M. Pomedli[*]

In the more than 500 years of contact between Europeans/post-Europeans and Aboriginal peoples, European approaches have been predominant. In this article I demonstrate a different interaction, namely, Ojibwa influences on a European clergyman. I argue that the Ojibwa changed some of the perspectives of Frederick Baraga, priest and bishop. The medium that transformed this cleric was auricular confession. In this sacramental exchange, the Ojibwa revealed their unique perspectives and their true selves. They disclosed, cumulatively, their linguistic idioms and their spiritual dispositions.

First, I will examine the original formative influences on Frederick Baraga and then the gradual transformative influences of the Ojibwa on him.

Frederick Baraga, civil lawyer and Roman Catholic cleric, spent 37 years (1831-1868) as "Apostle of the Lakelands" among the Ojibwa in an 80,000 square-mile triangular territory. This territory included areas of Minnesota, Wisconsin, Michigan, and Ontario.

The spiritual formation of Baraga in Austria and in his native Slovenia was important for him personally and for his mission work. During his studies at the University of Vienna, Baraga met and became one of the penitents of Redemptorist Clement Mary Hofbauer, the "Apostle of Vienna."[1] Later, in Ljubljana Seminary and during his seven

---

[*] Michael M. Pomedli, PhD, professor of philosophy at St. Thomas More College, University of Saskatchewan, Saskatoon, Saskatchewan, Canada, has a background in theology, phenomenology, and journalism; his specialty is Aboriginal thinking and treaty-making. He is the author of the following books: *Ethnophilosophical and Ethnolinguistic Perspectives on the Huron Indian Soul* and *William Kurelek's Huronia Mission Paintings*. He also translated and edited *Ojibwa Powwow World* by Dr. Sylvie Berbaum. He has published scholarly articles in many journals including *The American Indian Quarterly, American Indian Culture and Research Journal,* and *Laval théologique et philosophique.* Recipient of a Rockefeller Fellowship in the Native Philosophy Project, he has made many presentations at national and international scholarly conferences on topics such as Treaty Number Three, Aboriginal peoples and Christianity, and animals and the Midewiwin Healing Society.
[1] C. Wolfsgruber, "The Austro-Hungarian Monarchy," in *The Catholic Encyclopedia* (New York: Robert Appleton, 1907), 2:129. On Hofbauer's influence in

years of parish work in Slovenia, Baraga cultivated in part the spirituality of the 15th-century pietists called *devotio moderna,* a spirituality which spread through many parts of Europe and was embodied in *The Imitation of Christ.*[2] Baraga displayed aspects of this spirituality in his missionary work, including such practices as ensuring lucid instructional texts in the vernacular and leading a simple Christian life. In the spirit of the founder of the Redemptorists, Alphonsus Liguori, and that of Hofbauer, Baraga took to heart the spreading of the gospel to the poorest and most neglected in the world.[3]

Liguori had distanced himself from the ascetic Jansenistic, intellectualized and cold Christian lifestyle to embrace a warmer, more tender and personal piety[4] which sought a balance between rigor and laxity.[5] Other aspects of *devotio moderna,* which Baraga embraced and incorporated into his celebration of the sacrament of penance, include: a Christocentric approach emphasizing the humanity and virtues of Christ; a devotion to the Eucharist and the passion of Christ; a striving for perfection, that is, self-knowledge and the fulfillment of duties; the promotion of

Europe, see J. Magnier, "Clement Mary Hofbauer," in *The Catholic Encyclopedia* (New York: Robert Appleton, 1907), 2:44-45. On the direct influence of Hofbauer on Baraga, see Baraga's letter to Pope Pius IX, A0803, German, Sault Ste. Marie, MI, Oct. 25, 1865. Letters are from the Bishop Baraga Archives, Marquette, Michigan. Thanks to Elizabeth Delene, archivist, Ojibwa, Bishop Baraga Archives, Marquette, MI, for her helpful informative assistance, to Lawrence Martin, Ojibwa, University of Wisconsin Eau Claire, for encouragement, to Joan Halmo, University of Saskatchewan, Saskatoon, for discerning revision suggestions, to Stephen Pomedli, for diligent research assistance, to Rev. Achiel Peelman, OMI, Saint Paul University, Ottawa, for helpful comments, and to Msgr. Louis Cappo, Marquette, for gracious hospitality during my stay in Marquette.

[2] Graham A. MacDonald, "Baraga, a Habsburg Prelate in the New World," *The Beaver,* 74 (1994): 5-6.

[3] MacDonald, 6. The following instructional and devotional manual displays a likeness with Baraga's life, his sacramental ministry, and his writings: *The Mission Book: A Manual of Instructions and Prayers adapted to preserve the Fruits of the Mission drawn chiefly from the Works of St. Alphonsus Liguori* (New York: D. and J. Sadlier, 1858). This manual contains prayers and devotions both for preparing for confession, and for the act of confession, and prayers for contrition, and after confession. It gives details on the necessity to confess, the manner and frequency, and the practice of general confession.

[4] Frederick M. Jones, *Alphonsus de Liguori, the Saint of Bourbon Naples, 1696-1787* (Westminster, Maryland: Christian Classics, 1992), 291-292.

[5] Théodule Rey-Mermet, *Alphonsus Liguori, Tireless Worker for the Most Abandoned,* Jehanne-Marie Marchesi, trans. (New York: New York City Press, 1989), 465.

self-denial and efforts of the will, and the reading of the Bible both for edification and devotion.[6]

In Baraga's estimation, one of his most important and time-consuming missionary activities was "hearing confessions." The sacrament of penance along with the Eucharist became for him, as it was for Liguori and Hofbauer, an eminent means toward a devout Christian life.

Baraga, the Ojibwa, and Penance

First, let us examine in greater detail, Baraga's experiences of the sacrament of penance in an Aboriginal and missionary context. For Baraga, the confessional provided a unique source of factual information and knowledge about the affective dispositions of the Ojibwa.[7] From the confessional he derived a working knowledge of the penitents' and the community's character, a true confession! Already in Slovenia, the young priest had prized this sacrament, for he heard confessions late into the night and also very early in the morning. This traffic of penitents, "some of whom came from afar," and "were waiting at his confessional"[8] and outside the church created a disturbance and raised some protest from the other priests in the parish.[9]

Baraga continued this practice of marathon confessions with Aboriginal peoples soon after his arrival in L'Anse, Michigan. In 1831, before he mastered the Ojibwa language, Baraga used an interpreter to hear confessions, an interlocutor both the penitent and the priest trusted. (Many times, he heard confessions in the dark, an Ojibwa preference.)[10] Later, in 1837, he wrote in New York, on returning from Europe, that he heard "very many confessions" in German, and at Sault Ste. Marie, "I

---

[6] R. Garcia-Villoslada, "Devotio Moderna," in *New Catholic Encyclopedia* (New York: McGraw-Hill, 1967), 4:831. For tenets of the *devotio* which pertain to Baraga, see John Van Engen, *Devotio Moderna, Basic Writings* (New York: Paulist Press, 1988), 9, 10, 16, 25.

[7] Thanks to Rev. Charles Principe, CSB, University of St. Michael's College, Toronto, for this general insight.

[8] Joseph Gregorich, *The Apostle of the Chippewas, the Life Story of the Most Rev. Frederick Baraga the First Bishop of Marquette* (Chicago: The Bishop Baraga Association, 1932), 20.

[9] Regis Walling, "Bishop Baraga as a Model of Evangelization," *The Baraga Bulletin,* 46 (1992): 6. As a tribute to Baraga, his confessional in Metlika, Slovenia, is preserved in his memory; Regis Walling, "Positio of the Virtues of Bishop Frederic Baraga," unpublished manuscript, 1997, Bishop Baraga Archives, 106.

[10] Letter, A0438, German, Arbre Croche, Michigan, from Baraga to Leopoldine Society, Aug. 22, 1831.

have heard very many confessions, especially in English and Indian. The Indians now generally know that I speak the Indian language and they like to go to confession and they also like to make a general confession to me because they can express and reveal themselves correctly because they do not need an interpreter."[11]

Baraga had pastoral reasons for encouraging frequent confession. One reason was his role as pastor. Even when he had other duties ["a collision of duties," he writes], he felt obligated to "allow the Indians to visit me, [for] I am their father and counselor."[12] Another reason for the frequent celebration of penance was theological and spiritual. By means of the sacramental absolution of sins, penitents could achieve a closer union with God. In addition, Baraga considered himself the beneficiary of the sacrament, an "ineffable grace" of God,[13] which provided an indulgence both for priest and penitent.[14]

Baraga's approach to the sacrament of confession was in marked contrast to that of the Jansenists who gave absolution rather rarely and often prohibited the reception of communion. Instead, Baraga encouraged the frequent reception of both, for confession before communion and communion itself assured Natives that God loved and forgave them.[15] He also saw confessions as a means of preserving people from sin.

Baraga regarded confession as a consolation. As bishop he

---

[11] Letter, A0420, German, Sault Ste. Marie, Michigan, from Baraga to Amalia Gressel, Sept. 28, 1837.

[12] Maksimiljan Jezernik, *Frederick Baraga, a Portrait of the First Bishop of Marquette Based on the Archives of the Congregatio de Propaganda Fide* (New York: Studia Slovenica, 1968), 79, n.70. The term for penance in general use today in Roman Catholic theology is Sacrament of Reconciliation.

[13] Walling, "Positio," 105.

[14] References to confessions in Baraga's diary note that many people came "because of the plenary indulgences;" Regis M. Walling and N. Daniel Rupp, *The Diary of Bishop Frederic Baraga, First Bishop of Marquette, Michigan* (Detroit: Wayne State University, 1990), Dec. 13, 1856, 100. According to Henry Davis, "an indulgence is a remission of temporal punishment due to forgiven sin. . . .A plenary indulgence remits all the temporal punishment, that is, as the intention of the Church is concerned;" *Moral and Pastoral Theology, a Summary* (London: Sheed and Ward, 1952), 323. For a history of the development of indulgences and their controversy, see Bernhard Poshmann, *Penance and the Anointing of the Sick,* Francis Courtney, trans. (New York: Herder and Herder, 1964), 210-232.

[15] Letter, B0631, Slovenian, Rev. George Kallan, St. Martin's Parish, Kranj, Slovenia, to Bishop Anton Wolf, diocese of Ljubljana, April 21, 1828. Kallan criticized Baraga's "exaggerated zeal for confession."

wrote: "I know the Indians; I have spent 23 years among them, and I would still be among them if Providence had not called me to another place. But even now I am not entirely free of the Indians, and will not be as long as I live. At the Sault I have many Indians, all of whom come to me for confessions; and wherever I come on my visitations, I hear Indian confessions."[16]

He commented on how frequently he heard confessions. "The pagans [Aboriginal people] like very much to come to confession, and always more frequently," with 20-30 confessions on a single day and very few mortal sins![17] At L'Anse he wrote: "My dear children were very happy, for their sincere desire, to see me as a bishop, had been fulfilled. Here I remained 12 days.... [A]lmost all came to confession."[18] Confessions continued sometimes until 11:30 pm,[19] sometimes all day,[20] and at other times, 10 hours a day.[21]

He devoted himself to the confessional often at the expense of taking care of his personal needs. "I am so occupied with hearing confessions that I scarcely find time to eat, and for the necessary sleep."[22] He wrote that some "confession days" were so hot that the "candles melted."[23] On another occasion he heard confessions "all day" and "suffered much from constipation!"[24]

Baraga's approach to confession and its necessity reflects in part his theological formation and the theology of the early 19th century. This theology was contained in the diocesan statutes which, according to Regis Walling, offered "missionaries wise and prudent instruction for hearing confessions. Not only was the sacrament to forgive sin; it was also to encourage the practice of the virtue contrary to the sin, e.g., the avari-

---

[16] Letter, A0123, German, Cincinnati, OH, from Baraga to Leopoldine Society, Aug. 4, 1863.

[17] Letters, A0576, German, Arbre Croche, from Baraga to Amalia Gressel, March 8, 1832; A0433, German, Arbre Croche, Baraga to Leopoldine Society, March 10, 1832.

[18] Letter, A0114, Slovenian, from Baraga to the Slovenian people, Sault Ste. Marie, MI, Oct. 12, 1854.

[19] Letter, A0687, German, Sault Ste. Marie, from Baraga to *Wahrheitsfreund*, 21 (1858) 690, July 22.

[20] Letter, A0675, German, Sault Ste. Marie, from Baraga to *Wahrheitsfreund*, 23 (1860) 559, July 4.

[21] *Diary*, March 18, 1861, 223.

[22] Letter, A0563, German, Arbre Croche, MI, from Baraga to Amalia Gressel, July 29, 1833.

[23] *Diary*, June 22, 1858, 125.

[24] Ibid., Dec. 21, 1861, 252.

cious is to practice alms; the glutton is to fast; the proud are to learn humility and the tepid are to nurture their fervor."[25]

Bishop Baraga's directives to fellow missionaries highlight the importance of confession. These fellow priests are to pray daily for their penitents, go promptly when called for confession and be available at all times, and not only at set times.[26]

Theological manuals of Baraga's day which were directed mostly to the confessor can also give us some insight into the theology and spirituality of the sacrament. In 1866, H. E. Manning wrote that Jesus is present in this sacrament displaying the tenderness of a healing physician and the compassion of a good shepherd;[27] confession is a source of abundant gifts for the penitent. This sacrament, which is for the sinful, can become a means of self-knowledge through a self-examination of one's relations to others, can instill perfect contrition and pardon, and can lead to reparation and perseverance. In penance, Jesus Christ, through the priest, guides, sustains, and consoles the fearful and the tempted. Penance is a spiritual resurrection empowering those who confess to pursue virtues of sincerity, peace, and humility.[28]

The Counter-Reformation Council of Trent (1545-1563) had elaborated on the sacrament and had given directives. Paraphrasing the Council's treatment of the sacrament, Ladislas Orsy states that the "priest is in possession of the highest judicial privilege, which is to show mercy and to grant free pardon to the offender, provided he is repentant."[29] This sacrament is concerned with the internal dynamics that direct the life of the person,[30] much like the directions of a shaman or the vision quest, as

---

[25] Walling, "Positio," 109.

[26] Ibid.

[27] H.E. Manning, *The Love of Jesus to Penitents* (Dublin: James Duffy, 1866), ii.

[28] Ibid., 9, 11-12, 14, 15, 28, 33, 42.

[29] Ladislas Orsy, *The Evolving Church and the Sacrament of Penance* (Denville, New Jersey: Dimension Books, 1978), 123-124. For the Council's pronouncements on this sacrament, see *The Canons and Decrees of the Sacred and Oecumenical Council of Trent*, J. Waterworth, trans. (London: C. Dolman, 1848), 92-104. Dominic M. Pruemmer summarizes the purposes of penance according to the Council of Trent; *Handbook of Moral Theology*, trans. Gerald W. Shelton, (Cork: The Mercier Press, 1956 (1940)), 304: "Penance demonstrates to the penitent that grave sin deserves grave punishment; it helps the penitent become more cautious about committing additional sins; it can be a means of engendering good habits and avoiding sin; the penitent can become Christ-like, making satisfaction for sin."

[30] Orsy, *The Evolving Church*, 129.

we shall see later.

Baraga gradually acquired the knack for understanding the Ojibwa's language and heritage. He then put Christian truths within an Ojibwa framework. As Charles J. Carmody writes, "Since he was able to think in the native idiom, Baraga's Indian prayerbooks, catechisms, and sermon books are said to reflect the effective simplicity of Our Lord's parables.[31] For Baraga, who put much effort into providing the Christian Testament to the Ojibwa in their tongue, it was evident that penance and forgiveness were at the center of Jesus' preaching. In the Gospel of Mark, for instance, Jesus begins his messianic ministry with the words, "Repent, and believe in the Good News."[32] Baraga also followed Jesus' last commands to preach penance and the remission of sins to the whole world in his name.[33] Like the father in the parable of the prodigal son, Baraga felt that forgiveness knew no bounds.[34]

Baraga scrupulously kept the seal of confession, telling and writing no one about the secret matters occurring in the confessional between confessor and penitent. Grave sanctions were accorded those who broke the seal. But, positively, according to Canon Law the seal of confession protected the penitent from the dissemination of knowledge of his or her vices and character, thereby making the sacrament more approachable because of its confidentiality.[35]

Other characteristics of penance and the confessor relate to Baraga. The ritual for the sacrament, *De Sacramento Poenitentiae,* enumerates the traits of a confessor: "goodness, knowledge, prudence, and meticulous respect for secrecy.... No other ministerial work brings him into closer contact with souls; in no other work is he more intimately associated with the Holy Spirit. Other things being equal, the holier he is the better confessor he will be."[36]

Theologian Gerald Kelly mentions some negativities regarding confession from the confessor's standpoint: it is often a drawn-out experience, monotonous, distasteful, with a boring regularity and repetition

---

[31] Charles J. Carmody, "Apostle of the Chippewas," *The Priest Magazine,* 14 (1958): 329. Thanks to Rev. Demetrius Wasylyniuk, OSB, for this reference.
[32] Gospel of Mark 1:15 in *The Jerusalem Bible* (New York: Doubleday, 1966). All references are to this version.
[33] Gospel of Luke 24:47.
[34] Gospel of Luke 15:20f.
[35] Bertrand Kurtscheid, *A History of the Seal of Confession,* F. A. Marks, trans. (London: Herder, 1927), 309, 328.
[36] Gerald Kelly, *The Good Confessor* (New York: Sentinel Press, 1951), 7.

which can be construed as interfering with other work. It can deprive the pastor of pleasant recreation, can sap his energy, and fray his nerves.[37] Although Baraga wrote about some discomforts surrounding penance, he does not mention any of the above litany of woes.

Again, mostly from a western and psychological perspective, contemporary moral theologian Bernard Haering, a Redemptorist, writes that in penance the penitent discloses his or her entire body-soul and social personality. Such a disclosure can lead to self-knowledge and to maturity in which the missionary-penitent breaches the prison wall of self-enclosure and sin into freedom.[38] Haering makes the case that if there is no absolution from a confessor, then there is need for absolution from a psychiatrist![39]

Confession and the Ojibwa world

I would like to move beyond the consideration of penance from a Roman Catholic theological and institutional perspective to its intersection with Ojibwa lives, and with a few non-intersections or differences of perspectives. In accord with the Ojibwa's general liberal attitude to adopting things spiritual, the varied Aboriginal communities within Baraga's vast mission territory saw, as he also saw, several similarities between the practice of confessing and the vision/sound quest. Confidentiality and a uniqueness of relationships prevail both in the private confessional and in the quest, characteristics which served the Ojibwa well, for they preserved a one-to-one relationship and suited the dispositional reserve that many Natives had. In the sacrament, one speaks to a spiritual person, a representative of Manitou/God, who in turn returns words and gives directions. Also, in the quest, one approaches a search, often in a locale removed from the ordinary, with a spirit of openness and anticipation of insights and sounds. The confessional box is akin to the tree top or isolated spot where one might detach oneself from the everyday and become receptive to visits from spirits. Baraga was conscious of these Ojibwa contexts of the holy, for he pointed out Aboriginal peoples' sense of sacred places around Lake Superior, and the majestic walls of stone and the enormous rocks in areas where he ministered; he also noted their

---

[37] Ibid., 7.
[38] Bernard Haering, *The Law of Christ, Moral Theology for Priests and Laity,* Edwin G. Kaiser, trans. (Westminster, Maryland: Newman Press, 1963), 1:452.
[39] Ibid., 1:453.

fasting and vision quests.[40]

Baraga gave negative portrayals of some Ojibwa involved in spiritual matters, however, calling them tricksters *(jongleurs)*, imposters, and magicians *(magiciens)*, names with variant histories in Europe from the fifth century to his day.[41] According to Frank J. Warnke and Alex Preminger, a "jongleur [is] a wandering musician and entertainer of the Middle Ages...a name applied indiscriminately to acrobats, actors, and entertainers in general, as well as to musicians and reciters of verse."[42] While individual jongleurs as well as their fraternities attained court and societal prestige, many imitators were regarded as low fellows and held in contempt since they wore grotesque dresses, engaged in coarse buffoonery and read doggerel which appealed to vitiated tastes. For their unacceptable conduct, some were imprisoned, and condemned by the clergy as engaging in conduct "incompatible with true devotion, purity of life and sobriety of thought."[43] Baraga apparently had the base imitators in mind when he condemned reprehensible conduct among the Ojibwa.

To continue with wholesome and affirmative cultural convergences.[44] In this penitential sacrament, one bares one's inner self, trusts another, and receives directives and healing for one's life. One reflects on unsavory aspects of one's past, passes through a ritual which encourages change, seeks to be transformed and receives graces to live in a new way.[45] The Christian Testament calls this necessary transformation re-

---

[40] Frederick Baraga, *Abrégé de l'histoire des indiens de l'Amérique septentrionale* (Paris: à la Société des Bon Livres, 1837), 184; this is a translation of *Geschichte, Character, Sitten und Gebräuche des nord-amerikanischen Indier* (Laibach: J. Blasnick, 1837).

[41] Baraga, *Abrégé de l'histoire des indiens,* 184, 199-203, 209, 211, 213. Some of Baraga's early observations are based on his own experiences and others on secondary sources.

[42] Frank J. Warnke and Alex Preminger, "Jongleur," in *The Princeton Handbook of Poetic Terms,* Alex Preminger, ed. (Princeton: Princeton University, 1986), 110.

[43] Alfred Bates, ed., *The Drama, its History, Literature and Influence on Civilization* (London: The Athenian Society, 1903), 7:3-6, 13.

[44] The convergence of the sacrament of penance with one of the sacraments of initiation, baptism, is not investigated here.

[45] Under the title of "Puberty customs," Frances Densmore discusses rituals for both females and males; *Chippewa Customs* (St. Paul: Minnesota Historical Society Reprint, 1979 (1929)), 70-72, 84-85. Densmore recounts a healing song learned in the course of dreaming; *Chippewa Music* (Washington: Smithsonian Institution, 1929), Bureau of American Ethnology, Bulletin 45, 94-95.

pentance or conversion.[46] Basil Johnston considers a similar change for Ojibwa as necessary for a focused life: "No man begins to be until he has received his vision."[47] In his elaboration of the vision quest, Johnston notes what we might regard as further similarities between the seal of confessional and the vision quest. He writes that the quest is "personal not to be disclosed to others; nor were others to interfere with the vision or the quest of another person."[48] Johnston employs the Ojibwa term, *waussayauh-bindumiwin,* to denote a complete kind of vision entailing self-understanding, enlightenment of self, and at the same time, suggesting a destiny and even a career.[49]

While the outward forms of the sacrament of penance appear individualistic, that is, one individual sharing with another individual, there are communal elements within it. Both the penitent and the confessor come from varied communities, and are shaped by these communities. In the Roman Catholic tradition, the priest celebrates the sacrament in the name of the church community and acts as the community's representative. In Ojibwa traditions, the individual also brings communitarian ties, bonded with a tribe through cultural and sanguinary affinities, and also bonded with other individuals and groups by spiritual totemic ties.

Both priest and penitent share in the spirit world, that of the divine and Kitche Manitou, the world of saints and ancestors. The priest is a healer, an elder and counselor. But the sacrament also enlists the help of fellow human beings who have died and now form the communion of saints, as the guardian spirits also give "advice, knowledge and power."[50]

As Johnston elaborates on the characteristics of the vision quest, both the similarities and differences with the rite of penance come into relief. He writes of the power that the vision had to change conduct and even the character of the individual so that the individual could appropriate a different moral perspective. "Prior to this event, a man [or a woman] was, in a moral sense, incomplete, a half-being; by vision he gained purpose that conferred meaning upon his actions and unity to his life." Akin to this is the sentiment of contrition, a sorrow for not being in harmony with others, a purpose of amendment, and satisfaction for sins

---

[46] As we have seen in the Gospel of Mark 1:5.

[47] Basil Johnston, *Ojibway Heritage* (Toronto: McClelland and Stewart, 1976), 119.

[48] Ibid., 127.

[49] Ibid., 126.

[50] M. Inez Hilger, *Chippewa Child Life and its Cultural Background* (St. Paul: Minnesota Historical Society Reprint, 1992 (1951)), 167.

that forms the sacrament of penance.[51] Not to be omitted from this Ojibwa vision quest is the healing power of natural elements, of animals, and of places, often the homes of medicine manitous.[52]

Ojibwa neophytes often readied themselves for life with periods of fasting, also a Christian practice. These initiates sought completion of their quest with dreams, a practice not in agreement with Catholic spirituality. But, with Johnston, we can sense further convergences as Ojibwa prepared both their inner beings and their bodies. Preparation for the inner being in Ojibwa ritual, Johnston relates, took the form of "patience, discipline, silence, and peace," whereas preparation for the body resulted in "strength, endurance, agility."[53] Like the biblical spirit of *metanoia* (a Greek term for conversion, change of heart), the sounds and vision in the quest could lead to the birth of a new form of life by becoming an adult and no longer a youth. "At that moment, a man's acts and conduct assumed quality; purpose conferred character. Having received a vision, a man had then to live it out," a process sometimes more difficult than the quest itself. "That the Path of Life was tortuous was portrayed on birch bark scrolls--seven and sometimes nine branches digressed from the main road.... To avoid such a state, men and women went on annual retreat to review their lives to find where they had strayed, and to resume the true path,"[54] Johnston writes.

Other similarities are discernible between Ojibwa and 19th-century Roman Catholic spirituality: both the quest and the penitential sacrament are forms of prayer, a trait highlighted as we shall see in Bishop Baraga's pastoral letter. In its admission of women and girls, confession was open to both genders, an egalitarian practice like that of Ojibwa society.

In this penitential forum the Ojibwa provided Baraga with a unique and privileged insight into their inner beings, gave clues to their world, and helped him fashion an understanding of Ojibwa life. Baraga,

---

[51] Johnston, *Ojibway Heritage,* 120. The importance of contrition and satisfaction is highlighted by the Council of Trent; *Canons and Decrees,* 95.
[52] Grace Rajnovich notes that "'Medicine' had a great depth of meaning in traditional Indian usage; it meant something like 'mystery' and 'power' and included not only the activities of curing with tonics from plants and minerals, but also the receipt of powers from the manitous for healing, hunting and battle;" *Reading Rock Art, Interpreting the Indian Rock Paintings of the Canadian Shield* (Toronto: Natural Heritage/Nature History, 1994), 10.
[53] Johnston, *Ojibway Heritage,* 120.
[54] Ibid., 132-133.

the "Snowshoe Priest," used these disclosures in his translations of catechisms, prayer and hymn books, and in the compilation of a grammar text and dictionary.

Additional Ojibwa Influence on Baraga

The Ojibwa and Baraga had a mutual trusting relationship. Through the confessional box and in other ceremonial and everyday associations, the Ojibwa furnished Baraga with a deeper awareness of themselves and their needs. For Baraga, this expanded consciousness together with his legal skills empowered him to implore governments to honor treaty agreements, and to make land purchases on their behalf. While we can make the case that these dealings on behalf of the Ojibwa came from Baraga's Christian and humanitarian largesse, a parallel case can be made that they proceeded from his informed consciousness of the contextual needs of these people because they were Ojibwa. From his legal training he devised a way of ensuring a livelihood for the Ojibwa; one of these ways was to make land purchases and then turn the title over to them.[55] Other means that he employed included petitioning for annuities to be used in L'Anse for "the officers of farmer, blacksmith, and carpenter." He insisted that "their school, and oxen, and farming utensils be restored to them."[56] Joseph Gregorich mentions Baraga's manifold dealings with government concerning treaties, subsidies to schools, and funds for church construction.[57] In another instance, Baraga wrote a letter to the Indian Agent on behalf of Chief Shingob at Fond du Lac, demanding a "reasonable but permanent pay" for ceded mineral rights.[58] The letter "expresses the Indians' concern as they realize that they are very poor, that their hunting grounds are disappearing, and that their existing treaty with the United States government will soon expire, whereas other tribes have more advantageous perpetual treaties with the government."[59] In addition, from his association with the Ojibwa, Baraga deepened a communitarian awareness as he modeled, for instance, the L'Anse mission on

---

[55] Letter, A0645, English, L'Anse, MI, from Baraga to William A. Richmond, May 11, 1848.

[56] Letter, A0648, English, L'Anse, MI, from Baraga to Secretary of the Interior, U. S. Indian Affairs, March 10, 1853.

[57] Joseph Gregorich, "Life of Bishop Frederic Baraga," an extensive unpublished manuscript, c.1950, Bishop Baraga Archives.

[58] Letter, A0844, English, Nov. 20, 1847. This letter is signed by Chief Shingob and three "second chiefs."

[59] Gregorich, "Life of Bishop Frederic Baraga."

the Jesuit reductions in Paraguay; he moved the Catholic Natives to the west side of Keweenaw Bay in order to form their own community, build their own houses and farm their small plots of land, in other words, to have their own self-contained encampment.[60]

A general observation is often made that Europeans influenced Aboriginal peoples greatly, indeed dominated them and made them very dependent on European goods and culture. This is undeniable. There is, however, another side to this perspective. There are many instances in which the Ojibwa were the initiators, where their inner spirit and practical ways influenced and directed the missionary. The obvious example of this is the fact that Baraga learned the Ojibwa language from the people; in their linguistic formulations they revealed themselves to him. As we have seen, Baraga came to comprehend the native idiom. Since he had an understanding of the Ojibwa mind, he was able to translate oral expressions into the literal forms of prayers, catechisms, grammars and dictionaries. The Ojibwa took special pride in having these printed prayer books in their hands, books which contained many Christian truths previously expressed in European formulations but now given in Ojibwa. Baraga's European art works and articles of devotion, such as the Stations of the Cross, were framed in Ojibwa settings. His preaching and teaching, while often communicating European values, were adapted to Ojibwa life.

Baraga was ahead of his time in the Latin Church for insisting on the use of the vernacular, meaning, Ojibwa and Odawa, in Catholic ceremonies. Thus he commanded, despite contrary rubrical directives, that the vernacular be used in the sacraments, including the Eucharist, in instances where biblical texts were proclaimed.[61] We are not certain about the extent of this practice and when it began, but in one of his episcopal letters he forbids Rev. A. Van Paemel from saying (and/or singing?) the Gloria, Creed and Vespers in Latin rather than in Ojibwa.[62]

---

[60] Letter, A0645, English, L'Anse, MI, from Baraga to William A. Richmond, May 11, 1848. MacDonald notes that at L'Anse Baraga purchased the land for the mission and then deeded it to the Natives; thereby some of them were able to escape the removal process. "This early collaboration of ethics with title-in-fee-simple led eventually to the establishment of the Keweenaw Reserve," McDonald writes; "Baraga, a Habsburg Prelate," 8.

[61] Walling, "Model of Evangelization," 9.

[62] Entry on Nov. 20, 1854: "Nov. 20. Mackinac. Rev. A. Van Paemel. -- 'Gloria' and 'Credo' in Latin in your church? --Vespers also in Latin? -- This I forbid *sub poena susp.* [under penalty of suspension from ministry]." "Extracts

Baraga wrote about the importance of having the vernacular Bible for his mission work, a concern he shared with other Christian persuasions.[63] By displaying an enthusiasm for learning Native languages, and by making these languages the vehicles of instruction in the mission schools, Baraga revealed that he really appreciated the importance of the vernacular and Ojibwa culture.

The Ojibwa also helped Baraga expand his consciousness in matters spiritual. In his first pastoral letter, Bishop Baraga used the term, *Manitou,* that is, spirit. In employing this term, Baraga admitted the complexity of addressing an immanent or transcendent spirit, Christian or other, but at the same time, he expanded his awareness of spiritual beings beyond that of fixed characteristics. On one level, *manitou* can be seen as interchangeable with God, or with one of the persons of the Trinity. However, since human images and concepts cannot fully interpret the reality of this being/these beings, a less determinate name such as *manitou* was deemed appropriate, much as the name, Yahweh, remained unuttered in the Hebrew tradition. In an approach befitting the mystics, therefore, Baraga does not reduce the reality in question to a specific being, to named characteristics, or even to a conception.

The Ojibwa admitted the mysterious and hidden realities of the *manitous,* and they sought these realities through visions and dreams. Selwyn Dewdney tries to be specific about the various levels of the Ojibwa experience of *manitou:* "At the lowest level there were the powers potential in the simplest of natural objects, whether organic or inorganic. At a much higher level were the *manitos* that [A. Irving] Hallowell[64]...refers to as the 'masters.' ...Even among the Source Beings, as I prefer to call them, there were higher and lower ranks, partly determined by their importance as a food supply, partly reaching deep into traditional mysteries."[65]

Contemporary understandings of these manitou powers are in terms of creator/the creator, a term Baraga used in his pastoral letter. In this usage, Baraga is in accord with Johnston: "Manitou refers to realities

---

of Letters [those sent by Baraga]," 1854-1859, edited by Joseph Gregorich, unpublished manuscript, 1:29, Bishop Baraga Archives.
[63] Letter, B1251, German, Ann Arbor, MI, Rev. Frederick Schmid to Mission Center, Basel, Switzerland, Nov. 25, 1833; see Walling, "Positio," 110.
[64] A. Irving Hallowell, *The Role of Conjuring in Saulteaux Society* (Philadelphia: University of Pennsylvania Press, 1942), 7.
[65] Selwyn Dewdney, *The Sacred Scrolls of the Southern Ojibway* (Toronto: University of Toronto Press, 1975), 38-39.

other than the physical ones of rock, fire, water, air, wood, and flesh--to the unseen realities of individual beings and places and events that are beyond human understanding but are still clearly real. Kitchi-Manitou created the manitou beings and forces and infused them, to various degrees, into beings and objects."[66]

According to Baraga's interpretation, Kije Manito, or the Good Spirit's son, Menabojo,[67] made the earth. This spirit taught humans "how to lead an upright and happy life, to abstain from bad deeds, to be charitable, hospitable, kind and sincere."

Baraga notes, however, that this moral and theological interpretation of Menabojo relies on Christian influences.[68] According to Johnston, there is a meaning to Kitchi-Manitou in addition to that of power and creator: "The Great Mystery of the supernatural order, one beyond human grasp, beyond words, neither male nor female, not of the flesh.... What little is known of Kitchi-Manitou is known through the universe, the cosmos, and the world." Another meaning to *Manitou* is that of spirit within oneself, which one must seek, find and bring into reality, often through dreams and vision quests.[69]

Several additional issues could be considered. One of these is whether Baraga was a reductionist in his consideration of the Catholic religion, reducing it to Ojibwa conceptions. From his own religious stance, he was not. He was solidly at home with the truths of his religion as understood in 19th-century terms and did not deviate from them. He can be considered reductionistic toward Aboriginal spiritual perspectives, however, for he was a religious colonialist, a missionary who hoped to convert Aboriginal peoples to Catholicism; he, therefore, often relativized their spiritual approaches. He characterized the Roman Catholic religion as the norm and others as mirrors of that veridical norm. Another

---

[66] Basil Johnston, *The Manitous, the Supernatural World of the Ojibway* (New York: HarperCollins, 1995), xxi-xxii.

[67] Other spellings of the name of this narrative being are Nanabozho, Nannebush, Nanabush, and Winabojo, as employed by the Northeast and Subarctic Ojibwa. Michigan and Wisconsin Ojibwa use the name Manabozho and Menapus (Big Rabbit). Menabojo/Nanabozho is a complex trickster figure, often powerful and benevolent, but also deceitful and stupid; see Sam D. Gill and Irene F. Sullivan, *Dictionary of Native American Mythology* (New York: Oxford University Press, 1992), 340-341.

[68] Frederick Baraga, *Chippewa Indians as Recorded by Rev. Frederick Baraga in 1847* (New York: Studia Slovenica, League of Slovenian Americans, 1976), 34.

[69] Basil Johnston, *Manitous,* 2-3.

approach to different spiritual persuasions, somewhat similar to that of Baraga, and exemplified in the early 20th century by Charles de Foucauld, is that of living among them, convinced of the truth of one's own faith while hoping to convert others, but also willing to learn from their different beliefs. Still another way of dealing with variant religious convictions is to live firmly in one's traditions but, while encountering other persuasions, be willing to appreciate their worth and their practices. The challenge in such an inter-religious dialogue, which moves beyond mutual tolerance, is to acclaim what is holy in another, as Matt Vogel notes, "without trying to somehow baptize that person into our own tradition."[70] This was not Baraga's way.

Virtues and the Great Spirit

Baraga had many admirable qualities prior to his arrival in North America. We have already noted his devotion to the people through long sessions of hearing confessions in Slovenia and in North America, and the respect he accorded the Ojibwa's language and culture. But there are virtuous dispositions that Baraga learned quite directly from the Ojibwa. Walling notes that Baraga and other missionaries discovered or felt affirmations about the following virtues from the Ojibwa: "a reverence for life, a sense of the presence of the Great Spirit, and [a] dependence on the Great Spirit."[71]

Baraga's pastoral letter, written in Ojibwa during his first year as bishop, gives evidence of the pervasive feeling of the Great Spirit's presence and both the bishop's and people's reliance on the Great Spirit. He writes explicitly about the importance and centrality of Kije-Manito, Great Spirit, in his first pastoral letter addressed solely to the Ojibwa. Another pastoral letter in English was directed to other members of his diocese. A comparison of the two letters published during the same year is enlightening for the differences in tone and wording.

In the Ojibwa letter, the terms, "bishop," in the beginning and "your bishop," at the end of the letter is rendered *Kitchi-mekatewik-waniae* (Great Blackgown), without pretension, it seems, making an allusion to the Great Spirit whom Baraga was serving.[72] Baraga's love

---

[70] Matt Vogel, review of *Christian Hermit in an Islamic World* by Ali Merad (New York: Paulist Press, 1999), in *The Catholic Worker*, 69 (2002): 7.
[71] Walling, "Model of Evangelization," 8.
[72] P. Chrysostomus Verwyst, OFM, *Life and Labors of Rt. Rev. Frederic Baraga, First Bishop of Marquette, Mich.* (Milwaukee, Wisconsin: M. H.

for Native people is shown in the initial greeting, "to my beloved sons and daughters, my warmest greetings."[73] The English pastoral letter in contrast has a matter-of-fact and official heading: "Pastoral Letter of the Right Reverend Bishop Frederic Baraga."[74] The English letter provides a more formal setting by including Baraga's coat of arms and an ecclesiastically proper beginning: "By the Grace of God and the Favor of the Apostolic See, Bishop of Amyzonia, Vicar Apostolic of the Upper Peninsula of Michigan, to the faithful of his diocese, health and benediction."[75] In the English pastoral, Baraga spells out the duties of Christians, namely, that of faith, adoration, respect, obedience, and love. In this edition, there is no mention of Native people nor of Kiji-Manito, and he concludes as most contemporary pastoral letters did: "'The grace of our Lord Jesus Christ, and the charity of God, and the communication of the Holy Ghost be with you all. Amen.' Frederic, Bishop, and Vicar Apostolic of Upper Michigan."[76]

In addition to its more overtly affective tones, the letter in Ojibwa exhibits the identification Baraga had with Ojibwa life. He appropriates aspects of Ojibwa culture in obvious ways, giving evidence of the centrality of Kije-Manito.[77] In this pastoral, the Great Spirit is the creator who owns the earth, watches over it carefully, and gives blackrobes and bishops to the community of Native people. While missionaries obviously influence the Ojibwa, the influence of the Ojibwa themselves on Baraga is also evident as the bishop inserts the Christian message within the framework of nature: "Think of all the Great Spirit has done for you, making earth and sky and sending His Son to earth--doing it all for the glory of His Name and the happiness of man."[78]

Wiltzius, 1900), 431, 447. The latter part of this volume contains the Ojibwa version of the pastoral letter and Verwyst's translation based in some instances on the ecclesiastical terms of the day rather than on the actual Ojibwa words and expressions.

[73] A. Schretlen, SJ, "Unum est Necessarium, Pastoral Letter by F. Baraga, 1853," unpublished manuscript, Pickering, ON, 1986, 1, Bishop Baraga Archives. Schretlen gives a translation which corrects some of Verwyst's renderings.

[74] "Pastoral Letter of the Right Reverend Bishop Frederic Baraga," (Cincinnati: Catholic Telegraph, 1853).

[75] Ibid., 1.

[76] Ibid., 12.

[77] Verwyst, *Life and Labors*, consistently translates Kije-Manito with the hierarchical and biblical terms, "lord God," "Lord our God," "God," "Lord."

[78] Schretlen, 2.

As Baraga elaborates on the motto of the pastoral, "One Thing Alone is Necessary,"[79] he continues to intertwine Ojibwa and Christian spirituality: the necessary thing is "...to love and serve the Great Spirit well and so bring happiness to your spirit."[80] Baraga's interpretation is that the Great Spirit combines both the Lord, namely, Jesus Christ, and the Ojibwa Spirit. The intermingling of spiritualities to create a new one is also evident in Baraga's designation for the church: "Love your church-house *[mi sa Kije-Manito o wigiwam aking]*,[81] and cherish it, for on earth it is the house of the Great Spirit."[82] Baraga's appropriation of Ojibwa terms indicates a movement toward Ojibwa consciousness, as the Ojibwa also incorporate European perspectives. Both Ojibwa and Baraga, however, never leave their past entirely behind.

In tune with the expansive approaches of the spirited Ojibwa people, Baraga emphasizes that the Great Spirit is even greater than the priest. If one respects the priest, so much more should that person respect the Great Spirit. "Whatever you would not say or do in the presence of the priest, be sure never to say or do at all, for our Lord the Great Spirit is everywhere, and he sees and hears us at all times."[83]

For Baraga, Kije-Manito is ever present in his people. "Constantly in our hearts the Great Spirit is speaking to us, urging us to hate and to shun whatever is evil and to do instead only what is beautiful and good. If a Christian feels like doing something evil, the Great Spirit will whisper to him in his heart: Don't do that, it is evil. On the other hand, if a Christian feels like doing something good, instantly he is encouraged by the Great Spirit to do the good deed. Now that is the way the Great Spirit is constantly speaking to us in our hearts. Happy the Christian who constantly listens to what the Great Spirit is telling him."[84]

While the Great Spirit is greater than the priest, Kije-Manito can speak through this minister. "But still again the Lord speaks to us in sermons. When a Christian listens to a sacred sermon, he is of course listening to the Great Spirit.... Every time you confess your sins, gracefully accept whatever advice you are then given and do well everything

---

[79] Jesus' words during his visit to Martha and Mary, Luke 10:38-42, and Baraga's motto as bishop.
[80] Schretlen, 3.
[81] Verwyst, *Life and Labors*, 440.
[82] Schretlen, 6.
[83] Ibid., 7.
[84] Ibid., 8.

the Great Spirit then says to you."[85]

He concludes: "Accept and hold dear all that makes for your well-being, all that pleases the Great Spirit.... Amen, Frederic your bishop [Great Blackgown/*Kitchi-Mekatewikwanaie*]. "[86]

In his retranslated pastoral letter, A. Schretlen rightfully indicates Baraga's appreciation of Native spirituality. Baraga's contemporary fellow missionary, Chrysostom Verwyst, gives a translation which, in part, pits Christianity against Native spirituality: "And pay no attention to *Indian-religion (Indian paganism) [Anishinabe-ijitwawin]*. It is very foolish, God our Lord [Kije-Manito] hates it (Indian religion). A Christian acts very wrong and offends God [Kije-Maniton] much if he still minds or resumes what he renounced when he was baptized."[87] By translating this passage in words closer to the original, Schretlen shows how Baraga's passage is not meant to be offensive to the Ojibwa: "Never again bother about *man-made cults [Anishinabe-ijitwawin]*; they are particularly foolish and the Great Spirit loathes them. A Christian commits serious sin and offends the Great Spirit very much if he meddles with and picks up again what was rejected at Baptism."[88] Schretlen comments: "Baraga's message is quite unoffensive and makes no harsh unfair claims upon his native reader and listener. Like Christians everywhere on earth the native peoples were expected to renounce at Baptism whatever beliefs and practices that did not fit with the religion and/or prayer that Jesus Christ, Son of the Great Spirit, brought for all peoples everywhere."[89]

We have in Baraga's Ojibwa pastoral letter some indications of the Ojibwa's cultural and spiritual power in the formation of their bishop. Baraga affirms certain legitimacies in Ojibwa spirituality; the emphasis on the Great Spirit as preeminent and as creator is one of them. There are mergings of Ojibwa perspectives and Christian ones exemplified in the all-pervasive presence of the Spirit and its indwelling and impetus in individuals.

Virtues in addition to respect for the Great Spirit were present among the Ojibwa and had influences on the missionary. There was a reverence for one another in Ojibwa families and in their communities.

---

[85] Ibid.
[86] Ibid., 9. Verwyst, *Life and Labors*, 446-447.
[87] Verwyst, *Life and Labors*, 432, 433; emphasis added.
[88] Schretlen, 2; emphasis added.
[89] Schretlen, i.

This influenced Baraga or at least strengthened his disposition toward reverence for life. Early biographer, Verwyst, attested to Baraga's warm relationship with the Aboriginal peoples: "No Indian missionary of modern times was more beloved and revered by both Indians and whites than Baraga. He loved his Indians with a warm-hearted devotion which they reciprocated."[90]

Although Baraga had reasonable financial resources and privileged academic advantages prior to emigrating to North America, he became sensitive to the non-affluent conditions of his mission territory and diocese, and often adopted the demeanor of a destitute person. He thereby paralleled the poverty of the Ojibwa. To help relieve that poverty he used most of the funds, procured in his European excursions, for the Ojibwa directly and vigorously pursued the acquisition of additional funds by letter from the Leopoldine Society in Vienna.[91] Fellow missionary Rev. Francis Pierz attests to Baraga's virtue of poverty: "The missionaries whom I have learned to know personally...especially Mr. Baraga of whom even the Protestants and pagans praise, are sparkling pearls in the Church of Christ. All live in apostolic poverty and great humility, are inspired by an unsatiable zeal for the salvation of their neighbor and offer themselves to the great hardships of the office: but because of this they are held in great esteem by the people."[92] Later Pierz wrote to Baraga's sister, Amalia: "His boundless generosity will always preserve him in Apostolic poverty. The considerable sum of gold he brought with him last year from Europe has already been spent; consequently he will soon suffer from a lack of means of subsistence.... Their little establishment consists of 2 oxen, 2 good cows, 6 chickens, a cat, and no mouse."[93]

Another virtue present among the Ojibwa and formative of Baraga was a sense of community cohesiveness, conviviality and hospitality. Among the Ojibwa and in Baraga's life there was a celebratory joy

---

[90] Chrysostom Verwyst, "Frederic Baraga," in *The Catholic Encyclopedia* (New York: Robert Appleton, 1907), 2:283.

[91] Frederick Baraga, "A Diocese Without a Cent!" *The Baraga Bulletin*, 55 (2002): 11; this article is from his letter, A0117, German, from Sault Ste. Marie, MI, to the Leopoldine Society, Nov. 29, 1864. According to Walling, *Diary,* 162, n.215, "The Leopoldine Society, established in Austria in 1829, was a German benevolent society formed to advance missionary activities of the Catholic Church and German missionaries in the United States."

[92] Letter, B028, German, Rev. Francis Pierz to the Leopoldine Society, May 1, 1836; Leopoldine Society Archives, XIV/VI/15.

[93] Letter, B0822, German, June 20, 1838.

that took many forms and one was that of song. The mood engendered by singing, coupled with Baraga's delight in acoustical expressions, resulted in song fests that sometimes lasted throughout the night. He also used many European melodies and joined these with Ojibwa texts to form hymns which the Ojibwa could sing and thereby learn about Christianity.[94] His sister Antonia writes of the great happiness that the Ojibwa provided him: "He wrote me this with joy in his soul, and I am very sad with the knowledge that I cannot see him among these joyful Indians, because he is a completely different person when he is among his people. ...In all his travels I had never seen him so cheerful as when he sat among the Indians here in Mackinac and sang from the newly-printed books.... [He] would often sing along with them until late into the night, until he would lose his voice and not be able to speak."[95]

Baraga recounted the noticeable hospitality of the Ojibwa. "Strangers are announced as soon as they are perceived.... When he comes in, the Indian stretches out his hand towards him with a hearty *'bon jour'!* which he repeats four or five times. If the visitor is a relative of the family, they all kiss him, calling him by the term of relation.[96] The place for the visitors is the bottom or hind part of the lodge, opposite the door, where a fine new mat is spread out for them. The Indians are remarkable for hospitality; they always give the best they have to the visitors; they prefer to starve themselves, than to let the stranger want

---

[94] Walling, "Model of Evangelization," 10.

[95] Letter, B1327, English, Oct. 6, 1837. Baraga notes that the assembly sang Vespers on the missions with a "delightful melodion;" Letter, B1327, German, Mackinac, MI, Antonia von Hoeffern to Amalia Gressel (both sisters to Baraga), Oct. 6, 1837. The assembly also sang Vespers at Christmas (Letter, A0661, English, Arbre Croche, Michigan, from Baraga to *Detroit Catholic Vindicator,* 3 (1855) 39, 2; Dec. 26, 1855. See also, Letter, B1103, German, La Pointe, Wisconsin, von Hoeffern to Gressel, Oct. 4, 1838, where he writes specifically about Vespers at Christmas. Fr. Zephyrin, OFM, authored *Anishinabe Negamod, a Collection of Hymns, Ottawa and Chippewa Languages* (Harbor Springs, Michigan: Holy Childhood School Print, 1901), a compilation of hymns from many sources including Baraga. The following Ojibwa prayer book and catechism contains the words to many hymns and gives reference to the French medodies and Latin chants for each one: *Katolik Anamie-Masinaigan Wetchipwewissing,* fourth edition (Detroit: Munger and Pattison, 1849).

[96] Baraga makes this greeting more specific later on: "They never greet each other by name, but always employ the terms of relationship in which they are to each other. Often they employ these terms without being relatives, or without being so *nearly* related. Indians who are not relatives at all greet each other with *nidji,* my comrade, my friend, my equal. The females greet each other with *nin dangwe,* my sister-in-law;" *Chippewa Indians,* 55.

food. Invitations to meals are frequent in the Indian camps and villages, even without an apparent occasion, because they are social and like company. The custom to send small sticks like pencils, as invitation cards, is general in this tribe. Hospitality is seldom denied; and Indians who are not hospitable are denoted as avaricious and mean fellows."[97]

And again, Baraga wrote: "The finest characteristic of an Indian is his hospitality, the old patriarchal virtue. The Indians possess it in a high degree and practice it not merely among themselves, but also towards strangers and even towards those who have acted unfriendly towards them."[98] In cases of doubt, the tendency was to celebrate a meeting, as Baraga noted, with ceremony, dance, chant, and invocations.[99]

Animals and the rest of nature elicited an ethical response from Baraga. He learned of beauty, harmony, balance, solitude, and respect emanating from individual beings. Walling suggests that beings of nature can act as agents and elicit ethical dispositions, just as the Ojibwa as agents elicited virtue from the bishop.[100] "Baraga may have found certain natural virtues more prevalent among the Native people. Life lived close to nature fosters respect for human and animal life, an appreciation for the beauty of nature, an appreciation for solitude. When a person fishes there is that solitude, no matter from what culture a person comes. Everyone who fishes, who walks in a forest, who watches the sun and moon rise and set, enters that beautiful solitude."[101] Baraga felt the importance and influence of nature for personal life. As noted above, he wrote about Aboriginal peoples' sense of sacred places around Lake Superior, with their majestic walls of stone, and the enormous rocks.[102]

In the Ojibwa pastoral letter there is an exchange of a reciprocal awareness, Baraga appropriating the Ojibwa and the Ojibwa embracing

---

[97] Ibid., 50.
[98] A lecture given by Bishop Baraga in Cincinnati, Aug. 23, 1863, and printed in *Der Wahrheitsfreund,* 27 (1863): 18-19. This lecture was translated by Rev. John Zaplotnik as "The Customs and Manners of the Indians," *Acta et Dicta,* 5 (1917): 101.
[99] Baraga, *Abrégé de l'histoire des indiens,* 281.
[100] I do not want to soften or deny the effects of colonialism and thereby absolve its practitioners and deny the pain inflicted. For a more explicit examination of Native agency and alibis for colonialist denials, see Robin Brownlie and Mary-Ellen Kelm, "Desperately Seeking Absolution: Native Agency as Colonialist Alibi?" in *Out of the Background, Readings in Canadian Native History,* Kenneth Coates and Robin Fisher, eds. (Toronto: Copp, Clark, 1996), 211-212.
[101] Walling, "Model of Evangelization," 9.
[102] Baraga, *Abrégé de l'histoire des indiens,* 184.

the European. The formative influence of the Ojibwa on Baraga should not be overstated, however. Baraga remained European in his mindset. He continued to use as the basis of his translations into Ojibwa, the Roman catechisms, prayer books, the Ten Commandments, and Precepts of the Church. He did not impose, however, all forms of European civilization on the Ojibwa; for instance, he did not expect them to learn a European language. Here his approach was akin to the Jesuits in 17th-century New France, who generally sought to preserve whatever was good in the culture. This preserving and adapting approach was unlike the missionaries in New England, who often sought a thorough renunciation of Native cultures and a conversion to European forms of culture and Christianity.[103]

Baraga built a bridge between the oral tradition of the Ojibwa and the European/North American education process of reading and writing. Several accounts narrate the delight the Ojibwa had with their catechisms and prayer books. As Walling notes, "They would carry them with them and in the evening, after everything was done, they would sit and read their books. In a sense he made them or helped them to be responsible for their on-going growth in the faith."[104]

In the exchanges in the sacrament of penance, the Ojibwa furnished unique insights into their own conscience, into their world, and into their consciousness, indeed, true confessions! Baraga received further insights during counseling sessions, from visits and from the rapport in imploring governments on their behalf. Such lived sharing gave him an understanding of Ojibwa life which led him to grasp the nuances in their language and compile a dictionary and grammar which remain important today.

---

[103] James Axtell, *After Columbus: Essays in the Ethnohistory of Colonial North America* (New York: Oxford University Press, 1988), 58-59.
[104] Walling, "Model of Evangelization," 10.

THE INFLUENCE CHRISTIAN MISSIONARIES HAD ON POSITIONS OF LEADERSHIP IN IROQUOIS SOCIETY UP UNTIL THE WAR OF INDEPENDENCE

Brian Rice[*]

It is the writer's opinion that most history that is written is colored by the historian's cultural background, and this is especially true when it pertains to the history of Aboriginal people. Consequently there is always a certain bias in the interpretation and the reporting of events. The omission of Aboriginal world-views when interpreting historical events is a testament to what is lacking in most history about Aboriginal people. In other words, there is a difference between Aboriginal history as known by Aboriginals and the historical study of Aboriginals by people of European descent. In order to reflect Aboriginal interpretations of history, they must be derived from how Aboriginal people have conceptualized through their particular worldviews as to why certain events have occurred, especially when dealing with catastrophic situations such as the loss of a homeland, traditions and culture, languages, and, in the case of this paper, traditional leadership roles.

Much of this paper will show how the national interests of the various clergy who interacted with Iroquois society throughout the 17th and 18th centuries colored their agenda of missionary work which was to proselytize the Iroquois, with their own, nationalist interests. These interests included trade, warfare alliances, signing of treaties, and land appropriation for both national and personal use while trying to subvert the Iroquois worldview. The missionaries accomplished this in part by undermining the traditional teachings about the Iroquois cosmology and tried replacing them with Judeo-Christian ideologies. There was a disruption of traditional leadership positions that had included both men and women in positions of equal authority, in favor of Christianized male chiefs, who would eventually usurp the authority of the traditional he-

* Dr. Brian Rice is of Mohawk descent. He graduated from an Aboriginal Doctoral Program with a degree in Traditional Knowledge out of the Transformative Learning Division at the California Institute of Integral Studies. He wrote part of his traditional history of the Haudenosaunee while walking from Tyendinga Ontario, to Albany New York, and finishing at Ganondagan New York, visiting many of the sacred and historical sites of the Haudenosaunee. Dr. Rice has taught in the Departments of Native Studies, Religious Studies, International Development Studies, and Conflict Resolution Studies over the last twelve years, teaching courses on Aboriginal Culture, History, Social, and Political Issues. Presently Dr. Rice is a Director of an Aboriginal Governance Program within the Continuing Education Division at the University of Manitoba. He continues to teach courses on Aboriginal issues at the University of Winnipeg and Menno Simons College.

reditary leaders, both men and women.

Contemporary hereditary leader and an expert on the oral traditions of the Iroquois people, the late Jacob Thomas 'Hadagihgrenhta,' used to teach his students that, during the periods of the 17th and 18th centuries, the warriors had become difficult to control. According to Jacob Thomas, they stopped listening to the council of the hereditary chiefs and clan mothers all of whom were appointed leaders of the communities, which resulted in the destruction of the political system of the Iroquois confederacy. He blamed, in part, the acceptance of Christianity by Iroquois men for this occurring.[1]

It does appear from early, recorded land transactions during the late 17th century, which occurred between the Iroquois and the English, that Iroquois women were part of most negotiations concerning the transaction of land. This bears out an oral tradition in which women were as influential as men in the decision making of their society during the early colonial period. By the early eighteenth century, the signatures of women are omitted from any documentation concerning land transactions, although, in Iroquois society, they are considered to be the landholders. Therefore, women's leadership positions were the first to be undermined.

The loss of power, first by traditional female and then by male leaders, would have a profound effect on the decision making process of Iroquois society. During this period we see the beginning of the inception of patriarchy as a result of Christian, colonial administrators refusing to allow Iroquois women to be participants in negotiations, and eventually individual Iroquois males being selected and educated in the fundamentals of a Christian patriarchic-based education and promoted into leadership roles.

In order to understand how this transition affected Iroquois society in the colonial era, it is important to begin by understanding some principles of Iroquois tradition and cosmology, and how it has influenced the development of traditional leadership roles. To begin, most Aboriginal epistemologies, including that of the Iroquois, are based on a concept of living in balance within the particular eco-system they inhabit. This balance is a necessity for their survival. In the case of the Five, later Six Nations Iroquois, whose traditional name Rotinonshonni 'Longhouse People,' the name itself signifies the territory that was inhabited, governed, and kept in balance by them, until their displacement by the Euro-American in the late eighteenth century.

Paramount to their being able to maintain balance was the continuance of the culture passed down in oral teachings over many thousands of years. Included in the oral tradition was the development of

---

[1] Jacob Thomas, *Oral Recital of the Great Law of Peace*, Jake Thomas Learning Center, Oshwegan, Ontario, 1992.

Iroquois governing practices which required that balance be maintained between hereditary chiefs, clan mothers, and war chiefs, with the power of hereditary chiefs and clan mothers being more influential over the decision making process of the society than the war chiefs. Following contact with, and the influence of, Christian missionaries of various denominations, a shift in power occurred towards war chiefs who had been Christianized. This power shift would have repercussions affecting leadership positions and those repercussions have lasted onto this day.

According to the oral traditions of the Iroquois, the spiritual forces that guided the destiny of the world and the Iroquois people were the twins Teharonhiawako 'Holder of the Heavens' and Swiskera 'Flint Like Ice.' Teharonhiawako is believed to be a spiritual entity who created and allowed everything in the world to live out its natural cycle to perfection, while his twin brother ,Sawiskera, is an entity who continually tries to malign Teharonhiawako's creative works by bringing ice storms, death, warfare, and disease to the earth. After many contests between the two brothers over who would have supremacy over creation, Teharonhiawako eventually gets the upper hand. Sawiskera, whose power, although still substantial, is then limited. Sawiskera was subsequently relegated to reside across the great sea, where he would create the forces that would one day return and destroy Teharonhiawako's creation. From a traditional Iroquoian perspective, even from his distant abode, Sawiskera continues to try to effect change that would be detrimental to both the e4nvironment and to Iroquois society.

Among Iroquois in the past as well as the present, the coming of the Europeans, the introduction of the Christian belief system, the loss of traditional lands, and the destruction of the environment are viewed as products of Sawiskera's continuing influence and power over the world. This offers Iroquois an explanation as to why there are few of them residing in their homeland performing the societal functions that are required to live in harmony and balance within their traditional territory. Some Iroquois believe this to be testament to Sawiskera's continuing influence over the affairs of the world and, as predicted in Iroquois prophecy, will eventually result in the world's destruction, with Teharonhiawako eventually restoring it back to its natural order through a process known as purification.

In former times, the Iroquois as a confederacy of Five Nations comprised of the Mohawk, Oneida, Onondaga, Cayuga, and Seneca, had been governed by 50 hereditary male leaders and 50 clan mothers who oversaw the functions of their society. A sixth nation referred to as the Tuscarora, would join the other five nations in the early eighteenth century. Originally, the hereditary leaders and clan mothers were divided among the original Five Nations Iroquois and governed through their respective clans at a local, regional, and national level. The war chief had a subordinate role except during times of war when he was called upon as a last resort to take over the protection of the community. Once the danger ended he was relieved of all of his authority.

There is an ongoing debate among contemporary traditionalists as to whether the title of war chief existed after the founding of the Iroquois confederacy or whether it was abolished in favor of a deputy chief who acted on behalf of the hereditary chiefs and clan mothers. Some oral traditions relate that all of the original hereditary chiefs were at one time war chiefs who were relegated to the role of peace chiefs after the founding of the Iroquois confederacy. Therefore the role of war chief ceased to exist after the founding of the Iroquois confederacy. The only two chiefs who were given a task that could in any way resemble that of a war chief were the two Seneca hereditary chiefs Teionhokara 'Keeper of the Entrance' and Kanonkeritawi 'Hair Taken Off.' Those two sat at the western door of the Iroquois confederacy in order to oversee who entered the territory of the Longhouse of One Family. According to some traditionalists, the role of war chief became reestablished only during colonial times when the society was once again threatened with extinction.

The development of the governing structure of Iroquois society was said to be a result of a male individual known as the Peacemaker, who had been born of a virgin, and was chosen by Teharonhiawako to end the strife and war that had enveloped the Five Nations Iroquois prior to the arrival of the Europeans. Along with two other individuals, a male named Ayenwentha 'He Was Awoke' and a female named Tsakonsase 'Cat Face,' they formulated the laws that were established and which would last for many years among the Five Nations which became known as the Kayenera Kowa 'Great Law of Peace.' Even to this day, individual Iroquois greet one another by saying skenen kowa ken which means, are you still living within the great peace?' Within this matrix of laws and traditions were the foundations of the governing structures of Iroquois society. There are various dates given as to when the laws of peace within the Keyenera kowa were formulated, but the one that appears to be the most likely is1100 a.d.[2] With the arrival of the Europeans and Christian missionaries the durability of leadership positions formulated from the Keyenera kowa would be tested.

Christian missionaries of all denominations would become an important influence in the change in the power base of Iroquois society from hereditary chiefs and clan mothers to war chiefs, most notably in the late eighteenth century when Iroquois society became divided in war, and most Iroquois were dispersed from their homeland in what is now referred to as central New York State. Several Christian denominations, with competing mission and national aspirations, would be influential in first dividing Iroquois society at the local level, and then dividing the Six

---

[2] Doug George, *Iroquois Culture & Commentary*, (Santa Fe New, Mexico: Clear Light Publishing, 2000), 28.

Nations at a national level. According to the prophetic tradition of the Iroquois, much of what happened had been predicted and was due to the influence of Sawiskera.

Iroquois positions of leadership began to be transformed soon after initial contact. Change may have had its beginnings in 1609 with an attack by Samuel De Champlain on a delegation of the turtle clan sent out, most probably, by the Mohawk community of Tionontoken to greet him. Included in the delegation were three hereditary chiefs wearing their ceremonial headdress, Gustowah. War chiefs traditionally do not wear Gustowah when waging war. The Gustowah is an important ceremonial component of a hereditary chief's attire, and hereditary chiefs do not go on war expeditions.

In his journals, Champlain claims that the Mohawks and their leaders had come to battle. However, would it be more likely that they were following Iroquois protocol, which was to meet a visiting delegation at the wood's edge and to console them for their losses on their journey. This was a customary practice of the Iroquois when visited by a delegation from elsewhere. Instead of meeting that evening, the two parties were to greet each other the next morning. This is also in line with Iroquoian cultural practice, which disallows for any discourse to take place once the sun begins its descent in the sky.

The next day, as the Iroquois delegation approached Champlain, his men fired upon them from canoes, killing three hereditary leaders and as many as fifty others. This action sowed the seeds of strife between the Mohawk and the French which continued for the next 150 years. This event would set the stage whereby Iroquois society would be affected by a siege mentality, eventually resulting in their accepting terms of peace which allowed for Christian missionaries to enter their society and begin an internal war against Iroquois cultural practices and beliefs, which was divisive for the society as a whole, and resulted in eventual ruin. The outcome of these events would be the breakup of Mohawk society in the seventeenth century and the destruction of the Six Nations as a politically- coordinated, national entity during the next.

The tactics that were used to divide the Iroquois began with the Roman Catholic Jesuits in the 17th century. The first to be affected by their divisive tactics were the Huron.

Triggar explains how the Huron confederacy was the first to be destabilized by the Jesuit missionaries, who fomented divisions between Christian converts and Huron traditionalists by trading only with the converts.[3] This resulted in a discrepancy of wealth and an imbalance of power between the Christian minority and traditional majority, a move

---

[3] Bruce Triggar, *Natives and Newcomers: Canada's Heroic Age Reconsidered.* Montreal, (Quebec & Kingston, Ontario: McGill–Queen's University Press, 1985), 255.

from an egalitarian society where everyone shared equally in the wealth of the society, to one that resulted in the development of an elite class and under class of Huron who were in conflict with each other. It created bitter feuding between the two groups, which led to their eventual demise, with two thirds of their population succumbing to disease brought by the priests, and then warfare with the more unified Iroquois.

In his award-winning article named *The Warrior and the Lineage: Jesuit Use of Iroquoian Images to Communicate Christianity* Steckly explains how the Jesuits used the decimation of Huron society by disease and the threat of war to convert them to Christianity by utilizing frightening images of God, Jesus and the Devil, and incorporating these images into their theology and who, as ultimate warriors, were said to be able to surpass the cruelty of their Iroquoian counterparts.[4] One example is, Jesuit, Father Pierson's explanation of Jesus 'as the one who bears the war bundle':

> I am talking now of one who bears the reed mat of war, Jesus. He returned to the sky. He goes about overcoming them, killing the spirit and with it bringing the death of all sinning. All of us are enemies of the spirit. Jesus, the master will help us. He will wish that we overcome the spirit too. We will have the forces and ability by means of attachment to him.
>
> Jesus will also do this. Onontio (the French Governor) will overcome the Seneca when he goes with his troops. The one who bears the reed mat of war will do it, as I have said this day. All overcoming is such.
>
> We should congratulate Jesus, our master, as he overcame them. It would encourage our forces, so it would be certain that we will overcome the spirit who bears us ill will, and sinning. He fights for us also in that he discourages those spirits who are our enemies, who pursue us and bring us bad fortune. On this day he will take the group to the sky. He goes about seizing them, making them disappear, when he overcomes them.[5]

The Jesuits utilized these images and played on the psychology of the Huron as they expired in large numbers from disease and by war-

---

[4] John Steckly, "The Warrior and the Lineage: Jesuit Use of Iroquoian Images to Communicate Christianity, " in *Ethnohistory*, Vol 39, No.4, Fall 1992 (Duke University Press, 1992), 478-509.

[5] Pierre Potier, *The Fifteenth Report of the Bureau of Archives for the Province of Ontario for the Years 1918-1919*, (Toronto: Clarkson W. James, 1920), 539.

fare, in order to show the superiority of their deities over the Iroquoian ones, especially since the Jesuits were not affected by disease in the same way. Some Hurons converted to Christianity hoping they too would become immune to disease like the priests and that Jesus would look upon them in favor during war. Huron converts to Christianity were then placed in positions of power over their traditional counterparts by the Jesuits, and they were the only ones given access to the guns needed to repel their traditional enemy, the Five Nations Iroquois, especially the Mohawk and Seneca, which resulted in their being the best armed protectors of the society. This division weakened their ability to repel the enemy and led to their eventual defeat at the hands of the Iroquois.

With the demise of the remaining Huron by the Iroquois and the incorporation of many into the societies of the Seneca and Mohawk as replacements for their own losses, the Iroquois Confederacy would face its own destruction. The Christianized Huron were easily convinced by the Jesuits to help them in their quest to destabilize Iroquois society, and over the next few centuries into the present, Iroquois society would be threatened with extinguishment both externally through war, as well as internally through disease, displacement, and social upheaval. In the forefront of the upheaval of Iroquois society were the missionaries who, beginning with the Jesuits during the mid 17th century, would use the same psychological tactics of fear they had used on the Huron, to first divide Mohawk communities and later create divisions within the Five Nations Confederacy itself. In 1632, Jesuit Father Paul Le Jeune stated that "fear is the forerunner of faith."[6] By showing that their deity was superior in power to the Iroquois ones, the Jesuits could then begin the process of conversion.

By the year 1646, Jesuit missionaries began establishing themselves in Mohawk communities that had become vulnerable from disease and from continuous attacks by French forces, creating doubt in the viability of the Iroquois deities to protect them. It would eventually lead to a large group of Mohawks leaving the Mohawk valley to set up Roman Catholic villages along the Saint Lawrence River.

In 1666, after several devastating attacks by the French on traditional Mohawk villages, the Iroquois Confederacy decided to send ambassadors to sue for peace. Upon their arrival, the commander of the French, Tracy said to them:

> We want to have peace with you as well. However, your lands are our lands now. We claim it
> on behalf of the discoveries of Champlain and

---

[6] John Steckly, "The Warrior and the Lineage: Jesuit Use of Iroquoian Images to Communicate Christianity," in *Ethnohistory*, Vol 39, No.4, Fall 1992, (Duke University Press, 1992), 482.

the Black Robes who visited your Villages. You
will have to obey our laws and stop your attacks
on our allies.[7]

As a condition of peace, the French required that Jesuit priests be allowed to enter Mohawk communities. A Jesuit Priest named Fremen,
who arrived at the Mohawk village of Tionontoken soon after Tracy's attack, informed the hereditary chiefs that they must:

Stop your warfare and be men like us by
becoming Christians. If you kill any
Frenchmen, you will be hanged like the
wampum belt I have put on that pole.[8]

The obvious reason for the arrival of the priests was to pacify the remaining traditional Mohawk by both threat and by conversion and creating
more divisions amongst the Mohawks and their captive adoptees.
    It was during this period that a large contingent of Mohawks and
their Huron and Erie adoptees made their way towards the island of
Montreal, setting up the semi - Roman Catholic communities of Kahnawake and Kanehsetake. One of the first acts of the Jesuits was to
choose a war chief in the newly formed Catholic communities in order to
protect the French settlements from attack by traditional Iroquois. They
then chose a religious lay chief to administer the affairs of the settlements according to the wishes of the priests.[9]
    This strategy was used as a means of protection for the French
villages. Both Iroquoian and Algonquin Christian communities were established along river approaches to the island of Montreal so that they
would be a first line of defense for the French inhabitants of the island if
they were attacked. This is exactly what happened in 1637, when traditional Iroquois attacked the Christian Algonquin community at Sillery,
dispersing many of its Algonquin inhabitants, yet at the same time allowing the French inhabitants to bolster their defenses. Within a few years of
setting up the Roman Catholic communities, Jesuits would be coaxing
Christianized Mohawks to go out on war expeditions against other Iroquois under the threat of attack if they refused to obey the priests.
    By the 1680s, some Roman Catholic Mohawk's had helped the
French attack Seneca settlements. During a campaign against the Senecas
in 1687, (headed by Jacques Rene de Brisay, Sieur de Denonville), the

---

[7] Thomas Grassman, *The Mohawk Indians and Their Valley: Being a Chronology Documentary Record to the End of 1693*, (Schenectady, NewYork: Hugo
Photography and Printing Co., 1969), 250.
[8] Ibid., 443.
[9] Henry S.J. Bechard, *The Original Caughnawaga Indians*, (Montreal,
Quebec: International Publishers, 1976), 30.

French used Christianized Mohawk scouts from Kahnawake to lead them into Seneca territory. When a Mohawk from the Catholic settlement of Kahnawake was asked by a traditional Mohawk from the Mohawk Valley as to why he participated in a campaign that had destroyed Seneca villages and their much needed food supplies, he explained, "The priest forced us to go, by saying we would be imprisoned if we did not."[10]

Alfred mentions that the bitterness between Christian and traditional Iroquois became so great that Christian Iroquois were no longer recognized as members of the Iroquois confederacy. In response the Christian Iroquois, Mohawks, along with their Catholic Algonquin allies, under the auspices of the priests, would create a confederacy known as the Seven Nations Confederacy, which would align itself with French Interests. Traditional Iroquois remained allied with the interests of first the Dutch and then the English.[11]

Although the Jesuits remained influential in the affairs of the Christian Iroquois, it was under the direction of a Roman Catholic Sulpician, Father Francois Picquet, that the Christian Iroquois would become active participants in what became known as the Seven Years War, the largest war between the French and English involving Iroquois on both sides. In fact, Father Picquet was not only a counselor but also a soldier, according to Governor Duquesne, who was said to be worth ten regiments.[12]

By 1755, Mohawks from the Roman Catholic community of Kahnawake would be fighting against Mohawks from the valley in the battle of Lake George, a battle that would result in the death of the Anglican baptized Mohawk leader Hendrick, at the hands of Catholic Mohawks. Preceding the battle, the Catholic Mohawk and Mohawk from the valley faced off. In Mohawk Baronet, James Flexner relates:

> One of the Christian Mohawk from Kahnawake rose and asked, "Who are you and where are you going?"

> Hendrick answered, "I am a member of the Rotinonshonni, the greatest of all the onkwe honwe that live on turtle island."

> A Kahnawake Mohawk replied, "We are from the Seven Nation Confederacy, and we come with our father, the King of France, to fight the English; we have no quarrel

---

[10] Grassman, 443.
[11] Gerarld R. Alfred, *Heeding the Voices Of Our Ancestors: Kahnawake Mohawk Politics and the Rise of Native Nationalism*, (Toronto, Ontario: Oxford University Press, 1995), 47.
[12] Robert Choquette, Charles Lippy, & Stafford Poole, *Christianity Comes to the Americas*, (New York: Paragon House, 1992), 229.

with you. We therefore ask that you keep out of the way, lest we end of fighting one another."

Hendrick replied, "The Rotinonshonni have come to assist their brethren, the English against the French who are encroaching on our lands in the Ohio. The Kahnawake should join us in this worthy cause against them or keep out of the way."[13]

At that moment an over-exuberant Mohawk from the valley fired at a Kahnawake Mohawk. In a few minutes, forty Mohawk from both sides died, as they began killing one another. This was the first battle between respective members of the Iroquois nation. The Sulpician and Jesuit priests never advocated that, once they become Christian, the Iroquois remain passive in the wars between the French and the English, instead they reinforced their position that Catholic Iroquois fight on behalf of the French.

As the French remained influential with the Roman Catholic Mohawks throughout the seventeenth century and into the eighteenth century, the traditional Mohawk shifted their alliance in 1664 from the Dutch to the English, enemies of the French, thus beginning the process of Protestant evangelization among them. By the early 18th century Protestant missionaries had begun to visit Mohawk communities in response to a visit by a delegation to England in 1710 by four Mohawk leaders who required assistance in their battles with the French. The English asked that Protestant missionaries be sent to various Iroquois villages in return for their support. Upon arriving back in New York, Governor Hunter convened a meeting with Mohawk leaders advocating that they allow missionaries to be sent to their villages.[14] Within a few years, Protestant missionaries from various denominations were visiting various Iroquois communities. The national allegiances of these missionaries to both the English and the Americans would ring the death knell for the Iroquois Confederacy by the late eighteenth century.

It was during this period that young Iroquois men such as Joseph Brant, a Mohawk, were sent to be educated in the Protestant Christian tradition. Reviled today by his displaced people now living in Canada, Christianized Iroquois like Brant were a necessity for the English as a means to retain the Iroquois Confederacy as an ally in their wars against the French. Such men were used as pawns by both them and the Americans in their subsequent war against each other.

---

[13] James Thomas Flexner, *Mohawk Baronet: A Biography of Sir William Johnson*, (Syracuse, New York: Syracuse University Press, 1979), 170.
[14] John G. Garratt, *The Four Indian Kings*, (Canadian Cataloguing in Publication Data: Public Archives Canada, 1985), 13.

Brant, who came from a lineage with no political standing within the Iroquois confederacy, would be prompted up by his sister, Molly Brant's consort, William Johnson, and by Anglican missionary, John Stuart, as a leader and war chief of the Iroquois. He would also be given a Captainship in the English army. Hereditary Iroquois leaders in Canada still maintain that they never sanctioned the decisions that Brant made on behalf of the Iroquois Confederacy with the English, one of which was to side with the English during the American War of Independence.

In fact, it appears that during Iroquois Confederacy proceedings at Johnson Hall, where the destiny of the Iroquois and their lands were to be decided, few hereditary leaders showed up or were even invited to attend. Hereditary chief Hadahgihgrenhta maintained that war chiefs like Brant tried to circumvent the traditional leadership in favor of their own. During one council held at Johnson Hall, when William Johnson asked if any hereditary leaders had showed up, a war chief replied:

> The reason that you do not see many of our roy-
> aner here is because the weather and the roads
> are bad. They are not able to travel like we can.
> Therefore, negotiate with us, for it is we who are
> the leaders of consequence who manage the af-
> fairs of our people. Our royaner and clan
> mothers are a parcel of old people, who say
> much but do little. It is we who have the power
> and ability to settle matters with you, and we are
> determined to answer you honestly from our
> hearts to the fullest.[15]

The Oneida, who neighbored the Mohawk and were one of the Six Nations Iroquois, would make their own alliance with the Americans and fight against the English and other Iroquois allied with them during The War of Independence. They would fall under the influence of Reverend Samuel Kirkland, a Presbyterian missionary. He would convert to his form of Protestant Christianity an Oneida war chief named Skanandor, who would become influential in getting the Oneidas to side with the Americans against the other nations of the Iroquois Confederacy.

Kirkland was a strong proponent of abstinence and was one of the main attractions of the Oneida to his form of Christianity. After convincing the Oneidas to side with the Americans, he told them, "Go to the storehouse and take anything you want. There are barrels of rum waiting there."[16] The influence that Christian influenced war chiefs like Brant

---

[15] Barbara Graymont, *The Iroquois in the American Revolution*, (Syracuse New York: Syracuse University Press, 1972), 45.
[16] Ibid., 112.

and Skanandor had on the Six Nations Confederacy in taking apposing sides during the war, would eventually fracture the unity that had been established many years before with the Peacemaker and the Keyeneren kowa.

After the War of Independence, George Washington gave away most of the lands of the Iroquois to his soldiers and to his supporters. Others became land speculators acquiring large tracks of Iroquois land for themselves. Kirkland was one of those speculators. The Iroquois could no longer consolidate their decisions. Except for a few Oneidas and Onondagas it resulted in most of the Iroquois being dispersed from their homelands.

The loss of hereditary leaders' power base to Christianized war chiefs, was summarized by one hereditary leader. When asked what had happened; he replied:

> Times are altered with us onkwe honwe. For-
> mally the warriors were governed by the wisdom
> of their uncles, the sachems, but now they take
> their own way and dispose of themselves, re-
> building their village without consulting the
> royaner. While we wish for peace, they are for
> war; brothers they must face the consequences.[17]

---

[17] Ibid., 163.

FOUNDATIONS FOR A DINÉ (NAVAJO) CONTRIBUTION TO A THEOLOGY OF BEAUTY

John D. Dadosky[*]

As the title of this paper indicates, the topic is about the foundations for a theology of beauty. It builds upon a preliminary thesis I suggested in a previous article that the Diné (Navajo) might make a significant contribution to a theology of beauty.[1] Although this is not a historical paper *per se*, it is necessary to say something about the recent historical paradigm shifts in Catholic thought which provide the general context for this paper. I am thinking of: 1) the movement from a classicist to an empirical notion of culture, and 2) a dramatic shift in the Church's theology of mission, away from a defensive stance to a more positive valuation of other cultures and religions. These two paradigm shifts are inextricably related to each other.

An Empirical Notion of Culture. Dogmatic theology prior to Vatican II was part of what the Canadian theologian Bernard Lonergan (1904-1984) described as classicist. He states:

> On the older view [classicist view], culture was conceived not empirically but normatively. It was the opposite of barbarism. It was a matter of acquiring and assimilating the tastes and skills, the ideals, virtues and ideas, that were pressed upon one in a good home and through a curriculum in the liberal arts. It stressed not facts but values. It could not but claim to be universalist. Its classics were immortal works of art, its philosophy was the perennial philosophy, its laws and structures were the deposit of wisdom and the prudence of [humankind]. Classicist education was a matter of models to be imitated, of ideal characters to be emulated, of eternal verities and universal laws.[2]

[*] John D. Dadosky, PhD. is an assistant professor of theology at Regis College/University of Toronto. His recently published book is titled *The Structure of Religious Knowing: Encountering the Sacred in Eliade and Lonergan* (SUNY Press, 2004). He is interested in the interface between Christianity and traditional indigenous religions, issues in faith and culture, and inter-religious issues.

[1] John D. Dadosky, "Walking in the Beauty of the Spirit: A Phenomenological Case Study of a Navajo Blessingway Ceremony," in *Mission*, VI/2 (1999), 210-21.

[2] Bernard Lonergan, *Method in Theology*, (Toronto: University of Toronto Press, 1990), 301.

The classicist notion of culture was normative, universalist, with little room for pluralism—one simply presupposed what amounted to a sort of Platonic overarching form of culture (i.e. Western European), against which all other cultures were compared and judged. Christian evangelization, as Karl Rahner put it, was one of "European export."[3] Needless to say, such a notion of culture contributed to the cultural destruction of many of the indigenous peoples.

The paradigm shift of which we speak has reversed the classicist and has issued in an empirical notion of culture. The former was deductive in that the idea of culture was deduced from a universal conception of human nature. In contrast, the latter is inductive—and this makes all the difference. Our notion of culture is now informed and expanded by contact with the vast numbers of cultures throughout the world. As far as the Church is concerned, Rahner seems to imply that the notion of a 'Roman Catholic Church' is being supplanted by an emerging notion of 'world Church.'[4]

Transforming Mission. The second paradigm shift concerns that of mission in the Church. We have hinted at some of this already in the classicist culture. What one might call the classicist notion of mission fostered the missionary view that the Church brings God or Christ to a culture where it was believed that God does not exist. In contrast, Vatican II formally inaugurated the paradigm shift in the Church's relationship to other cultures and religions and sought to reverse such triumphalism. The *Declaration on Religious Freedom* (*Dignitatis Humanae*) insured that Christianity could no longer force the Gospel Message on another culture, and the *Declaration on the Relation of the Church to Non-Christian Religions* (*Nostra Aetate*) put forth a landmark positive valuation of non-Christian religions. However, the task remains for the Christian churches to fully grant traditional aboriginal religions the same status and respect as the so-called 'world religions.' In addition, the *Decree on the Church's Missionary Activity* (*Ad Gentes*) acknowledged that the Holy Spirit was present in the world prior to the Incarnation. This acknowledgement affected a shift in the Church's missionary emphasis. Where once the view of missionary work was that missionaries brought "Christ" to a culture, now following the paradigm shift, one recognizes that Christ (or the Spirit) is already present in the culture.[5]

While Vatican II may have formally inaugurated this paradigm shift, the foundations remain to be built upon, specifically with respect to how the Church can be enriched by its encounter with other cultures and

---

[3] Karl Rahner, "Towards a Fundamental Theological Interpretation of Vatican II," in *Theological Studies* 40 (1979), 717.
[4] Ibid., 717.
[5] On the paradigm shift in theology of mission, see David J. Bosch, *Transforming Mission: Paradigm Shifts in Theology of Mission* (Maryknoll, NY: Orbis Press, 1991), especially Chapter 10.

religious traditions. Bernard Lonergan states that theology mediates "between a cultural matrix and the significance and role of a religion within that matrix."[6] Robert Doran emphasizes that this mediation is one of "mutual self-mediation" between the religion and the cultural matrix.[7] Ideally, the interaction between culture and religion are mutually enriching, so that theology is continually renewed and brought up to date through the dynamic interplay of the two. In this way, the Diné notion of beauty may enrich the Church's theology of itself, especially with respect to the development of a theological aesthetics.

Contemporary Exigencies
The Swiss theologian Hans Urs Von Balthasar (1905-1984) decries the loss of transcendental *beauty* in contemporary theology (and philosophy).[8] Transcendental *beauty* is inextricably linked to the transcendentals of the *good* and the *true*. Hence, the eclipse of *beauty* leads to the relativity of truth and morality as well. Moreover, a division between or neglect of one of the transcendentals of *beauty*, *truth*, and *goodness* has ramifications in the human subject. For example, one of the effects of the bifurcation between *beauty* and *truth* is the inability to make aesthetic judgments. Consequently, one of the effects of this is that it becomes difficult to distinguish art from play. Likewise, the bifurcation between *beauty* and *goodness* can lead to a sort of split personality within the moral subject. One can think, for example, of some of the Nazis officers who had refined and developed aesthetic tastes while simultaneously committing depraved acts of immorality.

Concerning the eclipse of beauty Balthasar declares "if this is how the transcendentals fare because one of them [beauty] has been banished what will happen to Being itself?...The witness borne by Being becomes untrustworthy for the person who can no longer read the language of beauty."[9] In the limit, the eclipse of *beauty* ultimately leads to the diminishment of meaning, and with this our existence is threatened.

If Balthasar is correct in claiming that one of the chief ailments of modern theology has been the eclipse of transcendental *beauty* from

---

[6] Lonergan, xi.
[7] Robert Doran, "Lonergan and Balthasar Methodological Considerations," in *Theological Studies* 58 (1997), 65. I have applied this notion of mutual self-mediation to the issue of religious identity as related to the cultural matrix. See John D. Dadosky, "The Dialectic of Religious Identity: Lonergan and Balthasar," in *Theological Studies* 60/1 (1999), 1-22.
[8] Hans Urs Von Balthasar, *Seeing the Form*, Volume One, of *The Glory of the Lord: A theological Aesthetics*, trans., Erasmo Leiva-Merikakis, ed. Joseph Fessio, S. J., and John Riches (San Francisco: Ignatius, 1982), 18-19.
[9] Hans Urs Von Balthasar, *Seeing the Form*, Volume One, of *The Glory of the Lord: A theological Aesthetics*, trans., Erasmo Leiva-Merikakis, ed. Joseph Fessio, S. J., and John Riches (San Francisco: Ignatius, 1982), 18-19.

theological reflection, the restoration of *beauty* to its proper place in theological reflection may have ramifications beyond what Balthasar could have imagined. He had little to say about ecological concerns, perhaps because it was not an exigency in his time. However, let us assume for a moment he is correct in his analysis of the condition of *beauty*. We can apply his comments to the current ecological crisis by coming to understand that the loss of the transcendental *beauty* threatens the very *being* of our planet. That is, insofar as pollution, global warming, diminishing natural resources, etc. threaten to bring our planet to what Balthasar might describe as "a mere lump of existence."[10]

Moreover, since his formidable attempt at a theological aesthetics, there is an increasing awareness in contemporary theology of the potential contribution from other cultures and religions to provide categories and insights that enrich theological discourse. There is also a need for theology to take account of ecological concerns in such a way that it will instill a responsibility in all believers to be stewards of the Earth.

The ecological exigency follows from the recognition that much of theology is conditioned by an anthropocentrism which emphasizes the privileged place of humans in the cosmos. However, this has not always been the case. Peter Phan, a Catholic theologian, refers to Irenaeus and St. Francis as examples of people who promoted ideals that included an ecological motif.[11] The Protestant theologian Stanley Grenz suggests that the traditional Christian theology of sin contributes to ecological irresponsibility. He states:

> The destruction of community occurs on the level of our relationship to creation. As we noted earlier, sin means that we no longer live in harmony with the 'garden' in which the Creator placed us. Designed to enjoy fellowship with the rest of God's good creation, we now live in alienation from the natural world around us. Rather than seeing ourselves as creative beings under God, we seek to be the creator, to control nature and enslave it to serve us. We no longer see the earth as an organic whole which we serve on God's behalf. Rather, in our insatiable but misguided quest for a 'home,' we view the earth as the raw material for our transforming activity.[12]

Therefore, it would seem that a restoration of transcendental *beauty* into theological reflection could readily include an ecological component that

---

[10] Ibid., 19.

[11] See Peter Phan, "Eschatology and Ecology: The Environment in End-Times," in *Dialogue & Alliance* 9/2 (Fall/Winter, 1995), 99-114.

[12] Stanley J. Grenz, *Theology for the Community of God*, (Grand Rapids, MI: Erdmans, 1994), 207.

includes an embrace of the beauty in all creation. For Thomas Berry, who refers to himself as a *geo-logian* (rather than a theologian), the healing of the Earth is inextricably connected with embracing the beauty of God that is mediated through the Earth and all of creation. He states: "Intimacy with the planet in its wonder and beauty and the full depth of its meaning is what enables an integral human relationship with the planet to function."[13]

Balthasar wrote a multi-volume trilogy in order to construct a systematic theological aesthetics and to restore transcendental *beauty* to theological reflection. Although his contributions are brilliant, Balthasar may have never have imagined that the clues to the restoration of *beauty* lie within a non-western culture such as the Diné (Navajo), who possess a rich religious complex vastly different from Balthasar's European Christianity. Berry, one of the chief promoters of a theology that integrates ecological concerns, suggests that in order to heal the Earth we need to listen to the wisdom of indigenous peoples.[14]

These thinkers provide a context (or foundations) from a Western Christian perspective for a theology of beauty that could be enriched by certain insights from the Diné notion of beauty. The Diné notion of beauty is complex and will require more research, and this sketch will not do it justice. I will be content if I am able at least to demonstrate the provocative nature of this notion.

The Diné (Navajo) Notion of Beauty

The word for *beauty* in the Diné (Navajo) language is difficult to translate into English. The word commonly used is *hózhó*, and it signifies more than Westerners have traditionally ascribed to the word *beauty*. *Hózhó* can be glossed as *beautiful*, but it also refers to a peaceful, harmonious environment.[15] According to Leland Wyman, the term "includes everything that a Navajo thinks is good—that is, good as opposed to evil, favorable…as opposed to unfavorable or doubtful."[16] Gladys Reichard states that it refers to 'perfection as it is attainable' by human beings— the end towards which all beings (natural and supernatural) strive.[17] Clyde Kluckhohn claims that *hózhó* is the central concept in Diné philosophy and religious thinking. He states "in various contexts it is best translated as 'beautiful,' 'harmonious,' 'good,' 'blessed,' 'pleasant,' and 'satisfying.'" Part of the difficulty of translating the term into English,

---

[13] Thomas Berry, *The Great Work*, (New York: Bell Tower, 1999), xi.
[14] Ibid., 176-80.
[15] Robert W. Young and William Morgan, Sr., *Analytical Lexicon of Navajo*, (Albuqurque, NM: University of New Mexico Press, 1992), 459.
[16] Leland C. Wyman, *Blessingway*, (Tucson, Arizona: University of Arizona Press, 1970), 7.
[17] Gladys Reichard, *Navaho Religion: A Study of Symbolism*, Bollingen Mythos Series (Princeton: Princeton University Press, 1990) 45.

according to Kluckhohn, lies in the fact that the term simultaneously connotes moral and aesthetic value.[18]

Gary Witherspoon accepts the general interpretations of these researchers but argues that their interpretations rely heavily on the stem – *zhó*, rather than the emphasis on the prefix *ho-*.[19] This is significant for Witherspoon because *ho-* is a verbal prefix that connotes a reference to the larger environment as opposed to a more specific reference, which would use the prefix *ni-*.

> Thus when one says *nizhóní* [one] means 'it (something specific) is nice, pretty, good,' whereas *hózhóní* means that everything in the environment is nice, beautiful, and good. As verbal prefix, *ho* refers to (1) the general as opposed to the specific; (2) the whole as opposed to the part; (3) the abstract as opposed to the concrete; (4) the indefinite as opposed to the definite; and (5) the infinite as opposed to the finite.[20]

In this way, Witherspoon emphasizes that "hózhó refers to the positive or ideal environment. It is beauty, harmony, good, happiness, and everything that is positive, and it refers to an environment which is all-inclusive."[21] One begins to get a sense of the provocative nature of this notion for an environmental ethics.

Witherspoon contrasts *hózhó* to its opposite *hóchxó'* which can be glossed as "the ugly, unhappy, and disharmonious environment." These conditions are attributed to "evil intentions" and "evil deeds." When these afflict a person, a ceremony can restore one to the balanced condition of *hózhó*.[22]

The Diné notion of beauty is an important aspect of their ritual life and is integral to at least two ceremonies: the *Beautyway* and the

---

[18] Clyde Kluckholn, "The Philosophy of the Navaho Indians," in *Ideological Differences and World Order*, ed. F.S.C. Northrop, pp. 356-84 (New Haven: Yale University Press, 1949), 368-69.

[19] Gary Witherspoon, *Language and Art in the Navajo Universe*, (Ann Arbor, MI: University of Michigan Press, 1977), 24.

[20] Ibid.

[21] Ibid.

[22] John Farella accuses Witherspoon's interpretations of *hózhó* (and others like it) as being dualist because he believes they impose Manichean interpretations onto the Diné worldview and that they "reduce" the notion of beauty to one with moral connotations. See John R. Farella, *The Main Stalk: A Synthesis of Navajo Philosophy*, (Tucson, Arizona: University of Arizona Press, 1993), 35. This issue is complex and lies beyond the scope of this paper. Without going into detail, while I agree with some of Farella's concerns, in general I think his comments are somewhat dismissive.

Blessingway.[23] The latter comprises what John Farella describes as the "backbone" or "main stalk" of the Diné ritual life. Farella states: "Blessingway and Navajo culture are, from the native perspective, identical."[24]

The term *Blessingway* is a gloss (a poor one according to Farella) for the word *hózhǫ́ǫ́jí*, which contains the word *hózhǫ́*. The goal of the Blessingway, one could say, is to restore and/or promote the 'beautiful' conditions of health, happiness, long life, and harmony for oneself and one's people.

For the Diné, beauty is not something to be simply gazed upon but rather something to be integrated within one's life, and something that permeates all of one's life. Witherspoon states: "The Navajo do not look for beauty; they normally find themselves engulfed in it. When it is disrupted, they restore it; when it is lost or diminished, they renew it; when it is present, they celebrate it."[25] The ideal of such integration can be summed up in this following excerpt from a Navajo prayer:

> With beauty (hózhǫ́) before me, I walk.
> With beauty behind me, I walk.
> With beauty above me, I walk.
> With beauty below me, I walk.[26]

The goal of all of this is reflected in the phrase (or blessing) that is central to the Blessingway ceremony and to the Diné philosophical worldview: *Sa'a Naghái bik'e hózhǫ́*—traditionally glossed by some ethnologists as *long life and happiness* but it also can mean completeness, wholeness. These glosses do not capture the richness and depth of this fascinating and complex notion, but unfortunately it remains a subject for further study.[27]

In general, the ceremonial life of the Diné aims at restoring the afflicted individual to the path of *beauty* in cases where that individual has strayed from the path for one reason or another. In this way, one can say that the Diné ideal is to 'walk in beauty' in every aspect of one's life. Finally, the notion is provocative in that the restoration of an individual to the condition of hózhǫ́ (beauty) simultaneously affects the restoration of the community.

---

[23] On the Beautyway ceremony see Leland C. Wyman (ed.) *Beautyway: A Navajo Ceremonial*, Bollingen Series LIII (New York: Pantheon Books, 1957). On the Blessingway Wyman, *Blessingway*.
[24] Farella, 189.
[25] Gary Witherspoon and Glen Peterson, *Dynamic Symmetry and Holistic Asymmetry in Navajo and Western Art and Cosmology*, (New York: Peter Lang, 1995), 15.
[26] Ibid.
[27] For a more extensive and critical review this notion see Chapter 5 in Farella's *Main Stalk*.

Implications and Conclusion

As I have suggested, the Diné may offer some insights into the restoration of transcendental *beauty* for Western Christians primarily because: 1) beauty is a fundamental integral notion within Diné cultural and religious identity, 2) the Diné have not lost their notion of beauty as Balthasar suggests Western Christians have, and 3) certain insights from their notion may contribute to a restoration of transcendental *beauty* in a way that adequately meets the exigencies of ecological concerns. I will briefly expand on the third point.

We have inherited a rich philosophical tradition in the West. However, in its negative aspects, it lends itself to the dualism of mind and body and the separation of human beings from nature. This directly affects our relationship with the environment. Witherspoon explains:

> In the Western world, where mind has been separated from body, where [humans have] been extracted from nature, where affect has been divorced from "fact," where quest for and focus upon the manipulation and accumulation of things has led [humans] to exploit rather than to respect and admire the earth and her web of life, it is not surprising that art would be divorced from the more practical of affairs of business and government and the more serious matters of science, philosophy, and theology.[28]

In contrast, Witherspoon emphasizes the more integrated notion of beauty as expressed in art in the Diné worldview:

> In the Navajo world, however, art is not divorced from everyday life, for the creation of beauty and the incorporation of oneself in beauty represent the highest attainment and ultimate destiny of [humankind]. Hózhó expresses the Navajo concept of beauty or beautiful conditions. But beauty is not separated from good, from health, from happiness, or from harmony. Beauty—hózhó—is the combination of all these conditions. It is not an abstractable quality of things or a fragment of experience; it is the normal pattern of nature and the most desirable form of experience.[29]

---

[28] Witherspoon, *Language and Art in the Navajo Universe*, 151.
[29] Ibid.

We have noted that the Diné notion of beauty refers to the 'environment' holistically. This provides a fresh alternative to the dualism that permeates much of Western Christianity's philosophical and theological traditions.

Concluding comment. In his famous and intimate prayer to God, St. Augustine laments: "Too late have I loved you oh Beauty so ancient and so new." With the imminent environmental crises confronting our world today we cannot afford to be 'too late.' And it is not enough simply to put policies into place. Such policies need to be grounded within a larger more integrated worldview, one where *beauty*, *truth*, and *goodness* coincide in harmony. For Christians, this view will include a systematic theology that will adequately account for ecological concerns, and the Diné notion of *hózhó* (beauty) could provide an integral component for an ecological ethics and theology of beauty. Therein, the emphasis lies with human beings' recognition that the beauty of God is mediated through all creation and therefore they have a sacred responsibility to be stewards of all creation.

Admittedly, my reflections are far from exhaustive. Nor is it my intention to paint a nostalgic picture of the Diné worldview. Rather, I believe by listening to the wisdom of their tradition, they can assist us in a recovery of transcendental beauty so that we can begin, among other things, to heal the Earth from the use and abuse of humanity. In this way we may be able to say with the Diné:

> From the East beauty has been restored
> From the South beauty has been restored
> From the West beauty has been restored
> From the North beauty has been restored
> From the zenith in the sky beauty has been restored
> From the nadir of the earth beauty has been restored
> From all around me beauty has been restored.[30]

---

[30] Witherspoon, *Language and Art in the Navajo Universe*, 154.

PART IV

Christian Inculturation with the Cultures of Central and South America

Edited by
Bill Svelmoe
Saint Mary's College

THE KOGI MÁMA'S ECOLOGICAL ETHICS: LESSONS FOR CHRISTIANS

Dawn M. Nothwehr[*]

There is perhaps no better illustration of the relationship between ecology, ethics, spirituality, and the meaning of place than the life of the Kogi of the Sierra Nevada de Santa Marta mountain range in Northern Colombia. Their deep sense of place, as well as their intricate ecological wisdom and their profound awareness of social ethical responsibility is rooted in the narrative of their particular and intentional creation by Serankwa[1] according to $Sé$[2] to inhabit and care for "the heart of the earth," their unique region in northern Colombia. The law of $Sé$ legislates that everything must be in harmony from the beginning to the end of things. That is why, the Kogi say, our first step toward resolving the environmental crisis must be to recover the law of $Sé$, and fulfill it by paying proper tribute to the Guardians of the World. We must direct our thought toward $Sé$, (spiritual existence) through $alúna$.[3] The life of the Kogi is connected to the land and the knowledge and ways the Great Mother gave them in order to sustain their own life and flourishing and that of the entire world. In the Kogi worldview everything and everyone are spiritually interconnected from the moment of creation.[4] To step away from this *spiritual understanding* of their place is to invite disaster for themselves and for the entire world. The spiritual, ecological and social ethical duty of the Kogi is to maintain the harmony between themselves and the natural world and to banish from their life everything that would destroy it. For the Kogi, the world is a sacred place because the source of all is the same, the Great Mother, *Gaulcovaug.*

My aim here is to draw lessons from Kogi moral wisdom in or-

---

[*] Dawn M. Nothwehr, OSF, Ph.D. is Assistant Professor of Ethics at Catholic Theological Union, Chicago. Mutuality, feminist ethics of power, ecological ethics and Franciscan theology are her major interests. Her recent book is *Franciscan Theology of the Environment: An Introductory Reader,* (Quincy, IL: Franciscan Press, 2002).
[1] The one given the task of organizing the material world.
[2] Sé is spiritual existence. The law of Sé is the spiritual world that transforms material being.
[3] The spiritual amniotic sea of pure thought, memory, spirit, soul, mind, imagination.
[4] Gerardo Reichel-Dolmatoff, "The Loom of Life: A Kogi Principle of Integration," *Journal of Latin American Lore* 4/1 (1978), 12-27.

der to supplement and critique environmental ethics notions of the Christian West. To that end, in Part I, I briefly examine several of the main spiritual, ecological and social ethical notions vital for the Kogi culture. I begin with a brief historical survey of the Kogi people to set the context. Next, since the *mámas* are the primary authorities and the keepers of moral wisdom in this culture, I briefly examine their training and social role. Then, I address the reality that, even though this culture is entrenched in a feminine cultural mythic system, the role of men remains significant. After that, particular attention is given to the duty, according to the myth of The Great Mother, of men (and women) to maintain a balance between the masculine and the feminine. I then bring greater illumination to all of these elements by showing how the value and the relationship of the spiritual and material worlds are grounded in Kogi cosmogony and cosmology. I conclude this section of the paper by reviewing the classic case study by Gerardo Reichel-Dolmatoff of Kogi cultural change and environmental awareness. In Part II, I use a narrative approach to comparative religious ethics to glean significant truths from Kogi moral wisdom to supplement and critique Christian ecological ethics.[5] Please note, by holding up the positive moral wisdom of the Kogi, I in no way claim that they are a perfect moral society. There are many aspects of Kogi ethics that can be challenged by the Christian West. That challenge however, will need to be taken up at another time.

I. Spiritual, Ecological, and Social Ethical Notions

A Brief Historical Summary

The Kogi are the most intact living indigenous pre-Colombian nation directly descended from the Tairona civilization that flourished in the Sierra Nevada de Santa Marta region of Northern Colombia around 1,000 A.D. The Tairona civilization was highly developed and particularly skilled in spectacular gold-work, stonework, pottery, weaving, and engineering – building irrigation terraces, stone roads and houses that still function today.[6] "The Lost City" or Ciudad Perdida rediscovered in

---

[5] For more on narrative method in comparative religious ethics, see Darrell J. Fasching and Dell deChant, *Comparative Religious Ethics: A Narrative Approach* (Malden, MA: Blackwell Publishers, Ltd., 2002), especially 1-21.
[6] Gerardo Reichel-Dolmatoff, "Cultural Change and Environmental Awareness: A Case Study of the Sierra Nevada de Santa Marta, Colombia," *Mountain Research and Development* 2/3 (1982), 290. See Alan Ereira, writer and producer, *From the Heart of the World: The Elder Brother's Warning,* A BBC Television

the 1970's, bears witness to a civilization that rivals that of the Incas and the Aztecs. As we shall see, the Kogi have cherished Tairona wisdom and technology, though violence of all sorts has left its disorienting mark on their culture.

The Kogi bear the memory of the beginning of time and have vivid recollections of the Spanish conquest of 1498 (though they were never conquered), especially of Rodrigo de Bastidas (1525).[7] At first the peace-loving Kogi traded with the Spanish. However, about 1600 with the arrival of Catholic priests who forbade them to continue religious rites, and as conditions worsened under Governor Juan Guiral Velón, the Kogi recognized their survival depended on moving up into the mountains and isolating themselves.[8] This isolation served them well to the present day; they do not welcome others to their land, which they hold is sacred space.

Presently, the Kogi are one of three surviving Tairona groups. They live on the north and western sides of the Sierra Nevada de Santa Marta (See Maps I and II). Numbering about 6,000, they survive by focusing their energy on agriculture and the life of the spirit and the mind.[9] Unfortunately, ever since the Colombian government built a road linking Santa Marta with Venezuela, and after the re-discovery of the "Lost City" ecological destruction has skyrocketed along with "development."[10] It has become necessary for the Kogi, "the Elder Brother," to

---

production in association with the Goldsmith Foundation, New York: Mystic Fire Video, 1993, (sound, color, ½ inch, VHS videocassette): "Despite the punishing climate, these roads and stones still exist. One hundred and sixty inches of rainfall a year for five hundred years have not eroded these walls...The Kogi ancestors knew how to build with the forces of nature in mind, in contrast. . .our cities fight nature and if we abandon them they crumble."

[7] See Alan Ereira, *From the Heart of the World*, (videocassette). See also Gerardo Reichel-Dolmatoff, "Training for the Priesthood among the Kogi of Colombia," in Johannes Wilbert, ed., *Enculturation in Latin America*, UCLA Latin American Studies 37, (Los Angeles: UCLA Latin American Center Publications, 1976), 265-88.

[8] Donald Tayler, *The Coming of the Sun – A Prologue to Ika Sacred Narrative*, Monograph No. 7. (Pitt Rivers Museum: University of Oxford, 1997), 10. See Alan Ereira, *From The Heart of the World*, (videocassette). See also Gerardo Reichel-Dolmatoff, "Cultural Change," 290. In addition see G. Reichel-Dolmatoff, "The Great Mother and the Kogi Universe: A Concise Overview," *Journal of Latin American Lore* 13/1 (1987), 89-91.

[9] See Tairona Heritage Study Center, "Tribal Groups of the Sierra Nevada de Santa Marta in the 20th Century," < http://www.lamp.ac.uk/tairona/b2tribes.html > (July 31, 2002). See also Gerardo Reichel-Dolmatoff, "Cultural Change," 290.

[10] See Gerardo Reichel-Dolmatoff, "Cultural Change," 294-95.

communicate with the "Younger Brother" who threatens their survival.[11] On January 21, 1987 the Gonavindua Tairona was founded to link the Kogi with other indigenous peoples and to seek their legal independence and the autonomy of their traditional lands.[12] In 1989 the BBC's Alan Ereira was permitted to film a documentary on the Kogi, and in 1990 through his efforts, the Tairona Heritage Trust was established as a British non-governmental organization.[13] Administration of the Trust is currently done through the University of Wales anthropology department at Lampeter. The Trust's Tairona Heritage Study Center carries out educational and preservation projects on behalf of the Kogi. With this historical sketch in mind, we now turn to a brief examination of several key elements of the Kogi culture (See Appendix I and Appendix II).

Social Structure and the Role of the *mámas*

The real authority in Kogi society belongs to the *mámas* (the enlightened ones), the priests. The would-be *máma* gains his or her status through first, being selected as an infant by the current *mámas* through a sacred process of divination.[14] As soon as he or she is weaned, and for the next 18 years, the child is secluded from contact with anyone but the *máma* and the other apprentices and spends time learning ritual and esoteric knowledge according to a rigorous curriculum that includes:

(1) Cosmogony, cosmology, mythology
(2) Mythical social origins, social structure, and organization
(3) Natural history: geography, geology, meteorology, botany, zoology, astronomy, biology
(4) Linguistics: ceremonial language, rhetoric

---

[11] See Tairona Heritage Study Center, "The Political Milieu in which the Trust Works," < http://www.lamp.ac.uk/tairona/b4polmil.html > (July 31, 2002). The Kogi call themselves the "Elder Brother" and everyone else the "Younger Brother." See Alan Ereira, *From the Heart of the World*, (videocassette).
[12] See Tairona Heritage Study Center, "Threats to Kogi Society, and their Response – The Founding of Gonivindua Tairona," < http://www.lamp.ac.uk/tairona/b3thrts.html > (July 31, 2002).
[13] Tairona Heritage Trust , < http://www.eremite.demon.co.uk/kogi.htm> (July 31, 2002).
[14] See Gerardo Reichel-Dolmatoff, "Training for the Priesthood," 272-74. See also Tairona Heritage Study Center, "*máma* Barardo's Description of the Training of a *máma*," <http://www.lamp.ac.uk/tariona/b9mamab.html> (July 31, 2002).

(5) Sensory deprivations: abstinence from food, sleep, and sex
(6) Ritual: dancing and singing
(7) Curing of diseases
(8) Interpretation of signs and symbols, dreams, animal behavior
(9) Sensitivity to auditory, visual and other hallucinations.[15]

With such powers the *máma* then functions as priest, diviner, curer, village administrator, and judicial authority. All decisions — personal and communal — require divinations by the *máma*. The outcome of such divinations affects every action. The *mámas* regularly question the members of their community to determine whether the person has done anything to disturb the *Yulúka* or balance of life in the community. On the basis of these "confessions," the *mámas* not only exercise judicial authority but also gain an intimate knowledge of the community members and events that are important to their exercise of power.

Traditionally, some girls were selected by divination to be educated and trained by the wives of the *mámas* and older women to prepare "pure" foods, collect aromatic and medicinal herbs, and to assist in preparation for minor rituals.[16] However, women can also become *mámas*. In fact in this role, ritual actions by female *mámas* vividly portray the Great Mother cosmology. *Máma* Theresa exemplifies this point as she initiates a young boy:

> The point she wanted to stress was that it is woman who gives men their manhood. 'Yes, that's the way it is. I know how to give the *poporo* too. You put two coca leaves into the mouth of the boy and you bless them. And you also have to bless the *poporo* stick before you put it into his mouth. Just as the Mother first gave the *poporo* to men I also give it now. You have to be able to stay awake for four nights thinking of the Mothers and Fathers of coca and of the *poporo* stick and of the shells and of the *poporo*.'[17]

---

[15] Gerardo Reichel-Dolmatoff, "Training for the Priesthood," 278-79.
[16] Ibid., 277.
[17] Ibid.

Men and the Great Mother

It is the initiation rite in which the boy is given a *poporo* that signals his passage to manhood. The use of the *poporo* is accompanied by the chewing of coca leaves. The boy holds a hollowed out gourd (shaped like a penis, but which represents a womb) containing a powdery lime shell substance. He periodically licks the end of a stick and dips it inside, collecting a bit of the lime substance, and then eats it. He then rubs the wet stick on the mouth of the gourd, meditating as he does all of this. The combination of lime shell and coca leaf create a mild narcotic effect which helps achieve a state of mind making it easier to communicate with the ancestors.[18] According to Alan Ereira:

> [T]he powder of burned seashells inside is the essence of fertility, and for a boy to grow to manhood he must learn to feed on that. That, and the coca leaves, harvested only by women, will make him fit to father children and tend the land - to develop a relationship with a woman in the flesh, and with the Mother Earth. The *poporo* is the mark of civilisation. Eating from it reminds a man of what he is, and keeps him in harmony with the Great Mother.[19]

When their hands are not occupied with work, Kogi men will be seen "writing their thoughts" with the *poporo,* seeking harmony and balance with all of life.[20]

---

[18] Alan Ereira, *From the Heart of the World,* (videocassette): "The toasted leaf they chew is as far from refined cocaine as rye bread is from whisky. It has been a food for thousands of years for native Americans, giving them important vitamins, and enabling them to endure long periods without food and sleep."

[19] Alan Ereira, *The Heart of the World,* (London: John Cape, 1990), 209.

[20] Ibid., 209. See also Ibid., 90-91 where Ereira quotes *máma* Barardo's instructions to a boy being initiated: "When you have a wife you have to look after her, you have to work for her, make clothes for her, you have to care for her, you mustn't ever hit her or treat her badly. Now receiving this poporo you must think about these things. If you want a woman you have to speak well too, you have to talk to her parents asking their permission, then you can talk to the girl, ask her to give you water, speak well to her. Yes, you have to care for her a lot. You should take her with you to bathe, collect firewood for her, and get food for her. You must look after a woman well.... And now that you're going to receive a woman you should build your own house separately, you can't go on living with the other boys. You'll live separately with your wife, work for her, bring food for her, so that she can cook, you've got to look after your woman, you really have to care for her, you must bring her food, bring her meat, buy her

The Masculine and Feminine Balance and the Great Mother

The Kogi term, *Yulúka*, means the process through which balance is achieved. According to Reichel-Dolmatoff — it must be achieved within the individual, within society and within the world, and essentially it means the balance between the feminine and masculine principles.[21] Alan Ereira explains:

> When we look at the Kogi world, we do not see what they see. Men and women are not simply people, they are the embodiment of principles....The harmony and balance of the world is constructed out of the partnership of masculine and feminine, the dynamic process of weaving on the loom of life. All Kogi life is built around the complementarity of male and female. The Mother did not only create the physical world, but also shaped and peopled *alúna,* creating a Mother and Father for everything that exists. Life is meaningless without procreative energy, and whatever is alive must have a Mother and a Father— not only in physical fact, but also in *alúna,* the metaphysical world. The Kogi perceive life in many things which in our understanding are inanimate; any object which has purpose and meaning in the world has a metaphysical form in *alúna,* and therefore must be sustained by a balance of sexual forces, by its own Mother and Father.[22]

Unfortunately, with the encroachment of modernity this principle of *Yulúka* has been under siege. Hopefully, the many contradictions that have recently distorted the Kogi traditional vision of this balance will be halted and the tradition will be renewed to more practically reflect that

---

chickens and pigs so that she eats well. Give her animals, and when you go off to collect firewood come back quickly. Don't wander about looking after other women, other people's women. You've got your own woman and you have to look after her. When you've received your poporo, you have to act responsibly, you mustn't go on playing about with other children, you have to be responsible. Towards *mámas*, Comisarios and Cabos you have to act respectfully."
[21] See also Tairona Heritage Study Center, Alan Ereira, "Some Notes on the Status of Women in Kogi Society," < http://www.lamp.ac.uk/tiarona/b11womensoc.html > (July 31, 2002).
[22] Ibid.

ideal (See Appendix III). As Mary Ramos puts it:

> Woman is the focal point of Kogi culture since their cen-
> tral deity is the Great Mother. They are born from her
> and return to her uterus when they die. The Kogi horizon
> is not formed by mountains and valleys, but by the out-
> ward appearance of all that is feminine, for example, the
> green fields and the blue lakes are erotic visions, caves
> and lagoons are all considered to be hába's womb where
> they can leave offerings and make her fertile. (Hába
> means 'mother'.) Women therefore should be treated
> with the utmost respect.[23]

It is to the origins of this vision in the cosmology of the Great Mother
that we now turn.

Kogi Cosmogony and Cosmology: Spiritual, Ecological, and Social Ethical Roots

There are three fundamental dimensions to the Kogi cosmogony: a nine-
layered universe; a nine-tiered temple; and a nine months phased human
womb. The three components were simultaneous processes – first in
alúna; then, in what Westerners call reality.[24] Each of the three dimensions developed in distinct internal chronological phases. For example,
phases of the womb process are first, oceanic; second, therimorphic; and
third the androgyne. For the Kogi, these three components originating in
the Great Mother are the essential structures through which cosmogony,
embriogenesis, and architecture are intimately related.

The universe has nine layers that form a Cosmic Egg that is oriented within the seven points of reference – North, South, East, West,
Zenith, Nadir, and Center (See Appendix V). The egg is divided in an
upper and lower set of beehive shapes, each containing four spirit-
inhabited worlds. The upper half is benevolent life-preserving spirits and
the lower half is inhabited with malevolent and destructive spirits. The

---

[23] Ibid. See also Mary Ramos, "The Kogi – Guardians of the World" (Ph.D.
diss., University of Glasgow, Scotland, 1990).
[24] See G. Reichel-Dolmatoff, *The Sacred Mountain of Colombia's Kogi Indians*,
(New York: E.J. Brill, 1990), 10.

middle layer is our world.[25]

The first human was created when The Great Mother, as an androgyne, impregnated herself with the phallic hardwood stick she used to extract lime from a gourd container, and subsequently gave birth to *Sintána*. Later, *Sintána* had sexual relations with his Mother and numerous offspring were born. The first offspring were the Lords of the Universe and females who became the spouses of the lords. The daughters are identified with the nine distinct types of agricultural soil of varying fertility found in the Sierra Nevada de Santa Marta.[26] These figures were appointed as the chiefs, fathers, and mothers of various aspects of the created universe.[27] In subsequent incestuous relations with brothers and sisters, the Tuxe and Dake social patterns were established in Kogi society.

Rooted in this creation myth, the Kogi have developed a sophisticated spirituality that links the metaphysical and material worlds. According to Raman Gil, at the core of this system is *Sé*, spiritual existence.[28] The Great Mother originated spirit and thought, spinning out the first spiritual Parents (*Kaku Sé, Zaku Sé, Ade Sé, Abu Sé, Jawa Sé, Jante Sé*). Thus, everything was first created in spirit, in the non-material world as ideas. The Law of *Sé* is the spiritual world that transforms the material world. *Sé* holds everything that comes into being in a harmonious balance. From these diverse ideas, material existence and the vast world that exists only in the spirit, comes into being. Each species that emerges was given its specific function and a corresponding tribute that needs to be paid to keep it in harmony with all-else in the world. When the *mámas* meditate, they are communing with *Sé* and seeking to fulfill the Law of the Great Mother.

Sé, the Kogi believe, has the power to build or to destroy. If the law of *Sé* is not heeded, and because there is so much in *Sé* that has not yet been brought into being, destruction may well take place, and creation may simply begin again. This can be avoided, however, if humans

---

[25] See G. Reichel-Dolmatoff, "The Great Mother," 83-85. Also see G. Reichel-Dolmatoff, *The Sacred Mountain*, 10-12. The other two realms are explained in detail here, but will not be addressed in this paper.

[26] G. Reichel-Dolmatoff, "The Great Mother," 102-03.

[27] Ibid., 93-95. There are numerous versions of this account.

[28] Ramon Gil, a Colombian trained by the *mámas* as a spokesperson for the Gonavindua Tairona in Tairona Heritage Study Center, "Spirituality and Materiality - Ramon Gil Explains the Connection between the Two," < http://www.lamp.ac.uk/tairona/b14ramontext.html > (July 31, 2002).

will make the proper offerings and begin to work in the spirit. [29] The law of *Sé* covers every aspect of life. The name given the law of *Sé* is *Sentura Gwiawimundwa*; it is the thought that shapes our thought. It existed before the dawning of time and before the invisible became visible. Everything evolved from these spiritual depths. When thought dawned, the material world arose. As Raman Gil explains, the Kogi were, "given this law and the task of paying tribute for all that exists – the trees, the water, the stones, the rain, the sky, the lakes."[30] The role of tribute is particularly obligatory for the *mámas*. That is the reason all Kogi must be accountable to the *mámas*.

The *mámas* teach that it was *Serankwa* that organized and brought the material world into being through *Sé* (See Appendix IV). The first thing he did was organize the rock, the support and center column, of the world, *Gwi*. Then he put a string over the top and pulled up, raising the peak of Gonadindua. The *kadukwa, shukwákula,* and s*hendukwa* were placed at the cardinal points at each end of the world. Finally, he organized the four corners of the world and gave to each a guardian so that the material world would move in cycles, constantly revitalizing life. *Serankwa* gave each material thing its rules for coexistence and harmony, but there was no masculine and feminine until *Seynekun* (fertility, woman, fertile mountain) appeared and found *Serankwa*. Then together they gave shape to the spiritual Parents of all that exists. In *Seynekun* are the books that contain the law, the behaviors and functions of each thing that exists, and also the ways and offerings necessary for making pay-

---

[29] Ibid. Raman Gil provides some examples about what it means to work in the spirit:

> not to take things in thought to make something.
> not to remove quantities of things from mountains without paying tribute.
> not to covet a woman.
> not to want to kill, people or animals.
> not to steal women, money, crops.
> not to catch something without permission, such as fish from the river or the sea.
> not to build housing without making a spiritual payment.
> not to make a road without making a spiritual payment.
> not to think of getting drunk without making a spiritual payment.
> not to breathe the air without making a spiritual payment.
> not to accept the light without making a spiritual payment.
> not to work with lies or falsehood in thought.

[30] Ibid.

ment of tributes to each being's Parents.[31] Thus, it is in the conjunction between the masculine and feminine, *Serankwa* and *Seynekun* that the spiritual world becomes this material world. The Parents all have the task of communicating the Law of *Sé* to the *mámas* so that the Kogi will be able to maintain this world according to that deep spiritual principal. Therefore, if people are to live correctly, they need to attend to the spiritual aspects of life before they participate or use anything in the material world.

Any survey of Kogi material culture reveals a limited inventory of about thirty elements.[32] Concerning material goods, this Kogi expression is profoundly revealing: "Yes, our things are simple, but they live."[33] Kogi thought is highly sophisticated and objects and words are multireferrential and symbolic. As G. Reichel-Dolmatoff explains:

> Kogi thought operates mainly by analogy, sometimes by Paracelsian signatures, one might say, and thus creates chains of associations, usually on a specific level of categories. For example, on a geographical level a mountain peak is what a Kogi house represents on an architectural level. Both images, that of a mountain, and a house, furthermore correspond to that of a human body, to a knitted cap, to a constellation in the night sky, to a mythological being, and so on. Practically all objects of material culture thus constitute configurations of symbolic meanings which have to be read at certain levels of interpretation. The little lime figure eight-shaped gourd used as a lime container is an image of the cosmos, and the stick inserted into it is its axis. It follows, by Kogi logic, that the gourd is a womb, the stick is a phallus, the cocoa leaves to be chewed are female, and the powered lime is semen....the important point is that each artifact constitutes a mnemonic device, a teaching device, and is

---

[31] Ibid., Some examples of the spiritual Parents for objects of the material world are: Kalashé and Kalawia: the lords of the trees, of the forest; Nimaku and Nimekun: the authorities of water, of fish; Gonduwashwi: of the air; Mamatungwi: of the sun; Zareymun and Zairiwmun: of the sea; Zanani and Zarekun; of wild and domestic animals; Ulukukwi and Ulukun: of the snake; Seaga: of tigers and lions; Kakuzhikwi: of the ants.

[32] G. Reichel-Dolmatoff, "The Loom of Life," 9-10.

[33] Ibid., 9.

a constant reminder of rules and procedures, of norms, traditions, and cultural truths. Nature with its innumerable aspects are similarly coded and imbued with symbolic meanings. Mountains and rivers, animals and plants, wind and rain, and, of course, the human body itself are structured into significant units, forms, and clusters, the relationships among which can be understood only by those who know the polymetaphoric thought patterns of the Kogi.[34]

For the Kogi, this material world is primarily the Sierra Nevada de Santa Marta, a sacred place, "the heart of the World," not a territory to be exploited in a utilitarian manner. The Kogi are the guardians of this sacred space. They care for it according to their moral and social codes, all of which originate with the Great Mother.

The Law of the Mother: Spiritual, Ecological and Social Responsibility

G. Reichel-Dolmatoff's classical case study of the Kogi age old ecological and ethical system is the singular resource for us as we seek resolution to the numerous and complex issues of our environmentally threatened world.[35] Numerous insights can be drawn from this study. The Kogi have been engaged in horticulture for more than a thousand years and have preserved and developed an agricultural system that is quite intricate.

While in the Sierra Nevada de Santa Marta there are villages of up to a hundred straw-thatched, single-family houses, those are used primarily for ceremonial occasions (See Appendices VI and VII). The majority of Kogi life is lived in the family's homesteads that are scattered over the mountains, at various altitudes and sites where the family has plots to farm. Depending on fluctuating rain patterns, the carrying capacity of a field, or the cluster of neighbors, the constellation of each farming site varies from season to season. All Kogi families are semi-migratory, caring for several fields of various kinds of crops that thrive at various locations at different altitudes. Harvesting is done constantly, but there is never an effort to plant a surplus; Kogi farming is intentionally a subsistence proposition. Efforts are made to leave some fields fallow for

---

[34] G. Reichel-Dolmatoff, "The Great Mother," 78.

[35] See G. Reichel-Dolmatoff, "Cultural Change," 289-98. The following sections on the Kogi ethical and ecological practices draw heavily on this study.

a period of time, however that is not done with any defined consistency. This system "provides more spatial and temporal crop variety, an inter-linking of growth cycles, and has less dependence on rainfall since it is likely that even during drought some rain will fall at some spot in the mountains."[36]

Typical procedure is to clear a field (slash) in December and burn off the residual during February or March. The numerous blackened rocks testify to the effects of this slash and burn technique going on for centuries. G. Reichel-Dolmatoff explains that each field is typically on a slope and about two hectares of mixed crops. At about one thousand me-ters, the Kogi usually raise the following crops: plantains, bananas, sweet manioc, some maize, squash, sapote, pineapple, together with coffee and sugarcane as cash crops. At about one thousand five-hundred meters, beans are added to the mix; and, above that altitude, some maize, beans, arracacha, and sweet potatoes are grown; and higher still, fields of pota-toes and onions are set.

In many areas of Kogi territory one finds extensive archeological terraces with structural details similar to those found in ancient Tairona lands in the Santa Marta area. These are cleverly constructed with rows of boulders and varying sized rocks that serve the double purpose of col-lecting eroded topsoil and collecting the run-off water so it can be drained back by a slight lateral slope of the embankment. There are also contour terraces on slopes of forty-five degrees or more.[37]

Evidence clearly indicates the Tairona practices of agriculture were carefully attuned to the environment of the Sierra, and particularly situated to prohibit soil erosion. The modern Kogi are aware of the bene-fits of Tairona soil conservation and irrigation techniques, but practice these only in a limited manner. They have not integrated the ancient ter-races and irrigation channels into their present system. Today's Kogi know there are good soils in these ancient areas, but the lands are revered as sacred spots belonging to the ancestors. Reichel-Dolmatoff concludes: "....the Tairona reworked the natural environment and thereby increased its yield, the Kogi maintain their natural environment by planting their scattered fields and gardens with a mixture of subsistence crops."[38] Ar-cheological evidence shows that the Kogi also shifted their dietary habits from those practiced by the Tairona. Modern Kogi now rely on plantains

---

[36] Ibid., 291.
[37] Ibid.
[38] Ibid.

as their staple crop where their ancient ancestors relied on maize. Even though the Kogi needed to reorient their life from intensive irrigation agriculture to subsistence farming, they by no means failed. The Tairona diaspora that saw the disintegration of communal life "was overcome with adaptive mechanisms of great efficiency."[39]

Having been forced into ever-higher altitudes by the encroachments of various types of settlers and by climate changes caused by pollutants from modern technologies, present-day Kogi have achieved a highly complex knowledge of the intricacies of the ecosystems within which they live. They have a keen awareness of the soil characteristics, temperatures, plant covers, rainfall, drainage, slope exposures, and winds of their regions and have developed precise patterns, procedures and expectancies for each area. "In their sloping fields, the Kogi will plant a variety of species, but a small number of individuals, thus creating a generalized ecosystem, but on terraced ground near villages or on valley floors, they will do the contrary and create a specialized system by planting a small number of species like plantains, pigeon peas, sugar cane or coca."[40] In summary, Reichel-Dolmatoff quotes Janzen: "...the Kogi practice a sustained-yield, non-expanding economy within the carrying capacity of their environment."[41] The Kogi do not plant surplus crops, nor are there facilities for storage beyond a day or two. Sun-dried plantains are the exception and are kept for emergency use.

These adaptations are rooted in the spiritual practices of the Kogi, and the traditional laws of the Great Mother. The Kogi *mámas* possess the profound knowledge of astronomy, meteorology and ecology that was combined to give birth to an agricultural system and way of life that works in relationship *with* the forces of the natural environment, and that does not seek to exert control *over* it. Key to the agricultural and ecological adjustments made over the centuries is the belief in *Yulúka*, that there must be a balance between humans and nature, resources and water management, soil and forest conservation, but also a spiritual and moral balance to the individual – for the good of the society. Of equal importance is the belief that all food plants have "mothers" and "fathers" who are their guardians. Rituals and offerings to the spiritual beings insure crop fertility. Planting and harvesting is governed by the *mámas*

---

[39] Ibid.

[40] Ibid., 293.

[41] Ibid. See D.H. Janzen, "Tropical Agroecosystems," *Science* 182 (1973), 1212 – 1219.

divining to receive *sewá* or permission to fell a tree or dig a ditch.

The *mámas* and most adults are aware of the limits of the human population carrying capacity of the fields of their region, and are greatly concerned about undue population pressure. Large families are frowned upon, and complex birth control calendars are used. That it is sinful to "multiply like ants" is a moral tenet, and the model for reproductive frequency is the "squash plant which produces only here and there a clearly traceable fruit."[42] The *mámas* are equally concerned to maintain some areas of undegraded environment for emergency reserves.

The Kogi seek out the *mámas* divination about all aspects of life. In other cultures, so much power in the hands of the elite has proven problematic. However, the comprehensive Kogi religious and philosophical discipline of frugality, continence, obedience to a moral code, and meditation upon ultimate realities requires and enables the *mámas* to place themselves *within* the chain of all beings of the universe. The Kogi *mámas* do not have special resources nor do they gain any benefits from their work. They live as austerely as the rest of the people. For example, the *mámas* would possess only a standard Kogi wardrobe of two outfits – one thread-bear for everyday use and one newer one for ceremonial use.[43]

The Kogi are vividly aware of the fact that there are ecological limits to their system. They know that there is a critical two thousand meter limit beyond which they could not raise their staple, plantains. Their scattered field system has the advantage of keeping them in contact with their ancestral heritage – land outlined for them by the Great Mother — dotted with trails, houses, stone markers and ritually named landmarks. But, increasingly modernity's encroachments are making life more tenuous and endangering this sacred land. Five major threats are: (1) outsiders who grow illegal marihuana (2) the communications technology industry that perceives this area a strategic spot (3) local political insurgents (4) miners of one of the hemisphere's largest coal deposits at El Cerrejón, and (5) international tourists. As Alan Ereira explained:

> High in the mountains lies a region the Kogi call the *pa-ramo*. This is where the rivers are born. The rivers feed the oceans in an endless cycle that creates the clouds that bring the snows, giving birth to the springtime greenery

---

[42] G. Reichel-Dolmatoff, "Cultural Change," 293.
[43] G. Reichel-Dolmatoff, "The Loom of Life," 8.

of the *paramo.* But now, it's yellow. It should be green.
The water is gone. The *paramo* is dying out. There used
to be snow visible all around here. Now the snow is re-
treating – very rapidly. When the *paramo* dies, everything below that depends on it will have to die. That is
what the Kogi mean when they say that unless we do
something, the world will come to an end![44]

Unfortunately, recently even the science of "the Younger Brother" is
confirming what the Kogi *mámas* wisdom has taught for centuries about
the delicate ecological balance of the "heart of the world." The Elder
Brother's warning to the Younger Brother is urgent – for the sake of the
entire world, things must change! And as Reichel-Dolmatoff concludes:
"....the age old [Kogi] ecological awareness may contain important lessons. It is essential that specialists in all spheres of planning, training,
and research be made equally conscious of the cultural complexities of
the material conditions for survival."[45] It is to these potential lessons that
we turn our attention next.

II. Lessons From the Kogi *Mámas* for Christians

The Sacred –V- The Holy

No doubt Mircea Eliade would classify the Kogi belief system and moral
codes as fitting the categories of "primitive (tribal)" and "archaic (early
urban)" societies.[46] The Kogi cosmogony and cosmology certainly set
clear lines between the sacred and profane, and distinguish the "Elder
Brother" as morally superior to the "Younger Brother." Indeed, there are
particular spiritual powers and ways that rule all ecological, ethical, and
social relationships in their society. In Kogi society, ethics and ritual are
identical. As the saying goes, the "right" way is definitely, the "rite" way
– the ways of the Great Mother as taught and applied by the *mámas*. In
the terms of modern ethics, for the Kogi "is" equals "ought." The way of
the great Mother *is* the way things *ought* to be and *ought* to be done.

   A function of the Kogi belief system also fits what Emile Durkheim claimed to be the sole purpose of religious myth in a society. By

---

[44] Alan Ereira, *From the Heart of the World,* (videocassette).
[45] G. Reichel-Dolmatoff, "Cultural Change," 295.
[46] See Mircea Eliade, *The Sacred and Profane,* (New York: Harper & Row,
1957).

tracing the origins of customs to sacred myths the ways of a society become inviolable, thus stabilizing the society.[47] Given all of this, it might seem that the only alternative the Kogi present for the "Younger Brother" is to digress to the ways of the first millennium.

But, to the contrary! As the French sociologist Jacques Ellul observed, there is another function for religion and myth in a society, namely it can function to challenge the status quo and question the sacred order of society.[48] Indeed, beginning with Socrates, the role of ethics became a search for the truly "good," not merely a means of following a set order of things. In religious ethics we can seek ways of being and doing that promote order *and* create justice. To use Ellul's framework, we must distinguish between the sacred/moral and the holy/ethical. Or, as Paul Tillich explained, the experience of "the holy" calls into question any person, thing, or activity that would claim ultimate superiority, for "the holy" is "wholly other," not finite.[49]

It is from this later stance that comparative religious ethics finds value. In comparing the belief systems of the "Elder Brother" and the "Younger Brother"[50] both claim a fundamental value for the human person. The current ecological crisis violates the sense of justice held by both the Kogi and Western Christianity. Both ultimately appeal not to the social normative sense of the "sacred" but to the foundational moral experience of reverence for persons and their environment.[51] It is from this function of their belief system that the Kogi, the "Elder Brother," have issued a warning to the "Younger Brother" to "Stop what you are doing, or the world will come to an end!"[52]

When the Kogi speak of the death of the *paramo*, they level an ethical critique of the Christian West, the "Younger Brother:"

> We the *mámas* see that you are killing the world by what you do. We can no longer repair the world, you must....

---

[47] See Emile Durkheim, *On Morality and Society*, Robert N. Bellah ed., (Chicago: University of Chicago Press, 1973).

[48] See Jacques Ellul, *The New Demons* (New York: Seabury Press, 1975).

[49] See Paul Tillich, *The Dynamics of Faith* (New York: Harper & Row, 1957).

[50] Here I am presuming the Kogi referent is primarily Western Christianity, particularly Catholicism to which they were certainly exposed – for some good, but mostly ill. See Gerardo Reichel-Dolmatoff, "The Great Mother," 89-90.

[51] See Daniel C. Maguire and A. Nicholas Fargnoli, *On Moral Grounds* (New York: Crossroad, 1991).

[52] Alan Ereira, *From the Heart of the World,* (videocassette).

> The Great Mother gave us what we needed to live.... But
> now they are taking out the Mother's heart. She'll end,
> and the world will end if you don't stop digging and
> digging...What would they think if we *mámas* died....
> and there was no one doing our work. Well, the rain
> wouldn't fall, it would get hotter and hotter from the sky,
> and the trees wouldn't grow, and the crops wouldn't
> grow.[53]

Indeed, contrary to the Kogi ecological and moral wisdom that claims that everything is related, the "Younger Brother's" economy does not operate as if the Earth and its inhabitants are an interdependent whole. In fact, the prevailing economic theories view the earth as a series of interchangeable parts and machine like, rather than as an organic and communitarian whole. The general attitude toward the natural world in the West is that it is like a refrigerator that is raided and depleted only to be refilled with the better, tastier food of a new discovery. Ever new discoveries make the discoverer satiated and rich, enable her/him to move from place to place, and entitling her/him to limit the access of all others to even the most basic nutrition. In the meantime the "garbage" of all "meals" is randomly thrown (to that illusive place) "away" — which means, fundamentally — thrown into (another illusive place) "someone else's backyard," fouling air, water, and land, irreparably damaging ecosystems. This way of regarding the natural world and human ecology is a polemic opposite of the Kogi practice of carefully calculating the carrying capacity of their environment, and living within those limits.

In contrast to the Kogi practice of not raising surplus crops, the modern corporation further alienates us from understanding the earth as a community by shifting the goal and purpose of human activity from maximizing the quality of life for *all* the members of the household, to making the greatest profit and market share for a *few elite* stockholders and owners. Most recently technology and science have made it possible to shift wealth and resources from place to place and owner to owner within seconds, leaving no time for the "victim" to seek out other means of survival.

Unlike the Kogi economy that operates on the basis of sufficiency, the modern economy operates on the presumption of scarcity (of-

---

[53] Ibid.

ten artificially created). In contrast to the Kogi who teach their children the profound spiritual, ecological, and social value of a few material objects, Western television and other media teach children to value the latest invention for its own sake, and to be "good consumers." The modern economy views limits as negative and restrictive to maximizing profit. Such an attitude is increasingly being proven a false perception of reality. As Guy Beney has shown, it is no longer possible to flee to yet another place to escape the closed nature that is our *oikos*.[54] The long pattern of neglecting limits and respecting the cyclical patterns through which the natural world renews itself are catching up with this abusive pattern. We, "the Younger Brother," also now find our world in a condition of ecological crisis and vulnerability. Our own science is revealing that we have violated the household rules of our Earth, which required we recognize each member as having intrinsic value and thus, moral status. We now are reaping the results:

> Between 1500 and 1850 one species was eliminated every ten years. Between 1850 and 1950 the rate was one a year. In 1990 ten species a day were disappearing. By the year 2000 one species [was] vanishing every hour. The species mortality rate is speeding up constantly. Between 1975 and 2000 20% of all living species...have disappeared.[55]

The human species is not excluded from this sad picture. According to the United Nations Development Program, if the world population is divided into quintiles according to income, the richest 20% of the population receives 82% of the total income; the second 20% of the population receives 11.2% of the total income; the middle 20% receives 2.3% of the total income; the fourth 20% receives 1.9% of the income; and, the poorest 20% receives 1.4% of the income.[56] Globalization has become the force of exploitation and among the most threatened are the human poor, especially indigenous peoples.

---

[54] Guy Beney, in *Global Ecology*, ed., by Wolfgang Sachs (London: Zed Books, 1993), 181-82, cited by Larry Rasmussen, *Earth Community, Earth Ethics*, (Maryknoll: Orbis Books, 1996), 91-92.
[55] U.S. Worldwatch Institute cited in Leonardo Boff, *Ecology and Liberation: A New Paradigm*, (Maryknoll: Orbis Books, 1995), 15.
[56] The United Nations Development Project cited in Daniel C. Maguire, *Sacred Energies*, (Minneapolis: Augsburg Fortress, 2000), 27.

To be human and poor seems to be an oxymoron. To allow abject poverty to exist is a clear violation of the foundational moral experience of reverence for persons and their environment. Is there anything in the Western Christian tradition to assist us in responding to the Kogi ethical and ecological critique and the indictment of our economic and technological progress?

Leonardo Boff argues that liberation theology (that addresses economic and political oppression) and ecology must become partners in light of the current state of affairs of the world ecological crisis and the poor. He recalls that very soon after Ernest Haeckel first formulated the notion of ecology in 1866, a significant further development occurred. Ecology was soon understood as the unity of three ecologies.[57] Boff explains the elements of this unity:

> *Environmental ecology* is concerned with the environment and relations that various societies have with it in history.... and how human beings are integrated into it. *Social ecology* is primarily concerned with social relations as belonging to ecological relations; that is, because human beings (who are personal and social) are part of the natural world, their relationship with nature passes through the social relationship of exploitation, collaboration, or respect and reverence. Hence social justice - the right relationship with persons, roles, and institutions - implies some achievement of ecological justice, which is the right relationship with nature, easy access to its resources, and assurance of quality of life.... *Mental ecology* starts from the recognition that nature is not outside human beings but within them, in their minds, in the form of psychic energy, symbols, archetypes, and behavior patterns that embody attitudes of aggression or of respect and acceptance of nature.[58]

As classical liberation theologies claim, the human persons stand in need of a threefold liberation of the human person as: an earth creature (self actualization), a social being (political, economic, etc.), and a spiri-

---

[57] See F. Guattari, *As Três Ecologias* (Campinas: Papirus, 1988).
[58] Leonardo Boff, *Cry of the Earth, Cry of the Poor* (Maryknoll: Orbis Books, 1997), 105.

tual person. The three levels of liberation align well with the three ecologies (above). The human person thrives when s/he is at home, in a place where s/he is at peace with her/himself, in right relationship with God and neighbor, and respectful of the integrity of creation. Boff rightly contends that when these relationships are broken, we also see the emergence of poverty, oppression, ecological destruction, and injustice of all sorts.

The numerous public statements by the U.N. Interfaith Partnership for the Environment, The Parliament of World Religions, The World Council of Churches, Roman Catholic Bishops, and countless others around the globe reinforce the truth of Boff's claim concretely. For our purposes, the most striking thing about all of these statements is the return to the ecological and ethical vision articulated in the Jewish and Christian narrative of creation that the Earth is a "good" place, created by a generous God, and entrusted to humankind for care and nurturance.

In his well-known *Earth Community, Earth Ethics*, Larry Rasmussen makes much of the notion of the Earth as *oikos*.[59] He rightly claims that the Earth is first and foremost "habitat earth;" the natural content and context within which the *homosapiens (demens)* must live and hopefully, thrive. Drawing on the fact that the human is fundamentally social, he quickly moves to a discussion of *oikoumen,* the whole inhabited world. Everyone and everything in this world is interdependent with all else for surviving and thriving. Further, Judaism's *Shekinah* (the indwelling of God) concept and Christianity's notion of *oikonomia tou Theou* (the economy of God), have supplied the inner secret of the interdependent world, which in creation is the redemptive indwelling of God. Rasmussen observes that the overall message of Judaism and Christianity indicates, "God is 'home' here, as are we."[60] It is because of this indwelling that the world is indeed habitable and sacred. The earth is in fact a vast household of life — productive land, potable water, a hospitable atmosphere, and innumerable creations brought forth by *homosapiens (demens)* such as artistic expressions, forms of education, and spiritualities.

The habitat that is *oikos*, our home, is a closed space; sunlight is the only life form that comes to it from outside. Thus, for better or for

---

[59] See Larry Rasmussen, *Earth Community, Earth Ethics*, (Maryknoll: Orbis Books, 1996).
[60] Ibid., 90.

worse, all in this place, earth, is forever and always united in one house-hold (*eco-*). Earth beings are one family who must find the laws or rules (*nomos*) that will make possible the surviving and thriving of the entire family, if indeed any one being would live to its fullest.

Recent work by Australian theologian Denis Edwards provides important insights that may assist Christians in finding common under-standing with the Kogi concerning the inspired quality of the natural world. While space here does not allow development of his work, I offer two of his major theses as an indication of the possibilities for ethical dialogue between the Kogi and the Christian West. [61] The first thesis is: "The Spirit can be thought of as the power of becoming, the power that enables the self-transcendence of creation. The Creator Spirit is the pres-ence of God that empowers the evolution of life on Earth." The second thesis is: "The Spirit is the Companion to each creature. The Spirit is al-ready with every creature in the universe, loving and valuing each, bring-ing each into an interrelated world of creatures, holding each in the dy-namic life of the divine Communion. The Spirit of God delights in crea-tures in their beauty, their interrelated diversity and their fecundity as they already exist as self-expressions of the divine Wisdom." If Ed-wards' theses are correct, then how can Christians justify reckless exploi-tation of the natural world? Perhaps, it is at the level of metaphysics that the "Younger Brother" and the "Elder Brother" can find common cause.

The work of Rasmussen, Edwards, and Boff indicates interpreta-tions of the Christian narrative that is critical of the current ecological state of affairs. Similar to the Kogi, these Christians hold that the role of the human is to nurture and care for the Earth, and not foul the nest, be-cause to do so is to risk human life and the destruction of the harmonious good God created, the Earth itself. Such destruction is, ultimately, idola-try, to put our "knowledge" above divine wisdom concerning the mean-ing of this place we call home. This Earth, was created with generosity and superfluity; not selfishness and paucity. These versions of the Chris-tian narrative sing in concert with the teachings of the Kogi *mámas*, and what Boff calls "the permanent message from the original peoples" of

---

[61] Denis Edwards, unpublished paper "Making All Things New: An Ecological Theology of the Holy Spirit," given June 8, 2002, Catholic Theology Society of America, New Orleans, LA. For development of these theses and more see his: "For your Immortal Spirit Is In All Things," in *Earth Revealing, Earth Healing: Ecology and Christian Theology* (Collegeville, MN: The Liturgical Press, 2001), 45-66.

this Earth.[62] The Wisdom tradition of Judaism and Christianity shows us how we are connected to the Earth and one another. The mystique of nature must be given due importance; we must face the reality that science taken to its depths brings us to mystery, and mystery brought to intelligibility moves to concreteness. The issues of work, economics, spirituality, ecology, ethics and the Earth are intimately linked; Mother Earth, after all, nourishes and sustains everyone. Unlike the Kogi who walk barefooted in order to remain in touch with the Earth, people in the modern world of work remove themselves from the natural world, living in concrete jungles and cyberspace. If we are wise, we will find ways to touch the Earth from which we came.

There needs to be a return to the experience of celebration; for there is much to celebrate. Like the Kogi, we need to stand in the truth of awe and wonder; dance in joy of God's creation; and know ourselves for who we truly are, *adam*, "earth creature," again for the first time. It is in the intimacy of this dance, attuning body, mind, and spirit to the rhythms of this place we call home, that we also will come home to the heart of the one who created it all, home to a place in the heart of God.

It is true, as the Kogi tell us, our Earth is ill. It has been infected in many ways over time. We, as Boff rightly concludes, stand at a crossroads of three possible paths. One possibility is to continue the deepening of separation and competition of the 1990's fostered by the forces of globalization and neoliberalism. A second choice might be to attempt to minimize the effects of modernity by supporting "sustainable development" of this Earth. Or, we might heed the call of the Kogi and the Hebrew psalmist who reminds Jews and Christians [Ps. 24], "The Earth is the Lord's." We must make a radical turn to the Earth, choosing to make the deep conversion required to live *with* nature, not *from* nature. This will require that we take seriously the foundational moral experience, reverence for persons and their environment. It is this last alternative that Boff claims is the only real choice, if indeed, we are to avoid the fate of the dinosaurs. To that end, we might take into account the lessons of the Kogi *mámas*.

Lessons from the Kogi Mámas

According to the Kogi, one's life must be dedicated to the Law of the Mother, to learn the myths and traditions, the songs and the spells, and

---

[62] Leonardo Boff, *Cry of the Earth, Cry of the Poor*, (Maryknoll: Orbis Books, 1997), 123-27.

all the rules that regulate that ritual. They are equally compelled to learn tribal history, geography, ecology, animal and plant categorizations, and a fair knowledge of anatomy and physiology. The ultimate purpose behind all of this is to achieve the state of *yulúka,* a harmonic balanced state of agreement with all of life.[63] It is interesting to note that the book of *Proverbs* evokes a similar discipline for Christians and Jews to attend to the Law of the Lord.

The Kogi live with an eye toward sufficiency. A man for example, must not work for more material gain or acquire more property than he needs in order to properly clothe and feed his family.[64] General moral "counsels" are taught through numerous stories that prohibit: over-indulgence in food, sex, sleep, physical aggressiveness, theft, disrespectful behavior, cruelty to children and animals, or inquisitiveness by women and children. Praise and encouragement is given for economic collaboration, sharing food, sharing household utensils, respecting elders, and active participation in rituals.

The pace of life and the Kogi attitude toward all material things, especially the natural world, is governed by the belief that each object has the capacity to "speak" to the beholder; to answer life's questions and to guide one's actions. All objects are models and mnemotechnical devices that can communicate many messages at various levels of consciousness and meaning.[65] By attending to the natural world in particular, the Kogi have managed to find a way of life that is not destructive of it. They understand the needs of each part of their environment, at many levels. This knowledge is integrated with understanding of personal disposition and the possible consequences of particular stances and attitudes for the well being of the whole of the environment. As Alan Ereira explains, a man does not just suddenly decide to go and dig up some clay and make a batch of clay pots.[66] Rather, he will first go the *máma* for a *sewá* and follow the proper ritual preparation for extracting clay, "a secretion of the Mother," from the earth. Before giving the man permission to do the work, the *máma* will likely have the man make a "confession" to make sure he has the proper attitude and disposition to do his task properly. Then, with permission, the man will only take enough to

---

[63] G. Reichel-Dolmatoff, "Training for the Priesthood," 269.
[64] Ibid., 271.
[65] G. Reichel-Dolmatoff, "Loom of Life," 9-10.
[66] Jane Clarke, "Message from the Heart of the World — Alan Ereria Talks about his Encounter with a Remarkable People in the Mountains of Colombia," *Beshara Magazine,* (1991), 4.

make what he needs immediately. In this reflective preparatory action there is a moment of integration of the spiritual, physical, psychological, social, moral, and ecological dimensions of the man's life.

In this kind of existence there is no place for war, abusive sexual activity or aggression. Discipline and consideration of the good of the whole is at the center of all moral consideration. The way of the Great Mother is a way of generativity and life. For the Kogi, the overarching norm of life is that the world is alive, and they must do what is needed to cooperate with the fecundity of the Great Mother and to make life, live. This requires thought and discipline before any action takes place; the Mother, after all is both "memory and possibility."

In our ecologically threatened world, we would do well to heed the example of the Kogi. We, the "Younger Brother" of the Christian West, must recall the purpose of our existence given to us in the opening passages of *Genesis* and the *Gospel of John*...the earth and everything in it was created "good" and we are called by our incarnate God to "have life to the fullest." We are the sons and daughters of the Earth; we are the earth itself become self-aware. Like the Kogi, we need to allow ourselves time to reflect and to become aware of the non-linear dimensions of time and space that also affect our world and us. It is these dimensions that evoke in us the sacredness of the universe and the wonder of our own existence. Like the Kogi, we need to place ourselves in perspective with the vastness of the universe that boggles the mind. Each of us needs to realize how marvelous it is that we exist at all. With the Kogi, who see themselves as the creatures *within* a particular part of the world, we must discover ourselves as members of the species *homo sapiens (demens),* in communion and solidarity with all other species that make up the community of living beings. Like the Kogi, who recognize their uniqueness and possibilities *among* all of the creatures, we need to see our potential for good or for ill, and change our actions for the good. Finally, as the Kogi creation myth tells us – but also, the creation stories of the Bible and of modern science — we need to recognize that the choice for survival is ours. We are latecomers to the Earth; it existed before us, and it likely can exist after us.

Perhaps the lessons from the Kogi *mámas* can best be summarized in the words of the mediation hymn sung by the Kogi weavers:

> I shall weave the Fabric of my Life;
> I shall weave it white as a cloud;

I shall weave some black into it;
I shall weave dark maize stalks into it;
I shall weave maize stalks into the white cloth;
Thus I shall obey the divine Law.[67]

As the Kogi say, "A competent weaver is a good man, and a good piece of cloth is an achievement, something to be proud of; it is a well-lived life."[68]

---

[67] G. Reichel-Dolmatoff, "The Loom of Life," 13.
[68] Ibid.

Map I
Location: Sierra Nevada De Santa Marta

Source: Tairona Heritage Studies Centre, "Home Page,"
http://www.lamp.ac.uk/tairona/ (July 31, 2002).

MAP II

Distribution Of Tribes On The Sierra Nevada De Santa Marta

Source: Tairona Heritage Studies Centre, "The Distribution Of Tribes On The Sierra Nevada De Santa Marta," http://www.lamp.ac.uk/tairona/dtribes.html (July 31, 2002).

Appendix I

Kogi Community Structure

Traditionally, according to Reichel-Dolmatoff, the nuclear family was the basic social and economic unit of Kogi society and the most common household type.[69] The Kogi household functions as a property-owning, cooperative, economic unit. Kinship ties are reckoned bilaterally, but ownership and inheritance mainly follow male lines. Kinship terminology is of the Hawaiian type. For the Kogi, there exists parallel descent groups called Tuxe[70] and Dake.[71] The functioning and importance of these groups is not thoroughly understood because there has been a cultural breakdown and these structures are no longer fully intact.[72]

Beyond the family, the Kogi society is a kind of feudal system.[73] Households are organized into communities. Community authority is vested in the Comisario, or local secular headman, and the *máma,* or priest. Both receive weekly tribute from their subjects. While the Comisario holds office for one or two years (and is the authority recognized by the Colombian government) the real authority is the *máma* and the Comisario does nothing without first consulting the *mámas.* The duties and authority of the Comisario vary according to location, but includes settlement of minor disputes, overseeing communal labor, and mediating between the village and outsiders.

Cabos assist both the *mámas* and the Comisarios. Mayores are older reputable men who have some slight power over their kinsmen and the younger members of the community. The Mayores form a delibera-

---

[69] Gerardo Reichel-Dolmatoff, "Aspectos económicos entre los indios de la Sierra Nevada," *Boletin de Arqueología,* vol. II, nos. 5-6, (1949/50): 573-80. See also Gerardo Reichel-Dolmatoff, *Los Kogi: Una Tribu Indígena de la Sierra Nevada de Santa Marta, Colombia,* Vol. I, (Bogotá: Revista del Instituto Etnológico Nacional, Vol. IV, 1950), 1-320.

[70] This is a group formed of a man and his sons.

[71] This is a group formed of a woman and her daughters.

[72] Tuxe and Dake organization broke down at some time in the past, and Reichel-Dolmatoff's informants give conflicting information on the subject. See Gerardo Reichel-Dolmatoff, "The Great Mother," 102-04. Also see Gerardo Reichel-Dolmatoff, *Los Kogi: Una Tribu Indígena de la Sierra Nevada de Santa Marta, Colombia,* Vol. I, Second Edition, (Bogotá: Procultura, Presidencia de Republica, 1985) 157-213.

[73] Alan Ereira, writer and producer, *From the Heart of the World: The Elder Brother's Warning,* A BBC Television production in association with the Goldsmith Foundation, (New York: Mystic Fire Video, 1993), sound, color, ½ inch, VHS videocassette.

tive advisory body for the *máma*.

Appendix II

Marriage and Divorce

As in many societies that have a feminine cultural mythic system, contradiction in Kogi marriage ideals and practices resulted from demo-
graphic changes and from outside cultural contact.[74] Instead of marriage
representing the traditional balance between the masculine and feminine
principles, it has been reduced to support what Reichel-Dolmatoff claims
are the two major cultural themes of the Kogi, "food and sex/fertility."[75]
Traditionally these themes summarized a complex system where "each
partiline or matriline has many magical attributes and privileges that together with their respective mythical origins, genealogies, and precise
ceremonial functions, form a very elaborate body of rules and relationships."[76] Ideally, marriages are prohibited between close relatives, including cousins, and a man of a particular Tuxe should marry a woman
of a particular Dake. This is because certain lineage orders must be balanced for the good of society as a whole and arranged marriages allow
this balance to be brought about.[77] In marriage, the esoteric demands of
the Kogi's belief system and satisfying the natural order as taught by the
Great Mother are primary concerns.[78]

Kogi ideals stress fidelity and prohibit divorce. But sadly, a majority of the unions break up, and there is a high degree of infidelity. The
shortage of women is further exacerbated by the practice of polygyny
among older reputable men. Ereira says this about divorce:

---

[74] See Peggy Reeves Sandy's study: *Female Power and Male Dominance: The
Origins of Sexual Inequality*, (Cambridge University Press, 1981), especially
165-171.
[75] Gerardo Reichel-Dolmatoff, "Training for the Priesthood among the Kogi of
Colombia," in Johannes Wilbert, ed., *Enculturation in Latin America*, UCLA
Latin American Studies 37, (Los Angeles: UCLA Latin American Center Publications, 1976), 267-68.
[76] Ibid., 268.
[77] See Gerardo Reichel-Dolmatoff, "The Great Mother," 102-04. Also see Gerardo Reichel-Dolmatoff, *Los Kogi: Una Tribu Indígena de la Sierra Nevada de
Santa Marta, Colombia*, Vol. I, Second Edition, (Bogotá: Procultura, Presidencia de Republica, 1985), 213.-16.
[78] Ibid., 203-215. See Gerardo Reichel-Dolmatoff, "Training for the Priesthood,"
272-74.

Divorce among the Kogi is very simple: a woman simply switches her allegiance to another man, and symbolises that by accepting a piece of meat from him. If the woman leaves her husband, it will always be to enter into a new relationship - and men appear to have little trouble finding a new bride. But for an abandoned wife the problems are very serious. The balance has been destroyed, since neither sex can perform the other's work. A single mother is an anomaly: she has to become a dependent of her parents, part of their family once more. She may well be left with her own farm - indeed the *mámas* will generally ensure in a divorce settlement that the woman has enough land to sustain herself and her children - but she cannot work it without the help of her family.[79]

Marriage entails a one to two year period of bride service, following which the couple set up their own household, usually in the village of the bride. Husbands and wives are separated most of the time. The wife and children share a dwelling, while the husband either lives in a separate house nearby or spends most of his time in the *Nuhe*.

Appendix III

Roles for Women
Given the reality that Kogi cosmology is grounded in the myth of the Great Mother, *Gaulcovang*, one might assume that the status and daily existence of women might be equally honored and good. However, the Kogi have problems when applying the meaning of their central myth to social practices. This is apparent in both marriage practices, and in the division of labor within the society.[80] Women spin cotton but do not weave it - that is the men's role, as is its cultivation. Once woven, it is the women, and their daughters who make the bags and clothes whereas it is the men who make the pottery. In the horticulture, of this agrarian

---

[79] Gerardo Reichel-Dolmatoff, "Training for the Priesthood," 272-74.
[80] Gerardo Reichel-Dolmatoff, "Training for the Priesthood among the Kogi of Colombia," in Johannes Wilbert, ed., *Enculturation in Latin America*, UCLA Latin American Studies 37, (Los Angeles: UCLA Latin American Center Publications, 1976), 272-74.

society, the men will clear, break and prepare the ground but it is the women who sow, harvest and prepare the crops. Women do own land and daughters inherit from their mothers. Land ownership is normally a consideration in divorce and women are normally given enough to live from.

Interestingly, the Kogi believe that the Great Mother gave birth to all manifestation by thinking it into being. She was creator and teacher: "The Great Mother taught and taught. The Great Mother gave us what we needed to live and her teaching has not been forgotten right up to this day. We all still live by it."[81] It is this part of the Great Mother myth seems to have some practical influence in women's lives. According to Alan Ereira:

> Women rule the house, the domestic arena; men have an exclusive domain in the public arena, the ceremonial house. That is not to say that women have no say in public affairs; there are many stories of lengthy debates in the ceremonial house, lasting several nights, at the end of which a decision is reached on how to deal with some community problem. Then the men go home, tell their wives what has been decided, and the following day they reconvene somewhat shame-faced and agree a different solution. But in principle, it is the men who decide.[82]

Young girls move from childhood existence to marriage. From the time she has her first period, she is secluded. Once she has her second menstrual period, she is considered a woman and "ready to love." Then a man is selected for her through a divining process by the *mámas*. Each of the couple is first, interrogated by the *mámas* about their life to see if they are in proper harmony with the world both spiritual and material, and then the *mámas* make appropriate ritual payment. The woman is purified and cleansed, so she will have a pure mind, soul, and heart. Then

---

[81] Alan Ereira, writer and producer, *From the Heart of the World: The Elder Brother's Warning,* A BBC Television production in association with the Goldsmith Foundation, (New York: Mystic Fire Video, 1993), sound, color, ½ inch, VHS videocassette.

[82] Tairona Heritage Study Center, Alan Ereira, "Some Notes on the Status of Women in Kogi Society," < http://www.lamp.ac.uk/tiarona/b11womensoc.html > (July 31, 2002).

the *mámas* marry the couple.[83]

Appendix IV

The Kogi Cosmology – Creation Myth[84]

> *In the beginning there was blackness. Only the sea.*
>   *In the beginning there was no sun, no moon,*
>   *no people.*
> *In the beginning there were no animals, no plants. Only the sea.*
>   *The sea was the Mother.*
> *The Mother was not people, she was not anything.*
>   *Nothing at all.*
>   *She was when she was, Spirit.*
>   *She was memory and possibility.*
>   *She was alúna.*

The *mámas* say we don't remember the Great Mother. She is not a distant God. She is the mind inside nature. The Mother is fertility and intelligence.

> *Where does the idea of Earth come from? Where do*
> *we get the idea of water? Why do we have a word*
> *for it? These things were conceived from the begin-*
> *ning...from before the dawning. These were*
> *ideas....water and earth. We can only have ideas of*
> *things that have already been conceived in alúna.*
> *Before the dawning, before there was anything we*
> *were conceived in the waters of alúna....so were the*
> *trees, the mountains.... everything!*

And then the Mother began to spin out her thoughts. She threaded up a spindle...before the dawning...and the Mother spun out nine new worlds.

---

[83] Ibid.

[84] According to Reichel-Dolmatoff, "there is no such thing as an undiluted and "orthodox" Kogi cultural tradition. In the great diaspora from the Spanish (1600) numerous versions and variations concerning spiritual figures developed. What I utilize here is the "large kernel of truth" contained in most versions. See G. Reichel-Dolmatoff, "The Great Mother and the Kogi Universe: A Concise Overview," *Journal of Latin American Lore* 13/1 (1987) 77.

She gave birth to nine daughters. Each world had its own color. Then, She gave birth to sons – the Lords of Creation. One was Serankwa.

> *And then She wondered how would she create a liv-*
> *ing thing. It was hard to understand how to make a*
> *human. The Mother and her children had to think*
> *very hard. How does an eye work? How does a foot*
> *work? And it was done. And the ninth world was*
> *peopled. This was before the dawning. There were*
> *still no people. There were no plants, no animals, no*
> *sun....only the Mother. ...only alúna....*

The Mother bled. She had her period. She was fertile; and, the world was fertile. Her blood was gold, which remains in the earth. It is fertility. Gold and water; blood and water are necessary for the life of all things. And then the human beings were made to care for all living things....the plants; the animals....That is why people were made![85]

---

[85] Alan Ereira, writer and producer, *From the Heart of the World: The Elder Brother's Warning,* A BBC Television production in association with the Gold-smith Foundation, (New York: Mystic Fire Video, 1993), sound, color, ½ inch, VHS videocassette.

Appendix V

The Cosmic Egg

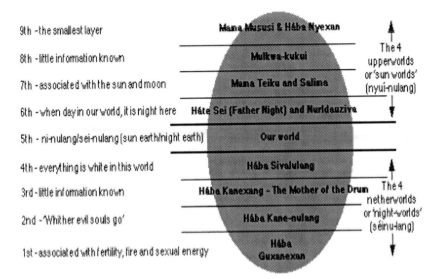

Names here are of the guardians of the particular levels.
Háte = Father, Hába = Mother

9th - the smallest layer — **Mama Mususi & Hába Nyexan**

8th - little information known — **Mulkwa-kukui**

7th - associated with the sun and moon — **Mama Teiku and Salina**

6th - when day in our world, it is night here — **Háte Sei (Father Night) and Nurldauziva**

The 4 upperworlds or 'sun worlds' (nyui-nulang)

5th - ni-nulang/sei-nulang (sun earth/night earth) — **Our world**

4th - everything is white in this world — **Hába Sivalulang**

3rd - little information known — **Hába Kanexang – The Mother of the Drum**

2nd - 'Whither evil souls go' — **Hába Kane-nulang**

The 4 netherworlds or 'night-worlds' (séinu-lang)

1st - associated with fertility, fire and sexual energy — **Hába Guxanexan**

Source: Tairona Heritage Study Centre, "The Cosmic 'egg'," <http://www.lamp.ac.uk/tairona/dcosmicegg.html> (July 31 2002).

Appendix VI

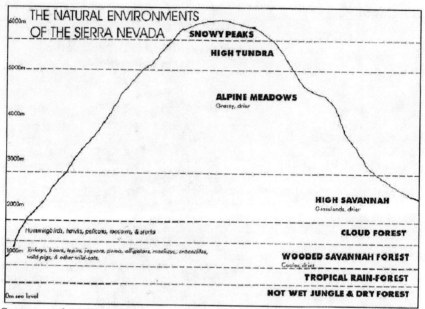

THE NATURAL ENVIRONMENTS
OF THE SIERRA NEVADA

6000m

SNOWY PEAKS

HIGH TUNDRA

5000m

ALPINE MEADOWS
Grassy, drier

4000m

3000m

2000m

HIGH SAVANNAH
Grasslands, drier

Hummingbirds, hawks, pelicans, macaws, & storks

CLOUD FOREST

1000m   *Turkeys, bears, tapirs, jaguars, puma, alligators, monkeys, crocodiles,*
wild-pigs, & other wild-cats.

WOODED SAVANNAH FOREST
Cooler, drier

TROPICAL RAIN-FOREST

0m sea level

HOT WET JUNGLE & DRY FOREST

Source: <http://weblife.bangor.ac.uk/rem/Kogi/diagram1.html > (July 31, 2002).

Appendix VII

The Sierra Nevada de Santa Marta

> Imagine a pyramid standing alone by the sea. Each side
> is a hundred miles long. It is a mountain, nearly four
> miles high. In its folds, imagine every different climate
> on earth. This is the Sierra Nevada de Santa Marta. The
> people hidden here call the Sierra the "Heart of the
> World." And themselves the "Elder Brothers."[86]

The Kogi live in the higher regions of the Sierra Nevada de
Santa Marta, mainly on the Northern slopes of the Palimino, San Miguel,
and San Francisco valleys. The soil and climatic traits of this area varies
greatly and thus numerous and the complex micro-environments are notable. Kogi communities are also on the Western part of the Mountain.
The Sierra Nevada is the highest coastal mountain in the world only 26
miles from the beach. It is located near the Equator, which means it has
no seasons. Day and night are of equal length all year round. All in only
30 vertical miles, and within 8,000 sq. miles, there are all nine biomes
that exist in the rest of Colombia (see chart). You can find coral reefs,
mangroves, arid deserts, rain and cloud forest, and in the higher eleva-
tions, plains and snow-capped peaks with temperatures close to –20 degrees. The highest peak (5,775 m.) is the Pico Simon Bolivar.

According to Alan Ereira, the Sierra is vital for the ecological
well being of the whole area. Thousands of creeks, streams, and rivers
flow from the peaks, through canyons and hills, forming 35 watersheds
along the way. These in turn can be divided into three major areas: the
Caribbean Sea, the Great Marshlands of Santa Marta, and the Cesar
River.[87] Approximately 20,000 indigenous people and 180,000 'colonos'
depend on this water, as well as the inhabitants of Santa Marta, Rio-
hacha, Valledupar, and ten municipalities, with their respective villages,
plus the watering canals of banana and cattle farms.[88] There are two main

---

[86] Alan Ereira, writer and producer, *From the Heart of the World: The Elder
Brother's Warning,* A BBC Television production in association with the Goldsmith Foundation, (New York: Mystic Fire Video, 1993), sound, color, ½ inch,
VHS videocassette.
[87] Alan Ereira, *The Heart of the World,* (London: John Cape, 1990), 209.
[88] Donald Tayler, *The Coming of the Sun – A Prologue to Ika Sacred Narrative,*
Monograph No. 7. (Pitt Rivers Museum, University of Oxford, 1997), 10.

seasons, the 'wet' from April to early December, and the 'dry' from late December to March. The effect of the prevailing winds means that these seasons are more marked on the northern and western slopes of the mountain. Here, the rainfall is heavier and forest cover is more extensive. The Sierra has been divided into three provinces, ten municipalities, two indigenous reserves (Arhuaco and Kogi-Malayo), and in 1977 two National Parks (Sierra Nevada and Tayrona) were created. In 1986, the region was named a Human and Biosphere Reserve by UNESCO.

THE DAWNING OF SOMETHING ANCIENT, YET NEW: RECONCILATION AND INCULTURATION IN THE GUATEMALAN HIGHLANDS[*]

Jean Molesky-Poz[**]

We are thankful for the arrival and commitment of the Jesuits who have motivated and encouraged evangelization from the relation of our *K'iche'* Maya culture in Santa Maria Chiquimula, Totonicapán. They have taught us to investigate our traditions and have illuminated our ways so that we have encountered that which is the most sacred of our grandparents: "to live as indigenous men and women."[1]

I want to give thanks to the people of *Tz'oljche'* (Santa Maria Chiquimula) for all they have taught me. I want to thank them because they have taught me the true face of God, Mother-Father. I want to thank them for teaching me to speak their language. But most of all, I want to thank them because at the same time they have taught me to speak their language, they have taught me to speak

[*] I am particularly grateful to Father Victoriano Castillo González, S. J. who has conversed generously and provided many important documents; to Eduardo León Chic, who has helped me understand multiple ethnographic layers of meaning in Santa Maria Chiquimula; and to my husband, Martin Poz Perez, for his extensive linguistic and culturally insightful contributions in this project. Further, I want to recognize and thank the University of San Francisco Jesuit Foundation for the financial support for fieldwork during the summer of 2002.

[**] Jean Molesky-Poz is Assistant Professor in Theology / Religious Studies and Latin American Studies at the University of San Francisco. She is completing her book, *A New Cycle of Light: The Public Emergence of Maya Spirituality*, an ethnographic work examining the contemporary praxis and theological underpinnings of Maya ancestral beliefs and practices through the narratives of Maya Ajq'ijab' (Calendar Keepers). Molesky-Poz received her Ph.D. from the Graduate Theological Union, Berkeley, in 1999. Previously she taught for fifteen years as a full-time lecturer in the Native American Studies Department at the University of California at Berkeley, specializing in Native Spiritual Traditions.

[1] Eduardo León Chic, "El Corazon de la Sabiduria del Pueblo Maya: El Calendario Maya y la Bioviersidad," *Cosmovisión Indigena y Biodiversidad en America Latina* (Cochoabambá, Boliva: Agroecologia Universidad, 2001), 131-2.

to God, Heart of the Sky, Heart of the Earth.[2]

The contemporary religious diversity of Guatemala has been shaped by multiple influences: legacies of traditional Maya religious beliefs and practices for thousands of years, the imposition of Spanish Catholicism on Maya communities during the colonial period, the introduction of Protestantism during the Liberal Years of 1871-1926, projects of Catholic Action in the 1950s, the more recent presence and dramatic rise of Pentecostals and evangelicals since the 1970s, and the most current public emergence of traditional spirituality among some Maya in Guatemala. Religious discrimination and religious conflict have marked this history in varied, and sometimes extreme, ways. Today this Central American country increasingly finds itself religiously pluralistic.[3]

Since 1985, there has been a public reclamation and florescence, a new dawning, of ancestral spirituality among Maya women and men in the highlands, a predominately indigenous region. This rejuvenation is marked by an increase of private and public communal ceremonies; the recuperation, reclamation, and daily use of the *Chol Qij*, the 260-day sacred calendar; and more women and men, of diverse ages and professions, backgrounds, from rural and urban areas, undertaking lives as *Ajq'ijab'* (Daykeepers, ritual practioners, keepers of the 260-day sacred calendar).

This emergence of Maya spirituality is due to the Maya reclamation of a singular universe of meaning which was submerged in and derived from a conscious reflection on Maya identities formed by colonial Catholicism, the intrusion of evangelism since 1976, the genocide and displacement of Maya, particularly during a civil war between 1978 and 1985. During this repression and war, more than 200,000 people, mostly Maya, were killed; 440 of their villages destroyed. Maya community and religious leaders (*Ajq'ijab'*) as well as Catholic priests and lay workers were frequent targets of state-sponsored repressions under the regimes of Lucas García, Ríos Montt, and Mejía Víctores. During and after the period of repression, Maya began organizing themselves, politically and

---

[2] V. Castillo González, S.J., *Ri Loq'Alaj K'utb'al: Rech Ri Relb'al Uk'u'x Ri Qajaw (Rituals of the Sacraments in the Language and Cosmovision of the Maya People)*, Tz'olojche: Ediciones Ik'laja, (1998), 8.
[3] For overview of religion in Guatemala, see T. Steigenga, "Guatemala" in *Religious Freedom and Evangelization in Latin America: The Challenge of Religious Pluralism*, Paul E. Sigmund, ed. (Maryknoll, New York: Orbis Books, 1999), 150-174.

culturally, asking questions of their identities and cultural heritage. The questions led them through the political and cultural, to something deeper: spirituality was the key of Maya identity, existence, and survival. In time, processes within Maya communities as well as national and international human rights policies and processes have opened a space for this public reclamation of indigenous spirituality.[4]

The response of the Guatemalan Catholic Church, an institution that has various degrees of religious-political control in the highlands over 500 years, to this emergence is varied, and deeply complex. As a Catholic and researcher investigating the public emergence of Maya spiritual practices in the Guatemala highlands for a number of years,[5] I have also been interested in the question of the *theology of inculturation*, that is, the *interaction* of the Gospel and Maya culture, among contemporary Maya Catholic Christians. I have come upon the parish of Santa Maria Chiquimula of the Birth of the Virgin Mary, located in the highland Catholic diocese of Quetzaltenango. In this parish, deliberate and courageous efforts have been made at *reconciling and healing the sufferings* of the K'iche' people caused by centuries of imposed racism, persecution and systematic marginalization, and at *building an inculturated evangelization* – that is, the Christian faith in a Maya symbolic universe- and praxis. Here in their indigenous setting, people have received Christianity and re-created it; they are carrying out their own inculturation process.

This paper begins with the K'iche' town of *Tz'olojche*, or Santa Maria Chiquimula, Totonicopán, with a brief overview of the religious-political history of the western highlands. We will then turn to more re-

---

[4] The Peace Accords of Guatemala recognizes "the importance and uniqueness of Maya spirituality" and promises "to respect its practices," in *Gobierno de la Republica de Guatemala y La Unidad Revolutionaria Nacional Guatemalteca, Acuerdo Sobre Identidad y Derechos de los Pueblos Indigenas* (Accords on the Identity and Rights of the Indigenous Peoples) (MINUGUA, 1995), 3; and "The State recognizes, respects and protects the right of identity for the Maya, Garifuna and Xinca people, their form of life, social organization, customs and traditions; the use of indigenous clothing and their distinct forms of spirituality, languages, dialects and the right to transmit them to their descendents," in Tribunal Supreme Electoral, Reformas a la Constitución Política de la República de Guatemala (Guatemalan Constitutional Reform of 1998), 1.
[5] Jean Molesky-Poz, *The Public Emergence of Maya Spirituality in the Guatemalan Highlands* (Ph.D. dissertation, The Graduate Theological Union, Berkeley, California), integrates historical, theological, cultural studies and ethnographic work among K'iche' Ajq'ijab'(Daykeepers) in the Quetzaltenango area of Guatemala.

cent events: the commitment in 1989 of the Society of Jesus (Jesuits) to this parish; the community's act of reconciliation in 1992; the theology of inculturation as it is worked out in ongoing ethnographic projects of cultural and linguistic recovery; educational and horticultural activities; modern communications; and communal, liturgical and spiritual practices. Analysis of this ethnographic data suggests that implicit in this deliberate undertaking are marvelous results: the community is experiencing a healing and unity among itself; excavating and reclaiming ownership of their ancestral ways; growing according to its own symbolic universe and values; and emerging as a community in confidence, flowering in inculturated liturgy, sacraments, catechesis and spirituality.

Historical Context

Tz'olojche', or Santa Maria Chiquimula, Totonicapán, is located in the western highland, an area populated primarily by ethnic and linguistic K'iche' and Mam, 50 kilometers northeast of Quetzaltenango. The municipality itself is situated on a flat mountain ridge; the pine tree canyons are carved by rivers, running deep and thin. The arid soil produces only beans, wheat and corn, so that the majority of households make their income as merchants. Santa Maria has 49,000 inhabitants, with one municipal village, ten *aldeas*, (hamlets) seven *caserios* (smaller hamlets) and 26 *parajes* (4-10 houses), the 36 outlining sites organized in 13 communities.

Historically, religious beliefs and colonial practices have taken on distinct shapes and processes in these highlands. In the late 1530s, the Spanish Crown sent specific mendicant orders - Franciscans, Dominicans and Mercedarians - into the highland Maya communities, unfavorable because of their geographical distance, high altitudes, and thus inaccessibility; secular clergy were sent to the eastern lowlands, near Ladino-populated areas such as Antigua and Guatemala City.[6] It is popular knowledge that the Franciscans, who originally founded the parish of Santa Maria, attempted to integrate Catholicism with Maya spirituality during the colonial period more than the secular priests or other orders.[7] For example, in Santa Maria while the Franciscans built the church over

---

[6] The most comprehensive overview of Catholicism in colonial Guatemala is Adrian C. Van Oss's *Catholic Colonialism: A Parish History of Guatemala, 1524-1821* (London: Cambridge University Press, 1986).
[7] Father Bascilio Chacach Tzoy, former pastor of Santa Lucia de La Reforma, personal interview by author, 2002.

a sacred site, a sacred temple, they had designed the large square plaza in front, with four *capellas* in the corners marking the four directions, and a large horizontal Maya cross, etched in the center space of the plaza. This quatrefoil cross, symbol and metaphor, is a way of entering Maya time and space. Most highland Maya fell subject to *congregacíon*, or resettlement, during the middle years of the sixteenth century. Imperial Spain pressured the largely dispersed highland Maya population to settle into *congregaciones* or *reducciones*, nucleated settlements designed to facilitate both the conversion of the Maya to Christianity and the extraction of native tribute and labor.[8] The Church established and maintained its power among rural indigenous highland communities with its large landholdings and its links to local leadership through the local *cofradias* or religious brotherhoods.

Given this hegemony of conquest and subjugation, Maya nativism continued to substantiate local communities in a number of ways. They developed religious and political structures, appearing as cultural syncretism. During the seventeenth century, Maya subverted the policy of *congregación* through the gradual dispersal, or *decongregación*. They applied their learning of the Roman alphabet to Maya produced manuscripts as the *Pop Wuj* and the *Annals of the Cakchiquels*, written in their own languages to preserve pre-Hispanic cosmology, mythology and history.[9] In time, the evolution of the colonial *cofradias* assumed a particular Maya identity. They allowed for the continuity of Maya religious belief and practice, and transformed them from an organization for personal salvation to one dedicated to promoting the general welfare of the entire community.[10]

Over time, many of these highland parishes were sparsely visited, neglected or abandoned so that the villages developed Christian teachings and rituals free from control of the Catholic hierarchy. As Watanabe writes, "Crown and Church in Guatemala administered the Maya

---

[8] G.W. Lovell, *Conquest and Survival in Colonial Guatemala: A Historical Geography of the Cuchumatan Highlands, 1500-1821*, (Kingston: McGill-Queen's University Press, 1985), 72-73; M.J. MacLeod, *Spanish Central America: A Socioeconomic History, 1520-1720* (Berkeley and Los Angeles: University of California Press, 1973), 120-122; van Oss, 14-17.

[9] J. Watanbe, *Maya Saints and Souls in a Changing World* (Austin, Texas: University of Austin Press, 1992), 54-55.

[10] D. Earle, "Maya Religion, Mayanist Ideologies and Forms of Conquest," Paper for Latin American Studies Association, Washington, D.C., 1995: 4; N.M. Farris, *Maya Society under Colonial Rule: The Collective Enterprise of Survival* (Princeton: Princeton University Press, 1984), 329.

more by visitation than by enduring presence."[11] When assigned Catholic clergy imposed their control, with charges of idolatry and sacrilegious acts, sometimes flogging the Maya then forcing them to work for the parish church,[12] many *K'iche'* maintained their practices clandestinely. Their strategy of resistance was to appropriate, when necessary, Catholic icons, rituals and social organizations, and at the same time, to maintain their beliefs and a religiously-based civil authority system in order to assure some relative cultural autonomy. In some cases, as in neighboring Momostenango, the continuity of traditional belief and practices is well documented.[13] Each highland village has its distinct religious history and story.

In the 1950s Catholic Action, a cold war strategy to wipe out communism, was launched as a large-scale catechist reform movement in the highlands. One aspect of the movement had been an attack on native religious organizations. Catholic Action zealots destroyed Maya altars; followers of *costumbre* were ridiculed and punished in public.[14] Father Bascilio, a K'iche' Catholic priest in the highlands and native of Santa Maria, explains, "I consider Catholic Action a second stage of imposition for rural people. They had satanized the *costumbres*. It divided the people." As Virginia Garrard Burnett explains, "it is clear that by the mid-1950s, traditional structures of authority and community cohesion in many locations were severely undermined, at least in a symbolic sense, and the culpability lay at the feet of Catholic Action."[15]

Don Pedro Calel, *chuchqajaw* (name in Santa Maria Chiquimula for the minister of the people, keeper of the 260-day calendar), Alcalde of the Cofradia of Cristo de las Escapules, relates the effect of Catholic Action in Santa Maria when a new priest had come to the parish in 1952. "He didn't appreciate the Maya ways. He threw the candles away. He even went to the municipal court, and we couldn't practice our religion any more. He stayed six to eight years." Don Pedro further relates, in K'iche' a language textured in metaphor, the effect of these processes in Santa Maria.

---

[11] Watanbe, 47.

[12] Lovell, 59, 86.

[13] B. Tedlock, *Time and the Highland Maya* (Albuquerque: University of New Mexico Press, 1982).

[14] Watanabe, 204.

[15] V. Garrard Burnett, "Tearing a Hole in the Sacred Canopy: Religious Conflict in Guatemala, 1944-1960," presented at the Latin American Studies Association meeting at Continental Plaza Hotel, Guadalajara, Mexico, April 17-19, 1997: 13.

After what happened in 1952, we were really hurt. It is like you were selling something, not just selling merchandise, but as if this selling is your whole way of living. Someone comes and throws it away. How are you going to eat? How are you going to live? Our religion was our way of surviving.

It's like the *barre*.[16] It ties and unties. After 1952, we were all tied up, and we were so sick. When someone is sick, you look at the *barre*; you measure it; you talk to it. But they took away from us, this business, this way to eat, this way to live.

Many people got sick because the Church authorities took away their lives. When you have a *barre*, it is your destiny.[17]

In 1989, a team of Jesuits (Society of Jesus) from the Central American province were assigned by the bishop of Quetzaltenango to minister among the people of Santa Maria Chiquimula. These Jesuits as companions of Jesus, must have asked the crucial question, "How is the Society's share in Christ's mission to be understood at this particular moment in history?" When the Jesuits arrived, the centuries-old severance, exacerbated by the Catholic Action practices of the 1950s, divided villagers between the Catholic community and traditional Maya practioners. In Don Pedro's words, "We people of *costumbre* would just sneak around the outside of the church, but we could never go in. We were too afraid. People began to go to other religions." Small evangelical chapels and communities had begun to dot the countryside.

Fr. Victoriano Castillo González, S. J. a Mexican national, was among the first group of Jesuits to arrive. He explained that in 1990 the parish administered a census, asking "'How many are evangelicals? How many are Catholics? How many are practicing *costumbre*?' There was no response to the question of *costumbre*." He noted a major changing moment in the community.

---

[16] A small bundle which contains 260 *tz'ite'* seeds (*Erithrina corallodendron*), crystals, rocks and herbs. It is considered the spiritual partner and protection of the *Ajq'ij*, and used in ritual practice.

[17] Interview with author, July 31, 2002, Santa Maria Chiquimula, audiotaped.

It all began in 1992, on the 500th anniversary of the invasion of Columbus in the Americas. Before October 12th, I had asked, "Well, what are we going to do here in Santa Maria Chiquimula?" And out of it came an act of reconciliation between the catechists and the people of *costumbre*. The catechists went door-to-door, calling on each of the *Chuchqajaw* (*Ajq'ijab'*), saying that on October 12th they wanted to have an act of reconciliation.

During the ceremony, we recounted the story of conflicts of Catholics with people of *costumbre*. People even of opposite sides, like a son whose parents had been very active in Catholic Action in the parish, asked pardon from the *Chuchqajaw* for all Catholics for their actions and attitudes. During the ceremony, hugs and reconciliations were exchanged. People rediscovered traditional values.

Before 1992, the theme of *costumbre* was taboo. Now the people of *costumbre* have a *cofradia* in the parish. In the 2000 census, over fifty percent of the people stated that they practice *costumbre*."

Fr. Victoriano continued:

"After the act of reconcilation in 1992, in confessions, people would say, 'Padre, I went to an *Chuchqajaw* to cure my son. Do you think it is all right?'"
"Do you think it is bad?'" I asked."
"Well, I don't know."
"Why did you go?"
"To cure my sick son."
"Is it wrong to go to heal your son?"
"No."
"Well, then it is not wrong."

Here in this dialogue between a worried parent and Fr. Victoriano, we see the underpinning of Jesuit spirituality: reflection on what it means to be human and responsible is liberating, and can lead to a conscious appropriation of who we are. Further, as the Society focused their mission in terms of the service of the faith and the promotion of justice, they broadened their focus to an indepth dialogue with the K'iche' religion. They encouraged and administered a community-based investigation into the town's culture that had for so many centuries been in conflict. In turn, they engaged with Santa Maria Chiquimula's culture and brought it into the light, which is essential for an effective presentation of and engagement with the Gospel, as we shall see in the following section.

Inculturated Evangelization

The first years after the Jesuits arrived at Santa Maria coincided with the Diocese of Quetzaltenango's pastoral letter, *In Communion and Participation*, which stated the Church's urgent need to share in the social, economic and political crisis that Guatemala suffered. Further, in the letter, the Church recognized the profound contents of faith in popular religion for the people.[18] On a larger scale, the whole Latin American Church, in its post-Vatican II perspective after Medellín (1968) and Puebla (1979) was infused with a fundamental concern: how to proclaim the Gospel in Latin America. This question of the inculturation of the Gospel emerged as one of the most salient points of the 4th General Conference of Latin American Bishops in Santo Domingo, January 1993. Different from the first evangelization in Latin America, where the colonial Church imposed Western culture in its proclamation of the Gospel, *inculturated evangelization* assumes the history, traditions, language, values and symbols of the various ethnic and indigenous communities – to incarnate the Word of Jesus in specific cultures.

"Inculturation is not the adaptation of the message, translating it and adjusting it to those receiving evangelization," notes Diego Irarrázaval, Latin American theologian, priest and vice president of the Ecumenical Association of Third World Theologians (EATWOT), rather:

Inculturation is the *interaction* between the gospel and cultures. That is how it is explained in very clear passages at Vatican II (GS40-44), 58; AG 22), Puebla (400-407), and Santo Domingo: John Paul II has called (the inculturation process) the 'center, means and aim of the

---

[18] Secretariado Diocesano de Catequesis, En Comunion y Participacion Plan Pastoral Diocesano, 1990-1994 (In Communion and Participation: Diocesean Pastoral Plan), (1994), Questzaltenango: Vicaria de Pastoral, 37-38.

new evangelization.' Authentic Christian values, discerned and assumed in faith, are necessary in order to incarnate the gospel message and the church's reflection and practice into that culture."[19]

To embrace the inculturation is not simply to be reduced to religious values, customs, beliefs and matters. Rather, as Diego Irarrázaval continues, "the Spirit—author of inculturation—is present in nature and the world of today, in history, and in person."[20]

One fundamental point of the Santo Domingo conference was to recognize the values of indigenous peoples in Latin America. That is, the Gospel must be inculturated in the old cultures of the continent. "In its striving in history the Christian community interacts with the paschal event and evangelizes."[21] Further, the Santo Domingo conference called on the Church to "undergo a pastoral conversion."[22] Shortly after the Santo Domingo conference, the Quetzaltenango Diocesean Pastoral Assembly gathered and with the concern of inculturated evangelization promised to take on the history, traditions, language, values and symbols of the ethnic communities. But these processes, the hard work of inculturation, were already underway in Santa Maria Chiquimula.

As mentioned earlier, the Jesuits undertook an investigation into the life and culture of Santa Maria Chiquimula. In 1989, the parish set up a project to interview more than eighty women and men elders from different communities of the municipality. Village elders were interviewed about their understandings of the *Chol Q'ij*, the sacred Maya calendar of 260 days, and the number and day signs and symbols that correspond to the Maya calendar; the sacred earth, their mother; ways of education; the family; legends and old stories; traditional religion and ceremonies; dreams as a form of communication of God; the relation of the animal world with the person; and understandings of death and its rituals. In this ethnographic undertaking, an appreciation and new affirmation of Maya knowledge emerged in the community.

From this investigation, the community developed projects in which the people would inculturate their faith in K'iche' language, val-

---

[19] D. Irarrázaval, *Inculturation: New Dawn of the Church in Latin America* (Maryknoll, New York: Orbis Books, 2000), 229, 4.

[20] Ibid., 15.

[21] Ibid., ix.

[22] Gustavo Gutiérrez, *The Density of the Present: Selected Writings* (Maryknoll, New York: Orbis Books 1999), 117-118.

ues and worldview. For example, 60-70 promoters of inculturation met every two weeks to learn to read and write in K'iche', to translate the Mass, the rosary, the stations of the cross, the Bible, and a catechism for children; they promoted workshops to reflect on the signs and symbols of their culture, on themes of reconciliation, Maya vocations, on *Pop Wuj*, the K'iche' creation account, the Earth, their mother, and the Maya worldview. Further, they established projects in which the community would:

- Prepare and coordinate liturgy for all the parish fiestas (choir, reconciliation rites, reading of the Word of God in K'iche';
- Prepare the liturgy for the patron saints and to orient the people of their communities on the cultural ways of the grandparents. They established a process to select elders to interview and the themes of investigation in the communities;
- Coordinate and help prepare themes for the annual Youth Week that happens at the end of the year in Santa Maria – for 1200 indigenous youth of southern Mexico and Guatemala;
- Coordinate with a Center of Investigation "Qamam" where they can transcribe, edit and produce themes of investigation;
- Correct and adapt the way of speaking in Santa Maria Chiquimula, for forthcoming publications of URL about themes of education, stories, legends and poetry;
- Participate in workshops on spirituality and courses on liturgy and culture in other parishes;
- Coordinate work with other parishes, which have a similar vision and project.[23]

Inculturated Projects: Rooted and Emerging

On July 31, 2002, a *Chuchqajaw* kneels on the adobe floor of the parish church and lights 20 candles at a side shrine, as a procession of hundreds of Chiquimulans, part from the church, sing in honor of St. Ignatius of Loyola. The procession is led by the cofradia of San Ignacio, who incense and carry the statue of their patron saint, an arch of multi-colored balloons surrounding his head. They walk on the *alfombra(carpet)* of pine needles and flowers shaped as the Maya cross in front of the altar, down the aisles, out the door, into the plaza and village streets, and back to church 40 minutes later. Half a dozen *chuchqajaw* sit casually on the

---

[23] Chic, 129.

benches built into the east and south walls of the church plaza, as individuals consult with them.

A twenty minute walk away, in the cemetery situated on the hill, two sisters, in their seventies, have each walked ten miles to sit at their parents' graves, as they do every twenty days. Here they feed bits of tortilla, and pour a little coffee and a few black beans over their graves. "Whenever we feel sad, we come here to gather strength." In the center of the cemetery, a *chuchqajaw* is incensing the four *cerros*, the four altars, calling their *nawales*, their guardians, and binding them as a net, to come and strengthen the center of their prayer. On the other side of town, children run up the hills, their backpacks bouncing behind them to begin their classes, "*Maltiox.* Thank you, Heart of Heaven, Heart of Earth, for this day."

Numerous projects have taken root in Santa Maria Chiquimula: adult education classes in coordination with Instituto Guatemalteco de Educación Radiofónica (IGER), taught by 26 volunteers, nine of them trained teachers; a three year boarding school institute for young boys 14-17 of the *aldea* to learn welding, electricity and carpentry, as well as the values of K'iche', their culture and community; a K –6th grade school whose foundation is the richness of K'iche' culture and language; a woman's horticulture group; a Center of Inculturation, for the ethnographic recuperation and dissemination of language and culture; development of 13 Eucharistic communities, one in the town center, 12 in the *aldeas*, whose responsibility is development in faith, in sharing the Word, in Eucharistic services, each with its chapel, as well as every thirteenth Sunday, being responsible for the Sunday liturgy at the parish church; and the Youth Week where 1200 indigenous youth from diverse geographic and linguistic areas of southern Mexico and Guatemala attend a week long seminar, retreat and community building event.

In Santa Maria, the community-based ethnographic recuperation of cultural and linguistic values has been the fount of educational activities and of cultural productions, including written texts. This, too, mirrors the concluding statements of the bishops at Santo Domingo, that an inculturated evangelization has effective *educational activity* and *modern communications*. In Santa Maria, Eduardo León Chic undertook the ethnographic project of recording legends of the town's origin, village customs and the significance of the calendar, of the ceremonies, of the *Chuchqajaw* according to village elders. In 1996 Instituto Guatemalteco de Educación Radiofónica "IGER" published Chic's ethnographic and illustrated *Ri Ojer Taq Tzij Pa Tz' olojche': Old Kiche' Stories of Santa Maria Chiquimula*, in K'iche' and in Spanish. Since then, the incultura-tion team, coordinated by Eduardo León Chic, has founded *Ediciones Ik'laja* and published numerous handbooks: *Inculturación del Evan-gelico*, (*The Workshop of an Inculturated Liturgy), Arewa' Ri qakojb'al: Marco Doctrinal la fe de nuestras comunidades indigenas Zona Pas-toral de Totonicapán*) (*The Doctrinal Beliefs of our Community), Qono-jel ri oj oj alaxik (Key Stories of the Bible), Ministerios Originarios: los ministerios desde nuestra cultura maya (Original Ministers: The minis-ters of our Maya culture).* Father Victoriano Castillo González has writ-ten a most important text, *Ri Loq' Alaj K'Utbal (The Sacramental Rituals in the Language and Cosmovision of the Maya People),* also published by *Ediciones Ik'laja.*

The Sacramental Rituals in the Language and Cosmovision of the Maya People, is the first sacramentary in K'iche' – not a translation from Spanish, but one that emerges from the K'iche' worldview. In the introduction, he writes:

> From the beginnings of evangelization, the first mission-aries who brought the Word of God to this land, made efforts to translate the contents of the Christian doctrine. But no one translated the sacraments, nor adapted them to our culture. This is the great sin of our Church, that even though late, we want to repair.[24]

Fr. Victoriano explains that this text is not a literal translation because it would lose the profuse symbolism in the K'iche' language, rather that this text expresses the thinking, the cosmovision, of the K'iche' speakers. Further, he explains his second intention: that all who work among the K'iche' learn this indigenous language and enter their cosmovision. Mons. Victor Hugo Martinez C., Archbishop of "Los Al-tos" Quetzaltenango, Totonicapán, reinforces this need as he writes in his pastoral in the introduction of the book that he offers this text "as a vehi-cle to enter the mind and heart of our Indigenous people, through their language," and permits it to be used "AD EXPERIMENTUM."

As one enters traditional highland life, one encounters the impor-tance of the *Chol' Qij* , the 260-day sacred calendar. The ancient 260-day

---

[24] Castillo González, 12 ; translation mine.

calendar refers to two continuous repeating cycles, the count of 13 days, and the set of 20-day names; the combination of the day names and particular number designate the quality of the day. The *Chol' Qij* is used to connect and harmonize with the elements and forces of the universe. Each day is sacred and to be respected; further, the calendar is the paradigm through which people understand their capacities and navigate their lives, individually, communally and ceremonially. While at one time the ancient 260-day cycle calendar was in use in much of Mesoamerica, it now exists in communities in Veracruz, Oaxaca, Chiapas, and is utilized throughout the Guatemalan highlands.[25] Inherited from their predecessors, transmitted from generation to generation, clandestinely maintained throughout the colonial period, the calendar remains foundational to Maya practical life, discernment and ritual practices.[26] Eduardo León Chic, writes that the calendar is "the heart of the wisdom of the Maya people."[27]

In the past few years, Santa Maria Chiqumula parish has printed and distributed *Agenda: Cholb'al Q'ij: rech we junab' 5117* – the parish calendar. Here the sacred calendar of 260 days cycles with the Gregorian

---

[25] Tedlock, 92.

[26] Here I provide a selected number of studies which have addressed the 260-day calendar. Daniel G. Brinton, collects month and day names of the Maya stock and "subjects them to an etymological analysis and comparison with their correspondents in the Zapotec and Nahuatl tongues, and endeavors to read the symbolic significance of the Calendar a mythical record and method of divination," [Daniel G. Brinton, *The Native Calendar of Central America and Mexico: A Study in Linguistic and Symbolism* (Philadelphia: MacCalla & Company, 1893), 4]. Ruth Bunzel, *Chichicastenango* (Guatemala:Editorial Jose de Pineda Ibarra, 1981), 332-343, discusses the meaning of the days from her ethnographic work in Chichicastenango in the 1930s. Barbara Tedlock, *Time and the Highland Maya* (Albuquerque: University of New Mexico Press, 1982), discusses earliest records of calendar day signs, geographical locations in both Maya lowland and highland and the preservation and utilization of the calendar in various linguistic regions; from 107-131, she provides discussions of the significance of the individual days and use of the sacred calendar in the town of Momostenango. Walburga Rupflin Alvarado, *El Tzolkin es mas que un calendario*, 2d ed. (Guatemala City: Cedim, 1997), 73-160, provides contemporary interpretations of the days from ethnographic work with several *Ajq'ijab'*. Eduardo León Chic, *El Corzaón de la Sabiduría del Pueblo Maya* or *Uk'u'xal Ranima' ri Qano'jib'al* (*The Heart of the Wisdom of the MayaPeople*), (Iximulew: Cedim, 1999), provides contemporary interpretations of the sacred calendar and its uses from his ethnographic work among forty elder Chuchqajaw in Santa Maria Chiquimula, his native village. See Tedlock, 89-104, for more extensive ethnographic chronicling.

[27] Chic, 127.

calendar of 12 months. Each day is marked with the Maya day-sign and number; the day on the Gregorian calendar; the Church's liturgical readings for the day; and a remembrance of specific universal saints and Central American martyrs, massacres, and saints; and the phases of the moon. In a sense, in this aesthetic production, one can connect with and navigate multiple worlds.

The calendar is a spiritual guide for discernment, explains Father Victoriano in the introduction to the *Agenda 2001*. He writes that the sacred 260-day calendar, and the interpretation of the days, is but one of the elements that emerges from the Maya culture to discern the presence of God. Over time, Maya have developed other discernments - dreams, muscular contractions of "the lightening in the blood," traditional ceremonies, climatic changes - through which they understand the language, the presence of God. These are the inculturated ways that a people share in the immanent and transcendent experience of the Mystery of God.

Further, Fr. Victoriano not only discusses Maya time, but Maya space as he amplifies the cruciform, its directions, colors, levels, and significance in relation to Maya cosmovision, amplifying its philosophical and theological interpretations for a practical life.

Conclusion

We know that the journey towards globalization began in 1592, when Ferdinand Magellan circumnavigated the globe, subjecting the world to the influence of the West. In the Americas, indigenous peoples were inscribed into the hegemonic interests of the Western world. Anticipating the beginning of the Third millennium of Christianity and the Jubilee, in 1998, John Paul II issued "We Remember: A Reflection on the *Shoah*," recalling the horrible genocide of millions of Jewish people. Further, he called all Christians, and all men and women "to seek to discern in the passage of history the signs of divine Providence at work, as well as the ways in which the image of the Creator in man has been offended and disfigured."[28] The projects of reconciliation and inculturation among indigenous people are a step towards this healing. The Church itself is being called to be changed, to be founded anew.

There is no doubt that the result of major efforts of reconciliation and inculturation take place over the long run, but the crucial element is the small steps that are taken today and tomorrow. In 2001 the parish

---

[28] John Paul II, *We Remember: A Reflection on the Shoah*, March 16, 1998, www.be.edu.bc org/research/cjl/Documents/We%20Remember.htm, 1.

conducted a census of Santa Maria's 49,000 inhabitants. Thirty thousand, or 3/5 said they practiced both traditions - Catholic and *costumbre;* 20,000 said they were evangelical. Father Victoriano explains they learned that in the past ten years ninety-four families, who had not formerly associated with any church, joined the Catholic parish, and twenty-nine families joined the parish from evangelical cultures and twenty-four or twenty-five families went to evangelical cults. Many women and men I interviewed, stated that they had no conflict in Catholicism and traditional practices. "It's the same," they replied. "God is love. Jesus teaches how to love one another; our ancestors taught us how to pray, to respect life. It is all one." Fr. Victoriano explains that he has come to understand that:

> The spiritual life of the Maya is to give thanks, in attitude, in answering, waiting, in patience, in courage. All of this came from the Maya. One fundamental part of Maya existence is their spirituality. It is with this spiritual life that they have resisted economic and violent crisis...Spirituality is the key of Maya existence.

Let me refer back to the two opening quotes, one of Eduardo León Chic, the young ethnographer and parishioner who expressed gratitude to the Jesuits because "they have taught us to investigate our traditions and have illuminated our ways so that we have encountered that which is the most sacred of our grandparents: 'to live as indigenous' "[29]; and to Father Victoriano who writes, "I want to thank the people of *Tz'oljche'* (Santa Maria Chiquimula) because they have taught me the true face of God."[30] This is the aesthetic activity of dialogic activity – a compassionate understanding which enlarges consciousness. Further, the fruit of reconciliation becomes creative. In Father Victoriano's words:

> The West tries to understand and explain God. But the Maya way is to live God. God is the rain, the earth. Every act of life is an action of God.
>
> In the West, why is it so complicated? One asks why God is in the poor? How can God be suffering? For the

---

[29] Chic, 131-132.
[30] Castillo González, 8.

Maya, this is not a problem, for God is in all. That's why you need to respect, even the alcoholic. The reality is distinct.

For the Maya, the fundamental part of life is affective. It is to feel in the body, to embody in rituals this love. In the West, we reduce the experience of God to ritual. It is much more than this. It is a total expression of life. It is a relationship with God in the family, in plants and animals, in the cosmos. It is an experience of living Trinitarian faith.

As of May 2002, an asphalted road first reached Santa Maria Chiquimula. True, goods and people will be transported quicker and more safely. But other processes of globalization, tourism, and penetration of capital will engage people's lives. Perhaps, too, the good news of the processes and effects of an *inculturated evangelization* will travel among other Maya communities, and beyond, as Christian communities seek ways of "inculturation," a term for designating an old reality, which, for the Christian carries resonances of incarnation. Here we see that the Word's transcendence and immanence is not diminished as the Church undertakes projects of enculturation; rather, it is reaffirmed. It roots, flourishes and flowers.

INCULTURATED PROTESTANT
THEOLOGY IN GUATEMALA

Virginia Garrard-Burnett[*]

> Christian self-understanding must form [theologies] that
> stops coinciding with the historically determined West-
> ern traditions that represent merely the background
> against which traditions take note of their limitations and
> Eurocentric specificity.[1]

This paper will explore theological innovation and issues of
identity and resurgence among the indigenous Maya population of the
Central American nation of Guatemala. Specifically, this work will examine the efforts of Mayan Protestants to "inculturate" Christian theology; that is, to decontextualize Christian narratives from their Western
cultural references and reposition them within a Mayan *telos*, or "*cosmovisión.*" The parameters of this paper are specific, in that it will discuss an evolving theology that is intentional in its creation and Protestant
in its perspective. Although there is also a Catholic analog to this theology, known as "inculturation theology," both the Catholic version and
the Protestant theology to be discussed here today are distinct in both
form, intent, and practice from the older blends of Mayan and Christian
beliefs that are generally thought of, with some imprecision, as "religious
syncretism"[2] or "folk Catholicism."

---

[*] Virginia Garrard-Burnett is Senior Lecturer at the Teresa Lozano Long Institute of Latin American Studies at the University of Texas, Austin. She is the
author of a number of articles on religion in Latin America, and the author of
Protestantism in Guatemala: Living in the New Jerusalem (University of Texas,
1998), editor of *On Earth as it is in Heaven: Religion in Latin America* (Scholarly Resources, 2000) and co-editor of *Rethinking Protestantism in Latin America* (Temple, 1993).
[1] Jürgen Habermas, "Israel or Athens, or to Whom does Anamnestic Reason
Belong?" in *Liberation Theologies, Postmodernity, and the Americas*, David
Batstone, et al, eds. (London: Routledge, 1997), 251.
[2] The literature on the nature of "religious syncretism" is, of course, extensive,
and the term itself is problematic, suggesting a religious form that derives from
indigenous peoples' misunderstandings and misappropriation of religious forms.
Hans Seibers has recently suggested a better explanation of indigenous religious
forms is "religious creolization," a term which suggests a purposeful blending of
religious cultures that results from the intentional integration of means and symbols from two or more religious traditions. [Hans Seibers, "Globalization and

Protestant Mayanized theology is a direct and conscious response to the historic repression of Guatemala's native indigenous population and of the recent efforts by Mayan intellectuals to create a coherent political movement to represent pan-Mayan political, social, and economic interests. Because of the theology's overtly political genesis, some historical and ethnographic background is necessary to understand the context for its development. Guatemala is one of only two nations in Latin America with an Indian majority (Bolivia is the other). Upwards of 60% of Guatemalans are indigenous; but its indigenous population has historically been the object of a virulent racism that has left them with some of the lowest social indicators in the hemisphere. In terms of religious identity, the majority (60%) of Guatemalans are Catholic (both orthodox and practitioners of a Mayanized "folk Catholicism"), although the influence of US missionaries and the rapid growth of independent, local Protestant churches has also resulted in a sizable and expanding Protestant population that accounts for approximately 35% of the population, a figure that is higher in Mayan, as opposed to non-Mayan parts of the country.[3]

Power in the country is vested in a small elite of primarily European origin and in the *ladinos*, a term which applies both to persons of mixed Indian-European descent and to, acculturated indigenous people. Guatemala has historically been the richest nation in Central America in terms of economic and natural resources, but decades of political struggle severely retarded its economic advancement during the second half of the twentieth century. The nation suffered through an unevenly matched and bloody civil war between Marxist guerrillas (the URNG) and the military-controlled government from 1961-1996. Although the struggle

---

Religious Creolization Among the Q'eqchi'es of Guatemala," in *Latin American Religion in Motion*, Christian Smith and Joshua Prokopy, eds. (London: Routledge, 1999), 261-273]. A good discussion of the issues surrounding religious pluralism and community identity can be found in Robert S. Carlsen, *The War for the Heart and Soul of a Highland Maya Town*, (Austin: University of Texas Press, 1997).

[3] Solid statistics on religious affilation in Guatemala are difficult to come by. The national census does not ask for such information, and most figures of church membership and attendance are collected by partisen groups affiliated either with Protestant or Catholic churches. For more on this problem, see Henri Gooren, "Reconsidering Protestant Growth in Guatemala, 1900-1995," in *Holy Saints and Fiery Preachers: The Anthropology of Protestantism in Mexico and Central America*, James Dow and Alan R. Sandstrom, eds. (Westport, Connecticut: Greenwood Press, 2001), 169-203.

lasted for 36 years, the most concentrated period of violence took place between 1981-1983, when state repression and violence accelerated sharply, corresponding to the scorched earth campaign in the largely indigenous highlands. During this period alone, at least 20,000 Guatemalans died violently, upwards of 80% of whom were Mayan.[4]

This grim period of genocide of the early 1980s still leaves a strong imprint of terror and its repercussion in the country, but it also elicited a wide variety of political and social responses. For our purposes here today, the most significant of these are the development of 1) the Mayan movement, a political movement by and for Mayan people to assert their own cultural and political rights, 2) the Peace Accords of 1996, which conceded and protected, for the first time in Guatemala's history, specific cultural and political rights to the Mayan peoples.[5]

The Protestant *teología maya* (which I will call here in a somewhat facile shorthand, Mayanized theology), which is the topic of this paper, is a direct project of this history of political subordination, genocide, and cultural resurgence. By some measures, Mayanized theology is as much a political gesture as it is a theology, for the authors of the theology are fully aware of the ways in which Mayan people have, over time, been able to appropriate a powerful means of domination and subordination (Christianity) and inverted both the means and the message for their own strategies. In this sense the decolonialized theology is much like other types of "liberating" religious discourses such as liberation theology or other theologies tied directly to the political and cultural agendas of subordinate groups, such as the black theology promoted by such figures as James H. Cone in the United States during the 1960s or feminist theologians within the Catholic Church today. This convergence brings to mind David Batstone's suggestion that, "...political discourse [naturally] has its theological counterpart. The coincidence of the political and the theological should come as no surprise; after all, theological discourse is responding to the same material culture that finds expression

---

[4] Patrick Bell, Patrick, Paul Kobrak, and Herbert F. Spirer, *State Violence in Guatemala, 1960–1996: A Quantitative Reflection* (Washington, D.C.: AAAS Science and Human Rights Program, 1999), figure 4.1, http://hrdata.aaas.org/ciidh/qr/english/.

[5] See Edward F. Fischer and R. McKenna Brown, eds. *Maya Cultural Activism in Guatemala* (Austin: University of Texas Press, 1996).

in political discourse."[6]

Of central significance to this project is an examination of the ways that local innovators adapt and reorganize imported religious "systems" for their own ends.[7] It begs the obvious to state that Christian missionary enterprises in Latin America have been, from the first colonial contacts, grounded in asymmetrical power relations and in the desire to reconstruct not only people's identities, but also their very consciousnesses. In his work on colonial Christianity in South Africa, John and Jean Comaroff describe religious cultural encounters as "a complex dialectic of invasion and ropost, of challenge and resistance...a politics of consciousness in which the very nature of consciousness [is] itself the object of struggle."[8] Given these high stakes and deep asymmetries, religion has remained a contested venue in Guatemala, and the struggle has never been completely one-sided. The object of Mayan theology is to invert and reinterpret the power relations and identity issues implicit in the Christian "project" for their own purposes.

Yet it would be a mistake to think of Mayan theology as nothing more than political rhetoric. Because Christianity has such a long and contested history in Guatemala, religion has often been used as a measure and metaphor for the deeply-rooted contradictions and tensions that underlie so much of Guatemala's past and present, and, in fact, religion— and militant Christianity in particular—sometimes lie at the very heart of these contradictions. Obviously, the colonial, imperialist origins of Christianity, both Catholic (Spanish) and Protestant (North American), in a place like Guatemala carry enormous historical weight that cannot be overlooked. Yet Christianity in Guatemala long ago lost its foreign ac-

---

[6] David Batstone, "Charting (dis)Courses of Liberation," in *Liberation Theologies, Postmodernity, and the Americas*, Batstone, et al. (London: Routledge, 1997), 159.

[7] I use the phrase "religious systems" here with some caution, and with a caveat offered by David Lehmann, who writes, "...there are not grounds for taking the fixed integrity of a religious system for granted or even for believing that religious ensembles, sub-cultures or institutions can be thought of as systems at all. However, the self-image of a religious institution or subculture as possessing its own integrity, or the images it produces of the other as a distinct system, are interesting and important because religion in the modern world is evidently a marker of identity and a mechanism for the production of group / identarian boundaries. ["Charisma and Possession in Africa and Brazil," unpublished paper, Cambridge University, 2000, 2].

[8] John and Jean Comaroff, *Of Revelation and Revolution: Christianity, Colonialism and Consciousness in South Africa, vol. 1* (Chicago: University of Chicago Press, 1991), 250.

cent and acquired what R.S. Sugirtharajah calls a "vernacular hermeneutics," a local system of value, understanding, and interpretation.[9]

This brings us at last to the particulars of Mayanized Protestant theology. At present, theological innovation is being produced by the Conferencia de Iglesias Evangélicas de Guatemala (CIEDEG), a "liberal" Protestant organization that is dominated by Mayan Presbyterians. CIEDEG is headed by Vitalino Similox, a Kak'chiquel Maya Presbyterian pastor who was an important intermediary for ecumenical church people associated with the URNG and a pivotal negotiator during the Oslo Peace Talks which ended the long war. Similox has been involved as an activist in the Mayan movement, and he ran for vice-president of the republic for the ANN, a left-of-center party, during the 1999 presidential elections.

The Presbyterians' prominence in the movement to Mayanize theology is due not only to Similox's influence, but also to historical factors that underscored long-standing concerns within the denomination as to the cultural implications of religious conversion. The Presbyterian Church has a long historical presence in Guatemala, and it was the first missionary group to cede full control of the denomination to local leadership (1961). In the mid-1960s, the church carved out two Mayan (Kak'chiquel and Mam) synods (administrative districts) to reflect its respect for indigenous cosmovision and theological autonomy.[10]

Discursive analysis reveals that Guatemalan Mayans who are Presbyterians often express a highly heterodox body of belief that incorporates both conventional Protestant theology, Mayan ideas of sacred geography, culturally-encoded polymorphic notions of the nature of God(s) and a worldview that is consciously grounded in Mayan *cosmovisión*, alongside Protestant emancipation narratives.[11] Although the Presbyterians are a relatively small group in Guatemala and are greatly outnumbered by Pentecostal Protestants, they have a political and social presence in the country that belie their actual numbers. Moreover, the majority of Presbyterians in Guatemala are now Maya.

---

[9] Rasiah S. Surgirtharajah, *The Bible and the Third World: Precolonial, Colonial, and Postcolonial Encounters* (Cambridge: Cambridge University Press, 2001), 175.

[10] See Virginia Garrard-Burnett, *Protestantism in Guatemala: Living in the New Jerusalem* (Austin: University of Texas Press, 1998), 114.

[11] See David Scotchmer, "Symbols of Salvation: Interpreting Highland Maya Protestantism in Context," (Ph.D. dissertation, State University of New York at Albany, 1991).

Although CIEDEG is dominated by the Presbyterians, its membership also includes congregations from many other denominations, including Pentecostals (who make up the vast majority of Guatemala's Protestants, both Mayan and non-Mayan), non-pentecostal fundamentalists, and independent Protestant denominations. The common denominators of membership are ethnicity—virtually all congregations that belong to CIEDEG are Mayan—and a shared geography of terror, in that the participating congregations are all located near or in areas where military reprisals and massacres of civilians during the civil violence of the early 1980s took place and therefore loom large on the landscape of local memory.[12] While the founding mandate of CIEDEG was to help in the implementation of peace and reconciliation in the region, (*camino de Shalom,* or "Shalom road"), its leaders recognized a need to confront the implications of Guatemala's recent history in theological terms.[13]

The notion of creating a new, dewesternized theology thus grew out of the 1996 Peace Accords, specifically the *Acuerdo sobre Identidad y Derechos de los Pueblos,* which specifically offers protection of indigenous religious practices as a cultural right. As a political strategy, the primary purpose of the new theology is to encourage a religious system that supports indigenous cultural rights within the larger context of Mayan resurgence.[14] At the symbolic level, the Protestant Mayanized theology is an attempt to create an alternative theological paradigm for Mayan Protestants who reject the popular conflation of Protestant religion with westernization (a process known in Latin America has *mestizaje*) and with conservative politics.

Since the late 1990s, CIEDEG has generated workshops, study groups, literature for use by church groups, political documents and other means to engender a Mayan-based Christology that seeks to contextualize basic Christian beliefs within a larger system of Mayan cosmology, cultural values, and worldview. At the most basic level, Mayanized theology attempts to reconcile Protestant Christianity with the three central elements of Mayan spirituality: peace with the natural world that sustains life, peace with other people (including the dead) and peace with the de-

---

[12] See CIEDEG, "La Misión de la Iglesia Evangélica de Guatemala en la Etapa Post-Conflict (Guatemala City: Ediciones Alternatives, 1998), 5.

[13] Ibid., chapter 1.

[14] CIEDEG, "La justicia siembra la Paz, y da su fruto a los artesanos de la Paz." Pamphlet, 2001; Vitalino Similox Salazar, "Evangelismo protestante y espiritualidad maya en el Marco de los Acuerdos de Paz," in *Prensa Libre*, May 8, 1997 (Guatemala: CIEDEG, 1997).

ity/ies.[15] But the theology also demands a reexamination of fundamental Christian images, symbols, and archetypes through the lens of "traditional" Mayan cosmovision(s). This means, at the most basic level, that theology should be expressed in a language that can be easily understood - literally, in the most widely-spoken Mayan languages (Kak'chiquel, Mam, and Ki'ché), but also figuratively, through the utilization of symbols, myths, and iconography that are locally understood, valued, and interpreted.

The reasons for embedding Protestant theology within Mayan culture are partially strategic: "How can a Maya accept the Good News of the Gospel," a Mayan theologian asks rhetorically, "if the person who is evangelizing practically requires him to give up what is essential to the profundity of his life, and annul the spiritual and cultural heritage of his ancestors?" But it is also a postmodern reinterpretation of Christianity's claims to unique revelation through the person of Christ. Instead of a conversion narrative based on a traditional Protestant/fundamentalist salvation narrative (before and after salvation through Jesus Christ), Mayanized theology insists upon recognition of the "persistent historic presence of God in our cultures: in the myths, the rituals, the customs, in the community, the services, organizations, in the families, in the humanistic conception of the human being, and in the Earth, as a point of reference in the Universe."[16]

Yet Mayanized theology is by no means universalistic. It embraces a traditional Christology which affirms Jesus Christ as "the Savior; without Him there is no hope...without him there is no eternal salvation, there is no human face of God outside of Christ." However, within this understanding is the caveat that "the event of Jesus, the Christ is not the exclusive possession or the private property of any culture...the Gospel transcends whatever [human] forces attempt to contain it in...whether it be cultural or religious."[17]

In a pamphlet published in Guatemala's most widely-read daily newspaper, CIEDEG's Similox argued that Christianity not only tran-

---

[15] See David Scotchmer, "Life in the Heart: A Maya Protestant Spirituality," in *South and Mesoamerican Native Spirituality*, Garry H. Gossens and León Portilla, eds. (New York: Crossroad Publishing Company, 1993), 507.

[16] Vitalino Similox Salazar, "Algunos propuestas de la religiosidad Maya hacia un pluralismo religioso, en el marco de los Acuerdos de Paz" (CIEDEG: Guatemala City, 1997), pamphlet.

[17] Vitalino Similox Salazar, *Religión Maya: Fuente de Resistencia Milenaria* (Guatemala: CIEDEG, 1998), 146-147.

scends, but actually valorizes indigenous cultures. "God loves all cultures and his salvation does not signify the denigration or renunciation of cultural and historic identity. Evangelization does not signify the announcement of the 'absence of God' in a culture, but [rather]it is an announcement of the good news of 'his presence'... ."[18] An evangelical pastor stated the equation more simply: "God was already here," he explained, "when Columbus arrived."[19] Yet some take a more cautious view: "Christ is present in all cultures," writes Mónica Ramirez de López, "but [He] participates actively to transform them. We must rescue our culture, values, customs, and social actions that do not go against the Word of God. But we must reject those that openly or covertly go against Biblical absolutes. From there all culture must always be test[ed], tried, and judged by the Scripture."[20]

Even this more conservative vantage point, however, provides a point of departure for understanding Mayanized theology. In his 1998 treatise entitled, *Maya Religion: Source of Millenarian Resistance,*[21] Similox outlined areas for cultural recovery within Mayan Christianity, so that, in his words, "the Maya may drink from his *own* well."[22] Specifically, the theology demands the reconstruction of theology within the framework of five Mayan cultural paradigms. These include:

- *The recovery of Mayan cultural values, particlarly the emphasis on the community over the indvidual.* This would be expressed in a different emphasis on corporate, over individual sins: "The pastor condemns certain sins, for example, laziness, alcoholism...witchcraft, idolatry, but never [things like] poor payment for labor, exploitation, or other social sins."[23] Even more to

---

[18] Vitalino Similox Salazar, "Evangelismo protestante y espiritualidad Maya en el Marco de los Acuedros de Paz," in *Prensa Libre*, May 8, 1997 (Guatemala: CIEDEG).

[19] C. Matthew Samson, "Interpretando la Identidad Religiosa: La Cultura Maya y La Religion Evangélica Bajo Una Perspectiva Etngoráfica," paper presented at the Segundo Conferencia Sobre El *Pop Wuj*, Quetzaltenango, Guatemala, 30 May-4 June, 1999, 9.

[20] Mónica Ramírez de Lopez, "Statement on behalf of the Fraternidad Teológica Latinoamericana, to the Primera Consulta Nacional de CIEDEG," February, 1998.

[21] Similox Salazar, *Religión Maya.*

[22] Ibid., 128.

[23] Ibid., 118.

the point, Mayan religious expression is based upon communitarian expression. Within the Protestant context, the emphasis is placed upon the new community of *hermanos/hermanas* (brothers and sisters) in the faith.

- *Re-integration of religion into everyday life, not just relegated to the Sabbath.* Traditional Mayan spirituality is not so much a system of dogma, but more a systemic spirituality that touches every aspect of life; more a "way of being" than a religion per se.[24] "Protestantism has tended to compartmentalize the practice of religion, which is not the Maya way—we pray before we cut the soil to plant; we pray before we shoot an animal to eat," writes Similox.[25] Mayanized theology, by contrast, calls for a fuller integration of faith into the quotidian details of life.[26]

- *The abandonment of the most obviously foreign cultural elements in worship.* This refers to such practices as women and men sitting on different sides of the church rather than as families (a Spanish Catholic custom) and the use of culturally inappropriate hymns translated into Spanish for use in worship services. "Evangelization has been [tantamount to] acculturation," writes Similox. "We received hymns, not only in a different language, but also in another mentality."[27]

- *The creation of a "Mayan hermeneutics."* This includes the utilization of symbols, rites, myths of ancient Maya culture, whenever possible, to convey Christian allegory. This becomes, then, a double hermeneutic puzzle, because ancient

---

[24] Samson, 10. See also, Guillermo Cook, ed. *Crosscurrents in Indigenous Spirituality: Interface of Maya, Catholic and Protestant Worldviews* (New York: E.J. Brill, 1997).
[25] Similox, *Religión Maya*, 119.
[26] Ibid.
[27] Ibid., 124-125.

Mayan religious symbols and imagery are buried so deeply beneath the symbols and myths of the dominant culture. The task, then, is to "decode from Mayan sources, such as the ancient chronicles, to decipher the true meanings of the ancient messages."[28]

Within this Mayan hermeneutic, the theology calls for recognition of "the sacred duality, that God is both Father and Mother."[29] While this notion runs parallel to what are now standard Western understandings of God's dual-gendered "personhood," it also, within Mayanized theology, carries fundamental ecological implications. In the Mayan context, "The motherness of God is in the form of the Earth (*tierra*). The earth is a divine gift and the mother of the community...[but it also an embodiment] of the divine pact with Abraham. Conversely, the earth is not only a material symbol of God's covenant, but it is also, considered sacred as a physical entity."[30]

- *The theology also prescribes the incorporation of other integral material elements of Mayan culture as utensils of worship*; these might include the pine-resin incense, votive candles, pine branches, and grain alcohol to libate holy spaces that are normally utilized in syncretic rituals or in the ancient healing practices now known by many Maya as *brujeria* (witchcraft or magic). Because conventional Protestant practice eschews these material elements, their explicit inclusion marks a clear departure from "noninculturated" Mayan Protestantism .

---

[28] Ibid., 139.
[29] Ibid., 143-144.
[30] Ibid., 142-143.

Finally, the inclusion of a third material aspect of worship clearly sets Mayanized theology apart from "orthodox" Protestantism, and this is the integration of corn into Christian worship. In both ancient and contemporary Mayan life corn is considered to be not merely a staff of life, but also the veritable source of life itself, and the planting, harvesting, and consumption of corn is considered a sacramental act. (It is an interesting parallel that colonial Spaniards refused to eat corn, and insisted instead upon planting wheat, so that it could be made into bread and for the Host for the Mass). In a creation myth described in the ancient Mayan holy book, the *Popul Vuh*, the Lords of Xabalba created mankind from ears of corn (*"hombres de maiz"*, or men of corn); in ancient but also in contemporary times, the reproductive cycle of corn forms the nexus of Mayan public celebration and ritual, and corn, in all its varieties of preparation, still makes up the foundation of the Mayan diet.

Thus, it should come as no surprise that Mayanized theology reasserts the centrality of corn as a spiritual element, and the identity of Mayan Christians, too, as *hombres de maiz*. "The indigenous person who stops planting corn," exhorts Similox, "leaves behind so many cultural elements that she puts herself at serious risk." The centrality of corn in Mayanized theology is highly symbolic, but it is also strategic, because in both Guatemala and Mexico, Protestants have been widely reviled for their refusal to participate in community fiestas and public celebrations. Similox's insistence that Maya Protestants should both participate in community celebrations and in the sacred duty of planting corn signals a clear affirmation of ethnic valorization in a Protestant context.

Despite this valorization, it is the reaffirmation of the material aspects of Mayan religious culture that proves a sticking point for many Mayan Protestants regarding inculturated theology. Mayan Protestants assiduously avoid the use of such material "gifts and creatures" as incense, candles, corn veneration, and alcohol. They repudiate these elements as "idolatrous" practices associated with syncretism and, worse still—in their way of thinking—Catholicism, which many Mayan converts, justifiably or not, negatively associate with spiritual domination and a repudiated pagan past. As another Mayan theologian, Antonio Otzoy, explained, "It was not long ago when Protestantism came; we were all Catholics then, and they would tell us, 'you are all pagans because you are Catholics.'...The Protestant Church in Guatemala is an anti-

Catholic Church."[31] Otzoy has suggested that the sublimation of Mayan religious forms within Catholicism has produced a fierce Protestant bias against what he calls the "double paganization" (*doble paganización*) of Mayan spiritual imagery.[32] Thus, the task remains for Protestant Mayanized theology to reclaim the patrimony of Mayan religious language, rituals, and symbolism not so much from the pre-Christian past, but from its strong association with Catholicism.

This issue illustrates as well as any the disconnect that exists between the discourse of Mayanized theology, articulated as it is by well educated Mayan pastors and intellectuals, and everyday Maya believers, who as yet have been reticent in their acceptance of inculturated Protestant theology. This is most apparent among the Pentecostals, who recoil at any formal reconciliation between a type of spirituality that they now consider idolatrous, and the "Christian way" (*camino*). Yet there is growing evidence that at the grassroots level, even Pentecostals are beginning to accommodate their indigenous world view with Protestant beliefs. This is evinced by Pentecostal "*acciones de gracias*," prayer services held at the planting and harvest of corn, and in informal discourse, as Mayan Protestants contemplate their unique place in the Christian *koinonia*. The questions they raise and the answers they devise suggest a reconciliation of Mayan beliefs within a Christian cosmology, rather than the other way around. This is well illustrated in the explanation a rural Mayan evangelical pastor gave of his understanding of the relationship between the holy scriptures of Christianity and ancient Mayan religion, the Bible and the *Popul Vuh*:

> I found that in the Bible, it says you have to have respect, right? In the Bible, it also says to honor the father and the mother, no? And there is one God, God the father, etc. In Mam [the pastor's Mayan language group], that is "elder," right? But the concept is the same.... So I think that it is possible to see that the people before [pre-Christian Mayans] had the concept; it's much clearer that there was religion and there was faith in God [in the New World] maybe in the time of Abraham--we don't

---

[31] Antonio Otzoy, "Hermandad de Presbiterios Maya," *Primera Consulta, La Misión de la Iglesia Evangélica de Guatemala en la Etapa Post Conflict* (Guatemala: Ediciones Alternativas, 1998), 38-39.
[32] Ibid., 38.

know, right? Because unfortunately, we don't have the
dates. Our ancestors had a great book (the *Popul Vuh*),
but our enemies [the Spanish friars] burned [it], right?...
what I want to say is that in reading the Bible, I arrived
at the conclusion that they [the ancient Mayan ancestors]
had it, when they were here on the earth, carrying a faith
in the kingdom of God.[33]

The rural pastor's exegesis suggests that, although Mayanized Protestant
theology has been created around the political project of Mayan cultural
revitalization in the aftermath of the civil war, the larger object of "de-
colonializing" and reconciling long-held beliefs with their new religion is
quite compelling to many Mayan Protestants for reasons that reach well
beyond political expediency. As anthropologist Matt Samson has noted,
"If the Bible is seen as a source of primordial authority and as a point of
religious identity for Mayan Protestants, there also exists among them a
strong impulse to include the ancestors of the family with them now that
that are on what they feel is the right path, through their conversion."[34] It
is perhaps in this fashion that Mayanized theology is making the transition from its genesis as the theological counterpart to a political discourse, to a vernacular hermeneutics in which is embedded a culturally
meaningful narrative of salvation.

---

[33] Samson, 11-12. This is a paraphrase and translation of a much longer text that
is printed in full in Samson's article.
[34] Ibid., 12.

PART V

Interaction of Christian Theology and Ethics with Native Arts and Literature

Edited by
Cyriac K. Pullapilly
Saint Mary's College

THE VOLKSWARTBUND AND THE ARTS, 1907-1933[*]

Margaret Stieg Dalton[**]

The Organization: The Early Years

The Volkswartbund began as the Verband der Männervereine zur Bekämpfung der öffentlichen Unsittlichkeit (Association of Men's Organizations to Fight Public Immorality).[1] An association of associations, it was created in 1907 by the leaders of a group of men's morality organizations, most of which were located in places like Aachen, Koblenz, Cologne, Mainz, and Mönchengladbach, although there were a few from large cities, like Essen and Duisburg, and one or two from areas outside the Rhineland and the Ruhr, like Frankfurt am Main and Munich. These morality organizations typically kept themselves occupied by promoting educational lectures, supporting the resolutions of other morality organizations, and complaining to any civil or religious authority that would accept a complaint about immoral books, inappropriate advertisements, the sale of contraceptive devices, offensive slide shows in kiosks, material on sex education, unsuitable privately printed material, and nudity in art, on the stage, or wherever it was publicly visible.[2]

The leaders sought strength in unity. "How much more effectively, energetically, and successfully we would be able to combat public immorality, if it was not a single organization, in a single place, but an association of united organizations in all the large cities," read the report of the organizational meeting. They hoped that their new association would facilitate cooperation and work on a national level to advance

---

[*] This essay is a version of a chapter in Professor Dalton's book, *Catholicism, Popular Culture, and the Arts in Germany, 1880-1933*, © 2004 by the University of Notre Dame. Reproduced with permission of the University of Notre Dame Press.

[**] Margaret Stieg Dalton is the EBSCO/Bristol Professor at the School of Library and Information Studies of the University of Alabama. She has an A.B. from Harvard University, an M.L.S. from Columbia University, and a Ph.D. in history from the University of California, Berkeley. Her principal research interests are scholarly communication and the history of libraries and culture. Her most recent book, *Catholicism, Popular Culture, and the Arts in Germany, 1880-1933*, will be published by the University of Notre Dame Press.
[1] An excellent introduction to the general topic of moral regulation is Alan Hunt, *Governing Morals: A Social History of Moral Regulation*, Cambridge Studies in Law and Society (Cambridge: Cambridge University Press, 1999).
[2] "Cölner Männerverein z. B. d. ö.U.," *Volkswart* 2 (January 1909): 8.

their common goal.[3]

That common goal was opposition to the perceived moral emergency of their time. In 1903 Hermann Roeren,[4] a Cologne lawyer and Center Party politician, and a moving force behind the new association, had expressed a widely-shared view: "A few years ago those who asserted that even here in Germany morality was declining in the name of 'culture' and 'free art' were dismissed as benighted and called moral zealots,... but no one now argues that there is no moral decline." He was exaggerating only slightly; there was widespread agreement in imperial Germany that morality was not what it had been. For all its menace, however, immorality remained vague, defined only by example. The morality organizations offered as evidence of moral decline rampant prostitution, homosexuality, and alcoholism, the sale and use of birth control devices, the spread of immodest dress, trashy literature, and plays in which there was hugging on the stage—the lists were endless.[5]

The Cologne Männerverein, an organization that was a fundamentally Catholic organization,[6] had a particularly important role in the

---

[3] Ernst Lennartz, "Fünfundzwanzig Jahre Volkswartbund," *Volkswart* 25 (January 1932): 5-6; Historisches Archiv der Stadt Köln, Bestand Marx, Bd. 397, Bericht über die 11. März 1907 in Cöln stattgefundene Versammlung der Vertreter der Männervereine zur Bekämpfung der öffentlichen Unsittlichkeit.

[4] Hermann Roeren (1844-1920), Cologne lawyer, member first of the Prussian legislature, then of the Reichstag, wrote on economics, noted for his opposition to the Lex Heinze.

[5] Historisches Archiv der Stadt Köln, Bestand Marx, Bd. 397, Hermann Roeren, *Die öffentliche Unsittlichkeit und ihre Bekämfung* (Cologne: J.P. Bachem, 1903), 3-4; also pamphlet,published by the Volksverein, *Ist die Gesundheit unseres Volkes bedroht?*; "Satzungen des Verbandes der Männervereine z. B. d. ö. U.," *Volkswart* 2 (Organisationsnummer March 1909): 7.

[6] The third annual report of the Männerverein emphasizes that all the Catholic organizations of Cologne and its suburbs had been invited to the pre-organizational gathering and that the governing boards of seventy-three Catholic organizations had sent representatives. At the organization of the Verband der Männervereine, however, Roeren insisted to Pfarrer Bohlen of the Essen Männerverein, an interconfessional organization, that the character of the Cologne Männerverein was interconfessional. Roeren argued that this made easier the establishment of a Cologne Protestant group; one can also see the establishment of the Protestant group as a statement of the Cologne Männerverein's Catholic orientation. Historisches Archiv der Stadt Köln, Bestand Marx, Bd. 397, Bericht über die 11. März 1907 in Cöln stattgefundene Versammlung der Vertreter der Männervereine zur Bekämpfung der öffentlichen Unsittlichkeit; Historisches Archiv der Stadt Köln, Bestand Marx, Bd. 397, Kölner Männer-Verein zur Bekämpfung der öffentlichen Unsittlichkeit, III. Bericht über die Gesamttätigkeit des Vereins, 1903.

new association, providing it with both leadership and essential support. Hermann Roeren, who had founded the Cologne men's morality organization in 1898 and remained its chairman, was instrumental in the formation of the new Verband and Ernst Lennartz,[7] the secretary and vice-chairman of the Cologne Männerverein, became its chairman. The office of the Verband was established in Cologne. The Cologne Männerverein also served as a role model to the new local groups the Verband set out to encourage.

To permit local groups that were interconfessional to affiliate with it, the Verband was by statute interconfessional, but from the beginning it was Catholic dominated.[8] Its chairman, Ernst Lennartz, and the editors of its journal *Volkswart*, first Josef Pappers,[9] then Johann (Hans) Fröhlings, were all Catholics. Catholic activity on moral issues, such as the bishops' Easter pastoral letters of 1909 that discussed moral problems, was well reported in *Volkswart*. Catholic bishops provided subsidies and the Verband often sought to work through Catholic organizations like the Katholikentag. A comparable explicitly Protestant presence is simply not there.

Within a year the new association began publication of *Volkswart* (People's Watch), a monthly magazine, that combined news from the different local groups, hortatory calls to action, reports on legislation, and pseudo-scholarly articles on relevant topics. The magazine was, in a very real sense, the *raison d'être* of the association. Its articles educated the moral warrior, its regular column "Aus den Vereinen" (From the Organizations) assured him that he was not alone. But its significance to the association went far beyond the impact of any one issue. Because Dr. Marcour,[10] a leader of the Koblenz Männerverein, legislator and director of the Görres-Druckerei, arranged for his publishing firm to take over its publication, it was essentially independent of the "fluctuating income" of the organization and survived World War I and the drastic inflation of 1923 relatively unscathed. In 1925 Lennartz described the journal as both

---

[7] Ernst Lennartz (1872-1932), Cologne lawyer, wrote on law, current events.
[8] The report on the founding of the Verband der Männervereine states that Roeren responded to the concerns of Pfarrer Bohlen, representing the Essen Männerverein, by emphasizing the interconfessional character of the Cologne Männerverein. The 1903 report of the Kölner Männerverein, on the other hand, recounts that all Catholic organizations in Cologne and its suburbs had been invited to the large assembly that preceded the foundation of the Cologne Männerverein. There is no mention of anything Protestant.
[9] Josef Pappers (1877-1911), author, editor.
[10] Eduard Marcour (1848-1924), journalist, editor.

"root and fruit" for the association, root in that it nourished the association, and fruit in that it spread seeds that perpetually renewed the morality movement. The relationship of journal and association was synergistic and the journal's continuity gave the organization stability. Appropriately, it gave its name to the parent organization in 1927.[11]

Volkswart was the single most important service the Verband provided to its constituent organizations, but it was not the only one. Other early accomplishments of the new association included the foundation of a library of writings related to the "interests, tasks, work, and enemies of the organization" and the establishment of a secretariat.[12] By the beginning of World War I the Verband had at least fifty-seven associated organizations, the vast majority from the Catholic Rhineland, and had become a base for potential political action.[13]

To describe the Verband as solely a coordinating and advisory organization, however, is to misrepresent its ethos. Technically, it was a supra-organization, its work far from the unsavory streets where the real fight against immorality took place, although those involved in efforts to fight moral decline did not make such distinctions. To them, the movement to fight immorality was one movement. From the journal it is clear that the Verband regarded the activities of the local organizations as the Verband's activities, in fact, if not in theory.

Cultural Concerns

The doctrine of moral emergency was a complex of interconnected ideas and assumptions in which fear and anger were prominent. The vision of the world shared by moral militants featured strong men and pure women, faithful to their religion and loyal to their Kaiser. Each had a well-defined role within the family. Their children were likewise strong, pure, devout, and loyal, and, moreover, obedient to their parents. Sex

---

[11] J. Fröhlings, "Zum Geleit," *Volkswart* 25 (January 1932): 3-5; [Ernst] Lennartz, "Warum abonnieren und lesen wir den Volkswart? *Volkswart* 18 (January 1925): 2.

[12] The secretariat may have existed in name only. The editor of the journal probably doubled as the general secretary, but there are few reports of activity by the secretary. A general secretariat was planned from the beginning, but funds were scarce.

[13] Fröhlings, "Zum Geleit," 3-5; "Zur Gründung eines General-Sekretariats," *Volkswart* 2 (Organisationsnummer March 1909): 8-9; "Gründet Vereine!" *Volkswart* 4 (November 1911): 161-62; "Aus unseren Vereinen: Neue Männervereine," and "Aus unseren Vereinen: Alte Männervereine," *Volkswart* 6 (September 1913): 137-38.

took place only within marriage. In contrast to this vision stood reality, a society that seemed anything but virtuous. In the eyes of moral militants, society's afflictions were many, including, but not limited to, individualism, materialism, optimism, aestheticism, atheism, pantheism, and an obsession with the body. They found themselves confused by the ambiguities of their society. How could a Volk that claimed to be a people of poets and thinkers allow itself to be inundated by a flood of millions of trashy publications? They wanted to believe in the healthy instincts and good taste of the Volk, but that the Volk was an eager consumer of trash and worse could not be ignored.[14]

These men were living through a time when values rooted in tradition and institutional religion were being replaced by values that emphasized self-interest. They recognized the transition and did not like it. To them, modern times were not good times and for the Catholics among them, they were particularly difficult. To Catholics, the Middle Ages represented the apogee of civilization. They liked to think of the cultural splendor, presumed concern for the common good, and deep religious faith of the medieval period as synonymous with Catholicism. The Middle Ages was everything the nineteenth and twentieth centuries were not, yet that era, and by extension, the (comparatively) unchallenged Church and faith, only seemed ever more distant and impossible of restoration.

Culture was the crucial link between corrupting modern values and immoral behavior. In an address to the annual gathering of German Catholics in 1912 (Katholikentag) that was reprinted in its entirety in *Volkswart*, Josef Mausbach,[15] a professor of moral theology at the University of Münster, described the central role of culture: "The spiritual atmosphere in which we live is determined and governed most strongly by works of literature and art."[16] Culture not only influenced the outlook

---

[14] Historisches Archiv der Stadt Köln, Bestand Marx, Bd. 397, *Vierter Jahresbericht des Volksbundes zur Bekämpfung des Schmutzes* (Berlin: Geschäftsstelle des Volksbundes, 1908), 3; "Das Volk selbst über die Schundliteratur," *Volkswart* 2 (July 1909): 110.

[15] Josef Mausbach (1861-1931), moral theologian.

[16] Historisches Archiv der Stadt Köln, Bestand Marx, Bd. 397, Hermann Roeren, *Die öffentliche Unsittlichkeit und ihre Bekämpfung* (Cologne: J.P. Bachem, 1903), 5-11; "Hirtenschreiben der Bischofskonferenz, 12. August 1908," in Erwin Gatz, *Akten der Fuldaer Bischofskonferenz, III, 1900-1919.* Veröffentlichungen der Kommission für Zeitgeschichte, ed. by Konrad Repgen, Rei A: Quellen, Bd. 39 (Mainz: Matthias-Grünewald-Verlag, 1985), 121; Josef Maus-bach, "Der Kampf gegen die moderne Sittenlosigkeit," *Volkswart* 5 (September 1912):

of the age, it influenced behavior. Pornography and not quite pornography in literature, art, and the theater were frequently blamed for the social ills that were the targets of the moral militants. Hermann Roeren made a direct connection between immoral writing and pictures, shameless exhibits in shop windows, and the fact that 25% of German academic youth had sexually transmitted diseases. The 1908 Fulda Conference of Bishops gave Roeren's statistics a slightly different twist, but implied the same connection: 25% of academic youth examined by doctors were infected with syphilis and even more with spiritual (geistige) syphilis, the result of pornographic books and pictures.

By 1900 culture in Germany comprised three significant categories: high culture, Volk culture, and popular culture. Although innovation was an increasingly important element in high culture, high culture was what it had been for centuries, culture for the upper classes, created by self-conscious artists and writers who argued fiercely over theories and practiced distinctive styles. New themes and new topics might offend, but if they did, the moral militant could comfort himself with the knowledge that their impact was confined to the upper classes. Volk culture, too, remained much what it had always been, a largely unwritten culture of the lower orders, its content traditional. The only new feature of Volk culture was its discovery by the intelligentsia, who in the course of the nineteenth century had turned it into an object of veneration and study. Because the Volk[17] supposedly remained true to ancient German ideals,[18] Volk culture was now seen as a repository of semi-mystical Germanness. Finally, there was popular culture, which was a genuinely new phenomenon. Technological development, a newly literate population, increased disposable income and leisure time in the working class, and urbanization had combined to generate a mass culture, the principal purpose of which was to make money for its producers and purveyors. Unlike other forms of culture, popular culture was a purely commercial product. Its content, moreover, had few recognizable antecedents. To Catholics,

---

129-36.

[17] Volk was used by intellectuals and politicians as a collective noun to identify the German peasantry and working classes, although whether the industrial worker belonged there was uncertain. Virtue was presumed to reside in the Volk; it preserved an understanding of true Germanness that had been lost by the bourgeoisie.

[18] The praise of Tacitus for the chastity of German women was periodically mentioned. [Alfred], Graf von Oberndorff, "Der sittliche Niedergang des deutschen Volkes und die Aufgaben der Katholiken," *Volkswart* 24 (October 1931): 145; "Aus den Vereinen: Aachen," *Volkswart* 3 (March 1910): 43.

whether intellectuals or moral militants, it was the cuckoo in the cultural nest.[19]

The Fight against Schundliteratur

It was this popular culture that was the focus of morality organizations. Because it made no pretense of serving any ideal other than Mammon, morality was irrelevant to it. The form of popular culture to which the moral militants devoted the most effort was Schundliteratur, the lowest category to which the term literature applied. Schundliteratur, and its somewhat more disreputable partner, Schmutzliteratur, fell somewhere between "true" literature and pornography; Schund is the German word for trash, Schmutz for dirt. The Schund novel was pure entertainment, with no literary pretensions and less literary merit. It came with assorted settings, the more exotic the better. It was a genre novel and might be an adventure novel, a western, a detective novel, or a romance. Schmutz novels were highly suggestive novels that just missed being pornography. To classify such works properly required a definition of "true" literature, but the Verband, like most morality organizations, took the attitude, "We don't want to decide whether something is or is not artistic, but only whether it appears to be something that will wound the healthy feelings of shame and morality of our people."[20] If it did not wound, it was literature, and not their concern; if it did wound, it was Schundliteratur, and to be fought. What might be wounded included sexual morals, respect for the law and the Ten Commandments, aesthetic taste, intellectual potential, and a vast range of subtle social expectations like courtesy to one's parents. A favorite charge was that the reading of Schund encouraged criminality in the young by portraying it as romantic and serving as a kind of how-to manual. These fears reflect class prejudice, bourgeois values, and conservative political and religious views.[21]

---

[19] Those who disliked popular culture conveniently ignored the fact that high culture, too, was an economic phenomenon.

A great deal has been written on culture. For this paper Theodor W. Adorno's *The Culture Industry* (London: Routledge, 1991), written by a man who experienced German culture during the period, and Dominic Strinati, *An Introduction to Theories of Popular Culture* (London and New York: Routledge, 1995) have been particularly useful.

[20] Josef Pappers, "Praktische Winke zur Gründung von Männervereinen zur Bekämpfung der öffentlichen Unsittlichkeit," *Volkswart* 2 (March 1909, Organisationsnummer): 4.

[21] An account of the battle against Schundliteratur in English is Margaret F. Stieg, "The 1926 German Law to Protect Youth against Trash and Dirt: Moral

In Article 184 the 1872 criminal code of the new Empire outlawed pornography, but Schundliteratur was not pornography. It might be suggestive, but it was not sufficiently obscene to qualify as pornography.[22] By 1890, however, the enormous growth of Schundliteratur had made it a major public concern in which fear of the lower orders was prominent and there was considerable agitation to extend what was illegal to include what was morally undesirable. A loose alliance of teachers, librarians, religious leaders, youth officials, police, and reformers dedicated to a wide variety of causes composed the anti-Schund forces. In this agitation Catholics took a leading role, although the fight against Schundliteratur knew no confessional boundaries. At the 1885 Katholikentag, Dr. Haffner, soon to be bishop of Mainz,[23] spoke of the dangers of questionable novels, a category in which he included the novels of Zola. Haffner concluded that whoever read bad novels would lose their principles of faith and morality, but was more concerned for the lady who read such books than for those of the lower classes. The evils of Schundliteratur were a regular topic of discussion at Katholikentage throughout the 1890s.[24]

The organizations of the Verband der Männervereine played a major role in the fight against Schund by keeping the issue alive and before the public. In the January 1909 issue of *Volkswart* several groups reported their activities. Aachen had complained to a judge about a bookseller that sold a series, "What One Doesn't Say Aloud." The bookseller had been found guilty and fined 50.—M, although the fine had been reduced to 10.—M plus court costs since it was a first offense. The Breslau group had sponsored a lecture on how to fight immorality in youth, in which the speaker declared that the most effective ways to

---

Protectionism in a Democracy," *Central European History* 23 (1990): 22-56.
[22] For an introduction to censorship in the Wilhelmine period see R.J.V. Lenman, "Art, Society, and the Law in Wilhelmine Germany: The Lex Heinze," *Oxford German Studies* 8 (1973-74): 86-113 and Gary D. Stark, "Pornography, Society, and the Law in Imperial Germany," *Central European History* 14 (September 1981): 200-29. The definitive study of censorship in the Weimar period is Klaus Petersen, *Zensur in der Weimarer Republik* (Stuttgart, Weimar: Verlag J. B. Metzler, 1995).
[23] Paul Leopold Haffner (1829-1899), professor of philosophy at Priesterseminar, Mainz, became bishop of Mainz in 1886.
[24] [Paul Leopold] Haffner, "[Lektüre]," *Verhandlungen der XXXII Generalversammlung der Katholiken Deutschlands zu Münster i. W., 1885* (Münster: Commissions-Verlag der Actien-Gesellschaft 'Westfälischer Merkur', 1885): 338.

counter Schundliteratur were to buy folk tales and to support Catholic libraries. Mönchengladbach announced the publication of a pamphlet by the Catholic teachers' organizations intended to educate parents on the dangers of the Schundliteratur plague. Cologne had filed complaints about seven immoral writings and petitions about eleven. The Cologne Männerverein had also joined with the Protestant Cologne Männerverein to found an organization devoted solely to fighting Schundliteratur and its companion, Schmutzliteratur.[25]

The Verband der Männervereine contributed to the cause of fighting immorality primarily through its journal. Almost every issue of *Volkswart* had some kind of article on the subject of Schundliteratur. These articles ranged from one by Ernst Lennartz that discussed the role of school officials in the fight to a theoretical discussion of the relationship of morality and art. Some articles were quite practical. The report on the assembly of the Cologne Männerverein of 1910 included a detailed presentation of how those who sold dirty publications operated. The account of how the Berlin schools fought Sherlock Holmes and Nick Carter was a suggestion to others to do likewise. There was even a bibliography.[26]

But for all the sound and fury, for all the intensity and high seriousness, the successes of the anti-Schund forces in the battle against Schundliteratur were limited. Schund remained intractable, although prosecutions for pornography increased dramatically after the passage in 1900 of the so-called Lex Heinze that somewhat expanded the definition of pornography. Schund had not been illegal before 1900 and it was not illegal after 1900. The Verband and its members could only use what local ordinances were available and continue to press for a national system of censorship of Schmutz- and Schundliteratur. *Volkswart* reprinted a speech by Hermann Roeren to the Reichstag in 1910 in which he supported a resolution to prohibit Schmutzliteratur. By 1914 a bill was pending in the Reichstag that added Schundliteratur to the jurisdiction of the Reichsgewerbeordnung (national commercial regulations), but the

---

[25] "Aus unseren Vereinen," *Volkswart* 2 (January 1909): 7-8.
[26] Ernst Lennartz, "Schule und Schulbehörden im Kampfe gegen die Schundliteratur," *Volkswart* 2 (June 1909): 90-92; (July 1909): 105-107; F. Weigl, "Moral und bildende Kunst," *Volkswart* 2 (August 1909): 117-19; "Generalversammlung des Cölner Männer-Vereins z. B. d. ö. Unsittlichkeit am 10. März 1910," *Volkswart* 3 (May 1910): 75-78; (June 1910): 90-92; "Der Kampf gegen die Schundliteratur," *Volkswart* 2 (April 1909): 58-59; "Die Sittlichkeitsbewegung im Spiegel der Presse," *Volkswart* 4 (April 1911): 63-64.

outbreak of World War I put the proposed legislation on hold. The flood of Schund publications brought by the war were handled under the strict military censorship imposed by the imperial government.[27]

Fighting Schundliteratur was the Verband's highest priority in the prewar period, but it was not its only cultural concern. Parents were warned to supervise carefully their children's visits to theaters, where plays that treated sex, divorce, or the misery of the poor might be encountered. Museums were viewed with disfavor because they too often displayed paintings that pictured nude subjects. Interest in the cinema increased, reflecting its growing importance as a cultural medium. The growing number of articles about films in *Volkswart* invariably emphasized negative features.

The Postwar Period

Although the Verband der Männervereine was "significantly behind" in its work when World War I ended, it had survived intact. The immediate postwar years offered both scope and stimulus for moral activities. Cinema was now the primary object of attention. Its power and effectiveness as a medium made it particularly threatening. Before the war for a film to be shown, permission had been necessary from the local police, but in the breakdown of law and order that followed Germany's defeat, police were needed for more urgent matters. A flood of "enlightenment" films appeared. Masquerading as sex education, they were nothing but pornography. As one writer described the situation, it was "as if the demons of the world were loosed."[28]

The Weimar constitution excepted films and Schundliteratur from its principle, "No censorship shall take place." The Reichstag of the new republic immediately used the exception to pass a law to censor films. Debates on the film law were well reported in *Volkswart* and the morality groups supported it strongly. The law of 1920, however, fell short of their expectations and the Verband and its groups continued to press for greater limitation. A 1922 article gives some idea of their standards. In the previous year some 150 films had been viewed in the Cologne area by teachers and social workers from an organization known

---

[27] [Hermann] Roeren, "Der deutsche Reichstag im Kampfe gegen den Schmutz," *Volkswart* 3 (April 1910): 50-54.

[28] "Der Generalsekretariat des Verbandes zur Bekämpfung des öffentlichen Unsittlichkeit," *Volkswart* 15 (April 1922): 49; Johannes Hambröer, "Vom freien Kino," *Allgemeine Rundschau* 16 (1919): 774.

as the Volksgemeinschaft zur Wahrung von Anstand und guter Sitte (People's Organization for the Protection of Decency and Good Morals). Of the 150 films, only one, "The Wonder of the Snowshoe," was considered completely acceptable.[29]

This article incorporated most of the criticism of films by those concerned with morality. That films could help to develop the sense of home and convey the excitement of exploration, that they could assist in scientific and technological education, were recognized, but worthy films were usually only background or filler for more popular films, like those dealing with criminals. The vast majority of films were dismissed as "completely without value, their principal object to engage the desire for sensation of the crowd." Films were merely Schundliteratur in another form: "What Schundliteratur offers in printed form, they offer in livelier presentation." Films undermined the social order. To an audience that was primarily young and working class, films portrayed individuals in conflict with the law, always, of course, for the noblest of reasons. Bourgeois society was invariably portrayed as corrupt, anyone with property as lazy and dumb. Criminals and prostitutes were romanticized. Divorce was acceptable, infidelity humorous. Caricatures of the monastic life grieved Catholics. Unrestrained pleasure was all that mattered.[30] The film law of 1920 had not concerned itself with such matters.[31]

The exception in the Weimar constitution that allowed for censorship under certain conditions also brought a renewed sense of purpose to those who opposed Schundliteratur, since Schundliteratur was one of the special conditions. In the early 1920s the campaign against Schundliteratur resumed with new energy. Public demonstrations in which the Verband's member organizations participated were frequent, the one in Steele concluding with a bonfire in which a collection of Schund was burned. In February 1924 *Volkswart* began publication of a series on Schundliteratur by Dr. Albert Hellwig,[32] a Potsdam judge who had long been an advocate of censorship of Schundliteratur and films. Three months later *Volkswart* reported that a law to control Schmutz and Schund had been proposed which the Verband strongly supported. It submitted a petition that urged the Prussian administration to address the

---

[29] "Das Ergebnis der Kinobesuche," *Volkswart* 15 (March 1922): 33.

[30] Ibid., 33-35.

[31] *Volkswart* ran a series on reform of the film law that appeared in the January, March, November, and December 1925 issues and the March 1926 issue.

[32] Albert Hellwig (1880-1950), prolific writer on Schundliteratur, films, and censorship.

problem; the ministry of justice responded that it was already doing so.[33]

A coalition of conservative parties that included the Catholic party, the Center, passed a law to regulate Schund- and Schmutzliteratur on 3 December 1926 that went into effect two weeks later. The new law mandated the creation of a list of publications that would result from the adjudication of complaints by reviewing boards in Berlin and Munich. A higher board was responsible for informing the Reichsminister of the decisions of the reviewing boards and for hearing appeals. Nothing on the list could be sold, given, or traded to anyone under eighteen.

Initially, the law was greeted with rejoicing, but its flaws quickly became apparent. The most obvious was inherent in its limitation to those under eighteen; since the population over eighteen offered a rich and perfectly legal potential market for Schundliteratur, it did not disappear from the streets. Administrative problems were particularly frustrating. It took the reviewing bodies a year to define "Schundliteratur" and another year to define "Schmutzliteratur." Even after those basic steps were accomplished, the boards were slow to add publications to the list of what was unacceptable. And what were they adding? No one cared any more about Buffalo Bill and Nick Carter.[34]

Reorganization and Catholicization
In the meantime, the Verband der Männervereine had undergone a fundamental restructuring. Founded on an interconfessional basis, it had been reconstituted as a Catholic association. The announcement of the change in the December 1926 issue of *Volkswart* gave a few kind words to how effectively Protestants and Catholics had cooperated in the good fight, but declared firmly that new times required new "principles." The morality organizations of western Germany[35] had expressed their wish that the organization become confessional to ensure peaceful cooperation.[36] Within a few months the organization was renamed the Volks-

---

[33] Albert Hellwig, "Die gesetzgeberische Bekämpfung der Schundliteratur," *Volkswart* 17 (February 1925): 25-26; "Die Antwort des Preßischen Justizministers auf die Eingabe des Verbandes vom 25.11.1924," *Volkswart* 18 (March 1925): 55-57.

[34] [Michael] Calmes, "Schund und Schmutz in ihren vielfachen Erscheinungsweisen," *Volkswart* 21 (August 1928): 113.

[35] Western Germany was a term that obscured the fact that most of the organizations were in the Ruhr and the Rhineland, areas that were predominantly Catholic.

[36] In the article "Die Arbeitsgemeinschaft des Volkswartbundes und des Bundes für sittliche Volkswacht," *Volkswart* 24 (July 1931): 107-108 by Lennartz and

wartbund (People's Watch Federation), a name both more manageable than the former eight-word name and more militant.[37]

Although the man who succeeded Lennartz as the chairman of the Volkswartbund's board of directors wrote five years after the ending of interconfessional cooperation that it had been the Protestants who wished to end their connection with the association, the pressure for change appears, in fact, to have come from the Archbishop of Cologne, Karl Josef, Cardinal Schulte.[38] One factor in the Cardinal's thinking has to have been financial; he had been supplying the organization with much-needed support. At least equally relevant, the climate of the mid-1920s did not favor interconfessional cooperation. At about the same time that the Verband der Männervereine ceased to be interconfessional, the Bühnenvolksbund, a theater organization that Catholics and Protestants had jointly created during the war to improve the quality of what was offered on the stage, also became exclusively Catholic. The papal encyclical *Mortalium Animos* of January 1928 condemned ecumenical discussions and its general tenor has to have discouraged interconfessional cooperation. Catholics were warned not be deceived by "the outward appearance of good," no matter how worthy the objective seemed.[39]

The establishment of the Volkswartbund on a Catholic basis came at a time when Catholic concern with immorality was growing. In 1925 the Fulda Bischofskonferenz issued guidelines for Catholics "to counter the modern-heathen revolution in moral ideas and views to which our Volk more and more often falls prey to a tremendous extent." The guidelines explained in theological terms the relation of body and soul and provided specific rules on moral issues that ranged from gymnastics to fashion to socializing to trashy literature. Moral renewal was

---

Ammann, the years before 1914 were described as a model of cooperation.

[37] "Aus den Vereinen: Der Verband zur Bekämpfung der öffentlichen Unsittlichkeit," *Volkswart* 19 (December 1926): 180; "Volkswartbund: Katholishce Verband zur Bekämpfung der öffentl. Unsittlichkeit," *Volkswart* 20 (June 1927).

[38] Karl Josef Schulte (1871-1941), named bishop of Paderborn, 1910, archbishop of Cologne, 1920, cardinal, 1921.

[39] Schaefer, "Kundgebung der vereinigten Sittlichkeitsverbände im Rahmen der 70. Generalversammlung der Katholiken Deutschlands in Nürnberg am 28. August 1931," *Volkswart* 24 (October 1931): 151; Historisches Archiv der Stadt Köln, Bestand 1010, Fasz. 8, p. 199, Newspaper clipping, Obituary of Ernst Lenartz; Historisches Archiv des Erzbistums Köln, Generalia 23.30, Lennartz to Hochwürdigsten Episkopat Deutschlands zu Fulda, 10. August 1922; E. Lennartz to Kardinal Dr. J. Schulte, Erzbischof von Köln, 12. März 1927; "Mortalium Animos: On Religious Unity," Encyclical of Pius XI, January 6, 1928, http://www.papalencyclicals.net, viewed 15 July 2002.

the theme of the 1928 regional Katholikentag which took place in Cologne.[40]

The reorganization clarified the Volkswartbund's role. Its function was now "to work steadfastly in the Catholic faith for the application of Christian morality to the public."[41] At the same time it became part of a dense network of Catholic organizations that offered a base of support and a means to reach the engaged part of the Catholic Volk. Within this network, the Volkswartbund had a clear identity. It was the militant arm of Catholic morality, its task to fight—at one point it referred to itself as a storm troop—and work closely with other Catholic organizations, particularly the Borromäusverein, that were concerned with the same problems but had a different function. The terms positive and negative were frequently used: the Volkswartbund was to eliminate bad reading, the Borromäusverein was to provide good reading.[42]

The lot of the Volkswartbund improved in practical ways, as well. Cardinal Schulte became its protector and its finances became less precarious. The general secretariat was reopened in November 1927 and the energetic Dr. Calmes[43] appointed its director. New local organizations were founded. By 1930 the eight member organizations of 1927 had grown to fifty-three. It began to function more as the directing unit in a hierarchy and less as the agent of its member organizations.[44]

The Volkswartbund used this access of strength to intensify its activity. Renewed purpose, increased energy, and improved organization

---

[40] "Nr. 66, Moderne Sittlichkeitsfragen," *Kirchlicher Anzeiger für die Erzdiözese Köln* 65 (20 January 1925): 15-18; Historisches Archiv des Erzbistums Köln, Generalia 23.30.1, Kölner Bezirks-Katholikentag 1928.

[41] How much change this brought is debatable. Ernst Lennartz did not feel that the previous interconfessional by-laws needed to be revised. Historisches Archiv des Erzbistums Köln, Generalia 23.30, Lennartz to Hochwürdigsten Herrn Kardinal Dr. J. Schulte, Erzbischof von Köln, 12. März 1927.

[42] "Aus den Vereinen: Bericht des Volkswartbundes 1932," *Volkswart* 26 (March 1933): 41; "Vereinbarung zwischen Volkswartbund (Köln) and Borromäusverein (Bonn) zwecks Bekämpfung von Schund und Schmutz in der Literatur," *Volkswart* (May 1928): 74.

[43] Michael Calmes (1894-1958).

[44] "Aus den Vereinen: Der Verband zur Bekämpfung der öffentlichen Unsittlichkeit," *Volkswart* 19 (December 1926): 180; [Michael] Calmes, "Zur Geschichte und Arbeit unseres Generalsekretariates!" *Volkswart* 25 (January 1932): 6-7; "Aus den Vereinen: Rechenschaftsbericht des Vorstandes für das Jahr 1929," *Volkswart* 23 (July 1930): 103-104; "Aus der Arbeit des Volkswartbundes," *Volkswart* 24 (February 1931); Historisches Archiv des Erzbistums Köln, Generalia 23.30, Volkswartbund, Rechenscahftsbericht des Verbandsvorstandes für das Geschäftsjahr 1927.

are perceptible. The General Secretary worked to found new local groups, educate other groups with an interest in morality, and mold public opinion. A prime example of the new efficiency and outlook is the document, Zehn Gebote für Schundkämpfer (Ten Commandments for the Schund Warrior), prepared for distribution to local groups. The commandments simultaneously convey its vigilante outlook and elitist values:

- to bring immoral writings, prints, and representations to the attention of the public prosecutor immediately (the legal definition of immoral was provided)
- to present to the nearest police station writings and pictures that offended in a moral or religious sense
- to carry a copy of the Schmutz list (produced by the reviewing boards under the 1926 law against Schund and Schmutz) and point out to a storekeeper anything on the list that he was selling
- to inform police immediately of erotic writings with nudes on the cover
- to keep the local Schundkampfstelle (agency to fight Schund) informed of observations of kiosks, lending libraries, and Schmutz sellers
- to report bad, but not purely local, examples of Schmutz and Schund to the Volkswartbund in Cologne and never to destroy any advertisements of Schund
- to speak courageously against dirty literature at kiosks, bookstores, and hairdressers
- to participate in the oversight of kiosks and bookstores, a task that is not snooping but corresponds to the democratic principle of the duty of a concerned citizen
- to buy and support, above all, Catholic newspapers, magazines, and journals and to demand that they be available in railroad bookstores
- to handle oneself courageously and skillfully, but not with prudery.[45]

---

[45] Historisches Archiv des Erzbistums Köln, Generalia 23.30, 2, 10 Gebote für Schundkämpfer, stamped 9(?) Feb 1932.

Although the new Volkswartbund continued to concern itself with other forms of culture, especially films, Schundliteratur remained its highest cultural priority, which was now elevated in its rhetoric to the honor of being the greatest danger to morality. This concentration was influenced by the impact of the 1926 law against Schund-and Schmutzliteratur; the law simultaneously disappointed, yet held out hope that the nation was finally serious about the problem. Those who opposed Schundlitertur could believe that their efforts might have some effect.

The Volkswartbund became a prominent presence at the conferences of other Catholic organizations, such as the Katholikentag and the Borromäusverein. It had major responsibilities in the newly established Zentralarbeitsausschuß, created by the Fulda Bischofskonferenz to coordinate the attack on Schund. It worked with diocesan officials wherever they were willing; thick files of records relating to the Volkswartbund can be found in most diocesan archives. Several bishops established *consilia a vigilantia* with special responsibilities for Schundliteratur. There is, for example, an extremely interesting report on the reading of young adults that was prepared by the *consilium* of the archdiocese of Munich and Freising.[46]

In addition to this expanded cooperation with other organizations and institutions, the Volkswartbund continued its previous practices. Schundkämpfer were still encouraged to practice "self-help," a euphemism for the personalized oversight of neighborhood merchants enshrined in the Zehn Gebote für Schundkämpfer. Not everyone, however, found the group's officiousness commendable. At least one diocesan ordinary found it necessary to issue a request to clergy to use the legal means available, regardless of the lack of success.[47]

---

[46] Rottenburg-Stuttgart, Diözesanarchiv, G1.1 F2.4d, [Michael] Calmes, "Der kathol. Seelsorger im Kampfe gegen die öffentliche Unsittlichkeit," Mimeographed reprint from *Der Seelsorger*; "Vom diesjährigen Katholikentag," *Volkswart* 22 (November 1929): 166-69; Verein vom hl. Karl Borromäus, Bonn. *Jahresbericht, 1928* (n.p., n.d.), 8; Historisches Archiv des Erzbistums Köln, Generalia 23.30, Arbeitsausschuss der deutschen Katholiken zur Förderung der öffentlichen Sittlichkeit, An die Hochwürdigsten Ordinarien im Bereiche der Fuldaer Bischofskonferenz, 29. September 1928; Mainz, Dom- und Diözesanarchiv, Generalakten, Abteil 55, Consilium a vigilantia der Erzdiözese München und Freising, Rundschreiben Nr. 64, 25. November 1930, published as 'Was liest unsere Jugend?" *Volkswart* 24 (February 1931): 19-23..
[47] Rottenburg-Stuttgart, Diözesanarchiv, G1.1 F2.4d, Bischöfliches Ordinariat, Rottenburg, "Schund- und Schmutzbekämpfung," 18. August 1931.

Contemporary Perspectives

As the impossibility of their self-imposed task became increasingly clear, enthusiasm for the fight began to wane. Reconfiguration as a Catholic organization had not solved the organization's problems because the fundamental problems did not lie in the organization but in human nature and the imperatives of democracy. The Schundkämpfer had been forced to face the sad fact that the Volk *wanted* to read Schundliteratur, just as it wanted pictures that were not necessarily great art, and films that entertained rather than instructed. In a market economy, publishers, printers, and producers were going to give them what they wanted. The long anti-Schund campaign had produced a law, but not an effective one; in a democracy, no government was going to be willing to pass a law restrictive enough to eliminate Schundliteratur. The Volkswartbund had tried to convert the Volk to their way of thinking, but the failure of that strategy, too, was now apparent.[48]

By 1933, even the most stalwart morality fighters were discouraged. The annual reports of the Volkswartbund and other articles in *Volkswart* reflect growing dejection. In 1932 members were exhorted to overcome dominant pessimism with "true Catholic optimism." The 1933 report described worsening moral conditions with particular attention to, of course, Schmutz- and Schundliteratur. Ernst Lennartz himself, in his reflections on the twenty-five years of the Volkswartbund written shortly before his death, referred to them as years of much success but greater disappointment and wondered if it was not perhaps too late.[49]

The Volkswartbund was aware that not everyone appreciated their efforts. hey might be convinced of the righteousness of their cause, but many Germans were not only indifferent to their work, but openly hostile to it. Occasionally, Dr. Calmes found it necessary to suggest that members work as unobtrusively as possible to avoid rousing opposition.

---

[48] "Warum ist der Kampf gegen die Schundliteraur so schwer?" *Volkswart* 18 (December 1925): 179-80; [Michael] Calmes, "Neue Wege der Selbsthilfe im Schundkampf!" *Volkswart* 22 (January 1929): 1-2. Interestingly (presciently?), Calmes states that no dictator is needed to push through autocratic and strict laws, but that the goals of the morality movement can be achieved within a democracy.

[49] "Aus den Vereinen: Rechenschaftsberict des Vorstandes für das Jahr 1929 (9. April 1929 bis 10. Juni 1930)," *Volkswart* 23 (July 1930): 104; "Rechenschaftsbericht des Vorstandes für die Jahre 1930-1932," *Volkswart* 25 (May 1932): 70; "Aus den Vereinen: Bericht des Volkswartbundes 1932," *Volkswart* 26 (March 1933): 41-42; [Ernst Lennartz] "Fünfundzwanzig Jahre Volkswartbund," *Volkswart* 25 (January 1932): 6.

emonstrations against censorship and in support of freedom of expression had, after all, succeeded in gutting the Lex Heinze. The 1926 law against Schund- and Schmutzliteratur had been passed, but with reluctance. Many reservations about its potentially chilling effect on literature had been expressed.[50]

In the long term, the most significant opposition to the Volkswartbund and to what it stood for took place not in the streets, but in the pages of journals and newspapers that shaped public opinion. Even in Catholic journals, by the end of the 1920s articles regularly presented ideas very different from those the Volkswartbund so intransigently defended. Among the controversial cultural ideas candidly discussed in the Catholic media were should literature deal with the problems of modern life such as the unloved urban environment and the unwelcome social changes? Should Catholic church music be limited to Palestrina, the sixteenth century composer, and his contemporaries? Should artists use modern styles?[51] Increasingly, Catholic intellectuals would have answered, yes, no, and yes. The distinguished Catholic playwright, Leo Weismantel,[52] stated flatly that the long-sought 1926 Schund- and Schmutliteratur law posed a threat to the freedom of intellectual life and he did it in the pages of *Germania*, the newspaper of the Catholic Center Party. Jakob Kneip,[53] one of the younger Catholic writers, dismissed the criticism of the Kölnische Volkszeitung for printing a picture of the naked Christ child in its 1926 Christmas number as ludicrous. What the Schundkämpfer saw as purity others disparaged as prudery.[54]

The real issues, of course, were cultural change and what the response to cultural change should be. Concerned Catholics argued that the Church had to adapt; the Byzantine Church was a cautionary example to its Roman counterpart of what could happen to a church that refused to adapt to new times. Equally concerned Catholics, a group that included both the leaders and the rank and file of the Volkswartbund, argued that not one iota, not one dot, of the moral laws was to be changed because

---

[50] [Michael] Calmes, "Schund und Schmutz in ihren vielfachen Erscheinungsweisen," *Volkswart* 21 (August 1928): 115.

[51] Giovanni Pierluigi da Palestrina (ca. 1525-1594), Italian composer.

[52] Leo Weismantel (1888-1964), writer, dramatist, educator; member of the Bavarian Landtag, 1924-1928.

[53] Jakob Kneip (1881-1958), writer of Heimat novels.

[54] "Zum Schund- und Schmutzschriftengesetz," *Germania*, 20 November 1926; "Katholiken und Literatur—Eine Auseinandersetzung: Jakob Kneip: Dichtung und Kirche," *Schönere Zukunft* 2 (21. August 1927).

they came from Christ himself. Even if there was no recognition that Christ's laws were open to different interpretations, however, there was some understanding that the times were changing. Moral militants might not like the direction in which they were changing, but they could not halt the inexorable process and they were not without insight into what was happening. They recognized the beginnings of globalization in American films and that Germany was an increasingly diverse society. The basic issue in multiculturalism, for example, is addressed in a discussion in *Volkswart* about the difficulty with the requirement in the film law that religious sensitivities be respected. The author pointed out that there were Buddhists and Muslims who lived in Germany; did that mean that Islamic and Buddhist religious sensitivity also needed to be considered?[55]

Conclusion

Thus far, consideration of the Volkswartbund and its activities has been limited to the questions for which the documentary evidence provides at least partial answers: who, what, where, when, and how. Now it is time to attend to "why." "Why" has been a factor only within the framework of the rhetoric of the members of the Volkswartbund, their statements of the imperatives, their justifications for their actions. Scholarship on morality movements, however, has shown that such movements cannot be taken at face value.[56] Motivations, not to mention the problems the movements address, are usually far more complex than participants acknowledge. What do the seeming candor and simplicity of the Volkswartbund obscure?

Two major approaches characterize the study of morality movements.[57] In the first, morality movements are treated as reflections of societal struggles over moral issues. The second focuses on interests; disputes over moral issues are a surrogate for other conflicts of interest.

---

[55] Wilh. Kurthen, "Moderne Kirchenmusik," *Gregoriusblatt für katholische Kirchenmusik*, (1924): 42; "Zur Reform im Lichtspielwesen," *Volkswart* 19 (October 1926): 145-47; [Michael] Calmes, "Zur Geschichte und Arbeit unseres Generalsekretäriates," *Volkswart* 25 (January 1932): 6-7; R. V., "Aus der Filmzensur: Welche Filme werden verboten? *Volkswart* 19 (August 1926): 120-121.

[56] Alan Hunt, "The Purity Wars: Making Sense of Moral Militancy," *Theoretical Criminology* 3 (1999): 409-36 compares the insights of Nicole Beisel's 1999 book on the anti-obscenity campaigns of Anthony Comstock in New York, Boston, and Philadelphia with those of David Wagner's 1997 book on temperance.

[57] Alternative terms: moral emergency, moral panic, moral reform.

Both perspectives offer insights into the essence of the Volkswartbund.[58]

The rhetoric of the Volkswartbund demonized the philosophic trends of the period. Individualism, materialism, aestheticism, in short, the usual suspects, were comprehensively and ostentatiously rejected. In 1931 the Volkswartbund identified its principal opponents as:

- adherents of a view of this-world happiness that requires the unrestrained pursuit of instincts with an elevation of the body to deification,
- representatives of a world view that advocates freedom of scholarship and art, in which freedom and licentiousness are interchangeable, and
- a group that only wishes to serve Mammon capitalistically and exploits instincts without scruple.

Intellectuals were regarded as untrustworthy, the act of thinking was dangerous. The Volkswartbund did its best to replace thought with conditioning; a list of defining questions printed on the membership cards of the Mönchengladbach Männerverein was recommended to others for use as a "catechism."[59]

The Volkswartbund recognized that they were in conflict with prevailing intellectual and social trends; it was, after all, their *raison d'être*. That their objectives affirmed what are thought of as middle-class Victorian virtues was equally true, if less evident to them. They wanted readers to read educational and improving books instead of Schundliteratur. They wanted them to spend their money differently and use their their time profitably, as, of course, the moral militants defined profitably. They treated the act of reading Schund as a political act, because it flouted the authority of priest and teacher who so frequently denounced it. Not only could sexually transmitted diseases be the result of reading Schundliteratur, but social revolution might follow. The logic is not particularly strong, but it convinced the members.

---

[58] Nachman Beh-Yehuda, "The Sociology of Moral Panics: Toward a New Synthesis," *Sociological Quarterly* 27 (1986): 496.

[59] "Kundgebung der vereinigten Sittlichkeitsverbände ..." *Volkswart* 24 (October 1931): 152; Historisches Archiv des Erzbistums Köln, Generalia 23.30b, 1, J. Schaefer, "Unsere Ortsgruppen im Kampf gegen Schund und Schmutz im Rahmen des neuen Gesetzes," in *Schund und Schmutz: Gesetz und Praxis*, ed. by the Volkswartbund (Cologne, 1928), 11; "Eine praktische Mitgliedskarte," *Volkswart* 2 (July 1909): 107-108.

Militant morality groups, whether their particular demon is prostitution, drugs, pornography, rock music, or Schundliteratur, have much in common and many of the conclusions derived from the study of other groups apply to the Volkswartbund. Lakoff's moral conservative moral categories are the Volkswartbund's. Pally's description of the promotion of censorship as an elixir of safety in the United States corresponds to the Volkswartbund's rhetoric. Mosse's discussion of the ambiguities of the view of women in traditional morality applies to the Volkswartbund.[60] The following synthesis by Stanley Cohen could have been written about the Volkswartbund:

> ... a condition, episode, person, or group of persons emerges to become defined as a threat to societal values and interests; its nature is presented in a stylized and stereotypical fashion by the mass media; the moral barricades are manned by editors, bishops, politicians, and other right-thinking people; socially accredited experts pronounce their diagnoses and solutions; ways of coping are evolved, or (more often) resorted to; the condition then disappears, submerges or deteriorates and becomes more visible.[61]

Very similar, highly consistent, yes, but morality movements are not interchangeable. The Volkswartbund was a distinctively German organization. One could even go so far as to attribute to it a flavor that is uniquely of the Rhineland. Only in a land in which Protestants were dominant but Catholics a substantial minority would it have taken the particular form it did. Moral fervor is not exclusively Protestant, but the

---

[60] The Volkswartbund was an association of exclusively male organizations. Not until 1932, when Lennartz stepped down as chairman of the board of directors, was there a woman involved in the organization's direction. One Frau Freericks of Cologne took the place on the board of middle school teacher Schäfer, who replaced Lennartz. J. F., "19.Vertreterversammlung des Volkswartbundes," *Volkswart* 25 (May 1932): 67.

[61] George Lakoff, *Moral Politics: What Conservatives Know That Liberals Don't* (Chicago, London: University of Chicago Press, 1996), 163; Marcia Pally, *Sex and Sensibility: Reflections on Forbidden Mirrors and the Will to Censor* (Hopewell, N.J.: Ecco Press, 1994), 14; George L. Mosse, *Nationalism and Sexuality: Middle-class Morality and Sexual Norms in Modern Europe* (Madison, Wisc.: University of Wisconsin Press, 1985); Stanley Cohen, *Folk Devils and Moral Panics* (London: MacGibbon and Kee, 1972), 9.

strength of typically Protestant theology, with its emphasis on self-help and individual responsibility, fueled moral militancy. It is not coincidental that societies for the suppression of vice were characteristic of the United States and Great Britain in the late-nineteenth and early-twentieth centuries, but not of France or Italy.

In the Volkswartbund's case a common commitment to their new nation, now beset by so many evils, facilitated cooperation between the members of the two confessions to establish an organization to fight those evils. Twenty years later tensions within the German Catholic community ended the uneasy alliance. Members of a disadvantaged minority, many Catholics lived in what was called a Catholic ghetto. An economic and social construct, as well as a religious community, from cradle to grave Catholics could live almost completely isolated within this ghetto. But by the 1920s erosion of the restraints of the ghetto were clearly accelerating. The Catholicization of the Volkswartbund can be seen both as part of an effort to discourage Catholics from participation in the wider German society and as an attempt to strengthen the ghetto internally. The Volkswartbund did not use the language of war and militancy lightly.

Henry Steele Commager warns that the yearning for a single, usually simple explanation of the chaotic materials of the past is a sign of immaturity. Whether or not he is right, the federated structure, too-numerous priorities, and lack of focused activity of the Volkswartbund make such a single explanation impossible. Its historical balance sheet would have to read as a series of contrasts: high ideals and distasteful methods; grand ambitions and disappointing accomplishments; a great truth and a Volk that refused to see it; much illusion but a *soupçon* of realism. In his valedictory statement to the organization he had guided for twenty-five years, Ernst Lennartz captured its discordant message. He wrote of many successes, but more disappointments, of rise and decline, of renewal and renewed growth, of new disappointments, but also of new successes. It is appropriate to close with his hope that by the time another twenty-five years had elapsed, the organization would no longer be necessary because the Volk would have experienced a moral renewal. To an outsider, such an idea seems an illusion, but it was the faith that gave the Volkswartbund its strength.[62]

---

[62] Lennartz, "Fünfundzwanzig Jahre Volkswartbund," 6.

SYNERGISTIC ASPECTS OF NATIVE *PIETAS*

Marguerite Kloos[*]

From the perspective of historical theology, images that recall Jesus' descent[1] from the cross engender the universal interest in native beliefs associated with the bodies of those condemned to early death and the intersection of life and death with the Sacred as the primary spiritual dilemma of the human situation. These images recall funerary emotions, practices and roles within ancient Greek, Roman and Jewish contexts, while preserving an increasingly emergent focus on the limitations of the divine hero, testifying to the breadth and depth of suspicion cast upon the hero's divinity as salvific and victorious. Failed and fallen hero? Divine hero-savior? In what is one of Jerusalem's most defining historical moments, Jesus' descent from the cross began to cast itself into the recesses of religious imagination, taking twenty remarkable centuries to be revealed through artistic images.

The scriptures themselves are almost silent in their description of

---

[*] Currently an assistant professor of religious and pastoral studies at the College of Mount St. Joseph (Cincinnati, OH.), Kloos has been engaged since the mid-1990's in interdisciplinary investigations. Particularly interested in questions pertaining to mystery, freedom, justice and imagination within various cultural contexts, she has found visual art and music to contain critical clues about the way humans shape and express theological content as a social commentary. Kloos and professor-artist Loyola Walter initiated an investigation into *Pietas* while designing curriculum for a team-taught course, which eventually led to this particular study. Her interest and research in indigenous expressions of religious themes in art and music began while teaching in Zuni, NM., during the 1980's. Kloos' theological training is in contextual theology, with an emphasis on cross-cultural pastoral care. She holds a master's degree in theological studies from the University of Dayton and a doctoral degree in ministry from United Theological Seminary.

[1] The christological theme of Jesus descending to earth has "functioned" throughout Christianity. It recalls God's words to Moses in Exodus 3:8. "I have witnessed the affliction of my people in Egypt and have heard their cry of complaint against their slave drivers. Therefore I have come down to rescue them from the hands of the Egyptians and lead them out of that land into a good and spacious land, a land flowing with milk and honey, the country of the Caananites, Hittites, Amorites, Perizzites, Hivites and Jebusites." Within the oral tradition of first and second century Christianity, the image of Jesus' descent from the cross became symbolic of the longing of the early Christians for the return of Christ "from above." The descent of Jesus from the cross implies the christological claim that Jesus Christ was affiliated with the ultimate earthly mission of the Lord God who "came down" to earth for the work of salvation.

Jesus' descent from the cross[2] and burial. Yet, curiosity about the relinquishment and funerary care of this corpse has produced a plethora of images. An icon of *Epitaphios Threnos*, the sculpture of the *Pieta* by Michelangelo, or any one of numerous more contemporary renderings such as Kathe Kollwitz's *The Woman With a Dead Child*, Marc Chagall's *Red Pieta*, or Ding Fang's *Our Sighs and Tears* in part at least, reveal something of the native culture's struggle to comprehend the meaning of a lifeless body. The flesh of heroes, suddenly and permanently rendered lifeless, confounds as frequently as it comforts the artists who lavishly explore the theme. No piece captures the tension with more clarity and poignancy than that of Pablo Picasso's *Guernica*. In a similarly startling depiction, Wig Hansen, an espoused non-believer, examines the horror and fear of children, trying to hide from the world behind a mother's massive, protective presence in his *Pietas*, which graces the entrance to Herning Hospital in his native Denmark. Each artist claims for him or her self a personal identification with the historical moment when Jesus' body was passed from the crucifier to the condemned man's family.

The thesis of this study is that images of Jesus' decent from the cross synergistically interpret aspects of native Jewish and Roman burial rites, ancient native Greek and Roman "hero" themes, and the universal attempt to grapple with the meaning of death.[3] These images are inspired by three distinguishable contexts: those based on funerary practices within Jewish, Greek and Roman society; those which affectively demonstrate the Greek notion of *pietas*; and those which emerge in secular settings where unimaginable violence ensues. The dynamics evident in each stage have been woven and re-woven into images that exemplify the native behaviors of the grief following the death and preceding the burial of the mourner's protagonist. More specifically, *Pietas* are in and of themselves a synergy of memories, taking in a whole history of pious mourners and religious skeptics who found consolation, camaraderie, and

---

[2] Only Luke's gospel (LK.23:53) has Joseph of Arimathea taking the body down from the cross for burial. The other gospels refer only to the body of Jesus be given over to Joseph of Arimathea for burial. Mary is not mentioned.
[3] A. Vrame, *The Educating Icon: Teaching Wisdom and Holiness in the Orthodox Way* (Brookline, MA: Holy Cross Orthodox Press, 1999), 3. Vrame points out that the concept of synergy in Orthodox Christianity implies the coming together of human and divine will. His claim is that from the interchange of human and divine will brought together in the viewing of an icon, a new and liberating perspective finds its way into the tradition.

contradiction in Libitina,[4] Roman goddess and caretaker of corpses, and the Jewish mother of Jesus, Mary, who withstood the hours at the foot of the cross (John 19:25) but whose role in the burial is not defined within the context of the Christian scriptures.

Theme One: Synergistic Aspects of the Ancient Greek, Roman and Jewish Notion of Burial and Death in the Midst of Life

Jesus is the hero of Christianity. He has the distinction of being its exemplary *broken* hero. In the Hellenistic milieu of early Christianity, the broken hero took on special meaning, a meaning that most likely inspired the first Byzantine images of Jesus' descent from the cross. For the Greeks, as Gustavo Gutierrez remarks, history was merely "remembering," but for Christians history is a "thrust into the future." This is perhaps the most striking influence that differentiated the ancient Greek and earliest Christian images of a broken hero. Ancient Greek and Roman mythology was filled with remembrances about their broken heroes, while Christians looked ahead to what their broken hero would do for them in the eschatological future. Most likely little was written in the gospel about Jesus' descent from the cross because such a recollection could be misconstrued by a non-believer, causing an emphasis on the failure of the hero.

Drawing from one aspect of the classical hero themes of the Greek and Roman cultures, the New Testament writer Paul records what theologian Gregory Riley describes as the "early death in the midst of life."[5] This theme frames the climax of a hero-pilgrim's journey. Tombstones from the ancient world reveal that life rarely was extended beyond one's twentieth year for men and slightly longer for women. At thirty-three, Jesus was already of elder vintage. Yet, just beginning a flourishing ministry at the time of his persecution and death, Jesus shared a similar fate to that of the ancient Greek hero, Odysseus.

The Greek myth recalls that divine wrath swept over Troy after the temple was defiled, and Odysseus, the warrior king from Ithaka, was

---

[4] Libitina was the Roman goddess of death, associated with burial rites. She is the custodial companion of the corpse who was held in high esteem, especially by the poor. Her Temple was known as the gathering place for undesirables; most likely those who were too poor to afford the extravagance of a burial procession and so they waited until the dark of night to bury the dead. She was able to procure ritual items necessary for the burial.
[5] G. Riley, *One Jesus, Many Christs: How Jesus Inspired Not One True Christianity, But Many* (New York: Harper Collins Publishers, 1997), 90-91.

exiled to a miserable life in which his constant traveling brought him no consolation or homecoming. In his misery and destitution, he became un-recognizable. The hero's *moira*[6] as a benevolent wanderer in the midst of corruption, deception, infidelity and abandon, pointed toward the integrity of the hero and the justice imperative most precious to the ancient world. Upon his eventual return home,[7] he received hospitality from only a few. As a reminder that divine justice will eventually right all wrong, those who had rejected the hero were later destroyed.

Central to early Christian mythology about the heroic Jesus Christ's death was the focus on his temporal state of resting in the tomb as critical to his *moira*. His descent from the cross inaugurated a pilgrimage, during which Jesus Christ was believed to have transcended the limitations of history. The pilgrimage of the believer and the inevitable fate of the focus of their belief, namely the hero, were inextricably united in iconographic depictions. "They are fellow-travelers, strangers, anonymous or even unknown saints who sinned and repented, agonized over evil, and repaired their portion of the world," writes Megan McKenna of early iconographers.[8] Each icon that depicted Jesus' burial in some way shaped an interpretive insight and included the foundational expectation that a new Kingdom would root itself in human history, liberating its subjects from all earthly chains of injustice, corruptness, disease and poverty.

In his own time there was little interest in preserving images of Jesus' death, descent, burial or resurrection. Jews who were convinced that at the least Jesus was *from* God, abided by the tradition of Hosea who proclaimed, "and now, the Canaanites and the Babylonians add sin to sin, they smelt images from their silver, idols of their own manufacture, smith's work, all of it. 'Sacrifice to them,' they say. Men blow kisses to calves."[9] For the believers of Jesus' time, the more convinced

---

[6] The roots of the word "fate" can be traced to a Homeric term, *moira*, meaning one's "lot" or "portion."
[7] The use of the term "home" was important to the Greeks who believed that the "cosmic order" of the heavens , an astrological phenomenon that ultimately controlled the destiny of the individual, was a sanctuary against human and spiritual forces. The individual was a wanderer who sought safe haven against the evils and corruptions of the city-state in such a cosmic home. An interesting extension of this concept exists within icons, believed themselves to be symbolic of the house of God.
[8] Megan McKenna, "Icons: The Eye of God in the Eye of The Beholder," in *The Bride*, by Daniel Barrigan (Maryknoll, NY: Orbis Books, 2000), 12.
[9] Hosea 13:2. The first images within Christian Byzantium did not concern

they were about his divinity, the less interest they had in offending God by creating likenesses of him. The Gentile Christians also resisted initial urges to create images of Jesus' descent from the cross. In the tradition of Greek dualistic philosophy, the idea or remembrance of Jesus' burial ritual was of the mind and as such was spiritually inspired. The physical world, however, which included art and images, was of a lesser value. While the Gentiles had no rules against images of Jesus Christ, the belief that the end of time was near didn't warrant any reason for taking time to create images of their fallen hero. Images of his burial would have been particularly inappropriate, since they could conjure reflections about his human frailty. However, as the hopes faded that Christ's return was immanent, icons began to emerge even before the written gospels were completed. For this early Christian community, so heavily influenced by the Hellenistic world in which they lived and even as they continued to worship the many great gods and goddesses of their history, Jesus the Christ functioned as a unifying hero among disparate native cultures searching for a reliable hero.

Alas, it is most likely the Hellenistic religious practices centered on the ideas of "piety, mystery and gnosis"[10] that gave way to images, influencing the early iconographers and iconophiles,[11] who grappled with numerous theological questions, including the meaning of Jesus' burial. Devotion to the hero, found in Greek and Jewish culture inspired a layer of mythic detail and symbol to the early Christian claims about Jesus that can eventually be realized in every iconic image recalling Jesus' descent from the cross.[12]

---

themselves with questions of divinity, but rather the images of the first Christian martyrs and disciples were portrayed in iconophilic devotion and pre-date the emergence of non-abstract depictions of Jesus.

[10] B. Thurston, *Spiritual Life in the Early Church: The Witness of Acts and Ephesians* (Minneapolis, MN: Fortress Press, 1993), 4-9. Byzantine images focused on the particularly Greek fascination with the illusive and "higher" spirit realm. This realm was marked by its mysterious energy, sensed but not fully known by those who practiced piety. The subject of the piety was a particular god-man hero, like Jesus.

[11] The icons "instructed" these followers in "the way, the life and the truth" of Jesus Christ. Legend claims that the first icons came from the hand of Jesus Christ himself. The disciple Luke, then, took up the practice to keep the story of the hero alive.

[12] While the gospels reveal practically nothing regarding the deposition of Jesus' body from the cross, the Gospel of Nicodemus communicates an embellished recounting of the trial, death and resurrection of Jesus. Dated at approximately the mid-fourth century, numerous stories grew up around the details presented in

Earliest Byzantine images of the descent were not physical. Earliest Byzantine images of Jesus' descent from the cross were cast in ideological language; words which carried a particular ideological focus on the meaning of the event. Words communicated the central belief that the descent from the cross was itself a homecoming, the return of the dead hero's body to the grieving family."[13] Jesus' exile to the tomb was understood by the ancients as a period of waiting. At the least, there would be the period of decomposition and collection of the bones for the ossuary box. At the most, there was the growing hope of resurrection, at least by a few early disciples. Heroes often "waited out" the human sinners and their divine mentors by taking an arduous solo journey during which battles and epiphanies transformed those very same antagonists, now distant from the hero's influence. Within the ancient Jewish context, the body had to be received and then buried according to the Law if the mission of the Messiah was to fulfill the Old Testament scriptures. According to the native Jewish custom of his day, Jesus would have been wrapped in herbs and laid out across a body-length shelf fastened to the wall of a tomb-cave. Here he would remain for the duration of one year, decomposing. Then his remains would be transferred to an ossuary.

Early Byzantine architecture did not immediately use overt images of Jesus Christ but instead reveled in symbolic images. An elaborate *frieze*, or decorative band telling stories of the great Old Testament biblical heroes was frequently woven around a liturgical space, affirming the generations of believers who prophesied the coming of the Christian hero. These *friezes*, using the colors and materials of fourth century Byzantium, communicated abstract ideas about Jesus as the fallen, resting hero, not fixed in a particular time or historical context. For instance, in one *frieze*, Byzantine Christians recalled a story from Matthew 12:40 in which Jesus remembers Jonas who "was three days and three nights in the whale's belly." He then goes on to prophecy, "so shall the son of man

---

this gospel, including the image of loyal followers who remained at the crucifixion scene and took charge of the body.

[13] J.R. Levison, "The Roman Character of Funerals in the Writings of Josephus," *Journal for the Study of Judaism: In the Persian Hellenistic and Roman Period* 33 (3), (2002): 245-272.

(Levison, 2002).Livingston points out that within the boundaries of the ideal Roman and Jewish funerary rites, "the primary role of the nearest relatives" was emphasized, that of properly preparing the body for burial. This article is particularly helpful in sorting out the claims made by Josephus regarding Jewish funeral practices and the influence of presentism, pervasively coloring Josephus' historical documentation, which reflect Roman practices as well.

be three days and three nights in the heart of the earth." Wonderfully descriptive, the classical sea monster, or hippogriff, became symbolic not of Jonas, great Old Testament hero, but of Jesus Christ. Those who viewed the symbol were obliged to remember Christ's journey to the center of the earth inaugurated by his descent from the cross and burial ritual.[14]

Frescoes adorned the catacombs as a reminder to those who came to pray that they were part of the burial vigil, awaiting the resurrection of all those who had "fallen asleep in the Lord."[15] Frescoe-viewing was a helpful form of devotional prayer for the pilgrims who came to the catacombs, but not practical for each Christian who desired to view the holy images. Over the next three hundred years, images of the revered disciples who slept with Christ were translated onto portable smaller pieces of wood and stone, using fine gold trim and a never-to-be-effectively-reproduced process of mixing melted wax and pigment to create detailed designs.[16] Icons became the central aid to personal practices of piety.[17]

About three hundred years after the iconoclast controversy,[18] the

---

[14] W. Flemming, *Arts and Ideas* (New York: Holt, Rinehart and Winston, 1963), 161-162.

[15] The influence of catacomb frescoe stylizing on this theme can be found in a twelfth-century depiction in the San Francesco chapel in Assisi (c. 1325).

[16] N. Baynes, "The Icons Before Iconoclasm," *Harvard Theological Review* 44 (1951), 93-106.

[17] Derived from the Greek word, *epitaphion* meaning 'on the tomb.' The images created by iconographers recalled the period of lamentation between the death and the resurrection of Jesus Christ. Sadly, because of the iconoclast controversy that came in the eighth century, few early examples of icons recalling Jesus' descent from the cross and burial still exist. According to the *Grove Dictionary of Art*, the earliest images of *Epitaphios Threnos*, the particular Byzantine image of Jesus' descent from the cross, is "an eleventh-century ivory panel." This earliest example contains the mourning figures of Joseph of Arimathaea, Nicodemus, Mary and Mary Magdalene attending the lifeless corpse of Jesus.

[18] The ordinary believers' pietistic practice of praying with icons came into direct conflict with the representatives of hierarchical Orthodoxy between 726 and 843 C.E. Icons were by this time the catechetical and inspirational bond between the church and the ordinary believers. Pope Leo III viewed the whole devotion to icons as a matter of idolatry. His position eventually brought bloodshed to and outright defiance from many Byzantium believers. The image of Jesus' descent from the cross defined the mood of the era. John of Damascus wrote of the controversy. "We venerate images; it is not veneration offered to matter, but to those who are portrayed through matter in the images. Any honor given an image, it is God who is honored, even as the material image is the vehicle of grace and blessings. The icons themselves are holy objects; they are not mere sym-

image of *Epitaphios Threnos* emerges, [19] captivating the imagination of Byzantine iconographers for its raw and tragic revelations. In the earliest versions of this icon, Mary supports and caresses the head of Jesus, whose total body-weight seems to rest in her lap. This of course is reminiscent not of the post-crucifixion scriptures as would be expected, but rather of the depictions of the manger scene, which favored the Matthew 2:11 image of Mary actually holding the human child for the visiting Kings to admire. Of interest is the Lukan account[20] in which the manger, not Mary, holds the infant Jesus. His humanity as well as his divinity is set apart, distanced from even his mother. The dependence of the child on the mother is the summation of a relationship that undeniably was impressive to those living in the Byzantine world. It emphasized the Byzantine peasant belief that at the end of his life, there is no distance between Jesus and his mother. As the head of Jesus rests in a position suggestive of a child coming from its mother's birth canal, the grief-stricken Mary holds her son's head as she once cradled his entire body. This gives the impression of a helpless, yet present woman who is still mothering even in death.

Iconophiles of the eleventh century perhaps found images of Jesus' descent from the cross compelling because they explored the depths of human suffering and longing for liberation in native Byzantine cultures. The early Byzantine icons depicting Jesus' descent, there is a notable interest in surrounding the body with a number of disciples, as well as Mary. These followers participated in the preparation and entombment of the body. In Roman and Jewish practices, it would have been customary for a group to gather, accompanying the body in a pro-

---

bols." Approbation came to the iconophiles in March of 843 when Theodora, widow of the vengeful and strict iconoclast Theopholus and mother of the future emperor, called a council. With her diligent insistence, church hierarchy restored the veneration of icons, initiated an ecumenical council and liberated the imprisoned iconophiles. Her act is remembered on the first Sunday of Lent each year in the "Triumph of Orthodoxy" celebration. From this point forward, the Byzantium empire found itself in a long period of sustained peace, growth and economic prosperity, lending credence to the claims that objects prayed to could have particular powers that brought graces and blessings for the believers.
[19] Derived from the Greek word, *epitaphion* meaning 'on the tomb.' The images created by iconographers recalled the period of lamentation between the death and the resurrection of Jesus Christ. The earliest example that remains following the Iconoclast Controversy is from the 11th-century and contains the mourning figures of Joseph of Arimathaea, Nicodemus, Mary and Mary Magdalene attending the lifeless corpse of Jesus.
[20] Luke 2:6-7, 12, 16

cession formation to the burial site. Greek Byzantine practices included that of a chorus of men, women and children serenading the spirit. These images may well be suggesting a fidelity to such practices. They deny that their hero is in any way a criminal, but some images do suggest the possibility that this is the burial of a poor man, with some images of humans caring for the body and set against a dark night sky.[21]

Peasant life was difficult and unpredictable, and viewing an icon image permitted spiritual escapes from the agony and hopelessness of such life, in part because the ordinary believer could identify with the message the icon communicated. Burial rituals routinely challenged the Byzantium believers to find meaning in the early deaths of their mortal heroes. For this meaning, they looked to the traditional's exemplary broken hero, Jesus, and the iconic images of his burial. The socialization of these native Orthodox Christians, as Anton Vrame points out, relied on icons of Jesus Christ and other martyrs to facilitate communion with the Holy Trinity so that *theosis,*[22] or the ultimate destiny of human existence, could be achieved. Cautious to not worship the icon itself, Orthodox iconophiles associated holiness with *theosis.* Communion with the Trinity, a fruit of viewing an icon, inspired the ordinary peasants to have the courage and confidence to bear witness to God's love and redeeming activity in the world. Thus it was believed they were moving closer to the destiny of their "fated" hero, Jesus Christ, who had descended from the cross in order to reach his ultimate destiny of union with God.[23]

Theme Two: Synergistic Aspects of the Icon Tradition and Michelangelo's *Pieta*

The Renaissance gave rise to a renewed interest in ancient Greek and Roman humanism underscored by the plight of the hero. While ecclesial leaders were trying to unify the church around the "Roman ideal,"[24] ordinary believers began to leave behind the majestic images of Christ in

---

[21] Levison, 252-256.

[22] Mystic Christian perspective includes the idea of *theosis*, which literally means to immerse one's self in the journey of life so as to become God-like in the midst of creation.

[23] Vrame, 186-187.

[24] Constantine envisioned a glorious marriage between the law (policy) and the eternal glory promised by Jesus. The authoritative union between the pope (the Bishop of Rome believed to be in apostolic succession to Peter) and the patriarch (believed to be the heir to a grand earthly kingdom) was solidified as the underpinnings of the "idea of Rome." The classical remnant of the Rome of antiquity served as the guiding image for this idea.

kingly, priestly splendor. They sought ways to practice the virtue of piety that were more in keeping with the simplicity of Jesus' human sacrifice.[25] Native Italian Christian pilgrims found satisfaction and potency in these practices, which were based on the themes of pilgrimage and the notion of conversion, popularized during the Byzantine period. This shift is evident as various artists begin to assign the title *Pieta* to the image of the descent of Jesus from the cross.

The genesis of the word *pieta*s is complex. Its entailed history is that of an ancient Roman word, influenced by an even older Greek context. By the time Michelangelo's first and most revered *Pieta* was completed in 1500, the word had come to mean, "loyalty to the highest degree... a profound love that neither life nor death can destroy."[26] What is fascinating is how previous meanings of *pietas* that had emerged in earlier Greek and Roman native cultures seem to be intentionally captured within Michelangelo's sculpture, drawing from a tradition of mythological figures like Aeneas and Odysseus. In his article, "Pietas and the Origins of Western Culture" Gerald Malsbary describes four dynamic aspects of *pietas*. As he suggests, a secular composite of these aspects came to describe the hero as a family-oriented pilgrim, embodying the value of law and beauty, able to bridge the past and the future with humility. This composite was borrowed by those creating religious art. "Christian *pietas*, then, when used to describe human beings, means the quality of loving with the love of God the Father: because in this love, not that we loved God, but that He loved us first, and sent his Son into the world, to be the expiation for our sins."[27]

Pietas, as Malsbary reflects, has a "certain mysterious quality behind the changing and diverse manifestations the theme encompasses." Malsbary asserts that in the context of ancient Greek culture, *pietas* is first and foremost, the spirit of the contest (*kairos*),

> ...(which) revealed the ancestral quality of the victor's family, rooted in myths of heroes and gods; it revealed the active favor of one or more gods at the moment of victory; and it revealed the hard work, suffering, devo-

---

[25] D. Kelley, *Renaissance Humanism* (Boston, MA: Twayne Publishers, 1991), 62.

[26] R. Hupka, *Michelangelo Pieta* (Angers, France: Editions Arstella, 1975), 78.

[27] Gerald Malsbary, "Pietas and the Origins of Western Culture," *Logos* 4(2), (2001): 115.

tion, and self-sacrifice of the individual victor, and the precariousness of his humanity.[28]

In the spirit of the contest, it was customary to celebrate heroes in lengthy poems, funeral monuments or other expensive tributes to the efforts that brought both fame and fortune to the individual athlete and the athlete's family. Pindar's odes, for instance, celebrated the quality of relationships within the family. The spirit of Greek life lived within the context of one's family and community was visible in the athlete's victory, not so much for his ability to compete, considered to be a grace bestowed by the gods, but because the athlete carried the fate, fame and fortune of the entire community and family with him.

Giotto's *Pieta* (1306) bridged the iconographical tradition's focus on the heroic efforts of the divine majestic Christ and the Renaissance fascination with the human hero Jesus who, as the flesh and blood of Mary, became the ultimate human sacrifice. In what would become a typically Renaissance fashion, Giotto saw that there was beauty and positivism, even in the sacrifice. "In general, his figures moved about in the space Giotto created for them with greater suppleness than heretofore. His world was marked by a new and intelligible relationship between man and his fellow men, between man and nature, and between man and God."[29] This piece initiated the Renaissance imagination to the renewed exploration of Jesus Christ's "descent" into the journey between life and death. Art historians agree that Giotto uses dimensionality and beauty, two considerations not explored in the icon tradition but inspired by the art of humanist Greece and Rome.

In Michelangelo's *Pieta* (1500), the familial quality of the hero emerges as both a response to and a commentary on the religious hero of Christianity as well as the state of the believers in Michelangelo's time. Completed between 1499 and 1500, this work symbolically marked a new era in human history and belief, leaving behind the tumultuous century during which Pope John XXIII's[30] attempt to heal the Great Western

---

[28] Malsbary, 98.

[29] Flemming, 323.

[30] Pope John XXIII, elected in 1409 after his successor, elected during the Council of Pisa, died. The Council was called to heal the Great Western Schism. Initially thought to be a talented leader who could heal the schism, he soon found himself as one of three men claiming to be the Pope. He convened the Council of Constance in 1414, during which he, along with the other "popes" was deposed.

Schism failed miserably; the reform movements of John Wycliffe and John Hus were solidified; and the growing lay fervor was spurred on by such works as *The Imitation of Christ* by Thomas a Kempis. The native culture around Michelangelo was one of uncertainty, but there was confidence in the newly-revived humanistic ideology based on the Roman-ideal, in which the notion of *pietas* had a central and enduring place. This period was also remembered by Michelangelo and his contemporaries for the two hundred year struggle to overcome the devastation wrought by the Black Death (1340's), numerous and savage peasant revolts, and a growing distrust of the political and religious leaders of the time. Many Christian scholars were obsessed with predictions of the pending apocalyptic end, while others began to turn toward an intellectual focus on the Greek manuscripts that found their way into European life after the fall of Constantinople in 1453. The growing intellectual movements of the European Renaissance were a welcome invitation to explore the christic-center of the Christian enterprise, particularly its eschatological qualities set aside by those who had predicted a cataclysmic end to the world by 1500.

Michelangelo was well-versed in the *studia humanitatis*, "those studies which perfect and adorn man [sic]," during which "one was prepared to take up a life in society together with his fellow men, to communicate with them clearly and effectively, and to understand both the past and the principles on which his community's values were based." Jerrold E. Seigel points out that the beginning and ending point in such studies was the "life of man [sic] in society."[31] Raphael's painting, *The School of Athens*, places the poetic Michelangelo left-of-center at the bottom of the hierarchically situated marble stairs leading to an entry arch where Plato and Aristotle debate the nature of the transcendental over and above the earthly reality.[32] Michelangelo was an espoused neo-Platonist and in keeping with the paradoxical nature of Renaissance philosophy, his sculpture of the *Pieta* contemplates the height of humanity's perfection, beauty and goodness in Jesus Christ's heroic "descent" from the cross. So drawn to the theme was Michelangelo that he created four *pietas*.[33] Commissioned in 1498 by Cardinal Jean de Bilheres de Lagrau-

---

[31] R. Schwoebel, R, editor, *Renaissance Men and Ideas* (New York: St. Martin's Press, 1971), 4.

[32] M. Aston, *The Panorama of the Renaissance* (New York: Harry N. Abrams, Inc., 1996), 40-41.

[33] Hupka, 78.

las of France[34] during the height of the Roman Renaissance, Michelangelo's *Pieta* of 1500 recalls the elements of Florentine Renaissance art that inspired his technique. A skilled and sought after painter, it was his love of sculpture that motivated Michelangelo's passion for artistic perfection apparent in this piece.[35]

In this sculpted version of the *Pieta*, the anatomically fascinated Michelangelo added an element of realism to this subject matter. He used the riddle of the time, the Renaissance as "implying sleep and awakening, going down as well as coming up, darkness before light, losing before finding,"[36] to allow the humanity and divinity of Jesus to be mysterious and certain all at the same time. In keeping with the rediscovery of ancient Greek and Roman myths, the heroes of Christianity also embarked on a journey during which a time of long sleep preceded the awakening. The journey is at its lowest point before the hero rises into the heights; the journey itself is an escape from the chaos into the cosmic order of heaven; and at last, the legacy of the journey proclaims liberation to those who are willing to witness the very moment in history that was the crescendo of the Greek classical theme, *pietas*.

In one of his earliest reliefs, *Madonna of the Steps* (1491-92), Michelangelo began to study the relationship between Mary and Jesus. Perhaps the loss of his own mother at an early age left the grief-stricken young man with an eagerness to understand the primary human relationship that even death could not destroy. Her death haunted Michelangelo throughout his life. Unlike the iconographers who sought to understand the human experience in more universal terms, the personal, more intimate aspects of relationality characterized much of Michelangelo's sculptures, especially evident in the *Pieta* (1500). He intentionally placed the viewer in the center of the situation, to make us witnesses to the finality of the encounter between mother and son. In so doing, he may have cathartically been dealing with his own grief, but it is also possible he was addressing the pressing issue of nominalism in the church, a theological movement that "rejected all forms of mediation between God and humankind."[37] Theologically, Mary was not a mediator, or she would have restored life. She was, however, *theotokos*, the Mother of God.

---

[34] Cardinal Bilheres de Lagraulas was the French ambassador to the Holy See.

[35] Michelangelo was so proud of his skills as a sculptor, he signed his work on the ceiling of the Sistine Chapel, *Michelangelo scultore* (sculptor).

[36] Aston, 11.

[37] R. McBrien, *Catholicism* (San Francisco: Harper & Row Publishers, 1981), 632.

While vestiges of Dante's depiction of Mary as having self-willed influence throughout the universe lingered into the late 1400's, hints of the coming reformation movements cast doubt on Dante's generous interpretation of Mary's role in human affairs.[38] It would have been difficult for Michelangelo to avoid theological discussions about Mary given his friendship with the Medici family and prominent religious leaders of his time. This piece becomes a commentary on Michelangelo's early Marian claims.

Controversially, the vertical nature of Mary's posture places her at the highest point of humanity. Viewed by Eastern and Western Christians as the "redemptrix of captives, as refuge of sinners, as mediatrix between God and humankind,"[39] by the late 1300's, Western Christians, like their Eastern Orthodox brothers and sisters, were convinced of the miraculous power of Mary images. But, as previously mentioned, the restless reformers who were contemporaries of Michelangelo vehemently opposed any theological interpretation of Mary that placed her as a co-redeemer or mediatrix. Perhaps it was Michelangelo's' youth and the influence of the Medici family, but in the *Pieta* he espoused the image of Mary as a youthful goddess, incorruptible and untouched by the sin that destroyed Jesus.[40] Vertically, she literally sits as the bridge between God and the human reality that symbolically lies across her lap. If Michelangelo had been the least bit astute about Jewish burial laws, this posture could have functioned theologically in a different way as well. Michelangelo may have used the body of Mary as the entombment shelf upon which Jesus' body was placed. Unlike other mere mortals, Jesus' decomposition never came. Michelangelo has brought together in this one piece the christological and Marianist concerns of his time. The synergistic perspective he births in the *Pieta* is that of the hero's descent with honor, family, and an abiding loyalty to the viewer.

The professional difficulty for many artists, including Michelangelo, in dealing with this subject was the obvious problem of Mary's older female body needing to support the heavier, dead weight of a younger male. *Lamentation Over the Dead Christ* (not dated) is a chalk drawing with the nude, dead body of Christ centrally placed on the lap of Mary who is seated on the ground. Three additional sketchy figures ap-

---

[38] Dante Alighieri, *The Divine Comedy*.

[39] McBrien, 874.

[40] Michelangelo is purported to have been twenty-three years old when he completed the *Pieta*.

pear to be assisting Mary, which allows the weight of the male body to be more realistically dispersed. Contemporaries struggled with the same logistical tensions. In his *The Descent from the Cross*, (1435) Rogier van der Weyden has only the men lifting the body of Jesus, as Mary was being helped to the ground by the other women. Botticelli has an unconscious Mary suspending the body of Jesus over the weight of her knee while three other strategically placed figures assisted. The *Pieta* by Ercole de Roberti (c. 1485) was perhaps drawing from a similar inspiration to that of Michelangelo when he painted a Madonna in voluminous flowing robes. The layers of material attempt to bury the masculine body that would be needed to support the male body of Jesus, which Roberti dwarfs and stiffens to achieve the affect of a mother cradling the son. The Roman ideal of beauty and the masculine quality of strength applied to female heroes, as well. Michelangelo attempted to chisel a solution to the artistic dilemma of portraying obviously unlikely relationships of objects within space, while maintaining a spiritual integrity between the Roman ideal and heroic qualities in realistic ways.

Michelangelo, having had permission to visit the morgue while living in the house of Medici, eagerly studied human anatomy. He was fascinated by the pyramidal composition of the Florentine Renaissance. An ardent admirer of the two most renowned pyramidal composers, Leonardo da Vinci and Piero della Francesca, Michelangelo set out to create a structure that "holds the attention within the composition and obviates the necessity for such external considerations as niches or architectural backgrounds."[41] Mary's robe-covered body dominates the vertical space, giving Michelangelo the freedom to create the illusion of a muscular, well-fortified woman. Jesus' horizontal body layers across his mother's lap, giving dimensionality and depth to the piece. Significantly, this style of composition emphasizes the Roman use of *pietas* connoting the devotion of a hero to family, politics and religion at all costs, while demonstrating a loving care for the ancestors and heirs who inspired fidelity to the law. Gregory J. Riley points out the human situation most fundamentally defining of the hero is that "one can, apparently neither try to live nor try to die apart from one's fate."[42]

A much more modern demonstration of Malsbary's "secular composite" notion of *pietas* can be found in the work of Danish artist

---

[41] Flemming, 375.
[42] Riley, 46.

Wiig Hansen's *Pieta* (1976).[43] An espoused non-Christian, Hansen's image in clay preserves the integrity of the "family-oriented pilgrim" richly introduced in the earlier Michelangelo *Pieta*. Hansen believed in the abiding beauty and goodness of humans, not spurred along by divine intervention, but transformed by human nature's propensity for following the laws of the heart. Commissioned for the main lobby of Herning Centralsgehus, a hospital in Denmark, Hansen, who died in 1997, wrote of this piece, "Could my faith make this wall come alive, and still more, could my expressions become intelligible as I hoped, so that—precisely at this place, where so much life has its beginning and so much life comes to its end—my work could achieve lucid clarity and become a consolation, a joy. Or, would nothing be revealed, so that we might be left blinded in the glaring light of incomprehension."[44] As with Michelangelo, Hansen had in mind the viewer as a witness to the enigmatic forces of life and death. Hansen, however, anticipated a non-religious, yet mystical solution to the hero's fate. It is noted by several art critics that Hansen, famous for his harsh lines and imposing colors, adds an element of "softness" to the Hospital piece, indicative of his attempt to care for the viewer while challenging himself to dig more deeply into the mysterious forces of life and death.

In a helpful comparative analysis of Hansen's preliminary drawing and completed relief, Jesper Christensen observes that:

> ...the *Pietas* version (the completed relief) eliminates the raw image of a fight between two men and replaces it with a fairy-tale character, called Angstens Engel" [The Angel of Fear], whose mask with piercing eyes and wing-like hair is a variant of the tolling head of many spooky folktales. This shift of perspective, from violent realism to folklorish symbolism, has a softening effect, that is augmented by the protective mother figure, who is portrayed as the confident center of her children's world.[45]

Subtly the contrast between the violence of a child's death and the com-

---

[43] Svendd Wiig Hansen (1922-1997)
[44] Jesper Christensen, "The Artist's Vision in a Public Space," *Scandinavian Studies* 69 (4), (1997): 5.
[45] Ibid., 5.

forting Mother's protective embrace of the young hero is established.[46]

In the tradition of the *Epitaphios Threnos,* Hansen "crowds" the intimacy of the center "Madonna of the Day and the Night" with a second set of figures to companion the dead. Reminiscent of the Greek and Roman heroes, such figures as "The Thoughtful One" and "The Searcher" are poised for a long period of contemplation on the meaning of the child's death. In a final explosion of color and asymmetry, Hansen added bold intrusive figures suggestive of the natural entities. "The Tempest" and "The Sun" enter the funerary ritual as forces not fully disclosed to the young hero and his mother.

As with Giottos' *Pieta,* Hansen bridges two ideological poles. In a nod to the tradition of Madonna and Child images as capturing Christianity's great hope in the midst of great despair, Hansen's *Pieta* also sets in motion a more desperate secular perspective postulating the emptiness to which all life succumbs. While there is no evidence that Hansen was influenced by the Cubist-style of Marc Chagall's *Pieta,* there is a striking similarity in composition and inspiration.[47] Chagall animates his version with heavy-black-lined figures supported by generous splashes of red, the pigment of suffering. Hansen proposes a comparable stylization of characters, demanding a long, interpretive look on the part of the observer. Both pieces were commissioned for public spaces, yet each work

---

[46] Hansen played with the theme of "Mother Earth" for many years before he created *Pietas.* An Aztec art enthusiast, Hansen fashioned a number of Mother Earth images, including *The Earth Weeps* in which Mother Earth, worn down by the struggle to overcome an "empty existence" is depleted of energy to sustain her children. *The Earth Weeps* memorializes the awakening of the planet to the environmental crisis of the 1970's and is a permanent installation in the Nikolaj Church in Copenhagen.

[47] There are a number of similarities between the works of Hansen and Chagall, too numerous to explore in this study. But one is particularly significant because it gives us insight about artistic inspiration in the development of the *Pietas* theme. Chagall, like Hansen, was commissioned to create original art for a hospital. In 1962, the Hadassah Hebrew University Medical Center synagogue was dedicated. The windows, representing the ups and downs of the twelve sons of Jacob, were the work of Russian-Jewish artist Marc Chagall. Deeply touched by the history of suffering that marked Jewish life, Chagall commented during the dedication, "All the time I was working, I felt my father and my mother were looking over my shoulder, and behind them were Jews, millions of other vanished Jews of yesterday and a thousand years ago." His non-Christian approach to the *Pieta* memorializes the terror of Jewish persecution he described in the Hadassah windows, reminding Christian viewers that Jesus was to his very death a Jew. On some level, the Chagall *Pieta* serves as a corrective to anti-semitism, just as Hansen's *Pietas* functions as a corrective to human emptiness.

discloses a private perspective that simultaneously attracts and repels. In the tradition of *pietas* described by Malsbary, the mystique of the hero is brought to a dramatic conclusion in both pieces. The quality of the relationship between mother and child remains intact, while the more vaguely defined characters of doom threaten to extinguish all human virtue, especially those virtues which were most notable in the young hero. For Michelangelo, the characters are implied by his attempt to draw the viewer in as an active participant in the grief. For both Chagall and Hansen, the characters around Mother and dead-hero-child suggest that the future is far less about divine intervention in the revival of the dead hero and much more about those who lurk in the shadows.

Theme Three: Synergistic Aspects of the Mortal Social Hero and *Pietas*

The theme of *pietas*, once completely satisfying for its emphasis on the Roman ideal of divinity and humanity, has, in a third stage of evolution, found relevance in the more contemporary images reflective of the social injustices that mark the plight of so many native cultures in crisis. The horrors of modern war, glamorized in media images of large, powerful explosive machines carrying the imposing threat of excessive destruction, even annihilation, has inspired a new genre of *Pietas*: those expressive of social injustice. In this third stage of development, many *Pieta* images have taken on a dark and pervasively complex universality, in which the theme is recognizable through the torment and suffering of its subjects. They function against a backdrop of hopeless confusion in the midst of unparalleled human despair and helplessness, and stand in contrast to the religious orientation of earlier *Pietas*, which noted fidelity to the Christian enterprise. They are not explicitly anti-Christian images, but rather the new wave of *Pietas* explore the universal dilemma of suffering in frightening clarity. Heroism can be characterized only by grief and a final curiousness about "what if" death had not been permitted. Like Michelangelo's *Pieta* (1500), these images will most likely survive the test of time because they are inherently bound to humanity's unrelenting pursuit of divine power and the horrific consequences such a pursuit manifests.

Kathe Kollwitz (1867-1945), a Prussian artist living in Berlin, found herself overwhelmed by the suffering and death all around her. Kollwitz could not repress her social conscience. As she lived among the poor helping her husband with his medical practice, her art took on a tone of cynicism and pain. The social injustices of the period were numerous and this woman had a special talent for capturing the essence of devastation and loss that accompanied the period. In 1903, she produced a series of prints, *Woman with a Dead Child: Pieta*. Overwhelming for their simplicity and intimacy, Kollwitz had no idea of the prophetic nature of these prints. She herself was to lose two sons in World War I and a grandson in World War II. And in this way:

> ...the fundamental vision that I think Kathe Kollwitz provides us, is of the impossibility of forgetting and the impossibility of letting go of the guilt; for the responsibility of the old, for the sacrifice of the young. And here again, we have one of the oldest ideas in the Judeo-Christian tradition. The idea was the sacrifice of Isaac by Abraham wasn't necessary, and yet in the First World War, as Wilfred Owen put it in his poetry: "No, no Abrahams went down and slew the sons of Europe one by one." This sense that the old lived on and the young were slaughtered for their beliefs is what she caught.[48]

Her socialist views engaged her in a series of activities that caused her to lose her position at the Prussian Academy, the first such position held by a woman. She survived the Nazi regime, but was considered an enemy of the state because of her apparent ambivalence regarding Nazism. Much of her work was destroyed in the bombings of Berlin in 1943. One of the few surviving works is the *Pieta* series, worked and re-worked into effective lithographs. As she struggled to make sense of the horrors of Holocaust, poverty, and oppression she no doubt felt the strength of this inspired presentation. The image of sacrifice was a constant theme that guided her work with intensity and purpose.

In the lithograph, *Woman With a Dead Child: Pieta*, a woman's body draped in despair over the body of her dead son, pours forth a desperateness about the future which would hold no consequence for her dead son as a man-hero. Though tormented by the social realities of her time, she never relinquished herself to intimidation. Ironically, as scholars have asserted, her later works amazingly moved away from the

---

[48] J. Winter, *The Great War and the Shaping of the 20th Century: An Interview with Jay M. Winter*, (1996) < www.pbs.org/greatwar/interviews/winter13.html >, July 12, 2002.

subject matter of *Pieta* that had so inspired her early prints. Perhaps the loss of her sons and grandson left her with no other choice than to abandon the apocalyptic in favor of the eschatological future for herself and the world.

A second and equally disconcerting *pieta* was captured in the well-known work, *Guernica* by Pablo Picasso (1881-1975). Painted for the World's Fair Exhibition (Paris, 1937), Picasso, like Kollwitz, was not pursuing a religious theme when he included a pieta-like figure of a woman wailing in despair. Picasso's work came to fruition after a ten-year personal struggle to find meaning and direction in his art. On a larger scale, he was deeply impacted by the civil war in his native Spain. Generalissimo Francisco Franco, desperate to assert himself as a world leader in the midst of economic depression and unrest, engaged Hitler's army in military maneuvers that, among other atrocities, included bombing a northern Basque village of Spain called *Guernica*.

Overwhelmed with the inhumanity and the massiveness of what had happened, Picasso set out to create a piece that would capture the horrors of what happened to this tiny village where the fires of hell burned for three days, consuming sixteen hundred people. No son would grow to become a man. The cries of an inconsolable mother seemed to capture the fragility and desperateness of the entire country. From Picasso's perspective, the world could never be the same. The technology, so embraced by the organizers of the World's Fair who commissioned him to create a piece, was to its very core the essence of the apocalypse. Picasso saw no hope and the grotesque images that poured forth from the painting could not be controlled or understood. The German program at the World's Fair described *Guernica* as "a hodgepodge of body parts that any four-year-old could have painted."[49] For Picasso, *Guernica,* and the pieta embedded in her yet-unfolding meaning, was an attempt at purging the evil that plagued his time in history. The fallen hero was consumed by the inhumanity of those he set out to save. No doubt, this was an eerie sense in a world only flirting with Hiroshima and the Holocaust.

Eastern influences have begun to weave themselves into the story of *pietas* in works like *Our Sighs and Tears* (1996) by Ding Fang.[50]

---

[49] *Treasures of the World; Episode One: Gernica: Testimony of War,* prod. Barry Stoner, Stoner Productions, 1999, videocassette.

[50] Ding Fang began his formal studies at the Nanjiing Art Institute four years after the official end of the "Chinese Cultural Revolution" in 1980. He identifies frescos found in Shannxi and Shanxi as being particularly influential in his painting. By his own admission, he is not particularly grounded in a post-

His work is, as much of Eastern art is, an exercise in the experimentation of new indigenous insights. It is fundamental and exposed, much like China's incorporation of Christianity.[51] Indigenous influences from his native Shannxi Province permeate the work of this Chinese artist. His version of *pietas* is emblematic of the current tide of Chinese social experience, yet it journeys beyond this one context. Particularly Eastern considerations must be brought to bear on this piece by viewers, and in particular two questions: How, if at all, can the images be understood as Chinese while employing the embedded Western notion of *pietas*? Fundamentally, in what ways, if any, does this Christian Asian image bridge yet another shift in the tradition of *pietas*?

In contrast to the Michelangelo's incorruptible Jesus, Ding Fang projects a partially decomposed corpse, looking more like a skeleton than a fleshy, barely-dead human. The figure is awkwardly cradled by three women. While the piece is somewhat gruesome in its presentation, it also points toward the dilemma of Chinese Christians as they imagine China's future on the brink of resurrection. Ding Fang's art makes reference to the political and social shifts in the post-revolution era.[52] In many ways, his vision of *pietas* transcends the traditional Christian limitations of a caring mother, suggesting rather a mother who is cold, disappointed and disconnected; a mother who could be called, "Christianity," perhaps. The haunting universal mother, "Mother Earth," may also be implied. The failed hero, decomposing before her, could be a metaphor for the failure of the Christian enterprise to include the universal experience of an immanent, incarnate God-man within the indigenous Chinese context.

The image may also be projecting a prophetic commentary about the destruction of the universe around which all humans have gathered and ritualized. The power of the image, *Our Sighs and Tears*, relies on the synergy of Chinese pre-revolution oppression and post-revolution purposefulness. Ding Fang belongs to a group of indigenous artists who seek the wisdom of China's past while bringing forth a new expressiveness that attempts "to disturb the heart and mind," a primary purpose of Asian art, according to Asian art critique Suwarno Wisetrotomo.[53] The

---

modernist perspective, but rather would define his artistic vision along the lines of cutting edge post-revolution artists

[51] T. Min, "Ding Fang's Artistic Career," *China Today* 44 (6), (1995): 50-53.

[52] J. Clark, *Modern Asian Art* (Honolulu: University of Hawaii Press, 1998), 48-53.

[53] S. Wisetrotomo, "Weighing Religious Codes," *Asian Christian Art Exhibit* (catalog), Austrian Museum of Fine Arts, (2001), 1-3.

disturbance is only intended for the strong of character. A weak character is incapable of being enlightened by what he or she sees, so one must ask: Why "look" at all? Enlightenment happens when a lingering emotion cannot be set aside. The emotion is settled only by action. Asian aesthetics tend toward the experiential; in other words, the meaning is in the production of art and the act of viewing it. What is gained from the act of viewing is a process of the emotions, not the mind. The image simply *is*. In contrast, Western aesthetics tend to intellectually search for the meaning in the image, not really as concerned with the production or the emotional integrity with regard to viewing it. Michelangelo presented an interesting Eastern "solution" to his viewer. He did have a desire for the viewer to interact as a witness to the burial of Jesus for the emotional value of participating in this historical moment. It could be said, then, that Eastern *pietas,* influenced by both Western Christianity and Eastern aesthetics, represents a kinetic exploration of consciousness about death and life, culminating in natural action, or action. Action, for Ding Fang, must be appropriate within the natural ecology as well as in the context of human social institutions. He suggests, through his ambiguous use of images in the Pieta, that action must also be somehow related to the Christian gospel. Ding Fang's *Our Sighs and Tears* is infused with environmental sensitivity, as well as Christian symbolism. As a matter-of-fact most of Ding Fang's exhibited works deal with ecological themes, yet he considers himself to be an Asian Christian artist.

In his own words, Ding Fang reflects, "You may say that I went to a small town named Zhen Jing in Shannxi Province. I found people and earth are in the relation of the same construction. The formation and the lines are in a deep connection. For example, the clothes local people wear are made of hand-woven material; the drapes on the clothes are just like the lines of the mountains there."[54] The central image within this work is a grotesque decomposing body, which implies the earthiness of one's humanity; the space between being and not being. Christopher Smith of the Zacheta Gallery, Warsaw, comments, "Ding Fang's city of the future is a hideous gray, smoldering, post-atomic, post-ozone-layer nightmare." The implied affiliation with the humanly-constructed institution of Christianity betrays his more pervasive affinity for the broader construct of reality that is governed by the laws (and heroes) of the natural world as opposed to human laws and heroes. But is his attempt to

---

[54] Z.Qi, "A Conversation with Ding Fang," *Century Online China Art Networks,* http://www.chinaartnetworks.com/feature/wen05.shtml, (September 9, 2003).

place humanity in the larger scheme of redemption of creation? The explicitly Christian theme of *pietas* demonstrates the universality he wants to achieve in his image, thus pointing toward the particularity of Chinese Christian inspiration as a local venue for ecological renewal; quite a striking paradox for a country growing at the rate of six percent annually, with corresponding consumptions of natural resources.

This piece can be considered as a bridge between Western and Eastern *pietas* in as much as it carries the weight of Chinese history, and in particular the heroes who balance the burden of the dead corpse of Chinese history; yet it is open to deeper reflection about the current relevance of Chinese Christianity, which has wrought indignation in its missionary zeal. For instance, the three female images seem to support the corpse, yet they do not appear to be cradling as a mother cradles the child; they are perhaps not even touching the corpse. So, what is their relationship, one figure to another and with the viewer? In one compelling consideration, the viewer could imagine that they are perhaps pulling away from the long history of Christian foreign missionary influence and oppression. The three characters may be symbolic of the Three-Self Patriotic movement, a movement that has as its tenants Marxism, process theology, liberation theology and an affirmation of the "Cosmic Christ." Self-governance, self-support and self-propagation are the three key principles guiding the Chinese Protestant Christian reform movement which is attempting to "modernize" Chinese Christianity. Should the Western viewer suspect that Ding Fang is commenting on the death of Jesus, the tradition's hero, or the three aforementioned movement's principles?

The universal reality of the "early death in the midst of life" and the fated hero touch every native culture in some way. *Woman with a Dead Child: Pieta, Guernica* and *Our Sighs and Tears* have become the seeds of a new wave of artistic encounter with the descent from the cross. Picasso is quoted as having said, "A painting is not thought out and settled in advance. While it is being done, it changes as one's thoughts change. And when it's finished, it goes on changing, according to the state of mind of whoever is looking at it." Certainly the same could be said for interpretations of Jesus' descent from the cross, which extend into every indigenous culture in which Christianity has planted her roots.

References

Artz, Frederick Binkerd. *Renaissance Humanism: 1300-1550.* (Oberlin, OH: Oberlin Press, 1966).

Benesch, Otto. *The Art of The Renaissance in Northern Europe.* (London: George Gibbons, LTD., 1945), 153-170.

Betterton, Rosemary. *An Intimate Distance: Women, Artists, and the Body.* (New York: Routledge Publishers, 1996), 12-36.

Fang, Ding. Ding Fang's Artistic Career. (*China Today* 44 (6), 1995)1-3.

Jose, Nicholas. My Search for a Shaman: The Impact of 1989 on Chinese Art. (*AAP* 1(2), 1994) 78-83.

Kollwitz, Kathe. *The Prints of Kathe Kollwitz/Curated by Jack Rutberg.* (Galway
University of Galway Press, 1996).

Lucie-Smith, Edward. *Lives of the Great 20th-Century Artists.* (London: Thames & Hudson Publishers, 1999).

Noun, Louise.Rosenfield. *Three Berlin Artists of the Weimer Era: Hannah Hoch, Kathe Kollwitz, Jeanne Mammen; with Essays by Annelie Lutgens, Maria Makela, Amy Namowitz Worthen.* (Des Moines, Iowa: Des Moines Art Center, 1994), 40-83.

Prelinger, Elizabeth. *Kathe Kollwitz; with Essays by Alessandra Comini and Hildegard Bachert.* (Washington: Yale University Press,1992).

Slatkin, Wendy. *The Voices of Women Artists.* (Englewood Cliffs, NJ: Prentice Hall, 1993), 128-143.

Southern, Richard William. *Medieval Humanism and Other Stories.* (New York: Harper   & Row Publishers,1970).

Sullivan, Michael. *Art and Artists of Twentieth Century China.* (Berkeley, CA:University of California Press, 1996).

CONVERSIONS AND INCORPORATIONS: CROSSING GENDERS AND RELIGIONS WITH LOUISE ERDRICH'S FATHER DAMIEN

Sheila Hassell Hughes[*]

I. Introduction: Third Spaces and Double-Crosses[1]

With *The Last Report on the Miracles at Little No Horse*,[2] Louise Erdrich finally gives name to the imagined North Dakota Chippewa[3] reservation that has been the geographic and spiritual center for much of her fiction, and grants history to its priest, Father Damien Modeste. Published between 1984 and 2001, the existing novels in Erdrich's Matchimanito series[4] vary in their focus on white and/or Indian charac-

[*] Sheila Hassell Hughes holds an MA in English from the University of Toronto and an interdisciplinary PhD in Women's Studies from Emory University. She lives in Ohio, where she teaches American literatures and Women's Studies at the University of Dayton. Her research focuses on the intersections of gender, culture, and religion in women's writing, and she has published a series of articles on American Indian women writers (Louise Erdrich, Wendy Rose, and Joy Harjo). Currently, she is collaborating on a book about the representation of religion in Erdrich's work. Originally from Vancouver, by way of the Okanagan Valley, she still considers British Columbia "home."

[1] This essay has benefited from the support and critical feedback of a number of groups and individuals. The initial research and writing was supported by a grant from the Forum on the Catholic Intellectual Tradition and the Research Council at the University of Dayton. Members of the Forum also served as an early audience for these ideas. My colleagues on the "Literary Imagination and Historical Truth" panel at the Conference on Christianity and Native Cultures—Donna Carter, Rick Waters, and, especially, Betty Booth Donohue, who offered an insightful response to our presentations—deserve thanks as well. Finally, I am grateful to Christine Modey, John McCombe, Rebecca Potter, and Miriamne Krummel who served as helpful readers of an early draft of this essay, and to Elizabeth Wardle, who offered proofreading assistance.

[2] Louise Erdrich, *The Last Report on the Miracles at Little No Horse* (New York: Harper, 2001). Subsequent citations of the novel will use the abbreviation *LR*.

[3] The terms "Chippewa," "Ojibwe," and "Ashinaabe" all refer to the same people group. There are also variations in spelling for the last two terms. For consistency, I use the spellings Erdrich employs in the novel. (Although "Chippewa" and "Ojibwe" can be used to distinguish groups in different regions, they are both applied to the population about whom Erdrich writes.)

[4] Peter G. Beidler and Gay Barton refer to *Love Medicine, The Beet Queen, Tracks, The Bingo Palace*, and *Tales of Burning Love* as the "Matchimanito

ters, but all of them explore the truths of narrative and identity as communal creations. Damien makes minor appearances in the other novels as a beneficent if mildly effective missionary, but in this recent version Damien's life and perspective are fore-grounded and his priestly role as intermediary takes on new meanings. While *The Last Report* continues Erdrich's practice of weaving together multiple voices and perspectives, the novel is somewhat unusual in its sustained focus on a single character. Even this singularity is tricky, though, for Damien proceeds to double before our eyes and ultimately embodies a third space altogether.

The priest's identity is doubled, or crossed, in at least two significant ways. We discover in the first pages of the novel that gender is one field of identity radically tra(ns)versed by Damien, as we read of the elderly man undressing in the dark. As "he ... unw[inds] from his chest a wide Ace bandage," the narrative reveals that "[h]is woman's breasts [a]re small, withered, modest as folded flowers."[5] In this description of unbinding we see, paradoxically, two genders enwrapped. The possessive pronoun indicates that the female body belongs to the man, even as Father Damien is "her creation," as we read in a later chapter.[6] Extreme old age, celibacy, and life as a man have all shaped the attitude of the "folded" breasts, which remain, nevertheless, a "woman's." This image is telling of the complex life about to be unfolded. In the chapters that follow, Father Damien discloses more about his other self—his "beloved sister" and "twin," Miss Agnes DeWitt—and about the impetus for her recreation in her "masterwork, her brother," Father Damien Modeste.[7] Although the story appears, in some ways, to begin as a narrative of identity exchange and gender "conversion," it becomes increasingly clear that both genders and personae live on, achieving a kind of transgendered integrity over the course of eighty-some years together.

Part of what this essay will do, then, is to offer a "transgendered reading" of the novel's protagonist, exploring ways in which the complex gender negotiations of Agnes/Damien model a third way for imag-

---

saga." They differentiate from this *The Antelope Wife*, which is set primarily in Minneapolis and introduces a new set of characters. Beidler and Barton, *A Reader's Guide to the Novels of Louise Erdrich* (Columbia: U of Missouri P, 1999), 2. Since the drafting of this essay, another novel, *The Master Butcher's Singing Club* (New York: Harper, 2003) has been published. It also focuses on a set of white (German immigrant) characters in the nearby town of Argus.
[5] *LR*, 8.
[6] Ibid., 77.
[7] Ibid.

ining gender—a way that exceeds or eludes the dominant binary-thinking of dominant Western and Christian epistemologies. To this end, I will consider the transgendered priest from the perspective of the two cultural and religious traditions s/he actively engages: Christian and Native American. Reading Agnes/Damien first according to the tradition of the Catholic "transvestite saint," I will show how this postmodern transgendered saint both fulfills and exceeds the received model. The Native American "two-spirit" figure offers another important point of "contact" for reading the life of our priest, however, and so I also examine his/her life through the lens of that indigenous, sacred tradition of gender diversity. From this perspective, Agnes/Damien appears as a Christian missionary uniquely acculturated to tribal traditions by virtue, in part, of her ambivalent gender identity.

Ultimately, however, I employ these transgendered reading strategies in pursuit of related questions about religious identity--for the second field of Damien's identity multiplicity is religious. In both personal belief and public ritual, Father Damien increasingly fuses Christian and traditional Ojibwe religious systems. Somewhat ironically, it is this Roman Catholic priest, more than any of Erdrich's Native or "mixed-blood" characters, who most dramatically embodies the kind of religious syncretism--the "fus[ing]" of "two belief systems to form a third, new reality"—that theologian Achiel Peelman attributes to Native North Americans.[8] As radical integrations of vision, rather than mere adoptions of traditional Christian symbols and sacraments, such practices hold the potential to realize Christ's presence: to newly "inculturate" Christ to Native ways of seeing, doing, and being. In this kind of inculturation, the cross of Christ is re-imagined as the Tree of Life, the transformative axis of a four-directioned universe.[9] As a cross-cultural symbol of mediation, connection, and transformation that is essentially integrative, the syncretized cross exceeds its traditional Christian parameters.

Agnes/Damien glimpses and also embodies the transgressive and transcendent values of such a "double-cross." This becomes most apparent in the priest's struggle with and eventual rejection of the missionary mandate to convert Indians. Instead of seeking converts, Damien adopts a model of loving, expansive, and mutually transforming absorption—the same kind of personal "incorporation" we have seen at work in his/her

---

[8] Achiel Peelman, *Christ is a Native American* (Ottawa: Novalis-Saint Paul U, 1995), 66.
[9] Ibid., 211-212, 217.

transgender practice. Our protagonist's religious "double-cross" is thus aided and abetted—indeed, I argue, brought into the realm of the imaginable for both the priest and the reader—by the transgenderism, or "gender syncretism," already made manifest in his/her life.

II. Transgenderism as a Model for Religious Integration

The term "transgendered" potentially includes all those who are, in Kate Bornstein's terms "transgressively gendered."[10] The term is most often used, though, to identify those who live their lives as men or women in contradistinction to their biological sex, without having opted for sex reassignment surgery. This includes people who live "full time" in one gender and also those who move back and forth between genders.[11] Although there is some debate about whether transgender identities actually exceed or challenge the two-gender system, I employ the term here to suggest a third space of gender identity akin to the "third new [religious] reality" identified by Peelman.

"Transgender" as a third term

For some theorists, the question of whether transgenderism actually disrupts the gender binary rests on whether sex is seen as a key to gender identity. If sex is irrelevant, then transgendered people simply inhabit a pre-existing gender identity. As Evelyn Blackwood argues, "Transgenders do not change the gender system unless their identity is different than either masculine or feminine. Men without penises or women without vaginas are still men and women. On the other hand," she explains, "if transgenders are neither masculine [n]or feminine, then American society could be said to have a multiple gender system."[12] This exclusionary approach to gender identity (either/or; neither/nor) is not the only way of distinguishing categories, however. Irreducible difference can be manifest in both/and relationships as well as neither/nor ones. As ethnic studies have shown us, the hyphen in hyphenated identi-

---

[10] Quoted in Virginia Ramey Mollenkott, *Omnigender: A Trans-Religious Approach* (Cleveland: Pilgrim, 2001), 40.

[11] Jason Cromwell, "Traditions of Gender Diversity and Sexualities: A Female-to-Male Transgendered Perspective" in *Two-Spirit People*, ed., Sue-Ellen Jacobs, Wesley Thomas, and Sabine Lang (Urbana: U of Illinois P, 1997): 119-159. 158.

[12] "Native American Genders and Sexualities: Beyond Anthropological Models and Misrepresentations" in Jacobs, Thomas, and Lang 284-94. 292.

ties (such as "Asian-American") itself comes to stand for a third element and a new site of psychic, familial, cultural, and political interrelation. The "trans" in "transgender," like the hyphen and the more recently much-theorized "border," similarly signals an other space of betweenness as well as connection that is both personal and social. As Judith Halberstrom suggests, "'Transgender' may, indeed, be considered a term of relationality [...for] it describes not simply an identity but a relation between people, within a community, or within intimate bonds."[13] I consider the term "transgender," then, to indicate an identity that may bear a both/and or a neither/nor relationship to the categories "man" and "woman," and therefore, by either exceeding or eluding the binary system of gender difference that so rigidly structures Western society, to constitute a third term. Whereas the two-sex system has generally functioned in the West to support the ascendancy of the One (the singular Man from whom woman is derived and assumed), a third term introduces the possibility of transformation. "The third sex," Marjorie Garber explains in *Vested Interests: Cross-Dressing and Cultural Anxiety*, "is a mode of articulation, a way of describing a space of possibility. Three puts in question the idea of one: of identity, self-sufficiency, self-knowledge."[14]

A Transgendered Reading

To read Agnes/Damien as "transgendered" turns the cross-dressing plotline from one of simple gender disguise to one of gender transformation. By destabilizing the presumed identicality and autonomy of personal identity, such an approach shifts our interpretive focus from questions about the cross-dresser's primary integrity (*How could she live this lie?*) to ones about the method and meaning of integration. As Halberstrom concludes in her analysis of transgender biographies, "When we read transgender lives it is necessary to read for the life and not for the lie. Dishonesty, after all, is just another word for narrative."[15] Such instruc-

---

[13] Judith Halberstrom, "Telling Tales: Brandon Teena, Billy Tipton, and Transgender Biography," *Passing: Identity and Interpretation in Sexuality, Race, and Religion,* Ed., Maria Carla Sanchez and Linda Schlossberg (New York: NYUP, 2001), 13-37. 15. Interestingly, Erdrich herself cites Billy Tipton's biography in one of her "Endnotes" to *Last Report* (357).
[14] Marjorie Garber, *Vested Interests: Cross-Dressing and Cultural Anxiety* (New York: Routledge, 1992), 11.
[15] Halberstrom, 36.

tion is especially relevant in approaching *Last Report on the Miracles at Little No Horse*, because, like so much of Erdrich's work, it is also a story about narrative itself.[16] The life story of our priest unfolds, then, not as the successive disrobing of one apparent person to reveal a second, singular identity beneath, but rather as the accumulation and enfolding of multiple selves into a growing mass of identity. Though they be foreign when "put on," the vestments, postures, and performances ritualized in the daily life of the priest become part of the self, related to the body in abiding ways. By living publicly as Damien for more than eighty years, Agnes ultimately fully incorporates him, and the two become one—a third, new creation.

While a transgender reading of the novel has merit of its own, part of my intent in applying it here, as I have indicated above, is to enlighten issues of religious transformation. Because cross-dressing highlights the permeable nature of identity borders in general, Garber points out that in literature it often "indicates *a category crisis elsewhere.*"[17] In *The Last Report*, I argue, the primary category in crisis is the religious. Damien's gender status and identity[18], in fact, bear religious weight in relation to a community at the crux of cultures. The priest's transvestitism, and the transgender identity it supports, are like material icons through which we perceive religious realities. A reading faithful to the shifting and relational quality of the "trans" leads us through gender to other issues of identity and relation. I reiterate, the deepest questions are not those raised by the novel's beginning: *Is Damien really a woman? And, if so, what is a woman doing disguised as a priest?* The more profound problems are those with which the novel leaves us: *Is Damien really a saint? And what is s/he doing in and to the*

---

[16] See Erdrich's own "Endnote" to the novel (358) for a playful reminder of the politics of storytelling. The Native American novelist, it seems, has re-appropriated and fictionalized the private, oral confessions of the Ojibwe people which Damien inappropriately recorded and sent to the Vatican with his reports.

[17] Garber, 17.

[18] The relationship between gender status (which is attributed to one by society and involves both role expectations and a social location) and gender identity (or one's internal identification with or against the status and roles socially ascribed to one) might be likened to religious terms. As historians at this conference have amply demonstrated, the state of a soul, Indian or otherwise, cannot be easily inferred from official church documents or even records of religious practice. When missionaries see conversion as an either/or proposition but Natives understand it as supplemental or complementary, the possibilities for "misreading" are plenty.

world of the Anishinaabeg?[19]

 To begin to address such essentially religious questions, and to help us imagine a reality—both spiritual and physical—that exceeds or eludes the either/or dualities of much Western thought and Christian tradition, we need to do more preliminary and comparative work. To that end, I will examine Damien's identity in terms of two gender traditions, both of which carry spiritual significance: the Christian "transvestite saint" and the Native American "two-spirit" figure. Exemplifying and adapting both traditions, the priest's story indicates that transformations across lines of difference should look to a "trans" model of syncretism as relational and mutual incorporation, rather than to a conversion model of oppositional and sacrificial exchange.

Religious Syncretism as a Structural Model

Before exploring these two traditions, though, I want to flesh out the broader issues of transgender identity more fully by turning my analogy inside-out and considering religious syncretism as a model for gender transformation. One way of understanding Native people's historical interactions with the colonizer's religion, after all, is to see Christianity as a mask or cloak taken up to protect threatened indigenous traditions. Peelman calls this response, which depends upon a radical split between "external assent" and internal beliefs, "dual acceptance."[20] Apparent conversion, in this case, would really be simple religious cross-dressing and identity passing. Similarly, we could read the priest's cassock and the identity of Father Damien as a kind of protective mask. After all, the sexual difference of the woman Agnes endures beneath this cloak, unremarked upon in an institution where women remain otherwise marginalized by masculine authority structures. In this interpretive scenario, Agnes functions as a sort of trickster-figure. She plays with and to the expectations of others, but never surrenders wholly to them. She stumbles into the male identity by sheer luck and, riding the current of chance, shape-shifts as needed, a perpetual survivor. This is a legitimate interpretation that opens both the religious and gendered meanings of the novel in helpful ways. But such "dual acceptance" or masking cannot account for the more deeply embodied shifting that Agnes undergoes.

 While her gender change is not absolute—not the kind of exact exchange of identities and affiliations implied by the term "conversion,"

---

[19] See footnote #3.
[20] Peelman, 66.

for instance—it is definitely more fundamental than a mere disguise. Agnes/Damien is not simply a duplicitous figure, a wolf in shepherd's clothing—appearing as one thing while really being the opposite. If s/he is a shape-shifter of sorts, it is because of a deeper multiplicity. What Agnes undergoes in her incorporation of Damien's persona is a fusion of masculine and feminine identities to form a third, new gender reality. Just as Damien's acculturation among the Anishinaabeg shifts his whole relation to the world and to God, so Agnes's embodiment in/of Damien involves a profound re-orientation of the self. The transvestitism in the novel unfolds to reveal a yet more profound transgender identity. And this ambivalent "trans"—a prefix which suggests not only crossing over from one to another, but also passage between, carrying over, rising above, and crossing out—carries religious weight in the novel.

From a religious studies perspective, then, the subsequent spiritual transformation of Damien provides a structural model for understanding Agnes's gender change. Damien becomes acculturated to the Ojibwe, altering his sense of self and world to fit another cultural vision—a vision that is, at its core, sacred. While this acculturation challenges his prior religious commitments and sense of vocation, it does not estrange him from the core of his Christian faith. In fact, Damien finds Christ revealed among the Ojibwe: most overtly in the person of his housekeeper and friend, Mary Kashpaw, whose mystical transfiguration, or shape-shifting, he witnesses.[21] The pattern of Damien's experience and apprehension of transformation demonstrates how the binary system, the insistence on either/or realities, deconstructs under pressure. It thus also shows something of the promise of Christ's inculturation—"a sort of 'reactualization,'" in Peelman's terms, "in [another] time and space, of the unique mystery of God's incarnation."[22] In this, the most mutually transformative kind of syncretism, transcendent Love—an empathetic self-opening to and incorporation of otherness—manifests as the third, irreducible term. Radically multiple and relational, Agnes/Damien's new gender identity—which is both a deconstructive refusal of singularity and a loving re-fusion of differences—is likewise a third term. At times the transgendered priest appears as neither male nor female, rising up in a transcendent refusal of gender itself. At other times s/he seems to be "both/and," sinking into an ecstatic fusion of difference. Both visions are helpful, I think, as we track towards a clearer picture of the third, trans,

---

[21] *LR*, 123.
[22] Peelman, 92.

identity.

What I primarily want to argue here, is not that religious practices and identities can provide a model for understanding those of gender (though clearly they can do so helpfully) but rather that gender realities work in Erdrich's novel to re-inform religious ones. The Agnes-Damien identity, I mean to show, provides a physical and social corollary for the deep religious syncretism at work in the novel. Drawing on and revising both Christian and Indigenous traditions of gender diversity, the profoundly fluid and relational transgender self in Erdrich's *Last Report* serves as the embodied realization of a new spiritual experience—as an icon of Christ, double-crossed and inculturated .

III. The Priest's Story: Damien Incorporated and Acculturated[23]

Before we consider *Last Report on the Miracles at Little No Horse* as a postmodern sort of transgender hagiography and as two-spirit biography, we need to sketch out some of the central developments of plot and character, from Agnes's initial gender-crossing to Agnes / Damien's final "crossing-over" to the "other side." The novel begins with an account of how Agnes becomes Damien in the first place. We learn this from Damien when, as the novel opens in the year1996, he drafts another in a long series of as-yet-unanswered letters to the Pope. In this epistle, which recounts the remarkable life of the priest's alter ego, Miss Agnes DeWitt, the centenarian reveals what he has kept hidden in all his previous reports. Sometime around 1911, we learn, Agnes encountered the infamous criminal, Arnold "the Actor" Anderson, in disguise for a bank heist. Agnes, formerly a Catholic novice (with yet another identity, "Sister Cecilia"), notices his wrinkled cassock and "Episcopalian brown shoes." Boldly, she inquires, "Sir, why this pretense? You are not a priest!"[24] She is then taken hostage and shot twice in the ensuing chase. Subsequently, when her common-law husband is killed in a rescue attempt, her home soon after washed out by a flood, and she swept away on the lid of her treasured piano, she is multiply and variously lost—literally transported and disoriented.

As a result of all this trauma, which includes a split skull from

---

[23] Because traditional tribal cultures like the Ojibwe are inherently "religious"–bearing no sharp distinction between the sacred and the secular—observations about the missionary's acculturation necessarily bear religious significance.

[24] *LR*, 25.

the second bullet, Agnes suffers the severing of key mental and spiritual connections. She forgets her musical and sexual passions—two gifts which have always been linked for her. As a young woman, she was a remarkable pianist who could stir herself and others—even the nuns—to states of emotional and physical ecstasy with her renditions of Chopin. Music has always been, for her, deeply erotic, in the sense of a profound human yearning for connection and personal transcendence through connection. This eroticism is tied to the feminine persona of Agnes, and it is the first strand pulled loose from the fabric of that early identity.[25]

Swept down the river, Agnes attempts to sink herself with the beloved piano, but her billowing nightdress buoys her up. Ultimately reclaimed by the shore, Agnes then finds the bloated body of a missionary priest dangling from a tree. Carried away by coincidence, she appropriates his costume before shrouding and burying him in her own. Now it is the reader's turn to ask, "Why this pretense?" If the first false priest robs her of full identity, the garb of the second cleric seems to promise its return, for Agnes becomes a method actor, par excellence, re-imagining and re-inventing herself under new conditions. She initially passes as the drowned priest in order to fulfill her own spiritual calling, which the convent left unfulfilled, and it is on these terms that she makes the journey to Little No Horse as the new Damien. In later years, she maintains the masculine persona to sustain Damien's personal commitments to the Ojibwe, who have by then become his people.

Unlike the self-serving criminal Actor, who "erase[s] his character" with the wave of "a hand across his face,"[26] our gender performer supplements and deepens her own character with the assumption of a new role. Erdrich artfully balances two personae in one person, such that neither male nor female identity is ever fully disclaimed. In an interview, the author explains that she had originally planned to do away with the female persona, but inevitably found that she "couldn't admit to Agnes being lost. It didn't seem realistic." Method acting as inhabitation, it

---

[25] Erdrich describes the eroticism of her text as a sort of personal transcendence that encompasses the yearnings of faith, rather than something merely sexual. (*Interview with Louise Erdrich*
< http://www.harpercollins.com/hc/readers/erdrich_interview.asp >, October 27, 2003. Audre Lorde's description of the erotic as a yearning for connection, integrity, and excellence that is "firmly rooted in the power of our [generally] unexpressed or unrecognized feeling" also applies perfectly to Agnes ("Uses of the Erotic: The Erotic as Power," *Sister Outsider: Essays and Speeches*, New York: Norton, 1984. 53).
[26] *LR*, 25.

seems, does not "mean changing oneself." Instead, Agnes "enlarges" herself "so that," in Erdrich's words, "she bec[omes] two people. She bec[omes] twice the person she was."[27] It is, then, Agnes/Damien's refusal either to "kill off" the old self or to remain "really a woman" in the end, rather than the apparent success of the gender "exchange," that enables transcendence. Her gender transformation is an expansion and incorporation, rather than a conversion. And it sets the stage for the questions of missionary conversion that follow.

We see the coincidence of genders most clearly in scenes of prayer. The narrator tells us that in the first years of mission work, "Agnes and Father Damien became one indivisible person in prayer. That [the] poor, divided, human priest enlarged and smoothed into the person of Father Damien."[28] While this might seem to suggest the silencing of all but the official, masculine, and orthodox voice, that is not our priest's spiritual trajectory at all. Over the next decade, in fact, the description of such prayers alter somewhat, becoming both more androgynous and more religiously syncretic. Indeed, gender incorporation and acculturation follow twin paths in the novel. "Four times a day," we are told:

> ... Agnes and Father Damien became that one person who addressed the unknown. The priest stopped what he was doing, cast himself down, made himself transparent, broke himself open. That is, prayed. He prayed that the seething factions [among his parishioners] merge and dissolve their hatred. He prayed, uneasily, for the conversion of Nanapush, then prayed for his own enlightenment in case converting Nanapush was a mistake. Agnes asked for a cheerful spirit and that her dangerous longings cease. She asked for answers, and for the spirit of the language to enter her heart ... [S]he preferred the Ojibwe word for praying, anama'ay, with its sense of a great motion upward. She began to address the trinity as four and to include the spirit of each direction—those who sat at the four corners of the earth. Wherever she prayed, she made of herself a temporary center of those directions. There, she allowed herself to fall apart. Disin-

---

[27] *Interview with Louise Erdrich*, 2.
[28] *LR*, 110.

tegrated into pieces of creation, which God might pick
up and turn curiously this way and that to catch the
light.[29]

Clearly, both voices and consciousnesses remain. The priest's
posture here is remarkably feminine, but insofar as his prayers concern
the parish, they remain Damien's. Agnes appears here, as elsewhere, as
the more private self, yet her part of the prayers is also more clearly
shaped by the indigenous culture and religion. It is her erotic openness,
her willingness to be disintegrated in the face of "the absolute,"[30] however, that also keeps the priest tentative and culturally mutable himself.
Just as Agnes addresses the Trinity as four, so Damien prays four times a
day. Her approach to learning the language is not to pin down precise
translations, but rather to open her heart to change from within. Damien's approach is more rational (requesting "enlightenment") and
political (hoping to "dissolve" the "factions") than is Agnes's contempla-
tive approach (centering the directions and "catch[ing] the light" in
God's hand), but both succeed in opening themselves to change from
without. Agnes wants answers, but she also desires to learn the very language of new questions, as well. Damien prays for conversion, but his
prayer also includes its own self-questioning and undoing. Indeed, in
prayer both figures undo themselves as bounded individuals, and this is
what enables them to "smooth" into "one indivisible person." Fused in
prayer, the two personae are integrated even as they individually disinte-
grate before the Great Mystery. The priest is most truly transfigured—
becoming one, incorporative both/and identity—only in those moments
when each persona is disassembled, and so s/he simultaneously achieves
a neither/nor transcendence of gender and personality.
　　Such prayer gives us another image of "third space." It articu-
lates a love—for God, for others, for all of creation—that unsettles the
boundaries of individuals. It is what Jeanne Smith identifies as the value
of "transpersonal selfhood" underlying Erdrich work.[31] Smith finds in the
conclusion to *Love Medicine*, for instance, "the paradoxical idea that
identity depends on blurring the boundaries between self and other. Isolated and self-contained, the individual has no meaning. Her characters

[29] Ibid., 182.
[30] *Interview with Louise Erdrich*, 2.
[31] Jeanne Smith, "Transpersonal Selfhood: The Boundaries of Identity in Louise
Erdrich's *Love Medicine*," *SAIL* 3.4 (1991): 13-26.

gain power and force only in surpassing personal boundaries, allowing themselves to blend with what is outside."[32] Both integration—of two personae in one person—and disintegration—letting go of the boundaries of identity in the midst of something larger—suggest, as we see them here, the relational nature of the self. These images also speak to the boundaries of religious traditions and institutions. For surely love and truth exceed and blur both. In contrast to these terms, conversion—literally a turning away or against, and also a term for exact exchange—de-emphasizes both connection and continuity and suggests a more contained view of the person and of spiritual reality.

IV. Agnes/Damien as Transvestite Saint

As a cross-dressed priest considered for canonization, Damien's life speaks directly to the tradition of "transvestite saints," but, as I have been suggesting, the novel ultimately presents us with a more radically "trans" vision than that found in the tradition and so also remakes it. The deeply relational selfhood that sustains Agnes's transvestitism accounts for some of her difference from the cross-dressing heroines of Catholic tradition, for whom gender was generally experienced as an either/or prospect.

The many "holy transvestites" unearthed by Valerie Hotchkiss's study of Christian cross-dressing in medieval Europe were primarily, like Agnes, women who dressed as men. And, in many cases, male garb similarly enabled these females to live otherwise-precluded lives as monks, eunuchs, missionaries, or crusaders.[33] Saint Joan (Jeanne d'Arc) was certainly the most famous of these, and for her, as for Saint Paul's companion Thecla,[34] putting on masculine dress seemed to serve as a sign of conversion—evidence of an inner turn away from feminine, private, and material concerns. As Hotchkiss concludes, "[b]y distancing her from her sex without concealing it, cross dressing became Jeanne's trademark, so to speak; it was the outward sign of transcendence and uniqueness."[35] There were many other women for whom men's clothing offered a more literal disguise and enabled thorough gender passing. For a number of

---

[32] Ibid., 23.
[33] Valerie Hotchkiss, *Clothes make the Man: Female Cross-Dressing in Medieval Europe*, The New Middle Ages 1 (New York: Garland, 1996), 13. Hotchkiss identifies "holy transvestites" as "protagonists in over 30 legends."
[34] Ibid., 20-22.
[35] Ibid., 51.

young women, it enabled escape from some of the social burdens of their sex: many, like the 5th-century Euphrosyne/Smaragdus and 14th-century Agnes of Moncada, donned male garb to flee unwanted marriages; others, like Glaphyra in 4th Century, did so to avoid other kinds of sexual advance. Still others passed as men to liberate themselves from the religious control of the patriarchal household (e.g. Domna, 4th C.).[36] Despite the range of contexts and specific motives, in most all of these cases, Hotchkiss concludes, the cross-dressed woman appears in male-written hagiography as motivated by a desire to "improve" herself by becoming more like a man, and therefore closer to God.[37] Hotchkiss concludes that "[a]s actualizations of male metaphors for faith, cross-dressed women symbolically depict the power of Christianity to 'transform' its adherents."[38] In traditional transvestite hagiography, then, as I am arguing is true in Erdrich's novel, gender-crossing signals religious change. Hotchkiss notes this connection, as well. "Radical transformation—water to wine, death to life, male to female—", she continues, "informs Christian doctrine on many levels."[39] Because Agnes/Damien exemplifies all three types of transformation identified by Hotchkiss—though the gender cross is a *trans*-action achieved more through incorporation than exchange, and the transcendence, an effect of a willingness to ride the divide between sexes, cultures, and religions—this character exceeds and revises the long if little-known, Christian tradition of transvestite saints.

Agnes's gender transformation—Hotchkiss's third category, but noted as "Miracle the First" among Damien's reports—is remarkably successful. Although we ultimately discover that she has duped few of the full-bloods, who are more attuned to gender variations than the white characters, Agnes actually succeeds in fooling all the missionaries who venture to the Little No Horse reservation, including her temporary assistant, Father Gregory (at least until he becomes her lover). Agnes's change in gender role and status is primarily performative, but it is not thereby merely superficial. There is a concomitant alteration and alternation in identity itself (as the prayer passage discussed above suggests). This is accomplished in large part through a process of internalization. Agnes begins with a list of "Some Rules to Assist in My Transforma-

---

[36] Ibid., 131-141. These saints lives are sketched in Hotchkiss's "Hagiographic Appendix."
[37] Ibid., 12.
[38] Ibid., 19.
[39] Ibid., 19.

tion"— including such masculine behaviors as "[a]sk[ing] questions in the form of statements" and "[a]dmir[ing] women's handiwork with copious amazement."[40] Her powers of observation aid in her gender disguise and absorption of a masculine identity, and her new postures and practices gradually become deeply habitual, literally reshaping, over the better part of a century, the body itself. As Ann Fausto-Sterling explains in *Sexing the Body*, even "brains and nervous systems are plastic" and the human body continues to change in relation with environment into adulthood, so that "nervous system and behaviors [continue to] develop as part of social systems." It is "plausible," she argues, "that the body can incorporate gender related experiences throughout life" and science makes it now "possible to imagine mechanisms by which gendered experience could become gendered soma."[41]

Erdrich's character exemplifies such a re-gendering of the body itself to some degree. Agnes cuts her hair and binds her breasts, of course, but her posture also changes as she retrains herself not to use her hips to open doors or balance heavy objects.[42] More remarkably, in her early days on the reservation she practically ceases to menstruate— something Agnes receives as a divine gift in answer to her prayers, but also as an "eerie rocking between genders."[43] And over time the body continues to transform in various ways. In later years, "age had thickened her neck and waist so that the [gender] ambiguity [of her youth] now was a single and purposeful power."[44] The man takes shape in Agnes's own body and becomes far more intrinsic to her being than a mask that could be removed at will. Agnes, the woman, never disappears entirely, and though her identity is bound and stunted in some ways, in others she grows fully into herself. Towards the end of their mutual life, for example, we read that "[t]he job of becoming Father Damien ... allowed the budding eccentricities of Agnes to attain full flower."[45] Nevertheless, our central character also becomes fully a man. Accepted and functioning as a Roman Catholic priest, Damien is a man by gender status and role. Even his gender identity is masculine to the degree, for instance, that he thinks, writes, and prays privately as Damien. Both man and woman in

---

[40] *LR*, 74.
[41] Ann Fausto Sterling, *Sexing the Body: Gender Politics and the Construction of Sexuality* (New York: Basic, 2000), 239-40.
[42] *LR*, 74.
[43] Ibid., 78.
[44] Ibid., 301.
[45] Ibid., 344.

embodied experience, Damien/Agnes achieves the miraculous transformation indicated by Hotchkiss, but through a process of incorporation, rather than exact exchange.

The second "miracle" reported by Damien—"the Divine Rescue of Miss DeWitt / 1912"—would seem to be of the death-to-life variety identified by Hotchkiss. Having reached the river bank, the young Agnes falls into a deep sleep, and, we are told, "That cessation of awareness proved a bridge between her old life and her new."[46] Upon awakening, she finds herself rescued, sheltered, and fed in the arms and bed of a mysterious man she soon recognizes as her divine husband, in the tradition of the erotic theology of medieval women mystics. This perspective melds with a sense of public vocation like of St. Joan, as we see in Damien's letter to the Pontiff:

> …having known Him in a man's body, how could I not love Him until death? How could I not follow Him? Be thou like as me, were His words, and I took them literally to mean that I should attend Him as a loving woman follows her soldier into the battle of life, dressed as He is dressed, suffering the same hardships.[47]

Because this letter is signed with Damien's surname, "Modeste," it also ironically highlights the feminized role of Christian priests who represent the Church as the "Bride of Christ." The born-again Agnes dresses as a man to follow her divine husband into battle; Damien, of woman doubly-born, experiences divine mystery as a woman in order to commune with a masculine God. Together, the two personae constitute a kind of spiritual and gender double-cross.

Although Agnes actually undergoes a whole series of physical near-deaths, the river rescue is the most clearly Christian example of rebirth, and it fits quite neatly into the model of saintly calling outlined by Hotchkiss. A "connection between baptism and maleness is stressed frequently in early Christian writings," she points out, as in Paul's image of "putting on Christ." And so Thecla, probably the earliest example of a woman cross-dressing in Christian literature, initiates the pattern of "assum[ing] ... male clothing after baptism" in order to accompany Paul in

---

[46] Ibid., 43.
[47] Ibid., 43-44.

mission work.[48] Our fledgling transvestite also appears to "bury the old self" in Pauline baptismal terms, by shrouding the first Damien in her own nightdress, in a section entitled "The Exchange."[49] But this model of sacrificial exchange is to be challenged and revised by the new Damien's encounters with Ojibwa spirituality, ultimately leading him/her to a more expansive and incorporative approach.

Even in this highly Christianized passage of the novel, in fact, we can detect the seeds of another vision. A great flood is the starting point for the Ojibwe creation myth, after all, and the new world that emerges is likewise built upon sacrifice.[50] The image of a bridge between the old life and the new also comes from the cosmic architecture of the Ojibwe. After death, the Anishinaabeg must cross a bridge over water to the afterlife. This is the source of the traditional Ojibwe belief that drowning is the death most to be feared. It is significant, then, that Agnes's life as Damien is bracketed by two failed attempts at suicide by drowning. In this first scene, the young Agnes is washed ashore into the robes of Damien. She escapes death and successfully maneuvers to an "afterlife" as the priest. From a tribal perspective, of course, there is no radical discontinuity between worlds. Hence, the spirit of Agnes can continue to haunt Damien, accompanying and aiding him in his work as a priest—and eventually reintegrating her spirit with his more fully.

Despite the return to exclusively feminine references in the final chapter of the novel and of the protagonist's life, Agnes and Damien both remain strongly present. The chapter, which records Agnes's preparations for death, after all, is titled "Father Damien's Passion / 1996." Indeed, another way in which our hero/ine departs from the hagiographic tradition of transvestitism, therefore, is in not "remain[ing] a woman in the narrator's (and reader's) mind" as Hotchkiss puts it.[51] As I have argued, this character truly lives in both genders. Insisting that "passing"—gender, racial, or otherwise—"is not simply about erasure or denial," Linda Schlossberg claims that it is, rather, "about the creation and establishment of an alternative set of narratives. It becomes," she explains, "a

---

[48] Hotchkiss, 20.
[49] *LR*, 44.
[50] Muskrat dives to the bottom of the great waters and, though he drowns as a result, manages to surface with the pawful of earth necessary to building a new world upon Turtle's back ["Ojibwe Creation Story." *Ancestral Trails*, (2002), http://www.ancestraltrails.org/ojibwe.html, September 23, 2003].
[51] Hotchkiss, 26.

way of creating new stories out of unusable ones ..."[52] The Passion of Agnes/Damien includes multiple lines of narrative, spanning genders, cultures, and faiths. Although preference is given to male and Christian as the "official and public" identities of our priest, much that is feminine and Native is woven in—and in our priest's own reports or "confessions" to the Pontiff, we find a version of self that is truly absorptive and expansive. S/he does, indeed, lead a "huge life,"[53] despite a series of near physical, spiritual, and gender "deaths."

At the novel's close, we have a second failed drowning, which functions as an answer and echo to the early scene of baptism and "exchange." An ancient Agnes sits alone on the shore of Matchimanito, preparing to sink herself secretly (and so escape discovery), but she suffers a stroke before she can do so. First "one side of the world [goes] dark," then the other. Damien's trusty Chippewa housekeeper and spiritual friend, Mary Kashpaw, soon appears to fulfill his final wish by sinking the dead body. But Agnes, of course, is spared the danger of actually drowning, having already made her final "crossing":

> Trusting, yearning, she put her arms out into that emptiness. She reached as far as she could, farther than she was capable, held her hands out until at last a bigger, work-toughened hand grasped hold of hers.
> With a yank, she was pulled across.[54]

Whether this hand is human or divine, white or Indian, Berndt's, Nanapush's, Fleur's, Christ's—or even Damien's—is unclear, for this latter scene is perhaps the most ambiguous in the whole novel.[55] Whether Damien has found the place he seeks in the Chippewa heaven, or Agnes meets her divine Maker...or whether there might be a third space of transcendence altogether—all this is as muddy as the waters of Matchimanito itself. This final image of crossing does reinforce, however, that even in death—the experience at once most uniquely individual and most identity-dissolving—the self is profoundly relational.

---

[52] Linda Schlossberg, "Introduction," Sanchez and Schlossberg, 4.
[53] *LR,* 349.
[54] Ibid., 349, 350.
[55] The students in my first year Berry Scholars seminar made compelling cases for a number of options: Agnes's common-law husband, Berndt Vogel; Nanapush; Fleur Pillager; Mary Kashpaw; Christ; and even Damien himself (since the stroke seems to divide the two halves of the brain).

A third set of transformations qualify as Hotchkiss's "water-to-wine" sort of miracles and these, like the near-drownings, serve as "book-ends" to Damien's sainted life. Upon first arriving at the mission, exhausted and famished, Damien finds the nuns in a worse state of starvation. Stumbling through the Mass, he experiences the mystery of transubstantiation in concrete and miraculous terms: the wafer and wine actually become meat and blood for the protein-deprived communicants. Agnes is bewildered and wonders whether this is the common experience of priests, but readers may detect here a theological corollary for her gender transformation.[56] The "real presence" of Christ among the communicants materializes the transgender relationality Damien brings to the table—something which is itself incorporative, communal, and transcendent.

In the last months of her life, when Agnes is "old, truly old, of an age she'd never imagined ... and her brain flicker[s], drop[s] things, seize[s] others," we witness her second water-to-wine miracle. Overcome by unbearable thirst after an evening Mass, she stoops "[i]nstinctively" and drinks deeply from the baptismal font. Later that night she is awakened from a deep sleep with "a sense of overwhelming blessedness—from within" and, stumbling upon the piano, she plays like a young, impassioned woman again: "For an hour, two hours, almost three of her waning life, Agnes lived fully and intimately in a state of communion."[57] The erotic ecstasy of her youth returns briefly as divine connection. It is one of the strands of memory torn loose by an act of evil—a memory she tells the devil she has "spent [her] whole life gathering ... back."[58] This late-night rejuvenation, then, restores, sustains, and helps integrate the saint in a miracle that is rooted in but exceeds the body. And, like the flesh and blood of the early Eucharist, it strengthens Agnes for the trials ahead (she is visited by the devil-as-black-dog later that night). In the morning, Father Jude playfully accuses Damien of having been "distinctly intoxicated" the night before, despite no evidence of wine. To this, Damien replies, "[l]ike [Saint] Portrarus's, my drunkenness is not of this world." He also confesses that his choice of "a life of denial" was "made with lust. Passion over passion. Hungrier for God, I came here...".[59] Consuming and incorporating sacramental realities, the

---

[56] *LR,* 67-69.
[57] Ibid., 306-7.
[58] Ibid., 310.
[59] Ibid., 312-3.

priest thus quenches the lusty thirst of Agnes and the two commune in forbidden miracles.

These and other miracles, spiritual visions, heroic acts of virtue, and a daily life of humility, devotion, and kindness, ultimately make Damien a candidate for sainthood—in the eyes of Father Jude[60] and perhaps in those of readers as well. Significantly, each of the saintly signs is tied to the priest's trans-gendered identity—his/her absorptive openness to multiplicity, to transformation from within and without. Given that "Agnes" was also one of the names given to the "female Pope" of medieval legend,[61] our character provides a 20th-century candidate for the tradition Hotchkiss documents in her "Lives of Transvestite Saints."

Such "third kinds," according to Garber, "put into question ... the very kinds of signifying practices (like for example, celibacy...) that create and police religious faith," and so might pose a challenge to Christian views of gender and sexuality. But most often they function merely as the "exceptions that prove the rule." Despite the existence—even the acknowledgement—of apparently transgressive gender identities, Western religions remain largely "oppositional structures that depend ... on discriminating between insiders and outsiders and upon sharply delineated male and female spheres ..."[62] Identity passing unsettles epistemological categories only quietly, after all, and so tends to leave intact the oppositional structures that prompt it. To further demonstrate how our priest's status as a "third" challenges the either/or thinking of much Western Christianity, therefore, we need to consider how Damien also fits the American Indian "two-spirit" tradition—a transgender identity model that, because of its long-esteemed place in traditional Native cultures, does not depend upon the kind of erasure required by identity passing.

V. Damien as Two-Spirit

"Two-spirit" is a modern, pan-Indian gender identification, generalized from a variety of tribal traditions of gender diversity. Like the term "transgender," it is often taken to imply homosexuality, but, according to Sabine Lang and others, the "two-spirit" identity is "not a matter of sexual orientation but of occupational preferences and special person-

---

[60] Ibid., 341, 352.
[61] Hotchkiss, 69.
[62] Garber, 212.

ality traits."[63] It is understood to be determined by neither genes nor culture but by the particular spirits attending a life. Being "two-spirit," then, is seen not so much a departure from social norms as it is a following of spiritual directives.

Lang's explanation of "gender-mixing," a category that she states "does not exist in the West," perhaps best fits the experience of Agnes/Damien, who would, according to Lang's framework, constitute a "man-woman." "Men-women" as well as "women-men," Lang states, are those "of usually physically unambiguous sex who voluntarily and permanently take... on the culturally defined activities and occupations of the opposite sex, and who ha[ve] a special (ambivalent) gender status assigned to [them] by [their] culture." Such a change of "gender status"— that is of one's social position within a particular culture—is not a simple exchange of public identities, she explains, and "is more likely to result in an ambivalent status than in the status of the opposite sex."[64]

Damien presents an interesting case in this regard—for we might question from which culture his gender assignment derives. Although he clearly remains a male priest in the eyes of many of his parishioners (hence Damien's fear that exposure would "un-do" the marriages, baptisms, and blessings he has performed and the faith such acts have fed[65]), it could be argued that, by virtue of celibacy and cassock, the priest is something of a "third" gender category even in Christian terms (despite the Roman Church's failure to see how this challenges male prerogative). Even more significantly, a number of Anishinaabeg themselves assign Damien an ambivalent gender. Nanapush, Margaret, Fleur, and Old Kashpaw all question the priest's precise gender status, and the trickster-elder Nanapush is intrigued finally to determine that Damien is "a man-acting woman" rather than a "woman-acting man." "We don't get so many of those lately," he states matter-of-factly; "Between us, Margaret and me, we couldn't think of more than a couple." In response to Nanapush's initial query, "What are you? ... A man priest or a woman

---

[63] Sabine Lang, "Various Kinds of Two-Spirit People: Gender Variance and Homosexuality in Native American Communities" in *Two Spirit People: Native American Gender Identity, Sexuality, and Spirituality.* Ed., Sue-Ellen Jacobs, Wesley Thomas, and Sabine Lang (Urbana and Chicago: U ofIllinois P, 1997), 101.
[64] Lang, *Men as Women, Women as Men: Changing Gender in Native American Cultures,* Transl., John L. Vantine (Austin: U of Texas P, 1998), 10, 47, 12.
[65] *LR,* 276.

priest?" Damien replies, "I am a priest." [66] We might therefore conclude that, for him, priest is a third gender category. We see a similar response when Agnes' brief affair with Father Gregory is coming to a close because she refuses to forgo the priesthood to become his wife. She tells him, "I cannot leave who I am," and, when he reminds her that she is "a *woman,*" she insists, "I am a priest." He counters,"a woman cannot be a priest," invoking the old Western double-standard that imagines women as less able to transcend the materiality of sex. But she again demurs, "No, ... I am nothing but a priest."[67] Religious identity appears to subsume sex here, creating an ambivalent status in which the priest is bride to Christ, Father to the faithful, and neither husband nor wife to any on earth. Whereas Agnes's sexuality has been a private affair, her spirituality *is* her public persona and constitutes her social gender.

To consider Damien as a true "two-spirit" person, however, we need to bracket off his Christian status to some degree. To that end, we could consider him an incorporated part of the tribal community he tries to serve. He is no superficial Indian "wannabe,"[68] but he is clearly welcomed into the family old Nanapush reconstructs with his adopted daughter, Fleur Pillager—another who, like the elder, has lost her immediate family to disease. As another adoptive father-figure for Fleur's girl Lulu (on whose baptismal record he accidentally records his name as both priest and father,[69] and for whose soul he barters his own with the devil), Damien establishes new relations that tie him to the people with spiritual bonds. Paula Gunn Allen explains that "spirit-related persons are perceived" in Native cultures "as more closely linked than [the] blood-related"[70] and it seems reasonable to conclude that Damien has found or made a new set of "spirit relations" for himself. Indeed, he announces (albeit to the devil) that he is converting to the tribal religion because everyone he wants to see is already in the Ojibwe heaven.[71]

It is by virtue of these new relations, perhaps, that Agnes' story shows parallels to the trajectory of Paula Gunn Allen's "medicine-dyke"

---

[66] Ibid., 232.

[67] Ibid., 206-7.

[68] As in "want to be"--i.e. those who, looking for an easy way to transcend the sterility of their Euro-American experience, "discover" or invent an indigenous ancestry for themselves.

[69] Nanapush has also gotten his name on the baptismal certificate—making his cultural paternity a legal, biological "fact."

[70] Paula Gunn Allen, *The Sacred Hoop: Recovering the Feminine in American Indian Traditions* (Boston: Beacon, 1986), 247.

[71] *LR,* 310.

or "ceremonial lesbian"—a transformational woman with special powers who is attached to a particular spirit. Tribal stories about such figures, Allen explains, "all point to a serious event that results in the death of the protagonist, [and] her visit to the Spirit realms from which she finally returns, transformed and powerful. After such events, she no longer belongs to her tribe or family, but to the Spirit teacher who instructed her." Her initiation requires her "to pass grueling physical tests, to lose her mundane persona, [and] to transform her soul and mind into other forms."[72] Agnes/Damien actually undergoes more than one near and symbolic death, as we have already seen, and a number of encounters—from her initial sojourn with the divine husband, to her later drug-induced sleep-journey down death's road—could be read as "visit[s] to the Spirit realms." Her battle with the Actor, her ride down the river, her journey to Little No Horse, and her subsequent encounters with disease, starvation, and the devil himself (in the form of a black dog), all constitute "grueling" physical as well as spiritual tests. Finally, her "mundane persona" is publicly suppressed, if not lost, when she takes on Damien's "other form." The priest might even be seen, in some sense, to "bon[d] with women to further some Spirit and supernatural directive"[73] in so far as the mission itself is inhabited primarily—and often entirely—by women.

Damien's also appears to find a traditional tribal Spirit-guide in the form of an animal that is emblematic of the kinds of life and death transformations we've considered from a Christian perspective. His teacher and guardian is the snake.[74] When she first recovers her musical gift, after all, her playing calls out the nest of snakes sleeping under the church's rocky foundation, and they mark and bless her erotic and musical re-birth. She even preaches them a sermon on divine love and identifies with them as her "friends."[75] The snakes upon which Damien's church is founded would seem to constitute an "ethnic sign" in Catherine Rainwater's terms: that is, as a figure open to multiple symbolic interpre-

---

[72] Allen, 257.

[73] Ibid.

[74] To a lesser degree, Damien also exhibits some spiritual connection with the bear, an animal associated with the medicine woman Fleur Pillager. On the way to baptize Fleur's baby, for instance, the priest stumbles across a bear (likely the same one who charges into the birth house in *Tracks*), and, again employing blessed water with "perfect instinct," baptizes the animal as well (*LR*, 183). Owing to its death-like hibernation, the bear is considered a figure of mediation between worlds.

[75] *LR*, 227.

tations that serves as a sort of test to separate cultural insiders from outsiders. These snakes certainly function to disorient the typical white reader whose first inclination is to recoil at the apparently satanic image. Although Rainwater dismisses Damien as a Christian dupe of the ethnic sign in *Tracks*, calling him "well-intentioned but meddlesome" and "ethnocentric,"[76] here the priest appears to "get it," indicating acculturation and the emergence of a trans-ethnic fluency on his part. Damien has shed his skin of Edenic imagery and comes to accept the snakes as fellow tricksters, "curious and small," likewise hoping to "learn the secret" of divine love. In a subsequent transformation of the church itself, Damien is delivered a compellingly ugly Madonna who rests upon, but does not properly crush, the serpent at her feet.[77] This statue (modeled after the artist's prostitute-lover) figures a new relationship between woman and sexuality and between the church and the earth—a relation rebuilt upon the rock of indigenous tradition. Once we begin seeing doubly (and Damien claims that he never saw the truth without crossing his eyes[78]), it is evident everywhere that, in Connie Jacobs' words, "Erdrich infuses Western language with Chippewa epistemology."[79] Having been acculturated to a degree that his own spirituality and vocation are Ojibwe-inflected, Damien's identity can be helpfully assessed using a Native model.

Damien exhibits a number of other features more particular to the "two spirit" role, as well. Despite some problematic terminology, many of the characteristics Walter Williams attributes to the Native American "berdache" (generally understood to be morphologically male but socially androgynous) and the "amazon" (his term for the female equivalent), are relevant here.[80] Essentially transformational, such figures

---

[76] Catherine Rainwater, "Ethnic Signs in Erdrich's *Tracks* and *The Bingo Palace*" in *The Chippewa Landscape of Louise Erdrich*, ed. Allan Chavkin (Tuscaloosa: U of Alabama P, 1999), 144-60.

[77] *LR*, 226.

[78] Ibid., 135.

[79] Connie Jacobs, *The Novels of Louise Erdrich: Stories of Her People*, American Indian Studies 11 (New York: Peter Lang, 2001), xii.

[80] The term "berdache"—taken from a French term derived from the Arabic for "kept boy" or "male prostitute" (Lang, *Men as Women*, 6)—has been rejected by Native Americans themselves and by most recent scholarship because of its inaccurate and negative implications (Jacobs, Thomas, and Lang, "Introduction," 6). Jacobs, Thomas, and Lang explain, "The English phrase *two-spirit*, which originated primarily in urban Native American/First Nations contexts where English serves as a lingua franca to bridge cultural and linguistic differences" is "a generic term for Native American gays, lesbians, transgendered individuals

"mix together much of the behavior, dress, and social roles of women and men. [They] gain social prestige by their spiritual, intellectual, or craftwork/artistic contributions, and by their reputation for hard work and generosity. They serve a mediating function between women and men, precisely because their character is seen as distinct from either," as well as "between the physical and the spiritual."[81] They are also understood to possess a sort of "double vision,"[82] perceiving, as Claire Farrer puts it, "as both men and women—and both the everyday and mythic reality."[83] Indeed, in many tribes, the role signifies "an individual's proclivities as a dreamer and a visionary."[84] Two-spirit people can also be associated with luck[85]—as those who, in Chippewa terms, can ride the current of chance and grasp the power of change.[86]

The Agnes/Damien character in *The Last Report* exhibits every one of these characteristics. Agnes literally rides the current of chance into the priest's cassock and then discovers among the Chippewa that she is "unusually lucky" as a gambler.[87] A transformational figure from the start, Damien clearly mediates between people and between realms as a priest, and his guardian, the snake, is "wrapped around the center of the earth [to keep] things from flying apart," as Nanapush explains.[88] Not even the rigidity of extreme old age renders Agnes immutable, for she is likened to the agate which, though a stone, is "made translucent by pressure,"[89] and Father Jude finds Damien likewise "impossible to penetrate one day, all too transparent the next."[90] But Damien has other gifts as

and other personals who are not heterosexual or who are ambivalent in terms of gender." The authors caution against translating the term directly into Native American languages, since doing so can significantly change its meaning (3).

[81] Walter Williams, *The Spirit and the Flesh: Sexual Diversity in American Indian Culture* (1986), With a New Introduction (Boston: Beacon, 1992), 2-3.

[82] Ibid., 41.

[83] Claire R. Farrer, "A 'Berdache' by Any Other Name ... Is a Brother, Friend, Lover, Spouse: Reflections on a Mescalero Apache Singer of Ceremonies," Jacobs, Thomas, and Lang, 248-9.

[84] Williams, 25.

[85] Anguksuar [Richard LaFortune], "A Postcolonial Colonial Perspective on Western (Mis)Conceptions of the Cosmos and the Restoration of Indigenous Taxonomies," Jacobs, Thomas, and Lang, 217-22. 220.

[86] John Purdy, "Against All Odds: Games of Chance in the Novels of Louise Erdrich," Chavkin, 8-35. 17-18.

[87] *LR,* 190.

[88] Ibid., 220.

[89] Ibid., 303.

[90] Ibid., 316. In this regard, s/he functions as a trickster figure as well. In her radical openness to chance and to the other and in her pure, scrappy endurance,

well: he is a scholar of culture and language, an amazing musician ("intellectual" and "artistic contributions"), and tireless servant of others ("hard work"). Agnes also has a special angle of vision into gendered behavior (worrying, for example, if Damien ever condescends to women the way Gregory unselfconsciously does to her), an eye for paradox ("double-vision"), and a unique gift of generosity in forgiveness.[91] She mediates not only between masculine and feminine, material and spiritual, but also been religious traditions themselves. God meets Damien in the miracle of the Eucharist and also in the sacrament of the sweat lodge. Voices speak to him "sometimes out of the wind and other times from the pages of religious books."[92] As a "dreamer and a visionary," he has face-to-face encounters with spiritual beings, and even ventures to the spirit world and back in a dangerous drug-induced sleep.[93] According to Nanapush, the cross-dressing may be trickery, but it is also part of doing "what [her] spirits [have] instructed [her] to do."[94]

Upon surveying the literature on both transvestite saints and two-spirit people, one might conclude that Damien fits better into this latter mold. Indeed, by the end of the novel—and of Damien's life—we may even question whether the priest really embodies a third space at all, for in many ways he appears to have "gone Native." But if Damien has ultimately "been converted by the good Nanapush," as our narrator claims,[95] it is a conversion based on incorporation rather than exchange. His prayers, over the years, turn increasingly mixed, and "His [spiritual] bedrock [becomes] aggregate."[96] Damien embodies the spirits not only of the two sexes, then, but also of two religions. Just as Agnes can never be wholly excised from the man, neither can the Christian be expelled from the Objibwe traditionalist. S/he poses the possibility of a German-

---

Agnes appears from the first as a "woman created of impossibility" and bound "to survive" (*LR,* 28)—another characteristic of the trickster. Able to metamorphose, or shape-shift, mythical tricksters like Nanabozho, after whom Agnes/Damien's dear, tricky friend is named, embody a particular kind of power: "ultimate control of one's own physical boundaries" (Smith, 20). Nanapush acknowledges this power in Damien when he puts the question of his gender to him at last—done to distract him at chess, in true trickster style. Damien complains, "You tricked me, old man," to which his friend replies, "Me! ... You've been tricking everybody!"(*LR,* 232).

[91] *LR,* 303, 309.
[92] Ibid., 266.
[93] Ibid., chapter 11.
[94] Ibid., 232.
[95] Ibid., 276.
[96] Ibid., 266.

American-Catholic-Ojibwa two-spirit, man-acting-woman. The hyphens, the transitions and transmissions of spirit, gender, and culture, multiply.

VI. Conversions and Incorporations: the transgender's religious double-cross

Despite his acculturation, Damien's role as a priest among the Anishinaabeg also remains somewhat problematic. The cassock that brings Agnes a new life does, after all, serve as a sort of "death robe" for others, and Damien himself no longer believes that conversion can redeem what has been lost to the Ojibwe. In the long run, therefore, he *must* practice a duplicity in faith. The priest who determines in his first weeks to be "a thick cloth" to "accept and absorb"[97] now realizes that the Church offers no ultimate redress and that he is inextricably "knit into the fabric of the damage." He continues in the priest's dress, therefore, to "clean up after the effects of what [he] helped destroy."[98] The final struggle for Damien, then, is how to undo the damage without undoing the relational connections—in both the physical and spiritual realms. To "undress" and remove the priest's robe would strip Agnes not only of her institutional role but also of her public self and all its social ties. Instead, Damien's primary strategy for healing, as I have been suggesting, is to opt for an ethic of erotic and relational expansion, incorporation, and mixing, rather than for straightforward conversion.

This is one crucial way in which Damien differs from Sister Leopolda—the novel's other potential saint and "trans" figure. Born Pauline Puyat, a mixed-blood, her story is scattered throughout a number of Erdrich's novels. She, like Damien, disappears in death--miraculously assumed into heaven according to her devotees. In *The Last Report*, Father Jude Miller has come to the reservation to investigate her possible sainthood, and he is deep into the writing of her passion before he considers Damien's own. Readers know, of course, that she has borne and denied a child out of wedlock, tortured the unsuspecting child in the convent, and murdered its father by strangulation with a barbed-wire rosary. Although Leopolda tries to blackmail Damien into silence, the elderly priest eventually reveals all this to Father Jude, as well as the fact that the bizarre features of her miraculous transfixation were actually symptoms

---

[97] Ibid., 74.
[98] Ibid., 239.

of tetanus, contracted from the rusty wire.[99] In his manuscript on Leopolda, Jude writes the following:

> In an attempt to reconcile the two worlds from which Leopolda drew spiritual sustenance, the young novice mistakenly, but with a fervent heart and pure intentions, attempted to graft new branches onto the tree of Catholic tradition ... When her efforts to meld the two cultures failed, she chose decisively for the one true church and diverted the fever in her soul to the zeal of conversion.[100]

When Leopolda fails to achieve a satisfying syncretism, readers of *Tracks* know, she re-invents her ancestry as wholly white, denying her own mixed identity, and becomes, increasingly, an agent of death on the reservation. She thus comes to embody the violent effects of conversion on personal identity and cultural continuity.

The problems of conversion—as a supposedly even exchange that ends up meaning both cultural and material theft--are laid out early in *The Last Report* when the powerful traditional woman Mashkiigikwe accuses Damien of wanting to steal "all that makes us Anishinaabeg. Everything about us. First our land, then our trees. Now husbands, our wives, our children, our souls."[101] He has no answer for her, and when, decades later, Damien encounters a much-diminished Mashkiigikwe panhandling in Fargo, he defends himself personally, but not the missionary vocation.[102] It is conversion as exchange that poses the greatest problems. Nanapush exemplifies this in the darkly humorous story he tells the young Damien in which "Nanabozho Converts the Wolves" by preaching to them and offering poisoned fat as a sort of "communion." In the end the animals are converted all right—into cash for their pelts. But, to the delight of Nanapush, namesake to the trickster-manitou, Damien is not rattled by the tale—giving more credit to both his parishioners and to himself. Perhaps, also, "the unmanly priest"[103] recognizes that such forceful erasure of identity is not the only means of personal transformation.

---

[99] Ibid., 326-328.
[100] Ibid., 339.
[101] Ibid., 100.
[102] Ibid., 309.
[103] Ibid., 85. This is Fleur's phrase.

Instead of seeking converts, he focuses on listening and freely dispensing absolution—his own special gift. Notably, it is in the chapter immediately following Damien's final confrontation with Mashkiigikwe in Fargo that Agnes comes to terms most clearly with her/his vocation. When the devil suggests that the priest's mercy has "opened many a door" to his powers, Agnes finds strange comfort in the fact:

> It was then that Agnes was assured that her Father Da-
> mien had done the right thing in absolving all who asked
> of forgiveness ... Here it was—the reason she'd been
> called here in the first place. ... This was why she con-
> tinued to live... She saw that forgiveness as a long, slow,
> soaking rain he had caused to fall on the dry hearts of
> sinners. Father Damien had forgiven everyone, right and
> left... All except for Nanapush, who had never really
> confessed to any sin, but had instead forgiven Damien
> with great kindness for wronging him and all of the peo-
> ple he had wanted to help, forgiven him for stealing so
> many souls. Nanapush! [104]

It is in forgiving, then, that Damien is forgiven, and in failing to convert that he receives mercy.[105]

Acting in response to the ultimate mystery of Love, the priest thus incorporates the lives around him, going on to live a "huge" and au-thentic life. He, in turn, is incorporated by them—a Christian branch grafted onto the Ojibwe tree of life. In the midst of drafting the excerpt from "Leopolda's Passion" quoted earlier, Father Jude himself catches a startling glimpse of this vision. Having written the line about "graft[ing] new branches onto the tree of Catholic tradition," he pauses:

> ...imagin[ing] the great rooted base of an oak spreading
> wide and the branches reaching hungrily toward light,
> one among them boldly colored, beaded entirely, and
> ribboned. He lean[s] back... and close[s] his eyes. Sud-
> denly, he [sees] that he [is] mistaken. The picture

---

[104] Ibid., 309-310.
[105] I am thinking here of Jesus's words in the Sermon on the Mount: "Judge not, and ye shall not be judged: condemn not, and ye shall not be condemned: for-give, and ye shall be forgiven" (Luke 6:37, KJV).

shift[s]. The tree is beaded all the way down to the center of the earth and the branch of his own beliefs, the
dogma and history of the Catholic Church, not even a
branch but a twig not strong enough for a bird to perch
on, just a weak and slender shoot.[106]

Radically re-situating the missionary endeavor, this vision—in which
Christianity is incorporated into the body of Native tradition and practice—suggests something closer to the inculturation of Christ than the
conversion of anyone. For while it is Church "dogma and history" that is
diminished here, the image of "a weak and slender shoot" also recalls the
"suffering servant" of Isaiah 53, in whom Christians recognize an image
of their Savior. If the shoot itself cannot bear Damien's own weight in
this context, then perhaps we might imagine him supported by the fork of
these branches, since he feels free to "ke[ep] the pipe, translat[e] hymns
or br[ing] in the drum ... [and is] welcome where no other white man [is]
allowed." And it is "apparent, to the people, that the priest [is] in the service of the spirit of goodness, wherever that might evidence itself."[107]

Clearly, *The Last Report on the Miracles at Little No Horse* is
about much more than cross-dressing and gender fluidity. Agnes is initially "carried by the flood of her being into this priest's garments," in
Erdrich's words,[108] and then devotes much of her energy in the early
years to transforming her public self into a man of the cloth. This instinc-
tive and practiced transvestitism and the transgender identity it shapes
ultimately stand for all kinds of other "(in)vestments," though—ones that
unsettle the dualities of saint/sinner, sacred/secular, Christian/pagan, and
white/Indian. Agnes's gender crossing opens the way to a profound religious syncretism, and, as she recovers her memory and grows into a self-
knowledge exceeding the boundaries of individuality, s/he does indeed
"absorb" the spiritual and material realities of the Anishinaabeg.[109] Our
priest may not thus be able to redeem what has been lost to the Native
converts and their descendents, but s/he and the Church may be sancti-
fied in the relational process. If Erdrich's cross-dresser thus double-
crosses Christian institutions, s/he does so, it would seem, in the transformational power of the inculturated cross.

---

[106] *LR,* 339.
[107] Ibid., 276.
[108] *Interview with Louise Erdrich,* 1.
[109] *LR,* 74.

INDEX

N

O